# *Real Communication* makes sense of the human communication course.

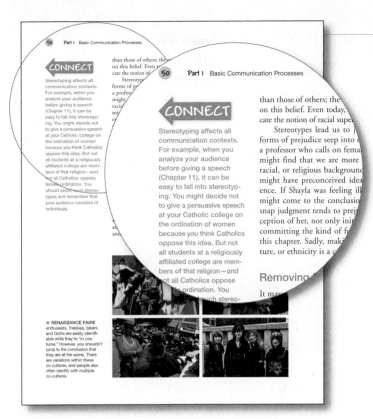

- *Real Communication* **covers all the basics — communication fundamentals plus interpersonal communication, group communication, and public speaking — and goes a step further by highlighting the connections among them.** Throughout the text, marginal CONNECT notes show how communication concepts discussed in one part of the book support and inform concepts discussed elsewhere.

# *Real Communication* provides the best study tools for success.

### REAL REFERENCE A Study Tool

**Now that you have finished reading this chapter, you can**

Understand how our personal perspective on the world influences our communication:

- ▶ **Perception** is the cognitive process that helps us make sense of the world (p. 38).
- ▶ **Communication processing** is the means by which we gather, organize, and evaluate the infor-

- ▶ The failure to see bey cumstances, or **cultu** native points of view
- ▶ **Stereotyping**, or gen our ability to see the **prejudice**, ill will

- **Study tools in each chapter and online reinforce the most important terms and ideas.** The flexible REAL REFERENCE study tool in each chapter allows one to review the chapter concepts, prepare for in-class discussions, and study for examinations. See the inside back cover or visit **bedfordstmartins.com/realcomm/ catalog** to learn more about the extensive online study tools.

# Real
# Communication
## AN INTRODUCTION

# Real Communication
## AN INTRODUCTION

**DAN O'HAIR**
University of Oklahoma

**MARY WIEMANN**
Santa Barbara City College

Bedford/St. Martin's
Boston • New York

**For Bedford/St. Martin's**

*Executive Editor for Communication:* Erika Gutierrez
*Developmental Editor:* Karen Schultz Moore
*Contributing Editor:* Ann Kirby-Payne
*Associate Editor:* Ada Fung
*Associate New Media Editor:* Jessica Chesnutt
*Production Editor:* Jessica Skrocki
*Senior Production Supervisor:* Nancy Myers
*Market Development Manager:* Sally Constable
*Marketing Manager:* Adrienne Petsick
*Marketing Assistant:* Melissa Famiglietti
*Marketing Development Assistant:* Melissa Esner
*Art Director:* Lucy Krikorian
*Text Design:* Jerilyn Bockorick
*Copy Editor:* Bruce F. Emmer
*Indexer:* Kirsten M. Kite
*Graphics:* Burmar Technical Corporation
*Photo Research:* Susan McDermott Barlow
*Cover Design:* Billy Boardman
*Cover Photos:* © Getty Images and care of Mary Wiemann
*Composition:* Nesbitt Graphics, Inc.
*Printing and Binding:* R.R. Donnelley & Sons Company

*President:* Joan E. Feinberg
*Editorial Director:* Denise B. Wydra
*Director of Development:* Erica T. Appel
*Director of Marketing:* Karen R. Soeltz
*Director of Editing, Design, and Production:* Marcia Cohen
*Assistant Director of Editing, Design, and Production:* Elise S. Kaiser
*Managing Editor:* Shuli Traub

Library of Congress Control Number: 2008929045

3 2 1 0 9 8
f e d c b a

For information, write: Bedford/St. Martin's, 75 Arlington Street, Boston, MA 02116   (617-399-4000)

ISBN-10: 0-312-24848-2
ISBN-13: 978-0-312-24848-2

**Acknowledgments**

Acknowledgments and copyrights appear at the back of the book on pages A1–A4, which constitute an extension of the copyright page.

# preface

**N**ow is a fascinating time to teach human communication. The field of interpersonal communication is evolving as new channels for communication develop; mediated communication is redefining the term *group,* making organizations flatter and generating new challenges for leadership and conflict management; and as social and professional networks spread out over the globe, public speaking is becoming a more crucial communication skill than ever before. Our goal for *Real Communication* was to create a textbook that captures the dynamic nature of the discipline in a way that truly engages students while encouraging them to assess their own communication experiences and to consider the communication concepts at work in the world around them.

As scholars, we see communication concepts at work every day—in our interactions with others, in the screenplays of the films and TV shows we see, in the carefully choreographed language of political campaigns, and in the subtle and blatant messages of advertising and marketing. But as instructors, we know that making these connections clear to students can be a challenge, especially in a course that requires us to cover diverse fields within the discipline—communication basics, interpersonal communication, small group communication, and public speaking—all in approximately fourteen weeks. But perhaps the most shocking comment we hear—one that comes spontaneously from students and has been reiterated by colleagues who find themselves pressed for time and depending on their textbook to cover the basics—is that the course doesn't reflect real life or the real world. As one student told us years ago, "I just don't see myself or anyone like me in the book we used. It's filled with examples about fake people. It's not real."

And so over the past decade, we've sought to reimagine the course and what an effective textbook for it might look like. The answer came in addressing the course challenges: we have to make it real, make it relevant, and help students make sense of the course. This was the birth of *Real Communication: An Introduction,* inspired by that student, wherever she might be today, who reminded us that books about hypothetical people will never drive home the point that effective, appropriate, and ethical communication can truly change our personal and professional lives.

The content of the book itself is the result of years of interactions, of communicating with students to gather information and develop a book that looks at communication scholarship from a real-world perspective. We talked to students, instructors, and professionals from around the country, seeking personal stories about how they used what they learned in the classroom. And we combed through countless media sources seeking inventive and intriguing ways to illustrate communication concepts at work—the ways in which we see communication playing out in the world around us, whether in scenarios on reality television programs, in national political campaigns, or during a visit to the grocery store. We involved instructors from all over the United States in various reviews and discussion groups to get a true sense of what they want and need from a communication textbook. And as we followed up with students, both in our own classrooms and in focus groups around the country, we found them excited to engage with the scholarship and practice key skills in their own lives, making the discipline *relevant* in a whole new way. Throughout the process, we looked for opportunities to draw more clear-cut connections between the various parts of our discipline. For example, nonverbal communication influences interpersonal and group communication and plays an important part in public speaking. Why limit it to a single chapter? Our research activities, along with the process of writing this book, have given us a new energy and appreciation for the human communication course—and we hope that students will enjoy a similar excitement for all that this slightly quirky and sometimes maddening but always interesting introductory course has to offer.

## Underlying Principles of *Real Communication*

Throughout *Real Communication*—and throughout our work on it—these guiding principles helped us create a practical teaching tool that is scholarly yet relevant and engaging for students.

▶ *Real Communication* **reflects basic communication scholarship as well as the latest research on today's hot topics.** All of the information you have come to expect from a human communication textbook is presented here, including coverage of self, perception, language, nonverbal communication, listening, interpersonal relationships, interpersonal conflict, small group communication, and the fundamentals of public speaking. But we've also included topics and research relevant in today's fast-changing world: organizational ethics and human trafficking, cultural myopia, physical ability and public speaking, geography and language, nonverbal cues, mediated communication, and much more.

▶ *Real Communication* **offers the idea of** *competence*—**effective and appropriate communication—as a practical tool to help students assess and understand communication.** To improve communication, we want students to remember that it is not enough to look at the messages they send. They must think about their verbal and nonverbal messages in light of their cognitions and the feedback they receive from their communication partners in the larger relational, situational, and cultural contexts. What is appropriate and effective communication with a cousin at a birthday party around religious family members may not be effective or relevant when leading a small group at work in a business environment.

▶ *Real Communication* **presents communication scholarship within the realm of students' shared experience.** Today's students are interconnected as no generation has ever been. The shared experience of popular culture—novels, film, and TV, but also the viral language of the Internet, the borderless interactions of online social networking, and the influence of current events in an age of round-the-clock news—this is the cultural context from which we've approached the scholarship of communication. This perspective informs the examples, features, and overall voice with which we present this basic introduction to the discipline.

▶ ***Real Communication* connects different areas of the discipline.** We've made it a point to look at the introductory human communication course holistically and developed a feature set that helps students clearly see the countless connections among the seemingly far-flung fields of the disciplines we cover. Further, we've incorporated running examples that in some cases span several chapters.

▶ ***Real Communication* is, well, real.** We've culled stories, tales, and interviews with former communication students as well as colleagues, friends, and just about everyone we've met to create boxes, examples, and features that will ring true because they are true. And we've invited readers to the party with a number of self-examination features that allow students to consider their own experiences and evaluate their own communication skills.

## Features of *Real Communication*

*Real Communication*'s guiding principles are supported by a solid program of special features.

▶ **Attention-grabbing opening and closing vignettes capture students' interest and frame the chapter content.** Each chapter of *Real Communication* is bookended with a topic that we think will resonate with students. In Chapter 2, for example, issues of self and perception are explored in the experience of Matisyahu, the innovative Hasidic musician who manages to reconcile his Orthodox Jewish beliefs with his love of reggae. In Chapter 3, on language, we relate real-world anecdotes about the confusion that can be caused by introducing someone as your "partner." In Chapter 9, the differing types of leadership are examined using characters from the television show *Lost* to crystallize the ways in which leadership is developed and managed. These stories get students thinking about a topic even before they begin the chapter, and the use of familiar faces—from *Lost*'s Jack Shephard to Comedy Central's Stephen Colbert—immediately shows them that they're about to think about something familiar in a new way. At the end of the chapter, we revisit the opening story and apply the chapter concepts to it so that students can consider how their thoughts have evolved in light of what they have learned.

▶ **Engaging examples make use of the world around us—politics, current events, television shows, movies, and so on—to help students understand communication theories and skills.** What do speed dating, Harry Potter, Jennifer Garner, the Amish community, *Family Guy*, and stories about our own families, friends, and students have in common? They all serve as very real and relevant examples for studying how and why we communicate.

We've striven to incorporate familiar and relevant examples not only in boxes and opening examples but throughout the narrative to help students see communication at work in a familiar way.

▶ **Critical thinking boxes on ethics, culture, and technology address issues in an ever-changing, fast-paced world.** From "pretend" cell phone use in public spaces to the ethics of critiquing a speaker's physical ability and the struggle to create group cohesion on a multilingual hockey team, the boxes in *Real Communication* offer students the opportunity to think critically about the ways in which communication concepts play out in a variety of situations. We include critical thinking questions with each box to help students make sense of these complicated communication scenarios.

▶ **Marginal CONNECT boxes make sense of the human communication course.** *Real Communication* answers students' common question, "Why do we study communication fundamentals, interpersonal communication, group communication, and public speaking in one class in one semester?" The answer is that the different areas of our discipline support and inform one another, and they offer vital concepts and skills that students can apply to their own lives and careers. Throughout the text, marginal CONNECT notes make this very point, showing students that understanding interpersonal conflict can lead to improved leadership in a small group, that the steps they take to organize a speech can help them organize a group meeting, or that an awareness of their nonverbal communication can clearly enhance their competence as listeners.

▶ **Unique features provide personal takes on communication.** These features show how communication concepts can make a difference in students' lives—and how they already have made a difference for individual students.

    **Real Communicator boxes** highlight how real people improved their lives by applying communication concepts. Interviews with students and former students explore the countless ways in which communication concepts inform our interactions in our personal lives and careers. From Bryan Au using persuasion to teach the benefits of raw food to Anna Capps overcoming her hearing challenges to deliver a killer speech, these boxes show students that communication theory and skills truly matter.

    **What About You? self-assessments** and marginal **And You? questions** prompt students to build self-awareness and assess their own communication in light of research. What are their stereotypes about nontraditional students or members of fraternities and sororities? Are they high or low self-monitors? What communication conflict are they most proud of addressing or resolving?

▶ *Real Communication* **reimagines the look of textbooks with a bold and friendly design and art program.** We are proud to offer a design that students have called "eye-catching" and "fun," with 250 images ranging from *American Idol* superstar Carrie Underwood winning it all to Tom Cruise using Oprah's couch as a trampoline. *Real Communication* looks more like a magazine than a textbook, encouraging students to engage with the scholarship rather than shrink away from it.

► *Real Communication* **provides the best study tools for student success**.

The **Real Reference study tool** at the end of each chapter contains a focused overview of the chapter's key concepts and terms, referenced to specific pages in the chapter. This flexible tool can be used before or after reading to reinforce the chapter concepts, as a quick refresher to prepare for in-class discussions, and to study for examinations.

Each chapter concludes with a series of simple, practical **Things to Try** activities that students can engage in to further explore the concepts and principles presented in the chapter. Our goal is to give students ideas for thinking critically about communication scenarios as they happen: Try watching a television show with the sound turned down, and see if you can figure out what's going on (Chapter 4); consider the way reporters pose their questions, the kinds of questions they use, and the way they sequence them at a press conference (Appendix: Competent Interviewing).

Each chapter also provides an **If You're Interested** list of readily available DVDs, books, and television shows relevant to the chapter material, with notes on how they illuminate specific chapter concepts. For example, watch HBO's series *The Wire* for an intense look at group communication as it plays out in politics, bureaucracies, police departments, and criminal organizations (Chapter 8), or take a look at the Criterion Collection DVD of Spike Lee's masterpiece *Do the Right Thing* and consider the way the film explores the nature of conflict on screen, as well as how its controversial nature prompted discussions of conflict beyond the theater (Chapter 7).

## Ancillaries

We are pleased to offer a complete set of print and online supplements to support instructors and students in the human communication course.

### Student Ancillaries

**Free and Open Companion Site at bedfordstmartins.com/realcomm,** content by Leah Bryant (DePaul University). The student-oriented portion of the companion Web site offers a host of useful tools and resources such as chapter outlines, multiple-choice questions, true-or-false questions, and essay questions.

**Real Communication e-book available free of charge when packaged with a new copy of the print text** or priced affordably as a stand-alone. The e-book includes the same content as the print book and allows students to add their own notes and highlight important information. Instructors can customize the e-book by adding their own content and deleting or rearranging chapters. In addition, accessing the e-book also gives students access to a host of premium resources, including these:

► *Video Central: Human Communication* offers students short video clips of *Real Communication's* most important vocabulary terms as well as clips from hundreds of speeches, allowing students to visualize and retain what they read in the text.

▶ *The Bedford Speech Outliner* walks students through the sometimes overwhelming process of building an outline and offers targeted feedback.

▶ *The Audio Relaxation Download* helps students calm their nerves before giving a speech. This great feature can be downloaded onto students' personal MP3 players.

▶ All material from the Free and Open Companion Site is included as well, from multiple-choice questions to chapter outlines.

To order the book plus e-book package, use ISBN-10: 0-312-57492-4; ISBN-13: 978-0-312-57492-5.

**Powerful Video Theater 3.0 Interactive CD-ROM available free of charge when packaged with a new copy of the print text.** We designed the student CD-ROM to provide examples and tools that a text alone cannot. The innovative Video Theater 3.0 offers full student speeches—informative, persuasive, special-occasion, and demonstration—along with professional speech clips. These video examples work not just as models but also as powerful teaching tools. For each full speech, we offer an outline, the text, and much more. We analyze each speech in five areas—audience analysis, content and supporting ideas, introduction, transitions and conclusions, and delivery and visual aids—and offer "hot links" so that while reading about a specific example, students or instructors can click and see the point exemplified. The CD-ROM also offers a tutorial to help students use visual aids effectively. To order the book and CD-ROM package, use ISBN-10: 0-312-57490-8; ISBN-13: 978-0-312-57490-1.

*The Essential Guide to Intercultural Communication* (ISBN-10: 0-312-55190-8; ISBN-13: 978-0-312-55190-2) by Jennifer Willis-Rivera (University of Wisconsin, River Falls). This useful guide offers an overview of key communication areas, including perception, verbal and nonverbal communication, interpersonal relationships, and organizations, from a uniquely intercultural perspective. Enhancing the discussion are contemporary and fun examples drawn from real life as well as an entire chapter devoted to intercultural communication in popular culture.

*The Essential Guide to Rhetoric* (ISBN-10: 0-312-47239-0; ISBN-13: 978-0-312-47239-9) by William M. Keith (University of Wisconsin, Milwaukee) and Christian O. Lundberg (University of North Carolina, Chapel Hill). This handy guide is a powerful addition to the public speaking portion of the human communication course, providing an accessible and balanced overview of key historical and contemporary rhetorical theories. Written by two leaders in the field, this brief introduction uses concrete, relevant examples and jargon-free language to bring concepts to life.

*The Essential Guide to Presentation Software* (ISBN-10: 0-312-53819-7; ISBN-13: 978-0-312-53819-4) by Allison Ainsworth (Gainesville State College) and Rob Patterson (James Madison University). This guide shows students how presentation software can be used to support but not overtake their speeches. Sample screens and practical advice make this an indispensable resource for students preparing electronic visual aids.

*Outlining and Organizing Your Speech* (ISBN-10: 0-312-53817-0; ISBN-13: 978-0-312-53817-0) by Merry Buchanan (University of Central Oklahoma). This student workbook provides step-by-step guidance for preparing informative, persuasive, and professional presentations and gives students the opportunity to practice the critical skills of conducting audience analysis, dealing with communication apprehension, selecting a speech topic and purpose, researching support materials, organizing and outlining, developing introductions and conclusions, enhancing language and delivery, and preparing and using presentation aids.

*Media Career Guide: Preparing for Jobs in the 21st Century, 6th edition* (ISBN-10: 0-312-46914-4; ISBN-13: 978-0-312-46914-6) by James Seguin (Robert Morris College). Practical and student-friendly, this guide includes a comprehensive directory of media jobs, practical tips, and career guidance for students considering a major in communication studies and mass media.

*Research and Documentation in the Electronic Age, 4th edition* (ISBN-10: 0-312-44339-0; ISBN-13: 978-0-312-44339-9) by Diana Hacker (Prince George's Community College) and Barbara Fister (Gustavus Adolphus College). This handy booklet covers everything students need for college research assignments at the library and on the Internet, including advice for finding and evaluating Internet sources.

## Resources for Instructors

**Instructor's Resource Manual** (ISBN-10: 0-312-53603-8; ISBN-13: 978-0-312-53603-9) by Diane Ferraro-Paluzzi (Iona College) with introductory material by Leah Bryant (DePaul University) contains helpful tips and teaching assistance for new and seasoned instructors alike. Content includes learning objectives, lecture outlines, general classroom activities, advice for teaching from the boxed pedagogy and CONNECT features, review questions, and additional resource films, as well as suggestions for setting up a syllabus, tips on managing your classroom, and general notes on teaching the course.

**Print and Electronic Test Bank** (print: ISBN-10: 0-312-53604-6; ISBN-13: 978-0-312-53604-6; electronic: ISBN-10: 0-312-53606-2; ISBN-13: 978-0-312-53606-0) by Al Golden (Joliet Junior College). *Real Communication* offers a complete testing program, available in print and also for the Windows and Macintosh environments. Each chapter includes multiple-choice, true-or-false, short-answer, and essay questions keyed to various levels of difficulty.

**Instructor material** at bedfordstmartins.com/realcomm provides a host of useful teaching tools. In addition to content for course management software, professors can obtain a downloadable version of the Instructor's Resource Manual, useful PowerPoint slides for each chapter of the text, a copy of our *Teaching Human Communication* newsletter (filled with teaching tips and advice from the trenches of the course), an electronic grade book, and ideas for classroom activities and discussions.

**PowerPoint Slides** by Bobette Wolesensky (Palm Beach Community College) provide support for key concepts addressed in each chapter, including graphics of key figures and models for class discussion. The slides are available for download from the instructor area of the Web site at bedfordstmartins.com/realcomm.

*ESL Students in the Public Speaking Classroom: A Guide for Teachers*
(ISBN-10: 0-312-53814-6; ISBN-13: 978-0-312-53814-9) by Robbin Crabtree
(Fairfield University) and Robert Weissberg (New Mexico State University). As
the United States increasingly becomes a nation of nonnative speakers, instructors must find new pedagogical tools to aid students for whom English is a second language. This guide specifically addresses the needs of ESL students in the
public speaking arena and offers instructors valuable advice for helping students
deal successfully with the unique challenges they face. Free to adopters.

**Professional Speeches** (ISBN-10: 0-312-19222-3; ISBN-13: 978-0-312-
19222-8). Available in DVD and VHS formats, Volume 19 of the esteemed Great
Speeches series offers dynamic contemporary speeches for today's classroom. The
most recent in the series, this video features compelling speeches including President Clinton's 1998 State of the Union address, Madeleine Albright's first speech
as secretary of state, Christopher Reeve's address to the 1996 Democratic National
Convention, and a speech on spirituality by the Dalai Lama. Additional videos
are available from the Bedford/St. Martin's Video Library. Free to qualified adopters. Please contact your sales representative for more information.

**Student Speeches** (ISBN-10: 0-312-39300-8; ISBN-13: 978-0-312-39300-7).
Three videotapes of student speeches provide models for study, analysis, and inspiration. Included are a variety of speeches that fulfill the most common assignments in public speaking—informative and persuasive speeches—by students of
varying abilities from Texas Tech and the University of Oklahoma. Free to qualified adopters. Please contact your sales representative for more information.

## Acknowledgments

First and foremost, we owe a great deal of gratitude to our families and friends who
supported us and listened to us as we worked through ideas for the book, who made
us laugh during bouts of writer's block, and who were understanding when we had
to cancel plans to meet deadlines. So thank you, Mary John, Erica, and Jonathan, as
well as John, Molly, Chad, William, John, and Andrea. You will always remain our
litmus tests for just how real our communication is across its many applications. In
addition, we both wish to credit and thank Gus Friedrich and John Wiemann,
whose contributions to this book and our discipline are far too many to list. And of
course, we must thank our students—including Daniel Bernard, Cory Cunningham, Kim Potts, and Michel Haigh, among countless others—who continue to inspire us as teachers. We're grateful for the frank discussions that have opened our
eyes to many of the challenges of this course from your point of view, and we are
grateful for your helpful and thoughtful suggestions on examples. (Special thanks to
Ben and Jason for being experts on *Family Guy*, *South Park*, and *Futurama*!)

We would also like to thank everyone at Bedford/St. Martin's who helped
make this book possible, including President Joan Feinberg, Editorial Director
Denise Wydra, Director of Development Erica Appel, and Director of Production Marcia Cohen. We owe a particular debt of gratitude to our editorial colleagues at Bedford: to Executive Editor Erika Gutierrez for her calm leadership
and passion for education; to Development Editor Karen Schultz Moore for her

creativity, tenacity, constructive advice, calmness, and vision to create a book that truly reaches students; to Contributing Editor Ann Kirby-Payne for her talent, dedication and sense of humor that can be felt on each page of the book; to Associate Editor Ada Fung for her artistic eye in organizing and executing our stunning art program; to Media Editor Jessica Chesnutt for managing all of the video material with professionalism and grace; and to freelance editor Valerie Raymond, for helping us complete each chapter's Real Reference. Without the production staff at Bedford, this manuscript would be nothing more than black words on white paper fresh from our printers (with quite a few typos to boot!). So we thank Managing Editor Shuli Traub for her leadership; Project Editor Jessica Skrocki for her calm dedication and superior organizational skills; Assistant Director of Editing, Design, and Production Elise S. Kaiser; Production Manager Marilyn Doof; and Senior Production Supervisor Nancy Myers for making a seemingly impossible schedule actually happen. Also, we credit our copy editor, Bruce Emmer; our proofreaders, Judy Kiviat and Eric Raetz; Art Director Lucy Krikorian; cover designer Billy Boardman; the designer of this beautiful book, Jerilyn Bockorick of Nesbitt Graphics; our permissions specialist, Sandy Schechter; and our capable photo researcher, Sue McDermott Barlow. Finally, we wish to thank Bedford's extraordinary marketing staff for their incredible commitment and excitement about our book—and their willingness to share that excitement with others: Director of Marketing Karen Melton Soeltz, Marketing Manager Adrienne Petsick, Market Development Manager Sally Constable, Marketing Assistant Melissa Famiglietti, and Marketing Development Assistant Melissa Esner.

We both feel lucky to have had the opportunity to benefit from the creativity of several of our colleagues who served as contributing writers on this edition of the book. Michele Wendell of Northern Virginia Community College, Woodbridge campus, researched and wrote the Culture boxes; Celeste Simons of the University of Texas at Austin provided numerous thought-provoking ethical dilemmas—many drawn from her students' own experiences—for our ethics feature; Bobette Wolesensky of Palm Beach Community College provided ideas, suggestions, and drafts of the CONNECT feature that is unique to this book; Charee Mooney of Arizona State University provided research and examples for our Culture and Conflict section (Chapter 7); and Marion Boyer of Kalamazoo Valley Community College wrote outstanding scenes for our *Video Central* content, which was brought to life by our talented crew of actors. And we cannot forget Matthew Burgess, a teaching assistant at the University of Minnesota, who interviewed all of our Real Communicators and brought their stories to life.

Finally, books simply do not happen without the feedback and suggestions of respected colleagues who read drafts of every chapter and tell us what works and what doesn't. Thank you for being part of this process: Allison Ainsworth, Gainesville State College; Susan D. Allen, University of Maryland; Doreen K. Baringer, Shippensburg University; Peter J. Bicak, Rockhurst University; Shereen Bingham, University of Nebraska at Omaha; Karen S. Braselton, Southern Illinois University; Jin Brown, University of Alaska Fairbanks; Jo Anne Bryant, Troy State University; Leah Bryant, DePaul University; Greg Carlisle, Morehead State University; Mindy Chang, Western New England College; Leeva Chung, University of San Diego; Tim Cline, College of Notre Dame of Maryland; Tim

Cole, DePaul University; Jean M. DeWitt, University of Houston–Downtown; William Donohue, Michigan State University; Steve Forshier, Pima Medical Institute; Diane Ferraro-Paluzzi, Iona College; Jodi Gaete, SUNY Suffolk; Randa Garden, Wayne State College; John R. Gillette, Lake City Community College; Al Golden, Joliet Junior College; Kelby K. Halone, University of Tennessee; Mike Hemphill, University of Arkansas, Little Rock; Emily Holler, Kennesaw State University; Angela Cooke-Jackson, Eastern Kentucky University; Maria Jaskot-Inclan, Wright College; Pamela Kalbfleisch, University of North Dakota; Charles Korn, Northern Virginia Community College, Manassas; Gary Kuhn, Chemeketa Community College; Betty Jane Lawrence, Bradley University; Amy K. Lenoce, Naugatuck Valley Community College; Lois Leubitz, Cedar Valley College; Shirlee A. Levin, College of Southern Maryland; Louis A. Lucca, LaGuardia Community College (CUNY); Shana M. Mason, Dona Ana Community College; Joseph McGlynn III, University of North Texas; Carol Montgomery, LaGuardia Community College (CUNY); Michael R. Moore, Morehead State University; Thomas P. Morra, Northern Virginia Community College; Alfred Mueller, Pennsylvania State University at Mont Alto; Donald Nobles, Auburn University Montgomery; Jessica A. Nodulman, Bowling Green State University; Kekeli Nuviadenu, Bethune-Cookman University; Penelope J. O'Connor, University of Northern Iowa; Jim L. Parker, Volunteer State Community College; Daniel M. Paulnock, Saint Paul College; Sandra L. Pensoneau, Wayne State University; Lisa Peterson, Boise State University; Evelyn Plummer, Seton Hall University; Dan Rogers, Cedar Valley College; Lori Forneris Schahrer, Joliet Junior College; David C. Schrader, Oklahoma State University; Celeste DC Simons, the University of Texas at Austin; Sarah Smitherman, James Madison University; Debbie Sonandre, Tacoma Community College; Terri K. Sparks, Mesa Community College; Mark Steiner, the College of Wooster; Jane Sullivan, Jefferson College; Carol Teaff, West Virginia Northern Community College; Jason Teven, California State University, Fullerton; Stephen Thompson, College of DuPage; Hank Tkachuk, Concordia College; Mary Anne Trasciatti, Hofstra University; Kristen P. Treinen, Minnesota State University; Judy Truitt, Volunteer State Community College; Tasha Van Horn, Citrus College; Jayne L. Violette, Eastern Kentucky University; Scott M. Vitz, Purdue University, Fort Wayne; Michele Wendell, Northern Virginia Community College; Jennifer Willis-Rivera, University of Wisconsin–River Falls; Jim Wilson, Shelton State Community College; Bobette Wolesensky, Palm Beach Community College; Alan Yabui, Bellevue Community College; Gustav Yep, San Francisco State University; and Joe Zubrick, University of Maine at Fort Kent.

We also offer a special thanks to our student reviewers who suggested examples, offered honest feedback about chapters, and unknowingly provided a great deal of encouragement. We may not know you personally, but we hope you feel personally invested in this project: Keegan Carroll, Cedar Valley College; Chris D'Aprix, Palm Beach Community College; Crystal Rubio, University of Houston; Carla Parisi, University of Northern Iowa; Patrick Puckett, Eastern Kentucky University; Lazya Silva, University of Houston; Victoria Skrip, Eastern Kentucky University; Jill Sweeney, University of Northern Iowa; Bill West, Palm Beach Community College; and Philip L. Griffith, Meghan Hill, Tracy Mayfield, David Preston, and Alejandro Ramirez, from Gainesville State College.

# about the authors

**D**an O'Hair is presidential professor in the Department of Communication at the University of Oklahoma and past president of the National Communication Association. He has cowritten or coedited fifteen communication texts and scholarly volumes and has published more than eighty research articles and chapters in dozens of communication, psychology, and health journals and books. He is a frequent presenter at national and international communication conferences, is on the editorial boards of various journals, and has served on numerous committees and task forces for regional and national communication associations.

**M**ary Wiemann is an associate professor in the Department of Communication at Santa Barbara City College in California. Her book chapters, journal articles, student manuals, instructor manuals, and online instructional materials all reflect her commitment to making effective communication real and accessible for students. A recipient of awards for outstanding teaching, she is also a communication laboratory innovator and has directed classroom research projects in the community college setting. She is a frequent presenter at the National Communication Association convention and has held a number of offices in the Human Communication and Technology Division of that organization.

# brief contents

# contents

**chapter 4**

# Real Communication

## AN INTRODUCTION

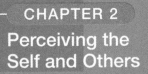

New Orleans's plea for help fell largely on deaf ears.

# chapter

**1**

# Communication: Essential Human Behavior

**When Hurricane Katrina, a category 5 storm,** hit the U.S. Gulf Coast at the end of August 2005, it destroyed countless buildings, flooded cities, and left nearly 2,000 Americans dead and thousands homeless. But the natural disaster was only a part of the heartbreak of Katrina. The ways in which state and local authorities and the federal government handled the storm shook the nation to its core.

When the levees in New Orleans failed, sending floodwaters through the city, the news media broadcast dire images of residents standing on rooftops and bodies floating in flooded streets. On September 1, news organizations broadcast Mayor Ray Nagin's plea for help from the city's convention center, where thousands were stranded without food, water, or electricity. "This is a desperate SOS," Nagin said ("Relief Workers," 2005).

Shaken by these images, Americans in other parts of the country looked on in shock when, hours after Nagin's plea was broadcast, Federal Emergency Management Agency (FEMA) director Michael Brown told CNN's Paula Zahn that the federal government was unaware of the situation at the convention center. "Sir," a stunned Zahn said in an interview with Brown that Thursday night, "you aren't telling me you've just learned that the folks at the convention center didn't have food and water until today, are you?" Brown replied, "Paula, the federal government did not even know about the convention center people until today" (Lipton & Shane, 2005). How was this disconnect possible? As the public watched the communication gap widen between what official sources said and what the media presented, the costs of communication failures became obvious—and tragic (Durham, 2006).

**After you have finished reading this chapter, you will be able to**

○ Define the communication process

○ Understand the functions of communication

○ Assess the quality, or communicative value, of communication by examining its six characteristics

○ Define what communication scholars consider to be competent communication

○ Describe the various visual representations, or models, of communication

○ Understand the ways in which communication is vital to everyone

Before we can analyze how communication failures affect our lives, we must be clear that **communication** is the process by which individuals use symbols, signs, and behaviors to exchange information. Or as communication scholar Brent Ruben (2005, pp. 294–295) puts it, "Communication is the process through which the social fabric of relationships, groups, organizations, societies, and world order—and disorder—is created and maintained." Successful communication allows us to satisfy our most basic human needs, from finding food and shelter to functioning in our communities to developing meaningful relationships with others.

But because communication is such a natural part of our daily lives, we often take it for granted and dismiss theories of communication as little more than common sense. Yet every day, communication failures lead to isolation, misunderstandings, hurt feelings, mistakes, and sometimes even disasters. Although Katrina was a horrific act of nature, a good deal of the death and devastation left in its wake—particularly in the city of New Orleans—was largely the result of failed communication. In fact, Roger Smitter, the executive director of the National Communication Association, points out that the Katrina disaster brings several questions about effective communication to the forefront: Why were evacuation messages ineffective in moving some Gulf Coast residents to flee the storm? How is it that organizations devoted to providing rescue and aid in disasters can become dysfunctional in their collaboration? What long-term impact will the televised images of Katrina's aftermath have on the public trust in government? And what forms of technology are best suited to deliver the messages needed in a crisis? (Smitter, 2005). As this disaster and others like it show, if communication were just common sense, then communication failures wouldn't be so common or so potentially devastating.

Throughout this chapter—and this book—we want you to take advantage of what you already know: your personal theories of communication and how communication works. But we also want you to question and evaluate your theories against what social science tells us about the very complex communication process. In this way, you'll make the social science theories real for yourself and apply the best of what they have to offer to your personal communication situations. By doing this, you'll be better able to predict how your communication choices will affect *others* and why *their* communication choices affect *you* as they do. So let's get started by looking at why we communicate, how we communicate, and what it means to communicate well. Then we'll look at a few helpful models that assist in visualizing the communication process and provide an overview of the history of this very rich discipline.

## We Must Communicate: The Functional Perspective

All over the Internet, new "daddy blogs" and "motherhood diaries" are popping up where moms and dads share all of the sleepless nights, dirty diapers, first words, first steps—and even first dates—that accompany being a parent. And we're sure that it comes as no surprise that parents, especially parents of newborns, spend a lot of time talking about crying babies. Which kind of cry clearly reveals a hungry baby? And that specific whimper must surely be a sign of exhaustion—or is it gas? What these parents are discovering, often at 2:00 A.M., is that we communicate from the moment we're born. A baby's cry lets everyone within earshot know that something isn't right: there's an empty stomach or a missing blanket or an impending ear infection that needs to be taken care of. Throughout our lives, we'll each dedicate a huge amount of time to the essential task of communicating with others in order to make sure that our needs are met (albeit in more sophisticated ways than a newborn).

This example also illustrates the **functional perspective** of communication, which examines how we use communication to help us begin, maintain, and end relationships. **Relationships** are the interconnections, or interdependence, between

---

Everyone has ideas about what constitutes good communication. But just how correct are those ideas? Do your personal theories of communication match what social science tells us about the way we communicate? Consider the following questions:

▶ *Does talking equal effective communication?* Have you ever sat through a lecture only to find that your instructor was boring, unclear, disorganized, or even offensive? Talking is one way of giving information, but it isn't always effective on its own. To communicate effectively, we need to be thoughtful and to use silence, listening skills, and symbols other than words. We cannot rely entirely on the spoken word. And when we do speak, we need to ensure that our words are effective.

▶ *Do body movements (often called "body language") constitute a language?* As you will learn in Chapter 4, nonverbal communication is important and useful, but there is no direct translation for what body movements mean. Because nonverbal communication can be interpreted in many different ways, it is not a true language.

▶ *Is more control necessarily better in communication?* While we admire people who can articulate their point of view, if we think they are trying to trick us or force us, we often resist what they are saying. Your father may stay on topic and clearly state his case against your choice of a major, for example, but he still can't make you do what he wants no matter how refined his intellectual skills may be.

▶ *Are most communication behaviors inborn and entirely natural?* No. Although we are certainly born with some ability to communicate, most of the skills we need in order to communicate must be learned—otherwise, we'd go through life crying whenever we needed something. We begin learning how to communicate during the first days of our life, and the best communicators never stop learning.

▶ *Is speaking well more important than listening?* An old conundrum asks, "If a tree falls in the woods and no one is there to hear it, does it make a sound?" Similarly, if you talk and nobody listens, has communication taken place? Communication is a two-way street, and listening is a crucial part of the process.

BOX 1.1

**COMMUNICATION IS *NOT* JUST COMMON SENSE**

two or more people that function to achieve some goal. As the definition states, our relationships involve **interdependence**, meaning that what we do affects others and what others do affects us. For example, Jamie flips burgers to get a paycheck to help pay for college—that's her goal. Her boss depends on Jamie to do her job well and keep the business profitable. And the customers, who just want an inexpensive and quick lunch, depend on both of them. Jamie, the boss, and the lunch customers are interdependent. Along the same lines, a communication relationship is one in which the interdependence is specifically based on the exchange or sharing of symbolic information. This kind of interdependence is obvious between friends, coworkers, and family members, yet in the course of a typical day, we also engage in countless relationships that are less personal in nature: with salesclerks, delivery persons, bus drivers, or Starbucks workers. Such minimal relationships last only momentarily, but they are in fact quite important to our overall well-being. (How else could we get that mug of black coffee or venti soy chai latte that gets our day off to the right start?)

A long line of research conducted in a variety of contexts—including work groups, families, and friendships—has found that virtually all communication behavior serves one or more primary functions, such as expressing affiliation, achieving goals, or influencing others (Wiemann & Krueger, 1980). Let's take a closer look at each of these functions of communication, keeping in mind that they can often be intertwined (for example, our influence over others can affect our affiliation with them).

## Expressing Affiliation

**Affiliation** is the affect, or feelings, we have for others. We show how much we want to be connected to or associated with someone by expressing liking, love, or respect—or, alternatively, dislike, hatred, or disrespect. This love-hate

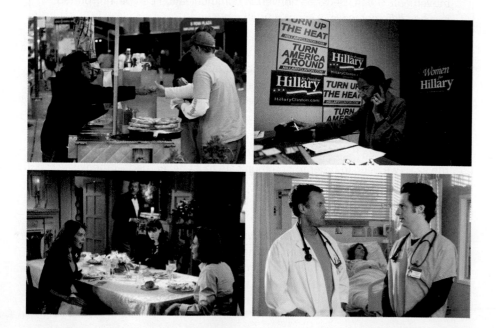

● **ALL COMMUNICATION RELATIONSHIPS,** whether fleeting like a canvasser's relationship with a voter or more permanent like a familial relationship, involve interdependence.

continuum functions to establish and maintain relationships happily (or unhappily).

Affiliation serves a number of beneficial functions. We may express our feelings to fulfill practical needs, as when we marry someone we believe can offer a stable and secure life. Other relationships and affiliations fulfill emotional needs, offering companionship or intellectual stimulation (or both). Consider "A Head in the Polls," an episode of the popular cartoon *Futurama* in which the slightly pathetic Fry is trying to decide which political party to join before an upcoming presidential election: Which party can he be the most excited about? Where will he fit in? He's most attracted to the "Voter Apathy" party, but when his enthusiasm to join the group ("Now *here's* a party I can get excited about!") proves that he's not apathetic enough, the party insiders turn him down. When he responds to the rejection casually, he's immediately admitted to the group. But once again, when Fry appears too pleased with his success, he's done. Luckily, he still has an affiliation with his coworkers and friends Leela and Bender at the Plan Express delivery company to fall back on.

● **EVEN IF LEELA** and Bender are annoyed by Fry from time to time, they still have an affection for him and consider him a friend.

## Achieving Goals

Without communication, such things as becoming educated, getting a job, and completing a variety of tasks, from simple business transactions to huge group-oriented projects, would be impossible. We rely on communication in order to accomplish particular objectives, a function we call **goal achievement**.

Communication that is highly goal- or task-oriented focuses on being practical and getting the job done. The goal (or goals), however, may change over the course of the communication encounter. For example, in the movie *How to Lose a Guy in 10 Days*, journalist Andie Anderson is stuck writing boring "how-to" articles for *Composure* magazine. She finds herself working on an article titled "How to Lose a Guy in 10 Days" and receives assurances from her boss that she'll be given more interesting assignments if she can actually follow her own advice. Meanwhile, advertising executive Benjamin Barry tells his boss that he can make any woman fall in love with him in ten days. His boss counters that if he can actually succeed at this seemingly impossible task, he'll have a chance to head up the advertising for a new diamond company. As Hollywood would have it, Andie and Ben cross paths, and the adventure ensues, ending (of course) with the couple abandoning their initial goals, falling in love with each other, and establishing a romantic relationship (a new goal).

● **ANDIE PRETENDS** to be a vegetarian and makes a big fuss when Benjamin cooks her lamb for dinner, hoping that he'll be disgusted by her behavior and break up with her.

You set communication goals when you decide that you want to influence someone and determine what you want to get from the target of your attempts. Often the same goal can be achieved in a variety of ways. In one episode of *South Park*, Kyle decides not to invite his friend Cartman to join him for his birthday trip to the Casa Bonita theme park

**AND YOU?**

Consider a communication situation that you were in today. What functions did it fulfill? Did it accomplish your goals? Did it meet your influence and/or affiliation needs?

because Cartman is mean and obnoxious. Cartman is outraged and sets a goal: to show Kyle how nice he is in order to get invited. First, he beats up a kid at school, claiming that this individual was calling Kyle names. But Kyle points out that this is hardly nice behavior. So Cartman shows up at Kyle's house dressed nicely—but Kyle points out that dressing nicely is not the same as *being* nice. Finally, Cartman approaches Kyle and apologizes, noting that he thought being mean was just part of their friendship. Kyle finally relents and invites Cartman. While the goal (proving his niceness and getting an invite) is the same in each case, the different strategies for achieving the goal present different obstacles. Not all are ethical (see Wiemann & Daly, 1994), and not all allow Cartman to maintain self-respect and dignity (assuming that *South Park* characters can have such feelings!).

## Influencing Others

One of the most important functions of communication is the ability to influence people. Virtually every communication is influential in one way or another: a politician's behavior during a press conference influences the way voters perceive her; Michael's lack of eye contact and quiet voice influence his professor's opinion of him during their interaction after class. You don't need to *decide* to influence someone; influence can be completely unintentional.

The ability of one person, group, or organization to influence others, and the manner in which their relationships are conducted, is called **control**. Unlike affection, which we can give and receive infinitely, control is finite: the more control one person has in a relationship, the less the other persons have. The exact distribution of control in relationships is worked out between the relational partners through communication—by the way they talk with each other, the content and structure of the conversations, and the timing and frequency of their interactions. While this negotiation of control may at times seem like a power struggle,[1] it is a necessary aspect of every type of relationship: family, friends, lovers, colleagues, doctors and patients, teachers and students, and advertisers and consumers.

The amount of control we have over others or they have over us varies; it is based on situation and status, allowing control to shift from one party to another as necessary. For example, as a new bank employee, Manny looks to his manager,

● **FOR A LEARNING** environment to be successful, teachers should have more control than students in the classroom.

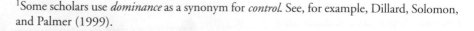

[1]Some scholars use *dominance* as a synonym for *control*. See, for example, Dillard, Solomon, and Palmer (1999).

# what about you?

## Assessing Your Control Needs

Answer these questions to understand how you negotiate control in certain situations.

1. You are unhappy with your roommate because you feel that he does not do his share of the cleanup in the kitchen. You
   A. continuously point out when it is his turn to clean up.
   B. tell him to forget it and do it yourself.
   C. give him the silent treatment until he realizes that you're upset.
   D. ask why he doesn't do the chores and consider reassigning tasks.

2. Your family is planning a summer reunion. You
   A. push to have it when and where you want.
   B. take over the planning yourself.
   C. announce that you're not going unless it's planned your way.
   D. participate in the decision process, volunteering to do your share.

3. You're assigned to a group project in class. You
   A. take leadership early, telling others what to do to get an A.
   B. give up trying to get everyone to cooperate and just do the work yourself.
   C. sit back and let others take leadership roles.
   D. help distribute tasks and work on a timeline with others.

4. You are in charge of reviewing an employee's performance. You
   A. speak to the employee about strengths and weaknesses and outline a plan to meet goals.
   B. deliver a written evaluation without a face-to-face meeting.
   C. avoid any formal evaluation and hope the employee figures things out.
   D. ask the employee for a self-evaluation and respond to it.

**If you responded "a" to most items:** You are comfortable exerting a lot of control, though you should express affiliation (respect, liking) so that others will realize you care about and respect them.

**If you responded "b" to most items:** You have a tendency to take control because you don't have much confidence in others. Instead, try having confidence in your ability to influence others so that you don't place all responsibility on yourself.

**If you responded "c" to most items:** You have a low control need. This often helps you avoid confrontation, but you're probably not getting your needs met in a number of areas.

**If you responded "d" to most items:** You are more willing to share control in relationships, making you more likely to accomplish goals with the cooperation of others.

Alexis, for direction and advice about how to do his job well. He expects to be told what to do and how to do it. The unequal control distribution is appropriate and meets both Manny's and Alexis's expectations of their job responsibilities. But as Manny becomes more comfortable in his new job, he will likely take more control, and Alexis will allow him to work more independently. This kind of redistribution of control is not so much a struggle as it is a natural process.

## How We Communicate

Consider this simple scenario: It's 8:45 A.M. in New York City. A woman walks up to a street vendor's cart, smiles and nods quickly at the vendor, and says, "Regular." Without hesitation, the man prepares her a small coffee with milk and two sugars. He hands her the coffee; she hands him ninety-five cents, says, "Thanks," and continues on her way.

With only two words spoken, an entire business transaction has been carried out to the satisfaction of both parties. But what exactly occurred? The characteristics of communication can explain.

## Characteristics of Communication

Communication is best illustrated by examining it in terms of six characteristics: the extent to which the message is *symbolic,* the extent to which the *code is shared,* the degree to which the message is *culturally bound,* the perceived *intentionality* of the sender, the presence of a *channel,* and the degree to which the process of encoding and decoding messages is *transactional.* That's quite a mouthful, so let us explain further.

As we discuss in Chapter 3, the most symbolic behavior is language. There is no particular reason why the letters *t-r-e-e* should represent a very large plant form, but they do. And in Chapter 4, you learn that gestures can serve a similar purpose. For example, joining the thumb and forefinger in a circle while extending the other three fingers stands for "OK" in U.S. culture. You likely don't need to be told what this gesture means.

### *Communication Is Symbolic*

Communication relies on the use of **symbols**—arbitrary constructions (usually in the form of language or behaviors) that refer to people, things, and concepts. The stronger the connection between symbol and object, the clearer the intended meaning, and vice versa. For example, our customer greeted the street vendor not with a hello but with a smile and a nod. In this encounter, her actions clearly indicated a greeting to the vendor.

People create and negotiate meanings in the course of their interaction. A symbol can take on a new meaning if at least two people agree that it will have that meaning for them. A romantic couple, for example, may create a symbol for their affection—perhaps a certain look, gesture, or joke—that no one else shares. Social groups, such as fraternities and sororities or sports teams, use this technique to establish their uniqueness and to create boundaries between themselves and the outside world; they might use a handshake or a password or clothing that sets them apart from others. We discuss the nature of symbols in more detail in Chapters 3 and 4.

## Communication Requires a Shared Code

Symbolic behaviors are grouped into patterns to create a **code**, a set of symbols that are joined to create a meaningful message. For communication to take place, the participants must share the code used to encode and decode messages.

---

# COMMUNICATIONACROSSCULTURES

THINK
ABOUT
THIS

### The International *Office*

Something about the BBC's show *The Office* struck a chord in the United Kingdom. The mundane goings-on at a small sales office of a large paper corporation seemed oddly familiar to audiences, from the endless clock-watching to dealing with pompous and annoying supervisors to unrequited romances between average, everyday coworkers. While the language and subtle humor were thoroughly British, the show was also universal enough to win over audiences abroad. It was soon exported, often dubbed or subtitled, to eighty countries. In the United States, it was broadcast on BBC America and quickly became something of a cult phenomenon. The little-known show sneaked up on homegrown programs like *Sex and the City* and *Will and Grace* when it snagged two Golden Globe awards in 2004, one for best TV comedy and another for a little-known actor (and series cocreator) Ricky Gervais, who beat out such established American stars as Bernie Mac, Matt LeBlanc, and Eric McCormack.

Fans of the original BBC sitcom were skeptical, to say the least, when NBC announced that it would be producing a version for American television, starring *Daily Show* alumnus Steve Carrell. Watered-down American versions of beloved British shows often tank in the United States, but gradually American audiences—both new viewers and fans of the BBC original—began to enjoy it. Within a few seasons, the American *Office* became a hit, taking home a number of awards of its own and reviving NBC's Thursday night comedy lineup. Meanwhile, back in Europe, the show has also been remade in France (where a dubbed version of the U.K. original failed) as *Le Bureau* and in Germany as *Stromberg,* with similar successful results.

Why is it that the simple concept of office life resonates in so many different cultures? And why does it seem that adaptations of the show, which typically don't work as well as the original, do even better? Liesl Schillinger, an American columnist and fan of both the U.K. original and the American *Office,* believes that it's because each show taps into the unique bleakness of office life within a particular culture. Life in the American cubicle, it turns out, is similar to life in an English office, but it's also different. And so jabs at office life must also be different. Many of the references on the BBC original are uniquely British in context, while American cultural references pepper the American version. "It's not that I don't like the U.K. *Office,*" Schillinger (2006) writes, "It's just that I don't like it as much. It doesn't reflect the reality of any U.S. workplace I know. The sexism is too blatant, and the inside jokes are often too, well, *inside.*"

**❶** What makes *The Office* so popular in the United Kingdom, the United States, and other countries? What is it about the show that resonates in so many countries? And how is it that three foreign remakes have found audiences as well?

**❷** Why do you think that *Le Bureau* has been successful in France, where the dubbed version of the U.K. *Office* was a failure?

**❸** Survey your friends to see who enjoys either the U.S. or U.K. *Office* and who does not. What is it about the shows that they find familiar? What do they find foreign? Do people who have worked in an office environment see the show differently than those who haven't?

Sources: Carter (2006); Schillinger (2006).

● **GETTING ALL DRESSED** up in the Colts' colors not only bands the fans together but also shows their alliance with the team.

**Encoding** is the process of mentally constructing a message for production, and **decoding** is the process of receiving a message by interpreting and assigning meaning to it. If the relational partners are using the same code, they are more likely to encode and decode messages more accurately and establish the shared meaning they are seeking to communicate.

Speaking a common language is the most obvious example of sharing a communication code, though it is certainly not the only one. Baseball teams, for example, develop elaborate codes for various pitches and plays, which are communicated through hand gestures and body movements that range from subtle (removing a baseball cap) to obvious (holding up three fingers and shaking them twice). Similarly, different groups share meanings for specific gestures, graphics, and other symbols. Consider the emoticons and texting and chat room shorthand we all make use of—especially when we're in a hurry.

● **A SUBTLE TAP** on the nose, a slight raise of a baseball cap: these are some of the signals baseball players use to indicate pitches or plays to their teammates.

## Communication Is Linked to Culture

If you've ever traveled abroad, or even through the different neighborhoods of a large city, you know that communication is difficult to separate from culture. **Culture** refers to the shared beliefs, values, and practices of a group of people. A group's culture includes the language (or languages) and other symbols used by group members as well as the norms and rules about how behavior can appropriately be displayed and understood.

Cultural groups vary in scale, and most people are members of several co-cultures simultaneously. **Co-cultures** are smaller groups of people within a culture who are distinguished by features such as race, religion, age, generation, political affiliation, gender, sexual orientation, economic status, educational level, occupation, and a host of other factors. Consider Anna, who identifies with a number of co-cultures: she is an American, a Native American, a Navajo, a midwesterner, a married lawyer with two children, a person with an income over $100,000 a year, and a Catholic. Each of these co-cultures carries different meanings for Anna and affects her communication, not only in terms of the languages she speaks but also in how she presents herself to others and how she interprets others' behavior (Chen & Starosta, 1996). Cultural identities can even form around common interests and shared opinions. Consider how two individuals with different interests might describe a piece of music. A music critic at *Blender* magazine might make distinctions between rock, soul, and hip-hop and might even break those styles down further, using terms like *old-school, freestyle, classic, punk, techno,* and *R&B.* For someone less involved or less interested in the music scene, such distinctions might seem unimportant—it's all just popular music.

## Communication Need Not Be Intentional

One communication system is characterized by behavior that is primarily *symbolic* and *intentional,* such as IM-ing a friend to let her know you will be away from your computer using a mutually understood code (BRB! ☺). But there is also a second system, based largely on the expression of emotions and body movements. This widely shared code has few cultural boundaries, is *spontaneous,* and is therefore unintentional (Buck, 1988; Motley, 1990). For example, you communicate a message when you blush, even though blushing is an involuntary action. The distinction between the two systems can be seen as the difference between *giving* information and *giving off* information (Goffman, 1967).

These distinctions are important because we tend to see involuntary messages as more honest and reliable because the person giving off the information does not have the opportunity to censor it. It is useful to note, however, that while some spontaneous messages (for example, emotional outbursts of grief and anger) are highly reliable and readily interpreted, most are ambiguous and open to a variety of interpretations: Are you blushing because you're embarrassed? Or because you're angry? Or because you've had a glass of wine or a hot cup of tea? Or because you ran up six flights of stairs in uncomfortable shoes? Generally, information given off is interpreted by paying attention to many other surrounding cues, but even then, the final assessment is still questionable. The most successful communicators are sensitive to the fact that both intended and unintended messages have an impact on the people around them.

## Communication Occurs Through Various Channels

Once, the only means of communication was face-to-face contact. But as society became more sophisticated, other types of communication emerged: smoke signals, handwritten correspondence, telegraph, telephone, e-mail, and text messaging are all examples of communication channels. A **channel** is simply the method through which communication occurs. We must have a channel in order to communicate.

Relationships can be maintained through a variety of channels. The information superhighway, which electronically connects an ever-growing number of people to one another, has facilitated an increase in long-distance relationships,

**CONNECT**

As you learn in Chapter 4, our nonverbal communication is wrapped up in culture. In Mediterranean cultures, for instance, men tend to stand very close together, frequently touching during conversation. But in North American cultures, the appropriate conversational distance is generally about three feet—and men seldom touch each other during social interaction, except when they shake hands in greeting.

**AND YOU?**

Have you ever given off an unintentional message that was improperly decoded (for example, blushing during an argument because you're angry, while your romantic partner assumes it means that you're lying)? What did you do to correct your communication partner or partners? Was it effective?

including those between parents and children, siblings, close friends, and even marriage partners. Professional relationships can thrive over great distances as well; telecommuters around the globe remain connected by computer and audio and video media channels. The book that you are holding, for example, was produced by a team of authors, editors, proofreaders, designers, artists, and indexers working in offices and homes all over the United States.

Most people in technologically advanced societies use many channels to communicate, though they are not always proficient at adapting communication for the channel being used. Do you have a friend who leaves five-minute voice mail messages on your cell phone as though speaking directly with you? (Don't we all know someone like this?) We've even had students send us sarcastic e-mail messages, incorrectly assuming that we will understand their intent to be funny or witty. We all need to identify the channel that will work best at certain points in our relationships and then adapt our messages to that medium. For example, an insurance person might determine that prospective clients do not respond to e-mail contact but that current customers find e-mail very helpful for receiving updates on existing accounts.

## Communication Is a Transactional Process

In July 2006, the actor and director Mel Gibson was pulled over in Malibu, California, for driving under the influence of alcohol. Although he cooperated at first, he became aggressive and belligerent when he was arrested, making disparaging anti-Semitic comments against Jewish people. Over the next few weeks, Gibson offered two public apologies to anyone offended by his comments:

> There is no excuse, nor should there be any tolerance, for anyone who thinks or expresses any kind of anti-Semitic remark. I want to apologize specifically to everyone in the Jewish community for the vitriolic and harmful words that I said to a law enforcement officer the night I was arrested on a DUI charge. I am a public person, and when I say something, either articulated and thought out, or blurted out in a moment of insanity, my words carry weight in the public arena. As a result, I must assume personal responsibility for my words and apologize directly to those who have been hurt and offended by those words. ("Gibson," 2006)

Yet no amount of apologizing or regret could change the fact that Gibson made these remarks, and nothing could have prevented the consequences—Gibson's fallout in the media. That's because communication is a **transactional** process: it involves two or more people acting in both *sender* and *receiver* roles, and their messages are dependent on and influenced by those of their partner. Once a communication transaction has been completed—once a message has been sent (intentionally or not) and received—it cannot be reversed, nor can it be repeated in precisely the same way. This ongoing process can be immediate, as in Gibson's face-to-face encounter with the officer, or delayed, as in the case of an e-mail exchange.

As we illustrate throughout this book, when you engage others in communication, you are attempting to influence them in some way. Equally important, but perhaps not so obvious, is the fact that you are opening yourself to be influenced *by* others. For example, when you are working on an assignment in a class group, your classmates' comments and suggestions influence you and your comments and suggestions, and vice versa. All parties in an interaction are responsible for the outcome of communication, and they all have a hand in whether or not goals are met (such as the completion of the assignment). The burden of responsibility, however, is distributed according to the communication situation. In some situations, such as close friendships or romantic relationships, responsibility is often shared equally. In other situations, like public speaking scenarios, the speaker tends to assume most of the responsibility and is seen as the person attempting to influence the audience.

## Assessing Communicative Value

To understand communication more fully, you assess the quality, or communicative value, of your communication. You do this by examining communication as it relates to the six characteristics discussed earlier. If it is definitely symbolic, with a shared code, and definitely intentional, it has three characteristics that give it high communicative value; communication breakdowns are less likely.

For example, recall the coffee sale described at the beginning of this section. The woman and the street vendor share a clear, if unwritten, code: in New York City, "regular" coffee means coffee with milk and two sugars. The code is not universal; it has a cultural meaning that is unique to New York, and even within the city, it is somewhat specialized, limited to street vendors. Had she said the same word to the counterperson at a Seattle's Best coffee shop on the West Coast, she might have gotten nothing more than a perplexed stare. See Table 1.1 for a more detailed breakdown of this transaction.

| Characteristic | Behavior |
|---|---|
| Communication is symbolic. | Both parties speak English. |
| Communication requires a shared code. | Both parties understand the meaning of "regular." Both parties understand the smile and nod greeting. |
| Communication is linked to culture. | Both parties are New Yorkers. |
| Communication need not be intentional. | The woman knows the meanings of her words and gestures; they are not ambiguous to the street vendor. |
| Communication occurs through various channels. | This example uses the spoken word, gestures, and eye contact. |
| Communication is transactional. | The woman understands the message she is giving, and the man understands the message he is receiving. |

**TABLE 1.1**

**COMMUNICATION CHARACTERISTICS: ANATOMY OF A COFFEE SALE**
Approaching the study of communication through its characteristics will help you evaluate behaviors you encounter in terms of their communicative value. As you can see, the simple coffee sale described in the text is clearly communicative, meeting all six criteria.

● **WHILE JOHNNY CASH** (played by Joaquin Phoenix in the film *Walk the Line*) had a great connection and rapport with his fans, his first marriage was far less successful.

● **FOR DANIEL PLAINVIEW,** the ambitious oilman in *There Will Be Blood,* it's all about the win. He states, "I have a competition in me. I want no one else to succeed," and doesn't hesitate to "remove" anyone who poses a threat to his position.

## Communicating Competently

Most people can identify situations in which they wish they could communicate better. Communicating is inherently complex because people and situations vary. For example, the 2005 film *Walk the Line* depicts the singer-songwriter Johnny Cash as thoroughly at ease in front of an audience but falling apart entirely when communicating on the home front. Cash's relationship with his wife, Vivian, seems to be marked by a lack of understanding, dishonesty, and an inability to connect on a personal level. The Academy Award–winning film reveals that Johnny Cash has a set of useful and unique skills and talents but that he must adapt those skills to suit the needs of different people and situations—as he does in his second, successful marriage to June Carter Cash.

In studying communication, our goal is to become competent communicators. We do not mean merely adequate, average, or "OK"; communication scholars use the term **competent** to describe communication that is effective and appropriate for a given situation, in which the communicators evaluate and reassess their own communication process (Wiemann & Backlund, 1980). We examine each of these aspects of competent communication in the following sections.

## Competent Communication Is Process-Oriented

An old sports adage says, "It's not whether you win or lose; it's how you play the game." Essentially, this means that the *process* (how you play) is more important than the *outcome* (who wins and who loses). In communication, an **outcome** has to do with the product of an interchange: in a negotiation, for example, the outcome may be getting a good deal on a product or getting a contract signed. In many contexts, the discussion of outcomes tends to focus on winning and losing, showing little concern about the means to achieve those outcomes. Competent communication, by contrast, is more concerned with **process**, which measures the success of communication by considering the methods by which an outcome is accomplished. Although outcomes obviously still play a role in a process analysis, *what* is said and *how* it is said take on greater significance. From the process perspective, it is better to optimize outcomes for both partners or achieve the goals of both partners than to maximize outcomes for or fulfill the goals of either one. From this perspective, mutual satisfaction is used as the gauge of success (Wiemann, 1977). A study of fathers and daughters, for example, finds that the most satisfactory relationships involved a matching of needs (such as communicating with each other for pleasure) and a balancing of control (complying with wishes while still stating personal opinions) (Punyanunt-Carter, 2005).

Process becomes very important when when long-term relationships are involved. For example, Geoff may win most of the arguments he has with his partner, Ryan, but if Ryan increasingly sees Geoff as stubborn and uncaring, he may eventually end the relationship. So success is really in the process (the way they argue and resolve differences) and not in the outcome (the winning of a specific argument).

Ethical considerations are a crucial part of this process. **Ethics** is the study of morals, specifically the moral choices individuals make in their relationships

Questions of right and wrong arise whenever people communicate. Ethical communication is fundamental to responsible thinking, decision-making, and the development of relationships and communities within and across contexts, cultures, channels, and media. Moreover, ethical communication enhances human worth and dignity by fostering truthfulness, fairness, responsibility, personal integrity, and respect for self and others. We believe that unethical communication threatens the quality of all communication and consequently the well-being of individuals and the society in which we live. Therefore we, the members of the National Communication Association, endorse and are committed to practicing the following principles of ethical communication:

▶ We advocate truthfulness, accuracy, honesty, and reason as essential to the integrity of communication.

▶ We endorse freedom of expression, diversity of perspective, and tolerance of dissent to achieve the informed and responsible decision-making fundamental to a civil society.

▶ We strive to understand and respect other communicators before evaluating and responding to their messages.

▶ We promote access to communication resources and opportunities as necessary to fulfill human potential and contribute to the well-being of families, communities, and society.

▶ We promote communication climates of caring and mutual understanding that respect the unique needs and characteristics of individual communicators.

▶ We condemn communication that degrades individuals and humanity through distortion, intimidation, coercion, and violence, and through the expression of intolerance and hatred.

▶ We are committed to the courageous expression of personal convictions in pursuit of fairness and justice.

▶ We advocate sharing information, opinions, and feelings when facing significant choices while also respecting privacy and confidentiality.

▶ We accept responsibility for the short- and long-term consequences for our own communication and expect the same of others.

● **NICK NAYLOR,** the chief spokesperson for tobacco lobbyists in *Thank You for Smoking,* uses all sorts of un-ethical means in order to spin a positive image of cigarettes.

● **TOM CRUISE'S** couch-jumping moment on *The Oprah Winfrey Show* was so bizarre, he became the butt of comedians' and late-night show hosts' jokes.

with others. Your personal values, along with your culture's values (Casmir, 1997), provide guidance on how to construct your messages appropriately as well as how to analyze messages directed toward you (Christians & Traber, 1997). Ethical concerns arise whenever standards of right and wrong exert a significant impact on communication behavior (Johannesen, 1996). A political spokesperson may spin the truth in order to garner support for his candidate. Although he may achieve the outcome he wants (a jump in the polls, for example), his communication will not be considered competent if it is manipulative, exploitive, or unethical.

## Competent Communication Is Appropriate and Effective

Do you speak to your grandmother the same way you talk to your friends? Would a doctor ask her husband to do something the same way she would ask her office receptionist? What kind of response would you get if you addressed a toddler the same way you talk to your professors? Competent, successful communicators adjust their behavior to suit particular individuals and situations. To communicate well, we must ensure that our communication is both appropriate and effective.

### Appropriate Behavior

We may forgive very young children for making attempts to jump or climb on the furniture, but a grown man? A grown man in an interview . . . on national television? Yet in May 2005, the actor Tom Cruise didn't think twice about jumping up and down on Oprah Winfrey's couch as the popular talk show host interviewed him about his budding relationship with actress Katie Holmes.

Communication behavior is appropriate when it meets the demands of the situation, as well as the expectations of one's specific communication partner and any other people present. Most of us know that talk show interviews usually involve a host asking guests questions. For viewer interest, the host might play a clip from a performer's upcoming movie or ask a singer to sing. And usually there's some celebrity gossip. But using the host's couch like a trampoline? Tom Cruise defied Oprah's expectations, as well as those of the audience, the viewers, and even his production and distribution company, Paramount Pictures, which ended a long-term relationship with Cruise a year later, citing his erratic behavior and unacceptable conduct.

In almost all situations, cultural norms and rules set the standards for expectations. For example, it would be entirely acceptable to pray out loud in the presence of others while a worship band performs at a Pentecostal Christian church, but you'd be less likely to see that at a Catholic church. Similarly, research shows that women tend to feel more comfortable expressing emotional caring to one another, often outright (using words of sympathy and comforting gestures), while men often feel limited by cultural expectations that insist they show caring in less open ways (Burleson, Holmstrom, & Gilstrap, 2005).

A successful communicator needs to develop the ability to determine what is appropriate and what is not in a variety of cultures and situations. Your ability to have a number of behaviors at your disposal and your willingness to use different communication behaviors in different situations is known as your *behavioral flexibility*. So while you might love to talk about politics or your grades when you're with your friends, you might decide that it's just not appropriate at Passover dinner at your Aunt Myra's.

**CONNECT**

One skill that can help you communicate appropriately is *self-monitoring*. As you learn in Chapter 2, the ability to monitor yourself and your environment for clues on how to behave is quite powerful. At a party, you can assess how formal or informal a situation is, what types of messages are considered acceptable or off-limits, and so on. Such knowledge allows you to tailor your communication to be competent in your environment.

---

# EVALUATINGCOMMUNICATIONETHICS

## Gina's Confrontational Style

You and Gina have been friends since your first year of college. You both majored in marketing, you worked together often throughout college, and now the two of you are hunting for advertising jobs in Denver. You've always found Gina's authenticity refreshing and fun—she has a bold style of dress, a boisterous laugh, and a big and unbridled personality.

But lately you are noticing that Gina's brand of "authenticity" is becoming harsh and somewhat confrontational. When the two of you go shopping for interview clothes, Gina gravitates toward very short skirts and sweaters that are perhaps a little too casual for the workplace. When the saleswoman comments that she might want to appear a bit more conservative, Gina responds abruptly, "That is a matter of opinion."

You can see that people are not responding well to Gina's communication style, both in her way of speaking and in her manner of dress, but you're not sure if Gina is aware that it is a problem. You are sure that Gina could be more polished if she wanted to be, but you are hesitant to make suggestions. After all, what right do you have to tell your friend to change? Is it really Gina's problem anyway, or is it other people's problem for not appreciating Gina for the person she is? And who is to say whether your conservative manner is more likely to land you a job than Gina's brash attitude?

**THINK ABOUT THIS**

❶ What do you think is at issue here? List the multiple dynamics that could be involved in this ethical communication dilemma.

❷ Using your list, consider a fictional conversation with Gina. What are the ethical considerations you must keep in mind when confronting her?

❸ Imagine you are Gina. Would you want to know if others respond negatively to your communication style? What ethical considerations would you want for someone to keep in mind when raising a sensitive issue like this?

# WIREDFORCOMMUNICATION

**THINK ABOUT THIS**

## E-Mail Etiquette: How *Not* to Communicate with Your Professor

From: student@college.edu
Sent: Tuesday, September 9, 2008 11:42 A.M.
To: professor@college.edu
Subject: hey

hey, sorry i missed class today . . . i had a little too much fun last nite had a rough time waking up;)
can you E-mail me your teaching notes ASAP? Tnx.

• • •

E-mails, when used effectively, are a valuable educational tool. They allow college students to ask questions outside of class and let professors provide instant feedback, making instructors more accessible than ever before. And while that's a great thing, many professors are complaining that some student e-mails are getting out of control—they're written informally, address inappropriate subject matter, or are outrageously demanding. The sample e-mail reprinted here manages to be all three at once: it hits the trifecta of communication incompetence.

### Informal

An e-mail to your professor isn't like posting something on your friend's Facebook wall; different communication contexts carry different expectations. Your message should be formal. It should open with a salutation ("Dear Professor Smith") and close with a proper signature ("Best, Kate" or "Thanks in advance, Jacob"). The rules of grammar, spelling, and capitalization all apply. There should be a clear subject line that should be appropriate to the content of the e-mail (otherwise, your professor may reject your e-mail as spam).

### Inappropriate

The e-mail shown here is wholly inappropriate for student-professor correspondence. There's a halfhearted attempt at an apology and a thinly veiled reference to being hungover on the day of class. Here, as with any communication, it's important to analyze your audience. There are some things you can say to your friends that you shouldn't say to your professor. Review your draft before you send it; if you think you've written something that you think *might* offend your audience, take it out!

### Demanding

Many professors complain that student e-mails are becoming increasingly pushy in tone. Recipients of poor grades send nasty notes, absent students demand teaching notes, and many students send more than ten e-mails a day, expecting their professors to be available around the clock. This is partly due to the fact that the impersonality of e-mail makes it easier to act rudely; students are demanding things via e-mail that they wouldn't have the gall to demand in face-to-face interactions. But that, of course, is no excuse.

Some guidelines: don't clutter inboxes with a barrage of requests, and give recipients plenty of time to respond. Use the tools that your professor has provided, such as course syllabus, assignment sheets, or notes posted on a Web site; you may find that you already have what you need. And if you skipped class, don't ask your professor what you missed; that's what classmates are for.

**1** What is the value of an effective and appropriate subject line in an e-mail? In what ways might the subject line influence your instructor's impression of the message and its sender?

**2** Why might students tend to use e-mail when a phone call or an office visit would be more appropriate? In what ways does the choice of communication channel influence the content and style of the message?

**3** What are the advantages of e-mail over other channels of communication when contacting a professor? How might a student capitalize on those advantages?

## Effective Behavior

Behaving appropriately is not enough to ensure success in communication. Competent communication must also be effective—it must help you meet your goals. This might sound obvious, but in practice it is not always easy to know what messages will work best—and it gets even more complicated when you have more than one goal (Canary, Cody, & Smith, 1994). For example, Travis is in a conflict with his fiancée, Leah, over whose family they will visit at Thanksgiving. Travis wants to meet several competing—even conflicting—goals: he wants to see his family, but he also wants Leah to be happy, to join him with his family, and to see him as reasonable.

If you have some knowledge of your partner's expectations, you have a great advantage in deciding which messages will be relatively more effective than others. For example, if Travis knows that Leah would like to spend Thanksgiving with her family because she wants to see her elderly grandmother, he might suggest that they spend the four-day Thanksgiving weekend with his family but the longer Christmas–New Year holiday with hers. In addition, knowing that you have multiple goals and prioritizing them—a task that is not always easy—can help you construct effective messages. If Leah thinks that spending Thanksgiving with her family and visiting her grandmother is a more important goal than pleasing Travis, she can construct an effective message that lets him know that she's sorry to let him down but that she absolutely must return home.

What is effective might not always be appropriate communication in other contexts. For example, research shows that many students feel that their most effective teachers are those who are organized, logical, enthusiastic, and approachable (Kramer & Pier, 1999). But just because it works in the classroom doesn't mean it's always appropriate. If your roommate handed you a detailed syllabus of a day-by-day schedule of what you should read, write, and do for the next semester while in your apartment, you might be both puzzled and annoyed. Similarly, Lauren appreciates her best friend Morgan because they can share the most intimate details of their lives with each other as is appropriate in a close friendship. But if Lauren's manager, Allison, were to share the same kind of extremely personal information with her, Lauren might feel uncomfortable and conclude that Allison is an ineffective manager.

● WHILE *SEX AND THE CITY*'S Miranda might be able to discuss the details of her relationships with her girlfriends, it would be inappropriate for her to have the same conversation with her coworkers.

## Competent Communication Involves Communication Skills

Successful sports figures, actors, educators, public officials, and musicians all have a well-developed set of skills that allow them to do their work successfully, inspiring others in the process. But having exemplary skills in one area does not make an individual competent overall. A professional musician may excel at piano and guitar but may have a great deal of difficulty with a particular academic subject. The same idea is true for great communicators: a professor who excels at public speaking may deliver upbeat and eloquent lectures in front of a classroom but may falter in front of a small group of colleagues at an academic conference.

Communication skills are behavioral routines based on social understandings; they are used by communicators to achieve particular goals (such as asking for a raise, maintaining a relationship, or working successfully as a team member in an organization). You may know people who have few communication skills and do not use them in a very sophisticated manner but who are nonetheless in mutually satisfying long-term relationships. Conversely, even the most highly skilled communicator may be involved in an unsatisfying relationship.

People who are judged to be incompetent in some situations are often unaware that they are unskilled; their inflated image of themselves seems to keep them from adjusting their behavior to use more effective skills (Dunning & Kruger, 1999). For example, you may believe that you are a great team player and that working in a class group is easy. Imagine your surprise when evaluation time comes around and group members describe you as "bossy" and complain that you "micromanage" them. You may be very good at leading a team but less adept at working alongside others as an equal; you may need to learn new communication skills in order to be a competent group member. Simply having communication skills does not guarantee communication competence, although having a number of skills does increase your behavioral options, thereby boosting your odds of success.

## Modeling Communication

As we've stated at various points in this chapter, the communication process is infinitely complex. For this reason, scholars have generated different models, or visual representations, of the process so that we may have another helpful way to examine our communication. Studying these models allows us to improve on our own communication while helping us learn more about others and the situations in which we find ourselves. Let's begin with the most basic representation of communication, the linear model.

### The Linear Model

The simplest communication is linear. In a simple **linear model** of communication (see Figure 1.1), a **sender** originates communication, with words or action; those words or actions constitute the **message**. The message must be carried through a specific channel (air and sound waves, written or visual, over telephone

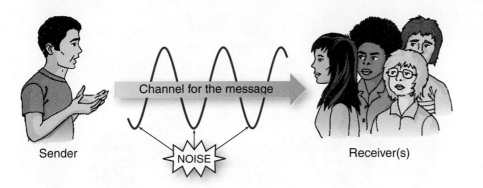

FIGURE 1.1
**LINEAR MODEL**

lines, cables, or electronic transmissions). Along the way, some interference, called **noise**, occurs, so that the message arrives (changed in some way from the original) at its target, the **receiver** (Shannon & Weaver, 1949).

The linear picture of communication is limited. A message is sent—end of story. There is no information on whether (or how) the message was received by anyone. This model illustrates how television and radio transfer messages to the public: the receiver does not play an active role. Linear communication can occur outside of media, though it is less common. The basic terms of the linear model are important to the building of more complex pictures of communication.

## The Interaction Model

An **interaction model** exhibits communication between sender and receiver that incorporates feedback (see Figure 1.2). **Feedback** is a message from the receiver to the sender that illustrates responses that occur when two or more people communicate. As with the linear model, noise occurs along the way.

Feedback can be a verbal message (your friend invites you to a party on Friday night, and you reply, "About nine?"), a nonverbal message (your roommate asks if you enjoyed the dinner, and you look up, smile, and nod), or both (you frown while saying, "I don't think I understand"). Communicators take turns sending messages in the interaction model.

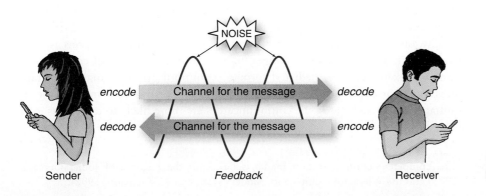

FIGURE 1.2
**INTERACTION MODEL**

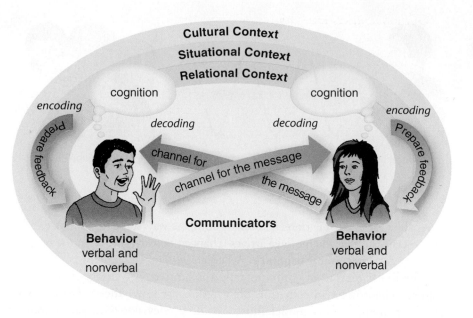

FIGURE 1.3
COMPETENT
COMMUNICATION MODEL

## The Competent Communication Model

Though each of these models is helpful in illustrating the communication process, neither manages to capture the complex process of competent communication that we talked about in the preceding section (Wiemann & Backlund, 1980).

To illustrate this complex process, we developed a model of communication that shows effective and appropriate communication (see Figure 1.3). This **competent communication model** is *transactional:* the individuals (or groups or organizations) communicate *simultaneously,* sending and receiving messages (both verbal and nonverbal) at the same moment in time, within a relational context, a situational context, and a cultural context.[2]

The link between communication behaviors is shown in this model by the arrows representing the messages being sent and received. In face-to-face communication, the behaviors of both communicators influence each individual at the same time. So the communicators are simultaneously encoding (sending) messages while decoding (receiving) communication behaviors. For example, Brianna is smiling and nodding at Cliff without saying anything as he talks about his golf game; she is sending messages of encouragement while receiving his verbal messages. Cliff is sending all sorts of messages about his putts and drives of the day, but he is also receiving messages from Brianna that he interprets as positive interest. This transaction changes slightly in different types of communication. For example, in a mediated form of communication—e-mail or instant messaging, for example—the sending and receiving of messages may not be simultaneous. In such cases, the communicators are more likely to take turns, or a delay in time may elapse between messages.

---

[2]The competent communication model is based on the research of John Wiemann (1977) and the Wiemann Competence Model (Wiemann & Wiemann, 1992).

Our model takes into account not only the transactional nature of communication but also the role of communicators themselves—their internal thoughts and influences as well as the various contexts in which they operate. There are four main spheres of influence at play in the competent communication model:

► The *communicators*. Two individuals are shown here, but many variations are possible: individual speaking to an audience, multiple individuals in a group communicating, and so on.

► The *relational context* in which the communication takes place.

► The *situational context* in which the communication occurs.

► The *cultural context* that frames the interaction.

Let's take a more in-depth look at each of these influences, as they are powerful and important considerations for effective and appropriate communication.

## The Communicators

The most obvious part of any communication situation is the communicators—the individuals who are engaged in communication. When sending and receiving messages, each communicator is influenced by **cognitions**, the thoughts that individuals have about themselves and others, including their understanding and awareness of who they are (smart, funny, compassionate, and so on), how well they like who they are, and how successful they think they are. We discuss this process in much more depth in Chapter 2, but for now, understand that your cognitions influence your behavior when you communicate. **Behavior** is observable communication, including both verbal messages (the words you use) and nonverbal messages (your facial expressions, body movements, clothing, and gestures). So your cognitions inform your behavior—the messages you encode and send—which are then received and decoded by your communication partner. The communication partner's own personal cognitions influence how he or she interprets the message before preparing feedback by encoding a new verbal or nonverbal message that is sent to you.

This constant cycle of communication can be seen in the following example. Devon knows that he's a good student, but he struggles with math, chemistry, and physics, and this embarrasses him because his mother is a medical doctor and his brother is an engineer. He rarely feels like he will succeed in these areas. He tells his friend Kayla about the fact that he failed his recent physics test and can't figure out why, since he studied for days beforehand. When he says these words, his eyes are downcast and he looks angry. Kayla, who likes to think that she's a good listener and who prides herself on the fact that she rarely responds emotionally to delicate situations, receives and decodes Devon's message, prepares feedback, and encodes and sends a message of her own: she calmly asks whether or not Devon contacted his physics professor or an academic tutor for extra help. Devon receives and decodes Kayla's message in light of his own cognitions about being a poor science student and feeling like he's always struggling with physics. He notices that Kayla made very direct eye contact, that she didn't smile, and that her message didn't include any

**AND YOU?**

Consider a recent difficult communication situation you encountered with one individual. How might your and your partner's behavior and cognitions have affected the communication? Does understanding this process make you more aware of these powerful forces?

words of sympathy, and he assumes she must be accusing him of not working hard enough. He prepares feedback and sends off another message—his eyes are large and his arms are crossed and he loudly and sarcastically states, "Right, yeah, I guess I was just too dumb to think about that."

Because communication situations can vary so greatly, successful communicators usually have a high degree of cognitive complexity. That is, they are able to consider multiple scenarios, formulate multiple theories, and make multiple interpretations when encoding and decoding messages. In this case, Kayla might have considered that Devon really just needed some friendly reassurance rather than advice; Devon might have realized that Kayla was just trying to offer a helpful suggestion.

### The Relational Context

All communication, from mundane business transactions to intimate discussions, occurs within the context of a relationship (represented by the inner sphere in the competent communication model). Every aspect of our communication is evaluated in terms of the relationship we have with the person or persons with whom we are interacting. A kiss, for example, has a different meaning when bestowed on your mother than it does when shared with your spouse or romantic partner. When you make a new acquaintance, saying "Let's be friends" can be an exciting invitation to get to know someone new, but saying "Let's be friends" to someone you've been dating for a year shuts down a whole lot of intimacy and could very well end the relationship entirely. The relationship itself is influenced by its past history as well as both parties' expectations for the current situation and for the future.

A relational history is the sum of the shared experiences of the individuals involved in the relationship. References to this common history (such as inside jokes) can be important in defining a relationship, both for the participants and for the participants' associates, because they indicate to you, your partner, and others that there is something special about this particular relationship. Your relational history may also affect what is appropriate in a particular circumstance. For example, you may give advice to a sibling or close friend without worrying about politeness, but you might be more hesitant, more deferential,

● **THE MEANING** of a kiss changes depending on context. A kiss between mother and son doesn't have the same meaning as a kiss between romantic partners.

or more indirect with an acquaintance, with whom you do not have an extensive history.

Our communication is also shaped by our expectations and goals for the relationship. Expectations and goals can be quite different. For example, high school sweethearts may want their relationship to continue (a goal), but at the same time, many couples know that going to college in different states may lead to a breakup (an expectation). With expectations and goals in mind, you formulate your behavior in the current conversation, and you interpret what your partner says in light of these same considerations. Clearly, our expectations and goals differ according to each relationship. You may have very specific goals and expectations for a conversation with the clerk at a shoe store in your local mall, for example, even if you don't expect the relationship to last beyond requesting a pair of size 14 Air Jordans to try on. On the other hand, both immediate and long-term goals may come into play in a conversation with a sister, a romantic partner, or a professor. Expectations and goals can and do change during the course of conversations, and they certainly change over the life span of a relationship.

## The Situational Context

Have you ever seen that episode ("Peter, Peter, Caviar Eater") of *Family Guy* where Lois inherits her deceased aunt's mansion in Newport, Rhode Island? Peter and Lois dine with their wealthy neighbors at the yacht club, but they get kicked out after Peter shares inappropriate stories, causing one man to become ill. Great dinner conversation. What happened here? Well, Peter failed to consider the situational context, which is determined by the particular circumstances surrounding communication, including social environment (a loud, boisterous party versus an intimate dinner for two), physical place (at home in the kitchen versus at Chicago's O'Hare International Airport), and specific events and situations (a wedding versus a funeral). The situational context (represented by the middle sphere in the competent communication model) also includes where you live and work, your home or office decorations, the time of day or night, and even the current events in the particular environment at the time.

For example, if Kevin gets home from work and asks Rhiannon what's for dinner and Rhiannon shrieks, Kevin might want to consider the context when he interprets her remark. Looking around, he might see that his wife is still in her suit, meaning that she only just got home from a long day at work. He might notice that the kitchen sink is clogged, the dog has gotten sick on the living room rug, and the laundry (his chore) is still sitting, unfolded, on the couch because he didn't get around to finishing it. By considering the context, Kevin is able to ascertain that Rhiannon is stressed because of these situational factors; if he doesn't consider the context, he might mistakenly conclude that she is mad at him.

## The Cultural Context

Finally, we must discuss the fact that all communication takes place within the powerful context of the surrounding culture (represented by the outermost

### AND YOU?

What relational, situational, and cultural contexts are influencing you as you read this book? Consider your gender, ethnicity, academic or socioeconomic background, and other factors. Have you studied communication or speech before? Have you taken a course with this professor before? What expectations and goals do you have for this book and this course?

Organizations also develop their own cultures, which have a huge impact on communication. You might work for a company that encourages casual dress, informal meetings, and the ability to openly share thoughts with your manager. Or you might work for an organization that is much more formal and hierarchical. Your communication needs to be adjusted to be competent in a particular *organizational culture*. We address this topic in Chapter 10.

sphere of the competent communication model). Culture is the backdrop for the situational context, the relational context, and the communicators themselves. As discussed earlier, culture helps determine which messages are considered appropriate and effective, and it also strongly affects our cognitions. For example, Hannah comes from a culture that shows respect for elders by not questioning their authority and by cherishing possessions that have been passed down in the family for generations. Cole, by contrast, was raised in a culture that encourages him to talk back to and question elders and that values new possessions over old ones. Both Hannah and Cole view their own behaviors as natural—their cognitions about elders and antique possessions have been influenced by their culture. But when each looks at the other's behavior, it might seem odd or unnatural. If Hannah and Cole are to become friends, colleagues, or romantic partners, each would benefit from becoming interculturally sensitive to the other.

Cultural identity—how individuals view themselves as a member of a specific culture—influences the communication choices they make and how they interpret the messages they receive from others (Lindsley, 1999). Cultural identity is reinforced by the messages people receive from those in similar cultures. In our example, both Hannah's and Cole's cognitions have been reinforced by their respective friends and family, who share their cultural identity.

## The Study of Communication

If you've never studied communication before, right now you might feel like you know more about messages and relationships and communication contexts than you ever thought you'd need to know! But there is still so much more to study that can have a profound effect on your friendships, romantic relationships, group memberships, career, and overall success in life. You've seen that communicating well—communicating effectively, appropriately, and ethically—is not innate, nor is it common sense; it is a process that we can all improve on throughout our lives.

So what's behind this discipline? What do communication scholars (like us) do? What do we study, and where did we come from? Well, in democracies from ancient Greece to the United States, scholars realized early on that communication was crucial to helping people participate in the government. Public speaking, for example, was taught in America's first universities, partly to reinforce the powerful effect that speaking out can have on society (Dues & Brown, 2004). A similar concern for the public's welfare was the reason for adding professional journalism courses to university curricula at the beginning of the twentieth century, when the sensationalistic excesses of the "penny press" highlighted the need for newspeople who were trained in both the technical aspects of reporting and the ethical responsibilities of journalists in a free society.

Today, communication continues to be a dynamic and multifaceted discipline focused on improving interactions and relationships, including those between two individuals, between individuals of different cultures, between speakers and audiences, within small groups, in large organizations, and among nations and international organizations. (Table 1.2 on p. 31 illustrates some of the major areas of specialization and the focus of each.) The research in our field draws

# real communicator

**NAME:** Vicky Sands
**HOMETOWN:** Queens, New York
**OCCUPATION:** Manager in the Analytics Department of Bloomberg
**FUN FACT:** I own a puffer fish named Shamu.

I came to college at the State University of New York at Oneonta wanting to get involved in student government. I was looking at courses my freshman year, and Introduction to Speech Communication looked like it might be helpful—there were sections on the syllabus devoted to group communication, listening, leadership, conflict, public speaking, things like that. Perfect.

The class changed my life. I know that sounds corny, but I loved it—I ended up majoring in communication. Before, I'd get into a group discussion and I'd just be participating. Since I took the class, it is like I'm in a different world, privy to all sorts of secrets and things that other people don't catch onto, from nonverbal cues to seating arrangements.

I ended up running for student government, and I won! My junior year, I was elected class president. And I never stopped using things I learned in that first communication course. Our executive board meetings—meetings with me, the vice president, the treasurer, and the secretary—were absolutely crazy. The VP had a lot of ideas, but he was terribly shy. The treasurer had a highly aggressive and dominating personality. And the secretary was so sensitive, she felt like the treasurer was always picking on her. Argue—that's all we did in those meetings.

But I started using some of the concepts I learned in class. I spoke to each of them individually. I knew not to surprise anyone in a group

setting. Plus, I knew that people aren't going to listen to you unless they feel like you're on their side. So when I talked to the VP, I asked him a lot of probing questions—how do you think things are going, stuff like that. I wanted him to feel as if he had a voice, a real say in things. When I met with the treasurer, I was careful not to point any fingers because if I had his kind of personality, I'd shut right off if people came at me full of blame and anger. And I took the secretary out to lunch. I let each of them believe that I had a personal interest in hearing them out—and I did; I had a student government to run!

I didn't tell anyone that I was also meeting with everybody else. I wanted each of them to feel as if I was their ally. At the next meeting, I made sure to sit between the treasurer and the secretary and I began by asking the VP a question. Of course, the treasurer butted in immediately, but I told him to hear the VP out. The change was dramatic. The VP stiffened his back; he felt empowered. When he started talking, I looked at the treasurer, and the treasurer winked at me. I turned to the secretary, and she gave me a knowing nod. Everyone in that room thought we were in cahoots! It was our best meeting ever.

And it was just a matter of putting myself in other people's shoes. That's the class's best lesson. It takes you out of being self-absorbed. You have to pay attention to everyone and everything around you. And it works!

clear connections between these assorted types of relationships, and the principles of communication laid out in this chapter can be successfully applied to various communication situations and contexts. For example, as technology advances, communication becomes more complicated, expansive, and sometimes unclear; for most of human existence, an interpersonal relationship was limited to face-to-face interactions, later enhanced by mediated communication via phone or letters. But today, individuals strike up personal and business relationships through e-mail, social networking groups, and phone contact across the globe, often without ever meeting in person.

Throughout this book, we'll draw connections (through our CONNECT feature) to show how communication skills, concepts, and theories apply to various communication situations and offer scholarship from four distinct areas of the discipline:

**AND YOU?**

Did you choose to take this course, or is it required? Regardless of why you're here, what do you hope to learn? What kind of communication most interests or intrigues you? What part of this book or course do you think will be most applicable to your life, future study, or professional career?

▶ *Basic Communication Processes.* All communication involves the basic processes of perception, language, nonverbal communication, and listening. Skills that we develop in these areas inform the way we handle communication in a variety of contexts, from talking with friends to making presentations in front of a class or a large public audience. In the remainder of Part 1 of the book, you will learn how these basic processes affect every communication situation.

▶ *Interpersonal Communication.* As social animals, human beings cannot avoid forming interpersonal relationships and interacting with other individuals. Interpersonal communication is the study of communication between **dyads**, or pairs of individuals. Most students find this study particularly relevant to their lives as they negotiate their friendships, romantic relationships, family relationships, and social interactions. We investigate the exciting, nerve-racking, fun, confusing, tulmultuous, and rewarding world of relationships and conflict in Part 2 of this book. An in-depth analysis of interviewing—one of the most daunting and important types of interpersonal communication—is offered in the Appendix at the back of the book.

▶ *Group and Organizational Communication.* If you've ever tried to run a meeting, manage a class or work group, or plan a day trip for a bunch of friends, you know that as the number of people involved in a conversation, activity, or project increases, communication becomes more complicated. By studying the nature of group interactions, communication scholars help create strategies for managing the flow of information and interactions among individuals in small groups.

Organizational communication, as it is studied and practiced today, grew out of attempts to create optimal work conditions for the factory workforce during World War II. With most of the men on the battlefront, old-line managers found themselves uncertain about how to motivate their new workforce, which was suddenly largely female. Efforts to learn about management and motivation turned into concerns for the quality of the work environment. This fast-growing area of the discipline is becoming more and more important as communication technology redefines the very nature of organizations in terms of size and proximity. We'll explore this in Part 3 of the book.

▶ *Public Speaking.* Don't panic! We're going to provide a lot of help and guidance to assist you as you become a competent public speaker. Even if you've never had to speak in front of a group before, in Part 4 you'll learn not only how to research and develop a presentation but also how to connect with your audience on a personal level. We also offer tips on becoming a more critical audience member whether you are engaged with a speaker in a lecture hall, a protest rally, or a professional conference.

| Area of Study | Focus of Study |
| --- | --- |
| Rhetorical theory and criticism | Analyzing speeches and other public messages |
| Argumentation and debate | Persuasion, reasoning, logic, and presentation |
| Interpersonal communication | Basic two-person (dyadic) processes |
| Relational communication | Interpersonal communication in close relationships such as romances, families, and friendships |
| Small group communication | The function, dynamics, and performance of group members |
| Organizational communication | Communication efficiency and effectiveness in business and other organizations |
| Mass communication and media studies | The design and production of media messages and the identification and evaluation of media effects |
| Political communication | The study of politicians, voters, and audiences and their impact on one another |
| Public relations | The production of messages designed to improve the image of individuals and organizations |
| Intercultural communication | Communication rules and values across cultures and co-cultures |
| Family communication | Communication between parents and children and between generations |
| Health communication | The communication messages of health care providers and patients |
| Conflict management | Reducing adversarial messages in personal, organizational, and community contexts |
| Nonverbal communication | Nonlanguage codes that communicate |
| Communication technology and telecommunication studies | Development and application of new technologies in all communication situations |

**TABLE 1.2**

**COMMON AREAS OF SPECIALIZATION IN COMMUNICATION RESEARCH TODAY**

We are confident that this book will provide you with an enjoyable reading experience as well as help you improve your communication (and thus your life, your work, your relationships, and your ability to speak out).

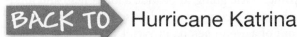

## BACK TO Hurricane Katrina

At the beginning of this chapter, we looked at the massive communication failures that contributed to the devastation and loss of life during and after Hurricane Katrina hit the U.S. Gulf Coast in 2005. Let's consider some of these issues in light of what you've learned in this chapter.

▶ Lack of communication was a crucial error before, during, and after the Katrina crisis. FEMA studies completed years prior to the hurricane warned of the potential for such a disaster in New Orleans but weren't publicized or acted on by the state or federal government.

▶ As Katrina approached, residents of the city refused to heed orders to evacuate, or were unable to leave because of sick relatives or a lack of transportation.

▶ In the aftermath of the storm, agency heads blamed citizens for ignoring broadcasted warnings, while the media criticized the government for ignoring images it was broadcasting of people in need.

▶ Cultural and situational contexts also played a role. Removed from the cultural and situational contexts, federal agencies in Washington may have underestimated the damage or assumed that the advance warnings were enough to persuade New Orleans residents to evacuate.

▶ Consider the effectiveness of the messages being sent regarding the storm. While the messages the media were sending from New Orleans clearly conveyed the degree of devastation, the messages sent by the government warning residents to evacuate prior to the storm were less effective.

## THINGS TO TRY

1. Think of someone (a family member, a celebrity, a politician, a friend, a professor) who exhibits competent communication in a particular context. What behaviors does this person exhibit that make him or her particularly effective? Would you want to model some of your own communication behavior after this person? Why or why not?

2. Keep a log of all the different channels (face-to-face, written, computer-mediated, telephonic, others) you use to communicate during the course of one day. Do you regularly communicate with a particular person via a specific channel (for example, you talk to your mother mostly over the phone, your romantic partner through text messages, and your childhood best friend via Facebook postings)?

What channels do you prefer to use when sending different types of messages (long and short messages, positive and negative messages, business and personal messages, and so on)?

3. Describe two communication situations, one in which someone was appropriate but not effective and one in which someone was effective but not very appropriate. Analyze these situations, considering the situational and relational contexts involved.

4. Consider a scene from a favorite film or novel. Imagine how it would change if you had not seen the rest of the film or read the entire novel. Would you come away from it with the same meaning if you did not understand the relational context between the characters or the situational context within the larger story?

## IF YOU'RE INTERESTED

*The History of Speech Communication: The Emergence of a Discipline, 1914–1945,* by Herman Cohen (Annandale, VA: Speech Communication Association, 1994)

A detailed history of communication in the beginning of the twentieth century, this book describes the people and organizations that led to the emergence of a true communication discipline. History buffs will enjoy the details and colorful depictions of the people who built communication today. Those of you who want to see how teaching communication developed will also find this an interesting read.

*Boxing Plato's Shadow: An Introduction to the Study of Human Communication,* by Michael Dues and Mary Brown (New York: McGraw-Hill, 2004)

This short history of the roots of communication study spans centuries. It includes views of communication from both humanistic and social perspectives and addresses the communication challenges facing us today and in the future.

*"Miscommunication" and Problematic Talk,* edited by Nikolas Coupland, Howard Giles, and John M. Wiemann (Newbury Park, CA: Sage, 1991)

Debunking the myth that communication is just "common sense," the fifteen chapters in this book address the failures of communication. The contributing authors examine "miscommunication" based on the challenges presented by gender, age, disability, culture, and profession.

*Sideways* (Fox Searchlight Pictures, 2004)

Follow the communication styles of two old friends as they spend a week before a wedding touring the Santa Barbara, California, wine country. Examine the ways in which they communicate as friends; consider the situational context and their relational history. Compare their communication with each other with their communication behavior with the women in their lives.

*Erin Brockovich* (Universal Studios, 2000)

Based on the true story of a Pacific Gas & Electric cover-up of contaminated water, this movie follows an inexperienced but tenacious woman as she pursues justice for the citizens of Hinkley, California. Erin illustrates how important effectiveness and appropriateness are to competent communication; she relentlessly pursues the facts and is not afraid to use her sexuality to help her get what she wants.

*Hitch* (Columbia Pictures, 2005)

This comedy romance features Alex "Hitch" Hitchens, a New York City "date doctor" who helps men woo the women of their dreams. Examine the goal orientation in the communication of the actors here. Hitch wants to remain anonymous to continue his work, but his control and affiliation needs can only be fulfilled with the cooperation of others, especially the gossip columnist that he falls in love with.

*The Break-Up* (Universal Pictures, 2006)

Although this is a comedy, it is also a serious look at the complexities of control and affiliation in a romantic relationship. Romantic partners Brooke and Gary call their relationship quits after a series of disputes, but neither will move out of the condo they have shared. Each of them exerts control in a variety of ways (some from their own ideas and others from friends trying to help them solve their problems) that illustrate that control is shared and cannot be forced on the other. Most important, Brooke and Gary discover that more control is not necessarily better and that their affiliation needs may be more important than being in control.

# REAL REFERENCE ▶ A Study Tool

**Now that you have finished reading this chapter, you can**

Define the communication process:

▶ **Communication** is the process by which individuals use symbols, signs, and behaviors to exchange information (p. 4).

▶ Communication is much more complex than "common sense" (p. 5).

Understand the functions of communication:

▶ The **functional perspective** examines how we use communication in **relationships** (p. 5).

▶ Relationship **interdependence** means that what we do affects others, and vice versa (p. 6).

▶ A communication relationship is based on sharing symbolic information (p. 6).

▶ There are three primary functions in communication:
  • Expressing **affiliation**, or the feelings we have for others (p. 6).
  • Relying on communication to accomplish particular objectives, or **goal achievement** (p. 7).
  • Negotiating **control**, the influence one individual, group, or organization has over others (p. 8).

Assess the quality, or communicative value, of communication by examining its six characteristics:

▶ Communication relies on **symbols**, arbitrary constructions related to the people, things, or concepts to which they refer (p. 10).

▶ Communication requires a shared **code**, or a set of symbols that create a meaningful message; **encoding** is the process of producing and sending a message, while **decoding** is the process of receiving it and making sense of it (pp. 11–12).

▶ Communication is linked to **culture**, the shared beliefs, values, and practices of a group of people, and **co-cultures**, smaller groups within a culture (p. 12).

▶ Communication may be intentional or spontaneous (p. 13).

▶ Communication requires a **channel**, the method through which it occurs (p. 13).

▶ Communication is a **transactional** process: you influence others while they influence you (p. 14).

Define what communication scholars consider to be **competent** communication:

▶ Competent communication is concerned with the **process** more than the **outcome** of communication (p. 16).

▶ **Ethics** is the study of morals (p. 17).

▶ Communication is appropriate when it meets the demands of the situation (p. 18).

▶ Communicators must determine what is appropriate in a situation, demonstrating behavioral flexibility (p. 19).

▶ Communication is effective when it achieves desired goals (p. 21).

Describe the various visual representations, or models, of communication:

▶ In the **linear model**, a **sender** originates the **message**, which is carried through a channel—perhaps interfered with by **noise**—to the **receiver** (pp. 22–23).

▶ The **interaction model** expands on the linear model by including **feedback** between the receiver and the sender (p. 23).

▶ The **competent communication model** is a transactional model incorporating three contextual spheres in which individuals communicate (p. 24).
  • *Communicators:* **Cognitions**, thoughts communicators have about themselves, influence **behavior**, observable communication, and how the message is interpreted before preparing feedback (p. 25).
  • *Relational context:* Communication occurs within the context of a relationship and is influenced by the relational history (p. 26).
  • *Situational context:* The circumstances surrounding communication, including social environment and physical place, influence communication (p. 27).
  • *Cultural context:* Cultural identity, how individuals view themselves as a member of a specific culture, influences communication choices (p. 27).

Understand the ways in which communication is vital to everyone:

▶ The discipline of communication grew out of the need to have informed citizens aware of the power of speaking out (p. 28).

▶ The discipline focuses on improving interactions and relationships between **dyads**, groups, organizations, and speakers and audiences (p. 30).

**Matisyahu:** Hasidic Jew or reggae star? Why not both?

# Perceiving the Self and Others

**In the heart of Brooklyn, New York,** an enclave of immigrants from Jamaica, the West Indies, and other islands lend the diverse neighborhood of Crown Heights a distinctly Caribbean flavor. But it was surprising to many in the music industry when in 2006 a new star emerged from one of Crown Heights' other ethnic enclaves. Matisyahu was suddenly one of the most popular reggae acts in dance halls and on alternative rock radio, and the video for his song "King Without a Crown" was in heavy rotation on MTV. His sound was unique, influenced by hip-hop grooves and folk music as well as roots reggae. But his look—and the beliefs it reflects—was probably the most surprising thing: Matisyahu is a Hasidic Jew. In his dress and in his lifestyle, Matisyahu adheres to strict religious customs. He wears the traditional long beard, black coat, and brimmed hat worn by most Hasidic men. And he lives by the rules of Talmudic law: he studies the Torah, keeps kosher, prays three times a day, and will not perform on the Sabbath; he points out that he cannot stage-dive during concerts because of restrictions on touching women who are not related to him. Matisyahu's music, steeped in Old Testament imagery, Hebrew language, and condemnations of secular life, ran counter to what most people expected to hear paired with traditional Caribbean beats.

While the notion of a Hasidic Jew performing music traditionally associated with Caribbean blacks might seem novel, to the singer it was a natural fit. Born Matthew Miller and raised in the New York suburbs, Matisyahu is a *baal teshuvah*, a secular Jew who discovered Orthodox Judaism in his twenties. His music blends the influences of his dreadlocked youth—much of it spent listening to reggae masters like Bob Marley and following the jam band Phish around on tour—with his newfound spirituality and lifestyle. To the artist, the connection between the two worlds is not strange at all.

**After you have finished reading this chapter, you will be able to**

○ Understand how our personal perspective on the world influences our communication

○ Explain how we use and misuse schemas when communicating with others

○ Discuss how and why we use attributions to explain behavior

○ Understand how cultural differences influence perception

○ Identify how our self-concept—who we think we are—influences communication

○ Describe how our cognitions about ourselves and our behavior affect our communication with others

**W**e all have a unique way of perceiving ourselves, others, and the world around us. As we discussed in the first chapter, **perception** is a cognitive process through which we interpret our experiences and come to our own unique understandings. Our thoughts and cognitions influence how and what we communicate to others and at the same time influence the way that we interpret the behaviors and messages that others send to us. We perceive, and others around us perceive at the same time, though we may not perceive the same thing. Consider, for example, how different individuals' perceptions about reggae music and Hasidic Jews might influence the way they receive Matisyahu's music. Think also about how Matisyahu's perceptions of music and religion have shaped his art. As you can see, understanding the perception process—and its role in communication—is crucial to our success as communicators. In this chapter, we look at how we see ourselves, how we see others, and how culture affects both of these processes.

## Perception: Making Sense of Your World

It's eight o'clock on a Wednesday night, and a roomful of singles are gathered at an Atlanta hot spot for an interesting event: over the next hour and a half, each woman will be introduced to no fewer than twenty eligible men. The problem: she'll have only three minutes with each of them. Each pair will divulge their first names, perhaps their occupations, where they're from, and why they're there (or at least why they say they're there!).

Speed dating is a hot trend in many metropolitan areas.[1] Organized by up-start companies that promise to screen applicants and put together large groups of potentially compatible singles, the event is arranged so that each single person is introduced to anywhere from ten to twenty potential mates, with whom they spend a short interval of time (usually less than ten minutes) to see if there is any "chemistry." But how much can one person learn about another in three minutes? Or even ten minutes?

The truth is that for better or for worse, you glean quite a bit of information from first impressions. Irina might tell Adam that she's thirty-one, is a public relations executive, was born in Milwaukee but has lived in Atlanta for nine years, and has a passion for *film noir*. Adam might hear all this but also notice that Irina is quite tall and very attractive, that she meets his gaze with steady eye contact, and that she appears quite assertive in her mannerisms. This information might lead him to make certain conclusions about her: "She is probably quite successful in her job," he thinks. "She might even make more money than I do." Adam might also notice that Irina is what he considers a "funky" dresser—she wears lots of brightly colored bead jewelry along with her conservative business suit. This, and her mention of *film noir*, puts him off a bit—Adam wonders if she's an "artsy" type. His last girlfriend was into art and was always dragging him off to gallery openings that he found painfully boring and pretentious. He feels a little intimidated by Irina and decides that they probably aren't compatible.

---

[1]This speed-dating trend is found not just in the United States. It is also popular in England and India (Doshi, 2005, p. 60).

Even during the briefest of encounters, you are barraged with information: the exact words of the message, the person's tone of voice, his or her facial expression, the level of eye contact. As all this information comes at you, you take in only part of it. **Communication processing** is the means by which you gather, organize, and evaluate the information you receive. Although you receive information through your basic senses, receiving information is just the beginning of the process. As with Adam's evaluation of Irina, your ability to process communication goes far beyond what you can see, hear, or touch and involves a number of highly personal factors. Whether you are looking at a painting, making a new acquaintance, or recounting the details of a specific event, your interpretation of what you see, hear, or experience will be unique to you, at least to some degree, because of the ways in which you select, organize, and interpret information.

● **WHEN OTHERS** approach you at a speed-dating event, you immediately start forming opinions about them. How they're dressed, the sound of their voice, and their smile all play into whether or not you feel a connection with these potential partners.

## Selecting Information

If you've ever listened to testimony at a trial (or seen one on TV), you may have been struck by how one witness will remember the exact time of the accident or the color and make of the cars involved, while another witness will describe the scene and note the sequence of events. They both saw the same accident but selected different parts of it to remember. In any situation, we are faced with a great deal of information, which we must sift through to determine what is important. In our speed-dating example, Adam is taking in some of the information Irina provides: what she says, how she says it, what she looks like, and how she presents herself. But just as he has chosen to pay attention to some information, other information may have escaped his notice. The next man Irina meets might notice entirely different things that Adam didn't see at all. For example, Ben might note that Irina's nails are bitten to the quick and that she nervously shakes her leg throughout their conversation and conclude that she's a high-strung person or even a little neurotic. Of course, it is possible that Ben and Adam were exposed to different information: perhaps Irina was nervous with Ben but not with Adam. But often people can come to vastly different conclusions even in the exact same circumstances. This is because each individual organizes and adapts his or her perceptions into existing memory bases called *schemas*.

## Schemas: Organizing Perceptions

As you receive information, you have to make sense of it. To do so, you rely not merely on the new information but also on how it fits with information you already have. For example, in evaluating Irina, speed dater Adam makes associations with his own experience and his own feelings. He compares Irina to his old girlfriend ("artsy") and to himself, guessing about her career and income. Adam, like all of us, is making sense of the endless inputs he receives through **schemas**, mental

## AND YOU?

Think back to your first impressions of two different people, one whom you immediately liked and one who made a more negative impression. What role might your schemas have played in these first impressions? Did these individuals remind you of other people you like or dislike? Did they exhibit traits that you have found attractive or unattractive in others?

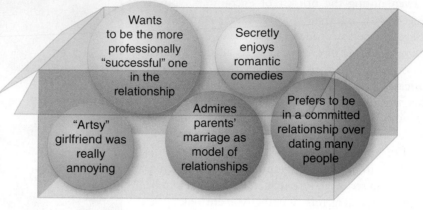

**FIGURE 2.1**

**ADAM'S SCHEMA ABOUT DATING AND RELATIONSHIPS** Our schemas affect our communication and our relationships. Here is Adam's schema for dating and relationships, represented as a box containing pieces of information from various sources in his life.

structures that put together related bits of information (Fiske & Taylor, 1991) (see Figure 2.1). Once put together, these chunks of information form patterns to create meaning at a more complex level.

## The Function of Schemas

In essence, schemas help you understand how things work or anticipate how they should proceed. Communicators retrieve schemas from memory and interpret new information, people, and situations in accordance with those schemas. For example, imagine that during your walk across campus, a classmate approaches and says, "Hey, what's up?" An existing schema (memory of past encounters) tells you that you will exchange hellos and then, after some small talk, go your separate ways. Your expectations for the interaction come from your schemas. Thus your schemas assist your perception process. When you recognize one component of a schema, the entire schema is activated and tells you what will most probably happen next.

As you go through life, you continually perceive new bits of information that help you structure and understand different situations. Your schemas adjust and enrich themselves through this process. Consider the popular *Harry Potter* books, in which author J. K. Rowling creates a world that continually challenges readers' (and Harry's) preconceived schemas. When young Harry first arrives at Hogwarts, he is both taken aback and delighted by his new environment: candles float, broomsticks fly, chess pieces move by themselves. Such magical objects and situations do not fit Harry's existing schemas of how things work. Yet as he moves through his seven years at Hogwarts, his schemas evolve: things that surprised him in year one no longer raise an eyebrow in year six.

## Challenges with Schemas and Perception

The schema process is a critical part of communication competence. To send and receive messages that are effective and appropriate, you must be able to process information in a way that makes sense to you but also has a high likelihood of being accurately perceived by others. Schemas can help you do all of these things. However, sometimes schemas can make you a less perceptive communicator; they may cloud your judgment or cause you to rely on stereotypes (which

● **SEEING** "Mad-Eye Moody" use the Unforgivable Curses in Defense Against the Dark Arts in *Harry Potter and the Goblet of Fire* shocked Harry and made him feel uncomfortable. However, by the seventh book, hearing them no longer seems jarring.

we discuss later in this chapter) or misinformation. Communication researchers note that schemas present three key challenges to competent communication: mindlessness, selective perception, and undue influence.

### Mindlessness.
To communicate competently, you must be focused on the task at hand, a process referred to as *mindfulness*. Schemas, however, may make you a less critical processor of information by producing a state of **mindlessness**. Mindlessness has its perks: it allows you to go through certain communication transactions automatically; you do not have to consciously think about how to greet a friend on campus every time you run across one or consider how to place an order every time you go to a restaurant. But mindlessness can be problematic. The noted communication professor and consultant Michael Roloff (1980) describes three signs of mindlessness: reduced cognitive activity, inaccurate recall, and uncritical evaluation. First, reduced cognitive activity means that when schemas take effect, you will simply think less or have fewer thoughts. A second sign of mindlessness is the inaccurate recall of information. Your friend wants to know all the details about the party she missed, but you were "on automatic pilot" to such an extent that you can't give the names of all the people there or specifics about their interactions. The third sign of mindlessness is the uncritical evaluation of what is processed. A mindless processor will not question the information that is being received and will react to the situation passively or lazily.

### Selective perception.
A second and related perceptual challenge facing communicators is succumbing to the biased nature of perception, referred to as **selective perception**. Whereas mindlessness is passive, selective perception is usually active, critical thought. If a group of five people watch a televised debate between two political candidates, they will likely have five different interpretations of what took place and what was important. Based on their existing schemas, one person might focus on budget deficits; another might be most concerned with foreign affairs, while a third might be intrigued only with the candidates' physical appearance. Their discussion of the debate will often result in arguments. Selective perception can be explained in part by the presence or absence of schemas. A person who is keenly interested in economics likely has a schema for ideas on balancing the federal budget and will pay attention to political opinions about it. By contrast, someone with no understanding of or interest in economic matters may not pay attention to something a speaker says about balancing the budget.

### Undue influence.
A third perceptual challenge that communicators deal with is resisting the **undue influence** of other people. Undue influence occurs when you give greater credibility or importance to something shown or said than should be the case. People have a tendency to give undue influence to male friends when discussing the topic of sports. Others may allow undue influence from their parents simply because people we regard highly have a greater chance of influencing our perceptions regardless of their accuracy, motives, or intentions.

Even the media can be a source of undue influence. Research has shown that people who watch talk shows develop perceptions that overestimate deviant behavior in society and develop less sensitive views of other people's suffering

**CONNECT**

If you've ever found yourself saying "Uh-huh" at the wrong time because you weren't paying attention during a conversation with a friend, you know that listening and mindlessness are a bad combination. In Chapter 5, you learn that competent listening involves being an *active,* rather than passive, participant in your communication situations and requires that you make conscious choices to decode your friend's message.

**AND YOU?**

What are your thoughts on the research showing that the media influence perception? Do you believe that you give undue influence to what you see on television or read about in magazines or the newspaper? Why or why not?

● GRAPHIC NEWS STORIES of muggings, murders, and brutal assaults might make you more likely to lock the doors and look repeatedly over your shoulder when you're out alone.

(Davis & Mares, 1998). Local media coverage of crimes also influences the perceptions that potential jurors have toward defendants. People who have been exposed to media reports are much more likely to perceive the defendants as guilty (Wright & Ross, 1997).

## Attributions: Interpreting Your Perceptions

When perceiving others, we often try to explain why they say something or act in a certain way, especially if their behavior does not exactly fit our existing schema. Personal characteristics that are used to explain other people's behavior are known as **attributions** (Jones, 1990). You make attributions to understand the causes of a behavior and to justify your perceptions, thus giving you greater control of the situation. Consider the following exchange:

EMMA    I'm heading over to Mark's place to help him study for our midterm. He has really been struggling this semester.

CALEB    Well, he was never exactly a rocket scientist.

Emma might be a bit surprised by Caleb's comment because he is not usually so blunt—or so mean! But if Emma can attribute his comment to his personality ("Caleb is jealous of my relationship with Mark"), she feels that she understands the situation more fully and that her perceptions are justified.

We make attributions about people all the time, and once we make an attribution, it exerts a very powerful effect on our communication. That is not, however, to say that our attributions are set in stone. Events or simply time can change how people perceive others. Seeing someone do something you thought the person incapable of, such as an unexpected act of kindness, can alter how you feel about the person, and such instances can change your attributions. **Interaction appearance theory** helps explain how people change their attributions of someone's physical appearance the more they interact (Albada, Knapp, & Theune, 2002). This theory suggests that as we get to know people better through positive interactions, we find them more socially attractive, which then leads to greater physical attraction. This is an interdependent process, in which the social interaction and relational attraction feed each other.

If you think back to past relationships, you may remember finding someone more attractive after you discovered, say, the person's quirky sense of humor. In this case, attributions work for the good of the relationship.

Attributions can be problematic too. One attribution pitfall is the **fundamental attribution error** (McLeod, Detenber, & Eveland, 2001; Ross & Nisbett, 1991), which explains our tendency to overemphasize the internal and underestimate the external causes of behaviors we observe. That is, when we see someone doing something wrong or inappropriate, we are likely to believe that the person has a character flaw (internal) rather than attribute that person's behavior to circumstances beyond his or her control or external factors ("Carla failed the midterm because she was too lazy to study"). When it comes to ourselves, however, the opposite effect is attributed. We usually attribute our own failures or negative circumstances to situational effects (external) and downplay our own culpability in the attribution ("I failed the midterm because my professor stinks").

## Improving Your Perceptions

It is not always easy to make accurate perceptions. For example, in the classic basketball film *Hoosiers*, Gene Hackman plays Hickory High basketball coach Norman Dale. Dale's small-town players are intimidated by the cavernous arena where they are to play for the Indiana state championship. Though they are aware that the basketball court is supposed to be regulation size, it looks enormous to them. It isn't until Dale uses a tape measure in front of their eyes to measure the height of the basket and the distance from the foul line that they start to perceive that the distances are no different from those in their tiny gym. This corrects their selective perception and restores their confidence.

We all tend at one time or another to perceive selectively or to be mindless. How do we overcome these tendencies? The following suggestions can help you improve your perception abilities and thus become a better communicator.

▶ *Verify your perceptions.* It may be natural to jump to some conclusions—to depend to some degree on existing schemas—but it is crucial that you take the time to confirm (or debunk) your conclusions about other people and events. At a park, you might see a parent yell at a small child and grab the child's arm. Your initial perception might be that the parent is extremely harsh and possibly even abusive. But look more closely—the child may have been about to reach for a sharp piece of a broken bottle on the ground.

▶ *Be thoughtful when you seek explanations.* Mindlessness causes us to rely on lazy forms of explanation for others' behaviors. Resist the natural tendency to fall back on the most obvious explanation for what you observe. For example, scuffles occasionally break out among players in college and professional sports. Your tendency may be to assume that the person who threw the first punch instigated the fight. Frequently, however, a fight starts when someone else says or does something that the fans cannot easily perceive: a hockey player might have thrown his stick high in the face of another player or may have uttered an offensive or derogatory term. In these situations, you need to ask yourself whether some event or action might have preceded or provoked what you observed.

▶ *Look beyond first impressions.* A third way to improve the accuracy of your perceptions is not to rely completely on your very first impressions, which often lead to inaccurate conclusions. Consider Meghan, who frequently comes off as gregarious and loud when people first meet her. Meghan is actually quite thoughtful and kind—she just loves meeting new people and is exuberant when asking questions while getting to know them. Whenever possible, it is wise to delay reaction or judgment until further perceptions are made.

## Perception in a Diverse World

A few generations ago, our great-grandparents may have gone months without coming into contact with someone from a different village or neighborhood; a wheelchair-bound child may have been unable to attend public schools; and in parts of this country, white and black Americans were not permitted to sit at the same lunch counter. In modern society, people from all walks of life learn, work, and play together; we continually interact with people from a vast array of cultural and ethnic backgrounds, lifestyles, and abilities. Through the use of technology, we are able to communicate with others across vast distances. A student in Louisville, Kentucky, can chat online with a student from Bangladesh; a salesman in Omaha, Nebraska, may have steady working relationships with clients in Tokyo. Our perceptions are inextricably linked to the wide diversity we encounter in the world.

● **DO YOU SHARE** a cultural identity with any of these individuals? Factors such as age, race, social class, gender, religious beliefs—even where we grew up—affect our own perceptions and the perceptions of others.

## The Cultural Context

As you likely know from experience, culture is an incredibly powerful context in communication: it has a profound effect on the way we perceive ourselves and the people around us. Think back to the model of competent communication presented in Chapter 1. The ring that comprises the cultural context is made up of all sorts of variables that make our perceptions unique: race, ethnicity, religion, politics, gender, sexual orientation, age, education, role, occupation, abilities/disabilities, geography, and so on. These differences are known as *diversity* (Loden & Rosener, 1991). They are the co-cultures defined in Chapter 1. To communicate effectively and appropriately in today's world, you must possess an understanding of and appreciation for people who perceive differently than you do. It's also important to understand the way your own unique background affects your perceptions. Let's look at an example.

In 2006, the publication of a dozen caricatures of the Islamic prophet Muhammad in a Danish newspaper sparked riots throughout the Muslim world. As fires burned in Middle Eastern cities, Westerners shook their heads in disbelief over what many perceived as an overreaction to a harmless editorial cartoon.[2] How did such a vast difference in perception come about? It is a complicated matter to be sure, but religion and geography are at the center of it. Religious beliefs can play a large role in shaping individuals' attitudes and values—they can imbue followers with a strong sense of right and wrong and inform their understanding of all aspects of life, from the creation of the world to restrictions on food and drink (Samovar & Porter, 2001). In this case, Muslims perceived a personal attack on their prophet and an affront to their religion, which prohibits any depiction of the Prophet. As Yunes Teinaz, spokesperson for the London Mosque and Islamic Cultural Center, noted at the time, "The European newspapers have published extremely offensive caricatures of the Prophet Muhammad. They are humiliating and racist. Muslims love the Prophet more than anyone—even their own families—and have a very strong belief that he is the messenger of God" ("Viewpoints," 2006). To many Westerners, however, the publication had more to do with freedom of expression and the right to critique individuals, governments, and religions. As the British journalist Munira Mirza pointed out, "There are a lot of British Muslims who I'm sure would not be offended by the cartoons. There are, of course, many who are upset and hurt but that's the point of living in a free society. No matter the price, the principle of freedom must be defended. Unless we stand up for freedom of speech, we are unable to engage freely and hold belief systems—of all kinds—to account" ("Viewpoints," 2006). At the center of this debate are two strongly held beliefs about what is sacred: the Prophet and the right to speak out about the Prophet (or anyone else for that matter).

You have likely encountered differing perceptions in your own life. Have you ever complained (or heard friends complain) about problems with closeness in a

**CONNECT**

To ensure that *diversity* is respected in professional situations, organizations (as well as the U. S. government) enact policies and codes of behavior to protect employees from hurtful, antagonistic communication regarding their sex, race, religion, national origin, sexual orientation, age, and abilities. This type of derogatory communication, known as *harassment,* is discussed in Chapter 10.

**AND YOU?**

What is your opinion on the scandal described here? Do you think that the newspaper was culturally insensitive? Do you think that some Muslims overreacted to the cartoon? Consider your answer to this question. How might your own co-cultures (gender, religion, age, and so on) influence your perception?

---

[2]American Muslims were more likely to share the perceptions of other Muslims rather than those of the majority of Americans. For example, the American Muslim Voice Web site (www.amuslimvoice.org) claimed that the publishing of the cartoons was hate speech, not freedom of expression, and likened the cartoons to the way that Nazi cartoons degraded Jews (Saeed, 2006).

friendship or romantic relationship with a member of the opposite sex? Even in the classroom, we get to hear all about it: "He doesn't listen to me," "All she ever wants to do is talk. She drives me nuts." Many people falsely wind up feeling that men and women are doomed to miscommunicate because we are essentially so "different." But much of the issue comes down to differences in perception. Julia Wood and Christopher Inman (1993) point out a "feminine bias" in portraying women as having more intense and emotionally rich friendships, prioritizing personal talk, and talking about feelings, thus having better communication. Wood

## COMMUNICATIONACROSSCULTURES

### Pregnancy, Perception, and Culture

Childbirth may have slowed down Jennifer Garner, but it didn't bring her life to a halt. Shortly after giving birth to a baby girl, Garner was greeting friends, meeting with personal trainers, granting interviews, promoting an upcoming movie, and getting ready for the final season of her TV show, *Alias*. Garner's case isn't all that unusual in America. In the United States, many mothers remain active after pregnancy. They hit the gym, return to work, and go on with their lives.

But in China, a new mom is traditionally expected to spend the first forty days after pregnancy behind closed doors in an effort to enhance her milk-producing ability. It's feared that chills might be harmful to healthy breast milk, and so windows must remain closed and bathing is forbidden. This practice is known as *zuo yuezi* (Tao, 2000). In order for *zuo yuezi* to succeed, household members and friends wait on the new mother, taking care of both her home and her personal needs. They are also expected to watch over and wait on the newborn infant. It is understood that the practice of *zuo yuezi* brings the women of the family, particularly the mothers, closer together.

Imagine how perceptions of women can be influenced by these two very different practices, were the two cultures to intermingle. In the United States, a woman from China might be regarded as lazy, rude, weak, or even superstitious by her American hosts because she is not attending to her own baby's needs. But in China, an American woman might be perceived as selfishly endangering the baby's health by not protecting the quality of her milk.

According to Pam O'Sullivan, the director of the BC Women's Birthing Program, significant cultural intermingling is occurring in her hospital in Vancouver, where there is a high density of both Chinese and Caucasian women (Williams, 2005). But once a hospital understands *why* certain practices are in play, it can execute policies to balance cultural differences and safety regulations. O'Sullivan explains, "We will push beds to the far end of the rooms to accommodate extended families and supply boiled water to Asian mothers who like to drink it to avoid stress. Although hygiene is very important, we will allow sponge bathing for women who traditionally avoid bathing and showering around births."

This kind of balance could not come about without first clarifying perceptions about a patient's culture.

**THINK ABOUT THIS**

❶ How might an American's perception of the *zuo yuezi* tradition lead to other perceptions about Chinese women and their home life, their friends, work, gender beliefs, and other matters? How might the reverse be true? How does one assumption often lead to others?

❷ Who has the responsibility to clarify perceptions?

❸ Are there instances in which making assumptions about another person's culture are helpful or necessary?

and Inman believe that both men and women seek close relationships and that they want these relationships to be meaningful, validating, and satisfying. Both sexes can benefit from understanding the gendered perceptions brought to the interaction. Masculine perceptions of closeness revolve around giving practical help or mutual assistance, doing things together (companionship), and engaging in activities that distract a loved one from troubles. Feminine perceptions of closeness are much more related to disclosing information and talking about personal topics—enjoying the simple process of talking in any manner. Both sexes can increase their communication competence by appreciating the perspective of traditionally gendered communication. Men can strive to share feelings more openly with close friends and romantic partners (traditionally feminine behaviors), while women can strive to share activities with friends and significant others and show care by doing things (traditionally masculine behaviors).

Although we cannot possibly look into every variable that constitutes the cultural context in perception, we would be remiss if we did not bring up one particular issue that has sparked lively discussions with our students: age. As instructors who work with many "traditional-age" college students (eighteen to twenty-three), we also see nontraditional students: parents in their thirties returning to start or complete their education, middle-aged adults looking to make a career change, and older adults seeking to learn something new. It is interesting to watch students of various ages interact and to call their attention to a few points. For example, young American adults often perceive older individuals as less vital, in sharp contrast to people from Eastern cultures, where older adults are considered wise and knowledgeable. Younger Americans often avoid interaction with older people (expecting to be uncomfortable and bored). Interestingly, older Americans often have a similar negative feeling about themselves. Why is this? One explanation is the influence of the media. Not many older adults are portrayed in a positive way in movies, on television, or in commercials, which may have a negative effect on people's perceptions of aging. Think about it: if young people are the ones experiencing adventure, romance, and intrigue in the media, what are the older people doing, sitting at home and feeling depressed? When older individuals are portrayed as strong, happy, and active, the result is a more positive self-image (Abhik & Harwood, 1997). Similarly, when younger individuals put aside their preconceptions and interact with their elders, they are often pleasantly surprised, and they are less likely to avoid communication with older adults if they perceive them as benevolent (kind, generous, wise) and personally vital (active, attractive, liberal, strong, healthy) (McCann, Dailey, Giles, & Ota, 2005). We see this in the classroom very often. When traditional and nontraditional students interact and work in pairs and groups, they often find much in common.

## Perceptual Barriers

Karl Krayer is an independent communication consultant who does diversity training for corporations, schools, and other organizations. Based on his experience, Krayer notes that successful intercultural communication requires mindfulness, being respectful of others, and maintaining an accurate perception of the situation. "Resistance to cultural diversity usually boils down to ignorance," Krayer says. "Once people understand other cultural groups better, it doesn't take long to see the fruits of the labor—that is, people working cooperatively together for a common cause" (personal communication, May 19, 2004). In our diverse world, perceptual challenges can give rise to potential barriers to competent communication, including narrow perspectives and stereotyping.

### A Narrow Perspective

In November 2005, Fox News commentator Bill O'Reilly and other broadcasters took to the airwaves to vent their rage over what they called the "war on Christmas." These critics complained that major department stores were ordering their employees to say "Happy Holidays" instead of "Merry Christmas" when helping customers. "I don't believe that most people who aren't Christian are offended by the words 'Merry Christmas,'" O'Reilly stated during his November 9 show. But when later in that same broadcast a marketing executive defended the practice of using more inclusive phrases, stating, "'Happy Holidays,' Bill, does not offend Christians," O'Reilly countered, "Yes, it does. It absolutely does. And I know that for a fact" (Media Matters, 2005).

Critics like O'Reilly may rail about the motivations behind what they think of as politically correct language, but acceptance or denial of diversity does play a role in how effectively we communicate. An inability to see beyond one's own beliefs and circumstances can make communication difficult. Individuals who fail to consider other cultural perspectives are said to suffer from **cultural myopia**, a form of nearsightedness grounded in the belief that one's own culture is appropriate and relevant in all situations and to all people (Loden & Rosener, 1991). Cultural myopia is especially dangerous when members of a dominant group in a society are unaware of or are insensitive toward the needs and values of members of others in the same society. Pundits like O'Reilly may make a living complaining about the nuances of political correctness, but they also blind themselves (and to some degree their audience) to alternative points of view.

We may experience myopia in conjunction with many aspects of cultural differences. Consider, for example, the shock that many Americans felt when Hurricane Katrina devastated the city of New Orleans in 2005, leaving countless residents trapped on rooftops or huddled in the Superdome for shelter. Many Americans watching this devastation on television wondered why New Orleans residents didn't just get into their cars and leave the city when the flood warnings were announced. Outsiders didn't understand the levee system or residents' strong allegiance to the city and its culture. For many upper- and middle-class Americans, the idea that a family might not own a car, might not be able to afford to stay in a hotel out of town, or might fear that its abandoned home would be looted never crossed their minds. They were blinded by their own circumstances, experiencing socioeconomic or geographical myopia.

AND YOU?

What is your opinion on Bill O'Reilly's comments? Is it insensitive to wish someone "Merry Christmas" if one is not sure that the individual celebrates this holiday? Should salespeople avoid messages about religion entirely? How might your religious beliefs—or lack of religious beliefs—affect your perceptions on this issue?

● MANY NEW ORLEANS RESIDENTS who did not evacuate for Hurricane Katrina found themselves without food, water, or shelter. They perceived their government as abandoning them, while outsiders perceived the residents as crazy for not leaving.

## *Stereotyping and Prejudice*

As you learned earlier in this chapter, we rely on schemas to organize information and create mental structures that suggest patterns and meaning. Yet schemas can be dangerous in a diverse society if we rely on them to make generalizations about people. **Stereotyping** is the act of fitting individuals into an existing schema without adjusting the schema appropriately; it involves organizing information about groups of people into categories so that you can generalize about their attitudes, behaviors, skills, morals, and habits. Stereotyping is an impression of a group of people that is fixed or set, so that when you meet an individual from this group, you apply your set of perceptions of the entire group to that individual.

Stereotypes may be positive, negative, or neutral; they may be about a group to which you belong or one that is different from your own. If you have a negative stereotype about corporate executives, for example, you may think that they are all greedy individuals participating in illegal financial activities (though many, if not most, are hardworking men and women who have climbed the ranks of the corporate ladder). Or if you have a positive stereotype about professors, you may revere all professors because of the work they do (though some will not deserve this reverence).

The effects of stereotyping can also be seen on a larger scale through the media. For example, marketers who craft their advertising messages to what they believe are the shared values of their audience practice stereotyping. Think of the television commercials for beer that air during sports telecasts. The advertisers are assuming certain stereotypes about their audiences—beer drinkers are primarily heterosexual males, and heterosexual males watch televised sports. This is why you see beer commercials involving highly sexualized women during football games. Little attention is paid to individual viewers—women, gay men, and men from cultures that discourage promiscuity are simply ignored.

Stereotypes lead to what is perhaps the most severe barrier to intercultural communication: **prejudice**, a deep-seated feeling of unkindness and ill will toward particular groups, usually based on negative stereotypes and feelings of superiority over those groups. These attitudes make it easy to protect your own group's attitudes and behaviors while abusing those of other people. At its most extreme, prejudice can lead to a belief that the lives of some people are worth less

● **IMAGINE BUDWEISER** advertising executives brainstorming this ad: "Who buys light beer?" "Women. They're always on a diet." Advertising campaigns generalize because they want to reach a large audience. Such tactics do not account for individual differences.

● IN *PRIDE AND PREJUDICE,* Elizabeth overhears Darcy dismissing her and quickly jumps to the conclusion that he is a pompous rich man. Only after getting to know him better and seeing the depths of his generosity does she change her opinion of him.

Stereotyping affects all communication contexts. For example, when you analyze your audience before giving a speech (Chapter 11), it can be easy to fall into stereotyping. You might decide not to give a persuasive speech at your Catholic college on the ordination of women because you think Catholics oppose this idea. But not all students at a religiously affiliated college are members of that religion—and not all Catholics oppose female ordination. You should avoid such stereotypes and remember that your audience consists of individuals.

than those of others; the entire institution of slavery in America flourished based on this belief. Even today, the cultural landscape is dotted with groups who advocate the notion of racial superiority.

Stereotypes lead us to judge others before we know all the facts. Subtle forms of prejudice seep into our communication all the time; we might notice a professor who calls on female students more than he does male students; we might find that we are more at ease talking to people who share our ethnic, racial, or religious background. Prejudice is not limited to groups, either. We might have preconceived ideas about an individual based on limited experience. If Shayla was feeling ill or grumpy on the day that Clark met her, he might come to the conclusion that she is sad or depressed all the time. This snap judgment tends to prejudice Clark toward Shayla and may color his perception of her, not only initially but in future communication as well. Clark is committing the kind of fundamental attribution error we discussed earlier in this chapter. Sadly, making these errors related to judgments about race, culture, or ethnicity is a common trap.

## Removing Perceptual Barriers

It may seem at times that the media and our own preconceived schemas combine to create a web of influence that makes it impossible to communicate effectively in a diverse world. Nonetheless, we can improve our communication skills to be more competent when we are interacting with people who are different from us. We must be mindful of the fact that although many groups share some experiences, individuals in each group have unique characteristics and experiences. A diverse society is knitted together from myriad co-cultures, and many individuals belong to a number of co-cultures at the same time. We

● **RENAISSANCE FAIRE** enthusiasts, Trekkies, bikers, and Goths are easily identifiable while they're "in costume." However, you shouldn't jump to the conclusion that they are all the same. There are variations within these co-cultures, and people also often identify with multiple co-cultures.

can improve our communication skills to be more competent when we are interacting with people who are different from us by taking the following steps to remove perceptual barriers:

▶ *Be mindful.* It is important to be mindful of the variations that exist within a group. Individuals are difficult to categorize. The open-minded and mindful process of emphasizing the unique qualities of each person (personality, intelligence, skills, and so forth), is one key to communication in a diverse world. These are the types of behaviors promoted by innovative race relations programs that promote more accurate knowledge of issues, attitudes, and behaviors related to race (Muthuswamy, Levine, & Gazel, 2006).

▶ *Consider multiple identities and co-cultures.* Do you describe yourself as a member of a specific group? For example, when asked to describe himself, Mike says he is "a techie and aspiring novelist from Ewing, New Jersey, who is obsessed with the band U2 and is an avid collector of DVDs." He doesn't even think to mention his sexuality or his ethnic background. Would you be surprised to learn that Mike is gay, black, and an immigrant from the Caribbean? In many communication situations, Mike might be judged first and foremost by those factors, even though he does not consider them the factors that define who he is. Acknowledging the many facets of a person's background and identity is crucial to avoiding fundamental attribution errors and stereotyping.

▶ *Expand your perspective.* Regardless of gender, age, sexual orientation, religion, or other characteristics, you can benefit from learning more about other groups. Plenty of experiences are available to you as a college student. Visit the Jewish Student Union's Sukkot service or the Christian Fellowship's Easter celebration; support the Women's Center in planning "Take Back the Night" on your campus. If your schedule permits, take a foreign-language class. And if you've always wondered about sushi but have never had it, give it a try.

▶ *Deconstruct your schemas.* You need to examine your own perceptions to see how you came to create schemas about different groups. Perhaps your thoughts about another group are influenced by stereotypes in the popular culture. Perhaps you subscribe to an idea about people of a specific race, ethnicity, age, or socioeconomic class based on images seen on television. Or perhaps you judge an entire group based on your experience with one or just a few individuals in that particular group. Understanding how your schemas were formed can help you modify them.

## Cognition: Perceiving Ourselves

In late 2004, pop diva Mariah Carey returned to the music scene with an odd request. She asked that her fans begin calling her by the nickname used by her closest friends: Mimi. Carey explained, "I am letting my guard down," noting that the name change was a celebration of "the fact that I've grown into a person and artist who no longer feels imprisoned by my insecurities or compelled to try and live up to someone else's version of Mariah Carey."

For some artists, changing their moniker is a way of signifying a new aspect of their music. But on some levels, name change pronouncements like Carey's reveal an attempt to change the person within, or at least to change the way we—and others—view our inner selves. On the heels of a very public nervous breakdown in 2001, Carey was struggling to come to terms with a more realistic and healthy view of herself; she wanted her public persona to reflect that change. And perhaps her more recent (2008) name change *back* to Mariah Carey is an attempt to reclaim a more formal relationship with the public.

Although the average individual would not consider a name change as quickly as a music star, to some degree we all must deal with the challenges of understanding who we are in order to become stronger communicators. Our view of ourselves is often so biased that we misinterpret or ignore information that we need in order to communicate effectively. Let's take a look at three important influences on our cognitions, or thoughts about ourselves: self-concept, self-esteem, and self-efficacy (see Figure 2.2 on p. 55).

## Self-Concept: Who You Think You Are

Think for a moment about who you are. You may describe yourself to others as a college student, a Hispanic male, a black female, a Christian, a biology major, an uncle, a parent, or a friend. But who you are involves much more. As we discussed in Chapter 1, your awareness and understanding of who you are—as interpreted and influenced by your thoughts, actions, abilities, values, goals, and ideals—is your **self-concept**. You develop a self-concept by thinking about your strengths and weaknesses, observing your behavior in a wide variety of situations, witnessing your own reactions to situations, and watching others' reactions to you (Snyder, 1979). You have views about yourself as cheap but intelligent, as active and scattered, as conservative but funny, as plain and popular—the list goes on and on. These are your cognitions. Remember from the model in Chapter 1 that both cognition and behavior make a communicator. In Chapter 1, we focused on cognitions about other people, places, media, and so on. But cognitions about self matter, too.

The self-concept has incredible power to shape our communication with others. It can shape what you think of other people because your perception of others is related to how you view yourself (Edwards, 1990). If attributes like honesty and wit are important to you, you will consider them important traits in other people; if you think that using foul language makes you appear cheap and vulgar, you are likely to think the same of others when they use such language. When you interact, self-concept is in play as well. It can affect how apprehensive you get in certain communication situations (McCroskey, 1997), whether or not you are willing to interact with others (Cegala, 1981), and how you approach someone with a request (whether you are meek and timid or strong and confident). People whose self-concept includes pride in their ability to communicate well often place themselves in situations where they are able to use their skills most effectively—Oprah Winfrey and Jon Stewart didn't become TV show hosts by accident! Similarly, people whose self-concept offers a less favorable view of their communication skills may shy away from opportunities (like seeking out a romantic partner or a new friendship) where such skills (or lack of them) would be in the spotlight.

So while your self-concept strongly influences how and when you communicate with others, the reverse is also true: when you interact with other people, you get impressions from them that reveal how they evaluate you as a person and as a communicator. This information gets reincorporated into your self-concept. In fact, many researchers believe that social interaction is key to developing one's self-concept because when you communicate with others, you receive evidence that you can then use to develop, confirm, or change your self-concept. *Direct evidence* comes in the form of compliments, insults, support, or negative remarks. For example, if a professor you admire tells you that you have great potential as a manager because you possess excellent leadership skills, you would probably make this information part of your self-concept. *Indirect evidence* that influences your self-concept might be revealed through innuendo, gossip, subtle nonverbal cues, or a lack of communication. For instance, if you ask a friend to evaluate your promise as a contestant on *American Idol* and he changes the subject or flat out laughs at you, you might get the impression that you are not such a great singer after all (not that such advice has stopped many terrible singers from trying out for this program!).

The media can also play an important role in how the self-concept is formed. We have a tendency to internalize our admiration for film and TV stars, models, famous athletes, and political figures by comparing what we like about them to our own self-concept. This is called **social comparison theory** (Bishop, 2000; Festinger, 1954), and it can influence how we think about ourselves and what we're willing to do to close the unavoidable gap created by this comparison. For example, women on television and in magazine ads are depicted as beautiful if they have a certain "look" (tall and extremely thin, with perfect skin, a perfect smile, and expensive clothing), and this look substantially influences how female viewers think of their own bodies (Bishop, 2000; Hendriks, 2002). Responses to the comparison between the look and the self have been chronicled in the news, with women resorting to diet pills and other forms of weight control. Eating disorders have also been linked to how the media portray the female body type (Bishop, 2000).

Clearly, the self-concept exerts a powerful influence on our lives, our relationships, and our communication. Struggles with self-concept—the way we see ourselves—are closely related to the way we feel about ourselves. Next, we examine how these feelings relate to communication.

## Self-Esteem: How You Feel About Yourself

**Self-esteem** refers to how one feels about oneself, usually in a particular situation. Self-esteem is essentially a set of attitudes that people hold about their own emotions, thoughts, abilities, skills, behavior, and beliefs

**AND YOU?**

Think about three characteristics that describe your self-concept and define who you are. Try to avoid characteristics that are obvious, such as "I am an Asian American female." How did you come to believe such things about yourself? What type of direct and indirect evidence led you to these beliefs? Do your loved ones support the view you have of yourself?

● **THOUSANDS OF AMERICAN IDOL** hopefuls audition every season for the chance to be the next Carrie Underwood (shown here with *Idol* host Ryan Seacrest). Their admiration for these "nobodies turned celebrities" and their desire to live the same fairy-tale story make them think, "Wow, I could be rich and famous too."

that fluctuate according to the situation or context. Self-concept and self-esteem are closely related: people need to know themselves in order to have attitudes about themselves. Consequently, many researchers believe that the self-concept forms first, and self-esteem emerges thereafter (Greenwalk, Bellezza, & Banaji, 1988).

You have probably noticed that people with high self-esteem have confidence in what they do, how they think, and how they perform. That's partly because these individuals are better able to incorporate their successes into their self-concept. For example, research shows that people with high self-esteem are more confident in their interpersonal relationships—perhaps because they are

## EVALUATINGCOMMUNICATIONETHICS

### Ethics and the Self-Concept

You and your romantic partner, Peyton, have been together for three years and have supported each other through many ups and downs, particularly in your professional lives. Both of you have successful careers and have made sacrifices to help each other achieve personal and professional goals. Most recently, the two of you moved to Washington, D.C., from Saint Louis so that Peyton could accept a promotion with a large financial investment firm. Since you were thrilled for Peyton's career opportunity and since you are able to work from a home office, you consented to the move. But it has been difficult because Peyton works long hours and your entire family and most of your close friends are still in Saint Louis.

Peyton comes home early one afternoon to announce that the investment firm has offered another promotion to a position that would require travel from Monday to Friday two weeks out of the month. Peyton talks excitedly about the increase in status and in pay and the new opportunities that the position would afford you both. Your immediate reaction is one of anger. How could Peyton consider taking a position that required so much travel, especially since this would leave you alone in a city where you know few people and where you work alone out of your home? Hadn't you sacrificed enough by moving halfway across the country for Peyton's career?

You confront Peyton, who is first surprised and then angry. "I thought we were working for the same thing—a better opportunity for our future," Peyton said. "I am good to you, and I give you everything you want. I thought I could count on you to support me in this. It is not like it will be much different from the way it is now since I work so late. After all, I'll be home every weekend."

You are hurt. You value harmony in your home and your relationships, and you value time spent with your partner. You believe that you are a flexible, reasonable person who appreciates joint decision making. You feel that you have been supportive and that you have made Peyton's career a priority in your home. Peyton's reaction, however, sends a much different message that makes you uneasy. You are upset by the different ways that you and Peyton perceive the situation and the ensuing communication difficulties.

**THINK ABOUT THIS**

❶ Consider the different elements that make up both your self-concept and your partner's. What do you each value? What are your goals and ideals? What are your thoughts and beliefs about work, relationships, and other important matters?

❷ How might your self-concept have affected the way that you perceived Peyton's message about the promotion? How might the message have affected your self-esteem?

❸ Now take Peyton's perspective. How might your partner's self-concept have affected the way that the news of the promotion was shared with you? How might your reaction have affected Peyton's self-esteem?

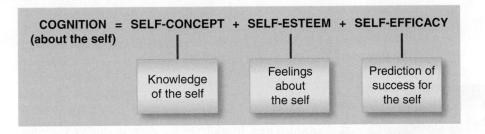

COGNITION = SELF-CONCEPT + SELF-ESTEEM + SELF-EFFICACY
(about the self)

| Knowledge of the self | Feelings about the self | Prediction of success for the self |

**FIGURE 2.2**

**UNDERSTANDING COGNITION**

more likely to believe that being friendly will cause others to be friendly in return (Baldwin & Keelan, 1999). Research also shows that people with high self-esteem do not feel the same need for public commitment from their relational partner as people with low self-esteem (Young & Acitelli, 1998). A man with low self-esteem might press his girlfriend to hold his hand or show affection in public in order to say, "Look! Someone loves me!" Someone with higher esteem would not need those public assurances.

Research suggests that some people have low self-esteem, or a poor view of themselves, because they either lack accurate information about themselves or mistrust the knowledge they do possess. For example, you may feel that you are a poor student because you have to study constantly to keep up your grades in German class. Your German professor, on the other hand, might find that your efforts and the improvement you've made over the semester reveal that you are a good, hardworking student. Low self-esteem may also result from an *inconsistent* view of oneself (Campbell, 1990). Some people who think they possess short-comings or negative traits may prefer to ignore them so that these traits will not affect their more enduring self-esteem. A satirical example of this kind of denial is provided in the character of Michael Scott on the TV situation comedy *The Office*. A horrible communicator who manages to be irritating, distracting, and offensive—often at the same time—Michael ignores his own shortcomings and instead convinces himself that he is in fact an especially effective communicator and a beloved boss. Small insights into Michael's life reveal that he is very lonely; he doesn't accept that he can or should improve his social skills because he needs to believe that his coworkers are already his friends.

People with low self-esteem are particularly sensitive to how others view them. Because they have less confidence in their abilities and skills, they are more likely to emphasize weaknesses instead of focusing on strong points, to believe negative information about themselves, to attempt to lower other people's expectations about their potential performance, and to communicate less confidence about their future behavior (Schlenker, Weigold, & Hallarn, 1990). Negative attitudes about ability can lead to poor performance, which can then reinforce existing negative attitudes about ability.

## Self-Efficacy: Assessing Your Own Abilities

You have an overall view of all aspects of yourself (self-concept), as well as an evaluation of how you feel about yourself in a particular area at any given moment in time (self-esteem). Based on this information, you approach a communication situation with

● **MICHAEL SCOTT** from the TV sitcom *The Office* is convinced that he is a lovable boss and an effective communicator. However, his colleagues might beg to differ.

an eye toward the *likelihood* of presenting yourself effectively. According to Albert Bandura (1982), this ability to predict actual success from self-concept and self-esteem is **self-efficacy**. Your perceptions of self-efficacy guide your ultimate choice of communication situations, making you much more likely to avoid situations where you believe your self-efficacy to be low. For example, Amanda tends to feel shy and unsociable in large crowds and so chooses not to go to large parties or crowded bars. Instead, she socializes in smaller, more formal group settings, joining various volunteer organizations, attending functions at her synagogue, and meeting people through friends, colleagues, and family members.

● **ON A REALITY TV** competition like *Project Runway*, contestants need to have great confidence in their own skills. But they must also size up their competition and maintain enough uncertainty that they don't get too cocky and slip up.

Even though a person's lack of effort is most often caused by perceptions of low efficacy, Bandura (1982) has observed that people with very high levels of self-efficacy sometimes become overconfident. Consider Lindsay Jacobellis, the 2006 gold medal favorite in women's snowboardcross. With a large lead, Jacobellis decided to throw in a stunt on her second-to-last jump in the competition. She wound up slipping and losing the gold. Bandura recommends that people maintain a high level of self-efficacy with just enough uncertainty to cause them to anticipate the situation accurately and prepare accordingly: a professional athlete might review footage of an opponent's best plays, for example, to keep a keen edge.

## Interpreting Events

Self-efficacy also has an effect on your ability to cope with failure and stress. Feelings of low efficacy may cause you to dwell on your shortcomings. A snowball effect occurs when you already feel inadequate and then fail at something: the failure takes its toll on your self-esteem, causing you to experience stress and negative emotional reactions. These feelings then contribute to lower self-esteem, which in turn sends your self-efficacy level even lower. For example, Jessie is job-hunting but worries that she does not do well in interviews. Each job she doesn't get reinforces this assessment; with each failed interview, she lowers her expectations for herself, and her interview performance worsens as well. By contrast, individuals with high self-efficacy are less emotionally affected by failure because they usually chalk up their shortcoming to a "bad day" or some other external factor. When Erin doesn't get a job she interviewed for, for example, she might conclude that another applicant was better suited to the position or that she'd stumbled on her words this time because she wasn't as well prepared as she usually is. Rather than dwelling on those notions, she simply vows to be better prepared for the next interview that comes up.

## Self-Fulfilling Prophecies

Inaccurate self-efficacy may lead to a **self-fulfilling prophecy**—a prediction that causes an individual to alter his or her behavior in a way that makes the prediction more likely to occur. If your friend Josh goes to a party believing that others don't enjoy his company, for example, he is more likely to stand in a corner, talk to few people, and feel even more anxious about his social skills or personality. Very few people come up to talk to Josh because he doesn't make much effort to be friendly, and thus Josh's prophecy is fulfilled: others don't like him. Josh's problem began before he even reached the party. He had anticipated that the party might turn out poorly for him based on his understanding of his likability. Self-efficacy and self-fulfilling prophecy are therefore related. When you cannot avoid situations where you experience low efficacy, you are less likely to make an effort to prepare or participate than you would for situations in which you are comfortable and perceive high efficacy. When you do not prepare for or participate in a situation (as Josh did not participate in the party), your behavior causes the prediction to come true, creating a self-fulfilling prophecy (no one talked to Josh at the party) (see Figure 2.3).

## Assessing Our Perceptions of Self

As a communicator, you are constantly assessing your competence level for strengths and weaknesses. These assessments of self are important before, during, and after you have communicated, particularly when you've received feedback from other people. You evaluate your expectations, execution, and outcomes in three ways: self-actualization, self-adequacy, and self-denigration.

### Self-Actualization

The most positive evaluation you can make about your competence level is referred to as **self-actualization**—the feelings and thoughts you get when you know that you have negotiated a communication situation as well as you possibly could. At times like these, you have a sense of fulfillment and satisfaction. For example, Shari, a school psychologist, was having problems with the third-grade teacher of one of the students she counsels. The teacher seemed to act uninterested in the student's performance, would not return Shari's phone calls or

CONNECT

Self-fulfilling prophecies are deeply tied to verbal and nonverbal communication. If you believe you will ace a job interview because you are well prepared, you will likely stand tall and make confident eye contact with your interviewer (Chapter 4) and use appropriate and effective language (Chapter 3) to describe your skill set. Your confidence just may land you the position you want!

**Self-Fulfilling Prophecy (SFP)**

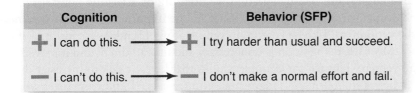

| Cognition | Behavior (SFP) |
|---|---|
| ✚ I can do this. | ✚ I try harder than usual and succeed. |
| ━ I can't do this. | ━ I don't make a normal effort and fail. |

Self-fulfilling prophecy imposed on others:

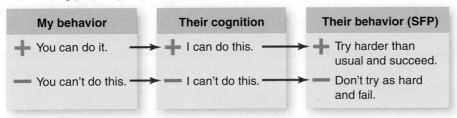

| My behavior | Their cognition | Their behavior (SFP) |
|---|---|---|
| ✚ You can do it. | ✚ I can do this. | ✚ Try harder than usual and succeed. |
| ━ You can't do this. | ━ I can't do this. | ━ Don't try as hard and fail. |

**FIGURE 2.3**

**THE SELF-FULFILLING PROPHECY**

e-mails, and seemed curt and aloof when they did speak. Shari finally decided to confront the teacher. Although she was nervous at first about saying the right thing, she later felt very good about the experience. The teacher had seemed shocked at the criticism but offered an apology. At the end of the meeting, Shari was quite content that she had been honest and assertive yet fair and understanding. This positive assessment of her behavior led to a higher level of self-esteem. When Shari needs to confront someone in the future, she will likely feel more confident about doing so.

### Self-Adequacy

At times you may think that your communication performance was not stellar, but it was good enough. When you assess your communication competence as sufficient or acceptable, you are feeling a sense of **self-adequacy**, which is less positive than self-actualization. Feelings of self-adequacy can lead you in two directions—either to contentment or to a desire for self-improvement.

Suppose that Phil has been working very hard to improve his public speaking abilities and does a satisfactory job when he speaks to his employees about the company's goals for next year. He might feel very satisfied about his speech, but he realizes that with a little more effort and practice, he can become an even better speaker. In this case, Phil's reaction is one of *self-improvement*. He is telling himself that he wants to be more competent in his communication, regardless of his current level.

While self-improvement is a good motivation, in some circumstances being satisfied or content with your self-adequacy is sufficient. For example, Lilia has a long history of communication difficulties with her mother. Their relationship is characterized by sarcastic and unkind comments and interactions. But during her last visit home, Lilia avoided conflict and felt good about her communication with her mom. The two didn't become best friends or resolve all the old problems, but Lilia thought she communicated well under the circumstances. She was content with her self-adequacy.

### Self-Denigration

The most negative assessment you can make about a communication experience is **self-denigration**. Self-denigration is criticizing or attacking yourself. It most often occurs when communicators place undue importance on their weaknesses or shortcomings ("I knew I'd end up yelling at my friend; I was just out of control"). Most self-denigration is unnecessary and unwarranted, and it prevents real improvement. Hunter, for example, thinks that he can't talk to his sister; he perceives her as stubborn and judgmental. Hunter says, "I know my sister won't listen. I can't do anything right in her eyes." Hunter needs to assess his communication behaviors: what specific words and nonverbal behaviors (like tone of voice) does he use with his sister? He must also avoid self-denigration by focusing on times when he had positive communication with his sister; he can also plan for communication improvement ("Next time, I will listen to my sister completely before I say anything back to her"). Thus our assessments of our competence run from self-actualization on the positive end to self-denigration on the negative end (see Figure 2.4).

**AND YOU?**

Think about a communication situation in your own life in which you believe that you achieved self-adequacy. Were you content with the outcome of the situation, or did you desire self-improvement? Why? Is it possible to feel both contentment and a desire for self-improvement in your communication situation?

**CONNECT**

To avoid self-denigration, consider the situational and relational contexts discussed in Chapter 1. You may judge yourself harshly for not communicating as easily with your Aunt Irma as you do with your friend Joe, but different environments—as well as unique relational histories with different individuals—may make that goal impossible. Rather, assess your communication with your aunt in light of the constraints of that particular situation and relationship.

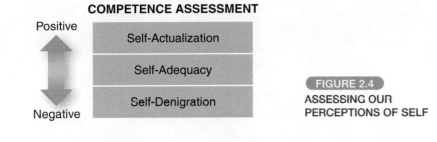

FIGURE 2.4
ASSESSING OUR
PERCEPTIONS OF SELF

## Behavior: Managing Our Identities

Recall our discussion of Mariah Carey's self-described transformation. As you've learned, you define yourself internally, through your self-concept and your ideas about self-esteem and self-efficacy. These are your cognitions, introduced in Chapter 1. But you also make decisions about how to share your internal view with others; this is manifested in your behaviors, both verbal and nonverbal. Cognition and behavior play roles in the way you perceive others and the way that others perceive you. Carey felt a need to change her own perception of herself and chose to share her desired self-concept with her fans and the public at large; by inviting the public to know "Mimi," she was asking them to look at her differently. And perhaps her return to "Mariah Carey" is yet another request to observe difference.

We all have aspects of ourselves that we want to share and aspects that we would rather keep private. Many of the choices we make in our communication behavior, from the clothes we wear to the way we speak, are determined by the way we want others to perceive us. Here we'll look at how we let the world know just who we think we are and how our communication with others can shape the ways in which they view us.

Let's examine the process illustrated in Figure 2.5 (see p. 60) for a moment. At the core of this process is the self. The self has cognitions (about the self) that consist of self-concept (knowing and understanding the self), self-esteem (evaluating the self), and self-efficacy (predicting success), all of which we've discussed. These cognitions influence our verbal and nonverbal behavior, which are comprised of self-presentation and self-disclosure, two terms we will explain in a moment. Our behavior generates feedback from others, which leads to our assessments of self-actualization, self-adequacy, and self-denigration. These judgments of our performance then affect our cognition. As you read about self-presentation, self-disclosure, and feedback in the coming pages, refer to this illustration as a reminder of their roles in our continuously evolving interactions with others.

### Self-Presentation

You let others know about yourself through **self-presentation**, intentional communication designed to show elements of self for strategic purposes. For example, if you want to create an impression among your coworkers that you are competent at your job as an editor, you might mention during conversations the

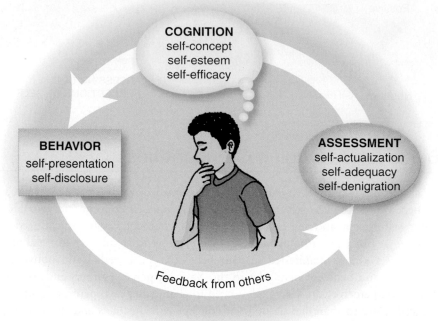

FIGURE 2.5

**THE SELF** The self is composed of our cognitions, our behavior, and our self-assessments. These factors work together to affect our communication.

**AND YOU?**

Like Julie, you have probably encountered situations in which you chose to engage in either face-to-face communication or mediated communication (text messaging, posting on a Facebook wall, e-mail). Why did you choose a particular channel? If you chose a mediated channel, did you feel safer from an unknown reaction as the research suggests? Why or why not?

names of popular authors you've worked with or tell stories about hilariously terrible errors you've found in various manuscripts you've worked on. According to Dan Canary and Michael Cody (1993), people tend to focus on self-presentation more when their social identity is being evaluated (formally or informally) by others. This is why you'll usually act differently in a situation where you're trying to impress someone (for example, if you are meeting your significant other's parents for the first time) than you will in a situation where you feel entirely comfortable with the way others view you (hanging out with your own friends or family).

Self-presentation comes in many forms. You can present yourself through face-to-face conversation, through e-mail or text messaging, and on social networking sites like MySpace and Facebook. You may even have a preference for one of these channels of communication when self-presenting. For example, many people will use asynchronous channels (e-mail, voice mail, cards) when they are unsure of the reaction they will get when they present themselves (O'Sullivan, 2000). For example, Lance and Julie had a heated disagreement and weren't speaking to each other. Julie finally realized that she was wrong, and wanted to apologize. Because she was uncomfortable in making this self-presentation to Lance over the phone or in person, she chose to send him a text message when she knew that he would be in a meeting (and would have his phone turned off).

Knowing how to present yourself in the best way usually involves paying attention to your behavior and that of others. **Self-monitoring** is your ability to watch your environment and others in it for cues as to how to present yourself in a particular situation (Snyder, 1974). High-self-monitoring individuals try to portray themselves as "the right person in the right place at the right time." These people watch others for hints on how to be successful in social situations and attempt to produce the verbal and nonverbal cues that seem most appropriate. You may know someone who is a high-self-monitoring communicator. During class, this person always sits in a certain strategic position, gets involved in discussions when others do so, gestures in a similar manner to others, and when it is time to let others talk, is very strategic with silence. These "sufficiently skilled actors" are able to implement situation-appropriate communication behaviors (Snyder, 1974). They consider themselves alert and flexible, ready to tackle a number of communication situations with ease.

Low-self-monitoring individuals are not nearly so sensitive to situational cues that prescribe communication behavior. They communicate according to their deep-seated values or beliefs. They do not feel the need to adapt to situations or people; rather, they feel that people and situations must take them the way they are, at face value. If low self-monitors anticipate a communication situation that is different from their own self-presentation style, they will either avoid the situation or accept the fact that their communication may not please all the parties involved.

Communicating successfully involves finding the appropriate level of self-monitoring for the situation and the people involved. It might seem like high self-monitors are the winners in social interaction, but this isn't always the case. High self-monitors can drive themselves crazy by focusing on every little thing that they say and do; for example, they may be so concerned about behaving appropriately that they fail to reveal their concerns openly and honestly to their romantic partners, leading to lower relationship satisfaction (Wright, Holloway, & Roloff, 2007). Competent communicators will monitor self-presentation just high enough to present themselves effectively without forgetting that communication involves others.

● **PLACES OF WORSHIP** often have dress codes, whether they are explicitly stated or not. People may feel that you are being disrespectful and inappropriate if you ignore the rules and do things your own way.

The process of choosing what information to share with others (and when to share it) has long fascinated researchers. In Chapter 6 we examine the *Social Penetration Theory,* which uses an onion as a metaphor to show how we move from superficial confessions to more intimate ones. Your outer "layer" might consist of disclosures about where you are from or what your major is, but as you peel away the layers, your disclosures will become more private and personal.

## Self-Disclosure

Angelica is a stylish dresser; has a lovely apartment in Austin, Texas; eats out at nice restaurants regularly; and drives a new car. But she has a secret: she is drowning in debt, barely keeping up with her minimum credit card payments. She looks around at her friends, all the same age as she and living similar lifestyles. She wonders if they make more money than she does or if they too are over their heads in debt. One night while out for coffee with her best friend, Shawna, Angelica comes clean about her situation: she can't go on their upcoming trip to Cozumel, she tells Shawna, because her credit cards are maxed out. Angelica has self-disclosed to Shawna.

When you reveal yourself to others by sharing information about yourself, you engage in **self-disclosure**. To count as self-disclosure in a relationship, the disclosure must be important; telling someone you like snacking on raw vegetables is not self-disclosure, but explaining to them the deeply held reasons why you became a vegetarian is. The disclosure must be not easily known by others and must also be voluntary.

Self-disclosure can be a tool for confirming our self-concept or improving our self-esteem; it is often used as a tactic to obtain reassurance or comfort from a trusted friend (Miller, Cooke, Tsang, & Morgan, 1992). For example, Angelica might suspect that Shawna is also living on credit; if Shawna discloses that she is, she will reassure Angelica that it's OK to buy things she can't afford on credit because everyone else is doing it too. However, if Shawna reveals

# what about you?

### Self-Monitoring Test

To test your own perceived level of self-monitoring, complete the following items, being careful to answer them as accurately and truthfully as possible. Use a 5-point scale for your answers: 5 = strongly agree; 4 = agree; 3 = neither agree nor disagree; 2 = disagree; and 1 = strongly disagree.

_____ 1. I am concerned about acting appropriately in social situations.

_____ 2. I find it hard to imitate the behavior of others.

_____ 3. I have good self-control of my behavior. I can play many roles.

_____ 4. I am not very good at learning what is socially appropriate in new situations.

_____ 5. I often appear to lack deep emotions.

_____ 6. In a group of people, I am rarely the center of attention.

_____ 7. I may deceive people by being friendly when I really dislike them.

_____ 8. Even if I am not enjoying myself, I often pretend to be having a good time.

_____ 9. I have good self-control of my emotional expression. I can use it to create the impression I want.

_____ 10. I can argue only for ideas that I already believe in.

_____ 11. I openly express my true feelings, attitudes, and beliefs.

_____ 12. I'm not always the person I appear to be.

Add up your scores on items 1, 3, 5, 7, 8, 9, and 12. Now reverse the scoring on items 2, 4, 6, 10, and 11 (5 = 1, 4 = 2, 2 = 4, 1 = 5). Finally, add these scores to the sum you calculated from the first set of items. If you scored 43–60, you are a high self-monitor; if you scored 30–42, you are an average self-monitor; and if your score was 12–29, you are a low self-monitor.

Source: Adapted from Snyder (1974).

that she makes more money than Angelica or that she manages her money more wisely, Angelica's self-concept may be damaged. As you will recall from Chapter 1, information you receive about your self is termed feedback. The feedback Angelica receives from Shawna will be based on her self-disclosure; the same feedback—and how she interprets it—also influences Angelica's perception of herself.

## real communicator

**NAME:** Georgia Banks
**HOMETOWN:** Superior, Wisconsin
**OCCUPATION:** Master's degree candidate in social work
**FUN FACT:** I've lived in eight apartments and five states in the past three years.

I'm white. I grew up in a town in Wisconsin that you've probably never heard of. According to my East Coast friends, I talk funny.

I live in New York now and work in a predominantly black high school, mostly with kids who are dropout risks. It's my job to improve their attendance and keep them in school. Because I'm white, my students had some preconceived perceptions about me, some of which are true and some not.

They thought I was rich and that I go home to a luxury Manhattan apartment (wrong on both counts: I've got credit debt and live in Queens). They had this perception that because I am white, I must be constantly happy, never experiencing hardship, living one contented day after another. I can understand where this idea comes from. My kids live in this tough neighborhood where there aren't any white people, and when they do go to a nice neighborhood, all they see are white people. But their stereotypes made my job very difficult. To improve attendance, I need to find out why these kids aren't coming to school—what's going on at home, are they physically afraid of their ex-boyfriend, is their mom in the hospital? These are exceptionally personal, private things. When I first got here, my kids (adolescents who deal with racism every day of their lives) looked at me and said, No way, I can't talk about that stuff with her. I was a white person

coming into their world. I couldn't understand their world of gangs and violence and exceptional peer pressure. I couldn't relate.

I didn't disabuse them of their perceptions in a verbally aggressive way, angrily denying their assumptions. I engaged in self-monitoring, a concept I learned about in college. I took every opportunity to open channels of communication, remembering everyone's name, stopping kids in the hall to say hello and ask how they're doing. I was patient and looked for cues into their moods, their individual communication styles. When they wanted to talk, I listened. When they didn't, I was OK with that. There are plenty of things to do in my office—poetry kits, games—and kids can just come in, sit down, and hang out—no need to talk if they don't want to, no pressure to leave. I've built an environment of trust. I let my kids be who they need to be, and I don't judge them.

But they are right about some of their perceptions. There are things I'm never going to understand. I never went through the things they're going through. But I can be a sounding board for good judgment. My kids know that they can come to me and trust me; they know that I care and that I'll listen. I'm here to help them. And I do help them. I'm good at my job.

But who really knows? All of this is just my perception.

How you incorporate feedback into the self depends on several factors. One of the most important factors is your *sensitivity level* to feedback. Research demonstrates that some individuals are highly sensitive, whereas others are largely unaffected by the feedback they receive (Edwards, 1990). Presumably, people who are more sensitive to feedback are susceptible and receptive to information about their abilities, knowledge, talents, and the rest. Low-sensitive people would be less responsive to such information. For example, when Ian ignores suggestions that he dress in a more professional and appropriate manner for work (rather than in jeans and sweatshirts), he is being insensitive to feedback about his personal appearance. Ian has a low sensitivity level to feedback and is unlikely to realize that his behavior may need to

# WIREDFORCOMMUNICATION

## Avatars: Virtual Faces

The face of Huey Freeman, the ten-year-old black activist at the heart of the comic strip (and popular Adult Swim cartoon) *The Boondocks,* stares out from the screen, his face set in his signature scowl, his left eyebrow cocked, his towering Afro extending above. This is the avatar, or virtual face, chosen by Trey, a regular contributor to an online political forum.

Logging into an Internet forum, chat room, or game typically involves creating an online identity. You choose a user name, create a one-line catchphrase that you'll use as your signature, and carefully choose from among various avatars (commonly called "avs"). The avatars are typically little icons or pictures used to present a particular image of yourself. They can range from basic emoticons (smiley faces) to photos of beloved celebrities, cartoon characters, or images from nature and allow you to express your identity visually rather than through words alone. Avatars can be chosen for any number of reasons, including to draw attention to yourself, to give others a glimpse of your interests, or to capture some aspect of your personality (Suler, 2007).

The characteristics of selected avatars are important to both behavior and perception. Nick Yee and Jeremy Bailenson (2007) found that people's behavior was affected by the physical characteristics of the avatar assigned to them. For example, people who were assigned to more attractive avatars self-disclosed more and talked more intimately with others than those assigned less attractive avatars.

As graphic representations, avatars are open to a great deal of interpretation and thus rely heavily on the viewer's perceptions. For example, Trey's choice of Huey might be interpreted in several ways. Is Trey, like the fictional Huey, a militant black activist? Is he an aspiring cartoonist? Is he just angry, like Huey looks? The truth is that Trey loves the comic strip, and his friends joke that he and Huey must go to the same barber. On some level, Trey also identifies with Huey's activism, wit, and intelligence, but he would rather imply this association than say it out loud.

**THINK ABOUT THIS**

❶ How might the image of Huey be interpreted by someone who is unfamiliar with *The Boondocks*? Would a fan of the strip perceive Trey's online self differently?

❷ If Trey's postings clearly lean toward the political left or right, might readers' interpretations of his avatar change?

❸ If Trey is revealed to be black, would that influence the way the image of Huey is received? What if Trey is actually white? Buddhist? Female? A teenager? A senior citizen?

**BEHAVIOR  =  SELF-PRESENTATION  +  SELF-DISCLOSURE**
(verbal and nonverbal)

| Intentional communication to show elements of the self for strategic purposes | Revealing the self by sharing information about the self |

**FIGURE 2.6**
UNDERSTANDING BEHAVIOR

change if he is to be promoted in the organization. Figure 2.6 illustrates how self-presentation and self-disclosure constitute the behavior segment of "The Self," seen in Figure 2.5.

## Technology: Managing the Self Online

On MySpace, you might come across a profile of Candice, a twenty-eight-year-old fabulously wealthy marketing executive who has a spacious one-bedroom apartment in San Francisco. Her picture reveals that she is quite attractive, and the stories she posts on her blog tell of her exciting business and personal trips to exotic locations around the world. In reality, however, the author of the content of these postings is Alice, a twenty-year-old sophomore business major from Bangor, Maine, who is projecting a possible future identity and asking others to perceive her as this ideal.

In blogs, in chat rooms, and on dating sites around the world, the presentation of self can be more controlled than in face-to-face encounters. When you manage the self online, you can potentially control self-disclosure, more easily choosing what to reveal and what to conceal. You can choose to reveal or not reveal your gender, ethnicity, and race, as well as your religious or political preferences. What's more, you can edit, revise, and organize the information you do disclose before the message goes out. In this way, you can present an image that is smart, charming, and eloquent, even if you tend to be nervous or timid in face-to-face communication. Among adolescents in particular, the Internet presents an appealing opportunity to experiment with identity. Sherry Turkle, a technology researcher, notes that the online environment offers young people a virtual "identity workshop" where they can try on different identities with little risk. "Things get too hot, you log off," Turkle notes, "while in time and space, you have consequences" (quoted in Wallis, 2006).

Identity management using technology is not new. For decades, a communicator could choose to use the telephone to deliver bad news or to trick others by pretending to be someone else. Personal ads in magazines and newspapers are examples of planned identity management (Parrott, Lemieux, Harris, & Foreman, 1997). In like manner, online communicators plan identity management; as they interact, they socially construct their images and reduce their uncertainty about themselves and others. Communication connections can be made more easily; you find like-minded souls to date, to discuss your ideas, to share your experience, or to support your causes. You might present yourself while maintaining connections to your groups of friends through a site like Facebook.com, Gay.com, or Americansingles.com.

**AND YOU?**

When you meet someone online, whether through an online dating service, a networking or friendship site, or an online class, do you assume that the other individual is offering an honest depiction of himself or herself? Do you offer honest accounts of yourself, or do you, like Alice, prefer to use this venue to communicate alternative or ideal identities?

 Matisyahu

Recall our discussion of the Hasidic reggae artist Matisyahu at the beginning of this chapter. A Hasidic Jew from New York, he emulates music from the Caribbean while adhering to a strict religious doctrine that seems a world apart from the beliefs of most reggae artists. What kind of schemas about music, culture, and spirituality does Matisyahu challenge? How do his music and his appearance reflect or contradict commonly held perceptions? Consider the following:

▶ Hasidic Jews are a fairly small sect in the United States; their customs of dress might seem strange to those outside the group. To some extent, Matisyahu's somewhat exotic look may be part of his appeal, in the same way that Bob Marley's dreadlocks may have seemed strange and intriguing when he first brought Jamaican reggae to American shores in the 1960s.

▶ Matisyahu's spirituality might seem at odds with reggae, a music closely associated with the Rastafari religion. But the artist perceives things differently, finding inspiration in reggae's call to embrace one's own spiritual heritage. Referring to the Marley song "Rastaman Live Up," Matisyahu told *Rolling Stone* in 2005, "I realized he was really saying, 'Figure out your roots, and be true to them'"(Khazzoom, 2005).

▶ As a *baal teshuvah* who was not raised Hasidic, Matisyahu's musical experience prior to his conversion undoubtedly influences his music today. This fact might serve to confirm some people's schemas about Hasidic Jews as an insular group, casting doubts on whether he would have the same sound if he had been raised with them. Others might question his authenticity, wondering if this is merely a persona he has adopted, like the dreadlocks he wore in his youth.

## THINGS TO TRY

1. Describe how you managed an impression of yourself in two different situations. Choose a private versus public situation or a new impression you were trying to manage versus an old one you were trying to change. Describe your conscious preparations for this impression management, and then describe the outcome. What contributed to your successful or unsuccessful management of self?

2. Take a look at the coverage of a presidential speech online at www.whitehouse .gov. After reading the complete speech, consider how the speech is characterized in various sources (blogs, liberal and conservative news sources, late-night comedy and satires). How do perceptions of the speech change from one source to another? Does your perception of the speech change as you consider the points of view of these various sources?

3. Think about a co-culture (age, sexual orientation, socioeconomic status, race, religion, and so on) with which you identify. Then make a list of stereotypes that are associated with that group. In what ways do you conform to such stereotypes? In what ways do you not conform? Do you identify with more than one culture? If so, are there any stereotypes on your list that contradict each other? How might intersection of these cultures (for example, being a white, Christian, thirty-year-old stay-at-home dad or being a fifty-year-old Hispanic lesbian scientist) affect your perception of yourself as well as others' perceptions of you?

4. Watch some television programming that is typically geared toward a particular group. We discussed football (as geared to heterosexual men) in this chapter. But you might also check out soap operas, after-school children's programming or Saturday morning cartoons, or other genres. Pay close attention to the advertisements you see. Are they geared toward the groups that are expected to be watching the programming? If so, do you see instances in which the commercials allow for flexibility and mindfulness (for example, any advertising geared toward women during football games)? If you are a member of the group being targeted during such programming, do you find yourself more or less persuaded by the message based on stereotypes about your group?

## IF YOU'RE INTERESTED

*First Impressions: What You Don't Know About How Others See You,* by Ann Demarais and Valerie White (New York: Bantam Books, 2004)

This is a psychological look at impression management. Its "seven fundamentals of first impressions" lead into "tweaking your first impression style." The textbook-style self-checks and dialogues guide readers through material in a pleasant and easy-to-read manner that parallels many of the topics in this chapter (perception, self-disclosure, awareness).

*Sex Differences and Similarities in Communication,* edited by Kathryn Dindia and Daniel J. Canary (Mahwah, NJ: Erlbaum, 2006)

Set within the context of sex similarities to balance the popular press emphasis on sex differences, this edited text is rich and varied. Particularly relevant to this chapter is the coverage of the evolution of biological sex differences in communication, the perceptions of those who depart from the stereotypical sex roles in conversation, and the verbal and nonverbal sex differences and similarities in communication behaviors across contexts.

*My Freshman Year: What a Professor Learned by Becoming a Student,* by Rebekah Nathan (Ithaca, NY: Cornell University Press, 2005)

Occupation and role influence perceptions. In this book, an anthropology professor takes a sabbatical and enrolls as a freshman in order to understand the attitudes, values, and perspectives of college students. Drawing on her own experiences and national surveys of college life, Nathan chronicles the misperceptions, misunderstandings, and mistakes of educators and students that affect the college experience.

*A Lot like Love* (Beacon Pictures, 2005)

Opposites attract—at least that is the premise of this film, which follows two very different people, Oliver and Emily, as they meet up year after year in different places. They change careers and move in and out of relationships, and yet they always seem to be there for each other. Though there are many things that pull them apart, their ability to talk, laugh, and self-disclose draws them together.

*Mr. and Mrs. Smith* (20th Century Fox, 2005)

Just how accurately do you perceive your romantic partner? Keep that question in mind as you analyze the perceptions of John and Jane Smith, an ordinary suburban couple with an ordinary suburban marriage. In actuality (and unbeknown to each other), they are both highly paid assassins working for two different organizations. When they are hired to assassinate each other, we get an interesting (if highly unrealistic) look at occupation, marriage, and perceptions.

*Water* (Fox Searchlight Pictures, 2006)

This is a beautifully made film that deals with the life of women (and an eight-year-old girl) condemned by Hindu law to spend the rest of their lives in an institution because they are widows. Though this film is set in 1938, its investigation and reflection of religious and cultural beliefs is relevant today, especially as the women begin to question their allegiance to a religion that makes outcasts of the widows and relegates them to poverty.

*50 First Dates* (Columbia Pictures, 2004)

Marine biologist Henry Roth finds the perfect woman in Lucy Whitmore. Whitmore has a rare brain disorder that wipes her memory clean every night, so Roth must devise ways to address her disability and keep her interest in him. This film is an insightful look at differing perceptions and a gentle plea for the acceptance of difference, despite the bathroom humor, animal stunts, and crude language.

# REAL REFERENCE ➤ A Study Tool

**Now that you have finished reading this chapter, you can**

Understand how our personal perspective on the world influences our communication:

▶ **Perception** is the cognitive process that helps us make sense of the world (p. 38).

▶ **Communication processing** is the means by which we gather, organize, and evaluate the information we receive (p. 39).

▶ Because we are constantly bombarded with information in any situation, we must sift through it all to determine what is important and what to remember (p. 39).

Explain how we use and misuse schemas when communicating with others:

▶ **Schemas** are mental structures we use to connect bits of information together (p. 39).

▶ Schemas help us understand how things work as well as decide how to act; they evolve as we encounter new information and situations (p. 40).

▶ Schemas present three challenges that derail good communication: **mindlessness**, a passive, automatic response that may be inaccurate; **selective perception**, allowing bias to influence thought; and **undue influence**, giving other sources too much say (p. 41).

Discuss how and why we use **attributions** to explain behavior:

▶ When we need to explain why someone says or does something in a manner that does not fit into our schemas, we look to attributions to explain the cause of the behavior and justify our perceptions (p. 42).

▶ **Interaction appearance theory** explains how people change their perception of someone's appearance as they spend more time together (p. 42).

▶ **Fundamental attribution error** explains our tendency to assume that another person's wrong behavior is due to an internal flaw, while attributing our own failures to external causes (p. 43).

Understand how cultural differences influence perception:

▶ Effective communication depends on understanding how diversity, the variables that make us unique, affects perception (p. 45).

▶ The failure to see beyond our own beliefs and circumstances, or **cultural myopia**, blinds us to alternative points of view (p. 48).

▶ **Stereotyping**, or generalizing about people, limits our ability to see the individual and can lead to **prejudice**, ill will toward a particular group coupled with a sense of one's own superiority (p. 49).

Identify how our **self-concept**—who we think we are—influences communication:

▶ We are more willing to interact in situations where we feel we have strengths and our self-concept is confirmed or changed by responses from others (p. 52).

▶ We compare ourselves against idealized images in the media, according to **social comparison theory**, often to our own disadvantage (p. 53).

▶ **Self-esteem** relates to self-concept and is how we feel about ourselves in a particular situation (p. 53).

▶ **Self-efficacy** is the ability to predict, based on self-concept and self-esteem, one's effectiveness in a communication situation. Inaccurate self-efficacy may lead to a **self-fulfilling prophecy**, whereby behavior is altered to make the prediction more likely to come true (p. 56).

▶ We assess our communication performances and rate ourselves through the lenses of **self-actualization** (high performance), **self-adequacy** (adequate performance), and **self-denigration** (poor performance) (pp. 57–58).

Describe how our cognitions about ourselves and our behavior affect our communication with others:

▶ **Self-presentation** is intentional communication designed to show elements of self for strategic purposes; it's how we let others know about ourselves (p. 59).

▶ The tendency to watch our environment and others in it for cues as to how to present ourselves in particular situations is called **self-monitoring** (p. 60).

▶ Sharing important information about ourselves, such as with a close friend, is **self-disclosure** (p. 61).

▶ The presentation of self can be more easily controlled when communicating online than in face-to-face encounters (p. 65).

Which of these pairs are partners?

# chapter 3

# Language and Communication

**Anne Kerry was walking** to the bank in her San Francisco neighborhood when she suddenly ran into Scott, an old college friend, accompanied by another young man. "Anne," he said warmly, "I want you to meet my partner, Bryan." Anne was surprised—she hadn't realized that Scott was gay. She asked, "How long have you two been together?" Both men looked at her quizzically before they realized what she was thinking. "No," said Scott, "I became a police officer. Bryan and I work patrol together." "I was embarrassed," said Anne. "I didn't mean to misunderstand their relationship. I just figured that 'partner' meant love interest" (Anne Kerry, personal communication, March 7, 2008).

Like many words in the English language, *partner* has a variety of definitions: it can mean anything from "an associate" to "a dancing companion" to "a group of two or more symbiotically associated organisms." But like Anne, many of us immediately jump to another definition: "half of a couple who live together or who are habitual companions." Indeed, the term is widely used by gays and lesbians seeking a label for their loved one. Some heterosexual couples have also embraced the term to reveal their committed state, particularly when they feel that they've outgrown the terms *boyfriend* or *girlfriend* or are unwilling to use the terms *husband* and *wife*.

The fact is, the labels we choose for our relationships have a huge impact on our communication. The term *partner* can give rise to ambiguity—is the person you introduce with this term a business colleague, someone you play tennis with, or your "significant other"? That ambiguity makes it difficult for others to grasp your intended meaning. Perhaps that's why some Massachusetts gays and lesbians who wed after the state ratified same-sex marriages avoid the term *partner*. Bob Buckley felt the power of such labels when his partner, Marty Scott, needed medical treatment. When hospital administrators asked his relationship to the patient, Buckley was able to say, simply, "husband," and was immediately allowed to stay with Scott, since spouses are afforded this privilege but partners are not (Jones, 2005).

After you have finished
reading this chapter,
you will be able to

○ Understand the power
of language—the
system of symbols we
use to think about and
communicate our
experiences and
feelings

○ Identify the ways
communication
functions for people—
the five functional
communication
competencies

○ Recognize
communication
problems and how
to address them

○ Understand that
language reflects, builds
on, and determines
context

S top and think about the power of the words you use to describe your relationships. As you can see from our opening vignette, the name used to describe our connection with another person is significant and powerful. This goes beyond our romantic attachments. Calling your father "Dad" or "Father" can reveal a different level of formality in your relationship. In a stepfamily situation, calling your father's wife "Mom" or "Lisa" can indicate how close you and she feel. Choosing terms and using words can get pretty complicated. That's why we dedicate this chapter to studying **language**, the system of symbols (words) that we use to think about and communicate experiences and feelings. Language is also governed by grammatical rules and is influenced by various contexts.

Of course, communication is much more than pure language. Nonverbal behaviors that accompany the words we speak—pauses, tone of voice, and body movements—are an integral part of our communication. We look at nonverbal communication in Chapter 4, but for now just remember that language does not occur in isolation; it's always accompanied by a nonverbal component. We now examine the nature of language, the functions of language, some problems with language, and important contexts for language.

## The Nature of Language

In 1970, a "wild child" was discovered in California. Thirteen-year-old "Genie" had been chained in a small room with no toys and little food for nearly her entire life. And what seems even crueler is that her abusive father did not allow her to experience human interaction—no hugs, no words of love or affirmation, and no conversation. As a result, Genie never developed language. Medical doctors, linguists, and psychologists worked intensely with Genie for over seven years, hoping to give the girl a chance at life in a community with others. But despite their efforts, Genie never learned more than a few hundred words and was never able to form sentences of more than two or three words (Pines, 1997; "Secret," 1997). Genie's sad story is of great interest to researchers who study how we acquire language, but it also highlights the complex nature of language. What Genie will unfortunately never fully grasp is that language is symbolic, filled with multiple meanings, and informed by our thoughts. It is also ruled by grammar and bound by context. Let's examine each of these points in turn.

### Language Is Symbolic

What comes to mind when you see the word *cat*? A furry childhood best friend? Fits of sneezing from allergies? Either way, the word evokes a response because *c-a-t* makes you think about your four-legged friend (or enemy). That's because a word is a type of *symbol,* a sign used to represent a person, idea, or thing. Symbols form the basis of language—there's no particular reason why *w-a-t-e-r* makes you think of the cool refreshing stuff that comes out of your faucet or that *b-o-o-k* makes you think of the physical object you are currently reading. They do because we speakers of English agree that they do. And so we can use them to communicate ideas and thoughts dealing with those subjects.

● **THE WORD** *SCHOOL* has multiple denotative meanings: it is both the place where students learn and a group of fish.

## Words Have Multiple Meanings

As you saw in the opening vignette, a single word can have a lot of meanings. A dictionary can help you find the **denotative meaning** of a word—its basic, consistently accepted definition. But to be a competent communicator, you'll also need to consider the **connotative meaning** of a word, the emotional or attitudinal response people have to it. Consider the word *school,* which has several denotative meanings, including a building where education takes place and a large group of fish. But the word can also carry strong connotative meanings, based on one's attitudes toward and experience with school: it might bring back happy memories of class birthday parties in second grade, or it might make you feel anxious thinking about final exams.

Obviously, choosing words carefully is important. Not only must you make sure the denotative meaning is clear (using the word *ostentatious* with a bunch of six-year-olds isn't going to help you explain anything), but you also have to be aware of the possible connotative meanings of the words you use (Hample, 1987). Consider the terms *husband* and *wife.* For many people, these are simply words to describe a spouse who is either male or female. But for others, the words carry strong gender-role connotations: the term *wife* might imply a woman who does not work outside of the home, cooks all of her husband's meals, and does all of the household chores.

## Thought Informs Language

Jamal Henderson is getting ready to apply to college. He keeps his father, Michael, involved in the process because he values his father's opinion. They both agree that Jamal should attend a "good college." But Michael feels hurt when Jamal starts talking seriously about urban universities in another state, thinking that his son has ruled out his own alma mater, the local campus of the state university system. The problem stems from Jamal and Michael's different concepts of what a "good college" is. Their language and their thoughts are related in their own minds, and each thinks he is using the term appropriately.

Your **cognitive language** is the specific system of symbols that you use to describe people, things, and situations in your mind; it influences both language and message production (Giles & Wiemann, 1987); it is related to your thoughts, your attitudes, your co-cultures, and the society in which you live (Bradac & Giles, 2005). Michael may be thinking a good college is close to home, is involved in the local community, and offers small class sizes. Jamal may be thinking a good college involves the opportunity to live in a new city and the chance to study at an institution that has drawn an international student body.

Clearly, thinking affects the language you use, but language also affects thought. If you sum up a coworker as an "idiot" in your mind, you might use the word *idiot* to his face; it may influence things you will reveal to him (or not) and the kinds of messages you construct for him. Your evaluation of him may cause you to treat him abruptly, not give him a chance to respond, or avoid him altogether. Even the words you use *with yourself* about others affect your experiences with them. For example, a study of women who stayed in violent romantic heterosexual relationships found that they often concocted dark romance narratives or fairy-tale accounts to explain why the violence was their fault or that the violence was somehow an expression of caring and concern (J. T. Wood, 2001).

## Language Is Ruled by Grammar

In Alice Walker's Pulitzer Prize–winning novel *The Color Purple* (1982), Celie, who is black, struggles with learning to read from a primer written for white children. Being corrected numerous times confuses and frustrates her, and she says, "Look like to me only a fool would want you to talk in a way that feel peculiar to your mind" (p. 184). Does good grammar equal good communication? Is it necessary for Celie to master standard grammatical English in order to communicate well?

The answer to these questions is yes, *to some extent.* As your third-grade teacher probably drilled into your head, **grammar**—the system of rules of a language that serves as a mechanism for the creation of words, phrases, and sentences—is absolutely important. Using the correct grammar of a particular language helps ensure communication clarity. For example, no one is going to legally stop you from pronouncing the word *tomato* "tommy-toe" (as one of our cousins did as a child), but this doesn't mean that anyone will understand that you are referring to the red fruit that tastes really good on a hamburger. That's because grammar has *phonological rules,* or rules about how words should be pronounced.

Similarly, grammar has *syntactic rules,* or rules about the placement of words in a sentence. To prove this point, take any simple sentence, such as "I ran to the store to buy some milk," and place the words in a different order. Suddenly your sentence, and your message, becomes entirely unclear. The importance of grammar is also highlighted in our attempts to learn other languages. Native speakers of English, for example, often have to remind themselves that the grammar of Romance languages (such as French and Spanish) requires a different syntax. For example, in English, adjectives typically precede a noun ("I have an intelligent dog"), while in Spanish, they follow the noun (*"Tengo un perro intelegente,"* literally translated as "I have a dog intelligent"). But to communicate clearly in Spanish, an English speaker must adjust.

Nonetheless, excellent grammar will not automatically make you an outstanding communicator. Telling your professor in perfect English that her style of dress is a sorry flashback to the 1980s is still offensive and inappropriate. That's because competent communication considers the situational, relational, and cultural context.

## Language Is Bound by Context

Imagine a scenario in which your cousin prattles on and on about her wild spring break in Miami—how much she drank, how many parties she went to, and so on. Now imagine that she's talking to your seventy-year-old grandmother . . . at your niece's fifth birthday party . . . in front of a group of conservative, devoutly religious family members. There are many responses to this particular scenario, which underscore one of the more complicated aspects of language: it is bound by contexts such as our relationship with the people we're with, the situation we're in, and the cultural factors at play. Does Grandma really want to hear about your cousin's behavior? Is it really OK to talk about this at a kid's party? And what about respecting the beliefs and sensibilities of your family members? We examine the relational, situational, and cultural context later on, but for now just know that communicating competently involves understanding context as much as it means understanding grammar.

● **IT'S PROBABLY** a good idea to avoid regaling your grandmother with tales of your crazy spring-break shenanigans.

## The Functions of Language

One of the very first phrases that little Josie learned to use was "thank you." Had this eighteen-month-old toddler already mastered the rules of etiquette? Was she just picking up a habit from her parents? Or was she learning that the use of certain phrases would help her get what she wants: a compliment, a smile, a cookie?

Effective language use is essential for successful communication. You learn isolated words and grammar as you acquire language. Little Josie, for example, probably picked up the expression "thank you" from her parents, her older brother, or her babysitter. But to be a competent communicator, she must learn to use symbols appropriately. If Josie uses "thank you" as a manner of greeting or as a name for her stuffed bear, she's not using it appropriately, so she's not communicating effectively. **Communication acquisition** requires that we not only learn individual words in a language but also learn to use that language *appropriately* and *effectively* in the context of the situation. And just as Josie gets a smile from her parents for saying "thank you," we must use language competently to achieve our goals.

The language researcher Barbara Wood (1982) identified five functional communication competencies that focus on how language behaviors work or function for people. We all develop these when we're young by interacting with family and peers and observing television and other media (which give us a broader picture of the world). These competencies—controlling, informing, feeling, imagining, and ritualizing—remain important throughout our lives and are worth exploring in order to improve our communication.

Using language as an instrument of control is part of our *self-presentation,* discussed in Chapter 2. When you're on a job interview (Appendix), you'll want to use clear, professional language that highlights your skills in order to present yourself as a qualified candidate. Similarly, when delivering a speech (Chapter 13), your language choices should let your audience know that you're engaged with your topic and prepared to discuss it.

● **WE'VE ALL BEEN THERE:** a tourist asks you for directions and you mutter, "Um, yeah, you go a little bit up this way, and turn around that way . . ."

## Using Language as a Means of Control

Language is used as an instrument of *control,* to influence oneself, others, and the environment. Josie's use of the phrase "thank you" impresses her mother, who reassures her that using the term makes her a "good girl." Such appropriate use of language can make children seem cute, smart, or polite, giving them the ability to present themselves in a positive light.

Recall from Chapter 1 that *control* is actually a neutral term; it may be positive or negative but is in any event a crucial social skill. Josie will quickly learn that using "thank you" appropriately has positive repercussions. As she gets older, she may learn to use language to bargain ("I'll eat my peas if I can have ice cream") or manipulate ("You're the best, Dad—can I stay up until the movie ends?"). As an adult, Josie will be able to use language to control her environment by persuading others to vote for her favorite presidential candidate or against land development in her community. She'll be able to negotiate a raise in salary and bargain with a car dealer. It is important, however, that Josie avoid negative control strategies such as whining, ridiculing, insulting, threatening, or belittling, as they are not signs of a productive, successful communicator and can actually damage relationships.

## Using Language to Share Information

Have you ever asked a sick child to tell you "where it hurts," only to receive a vague and unhelpful answer? This is because young children are still developing the next functional competency, **informing,** or using language to both give and receive information. As an adult, if you've ever been asked for directions, you know very well that providing people with information that they can understand and in turn understanding the information others convey to you are equally important skills.

There are four important aspects of this informing competency: questioning, describing, reinforcing, and withholding.

▶ *Questioning* is a crucial step in communication that we learn at a young age and use throughout our lives. Young children hungry for information about their world quickly learn the power of the simple, one-word question "Why?"

▶ *Describing* helps us find out about the world and communicate our world to others. Parents and teachers may ask children to repeat directions to their school or their home or to detail the specifics of a story they've heard.

▶ *Reinforcing* information can be an important aspect of competent listening. We might take notes or simply repeat the information (to ourselves or to the other person) to confirm our comprehension.

▶ *Withholding* information or opinions may be the most useful thing to do in a number of situations. Knowing when to reveal information and when to withhold it may require a certain level of maturity—you may choose, for example, not to express your opposition to your manager's plan because you want to keep your job or not to reveal a piece of information that might embarrass a friend.

Together, these four skills form the basis of the informational competency that we use to communicate throughout our lives.

## Using Language to Express Feelings

Poets, writers, and lyricists are celebrated for using language to capture and express emotions. But most expressions of feelings are less elaborately composed than a Shakespearean sonnet or an angry protest song. In everyday conversation and correspondence, we use language to send messages to others to express how we feel about ourselves, about them, or about the situation. Young children can say, "I'm sad," and cry or laugh to communicate feelings. As we mature, we learn how to express liking, love, respect, empathy, hostility, and pride—a complex set of emotions. The functional competency of **feeling** is primarily relational. We let people know how much we value (or don't value) them by the emotions we express.

We all use language to express our feelings, but being competent at it requires that we do so in an appropriate and effective way. Many people find themselves unable to communicate well when it comes to their own emotions: Elliot might express his frustration with his staff by yelling at them; his staff might respond by raking Elliot over the coals at a local pub after work. Elliot could have said, "I'm feeling *worried* that we're not going to make the deadline on this project"; someone on his staff could have said, "I'm feeling *tense* about making the deadline, too, but I'm *confused* about why you yelled at me." There are also times when we choose to avoid expressing feelings that we judge to be inappropriate or risky in a given situation (Burleson, Holmstrom, & Gilstrap, 2005). For example, when Abby's husband tries to talk about starting a family, Abby might find herself changing the subject to avoid admitting that she doesn't think she's ready to take that step.

## Using Language to Express Creativity

What do Charles Foster Kane, Harry Potter, Wolverine, Lady Macbeth, and Special Agent Jack Bauer have in common? Each is the product of the imagination of a writer or storyteller. And regardless of whether they were conceptualized as part of a novel, comic book, or play, each character and his or her story was primarily expressed through language.

**Imagining** is probably the most complex functional competency. It is the ability to think, play, and be creative in communication. Children pretend to do something or to be someone (a superhero, a cartoon character, a person from a movie). Adults continue to enjoy this kind of creative communication. The way a song is worded, the way a play is scripted, and the way special effects coordinate with the message delivered in a film—these function to entertain us by stimulating our imaginations. On the job, imagining is the ability to use language to convey a vision for a project to your coworkers (such as an architect using words to

As indicated, sometimes competent language use means knowing when to withhold information or avoid topics. This is particularly important when developing and maintaining interpersonal relationships (Chapter 6). For example, *strategic topic avoidance* allows you to steer the conversation away from discussing your friend Emily's recent painful breakup until Emily feels ready to discuss it with you.

Using language to express feelings competently can be a powerful addition to your communication skills in a variety of settings. In a small group setting (Chapter 8), you need to express your frustration with the fact that you're doing most of the work. Similarly, in an organizational setting (Chapter 10), you might save your company time and money by effectively sharing your concerns about a project.

explain blueprints and models). In a debate, imagining skills enable you to think ahead of your opponent, to put words to each side of an argument, and to use language in ways that are logical and convincing.

## Using Language as Ritual

When little Josie said "thank you" for her cookie, it was a sign that she learned the fifth functional competency: ritualizing. **Ritualizing** involves learning the rules for managing conversations and relationships. We begin learning these rules as children: peekaboo games facilitate learning turn-taking in conversations. Learning to say "hi" or "bye-bye" or "please" means internalizing politeness rituals. Later, teasing, joke telling, and even gossiping may be early lessons in how to manage relationships.

In adulthood, ritualizing effectively means you say and do the "right" thing at weddings, funerals, dinners, athletic events, and other social gatherings. Too bad no one told Mitch (Luke Wilson) that in the 2003 movie *Old School.* As best man at the wedding of his friend Frank (Will Ferrell), Mitch gives a depressing speech on the topic of his own painful breakup rather than following protocol and toasting the happy newlyweds. Everyone feels the discomfort until Beanie (Vince Vaughn) steps in and takes over the speech.

● **RULE NUMBER ONE** for wedding toasts: don't talk about depressing breakups!

## Problems with Language

"I think we're still in a muddle with our language, because once you get words and a spoken language it gets harder to communicate" (Ewalt, 2005, para. 1). The famous primatologist Jane Goodall made this point when explaining why chimpanzees get over their disputes much faster than humans. They strike out at each other and then offer each other reassuring pats or embraces, and *voilà,* argument over. Not so with people: words can be really hard to forget.

As you've probably experienced, words can lead to confusion, hurt feelings, misunderstandings, and anger when we blurt things out before considering them (and their effects) carefully. We sometimes speak too vaguely and fail to consider the timing of our words. We sometimes use labels in ways others don't appreciate, reveal bias through our words, or confuse the difference between facts and opinions.

## Abstraction and Meaning

Language operates at many levels of abstraction, meaning that it can range from being very vague to very specific. You might talk in such broad, vague terms that no one knows what you are talking about ("Food is good!"), or you can speak so specifically that people may think you are keeping notes for a court case against them: "I saw you at 10:32 P.M. on Friday, January 29, at the right-hand corner table of Harry's Bar with a six-foot-tall, brown-haired man wearing black jeans, boots, and a powder blue T-shirt."

The famous linguist S. I. Hayakawa (1964) illustrated the specific versus the general levels of abstraction by constructing an **abstraction ladder** (see Figure 3.1). The top rungs of the ladder are high-level abstractions: these are the most general and vague. Lower-level abstractions are more specific and can help you understand more precisely what people mean. "Request something interesting from Netflix" is a high abstraction that allows a wide range of choices (and the possibility of some really bad movies). Saying "I'd like to watch a drama tonight" (lower abstraction) is more likely to get you something you'll appreciate, while naming the exact movie ("Get *Atonement*") ensures satisfaction.

But even though lower abstractions ensure clarity, high abstractions can accomplish certain communication goals. Here are a few examples:

▶ *Evasion.* We employ highly abstract language as a means of **evasion**, to avoid providing specific details. A teenager might tell her parents that she is "going out with some friends." Her parents might counter by demanding less ab-

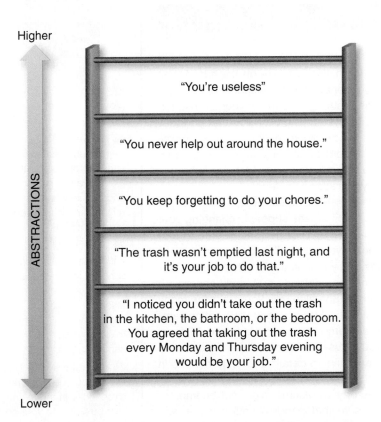

FIGURE 3.1

**THE ABSTRACTION LADDER**

Higher

ABSTRACTIONS

"You're useless"

"You never help out around the house."

"You keep forgetting to do your chores."

"The trash wasn't emptied last night, and it's your job to do that."

"I noticed you didn't take out the trash in the kitchen, the bathroom, or the bedroom. You agreed that taking out the trash every Monday and Thursday evening would be your job."

Lower

● **SKATEBOARDERS HAVE** their own jargon for their fancy flips and tricks. If you're not a skateboarder, an "ollie" might seem like a foreign concept.

stract answers: "Where exactly are you going to be? Which particular friends are you going with?"

▶ *Equivocation.* Another form of high-level abstraction is **equivocation**, using words that have unclear or misleading definitions. Equivocation may be used strategically to get out of an uncomfortable situation, as when a friend asks what you think of her new sweater—which you think is hideous—and you reply, "It's . . . *colorful.*"

▶ *Euphemisms.* Sometimes we employ highly abstract **euphemisms**, inoffensive words or phrases that substitute for terms that might be perceived as upsetting. For example, you might say that your uncle "passed on" rather than "died" or that your mother had a "procedure" rather than an "operation."

Abstract language can also say a lot about groups you belong to or identify with. For example, **slang** is language that is informal, nonstandard, and usually particular to a specific group; it operates as a high-level abstraction because meanings of slang are known only by a particular group of people

## EVALUATINGCOMMUNICATIONETHICS

**THINK ABOUT THIS**

### Résumé Language

You've just graduated with a B.A. in journalism and are on the hunt for an entry-level position as a writer or copyeditor at a local newspaper or news organization. You know that your résumé is strong in terms of your degree, relevant coursework, and good grades, but you're a bit worried that you may not have enough real-world news experience. Since you had to work full time to pay college expenses, you couldn't afford to take the kinds of unpaid internships that look so impressive on a résumé; you waited tables all through college instead and graduated in five years instead of four.

You discuss these concerns with a friend who suggests making some changes in the language of your résumé. First, she suggests changing your entry date for college to make it look like you finished the degree in four years. Second, when noting the articles you've published in your campus newspaper, *The Monitor,* she suggests that you omit the fact that *The Monitor* is a school-sponsored newspaper and that instead you simply describe it as a 7,500-circulation weekly newspaper. She also tells you to list the many articles you've posted on your sister's political blog among your writing samples, since your sister uses her married name and no employer would know you are related. Finally, she tells you to use your cover letter to describe yourself as "a team player" who is "attentive to detail" and "experienced in the newsroom."

You're worried that some aspects of your résumé might not be impressive enough, but you're not entirely sure that padding your résumé with vague language and empty jargon is the way to go. What will you do?

❶ Is it crucial that an employer know how long it took you to earn your B.A.?

❷ Will you follow your friend's suggestion to use vague expressions like "team player" or "experienced"? In what ways might you use more precise terms to describe yourself?

❸ Is it ethical to describe your college newspaper in a way that makes it sound like you worked there in a professional rather than voluntary capacity? Is intentionally misleading an employer the same thing as lying?

❹ Might there be ways in which you could use real experience in the restaurant business to your advantage here?

during a specific time in history. A rock concert might be described as "groovy," "totally awesome," or "off the hook"—each expression places the speaker in a particular time or place in the world. Related to slang is **jargon**, technical language that is specific to members of a given profession or interest group or people who share a hobby. Jargon may seem abstract and vague to those outside the group but conveys clear and precise meanings to those within

> **AND YOU?**
>
> What kinds of slang or jargon do you regularly use? How did you become familiar with these terms? And how would you go about explaining these terms to someone who is unfamiliar with them?

## real communicator

**NAME:** Snowden Wright
**HOMETOWN:** Meridian, Michigan
**OCCUPATION:** Administrative assistant at Columbia University Graduate School of Business
**FUN FACT:** I own a copy of every Pauly Shore movie made prior to 2002.

The orders came to me in two different ways. First, the waitresses screamed them through the window that connected the dining area with the kitchen. "Cheeseburger, bloody," they said. "Eighty-six the toms." Second, the orders came to me written on little white tickets. "G-C-squared, SP-SW," one read. "Healthy side, x basket." It was my first day working as a short-order cook, and I was already out of my league. The waitresses yelled louder and louder through the window. The little white tickets piled higher and higher. My problem wasn't that I couldn't keep up with the orders; my problem was that I didn't understand what the orders meant.

The Westside Grill, I soon learned, has its own language that relies on a lot of restaurant-specific jargon to convey information between the servers and the cooks. For example, when the waitresses say, "Cheeseburger, bloody, eighty-six the toms," they mean a customer has ordered a cheeseburger, cooked rare, hold the tomatoes. When an order ticket reads, "G-C-squared, SP-SW, healthy side, x basket," it means—through a series of acronyms—that a customer has ordered a grilled chicken wrap, cut in half, on a spinach tortilla, with Swiss cheese, a side order of fruit, and an extra basket.

I knew from my college courses on communication that if I didn't learn this language—quickly—I'd be having a pretty awful time at work. So I set about figuring it all out. On my first day, I reinforced the spoken information by repeating the orders aloud (hoping to confirm, in front of the waitresses, that I understood what they were saying), but I also withheld the fact that I did not understand them (again, hoping to confirm, in front of the waitresses, that I'm a pretty smart guy). Later that day, when things were slower in the dining area, I questioned the waitresses about what the orders meant, but rather than describing their answers, the waitresses gave me blank, humorless stares. "What?" they said. "You don't speak English?" Great. You can see how thought and language work in this situation. A "healthy side" seems like a pretty vague abstraction to me (aren't cucumbers and carrots healthy sides?), but to the waitresses of the Westside Grill, the words clearly mean "side of fruit". I had to keep this in mind as I set about making my summer job work out.

Through trial and error and sheer persistence, asking questions when necessary and observing my coworkers, I became fluent in the Westside Grill's language. I understood not only the words spoken by the waitresses but also those written on the little white tickets. My language skills grew so developed that I even introduced new vocabulary to the kitchen. "To hockey-puck" a burger, for example, means to cook it well done. Sometimes the waitresses hear the new words and ask me to explain them. "What?" I say. "You don't speak English?"

to situational factors, preferring to observe those factors rather than comment on each one. Individuals in **high-context cultures** (including Japan, Korea, China, and many Latin American and African cultures) use contextual cues—such as time, place, relationship, and situation—to both interpret meaning and send subtle messages. A Chinese person who disagrees with someone, for example, may not say anything; the communication partner must look for clues of disagreement in the context. These clues may include the amount of time that passes before a response or the nonverbal behaviors that occur or don't occur. A person from a high-context culture is also more likely to attribute a communication partner's behavior to factors related to the situation than to an individual's personality. In other words, people in a high-context culture would not assume that someone is rude for remaining silent; they would be more likely to think that the individual didn't respond because the situation called for restraint and politeness.

A **low-context culture**, by contrast, uses very direct language. The United States, Canada, Australia, and most northern European cultures tend to have this low-context style—they do not rely as much on the context of the communication situation for meaning. In the United States, for example, it would seem normal for someone to say, "Alex, I need a list of twenty items for the Allan project from you by five o'clock today." Someone from a high-context culture would more likely say, "We are starting the project," and would assume that Alex would have the list ready on time because Alex understands the situation as the speaker does. If Alex did not get the list completed on time, a boss in a low-context culture would blame it on his laziness or incompetence, whereas a manager in a high-context culture would blame it on situational constraints, such as Alex having too many projects to work on. High- and low-context styles are compared in Table 3.1.

### Gender and Language

In a scene from the 1996 cult film *Trainspotting,* two couples attending a dance club are chatting above the din of music. The women have gone off to the bathroom, the men stay behind, and both pairs are deep in talk about their relationships.

---

**TABLE 3.1**

A COMPARISON OF HIGH- AND LOW-CONTEXT CULTURES

| High-Context Cultures | Low-Context Cultures |
|---|---|
| • Rely on contextual cues for communication<br>• Avoid speaking in a way that causes individuals to stand out from others<br>• Avoid intruding on others<br>• Avoid saying no directly, preferring to talk around the point<br>• Usually express opinions indirectly<br>• Usually express disagreement by saying nothing<br>• Tend to find explanations for behaviors in the situation<br>• Admire relationship harmony | • Rely on direct language for communication<br>• Value self-expression<br>• Construct explicit messages<br>• State opinions and desires directly<br>• Persuade others by speaking clearly and eloquently<br>• Usually express disagreement clearly and directly<br>• Tend to find explanations for behaviors in individuals<br>• Admire verbal fluency |

When the women return and ask the men what they're discussing, the men quickly reply, "Football." When the men pose the same question, the women tartly shoot back, "Shopping."

The idea that men and women speak entirely different languages is popular fodder for comedy, talk shows, and pop psychologists. But actual research findings indicate that these differences between men and women are much smaller than the popular press indicates (Mulac, Wiemann, Widenmann, & Gibson, 1988). As Mary Crawford (1995) notes, studying language from a sex-difference approach can be misleading, as it treats women (and men too) as a homogenous "global category," paying little attention to differences in ethnicity, religion, sexuality, economic status, and other factors. These cultural factors deeply affect our thinking and perception of gender roles, and gender roles, in turn, are often inscribed with "different languages" for the masculine and the feminine (Gudykunst & Ting-Toomey, 1988).

Consider how social expectations for masculinity and femininity might play out in men's and women's conversation styles, particularly when negotiating power (who has more control in a given relationship). Powerful controlling language may be used to define limits, authority, and relationship. Less controlling language is used to express affection, defining the affiliation level in the relationship. Let's look at a few examples.

▶ *Interruptions.* Male speakers are thought to interrupt others in conversation more than female speakers, but the situation and the status of the speakers are probably better predictors of interruptions than biological sex (Pearson, Turner, & Todd-Mancillas, 1991). For example, female professors can be expected to interrupt male students more often than those male students interrupt the professors, owing to the difference in power and status. When status and situation are neutral, men tend to interrupt women considerably more often than women interrupt men, according to Zimmerman & West (as cited in Ivy & Backlund, 2004).

▶ *Qualifiers, hedges, and disclaimers.* Language that sounds hesitant or uncertain is often perceived as being less powerful—and such hesitations are often associated with women's speech. *Qualifiers* include terms like *kind of, sort of, maybe, perhaps, could be,* and *possibly*; *hedges* involve expressions such as "I think," "I feel," or "I guess" ("Oh, I guess maybe we could go to Chicago instead of London for vacation"). *Disclaimers* discount what you are about to say and are often used to head off confrontation or to avoid embarrassment: "It's probably nothing, but I think . . ." or "I'm likely imagining things, but I thought I saw . . ." (Borisoff & Merrill, 1998).

▶ *Tag questions.* Another sign of hesitancy or uncertainty associated with women's speech is the *tag question,* as in "That was a beautiful sunset, wasn't it?" or "That waitress was totally obnoxious, wasn't she?" Tag questions attempt to get your conversational partner to agree with you, establishing a connection based on similar opinions. Interestingly, some research reveals that tag questions are not always examples of hesitancy or uncertainty. As noted in a study by Spender (as cited in Ivy & Backlund, 2004), sometimes they come across as full-fledged threats—for example, "You're not going to smoke another cigarette, *are you?*"

CONNECT

Gendered language often affects mixed-sex small group settings. Women are socially encouraged to use affectionate language to keep the peace and share power (Chapter 8). Men are rewarded for taking charge of a group and using direct, action-oriented language. Competent communicators must be aware of these differences in style and must promote group communication that encourages all members to share and challenge ideas in order to achieve group goals.

### AND YOU?

What are your personal thoughts on sex, gender, and language? Do you think men and women speak different languages, or do you feel that we all speak more similarly than differently? How do your thoughts and opinions match up with the research we've cited in this chapter?

▶ *Resistance messages.* Date rape awareness programs advise women to use the word *no* when a male partner or friend makes an unwanted sexual advance. But a woman might instead say, "I don't have protection," choosing vague or evasive language over the direct no to avoid a scene or hurt feelings. Men, however, sometimes perceive an indirect denial as a yes. Women's use of clearer messages, coupled with men's increased understanding of women's preference for more indirect resistance messages, can lead to more competent communication in this very important area (Lim & Roloff, 1999; Motley & Reeder, 1995).

### Geography and Language

Our editor from New Jersey assures us that even in such a small state, it makes a big difference if you are from North Jersey or South Jersey. (The status of people from the middle part of the state remains unclear, at least to us!) People in North Jersey eat subs (sandwiches that you buy at 7-Eleven or QuickChek) and Italian ice (a frozen dessert); the night before Halloween, when shaving cream and toilet paper abound, is Goosey Night or Cabbage Night; and "the City" is, of course, New York City. People from South Jersey eat hoagies (typically from a convenience store called Wawa) and water ice; the night before Halloween is Mischief Night; and going to "the City" means taking a trip to Philadelphia.

As this example illustrates, even speakers of the same language who grow up a mere fifty miles apart find that the culture of their environment affects their language and their understanding of the world. Now, the world won't end if you walk into Wawa and order a sub (though you might get an irritated look from the person preparing your sandwich), but other examples are more extreme. A British friend moved to Ottawa, Canada, and needed to do some grocery shopping. Disappointed with the cuts of meat on display, she asked the butcher if he could give her a joint. The butcher stared back at her with a shocked look on his face, and she couldn't understand why. She, of course, wanted a large roast; he, however, thought she was asking if he could find her some marijuana. And then there's Ada, our associate editor, who kindly shared an embarrassing moment with us (and is allowing us to tell you). When she came to the United States from Hong Kong, she knew she had to give up some of her Britishisms in order to communicate more effectively with her American-born classmates at Wesleyan University. This was never more apparent then when she asked a classmate for a rubber to correct some mistakes in her notebook. She wanted an eraser; he thought she was asking for a condom. Needless to say, she was a bit perplexed by his response: "Maybe after class?"

### AND YOU?

Think back to where you grew up—whether in the United States or abroad. Are there any terms that you use that would cause confusion to others who speak your native tongue? Have you ever been in a situation where you've used a regional term that caused an embarrassing miscommunication?

● **IS THIS A SUB** or a hoagie? Perhaps a hero or just a plain old sandwich?

## Accommodation

One tool that can be helpful when we communicate with individuals from different cultures or co-cultures is **accommodation**, changing our communication behavior to adapt to the other person (Giles & Smith, 1979). If we accommodate in a positive way, we usually *converge,* seeking approval and showing solidarity by changing our language and vocabulary as well as our tone, rate, and pitch (to be discussed in Chapter 4) to be more similar to those of our communication partners. But if we emphasize differences by failing to accommodate or by refusing to adapt, we often experience a negative outcome.

Cultures and co-cultures signal their identification with their particular groups by using specialized language, accents, or vocabulary; they maintain or assert their group identity in this way, sometimes even exaggerating behaviors to keep others out or to signal their contempt for people in another group (Hecht, Jackson, & Ribeau, 2003). **Code switching** and **style switching** are types of accommodation in which communicators change their regular language and slang, as well as their tonality, pitch, rhythm, and inflection, to fit into a particular group. These language accommodations may be ways to survive, to manage defensiveness, to manage identity, or to signal power or status (Bourhis, 1985). A great example of this is Hugh Grant's attempt at being a Mafioso in the 1999 film *Mickey Blue Eyes*. When his character, Michael, becomes engaged to Gina, he also inadvertently becomes involved with her Mafia family. At first, it's just doing a few "favors" for her relatives, but soon he's helping bury bodies and forced into pretending to be the notorious "Little Big Mickey Blue" from Kansas. His future father-in-law coaches Michael to change his *t*'s to *d*'s and drop his *r*'s, hoping he'll be able to say *fuhgeddaboudit* like a true mobster. Although his attempts at Mafia-speak are terrible, Michael still manages to fool a few people.

● FUHGEDDABOUDIT!
The proper-British-speaking Michael fails miserably at talking like a mobster and blending in with the Mafia.

## Technology as Context

Have you ever sent an e-mail or a text message that was misunderstood by the recipient? It has happened to all of us—and that's often because our e-mails, text messages, and IMs lack the nonverbal cues and hints that we provide in face-to-face conversation. So if you text your partner to say that you both have to spend Friday night with your slightly quirky Aunt Ethel and he texts you back "Great," is he really excited? Is he being sarcastic? "Great" could mean either thing, but you can't see his nonverbal reaction to know if he's smiling or grimacing and rolling his eyes. That's why, when communicating in the context of technology, language must be very clear to be most effective (Walther, 2004). For example, language that is more intense (powerful, committed, strong, not neutral) gets more responses in e-mail surveys, likely because it directs attention to important points (Andersen & Blackburn, 2004). And people in computer-mediated groups who use more powerful language are seen as more credible, attractive, and persuasive (Adkins & Brashers, 1995).

● **ALTHOUGH MANY** of America's customer-service-representative jobs have been relocated to other countries, you should have no problems communicating in a common language.

But technology affects language use in other ways, including the proliferation of English as the language of the Internet. The Internet allows users to live in a global society. Individuals in Salt Lake City, São Paulo, and Stockholm can all communicate digitally, often in English, which has dominated the Internet, despite the fact that two-thirds of all Internet users are not native English speakers (Lievrouw, 2000). Similarly, critics claim that because English dominates the mass media industries, the values and thinking of English speakers are being imposed on the non-English-speaking world. Nevertheless, many non-Western countries have benefited from this proliferation, with countless jobs being relocated to places like India and Hong Kong. The emergence of a dominant language and digital connections have changed the communication—and subsequently, the economic—landscape (Friedman, 2007).

Despite the controversies surrounding English and the Internet and mass media, technology has, in some sense, created a language of its own. The language of text messaging and chat rooms frequently relies on acronyms (IMO for "in my opinion," LOL for "laughing out loud"), which have come to be used and understood in a variety of other contexts (see Table 3.2). The need for these acronyms is influenced by the fact that this context for communication is meant to be rapid and direct. Any system that reduces the number of keystrokes improves the speed and efficiency of the medium. At the same time, however, it's important to keep text language in its appropriate context. If your professor

**TABLE 3.2**

**THE LANGUAGE OF TEXT MESSAGING**

| | | | | | |
|---|---|---|---|---|---|
| Anything | **NTHING** | Later | **L8R** | Work | **WRK** |
| Are you OK | **RUOK?** | Love | **LUV** | Why | **Y** |
| Are | **R** | Mate | **M8** | You | **U** |
| Ate | **8** | Please | **PLS** | Happy | **:-)** |
| Be | **B** | Please call me | **PCM** | Very happy | **:-))** |
| Before | **B4** | Queue/cue | **Q** | Angry | **:-II** |
| Be seeing you | **BCNU** | Rate | **R8** | Confused | **%-)** |
| Cutie | **QT** | See/sea | **C** | Tongue-tied | **:-&** |
| Date | **D8** | See you later | **CU L8R** | Sad | **:-(** |
| Dinner | **DNR** | Speak | **SPK** | Saintly | **O:-)** |
| Easy | **EZ** | Tea | **T** | Laughing | **:-D** |
| Eh? | **A?** | Thanks | **THX** | Crying | **:'-(** |
| Excellent | **XLNT** | Thank you | **THNQ** | Surprised/ | |
| Fate | **F8** | To/too | **2** | shocked | **:-O** |
| For | **4** | To be | **2B** | Screaming | **:-@** |
| For your | | Today | **2DAY** | Kiss | **:-*** |
| information | **FYI** | Tomorrow | **2MORO** | Pig | **:@)** |
| Great | **GR8** | Want to | **WAN2** | Clown | ***:-)** |
| Late | **L8** | What | **WOT** | | |

Source: Nash (2008).

writes you an e-mail regarding your recent absences from class, it's probably not a good idea to respond with "NOYB, IMHO" (none of your business, in my humble opinion). It's inappropriate on several levels—it shows a lack of respect for your instructor (obviously!) but also a lack of understanding regarding context. E-mail etiquette requires more than just a string of acronyms; complete sentences are often appreciated by the message recipient.

## BACK TO  Our Partners

Our discussion of the word *partner* and its various meanings made it clear that the labels we choose are incredibly powerful—and can be fraught with communication complications.

▶ The word *partner* has several denotative meanings, as we discussed earlier. But it can also have powerful connotative meanings. Let's look at romantic couples who choose the term *partner*. When some people hear an individual refer to his or her "partner," they may assume the individual is gay or lesbian—and may have positive, negative, or neutral reactions based on their cultural background. Others may receive the term suspiciously, feeling that the individual is trying to hide his or her marital or legal status. Still others may react favorably, believing that *partner* is a term that marks equality in romantic relationships.

▶ Abstraction plays an important role in the use of the term *partner*. Saying "This is my boyfriend" or "This is my business partner" is a low-level abstraction, offering others a clear definition of your status. But the term *partner* is a high-level abstraction, keeping your status and relationship considerably more vague.

▶ Considering the relational, situational, and cultural context is one way to make the term *partner* less abstract and vague. If you let your chemistry professor know that your "partner" needs some help with an experiment, the instructor understands that you mean your lab partner rather than your romantic partner or the person you play tennis with. Similarly, when introducing the love of your life to your elderly great-aunt, you might want to use a less ambiguous term. Your aunt may be of a generation that did not use the term *partner* to apply to a love interest.

## THINGS TO TRY

1. Take a look at a piece of writing you've produced (an essay, your résumé, or an e-mail to a friend). Do you use high or low levels of abstraction? Is your choice of language appropriate for the communication contexts involved? (For example, is your essay written in a way that is mindful of your relationship with your professor and the academic setting?)

2. Describe the similarities and differences you find in the language you use and the language a close friend or family member of the opposite sex uses over the

course of a single conversation. What did you notice? Were there any misunder-standings or power struggles in this conversation? How do your findings match up with what the research we presented tells us?

3. Watch an episode of your favorite television show, paying special attention to the dialogue between specific characters. Does the dialogue reflect and reveal the characters' relationships with each other? Or is it primarily concerned with re-vealing plot details? Explain.

## IF YOU'RE INTERESTED

*Sex and Gender Differences in Personal Relationships,* by Daniel J. Canary and Tara M. Emmers-Sommer, with Sandra Faulkner (New York: Guilford Press, 1997)

This book injects sanity into the gender and language debate fueled by Deborah Tannen's view of gender as two cultures and John Gray's exaggerated sex claims about men and women coming from different planets. Canary and Emmers-Sommer hold that Tannen's and Gray's views about gender and language are simplistic; the authors detail a more complex and more accurate way of under-standing people and how they relate to each other.

*Language and Language Behaviors Series,* edited by Howard Giles (Newbury Park, CA: Sage, 1990)

You might find any one of the books in this series interesting: Adam Jaworski, *Power of Silence;* Sik Hung Hg and James Bradac, *Power in Language;* and Niko-las Coupland and Jon F. Nussbaum (Eds.), *Discourse and Lifespan Identity.* Another book in an extension of this series, by Michael L. Hecht, Ronald L. Jackson II, and Sidney A. Ribeau, is listed in the References.

*The N Word: Divided We Stand* [DVD] (MediaLink Entertainment, 2004)

This Peabody Award–winning documentary film takes a look at what is perhaps the most potent, volatile, and controversial word in American English. With historical insights into the evolution of the meaning of the word and its use over the years both within the black community and elsewhere, as well as personal accounts from figures from Chuck D to Bryant Gumbel, *The N Word* offers a thorough, thoughtful, and compelling examination of language and culture.

*Mockingbird Don't Sing* (Dorian Films, 2001)

This film tells the story of "Katie," a thirteen-year-old girl whose parents kept her locked in her bedroom tied to a chair. Inspired by the real-life events sur-rounding the young "Genie" we mentioned in this chapter, the film follows the fictional linguist Sandra Tannen in her attempts to teach Katie language and ba-sic communication skills.

# REAL REFERENCE ▶ A Study Tool

**Now that you have finished reading this chapter, you can**

Understand the power of **language**, the system of symbols we use to think about and communicate experiences and feelings:

▶ Words are symbols that have meanings agreed to by speakers of a language (p. 72).

▶ A **denotative meaning** is the accepted definition of a word; its **connotative meaning** is the emotional or attitudinal response to it (p. 73).

▶ **Cognitive language** is what you use to describe people, things, and situations in your mind (p. 74).

▶ Correct **grammar**, the rules of a language, helps ensure clarity (p. 74).

▶ Learning words and how to use them effectively is the process of **communication acquisition** (p. 75).

Identify the ways communication functions for people, the five functional communication competencies:

▶ As an instrument of control (p. 76)

▶ For **informing**, including four aspects: questioning, describing, reinforcing, and withholding (p. 76)

▶ For expressing **feelings**, letting people know how we value them (p. 77)

▶ For **imagining**, communicating a creative idea (p. 77)

▶ For **ritualizing**, managing conversations and relationships (p. 78)

Recognize communication problems and how to address them:

▶ The **abstraction ladder** ranks communication from specific, which ensures clarity, to general and vague (p. 79).

▶ Some communication situations may call for abstractions: **evasion**, avoiding specifics; **equivocation**, using unclear terms; or **euphemisms**, using substitutions for terms that might be upsetting (pp. 79–80).

▶ **Slang** is a group's informal language; **jargon** is a group's technical language (pp. 80–81).

▶ **Semantics** refers to the meaning that words have; **pragmatics** refers to the ability to use them appropriately (p. 83).

▶ We ignore individual differences when we place gender, ethnic, or other role labels on people (p. 85).

▶ **Biased language** has subtle meanings that influence perception; using **politically correct language** is an attempt at neutrality (pp. 86–87).

▶ **Facts** are verifiable, **opinions** involve personal evaluations, and **inferences** are conclusions based on facts (p. 87).

Understand that language reflects, builds on, and determines context:

▶ We use different **speech repertoires** to find the most effective language for a given situation (p. 88).

▶ We use language to create or reflect the context of a relationship (p. 88).

▶ Some situations call for formal language, **high language**, while in more comfortable environments, **low language**, often including slang, is appropriate (p. 90).

▶ The **Sapir-Whorf hypothesis** suggests that our words influence our thinking (p. 91).

▶ **Linguistic determinism** is the idea that language influences how we see the world; **linguistic relativity** holds that speakers of different languages have different views of the world (p. 91).

▶ Individuals in **high-context cultures** use contextual cues, such as time, place, relationship, and situation, to both interpret meaning and send subtle messages; in **low-context cultures**, language is much more direct (p. 92).

▶ Assuming gender differences in communication can be misleading, yet some differences in masculine and feminine language exist (p. 93).

▶ The culture of the geographical area affects language (p. 94).

▶ **Code switching** and **style switching**, changing language use as well as tone and rhythm, are two types of **accommodation**, changes we make to our language to adapt to another person's communication style (p. 95).

▶ Communication technology has made English the dominant world language and has created a global society (p. 96).

**Marlin and Dory's** bulging eyes and gaping mouths
are telltale signs that there's something scary out there . . .

# chapter 4

# Nonverbal Communication

**You're sitting in a darkened theater,** watching a little clownfish search the entire ocean for his lost son. And for ninety minutes, you are captivated by his story. You're rooting for Marlin and his forgetful friend Dory as they journey to Sydney, Australia, in hopes of finding Nemo. But what could make an audience of any age believe that a fish loves his offspring? Or that tropical aquarium fish spend their time plotting an escape from their glass prison? Making believable characters out of objects, animals, and imaginary creatures is something that the artists at Pixar Animation Studios—where modern classics such as *Finding Nemo* (2003), *Cars* (2006), and *Ratatouille* (2007) were spawned—have mastered.

The company's first short film, the Academy Award–winning *Luxo Jr.* (1986), featured a pair of desk lamps with humanlike nonverbal behaviors, in a short story about a parent and child playing with a rubber ball. There is no dialogue, but the lamps hop about, their shaded lightbulbs acting as heads, held up by articulated arms that resemble shoulders. The result is a few minutes of suspended disbelief: these are not two ordinary desk lamps; this is a hyperactive child being looked over by a somewhat exasperated parent. Creator John Lasseter noted that he knew that he had succeeded when he realized that audiences were more captivated by the story and the characters than they were by the then-novel computer animation that created them. "A dear friend of mine came up to me after it premiered and said, 'John, John, I have a question for you,'" Lasseter recalled. "I thought, 'He's going to ask me about the shadow algorithm, or something like that.' But he asked, 'John, John, John, was the parent lamp a mother or a father?'" (Lasseter, 2001, para. 22). The lamp doesn't speak. The lamp doesn't even look like a person. Yet when one hopping desk lamp shakes its head at a smaller one and seems to exhale with a shrug, we understand that there is a humanlike relationship between the two lamps and that Luxo Sr. disapproves of Luxo Jr.'s behavior.

After you have finished
reading this chapter,
you will be able to

○— Understand the power of
nonverbal communication

○— Outline the functions of
nonverbal communication

○— Describe the set of communication symbols that
are nonverbal codes

○— Understand the influ-
ences culture, technology,
and situation have on our
nonverbal behavior

As you learned in Chapter 3, language is a key component of human communication, but it is not our *only* means of communicating with others. Much of what we "say" about ourselves and what we learn about others comes from **nonverbal communication**—the process of intentionally or unintentionally signaling meaning through behavior other than words (Knapp & Hall, 2005). This definition includes a variety of actions, including gestures, tone of voice, and eye behavior. What animators at Pixar recognize is that these nonverbal behaviors are powerful communication tools. By giving a lamp the ability to shrug or Marlin the clownfish the ability to show despair in his eyes, the artists make them human for us, illustrating behaviors that we've used and emotions we've felt. Nonverbal communication is indeed powerful, so we dedicate this chapter to studying it, beginning with the nature and functions of nonverbal communication and moving on to particular nonverbal behaviors and their contexts.

## The Nature of Nonverbal Communication

A deaf woman signs a message to a companion. A colleague writes a note to you on a pad of paper during an excruciatingly boring meeting. A man taps his watch to signal to a friend that it's almost time for lunch. A father hugs his daughter when she falls from her bike and scrapes her knee. In all four instances, communication is taking place without a word being spoken. But are all these communication examples nonverbal? In this section, we'll find out about the essential nature of communicating nonverbally.

### Nonverbal Behavior Is Communicative

As we have noted, you are communicating nonverbally when you convey a message without using any words. But you also communicate nonverbally when you use nonverbal behaviors *in addition* to words: when you smile, frown, or gesture as you speak or when you speak using a particular tone or volume. For example, as a kid, you probably knew when your parents were angry with you because they called you by your full name while using "that tone."

With this information in mind, consider the examples we just gave. American Sign Language (ASL), a visual language with its own grammatical structure used by hearing-impaired individuals in the United States and English-speaking Canada, is still verbal communication. It may be *nonvocal,* indicating that the voice is not used, but it is still a language with gestures as symbols (rather than spoken words) and with its own strict grammar rules. Likewise, the note that your colleague writes to you uses words, so it too is a form of verbal communication. Only the third and fourth examples are nonverbal communication—tapping a watch and offering a hug signal meaning without any use of linguistic symbols. Yet the example of the two friends reminds us that nonverbal behavior and verbal communication are connected. Had the friends not made a verbal agreement to meet for lunch, the act of tapping the watch might be really confusing.

 **GIVING SOMEONE** a big hug is an example of nonverbal communication, but communicating with someone using American Sign Language is not.

## Nonverbal Communication Is Often Spontaneous and Unintentional

In the 1998 cult film *Rounders*, Matt Damon and Edward Norton star as two friends, Mike and Worm, who need to win some fast cash playing poker in order to pay off Worm's debts. If you've ever played poker, you know it's a game that requires you to keep an emotionless face—any hint of joy or frustration might reveal your hand to your opponents. That's exactly how Mike ends up beating Teddy KGB (John Malkovich). Normally an accomplished player, KGB suffers from a particular "tell" or indication that he has a bad hand: eating Oreo cookies. Mike figures out this nonverbal behavior and uses it to his advantage.

Was Teddy KGB deliberately trying to tell Mike about his lack of confidence in his hand? Of course not. Why would anyone do such a thing with so much money at stake? But this example illustrates that our nonverbal communication can often be spontaneous and unintentional—we can send nonverbal messages without even being aware that we are doing so. You might cry, slouch, or blush without meaning to display those behaviors; your voice might be harsh and loud when you find out some upsetting news, even if you don't want to come across as angry or upset.

## Nonverbal Communication Is Ambiguous

Confusing nonverbal communication is the stuff that sitcoms are made of. Think of any of your favorite TV comedies in which one character mistakes another character's blush for attraction or a particular look is supposed to signal a specific message between two friends, only to go horribly wrong. The fact is, nonverbal communication can be ambiguous. Blinking, stammering, or hesitations in speech can indicate deception. But they can also indicate

### CONNECT

You make sense of your world and decode nonverbal behavior through *schemas*, your accumulated experience of people, roles, and situations. So if you discover that your friend lied to you, you might suspect, on the basis of your relational history, that whenever he avoids eye contact with you, he is lying. But competent communicators must think beyond schemas when determining the meaning of nonverbal communication.

● **DOES THIS CARD PLAYER** have a good or bad hand? Who knows? His poker face reveals nothing.

anxiety or uncertainty. In many cases, you can pick up clues about the meaning of behavior from the situational context. If your friend is sighing deeply and blinking rapidly as she heads off to her biochemistry final exam, you're probably safe guessing that she's feeling anxious. But you can't know for sure. Perhaps her boyfriend broke up with her twenty minutes ago and she just doesn't feel like talking about it. This is why we tell our students to regard nonverbal behavior as cues to be checked out rather than as facts to be blindly accepted.

## Nonverbal Communication Is More Believable Than Verbal Communication

Imagine you're grabbing lunch with your brother. You're talking a mile a minute about all your exciting plans for after graduation, but he's staring off into space. Maybe you're just boring him, right? But when you look closer, you notice that his face is ashen, he isn't making eye contact with you, and he hasn't shaved in a few days. In fact, his hair looks kind of dirty too. You pause and ask, "Hey, is everything OK with you? You seem . . . not yourself." Your brother looks up somewhat startled, tries to smile, and says, "What? Oh! Yes, everything is great."

What just happened here? It's called **channel discrepancy**, the situation when one set of behaviors says one thing and another set says something different. In this case, your brother's verbal communication delivers a clear message: "My life is great. No problems here." But his nonverbal communication says something else: "I'm so upset about something that's going on in my life that I can't listen to you, I can't look at you, and I can't even groom myself." So which message do you believe? In most cases, you'll probably go for the nonverbal message, as you may believe that your brother has less control over nonverbal communication than verbal communication, thus making it a more reliable indicator of his feelings. Research supports these assumptions. For example, studies show that nonverbal behavior is often more important than verbal behavior when we express spontaneous feelings (such as crying), assess the motives of others and how they present themselves (such as trying to determine deceit), express rapport with others (such as showing liking), and figure out others' meanings when there are not many other behaviors to observe (Grahe & Bernieri, 1999). Another study of adult children and their mothers found that mothers perceived nonverbal signals of distress in their children as less intentional and less controlled and therefore more reliable indicators of social meaning than verbal behaviors (Burgoon & Hoobler, 2002).

**AND YOU?**

Have you ever ignored what someone said because the person's nonverbal behavior seemed to contradict the verbal message? Were you able to determine if the nonverbal communication was accurate?

# Functions of Nonverbal Communication

Now that we've established what nonverbal communication is and understand its essential nature, we can discuss how it works and how it helps us interact effectively in relationships. While it is impossible to discuss every purpose that nonverbal behaviors serve, we highlight here the most important ways that nonverbal behaviors work on their own and in combination with verbal behaviors to affect your communication.

## Reinforcing Verbal Messages

Nonverbal behavior often serves to clarify meaning by reinforcing verbal messages. It does so in three ways: repeating, complementing, and accenting. **Repeating** mirrors the verbal message, offering a clear nonverbal cue that repeats the verbal message. For example, you might hold up three fingers while saying "three" or shake your head at a toddler while saying "no." You can also reinforce verbal messages with **complementing**, nonverbal behavior that matches (without actually mirroring) the verbal message it accompanies. For example, when you pat a friend on the back while saying, "You did a great job," you reinforce the message that your friend has done well.

Nonverbal behaviors are also used for **accenting**, or clarifying and emphasizing specific information in a verbal message. For example, if you are leaving a message for your housemates that indicates your disgust with the condition of your shared kitchen, you might write, "Wash those dirty dishes <u>TODAY</u>!" By underlining and using capital letters and an exclamation point, you emphasize the urgency of your message: not tomorrow, not whenever, but *today.*

## Substituting Verbal Messages

Nonverbal cues can also be used for **substituting** or replacing words. For example, a traffic police officer's outstretched palm substitutes for the word *stop,* and wagging a finger at a toddler can indicate "no" without your saying anything. Substituting is common in situations where words are unavailable (as when communicating with someone who does not speak the same language as you) or when words are inappropriate (in situations that call for silence) or unintelligible (in noisy situations). You might also use substitution to signal information that you'd rather not say aloud—for example, raising your eyebrows at a friend seated across the table from you when the other friend you're dining with mentions (for the tenth time) that his current internship is paying him *really* well.

## Contradicting Verbal Messages

As we noted earlier, if a person's verbal and nonverbal messages seem at odds, we're more likely to look to the nonverbal behavior for the truth. That's because nonverbal communication also functions as **contradicting** behavior to convey meaning that is the opposite of the verbal

● **WHEN A TRAFFIC COP** holds out one hand, you know to stop; she doesn't have to scream "STOP!" to get the intended effect.

message. Sometimes this is unintentional, as when you clearly look upset but say that nothing is wrong and don't even realize your nonverbal communication is giving you away. Other times, though, contradicting behavior is initiated on purpose. This may be true of people looking for sympathy or attention—by sighing deeply and remaining silent, Carolina might be able to get Andy to ask, "What's wrong?" She can keep the attention coming by refusing to answer or simply stating, "Nothing," so that he responds, "No, really, I'm worried. Tell me what's up." While such tactics can be quite effective in getting attention, they are also somewhat deceptive, intending to take advantage of a partner or friend's concern for selfish purposes.

Contradicting behavior is also part of what makes joking around and the use of sarcasm (cutting remarks) so powerful. When you roll your eyes and state, "Wow, that was a captivating lecture," it lets your classmate know that you found listening to your professor about as interesting as vacuuming even though your verbal message indicates the exact opposite. Contradicting behavior can work positively as well, as when your friend calls to your beloved dog, "Come here, you smelly, ugly little monster!" Your friend's smile, high pitch, and open arms reveal instead that your dog is probably too cute for words.

● **OLIVE THE PUG.** A smelly, ugly little monster? Certainly not.

## Regulating Interactions

Nonverbal cues are also used in **regulating** or coordinating verbal interaction—they help us navigate the back-and-forth of communication in a constructive, appropriate manner. For example, when you answer the phone with "Hello" and then pause, you are offering the person on the other end a chance to identify himself and explain why he is calling. Face to face, you may hold your hand up as a sign that you are not finished with a task and do not want to be interrupted; slouching or sitting back may indicate that you are waiting for someone else to speak. Similarly, in the United States, most individuals conducting job interviews will extend a hand and pause when introduced to the interviewee. This allows the interviewee to extend a hand in greeting as well while polite pleasantries such as "It's nice to meet you" and "How are you?" are exchanged. Both the verbal and nonverbal behaviors allow the introduction and interaction to go smoothly and comfortably for both parties.

**AND YOU?**

Imagine that you are listening to a friend tell a long story in a face-to-face setting. How might you regulate the interaction to show that you're listening or that you'd like to interject a comment? Would these actions change if the conversation were taking place via instant messaging or in a chat room? How so?

## Creating Immediacy

Earlier in this chapter, we described a father hugging his daughter who fell from her bike as an example of nonverbal communication. In this case, the hug conveys a message of love and concern. The hug may be all that is needed, or it may accompany some soothing words: "Don't worry. We'll get you a *Dora the Explorer* bandage." This example illustrates another important function of nonverbal communication: it creates **immediacy**, a feeling of closeness, involvement, and warmth between people as communicated by nonverbal behavior (Prager, 2000). Such things as how close to others you sit or stand and how much you look at them, smile, turn and lean toward them, and touch them influence feelings of physical and psychological closeness.

Immediacy behaviors help you form and manage impressions, particularly if you want to have more social influence. The implications for interpersonal relationships are clear: physical contact, eye contact, smiling, and other gestures tell your romantic partner, your family members, and close friends that you love and care for them and that you want to be near them. But this is also true in group and organizational settings. Whether you're working on a group project for a biology course or designing a new ad campaign for your employer, you can show involvement and interest in what others are saying by allowing them the space to speak, nodding to show that you're actively listening to what they're saying, and using an engaged tone of voice when you speak. These behaviors communicate respect and dedication to your colleagues—and make you look like a pretty great colleague in return. A particularly powerful example of nonverbal immediacy in the professional world comes from a study of doctors and patients that found that physicians who engage in immediacy behaviors usually have patients who are less fearful of them and more satisfied with their medical care (Richmond, Smith, Heisel, & McCroskey, 2001).

## Deceiving Others

In our example from *Rounders,* KGB lost at poker because his nonverbal communication gave him away, and he failed to deceive his opponent. If we're honest, most of us will admit to engaging in **deception**—the attempt to convince others of something that is false—from time to time (O'Hair & Cody, 1994). Sometimes we deceive others in order to protect them, as when you tell your friend that she looks great while she's lying on the couch looking pale and ill from the stomach flu. Other times, we deceive because we are afraid. On one episode of *CSI: Miami,* Maria—an illegal alien—swears to her boss that she did not reveal any information about him to the police (even though she did). Her boss is abusive, and she fears that he will hit her or have her deported or possibly even kill her. And at still other times, deception can be out of simple malice. One of our neighbors was a recent victim of such viciousness. Barbara received a phone call from a really friendly guy who claimed to be "with the government." He wanted to make sure that everything was correct in her "file" so that she would begin receiving retirement benefits the next year. He asked for her Social Security number and for some other bits of personal information before hanging up. "I feel so stupid," Barbara confided. "I can't believe I fell for it. But he sounded so sincere . . ."

Like most of us, Barbara was drawn in by the sound of a warm, friendly voice. And this identity thief was certainly counting on his nonverbal behavior—as well as his words of concern and care—to trick her. Yet researchers tell us that most of us look for the opposite type of behavior to sniff out a liar (Canary, Cody, & Manusov, 2008). We look for people who appear or sound anxious, who avoid making eye contact, or who have frequent and awkward body movements. We might also suspect people who have dilated pupils and who raise their vocal pitch, as these nonverbal behaviors are less under conscious control, making them more believable than words or other, more controllable nonverbal behaviors (Burgoon, Buller, & Woodall, 1989; Goss & O'Hair, 1988). Research certainly supports the idea that such nonverbal behavior can point to lying and deception, but this is not always the case. As Canary, Cody, and Manusov (2008) note, "A liar may appear anxious only if he or she is concerned about the lie or about getting caught. If the lie is unimportant, a communicator may instead be relaxed and controlled. Further, someone who is accused of lying but is in fact telling the truth may show signs of anxiety" (pp. 82–83).

Does this mean that we're fated to be tricked by those who want to deceive us? Hardly. We can still look to the power of verbal messages—Barbara could have realized that someone from "the government" would probably have a more official title and would already know her Social Security number. And we can also look to the relational context and situational context of our interaction. If you suspect that your partner is lying to you and you have caught him or her lying in the past, you might have more reason to be suspicious.

## Codes of Nonverbal Communication

At this point, you've seen how complex nonverbal behaviors work together to accomplish a number of goals or functions. You also have a good sense of what types of actions constitute nonverbal communication—giving someone a hug, making eye contact, or pausing to let someone else speak. In this section, we examine these **nonverbal codes**, symbols we use to send messages without, or in addition to, words. Although we divide these codes into categories for simplicity and clarity, remember that nonverbal behaviors seldom communicate meaning in isolation. Usually, clusters of nonverbal behaviors convey a message—for example, raising your eyebrows and gasping show surprise or shock, with or without any accompanying words. The specific codes we examine here are gestures and body movements, facial expressions, eye behavior, voice, physical appearance, space and environment, touch, and time.

### Gestures and Body Movements

You've probably heard a lot of talk about "body language" and its implications for communication. A friend might let you know that so-and-so is into you because his or her "body language" makes it really obvious. However, the way we move our bodies is not a language at all—shaking your leg while you're sitting or slouching your shoulders has no universal definition. What's really going on when you "read" someone's "body language" is the observation of **kinesics**, the aspects of gestures and body movements that send various messages. When Eva turns her body to include Jane in a conversation, or Rodney walks into an interview with confidence, for example, we are witnessing kinesic behaviors—and research shows that we're all fairly good at deciphering the emotions of others from their gestures and movements (Montepare, Koff, Zaitchik, & Alberet, 1999).

There are five main categories of body movements that convey meaning: emblems, illustrators, regulators, adaptors, and affect displays (Ekman & Friesen, 1969).

▶ **Emblems** are movements and gestures that have a direct verbal translation in a particular group or culture. They substitute for verbal messages. An American might use the "OK" sign (meeting the thumb and index fingers in a circle and extending the other fingers) to indicate that things are going well, but in other cultures, this emblem stands for various derogatory or vulgar terms.

▶ **Illustrators** reinforce verbal messages and help visually explain what is being said. Holding your hands two feet apart while saying, "The fish was this big!" is an illustrator.

▶ **Regulators** help us manage our interactions. Raising your hand and lifting your head, for example, indicate that you want to speak.

▶ **Adaptors** satisfy some physical or psychological need, such as rubbing your eyes when you're tired or twisting your hair when you're nervous or bored. Adaptors are not conscious behaviors; they are used to reduce bodily tension, often in response to heightened emotional stimulation. They may be more frequent when someone is stressed, impatient, or bored, and are often interpreted as indicators of negative feelings (Goss & O'Hair, 1988).

▶ **Affect displays** are nonverbal behaviors that convey feelings, moods, and reactions. They are usually unintentional, reflecting the sender's emotions: slumping in a chair may indicate fatigue or boredom; a sad face may reflect a recent argument with someone. That's not to say that they're *always* unintentional, though: you may purposely set your jaw and hit your fist on the table to indicate your anger or frustration.

**CONNECT**

Kinesics are important in many situations. When you give a speech, your body movements should support your words. For example, illustrators help clarify a point for your audience; confident posture reassures your audience that you're prepared and organized. Certain adaptors, however, can leave listeners with the impression that you are bored with your own speech (no one enjoys a yawning speaker!). We discuss these issues further in Chapter 13.

## Facial Expressions

Jim Carrey is the man with an elastic face. (It's appropriate, then, that his first film was titled *Rubberface.*) If you've seen such Carrey films as *Ace Ventura: Pet Detective* or *Dumb and Dumber,* you've probably marveled at his ability to contort his eyes and facial muscles into bizarre poses. Part of the reason we laugh at Jim Carrey's antics is that he's able to exaggerate and play on some of the expressions that all humans, across all cultures, share (Ekman & Friesen, 1971). A smile, for example, indicates happiness whether you are a young midwestern girl, an elderly Middle Eastern man, or a "pet detective" in Miami searching for a missing mascot. In fact, Irenaus Eibl-Eibesfeldt (1973) observed that blind children, who cannot learn to mimic facial movements through sight, exhibited sadness, anger, disgust, fear, interest, surprise, and happiness in the same way that sighted people exhibit these feelings (see Figure 4.1 on p. 110). Eibl-Eibesfeldt concluded that these seven primary facial expressions are inborn, while a variety of other expressions seem to be learned from our culture.

But the fact that we're fairly adept at deciphering these seven common

● **JIM CARREY** is the master of exaggerated facial expressions.

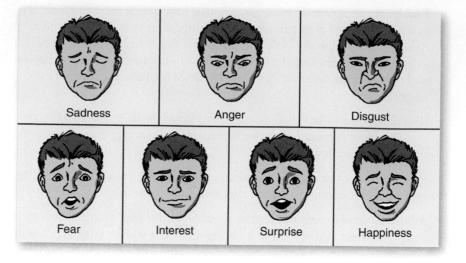

**FIGURE 4.1**

**CROSS-CULTURAL PRIMARY FACIAL EXPRESSIONS** Research shows that these seven expressions of emotion exist in all cultures and do not require one's ability to see in order to be learned.

expressions of emotion doesn't mean we're experts at decoding all facial expressions—especially since the human face is capable of producing over a thousand different expressions (and as many as twenty thousand if you take into account all of the combinations of the different facial areas) (Ekman, Friesen, & Ellsworth, 1972; Harrigan & Taing, 1997). This is partly because our emotions can be concealed by facial management techniques, ways of consciously manipulating our faces to give off a particular expression. One common facial management technique is **masking**, replacing an expression that shows true feeling with an expression that shows appropriate feeling for a given interaction. You use masking techniques when you smile while congratulating your best friend on her engagement, even though you think her fiancé is a nasty, pretentious snob (Richmond, McCroskey, & Payne, 1991).

## Eye Behavior

"Apprehensive Stepmother" wrote to *Slate*'s "Dear Prudence: Advice on Manners and Morals" columnist with an intriguing problem. She recently married a man whose adult daughter refuses to accept their relationship. Understanding that it takes time to blend a family, "Apprehensive" was willing to give her stepdaughter some space. But after she and her husband tried to deliver Christmas presents to her stepdaughter, "Apprehensive" fell apart. The stepdaughter refused to look at her or acknowledge her; she also refused to make eye contact with "Apprehensive's" mentally challenged son, who immediately picked up on the fact that he was unwelcome in his stepsister's home ("The Wicked Stepdaughter," 2008).

Most people reading "Apprehensive's" story immediately realize that the stepdaughter's behavior is rude. Why? Because **oculesics**, the study of the use of the eyes in communication settings, has a profound impact on our nonverbal communication. Researchers conducted studies on infants to discover whether or not

Many people feel uncomfortable with direct eye contact—particularly if their culture considers such behavior rude. However, eye contact remains an important part of giving speeches and succeeding in job interviews in the United States. In both situations, eye contact signals respect for your audience and confidence in your abilities and preparedness. You learn more about the challenges of eye contact, and how to move past them, in Chapter 13 and the Appendix.

**TABLE 4.1**

## THE POWER OF EYE CONTACT

| Function of Eye Contact | Example | Image |
|---|---|---|
| Influences attitude change | Looking at someone to get the person to trust you or comply with your wishes | |
| Indicates a degree of arousal | Glancing across a crowded room to signal attraction or interest; looking at a customer attentively in the interest of receiving positive evaluations—and sales (Ford, 1999) | |
| Expresses emotion | Soft eyes of loving looks; frightened eyes of a startled person; hard eyes of an angry person | |
| Regulates interaction | Looking more at a conversational partner when listening; regulating eye contact to assume or give up the speaking role (Wiemann & Knapp, 1999) | |
| Indicates power | Direct, prolonged gaze to convey dominance; avoidance of eye contact to signal submissiveness | |
| Forms impressions | Making eye contact with an audience to communicate confidence and sincerity | |

Source: Leathers (1986). Adapted with permission.

babies as young as two days old prefer direct or averted gazes from adults. When newborn infants (ages two to five days) were shown pictures of human faces on a screen—some making direct eye contact and looking forward, others looking away with averted glances—the newborns stared significantly longer at the faces offering a direct gaze. In fact, the babies also oriented themselves more often toward the face that made eye contact with them (Farroni, Csibra, Simion, & Johnson, 2002). Previous studies also confirmed that babies as young as three months old would smile less when adults averted their gaze, though the smiling would return when adults resumed eye contact (as cited in Farroni et al., 2002).

The human gaze remains important throughout the lifespan. You might make direct eye contact with a hiring manager in a job interview in the United States. And you will likely use eye behavior to send messages in more personal relationships. For example, the way that you look at a friend is likely not the same way that you look at your romantic partner and certainly not the way you look at someone you dislike immensely. Each glance can send a message of liking, loving, attraction, or contempt (see Table 4.1 on p. 111).

## Voice

At the beginning of the seventh season of *Scrubs,* a new batch of interns lands at Sacred Heart Hospital. Among them is Josephine, a petite woman whom the attending physician, Dr. Cox, offensively renames "Fun Size" (yes, like a small candy bar). It turns out that not only is she short-statured, but she also has a very high-pitched, squeaky voice. To Dr. Cox's ear, everything she says comes out sounding like a childish whine. Dr. Cox tells her that she has "a ridiculous speaking voice" and instructs her to write down anything she needs to tell him so that he never has to hear her voice again.

● **DR. COX HARSHLY JUDGES** "Fun Size" because of her high-pitched, childish voice. In fact, he is so annoyed by it that he demands she never speak in his presence.

Although this episode is intended to be humorous, it does reveal that we judge others by the qualities of their voice. Indeed, how we say something to someone matters just as much as what we say—sometimes even more. How and when we pause, the speed and volume of our speech, and the inflections we use are examples of powerful nonverbal vocal messages called **paralanguage.**

The human voice is capable of numerous qualities, and most of us fall somewhere on a continuum between extremes of these qualities. Consider the degree of hoarseness, smoothness, or deepness a voice might have. Or think about the differences implied in precise versus slurred speech or shrill versus soft speech. We all have preferences about which voices are most attractive—and while individual tastes do vary, research points to some general overall preferences. For example, we find angry, demanding voices annoying—and whiny voices *really* annoying (Sokol, Webster, Thompson, & Stevens, 2005). Look no further than your favorite radio DJs or newscasters to examine the vocal qualities people enjoy the most (after all, these people make a living with their voice!). They are not shrill or nasal, but tend to have smooth voices and find a middle ground between precise and fluid speech.

The ability of the voice to influence communication doesn't end there. We must also consider our **vocalizations**, paralinguistic cues that give information about the speaker's emotional or physical state, such as laughing, crying, sighing, yawning, and gasping. Vocalizations also add emphasis to our spoken words, as when you assure a friend by stating, "You did *great* today." Other vocalizations simply replace words or create nonword fillers in conversations. *Shhhh* is probably a vocalization most of us couldn't live without— and imagine how awkward an everyday conversation would be without *uh-huh* or *ah* or *uhhh*.

## Physical Appearance

Consider the following quote from *What Not to Wear* stylist Clinton Kelly: "I really don't care what the average person on the street is wearing. But if you're coming to me for a job, if you're coming to me to do my plumbing, to decorate my house, I'm going to take into account what you're wearing" (Wieder, 2003). Does what you wear—or your appearance in general—really speak to your ability as a student, a carpenter, or a teacher? Perhaps your appearance doesn't convey your abilities or define who you are as a person, but it communicates a message about you nonetheless. In fact, the initial impression your appearance makes may affect your future interactions with others (Burgoon et al., 1989).

Most people in Western society are well aware of the significance of appearance. Research shows that society affords attractive people certain advantages. For instance, attractive students receive more interaction from their teachers (Richmond et al., 1991); attractive defendants are more likely to be found innocent in a court of law (Efran, 1974); and "good-looking" job candidates have a three to four times greater chance of being hired (Molloy, 1983). Appearance affects not only perceptions of attractiveness but also judgments about a person's background, character, personality, status, and future behavior (Morris, 1985). In fact, the psychologist Nancy Etcoff (1999) claims that all cultures pursue and value attractiveness as a matter of survival.

These perceptions about appearance and attractiveness are inferred from physical characteristics like body shape and size, facial features, skin color, height, and hair color but also from the clothing you wear, which can reveal quite a bit about your status, economic level, social background, goals, and satisfaction (Crane, 2000; Sybers & Roach, 1962). For example, uniforms are often associated with lower-status jobs, such as working in a fast-food restaurant, while more formal attire (business suits) and specific uniforms (doctors' coats) are associated with higher-status occupations.

We also infer a great deal of meaning from the things we adorn our body with, known as **artifacts**—accessories carried or used on the body for decoration or identification. For example, the expensive Rolex watch that your uncle always wears sends a very different message about wealth and status than the ten-dollar watch your friend wears. Other artifacts, such as briefcases, tattoos,

Your ability to use vocalizations like "uh-huh" and "mm-hmm" can help others perceive you as an effective listener (Chapter 5). When a loved one approaches you to discuss a difficult situation, you want to allow the person to speak and not constantly interrupt with your own words. Vocalizations tell your friend that you're listening and that you're actively engaged in the process of communication.

Chapter 10 explains that the clothes and artifacts you exhibit in a professional setting both reflect and shape the organization's culture—its beliefs, values, and ways of doing things. An organization that permits employees to wear jeans and sneakers likely encourages a different culture than one that requires uniforms. Competent communicators must be mindful of the messages their clothing and artifacts send in light of the larger organizational picture.

earrings, nose rings, nail polish, and engagement and wedding rings, also convey messages about your relational status (married versus unattached), your gender, and even how willing you are to defy conventions (as in the case of, say, tongue rings).

## COMMUNICATIONACROSSCULTURES

**THINK ABOUT THIS**

### The Great Uniform Debate

Clothing can communicate social status, group affiliation, gender identity, and socioeconomic status, among other things. During adolescence especially, we use clothing to create messages that express who we are—or who we want to be. Today's adolescents wear everything from miniskirts to full-length jackets to T-shirts with sexual or explicit messages on them and often focus on brands and lines of clothing as defining individual status and identity. Such trends have given rise to some debate about proper attire in public schools in the United States. And while the argument sometimes centers on money and violence, a good portion of the dialogue focuses on what clothing communicates to other students and about the institution. However, in the past decade, this trend has been changing thanks to the adoption of uniforms by some school systems (Cox, 2005).

Proponents suggest that uniforms communicate more than just a preppy look. Uniforms communicate belonging by showing who is supposed to be in the school and who is not, as well as school pride (Wilde, 2008). What is more important is what uniforms do *not* allow to be communicated—gang affiliations and socioeconomic status (Caruso, 1996). A uniform, it is argued, forces students to leave such affiliations at the door of the school. As former President Clinton noted in his 1996 State of the Union address, which focused on stronger families and a safer world for children, "If it means that teenagers will stop killing each other over designer jackets, then our public schools should be able to require their students to wear school uniforms." By reducing negative messages, those in favor of school uniforms hope to encourage learning and allow students to reduce stereotyping.

But opponents suggest that uniforms communicate something negative—conformity and intolerance toward difference (Caruso, 1996). Such was the case in France in 2003 when two sisters were barred from entering a school building because their headscarves did not conform to the school's uniform policy. Their father contended that the dress policy encouraged religious intolerance in an area where about half the students were Muslim (Schofield, 2003). Some youth co-culture theorists, such as Dick Hebdige, even contend that clothing, along with other nonverbal indicators, assist youth in questioning the dominant culture and creating their own identity and self-esteem, a skill that is important to develop during adolescence.

Whatever the outcome of the uniform debate, one thing is clear: clothing in the youth culture communicates volumes about both the individuals and the corresponding institutions (Hebdige, 1999).

**①** What other items, besides clothing, nonverbally communicate information about a high school student?

**②** When you were in high school, what styles did you wear, and what did these clothing items communicate about you? If you now have or have had teen children, what do or did they seem to be communicating about themselves?

**③** Do you believe that uniforms reduce stereotyping by class and status in society? Explain your answer.

**④** Is this more of an issue in high schools and middle schools than in elementary schools? What would you do if your college or university suddenly adopted a uniform policy?

## Space and Environment

In addition to the messages your body, its movements, and its adornments convey, you also send nonverbal messages by the spaces that surround you and your communication partners. We examine three such factors here: proxemics, territoriality, and environment.

### Proxemics

A young man named Ben was recalling his first high school job at a local movie rental store (in the days before Netflix). Although Ben liked the job well enough, he had a serious problem with his coworker, Lucas. Lucas was a close talker—a person who stands very near when speaking to others. "During shifts when I'd be on with this guy, I'd always have to try to find some excuse to be away from the counter," Ben said. "If we were both behind the counter together, he'd talk so close that I'd end up completely backed into a corner, with the counter digging into my back, just hoping for someone to rob the place so there'd be an excuse to get out of the situation." Ben's intense discomfort with Lucas was due to **proxemics**, the study of the way we use and communicate with space.

Professor Edward Hall (1959) identified four specific spatial zones that we often use when communicating with others (see Figure 4.2).

▸ *Intimate* (0 to 18 inches). We often send intimate messages in this zone, which is usually reserved for spouses or romantic partners, very close friends, and close family members.

▸ *Personal* (18 inches to 4 feet). In the personal zone, we communicate with friends, relatives, and occasionally colleagues. This is perhaps the most intimate zone that Lucas should use to communicate on the job.

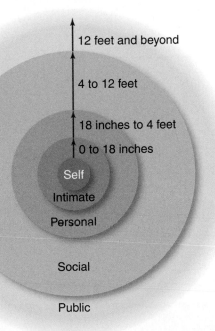

12 feet and beyond

4 to 12 feet

18 inches to 4 feet

0 to 18 inches

Self
Intimate
Personal
Social
Public

**FIGURE 4.2**
**ZONES OF PERSONAL SPACE** The four zones of personal space described by Edward Hall indicate ranges that generally apply across cultures.

# what about you?

## You and Your Artifacts

Take a look at the following list of artifacts. Do you make use of or wear any of these items? If so, what does the artifact mean to you, personally, about your identity? What messages might the artifact send to others?

| Artifact Type | What Does It Mean to Me? | What Does It Say About Me? |
|---|---|---|
| Jewelry (necklaces, rings, watches, cuff links) | | |
| Perfume or cologne | | |
| Body piercings (tongue rings, nose rings, eyebrow piercings) | | |
| Tattoos | | |
| Specific hairstyles (Mohawk, shaved, braided, long, disheveled) | | |
| Clothing labels or logos | | |
| Eyewear (sunglasses, eyeglasses versus contact lenses) | | |
| Other accessories (scarves, belts, high-heeled shoes) | | |

▶ *Social* (4 to 12 feet). The social zone is most comfortable for communicating in professional settings, such as business meetings or teacher-student conferences. This zone would be more appropriate for Lucas.

▶ *Public* (12 feet and beyond). The public zone allows for distance between the interactants, such as public speaking events or performances.

Your personal space needs may vary from these space categories (and these vary according to culture too; Hall "normed" these zones for different cultures around the world). How close or distant you want to be from someone depends quite a bit on whom you're dealing with, the situation, and your comfort level. You might well enjoy being physically close to your boyfriend or girlfriend when you are taking a walk together, but you're probably not going to hold hands or embrace during class. Some families use the intimate and personal zones frequently or exclusively; other families are more distant and formal. And sometimes characteristics of our personality affect our use of space (Harper, Wiens, & Matarazzo, 1978). For example, extroverted people require less space than introverted people, and highly anxious persons or shy people generally prefer to keep others at greater distances. But regardless of your personal preferences, violations of space are almost always uncomfortable and awkward and can cause relational problems. Just ask Ben! Because of Lucas's constant violations, Ben could barely tolerate speaking to him, making the working environment less productive.

### Territoriality

Closely related to proxemics is **territoriality**—the claiming of an area, with or without legal basis, through continuous occupation of that area. Your home, your car, and your office are personal territories. But territories also encompass implied ownership of space, such as a favorite living room chair, a seat in a classroom, a parking space, or a usual table in a restaurant. When territoriality is encroached on, the territory is usually defended by its claimant. If you've ever seen the *Family Guy* episode "One If by Clam, Two If by Sea," you've seen this point in action. After a hurricane, Peter, Quagmire, Cleveland, and Joe are distraught to learn that their favorite bar has been sold to an Englishman named Nigel Pinchley, who turns the venue into a British pub. Unable to find a new place to hang out and desirous to reclaim "their" space, the men attempt to ignite their own American Revolution by wreaking havoc at the pub. They do get their space back in the end . . . but not through their antics!

### Environment

Any home designer or architect knows that humans use space to express themselves. The layout and decoration of your home, your office, and any other space you occupy tells others something about you. For example, the way you arrange your furniture can either encourage interaction or discourage it; the décor, lighting, and cleanliness of the space all send messages about how you want interactions to proceed. The power of the environment on communication may explain, in part, the success of shows like *Extreme Makeover: Home Edition* and *Trading Spaces.* Episodes will often show a dreary and ignored living space that is

CONNECT

Territoriality can have an impact on group communication, as we generally feel more in control of situations on our own turf (Chapters 8 and 9). Think about this the next time a professor breaks you up into random groups. Do you enjoy moving across the room from your usual seat, or do you prefer your group members to come to you? Chances are good that a new "territory" will affect your communication behaviors.

# real communicator

**NAME:** Michael Rosenberg
**HOMETOWN:** Las Vegas, NV
**OCCUPATION:** Adjunct professor
**FUN FACT:** Someday I'm going to play major league baseball. Someday . . .

I teach creative writing at a large university in the Midwest. I use classical and contemporary short stories as models for plot, characterization, and description. But when I teach dialogue, I don't use any stories. Instead, I borrow an exercise from my college general education communication course: writing conversations between two characters and then altering or enhancing meaning with nonverbal communication cues. The fact is that to write dialogue that reads authentically, students must master this art.

First, I set a two-person scene—a father and daughter reuniting, a husband discovering that his wife is having an affair, two friends parting ways. Then I have my students write a 250-word conversation between the two, noticing how nonverbal cues interact with the words. For example, nonverbal communication can reinforce dialogue: *"Jane, great to see you,"* Tom said, *grinning.* Even better, it can substitute for verbal messages: *Tom grinned as Jane walked into the room. He threw the afghan off his aching body and spread his arms wide for a hug.* That line creates a picture in the reader's head, and it's an efficient way to break up any dialogue above or below it on the page. But it is perhaps most useful to the fiction writer when nonverbal communication contradicts verbal messages—particularly when it involves deception. Here's an example that introduces conflict nonverbally: *"Jane, great to see you," Tom said. Under the afghan, his arthritic hands balled up into fists.*

Balled-up fists are an affect display. And that's just one example of the kind of kinesic behavior that brings fictional dialogue to life. I ask my students to write facial descriptions of their characters and in particular to look out for any masking techniques those characters might employ. We then move on to eye behavior, which is a bit trickier to do well. Because we employ oculesics so often in our real-life communication, they tend to be overused in fiction. *Narrowed eyes, teary eyes, eyes cast down at the ground* are all written examples of eye behavior that unfortunately verge on clichés. After eye behavior, we work on nonverbal artifacts. What are some of Tom's props? He's got the afghan, but what else? Is he reading a book? Does he have any tattoos? Is he wearing a polyester suit? When writers makes choices about their characters' artifacts, they're building more specific characters. And as readers, we love specific, unique characters we can see in our mind's eye.

Finally, I ask my students to render their characters' paralanguage: pauses, speed, volume, inflections. When paralanguage is used well, readers hear exactly what the writer intended. Consider this line:

"Honey, stop asking me that question over and over, please."

It becomes more menacing if we add pauses and slow down the speed. We can do this using dialogue tags and punctuation:

"Honey," he said. "Stop asking me that question. Over and over. Please."

And it changes even more when we use italics to add inflection:

*"Honey,"* he said. "Stop asking me that question. Over and over. *Please."*

*Voilà!* By the end of the class, the students have turned a page of pure dialogue into a fully realized scene. And all I had to do was steal an idea from one of my college professors.

## Time

Imagine that you are [...] alize that you've prob[...] word—your lateness [...] punctuality and his o[...] pletely acceptable for [...] the person wait, you [...] have control.

**Chronemics** is th[...] they structure time in [...] nication because you [...] person's **time orient:** [...] time—determines th[...] tent, the length of th[...] tuality (Burgoon et a[...] mother, you're sendir[...] that you want to voi[...] her the time to finisl[...] she has to say. Simil[...] and interest. For exa[...] gether even when it's [...] friend Paul when yo[...] class, it's not the sam[...] you would when you [...] match.

## Influences or

Pick any individual [...] different things in di[...] tions. A kiss is a frien[...] of the same sex throu[...] is not necessarily the [...] to be saved for imm[...] might kiss your rom[...] than you would wh[...] eight-year old niece, [...] the emoticon :-X. C[...] context in order to [...] Here we consider h[...] influences on our nc[...]

transformed into a warm and vibrant room that everyone suddenly wants to be in. Similarly, on the show *Kitchen Nightmares,* chef Gordon Ramsay works with failing restaurants to fix menu, food preparation, and personnel problems. But as a savvy restaurant owner himself, Ramsay knows that a good part of the dining experience revolves around the look of the establishment. So he employs a professional design team to redecorate the space to create a specific atmosphere—a spartan, minimalist decor to attract a hip and trendy clientele, for example, or a warm, cozy space to attract couples looking for a romantic evening out.

The environment can also affect the specific messages that are communicated in a situation. For example, you're likely to send more romantic messages over an intimate, candlelight dinner than in a neon-lit bowling alley. Similarly, a politician might choose to give a speech on immigration reform on the southern tip of Manhattan, with Ellis Island and the Statue of Liberty—two strong symbols of the history of immigration in the United States—in the background.

● THE *EXTREME MAKEOVER: HOME EDITION* team changes the quality of people's lives when they transform drab and inhospitable houses into aesthetically pleasing, welcoming homes.

## Touch

Touch is the first communication experienced in life. A newborn baby is soothed in the arms of her parents; she begins to learn about herself and others as she reaches out to explore her environment. The study of touch as a form of communication is termed **haptics**, and it remains an important form of communicating throughout life. We hug our loved ones in happy and sad times, we reassure others with a pat on the back, we experience intimacy with the caress of a spouse, and we look for someone to hold our hand when we're feeling anxious or afraid.

There are as many different types of touches as there are thoughts and reactions to being touched. So we look to scholar Richard Heslin's intimacy continuum (1974) for insights into how our use of touch reflects our relationship with a communication partner:

▶ *Functional-professional touch* is used to perform a job. How would your dentist perform your root canal or your hairstylist get rid of your split ends if they didn't touch you?

▶ *Social-polite touch* is more interpersonal than functional-professional touch. It is often a polite acknowledgment of the other person, such as a handshake.

▶ *Friendship-warmth touch* conveys liking and affection between people who know each other well. Examples might be hugging your friends or offering your brother a pat on the back.

▶ *Love-intimacy touch* is used by romantic partners, parents and children, and even very close friends and family members. Examples include kissing (whether on the mouth or on the cheek), embracing, and caressing. This type of touch communicates deep closeness.

## Culture and Nonverbal Communication

Hold up one hand, with your thumb and two middle fingers folded, and wave it at a crowd of people. That's what President George W. Bush and members of his family did before cameras during inaugural festivities in 2005. The next day, newspapers in Norway ran photos of a smiling Jenna Bush holding her hand in the "Hook 'em Horns" salute to the University of Texas Longhorns, with a headline reading "Shock Greeting from Bush Daughter" (Douglass, 2005). Why all the fuss over a gesture of support for a college football team? Because the gesture carries different meanings in different cultures. In Norway, it is commonly understood as a satanic salute.

● JENNA BUSH thought she was showing her support for the University of Texas Longhorns—not giving a Satantic salute!

TABLE 4.2

**HOW PEOPLE TOUCH**

As this example illustrates, nonverbal communication is highly influenced by culture. What may be an innocent gesture in one group, context, region, or country can convey a different and possibly offensive message elsewhere. But culture's impact on nonverbal communication goes far beyond miscommunication through gestures. It affects everything from eye behavior and silence to time orientation, touch, and notions of physical attractiveness.

Consider the need to be sensitive to culturally linked nonverbal communication in the academic and professional world. For example, in the United States, we are accustomed to making direct eye contact when speaking to someone, whether a colleague, a supervisor, or a professor. Similarly, in the Middle East, engaging in long and direct eye contact with your speaking partner shows interest and is helpful in determining the sincerity and truth of the other person's words (Samovar, Porter, & Stefani, 1998). However, in Latin America, Japan, and the Caribbean, such eye behavior is a sign of disrespect. You can imagine the misunderstandings and negative perceptions that might take place during an interview between a hiring committee of professors at a university in Guatemala and their potential new colleague from Saudi Arabia.

Similarly, whether in an academic, business, or social environment, members of different cultures will use and perceive time differently. Edward Hall (1959) claims that three time systems operate in any culture: technical (scientific measurement), formal (the culture's system of measuring time), and informal (the casual time of a culture). Formal time involves the way a culture measures, values, and uses time. The phrase "time is money," used extensively in Western cultures, indicates how people value time, including their sense of urgency to have things done. Being "on time" in most Western cultures is part of competent behavior (Mast, 2002). Informal time involves punctuality and duration. For example, most Western cultures find it extremely rude to be late, but in most Latin cultures, lateness is entirely acceptable. Without this understanding, prompt executives in Boston may be extremely irritated by the perceived rudeness of their colleagues in the Caracas office who don't join a 10:00 A.M. videoconference until 10:15.

the potential to be even more persuasive th
group and interpersonal social interaction
volved and responsive (Bailenson, Beall, L
In task-oriented interactions (interperson;
sence of nonverbal cues may actually help
message more efficiently, so it is important
in electronic communication (Burgoon, B
Fischer, 2002).

## The Situational Context

Smiling at a funeral. Raising your Starbucks
long, steady, somewhat flirtatious eye contact

---

### WIREDFORCOMMUNIC

#### War Games Without Weapons, Sometimes Without Words

It's probably no surprise that soldiers bene
fered in computerized war games. But so
dodge more than bullets: in different culture
different norms and rules of nonverbal comn

American soldiers stationed in Iraq, fo
hard way that gestures that are innocent ir
offensive in Iraqi culture (and vice versa). I
of your feet is considered rude in Iraq; p
bowing, and handshakes can also lead to
stance, an Iraqi man gestured at a female s
gether. He was indicating friendship; she
sexual gesture.

This is where Tactical Iraqi, a virtual reality
comes in handy. *Wired* magazine reports tha
life scenarios by learning a set of Arabic phra
and taboos. . . . A speech-recognition syster
sponses. Accurate responses allow the sold
characters and advance to the next level" (C
soldiers understand the Iraqi gestures, as wel
to perceive gestures that are considered inno

Interestingly, the game, though intended
combat of any kind. It focuses instead on mut
attempting to gain the trust of their compani
communities. The game's technical director,
power of nonverbal communication in this p
moving the weapons and replacing them with

---

Similarly, much interesting research has been done on culture's effect on touch. Some cultures are **contact cultures** and depend on touch as an important form of communication, whereas other cultures are **noncontact cultures** and are less touch-sensitive or even tend to avoid touch. For example, Latin American, Mediterranean, and Eastern European cultures rely on touch much more than Scandinavian cultures do. Public touch, linked to the type of interpersonal relationship that exists and the culture in which it occurs, affects both the amount of touch and the area of the body that is appropriate to touch (McDaniel & Andersen, 1998). Social-polite touch, for example, involves a handshake between American men but a kiss between Arabic men. And as we learned from Hasidic reggae star Matisyahu in Chapter 2, some religions prohibit opposite-sex touch between unmarried or unrelated individuals.

Research has also offered some interesting insights into the relationship between gender and nonverbal communication. For example, women engage in more eye contact than men and initiate touch more often (Stewart, Cooper, & Stewart, 2003). Women have been shown to smile more than men and return more smiles (Hall, 1998). Yet is this difference necessarily biologically based? Learning gender roles may well play a large part in the development of nonverbal behavior. Judith Hall and her colleagues note that learning environments may foster difference, with mothers using more varied facial expressions with their daughters because they believe that women are more expressive (or are supposed to be more expressive) than men. A more emotionally expressive and varied environment in childhood may well lead to more opportunities for nonverbal skill development for women (Hall, Carter, & Hogan, 2000). Adult gender roles may also play a part. Since women are expected to look out for the welfare of others, smiling—as well as other affirming nonverbal behaviors—may help meet situational, gendered expectations (Hall et al., 2000). This very point may also help explain why women exhibit greater sensitivity to nonverbal messages. This marks women as more socially responsive, as they interrupt less and exhibit more signs of interest (such as head tilts and paralinguistic encouragers like *uh-huh* and *ah*). They also decode others' nonverbal behaviors more accurately, particularly those involving the face (Burgoon & Bacue, 2003).

One thing is clear: nonverbal behaviors traditionally associated with femininity are perceived as weak. For example, smiling women are more likely to be interrupted than either unsmiling women or men (Kennedy & Camden, 1983). The first female Speaker of the House of Representatives, Nancy Pelosi, was criticized for weeks following the State of the Union address of January 24, 2007. Pelosi's gentle gavel motion (call to order), sweet voice and smile, and light nervous laughter were noted as inappropriate behaviors for a person in her position. In addition, critics contrasted Pelosi's rapid blinking and tongue and mouth movements with the serious expression of Vice President Cheney as the TV cameras framed the two behind the president.

● NANCY PELOSI'S gentle mannerisms might be appropriate in other professions, but they were deemed inappropriate for the Speaker of the House of Representatives.

## Mediated

At a conference
cation and e-ma
sides. She asked
on the date they
her students, A
vented him fror
vided quality wc
and did not inte
know she had r
shocked to learn
a sign of annoya
In the end, Aarc
what you meant

As you've lea
to face, you've g
communication
*paralinguistic cue*
even in the absen
or text message,
language, and so

A whole seri
communication:

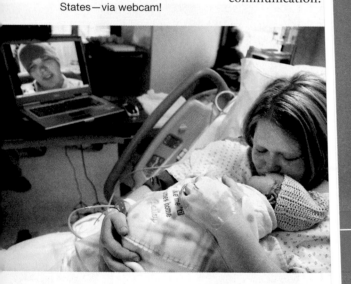

● **TECHNOLOGY HAS
BECOME** so advanced that
a father stationed in Iraq is
now able to witness his
child's birth in the United
States—via webcam!

tach or compress f
behaviors help cre
Lippert, 2004).

As technology
that our electronic
nels: videoconferer
have visual as well

○— **A doctor's** ability to effectively listen to a patient can
literally mean the difference between life and death.

# chapter 5

# Listening

**Picture yourself gearing up for an important interview.**
You've got some serious questions, the answers to which will certainly affect your life. Now picture that interview occurring in a brightly lit, sterile examination room. Oh, and you're wearing a paper gown that is entirely open at the back.

Communicating to your doctor about your health and treatment can be difficult for many reasons. The medical profession is afforded great prestige in the United States, and many patients feel inadequate in their understanding of their own health; they don't want to sound "silly" in front of their physician. Similarly, nervous patients can have a hard time expressing their thoughts. Doctors, in turn, can get flustered or impatient with their anxious patients and may interrupt them or prompt them for more information with jargon-filled questions. They, like all of us, sometimes forget that the language that is second nature in their profession sounds like a foreign language to outsiders. Couple these issues with the fact that doctors are frequently overbooked and expected to spend little time with patients, and you can see how such communication challenges can lead to potentially disastrous consequences.

That's why many medical schools and hospitals are now teaching students and staff clinical communication skills. Richard Frankel, the medical sociologist who developed a training program for Indiana University that focuses on teaching doctors to listen effectively to their patients, points out that doctors often make the mistake of focusing their attention on the first concern or symptom that a patient raises. But a worried patient might hesitate to mention the most serious concerns (such as suicidal thoughts, or a mole in an embarrassing spot) and blurt them out only at the end of a long list of minor problems (Franklin, 2006).

Research indicates that such training programs are beneficial for both doctors and patients. In one study, medical professionals who attended a three-day communication training session at the University of Sussex (2002) showed more empathy toward their patients and were more efficient in their consultations. Although the doctors spent the same amount of time with their patients, the patients felt that they had been given much more of their doctors' attention.

## chapter objectives

After you have finished reading this chapter, you will be able to

- Outline the listening process and styles of listening

- List the reasons why we listen

- Identify challenges to good listening

- Identify attitudinal and ethical factors that inhibit listening

- Describe how various contexts affect listening

On our kindergarten report cards, we are judged on our ability (or inability) to listen. "Listens well" and "Follows directions" are high praise for your average five-year-old. But somewhere in the years that follow, we stop thinking about listening as a crucial skill. "I listen well" probably isn't a line on your résumé, like being able to speak German or knowing the ins and outs of JavaScript. Yet professors, employers, and career counselors often note that effective listening is one of the most important skills a student or employee can possess. And for doctors and patients, the ability to listen well can have a profound effect on health: both parties must listen effectively in order to make accurate diagnoses and crucial decisions about treatment.

In this chapter, we'll examine the very nature of listening—how we hear, process, and come to understand the meaning of spoken information. We'll learn why listening is so important and why we so often fail to listen effectively. Throughout, we'll offer a variety of concrete tools and techniques that can be used every day to make us more effective and more competent listeners.

## How We Listen

How many times have you had the radio on, only to realize you weren't listening to it? You know you heard the music, and you may have sung along. But just moments after it ends, you can't recall the name of the song or how the DJ introduced it. You were thinking about something else or simply not paying enough attention to retain what you heard.

Although the two are often confused, hearing and listening are not the same thing. **Hearing** is, essentially, the physiological process of perceiving sound. It's a complex process through which sound waves are picked up by the ears and transmitted to the brain. Unless there is a physical reason why hearing does not take place, it is an involuntary process—you can't turn it on or off. But you can, to some degree, decide what sounds you're going to notice and attend to. This is where listening comes in. **Listening** is the process of recognizing, understanding, and accurately interpreting the messages you hear. It is much more than just hearing words or an ability to recall information (Todd & Levine, 1996). Listening involves *processing* what others say and do, paying attention, and understanding (Thomas & Levine, 1994), as well as *creating* messages that respond to the speaker and are directed toward achieving goals (Wiemann, Takai, Ota, & Wiemann, 1997). In this section, we'll examine how this crucial process works.

### The Listening Process

The listening process occurs so quickly that we may think of it as automatic, but in fact, listening involves a complex web of skills. We can develop and improve those skills by focusing on the voluntary parts of the process, as detailed in the following sequence of steps:

1. *Selecting.* Since hearing is involuntary, we cannot choose what we hear. When you are faced with competing stimuli—say, the sounds of the television in the

● **THERE'S A BIG** difference between hearing a song on the radio and listening to a friend express concern about a personal issue.

next room, the dishwasher running, and your roommate Brett complaining about his economics midterm—you will need to choose one sound over the others. This is a process called **selecting**.

2. *Attending.* Working hand in hand with selecting is **attending**—the additional step of *focusing attention* on your selected message or sound. Let's say you select Brett's voice (deciding that it's probably more interesting than the sound of the running dishwasher); the next step is to attend actively to his words and message. Attending is a particularly important step to be aware of, as it is not always easily achieved. Your other roommate, Elton, may have the TV tuned in to your favorite show, and you desperately want to hear the dialogue in the next room. That makes attending to Brett's message much more difficult.

3. *Understanding.* In the process of talking about his midterm, Brett mentions the disagreement he had with his professor over the wording of a particular essay question. He starts throwing around phrases like "aggregate supply" and "reciprocal demand." You've never studied economics, so you barely understand a word he's saying. **Understanding**—interpreting and making sense of messages—is a crucial step in the listening process because it is what enables us to interpret meaning. If you were an economics major yourself, you'd be better able to make sense of and understand Brett's dilemma.

4. *Remembering.* As a student, you know that it's important to hear and understand the messages you receive in class and also to recall them during an exam or when applying the content to real life. Thus **remembering** or recalling information is also part of the listening process. If you don't recall what happened in your conversation with Brett, he might be annoyed later on when he tells you about how things turned out with his professor.

5. *Responding.* Although we tend to think of listening as merely receiving messages, responding to messages is actually an important part of the process. **Responding** to messages involves generating some kind of feedback or reaction that lets others know that you have received and understood their message. So when Brett wonders if he should talk to his professor and you say, "That sounds like the best course of action given the importance of this exam for your grade," it lets him know that you fully comprehend his concern.

Empathic listening relies on appropriate nonverbal communication (Chapter 4). In addition to paraphrasing messages, you let your partner know you're listening by leaning in, nodding, and making eye contact. Your tone of voice and your vocalizations—like the supportive "mmm hmmm"— also show empathy. The combined effect of your verbal and nonverbal messages tells your partner that you care.

**empathic listening**, we are attempting to know how another person feels. It involves listening to people with openness, sensitivity, and caring. Empathic listening can provide emotional support for someone in need or comfort someone when tragedy or disappointment has struck. For example, on the animated TV series *Avatar: The Last Airbender,* archenemies Zuko and Katara are trapped in crystal catacombs underneath the city of Ba Sing Se. Their communication is initially marked by bitter, pointed language and a refusal to listen, but over time, they come to realize what they have in common—both lost their mothers directly or indirectly to war. The change in their communication after this revelation is dynamic as each begins to understand and empathize with the other's story. Listening gives them insight and compassion for each other—at least for a little while!

When you are listening empathically, it's important to **paraphrase** the thoughts and feelings being expressed. This involves guessing at feelings and rephrasing what you think the speaker has said ("It really sounds like you're overwhelmed by the amount of work you need to do"). That's because empathic listening is person-centered (Burleson, 1994). It recognizes and elaborates on the other person's feelings, giving them some degree of legitimacy. The empathic listener reflects the feelings and thoughts of the other without suggesting an answer or solution (Fent & MacGeorge, 2006).

### Appreciative Listening

The fourth goal of listening is enjoyment. **Appreciative listening** is used when your goal is simply to take pleasure in the sounds that you receive. Listening to music, poetry, narrations, comedy routines, plays, movies, and television shows for sheer enjoyment all qualify as appreciative listening situations (Christenson, 1994). Some people find this type of listening so important that they schedule time to do it—that's why we buy tickets to concerts and other performances or tell our family members to not bother us when *Lost* is on. Appreciative listening can also help relieve stress, unclutter the mind, and refresh the senses. We can't help but wonder if this is why credit card or health insurance companies play classical music while they keep callers on hold for twenty minutes—not that it works to keep most of us from being angry. Table 5.1 illustrates ways in which you can accomplish each of the four listening goals we have discussed in this section.

## The Value of Listening Well

So now you know how we listen and what types of listening we do, but let's face it, we're all busy. Listening is probably a skill we can sometimes do without or shortchange, right? Hardly. Listening is crucial to winning at Trivial Pursuit and running for class president, from knowing how to change a tire to knowing how to argue for a better grade or a pay raise. Put simply, listening affects more than your ability to communicate: it enables you to live a productive, satisfying, and healthy life.

● **SOMETIMES** we listen for the pure enjoyment of the sound of a jazz artist, a string quartet, or a rock band.

| Type | Description | Strategies |
|------|-------------|------------|
| Informational | Listening to understand, learn, realize, or recognize | Listen for main ideas or details; take speaker's perspective; use memory effectively |
| Critical | Listening to judge, analyze, or evaluate | Determine speaker's goal; evaluate source of message; question logic, reasoning, and evidence of message |
| Empathic | Listening to provide therapy, comfort, and sympathy | Focus on speaker's perspective; give supportive and understanding feedback; show caring; demonstrate patience; avoid judgment; focus on speaker's goal |
| Appreciative | Listening for enjoyment of what is being presented | Remove physical and time distractions; know more about originator (author, artist, composer); explore new appreciative listening opportunities |

**TABLE 5.1**

**LISTENING GOALS**

## Effective Listening Helps Your Career

Effective listening is greatly valued and rewarded professionally. Employers report that effective listening is related to job satisfaction, performance, and the achievement of the organization's goals (Cooper, 1997). In fact, surveys of *Fortune* 500 company personnel reveal that listening is one of the most important skills that a college graduate can possess (Wolvin & Coakley, 1991). In the professional world, employees who are good listeners are seen as alert, confident, mature, and judicious—qualities that result in professional rewards.

## Effective Listening Saves Time and Money

One of the reasons that professionals value listening skills so much is simply because good listeners save time by acting quickly and accurately on information presented to them. You comprehend more when you listen well (Rubin, Hafer, & Arata, 2000), so if you actively listen to your instructor's remarks about an upcoming exam, you can save time by studying more effectively. If you listen carefully when someone is giving you driving instructions to get from point A to point B, you'll be more relaxed and more likely to show up on time.

Good listeners can avoid costly errors: businesses lose millions of dollars each year because of listening mistakes alone (Steil, Summerfield, & de Mare, 1983). Repeated or duplicated tasks, missed opportunities, lost clients, botched orders, misunderstood instructions, and forgotten appointments can cost companies money and affect your personal budget as well: when Stephen leases a new car, for example, he fails to listen to the sales pitch, doesn't ask effective questions, and doesn't read the agreement carefully until after he's signed it. Only then does he realize that he'll be charged heavily for driving more than 15,000 miles a year.

**CONNECT**

Employees aren't the only ones who must listen well. In Chapter 10, you learn that successful managers take time to talk to employees, minimize distractions during those discussions, ask questions, and respond with appropriate verbal and nonverbal behavior, thus showing that they are truly listening to the employee's concerns.

**AND YOU?**

Can you think of a time when poor listening cost you something? Have you ever missed test instructions? Missed meeting a friend or a team practice? Do you think these lapses reflect the value (or lack of value) you placed on these events?

● **HOW WILL** your real estate agent help you find your dream home if he doesn't listen to and comprehend your desire for high ceilings and hardwood floors?

**CONNECT**

As relationships develop (Chapter 6), communication content changes, as do listening behaviors and goals. When you were in the *initiating* and *exploratory stages* of your friendship with Michelle, you likely used informational listening to discover her hometown or hobbies. But during the *intensification stage,* critical and empathic listening likely became more important as you sought to analyze, understand, and connect with her on a deeper level.

### Effective Listening Creates Opportunities

Good listeners don't just avoid mistakes; they find opportunities that others might miss. A real estate agent who truly listens to what a young couple is looking for in their first home and comprehends their financial constraints is more likely to find the clients a home that truly works for them. Even to write a textbook like the one you are reading involves listening. As authors, we must listen to our peers, who help us decide what topics and scholarship to include. We must listen to the students who have reviewed our manuscript to find out what kinds of examples and issues will make communication scholarship most relevant to them. And we must listen to our editors, who help us make the material clear and engaging.

### Effective Listening Strengthens Relationships

Throughout this book, we note that relationships depend on good communication in order to thrive. That means that we need to be aware of our perceptions and our verbal and nonverbal messages, but it also means that we need to understand the role that listening plays in our relationships. Have you ever had a friend who just talked about himself or herself without ever allowing you to share your own thoughts or concerns? Does your roommate or a colleague send text messages or type e-mails while saying, "I'm listening"? Perhaps they're hearing, but listening seems unlikely.

In new relationships, competent listening is required for partners to learn more about each other; a failure to do this usually results in less attraction and more negative emotions toward the other person or the relationship in general (Knobloch & Solomon, 2002). And as relationships progress, listening remains a top priority. For example, you won't be inclined to continue making self-disclosures to a friend who isn't showing you involved listening behaviors.

## Listening Challenges

Despite the tremendous benefits of listening well, we all fail to listen effectively at times. We may find ourselves unable to listen to material (or a speaker) that we find boring; we may have trouble focusing when we have a lot on our mind, are in a rush, or are coming down with a cold. **Listening barriers** are factors that interfere with our ability to comprehend information and respond appropriately. A variety of challenges affect our ability to listen effectively. We discuss several such factors in this section.

### Environmental Factors

In 2002, Verizon Wireless launched an ad campaign that you're probably quite familiar with. The quirky Verizon tech guy (played by Paul Marcarelli) roams through wheat fields, across snowy mountains, through airports, along highways, and into a bowling alley asking his signature question: "Can you hear me now?" According to the Yankee Group tracking firm, these ads helped Verizon increase business in the fiercely competitive cell phone market: customer numbers grew 10 percent to 32.5 million in the first year of the campaign alone (Howard, 2004). But why was this particular campaign so successful? Because the noise around us (like static and choppy phone reception) inhibits listening, which in turn makes communication quite difficult.

Noise is only one of the environmental factors that impair our ability to listen and sometimes even hear. For example, it's usually easier to listen in one-on-one situations than group settings because groups involve more people competing for your listening ear and attention (Beatty & Payne, 1984). It can also be difficult to listen when there are distractions in your environment: the TV is on, you've got a view of the beach out of your window on a sunny day, your baby is crying, your allergies are driving you crazy, or the acoustics of a room cause the speaker's voice to echo.

If you know that environmental factors will distract you from a listening situation ahead of time, there are several things you can do to increase your attention. There's a classroom on one of our campuses that is always cold, even if it's 90 degrees outside. So we warn our students to dress appropriately—freezing in a tank top is not an excuse for not listening and taking notes during a lecture! Similarly, if you know that a particular group meeting has lots of rowdy individuals making it difficult to listen to the speaker, try to get to the meeting early to pick a seat closer to the speaker. Seemingly small steps like this can boost your communication success quite a bit.

## Hearing Challenges

Environmental factors—like trying to talk on your cell phone at a construction site—can explain many situations where it is difficult to hear and therefore listen. But sometimes the difficulty lies not in the situation but in a physical or medical issue. For example, the ability to hear does decline with age (Bellis & Wilber, 2001), and this hearing loss affects not only the ability to hear words but also the nonverbal aspects of speech (tone, pitch, range, and so on) (Villaume & Brown, 1999). Stereotypes of older adults portray them as unable to engage in normal conversation because of cognitive decline when the reality is often that they have to work harder to separate the sounds they hear (Murphy, Daneman, & Schneider, 2006). And hearing challenges are not an issue faced solely by older people; accidents, diseases, or physical differences can also cause varying degrees of hearing impairment.

● **LISTENING** is not reserved for those with the ability to hear. These two friends are sharing ideas through sign language.

It's important to note, however, that hearing loss (even total hearing loss) does not mean that an individual is unable to listen competently. For example, deaf individuals often speak of "listening with their eyes," and research notes that those who cannot hear physically are quite competent at decoding nonverbal behaviors such as gestures, facial expressions, and eye behaviors that can reveal a speaker's emotions (Grossman & Kegl, 2007). In addition, individuals who use American Sign Language as a primary language also listen to each other and encode and decode messages in much the same way as two friends speaking Japanese, English, French, or any other vocal language.

## Multitasking

If listening well amid environmental distractions is difficult, it can be nearly impossible when your attention is divided among many important tasks. **Multitasking**—attending to several things at once—is often considered an unavoidable part of

## COMMUNICATIONACROSSCULTURES

### THINK ABOUT THIS

### Listening with Your Eyes

In the city of Rochester, New York, people listen differently. Movies are shown with captions of dialogue. Telephones flash rather than just ring. That's because the city hosts the nation's largest population of deaf and hearing-impaired residents and is home to the National Technical Institute for the Deaf, part of the Rochester Institute of Technology (RIT) (York, 2006). On campus and in the surrounding city, Deaf culture mingles with the larger culture of the hearing, and listening takes on a new dimension.

Deaf culture defines itself not by hearing ability (or lack of it) but through the shared code of language. American Sign Language (ASL) is the most common signed language in North America, and it is quite distinct from spoken language. For example, ASL is not a code of nonverbal gestures that translate word for word into spoken English but rather a completely different language, rich with unique meanings and nuances (Hott & Garey, 2007; Siple, 2003).

Among the deaf, eye contact, appearance, time, and touch play key roles in understanding others. When communicating, deaf people rely more heavily on nonverbal cues than most hearing people do. This can cause confusion. Most hearing people, for example, are uncomfortable maintaining eye contact for prolonged periods of time; but for a deaf person, breaking eye contact—or failing to make it in the first place—is a sign of indifference or disinterest. Deaf people use touch to greet one another and facial expressions, body movement, and gestures to convey meaning; from their perspective, the verbal communication of the hearing can seem lifeless and dull (Siple, 2003).

In fact, the visual nature of sign language has given rise to a unique form of poetry that must be performed rather than read. And just as written poetry makes use of devices like rhyming, line division, and alliteration, signed poetry takes advantage of the visual nature of sign—for example, repeating similar hand movements and orientations to make visual "rhymes" and incorporating facial expressions and other nonverbal cues.

❶ How can hearing people become better listeners when they communicate with deaf people? How can deaf people improve their listening skills in the hearing world?

❷ If you are able to hear, does it strike you as surprising that in Deaf culture, you might be labeled as deficient in the realm of nonverbal communication? How might this influence how you view your own communication skills?

❸ What kinds of mediated communication do both hearing and deaf people share? Can individuals use them to overcome communication barriers between hearing and deaf people?

❹ What kind of meaning might be lost if a poem born in ASL were to be translated into written form? Can a nonsigner truly appreciate the performance of a signed poem?

Source: Dirksen Bauman (2003).

modern life. We routinely drive, walk, cook, or tidy up while listening to music, talking on the phone, or watching television.

We may truly believe that we're giving fair attention to each task, but research shows that our ability to attend to more complicated chores—driving in an unfamiliar place, listening to a lecture, cooking a new recipe—suffers when we multitask. That's because our ability to focus is limited—we wind up toggling our attention between various tasks, alternating from one to another, and our efficiency and accuracy decrease substantially (Wallis, 2006). And while it's true that to some degree individuals who grew up in the electronic age surrounded by television, PlayStations, and iPods can multitask better than those who grew up without such distractions, it's still largely a myth that multitasking can be done well: regardless of age or experience, the brain is limited in its ability to process information during multitasking (Wallis, 2006).

**AND YOU?**

Do you routinely multitask? Do you agree or disagree with the research that states that such activities inhibit your ability to listen and process information?

## Boredom and Overexcitement

Sometimes it's just hard to listen to a speaker whose voice lulls you off to sleep or whose presentation is lifeless; it can be equally hard to listen to a perfectly competent speaker who is giving a presentation on a boring topic. The truth is, when something (or someone) seems overwhelmingly dull, we can wind up daydreaming. There are so many more interesting things to think about: weekend plans, that interesting person you met at a party on Friday night, what you want to do after graduation . . . Even creating a mental grocery shopping list might seem more interesting than listening to a particular speaker. Nonetheless, boring information may still be important information that is worth your attention. On the flip side of boredom, overexcitement may also distract us from listening effectively, even if the speaker is saying something that you might normally find really engaging. If you're consumed by plans for an upcoming wedding or a vacation or you're wondering how you're going to study for two midterms while writing a twenty-page paper and putting together a lab report, it can be difficult to listen to competing messages.

There are ways to improve your listening skills in situations where you are prone to boredom or overexcitement. You can be a better listener by becoming more conscious about the situation. Think about how *you* would deliver the information being discussed and how you would restructure it or give examples; in the process, you may find yourself listening much better and avoiding boredom. Avoid daydreaming by taking notes and relating the information to your own life examples. If you're in an interpersonal situation—and you're sick of listening to your friend Carla complain for the hundredth time about her problems with Professor Jones—you might discuss your concerns with her or try to put yourself in her shoes.

## Attitudes About Listening

You probably haven't spent much time analyzing your attitudes and feelings about the act of listening (who has?). Yet sometimes our attitude is the very thing that causes us to struggle when communicating with others. Let's examine three examples here.

### Talking Seems More Powerful than Listening

In many Western societies, people tend to think that talking is powerful, so *not* talking must be less than powerful. Because we fail to value the power of listening,

---

## WIREDFORCOMMUNICATION

### Multitasking: An Attention Deficit Epidemic

Alicia is sitting in a history lecture hall, typing notes as her instructor runs through a PowerPoint presentation detailing Santa Anna's siege on the Alamo. As her IM window pops up, she takes a moment to read a note from a classmate who missed yesterday's lecture and was hoping to borrow her notes; they exchange messages before she toggles back to her notes and tunes back in to the lecture. Alicia doesn't realize it, but in the time it took her to attend to that message, she missed five minutes of the fifty-minute lecture.

For many people, modern life means spending the bulk of one's time plugged in to any number of electronic devices, from iPods to cell phones to laptops. Many people like to brag about their ability to multitask, and with the right technology, we can do six things at once. But should we?

Some experts think not. According to cognitive researchers, the human brain doesn't really multitask, it just divides its attention. That means we're never really paying attention to more than one thing at a time; we're just constantly moving between tasks. And the more tasks, the more likely we are to make mistakes. "If a teenager is trying to have a conversation on an e-mail chat line while doing algebra, she'll suffer a decrease in efficiency, compared to if she just thought about algebra until she was done," notes one expert. "People may think otherwise, but it's a myth" (Wallis, 2006, p. 53).

One researcher has postulated that continued multitasking can lead to symptoms similar to those of attention deficit disorder (ADD), including distractibility, restlessness, impulsiveness, and irritability. The psychiatrist Edward Hallowell, author of *Crazy Busy: Overstretched, Overbooked, and About to Snap! Strategies for Coping in a World Gone ADD,* calls the condition attention deficit trait (ADT) and notes that it is caused by environmental factors: a person with ADD always has symptoms, but a person with ADT is able to relax when he or she is in the setting that induces the symptoms (Steptoe, 2006). Hallowell points to those who spend the bulk of their time responding to e-mails and voice mail and being interrupted by phone calls and IMs. Technology invades their lives and leaves them little time to process their thoughts. "What your brain is best equipped to do is to think, to analyze, to dissect and create," Hallowell notes. "And if you're simply responding to bits of stimulation, you won't ever go deep" (as cited in Gilbert, 2005). So for those of us who divide our attention between various beeps, buzzes, and other inputs, it might be worth taking some time to unplug and reboot.

**THINK ABOUT THIS**

❶ What kinds of activities do you know distract you and affect your ability to listen? Are there any tasks that you feel you can do without affecting your listening?

❷ Do you ever listen to music while you study? How carefully are you really listening to it? Is it just background noise that you actually tune out?

❸ Does it bother you when people attend to other things—checking e-mail, Web surfing, and such—when you are speaking to them?

we tend to neglect it. Michael listens only to plan what he's going to say next; he's not interested in what his wife has to say, only in making *her* listen to *him*. Katrina thinks she already knows what others will say; when her sister is speaking to her, she nods quickly and says, "Yeah, yeah, I know." Both Michael and Katrina would likely be better communicators and experience healthier relationships if they remembered that listening empowers.

A frequently recommended suggestion for listening well is simply to stop talking. Sounds simple, right? It's easier said than done; you have to adjust to a new speaking-to-listening ratio. That means you talk less and listen more, being sure to raise your awareness of your listening time. If a desire to dominate the conversation creeps up on you, just remind yourself that you are empowering communication partners to reveal their thoughts, insights, fears, values, and beliefs (Fletcher, 1999) and that you are freeing yourself to connect, enlarge, and comprehend multiple concepts and connections (Dipper, Black, & Bryan, 2005) through the act of listening. In the long run, you may even get more influence in relationships as people come to think you understand them, relate to them, and confirm them. As they feel more confident about your caring for them, they give *you* more influence.

### Overconfidence and Laziness

Randall walked into a status meeting certain that he knew everything that was going to be said. As he confidently sat through the meeting only half listening to his colleagues tossing ideas around, his boss began asking him questions that he was unprepared to answer. The root of Randall's problem lies in overconfidence—he assumed that he didn't need to pay attention because he already knew everything. Overconfidence frequently leads to laziness—we use our high expectations of ourselves as an excuse not to prepare or plan in advance or pay attention during the communication transaction.

### Listening Apprehension

You may be aware that many people suffer from public speaking anxiety (perhaps you suffer from it yourself). But did you know that many people also struggle with concerns about listening? **Listening apprehension** (also called *receiver apprehension*) is a state of uneasiness, anxiety, fear, or dread associated with a listening opportunity. Listening to your boss give you a reprimand about your performance, listening to someone else's personal problems, or listening to highly detailed or statistical information can trigger listening apprehension, which compromises your ability to concentrate on or remember what is said (Ayres, Wilcox, & Ayers, 1995).

Students with high listening anxiety have lower motivation to process information in the classroom, which can affect overall academic performance (Schrodt, Wheeless, & Ptacek, 2000); confident individuals usually understand information better than their less confident peers (Clark, 1989). So it is important to assess your ability to listen effectively and to spend time developing your listening confidence. What do you think about your own listening apprehension? You may have a better idea after you complete the self-assessment on page 148.

**CONNECT**

Believe it or not, public speakers must listen to the audience to help the audience listen to the speech. Chapter 13 describes the importance of interacting *with* the audience rather than speaking *at* your listeners: Are your listeners yawning or grumbling, looking confused, laughing, or nodding in agreement? By watching for such verbal and nonverbal cues, competent speakers can adjust elements of their speaking (rate, pitch, volume, and so on) to meet the audience's needs.

## Unethical Listening Behaviors

In addition to environmental factors, hearing challenges, multitasking, boredom, overexcitement, and attitudinal factors, our own selfishness and defensiveness can come into play in a major way when listening. We're all guilty of such behavior from time to time. We hope that this discussion will help you become aware of unethical listening behavior and improve your communication skills. The behaviors that we discuss in this section—defensive, selective, selfish, hurtful, and fraudulent listening—are all aspects of incompetent communication. They will not benefit you in any way personally or professionally. But with careful attention and the development of positive listening behaviors, they can be overcome.

## what about you?

### Your Listening Apprehension

Lawrence Wheeless has developed a test that identifies listening areas that can cause apprehension. Some of these areas are listed below. Answer the following questions to get an idea of your listening apprehension level.

Score your answers to the following questions according to whether you strongly agree (1), agree (2), are undecided (3), disagree (4), or strongly disagree (5).

_____  1. I am not afraid to listen as a member of an audience.

_____  2. I feel relaxed when I am listening to new ideas.

_____  3. I generally feel rattled when others are speaking to me.

_____  4. I often feel uncomfortable when I am listening to others.

_____  5. I often have difficulty concentrating on what is being said.

_____  6. I look for opportunities to listen to new ideas.

_____  7. Receiving new information makes me nervous.

_____  8. I have no difficulty concentrating on instructions given to me.

_____  9. People who try to change my mind make me anxious.

_____  10. I always feel relaxed when listening to others.

*Scoring:* Add up your scores for items 1, 2, 6, 8, and 10. Now add up your scores for items 3, 4, 5, 7, and 9. Subtract the total of the second set of answers from the first total to get a composite score. If your final score is positive, you have a tendency toward listener apprehension; the higher the score, the more apprehension you report. If your final score is negative, you have little or no apprehension.

Source: Wheeless (1975). Adapted with permission.

## Defensive Listening

Harry Potter can't stand Professor Snape; Professor Snape despises Harry Potter. If you've ever read the Harry Potter series of books or seen the movies, we don't need to tell you this twice! To some extent, the mutual dislike is earned: Snape often singles Harry out for punishment, and Harry frequently disrespects Snape. But when Snape must teach Harry Occlumency—the ability to block his thoughts from being read by Lord Voldemort—the two must attempt to put aside their differences. Harry finds Occlumency extremely difficult and becomes easily frustrated—he won't even listen as Snape urges him to practice, not give up, and understand that it is crucial for Harry to master this task. In Harry's eyes, Snape is picking on him yet again, trying to make him feel like a failure, so he simply shuts down and responds with anger. In this example, Harry is practicing **defensive listening,** responding with aggression and arguing with the speaker without fully listening to the message.

● **HARRY POTTER** and Professor Snape may have their issues, but Harry's defensive listening isn't going to help him learn Occlumency.

We've all been in a situation where a speaker or communication partner seems to be confronting us about an unpleasant topic. But defensive listeners who respond with aggressiveness and who argue before completely listening to the speaker experience more anxiety (Schrodt & Wheeless, 2001), probably because they anticipate not being effective in the listening encounter. If you find yourself listening defensively, we offer some tips to help you in Table 5.2.

| Tip | Example |
| --- | --- |
| Hear the speaker out | Don't rush into an argument without knowing the other person's position. Wait for the speaker to finish before constructing your own arguments. |
| Consider the speaker's motivations | Think of the speaker's reasons for saying what is being said. The person may be tired, ill, or frustrated. Don't take it personally. |
| Use nonverbal communication | Take a deep breath and smile slightly (but sincerely) at the speaker. Your disarming behavior may be enough to force the speaker to speak more reasonably. |
| Provide calm feedback | After the speaker finishes, repeat what you think was said and ask if you understood the message correctly. Often a speaker on the offensive will back away from an aggressive stance when confronted with an attempt at understanding. |

**TABLE 5.2**

**STEPS TO AVOID DEFENSIVE LISTENING**

Selective listening can also be influenced by our attributions—personal characteristics we use to explain other people's behavior. If you believe that your classmate Lara is lazy, you may listen only to messages that support your attribution. Competent communicators avoid selective listening by verifying their perceptions, seeking thoughtful explanations, and moving past first impressions in order to understand communication partners (Chapter 2).

### Selective Listening

When you zero in only on bits of information that interest you, disregarding other messages or parts of messages, you are engaging in **selective listening**. Selective listening is common in situations when you are feeling defensive or insecure. For example, if you really hate working on a group project with your classmate Lara, you may only pay attention to the disagreeable or negative things that she says. If she says, "I can't make it to the meeting on Thursday at eight," you shut off, placing another check in the "Lara is lazy and awful to work with" column of proof. However, you might miss the rest of Lara's message—perhaps she has a very good reason for missing the meeting, or perhaps she's suggesting that you reschedule.

Selective listening can work with positive messages and impressions as well, although it is equally unethical in such situations. Imagine that you're a manager at a small company. Four of your five employees were in place when you took your job, but you were the one who hired Micah. Since hiring well makes you look good as a manager, you might tend to focus and brag to your boss about Micah's accomplishments and the feedback from others in the organization on Micah's performance. He may well be a great employee, but it's important to listen to compliments about other employees as well, particularly when it comes time to consider promotions.

To improve our communication, particularly when we're feeling apprehensive or defensive, we must face communication messages honestly—that is, we must not avoid particular messages or close our ears to communication that's uncomfortable. Being mindful of our tendency to behave in this manner is the first step in addressing this common communication pitfall.

### Selfish Listening

Selfish listeners listen for only their own needs—or even for their own unethical purposes. Consider the film *Mean Girls,* in which Cady (Lindsay Lohan) attempts to break up the clique known as "the Plastics," consisting of friends Karen, Regina, and Gretchen. Cady's first strategy is to insert doubt into the friendships between the girls and then to listen as each girl approaches her with confidences and concerns. For example, Gretchen cries to Cady in the girls' bathroom about her frustrations with Regina—and in the process spills the beans that Regina is actually cheating on her boyfriend. Cady isn't listening to be a supportive friend; she's listening to gain information to use against Regina.

But selfish listening can also be **monopolistic listening**, or listening in order to control the communication interaction. Think again of Cady. Her actions to comfort her friend are clearly geared toward getting what she wants and allowing her more control in the conversation.

● **"THE PLASTICS"** may be mean and petty, but that doesn't excuse Cady's selfish listening in the film *Mean Girls*.

## Hurtful Listening

Hurtful listening also focuses on the self, but it's a bit more direct—and perhaps even more unethical—than selfish listening. *Attacking* is a response to someone else's message with negative evaluations ("Well, Leon, that was a pretty stupid thing to say!"); *ambushing* is more strategic. By carefully listening, the ambusher finds weaknesses in others—things they're sensitive about—and pulls them out at strategic or embarrassing times. So if Mai cried to Scott about the fact that she failed her calculus final and Scott is later looking for a way to discredit Mai, he might say something to the effect of "I'm not sure that Mai is the right person to help us draw up a budget. Math isn't exactly her strong suit, is it, Mai?"

At other times, our listening isn't meant to be intentionally hurtful, but we can still end up offending others or being inconsiderate of their feelings. **Insensitive listening** occurs when we fail to pay attention to the emotional content of someone's message, instead taking it at face value. Your friend Adam calls to tell you that he got rejected from Duke Law School. Adam had mentioned to you that his LSAT scores made Duke a long shot, so you accept his message for what it appears to be: a factual statement about a situation. But you fail to hear the disappointment in his voice—whether or not Duke was a long shot, it was his

## AND YOU?

Do you know any people who engage in the unethical behaviors described? Is it frequent behavior or a rare slip? How do these tendencies affect your interactions with those people? Do you ever find yourself engaging in such behaviors?

## EVALUATING COMMUNICATION ETHICS

**THINK ABOUT THIS**

### Listening When You're Sick of Hearing

You were happy to lend your friend Jamie a sympathetic ear as Jamie worked through a difficult divorce earlier this year. You were by Jamie's side when the divorce papers were filed; you went to the bank to help open up a bank account and hunted for a new apartment together. And of course, as a single person yourself, you were there to empathize as Jamie faced the prospect of heading back into the dating world. You agreed to be each other's date when attending parties with all of your coupled-up friends and made plans to check out a speed-dating party together as sort of a gag.

But now, only eight months after the divorce, Jamie is in the throes of a new romance with an attractive new coworker. You can't help but feel a bit jealous—you've been single for more than three years; it doesn't seem fair that Jamie should find love so quickly. What's worse is that Jamie insists on spending as much time as possible with this new love—often at the expense of time with you. You want to support and be happy for your friend, but you're finding it very difficult to listen to discussions about day hikes and movie nights and sports outings. You find yourself continually avoiding the subject of dating, and as a result, you notice that Jamie seems less interested in talking to you. Somewhat relieved, you start to avoid talking to Jamie at all. You're not all that surprised when Jamie suddenly asks you why you're mad. But you don't really know what to say. You know why you're avoiding your friend, but you're sort of embarrassed about your reasons. What should you say?

❶ Should you tell Jamie the truth? Is it ethical to hide your true feelings from a friend? What might happen if you just say, "I'm embarrassed to say that I'm feeling a bit jealous. I'm feeling bummed about my own love life, and I miss having you as my similarly single friend"?

❷ What are Jamie's ethical responsibilities here? Has your friend been listening to you? Should Jamie have been able to sense your sensitivity about the situation from the way you've responded?

❸ What kinds of unethical listening behaviors might be at work here? Are you avoiding? Is Jamie ambushing?

top choice as well as a chance to be geographically closer to his girlfriend, who lives in North Carolina. Had you paid attention to Adam's nonverbal cues, you might have known that he needed some comforting words.

### Pseudolistening

When you become impatient or bored with someone's communication messages, you may find yourself engaging in **pseudolistening**—pretending to listen by nodding or saying "uh-huh" when you're really not paying attention at all. One of the many downsides of pseudolistening is that you can actually miss important information or risk offending your communication partner and damaging the relationship. Homer Simpson is a pro at pseudolistening, particularly when it comes to communicating with his boss, Mr. Burns. Admittedly a cranky, unpleasant guy, Mr. Burns frequently attempts to discipline Homer, who is busier playing office games than getting his job done. But though he may give the faint impression that he is hearing his boss's words, Homer never listens. Instead, he daydreams, has conversations with himself inside his head, and imagines that Mr. Burns is morphing into various objects, in one case an ice-cream cone. This point may be amusing on television, but in real life, failing to hear your boss out—particularly when you're being corrected—can have some professionally disastrous results.

MATT GROENING

● **WHAT MIGHT** Mr. Burns be saying here? Homer Simpson doesn't know because he's pseudolistening.

## Listening in Context

Chances are, you've recognized bits of yourself or your friends scattered throughout this chapter. We have all, at one time or another, felt defensive, nervous, bored, or lazy and found that we were less effective listeners because of it. But you probably don't feel that way all the time. You might find yourself to be a great listener in certain situations and weak in others. That's because, like every other part of communication, our listening skills and abilities are affected by context. In this section, we examine the ways in which the context of a communication influences listening.

## The Relational and Situational Contexts

Imagine this scenario. You're a shy, introverted person, and you're standing in a crowd of people at a party or a conference. You positively hate events like this, vastly preferring interpersonal or very small group activities. The idea of walking up to someone you don't know (especially since everyone there seems to know each other) makes your heart race, and you begin to sweat bullets. The only person you do know—your friend Yvonne—is late. This is so like her. She's always late for everything. You've even given up on going to the movies with her since it's pointless to pay $12 for a ticket when you'll miss the first half hour of the film anyway. Suddenly, Yvonne rushes in, breathless. She seems out of sorts and begins a hasty explanation: "I'm sorry I'm late but . . ." You may well hear Yvonne's excuse, but are you listening?

The situation we're in and the relationship we have with other communicators at any given time have a profound effect on our communication (as you've likely discovered in Chapters 2, 3, and 4). When you're in a place you're unfamiliar with or when you're feeling uncomfortable with your surroundings or the formality of an event (such as a funeral, a wedding, or a professional conference), you may experience the sort of listening apprehension that we discussed earlier. And in some situations, such as a party, environmental noise can contribute to listening problems. We've all been in a situation where there are so many people talking or loud music playing that you literally have to scream to be heard, and it feels like it takes all of your energy and concentration just to make out a conversational partner's words. Clearly, such situations make communication more challenging.

The relational context is also at play in this scenario. Yvonne, as great a friend as she may be, has sent you messages through her nonverbal behavior of chronic lateness. You perceive her lateness as a sign that she does not value your time or friendship, whether or not that is the truth. So when Yvonne attempts to explain why she is late on this occasion, you hardly pay attention, offering no empathy and not thinking deeply about the message. Perhaps it's another excuse about car trouble or running into an old friend on her way to meet you, but perhaps it isn't. Maybe Yvonne got some bad news about her brother who is stationed abroad in the military or perhaps she wasn't feeling well earlier in the day. The only way that you'll find out is to listen actively.

## The Cultural Context

In various parts of the United States and abroad, you will encounter listening behaviors different from your own. As you travel or do business across the country or the world, you'll likely find it necessary to understand and adapt to listening differences.

When you think about traits and habits that make someone a "good" listener or a "bad" listener, you're often thinking about how your culture judges listening ability. For example, indirect styles of communication, common in Eastern cultures like China and Japan, require listener-responsible communication that saves face for the speaker. So a listener would be expected not to question the speaker directly, to construct meaning and understanding from the context of the situation, and to accommodate the speaker's needs more than the listener's (Lustig & Koester, 2006). Speaker-responsible listening, common in Western cultures like the United States and Canada, is more direct; the speaker usually tells the listener what he or she wants the listener to know. The listener can ask direct questions without offending the speaker, and both speaker and listener may be assertive without threatening the relationship or making the situation uncomfortable.

In addition to the actual listening behaviors themselves, *perceptions* of appropriate listening vary among cultural groups. One study of competence and listening found that Caucasians in the United States are perceived as approaching listeners who are expressive and exhibit nonverbal facilitators (like nodding, saying "mmm-hmmm," and the like). Caucasians also use more questioning techniques to clarify and comprehend the speaker's message. Hispanic Americans and Asian Americans are perceived as somewhat less expressive than whites, and African Americans are perceived as the least expressive listeners among these groups (Dillon & McKenzie, 1998). If you are comfortable or aware of only the preferred listening style of your own culture, miscommunication can occur. So Jennifer, a Colombian American, speaking with Jonathan, an African American colleague, might judge Jonathan as an ineffective listener if he is less expressive than she would hope as she complains about their mutual boss. She needs to remember that culture—including gender—is at play in this situation. In traveling around the globe, you will also find that expressiveness is viewed very differently in different cultures. Whereas many Westerners consider deep feelings private (or to be shared only with intimate relational partners), other cultures, including Hindus in Fiji and the Ommura in New Guinea, do not regard private feelings as sacrosanct; they communicate a variety of emotions to others in order to build shared experiences and expressions (Brenneis, 1990). Some suggestions that can help you communicate with people of different cultures are offered in Table 5.3.

A discussion of culture would not be complete without thinking about how we construe gender and how we're taught to think of masculinity and femininity. For example, our expectations of how men and women should behave powerfully affect our perceptions of listening competence. Men in the United States, for example, are discouraged from expressing intense emotions in public (Brody, 2000). This reluctance to react emotionally to information may give the appearance that men are not listening. Expectations about appropriate feminine behavior, however, encourage women to exhibit more verbal

**TABLE 5.3**

**TIPS FOR COMMUNICATING ACROSS CULTURES**

| Tactic | Explanation | Example |
|---|---|---|
| Recognize cultural differences | When communicating with someone from a different culture, keep in mind that factors such as country of origin, religion, gender, educational level, and socioeconomic status all play into our values and beliefs about communication. If you can, learn about the person's background, and ask questions. | If your future mother-in-law is a devout Catholic from France and you are a nonreligious person from St. Louis, you might want to learn more about French culture and Catholicism; you might ask your fiancée questions about how to get to know Mom. |
| Clarify behaviors as appropriate | Pay attention to the cultural needs of the listener. If you find that cultural differences are preventing good communication, tell the speaker or be silent to observe context and nonverbal behaviors. | "I don't think I'm understanding you correctly. Can you say that in another way for me, please?" |
| Adjust to differences | Ask more questions if necessary; ask the speaker to work with you to bridge the gap between cultural differences. | "I'm sure I'm not getting the complete picture. Can you give me an example of the problem to help me understand it better?" |

and nonverbal feedback when listening (Duncan & Fiske, 1977). Research notes that they nod and smile more, and use more encouraging filler words ("Really?" "Oh, wow," "Right"). You can see this point in action in the episode "I Am Peter, Hear Me Roar" of *Family Guy,* where Peter gets in touch with his feminine side. He calls his buddy Quagmire "just to talk"—he wants to listen to what's going on with his friend and have his friend listen to him in turn. Quagmire is so uncomfortable with this situation that he slams down the phone!

Such differences are not necessarily biologically based, however. Listener behavior is not consistent in all situations. For example, in brief debates, South African men engaged in more of these supportive verbal and nonverbal cues when they addressed female audiences, indicating that situational and relational context may be more powerful than gender expectations (Dixon & Foster, 1998).

● **THE GANG** from *Family Guy* believes that listening— and the verbal and nonverbal expressions that accompany it—is for women only!

## Technology as Context

How well do you listen to your text messages and e-mails? Are you skilled at listening to posts on your Facebook wall or your MySpace page? These might seem like strange questions, but we must in fact listen well when we decode messages sent through these channels. In some ways, listening to messages in various technological contexts requires a lot more effort than other forms of communication. For example, when you talk on the phone, you rely on verbal messages as well as vocal nonverbal messages (tone of voice, speaking rate, silences, and so on) because you lack other nonverbal cues such as body movement and eye behavior. But when you read your mom's e-mail or you text your significant other, you often lack both components.

For this reason, you must be sure to listen actively to the cues you do have at your disposal. When your friend Sheila capitalizes a word in an e-mail, she's giving emphasis to a particular point; you can show her that you've "listened" by making sure to address that particular point. In general, you show your communication partners that you've listened to their e-mails when you respond to all of the questions or concerns that they raised. You're not listening competently if you respond to your father's questions about when you're coming home next with an e-mail that details what you had for lunch. Similarly, you listen well when you enter a chat room and read the sequence of comments before responding (rather than blurting out a response to the first post you see).

And of course, using technology competently also involves consideration of the receiver of your message. Consider how your friend Eddie in Milwaukee would want to hear the news that you've broken up with his cousin whom you've been dating for two years: through a text message? on MySpace? over the phone? You'll want to choose the channel that is the most effective and appropriate for the occasion.

## BACK TO The Doctor's Office

At the beginning of the chapter, we discussed the unique question-and-answer dance that occurs between doctors and patients. Let's consider the ways that the listening barriers and skills discussed in this chapter affect communication when we discuss our health.

▶ Doctors in the 2002 University of Sussex study were trained to ask their patients more questions and to allow each patient to tell his or her own story. This made patients more involved in their own treatment and made them feel as though their doctors really cared about them.

▶ The nature of medical exams can make patients feel powerless. Consider the cues of clothing and artifacts: the doctor wears an official white lab coat, while the patient is naked beneath a paper gown. Even after the exam is over, it's hard for patients to reestablish their power in the communication relationship. One patient, a Harvard Law School graduate who has gone head to head with judges, juries, and opposing lawyers without a hitch, told the *New York Times* that when it comes to talking to her doctor, she's not so tough. "He's still the guy with the white lab coat behind the giant desk . . . and I still feel like the schlub in the paper dress" (Franklin, 2006, p. F5).

▶ Listening apprehension is a huge listening barrier for many patients. Patients may be concerned or preoccupied with anxiety about their own health, fears that their concerns will sound foolish, or even feelings of embarrassment or modesty during a medical exam. The situational and environmental context often serves to increase listening apprehension.

▶ Training programs like Frankel's are beneficial for both doctors and patients. When done well, listening contributes to the more accurate transfer of information to other health professionals. Patient records are more accurate, doctors make fewer mistakes, and patients feel better about their treatment (Eisenberg et al., 2005).

## THINGS TO TRY

1. Describe a time when you listened well. How do you know you listened well? Where were you? Who were you with? What were your goals? Did you adapt your listening to the situational, cultural, or relational context? What can you learn from this successful listening experience to guide you in future listening challenges?

2. Practice listening with your eyes as discussed in this chapter. When you go to your next class, observe your instructor or whoever is speaking. Form an overall impression of the speaker from nonverbal cues such as body movements, eye

behavior, and tone of voice. What emotions do they suggest? Do they match the verbal message being conveyed?

3. As you become a more critical listener, inquire about inconsistencies when you observe them in conversation. For example, if your friend offers you verbal and nonverbal messages that contradict each other, let him or her know. Be careful to avoid being defensive here. Instead of saying, "You're sending me mixed messages," say, "I'm confused about what you mean. You said you were happy with the decision, but you frowned and sighed at the same time."

4. Practice listening styles that are less familiar to you. Some people don't paraphrase well; others are uncomfortable being person-centered. The best way to try this out is to look back at the chapter and think about the discussions that made you feel uncomfortable ("I could never do that"). Then give it a try in a context that might benefit you. For example, if you tend to be an empathic, person-centered listener in group meetings and your meetings always run late because of it, try being more time-centered or action-centered.

## IF YOU'RE INTERESTED

*Perspectives on Listening,* edited by Andrew D. Wolvin and Carolyn Gwynn Coakley (Norwood, NJ: Ablex, 1993)

This book includes a perspective of listening skills, a discussion of the role of memory in listening, and a consideration of the difficulties experienced by individuals with listening disabilities. Chapters on empathy and listening as a relational process are useful for beginning students as they develop listening strategies and become more effective, competent communicators.

*Teaching Speaking and Listening in the Primary School,* by Elizabeth Grugeon (London: Fulton, 2005)

The premise of this book is that the way to literacy is through oracy (speaking and listening skills). Since most of us received very little elementary school training in either speaking or listening, this is a useful book to look at even if you are not an elementary school teacher. Internet access to this book is available through many libraries.

*The Queen* (Miramax, 2006)

In examining the perceptions of the public, the prime minister, and the queen of England following the death of Princess Diana in 1997, this movie reflects listening concepts. We see examples of unethical listening in early scenes when the queen clearly plans to limit the topics she will discuss with the newly elected prime minister, Tony Blair. Situational, cultural, and relational contexts affect efforts to communicate with the queen, who eventually engages in both comprehensive and critical listening to adapt to the needs of her constituents.

*The Secret Life of Words* (Focus Features, 2005)

Hearing-impaired and isolated, British factory worker Hanna turns off her hearing aid to isolate herself further from those around her; she almost never speaks.

Her boss forces her to take a vacation, so she goes to a coastal town in Northern Ireland, where she inexplicably volunteers to help a burn victim named Josef who is temporarily blinded from an accident. Although the movie's most powerful scene is Hanna's eventual opening up and confession to Josef, it is the process of the characters getting to that point that is relevant to this chapter. Silence, questions, timing, nonverbal sensitivity—this movie illustrates all of these powerful aspects of effective listening.

*The Fig Eater*, by Jody Shields (Boston: Little, Brown, 2000)

This murder mystery contains a lot of listening advice. The inspector in this novel believes that listening is one of the most important abilities an investigating officer can possess. He frequently quotes the philosopher Plutarch, who instructed men to listen in silence, without asking questions, and thoughtfully consider what they'd heard afterward. During interrogations, the inspector claims he can distinguish the different qualities of the witnesses' silence, as if it were a tone of voice. He even cites a text, to show how important it is to observe the listening behavior of others: "To observe how the person questioned listens is a rule of primary importance, and if the officer observes it, he will arrive at his goal more quickly than by hours of examination" (p. 147).

**Now that you have finished reading this chapter, you can**

Outline the listening process and styles of listening:

▶ **Hearing** is the physiological process of perceiving sound; **listening** is the process of recognizing, understanding, and interpreting the message (p. 134).

▶ We improve listening skills by focusing on the voluntary parts of the process: **selecting**, choosing one sound over others; **attending**, focusing on the message or sound; **understanding**, making sense of the message; **remembering**, recalling information; and **responding**, giving feedback (p. 135).

▶ **Active listening** involves making choices about selecting, attending, and so on, and is more competent than **passive listening** (p. 136).

▶ **People-oriented listeners** listen with relationships in mind (p. 136).

▶ **Action-oriented listeners** focus on tasks (p. 136).

▶ **Content-oriented listeners** carefully evaluate what they hear (p. 136).

▶ **Time-oriented listeners** prefer information that is clear and to the point (p. 136).

▶ Most people develop multiple listening preferences (p. 136).

List the reasons why we listen:

▶ **Informational listening** is used to understand a message (p. 137).

▶ In **critical listening**, you evaluate or analyze information, evidence, ideas, or opinions, and use critical thinking (p. 138).

▶ **Empathic listening** is an attempt to know how another person feels, often using **paraphrasing** to recognize and elaborate on the other's feelings (p. 140).

▶ **Appreciative listening** is used when the goal is simply to appreciate the sounds, such as music (p. 140).

▶ Effective listening is rewarded (p. 141).

▶ Good listeners save time and money by acting on information quickly and accurately (p. 141).

▶ Good listeners find opportunities others might miss (p. 142).

▶ Relationships depend on good communication, including listening, to survive (p. 142).

Identify challenges to good listening:

▶ **Listening barriers** are factors that interfere with our ability to comprehend information and respond appropriately (p. 142).

▶ Allergies and crying babies are examples of environmental factors that impair our ability to listen (p. 143).

▶ Hearing loss challenges can be overcome with understanding of nonverbal behaviors (p. 143).

▶ **Multitasking**, attending to several things at once, limits focus on any one task (p. 144).

▶ A boring speaker or a boring topic can be hard to follow, and on the flip side, overexcitement can be distracting (p. 145).

▶ Talking may be regarded as more powerful than listening (p. 146).

▶ Overconfidence may cause us not to pay careful attention during communication (p. 147).

▶ **Listening apprehension**, anxiety or dread associated with listening, may hinder concentration (p. 147).

Identify attitudinal and ethical factors that inhibit listening:

▶ **Defensive listening** is responding with aggression and arguing with the speaker, without fully listening to the message (p. 149).

▶ **Selective listening** is zeroing in on bits of information that interest you, disregarding other messages or parts of messages (p. 150).

▶ Selfish listeners listen for their own needs and may practice **monopolistic listening**, or listening in order to control the communication interaction (p. 150).

▶ **Insensitive listening** occurs when we fail to pay attention to the emotional content of someone's message and just take it at face value (p. 151).

▶ **Pseudolistening** is pretending to listen while not really paying attention (p. 152).

Describe how various contexts affect listening:

▶ Different situations (a crowded party, a professional conference) create different challenges (p. 152).

▶ The dynamics of the relationship between communicators can also change how you listen (p. 153).

▶ As in all aspects of communication, the cultural context affects listening behavior (p. 153).

▶ It may seem that we don't listen when we communicate electronically, but technology is an important context for listening (p. 155).

# Interpersonal Communication

**Fans make** new friends while celebrating their love of superheroes at Comic-Con.

# chapter

## 6

# Developing and Maintaining Relationships

**"I've been waiting for this for a year now!"** said one fan with glee as he headed in to the New York Comic Convention in February 2007. He was one of more than forty thousand fans who attended the celebration of comic books, science fiction, and fantasy (Ratner, 2007). And while plenty of attendees were there to meet the likes of Teenage Mutant Ninja Turtles creator Kevin Eastman or filmmaker Kevin Smith, they were also there to meet one another.

For most fans of popular fiction, the story ends when the novel closes or the credits roll. But for a large number of committed readers and viewers, the fantasy worlds they love take on lives of their own. Fandoms surrounding popular and cult-hit television shows, films, comics, and graphic novels are no longer secret subcultures: they are thriving communities that generate genuine relationships.

The Internet has allowed fans of various stories to connect in ways unheard of in the past. A few decades ago, a *Star Trek* fan had to trek to a convention to find the kind of camaraderie that can now be found with the click of a mouse. Online groups and forums allow fans to connect with one another in order to find companionship and stimulation. And those Web-based relationships can lead to in-person relationships, when fans meet each other at conventions.

The first science-fiction convention dates back to 1939—and so do stereotypes of science-fiction fans. Writer Frederik Pohl described guests at that conference as "toadish" and "loners" (Pollak, 2006). But the fact is, even loners need to find like-minded companions to experience life fully.

**After you have finished reading this chapter, you will be able to**

○ Explain key aspects of interpersonal relationships

○ Understand how and why we form relationships

○ See that every relationship has advantages and disadvantages

○ Consider how people in relationships choose to divulge or withhold personal information

○ Outline the predictable stages of most relationships

As you learned in Chapter 1, people need to be in relationships with other people, plain and simple. After all, relationships help us meet our needs for companionship and intellectual stimulation and also help us meet our physical needs. Could Frodo of *The Lord of the Rings* have survived without the help of his friend Samwise Gamgee, who provided him with the protection and the love necessary to stave off the evil effects of the ring? Of course not!

In this chapter, we'll focus on **interpersonal relationships**, the interconnections and interdependence between two individuals. But to understand these relationships, we need to be aware of the role communication plays in them. **Interpersonal communication** is the exchange of verbal and nonverbal messages between two people who have a relationship and are influenced by their partner's messages. You engage in interpersonal communication in your most intimate relationships—when you sit down to a heartfelt conversation with your significant other or when you catch up with your childhood best friend. But you also engage in interpersonal communication when you talk with your professor about your midterm grade and when you chat with your waiter at Chili's. Even though your relationship with your mom is probably more important to you than your relationship with a barista at Starbucks, competent communication in both relationships allows you to meet personal needs and achieve goals, whether it's support after a hard day's work or a cup of coffee.

So let's take a closer look at interpersonal relationships and the communication that takes place in them by examining the types of relationships we form, why and how we do so, and what happens once we're in them.

## Types of Interpersonal Relationships

Martin asks Pete, "Do you know my friend Jake?" Pete responds, "I've met him once or twice. He seems OK." In two short sentences, we gain a lot of information about relationships at play among these three men: to Martin, Jake is a friend; to Pete, he's just an acquaintance. Each of us is involved in multiple relationships, and we distinguish between them in countless ways. We have acquaintances, colleagues, friends, close friends, family members, romantic partners, virtual strangers we see all the time (like the Starbucks barista), and so on. In fact, every person has a complex **relational network** or web of relationships that connect individuals to one another. In this section, we'll focus on family relationships, friendships, and romantic partnerships, as well as online relationships.

### Family

Who's your family? For some people, the term *family* refers to immediate relatives who live in the same household. For others, it means a more extended family that includes grandparents, aunts, uncles, and cousins. Still others use the term to describe groups of people with whom they are intimately connected and committed, even without blood or civil ties. Participants in Alcoholics

Anonymous, fraternal organizations, and religious communities often consider one another to be family. But for our purposes, a **family** is a small social group bound by ties of blood, civil contract (such as marriage or adoption), and a commitment to care for and be responsible for one another, usually in a shared household.

Family relationships constitute the first and most basic relationships in our lives. From them, we learn communication skills and develop characteristics that affect how we interact with other people throughout our lives. Consider the success of TLC's reality series *Little People, Big World*. The show revolves around the daily family life of the Roloffs, led by parents Matt and Amy, who are both dwarfs (little people) and their four children. It is moving to learn about the struggles that Matt, Amy, and their son Zach (who is also little) face living in a world where everything is built for people over four feet tall, but what's truly endearing about the show are the relationships and communication between the family members. How does Zach relate to his average-height twin, who is nearly two feet taller than he is? How do Matt and Amy communicate about important family decisions when Matt is an idealistic dreamer and Amy is a logical planner? Through all of the soccer practices and mishaps around their Oregon farm, we watch the Roloffs deal with one another with openness, affection, discipline, humor, and sarcasm—qualities that reveal strong family communication according to contemporary research (see Table 6.1 on p. 166). Moreover, Matt and Amy reveal that they are highly invested in teaching their children family customs and traditions, beliefs and values, and the communication skills to face life's challenges; they want their kids to feel loved and secure so that they achieve success both professionally and personally (Ducharme, Doyle, & Markiewicz, 2002).

## Friendship

As individuals grow and begin to interact with people outside of their families, they are able to establish new, nonfamily relationships. **Friendship** is a

**CONNECT**

As you learn about interpersonal relationships, remember the competent communication model from Chapter 1. There is no right way to communicate with friends, family, or romantic partners because competent communication considers relational, situational, and cultural contexts. You may feel comfortable sharing personal information with your father; your friend Julie may not. You and your romantic partner may develop a communication style that simply wouldn't work for your brother.

● *LITTLE PEOPLE, BIG WORLD* depicts struggles and triumphs that any family can relate to while also representing dwarfism in mainstream media.

**TABLE 6.1**

**FAMILY
COMMUNICATION
QUALITIES**

| Communication Standard | Examples |
|---|---|
| Openness | • Being able to talk when something is wrong<br>• Talking about sensitive issues like sex or drugs<br>• Sharing feelings |
| Structural stability | • Having at least one person in the family whom everyone listens to and obeys<br>• Dealing with emotional issues only when everyone can handle them |
| Affection | • Being loving and affectionate with one another<br>• Saying affectionate things like "I love you" |
| Emotional and instrumental support | • Helping each other<br>• Being able to count on each other<br>• Knowing support will be there |
| Mind reading | • Knowing what's going on with each other without asking<br>• Understanding how the other feels without discussing it |
| Politeness | • Never being rude or inconsiderate<br>• Not talking back |
| Discipline | • Having clear rules for family members<br>• Knowing that there are consequences for breaking family rules |
| Humor or sarcasm | • Being able to tease other family members<br>• Poking fun at each other |
| Regular routine interaction | • Meeting regularly to discuss things<br>• Setting aside time to communicate |
| Avoidance | • Avoiding topics that are too personal<br>• Agreeing to skirt issues that are painful |

Dr. John Caughlin at the University of Illinois conducted three studies of 1,023 undergraduate students and found that people generally agree that these ten qualities constitute "excellent family communication" (2003).

**AND YOU?**

What characteristics do you consider most important in your friendships? How do they compare to the characteristics mentioned in the research? Do your friends meet your expectations? As a friend, do you exhibit the characteristics you listed as most important?

close and caring relationship between two people that is perceived as mutually satisfying and beneficial. Research has revealed many positive benefits from forming friendships with other people, including emotional support, companionship, and coping with major life stressors. Studies have also revealed that children who form successful friendships with others perform better academically and demonstrate fewer aggressive tendencies than those who do not (Doll, 1996; Hartup & Stevens, 1997; Newcomb & Bagwell, 1995; Rawlins, 1994; Weisz & Wood, 2005).

Although everyone has a personal opinion as to what qualities a friend should possess, research shows that people seem to agree on six important characteristics of friendship: availability, caring, honesty, trust, loyalty, and empathy (Pearson & Spitzberg, 1990).

▶ *Availability.* As simple as it may seem, one of the keys to building and maintaining a friendship stems from availability—your friend's ability to make time for you (and vice versa). If you and your friend seldom interact with each other, the relationship can deteriorate.

▶ *Caring.* The very nature of friendship is dependent on feelings of concern for each other. You and your friend likely care and perhaps even worry about each other's happiness and well-being.

▶ *Honesty.* Honesty is vital in all friendships. You want your friends to be open and truthful with you, even if that means that they sometimes need to tell you things that are hard to hear.

▶ *Trust.* You trust your friends to be honest with you, but you also trust them to maintain your confidentiality when you share private thoughts with them. A true friend will not blurt out your private matters or insecurities to the entire world.

▶ *Loyalty.* A friend who can be loyal in even the worst of times (a difficult breakup, unemployment, illness) is one worth keeping! Loyal friends manage to maintain relationships despite disagreements or arguments.

▶ *Empathy.* The ability to react with **empathy**—putting yourself in the other person's place in an attempt to understand his or her experience—is a valuable trait to find in a friend. Empathetic friends can respond with comfort and condolences and can offer the support and encouragement you need to get through difficult times, even if they've never been through what you're facing.

● *SUPERBAD'S* **BEST-FRIEND** duo, Seth and Evan, support each other through thick and thin.

The extent to which you and your friend share these characteristics helps build the relational context of your relationship, as you learned in Chapter 1. The amount of trust, loyalty, honesty, and other characteristics that you experience together affects you as you construct and decode messages.

## Romantic Relationships

What ideas, thoughts, and feelings come to mind when you think about romantic relationships? Passion, romantic dinners, jealousy, butterflies in your stomach? Some of the most popular movies and works of fiction revolve around the attainment of romantic love. Maybe you've read Charlotte Brontë's *Jane Eyre,* considered one of the most romantic novels of all time. Jane's sentiments when looking at her beloved Mr. Rochester have resonated with readers for 160 years: "My eyes were drawn involuntarily to his face; I could not keep their lids under control: they would rise, and the iris would fix on him. I looked, and had an acute pleasure in looking—a precious yet poignant pleasure; pure gold, with a steely point of agony."

*Love* is a word that we often throw around without thinking about what it means. Over the course of an average day, you might say things like "I love the Philadelphia Eagles" or "I love the seven-layer burrito at Taco Bell." But for our discussion, we'll define **love** as a deep affection for and attachment to another person involving emotional ties, with varying degrees of passion, commitment, and **intimacy**, or closeness and understanding of a relational partner (Sternberg, 1988). And there are many types of love that can characterize different relationships—or even the same relationship at different times. For example, is the love between Anna and Mario, married for fifty-seven years, the same as it was when they were first married? The Canadian researcher John Lee is noted for conducting experiments (involving hundreds of people) with the goal of determining the nature of categories of love. Lee (1993; see also Hendrick & Hendrick, 1992) found that love comes in six types: *eros* (erotic, sexual love), *ludus* (playful, casual love), *storge* (love that lacks passion), *pragma* (committed, practical love), *mania* (intense, romantic love), and *agape* (selfless, romantic love). These types of love are explained in detail in Table 6.2. Some relationships may be characterized by only one of these types of love, while others may move through two or more types of love over the course of time.

**TABLE 6.2**

**TYPES OF LOVE**

| Type | Description | Explanation |
| --- | --- | --- |
| *Eros* | Beauty and sexuality | Sex is the most important aspect of erotic love. This type of relationship is quite intense, both emotionally and physically. The focus is on beauty and attractiveness. |
| *Ludus* | Entertainment and excitement | *Ludus* means "play" in Latin, and the ludic lover views love as a game. Ludic love does not require great commitment. |
| *Storge* | Peacefulness and slowness | *Storge* is a type of love that lacks passion and excitement. Storgic lovers often share common interests and activities but rarely disclose any feelings about their relationship. |
| *Pragma* | Deed, task, work | In Greek, *pragma* means "life work." Pragmatic lovers are extremely logical and practical. They want a long-term relationship with an individual who shares their goals in life. |
| *Mania* | Elation and depression | This is the love that is often referred to as "romantic love." It exhibits extreme feelings and is full of excitement and intensity, but it reaches a peak and then quickly fades away. |
| *Agape* | Compassion and selflessness | In this type of love, the individual gives willingly and expects nothing in return. This type of lover can care for others without close ties; a deep relationship is not necessary for agapic love to develop. |

● ROMANTIC COUPLES, regardless of sexual orientation, age, race, or ethnicity, all enjoy similar benefits of being in a relationship: intimacy and commitment.

The complexities of romantic love can be astounding, but one thing is clear: the desire to attain it is as universal as it is timeless. In fact, the value of relationships and the characteristics that comprise love and commitment between two people are fairly consistent regardless of culture. Same-sex couples in long-term, committed relationships share the same benefits of meaningful commitment (such as life satisfaction and general well-being) as other romantic couples (Kurdek, 1989; Lipman, 1986), and cohabiting unmarried couples enjoy greater well-being than single people (though not as much as married couples) (Brown, 2000; Horwitz & White, 1998). Perceptions of love and romance are also somewhat consistent across cultures: one study found that among Americans, Chinese, Japanese, and Koreans, differences in notions of love were not pronounced, and respondents from all four countries reported that happiness and warmth were associated with love (Kline, Horton, & Zhang, 2005).

## Online Relationships

Holly and Delia's friendship began long before they met face to face. As regular readers of a social commentary journal, the two women began posting in the journal's chat rooms. Over time, they developed a friendly conversation that led to direct e-mail correspondence. When Holly found herself traveling on business to Delia's hometown of Phoenix, the two finally met.

Research shows that virtual relationships develop much like those that grow from face-to-face contact (Parks & Roberts, 1998). Interestingly, however, relationships that develop online may not be bound by many of the rules that govern other types of relationships. Because online interaction does not allow for nonverbal cues that are important to relationship development, online communicators may have exaggerated perceptions of their relational partners (Tidwell &

Walther, 2002). This phenomenon is called **hyperpersonal communication** (Walther, 1996). Also, the fact that these online relationships usually do not include the physical presence or even a visual image of the relational partner makes them less constrained than interpersonal relationships (Caplan, 2001). You can interact whenever you want, or you can just sign off if you don't feel like dealing with the other person (something that's often not possible if you live with a friend, family member, or romantic partner).

## real communicator

**NAME:** Bethany Talley
**HOMETOWN:** Brownwood, Texas
**OCCUPATION:** Public relations account executive at Weber Shandwick
**FUN FACT:** John and I are getting married in August!

John and I were high school sweethearts in Brownwood, Texas. When we graduated, I went to the University of Texas in Austin, and John enrolled at the University of Southern California, a whopping 1,400 miles away. We decided to try the long-distance thing. It hasn't been easy.

I never realized how hard it is to have a relationship over the phone. I've asked John, "When do you think you're going to come visit?" If he replies with "I'm not really sure," followed by silence, I assume that he doesn't care to come. Little do I know, he isn't saying anything because he is looking at his planner for a good weekend to visit. I get frustrated and say, "Well, if you don't want to come, just tell me." And then he's annoyed with me for getting mad at him over nothing.

Jokes have been even harder. I'd ask John, "Are you still coming to see me this weekend?" and he'd go, "You know what? I don't really want to see you this weekend!" He was joking, but without the nonverbal cues of face-to-face interaction, I couldn't know that. I couldn't see his smirk or the way he raises his eyebrows. I'd get upset, and he'd have to go through the awkwardness of explaining that he was just kidding. He was probably also thinking, "Why doesn't she get my jokes anymore?" We couldn't communicate the way we used to, and it was both frustrating

and scary. We were fighting more. "What's wrong with us?" we wondered.

I knew from studying interpersonal communication that we had to make some important changes in order for our relationship to survive. I particularly remembered a really intense class discussion about the importance of nonverbal communication in relationships. I talked to John about this, and he surprised me with a fantastic present: webcams for our computers! We could see each other and pick up on our nonverbal cues. We also started e-mailing more. In e-mail, you have to think about what you're saying more thoroughly. You can follow up sarcasm with something like a smiley face emoticon ☺. John started getting himself in less trouble with me.

But the most helpful thing was just acknowledging the situation. We were having trouble because we couldn't see each other. Identifying the problem and acknowledging it out loud really made a world of difference. We had different expectations, both in how we should say things and in how we should hear things.

Things have been great since we began working on our communication. We've been together for six years now, and when we graduate in May, we're hoping to live in the same city again. John wants to come back to Texas. I'm thinking I'd like to be in California. We still have to talk that one out.

Many relationships exist only in the world of chat rooms and e-mail; for others, online communication is part of a larger communication relationship. Research shows that different electronic channels (such as texting or posting on Facebook) indicate different types of relationships. Among people who use e-mail for social purposes, for example, heavy users have more social ties than occasional users. E-mail users also have a tendency to communicate face to face with the same people they write to, whereas chat room participants do not maintain the same relationships offline (Zhao, 2006). In either case, though, electronic channels provide a means for relationships to develop and be maintained.

## Why We Form Relationships

We've already established that romantic relationships are a timeless and universal desire. But what about other types of relationships like those you have with friends, colleagues, or family members? You might expect that collectivist cultures (like Japanese culture) would place more importance on relationships than fiercely individualistic cultures like we find in the United States. But most research fails to demonstrate large differences between these culture types, revealing instead that individuals value their relationships regardless of culture (Diener & Diener, 1995; Endo, Heine, & Lehman, 2000; Landsford, Antonucci, Akiyama, & Takahashi, 2005). So what is the power behind this truth that is so strong that it transcends cultural differences? In this section, we examine the reasons why we form relationships in general and the factors that influence the formation of particular relationships.

### Functions of Relationships

In United States prisons today, more than twenty-five thousand inmates are serving their time in solitary confinement—removed from the general prison population, isolated in small cells with little human contact (Sullivan, 2006b). It's a measure that prison officials feel is necessary to maintain order, but many people feel this constitutes cruel and unusual punishment. Why might isolating inmates be useful? Why might it be cruel? The answer to both questions is the same: because human beings need to form and maintain relationships in order to satisfy basic human needs—to provide companionship, to provide stimulation, and to meet goals.

### *Companionship*

Humans feel a natural need for companionship, and we all long for **inclusion**—to involve others in our lives and to be involved in the lives of others. Thus loneliness can be a real motivation—in some cases, the primary motivation—behind some people's desire for a relationship. In fact, psychological problems such as anxiety, stress, depression, alcoholism, drug abuse, and poor health have all been tied to loneliness (Canary & Spitzberg, 1993; Perlman & Peplau, 1981; Rubin, Perse, & Powell, 1985). Depriving prisoners of companionship

**AND YOU?**

Do you have any relationships that exist strictly online? Do you consider these relationships different from other ones in your life? Are they more intimate or less?

● **SOME PEOPLE** feel that solitary confinement for prisoners is an overly cruel measure because they see companionship as a basic human need.

may be an effective form of punishment, but it may also be damaging to them on a psychological level, dashing any hopes for eventual rehabilitation.

### Stimulation

People have an innate need for intellectual, emotional, and physical stimulation (Krcmar & Greene, 1999; Rubin et al., 1985). Nobody enjoys being bored! So we seek out diversions: watching TV or listening to music. But interaction with another person provides a unique kind of stimulation because it occurs on a personal level and frequently provides multiple types of stimulation at once.

Consider some of the communication relationships you have with various people over the course of a day. You might chat with your roommates or your family in the morning about the fact that you're nervous about an exam. You head off to a world literature course where you're confronted with ideas that you've not previously considered. And then you meet up with your significant other, who greets you with a warm hug after a long day. It's also possible, of course, for you to find multiple forms of stimulation in one person.

These innate needs for stimulation are what cause many people to feel that solitary confinement is unethical and immoral. And prisoners are deprived not only of intellectual and emotional stimulation but of physical stimulation as well. Even though we rarely give casual physical contact much thought, we tend to crave it when we do not have it. Prison inmates, for example, describe the "pinky shake"—poking their smallest fingers through holes in cell doors to make contact with others as they pass—as their only form of human contact during years spent in isolation (Sullivan, 2006a).

### Achieving Goals

Some people enter into relationships to achieve particular goals. Sometimes the goal is simply satisfying the needs we have discussed earlier: to alleviate loneliness, for example, or to provide stimulation. Other goals are more practical: if you have dreamed all your life about working in finance, you might seek relationships with influential people in that field through networking via your college alumni group or through an internship.

Often your initial motivation for developing a relationship with a particular individual is to see what that person can do for you or how he or she can help you. This is the argument that is placed forward by those who feel that solitary confinement is unavoidable. When particularly dangerous prisoners are kept in isolation, they are unable to form relationships that might help them to accomplish dangerous goals (such as gang memberships or terrorist networking) (Sullivan, 2006b).

## Interpersonal Attraction

In the 2006 film *Miss Potter,* Renee Zellweger stars as the famous children's author Beatrix Potter. The movie chronicles Beatrix's life (taking many Hollywood liberties when it comes to the facts!), from her rise as a writer to her life as a conservationist, buying up properties in England's Lake District to save them from development. An interesting relationship develops between Beatrix and the lawyer, William Heelis (Lloyd Owen), who helps her purchase her Lake District farms. The film shows flashbacks of William encouraging Beatrix with her stories and artwork as a child, though the two lost touch as their lives went in separate

**AND YOU?**

Do you rely on different relational partners for companionship, stimulation, or goal achievement? Do you have some relationships that provide all three functions?

directions. When Beatrix moves to the Lake District after the death of her fiancé, Norman (Ewan McGregor), they reconnect and find a shared passion for nature and the land. A quick friendship develops, and after several years, romance and marriage.

Why did it take so long for Beatrix and William to develop their relationship? As discussed previously, we seek relationships to meet basic needs for companionship, stimulation, and goal achievement. But our reasons for forming specific relationships are as individual and complex as we are and are rooted in our unique needs and motivations, which develop and change over the course of our lives (Westmyer, DiCioccio, & Rubin, 1998). Let's take a look at a few issues that influence our likelihood of establishing particular relationships.

## Proximity

As practical and unromantic as it sounds, one of the first criteria of relationship formation is simple **proximity**, or nearness. We must be able to interact with someone in some way in order to form a relationship. In other words, we can't have a relationship with someone we haven't met (so for most of us, the chances of a relationship with Halle Berry or Patrick Dempsey are, unfortunately, quite slim) or someone we are not in contact with over time. This is one reason why Beatrix and William did not establish their love until much later in life. They simply weren't around each other for several decades and had lost touch.

Physical proximity was once the most important factor in determining relationships: if you were to move away from a neighborhood, switch schools, or change jobs, you would likely lose touch with old friends and eventually make new friends in your new surroundings. While this still can and does happen, modern technology, from Facebook to text messages, allows us to maintain virtual proximity with people who are physically quite far away. Nonetheless, if a person is not in physical proximity and fails to establish and maintain virtual proximity, the chances of forming or maintaining a long-distance relationship dwindle.

## Physical Attraction

If you've ever watched a makeover show like *What Not to Wear* or *How to Look Good Naked,* you've no doubt seen at least one client who expressed a belief that an improved physical appearance would enhance his or her prospects for love and career success. And as you've learned in earlier chapters, your physical appearance does indeed play an important role in attracting others, especially in the very early stages of a relationship, when first impressions are formed. People who are considered beautiful or attractive are often perceived as kinder, warmer, more intelligent, and more honest than unattractive people. And according to the researchers Dan Canary, Michael Cody, and Valerie Manusov (2008), they have earlier opportunities for dating and marriage.

But before you wonder if your social worth is based solely on your physical attractiveness, we want to echo Canary and colleagues' additional research and point out two things. First, beauty is largely defined by cultural standards. For example, among the Padaung tribe of Southeast Asia, women wrap rings around their necks to push down their collarbone and upper ribs, giving the illusion of

● **PROXIMITY AND SIMILARITY** helped children's author Beatrix Potter find true love.

While culture plays a powerful role in our ideas about physical attraction, it's important to remember that we all have *schemas* about attractiveness (Chapter 2). So while you might find Jordan very attractive, your friend Cameron might not because Jordan reminds her of a previous awful romantic partner, or because Jordan is the spitting image of Cameron's brother.

● **STACY AND CLINTON** on *What Not to Wear* quickly convince their "fashion victims" that an overhaul of their wardrobe will also get them out of their love or career rut.

an extremely long neck. While there are many interpretations of where this custom originated and why it continues today, the most commonly accepted explanation is that a long neck is considered a sign of beauty and wealth. Western tourists who visit the Padaung, bringing very different standards of beauty, might disagree. In addition, our *communication* has a large impact on perceptions of beauty. For example, Levinger (as cited in Canary, Cody, & Manusov, 2008) notes that "initial impressions of a beautiful person are outweighed by subsequent interaction" with the person and that "an ugly person may gradually or suddenly become attractive for reasons other than a change in physical appearance" (p. 250). So your ability to use verbal and nonverbal messages appropriately and effectively probably has a lot more to do with your attractiveness than perfection of your smile or the size of your jeans!

## Similarity

Long before her days as the "nice" judge on *American Idol*, Paula Abdul recorded the hit song "Opposites Attract," detailing the great attraction between people who are fundamentally different. Well, as Simon Cowell might tell you, Paula isn't a social scientist. Not to offend any of you romantics out there, but research shows that our attraction to others is often based on the degree of *similarity* we have with another person, whether through shared hobbies, personality traits, backgrounds, appearance, attitudes, or values. In short, people look for others who are, in one way or another, like themselves. Beatrix and William, for example, found that they shared a passion for nature, the land, and farming. These similarities gave them a solid grounding for friendship and eventually marriage.

Communication researchers have been busy trying to gauge how much interest one relational partner has for another based on an estimation of similarity between the two. Several concepts have flooded the landscape of relationship research, including the attraction-similarity, matching, and genetic similarity hypotheses (Amodio & Showers, 2005; Berscheid, 1985; Byrne, 1971; Fehr, 2001; Morry, 2005; Rushton, 1990). The **attraction-similarity hypothesis** suggests that the extent to which we project ourselves onto another person is the direct result of the attraction we feel for that person. Greater attraction to an individual leads to perceptions of greater similarity. The **matching hypothesis** also deals with attraction, positing that we seek relationships with others who have comparable levels of attractiveness. Finally, the **genetic-similarity hypothesis** argues that two individuals who hail from the same ethnic group are more genetically similar than two individuals from different ethnic groups. The impact of the hypothesis is that we tend to help, favor, and form relationships with people from our own ethnic group (Rushton, 1980).

What remains clear from the research, however, is that it is our *perception* of similarities that counts most (Morry, 2005). For example, consider close friends Liza and Cheryl. Liza is an African American student from Illinois, a literature major; Cheryl is a white student from Boston, majoring in engineering at the same school. To an outsider, they seem like a mismatched pair: Liza is obsessed with the Chicago Bulls, and Cheryl hates sports; Liza loves fashion, and Cheryl couldn't care less. But ask either of them what they have in common, and they'll roll off a list of similarities: both grew up in urban neighborhoods, attended Catholic high schools, love indie rock, are politically active, and take great pride in being able to quote Tolkien on cue. So long as the relational partners feel that they have much in common, as Liza and Cheryl do, they can come to enjoy the attraction afforded by this interpersonal phenomenon.

**AND YOU?**

Consider someone with whom you share a very close relationship. In what ways are you similar to this person? Are those similarities what attracted you in the first place?

## Managing Relationship Dynamics

The columnist Carrie Bradshaw (along with her real-life counterpart and creator, the writer Candace Bushnell) makes a living dissecting and examining the dynamics of relationships. Viewers tuned in to *Sex and the City* to watch Carrie and her friends stumble through romances with myriad men, as well as to watch the relationships among the four women themselves grow and adapt to changing life circumstances. Through it all, Carrie offers observations on the nature of relationships; and although her musings may offer some interesting insights, communication researchers have been exploring the way we manage relationships in a far more scientific way. In this section, we'll explore the dynamics of relationships, on the assumption that our connections to others are constantly changing, growing, and evolving throughout our lives (Conville, 1991; John-Steiner, 1997).

### Costs and Rewards

Every relationship has advantages and disadvantages for the parties involved. A close friendship may offer companionship and intimacy, but you will also need to accept your friend's negative personality characteristics and invest time in working through difficult situations together. This process of balancing the advantages and disadvantages of a relationship is called a **social exchange of costs and benefits** (Cook, 1987). Irwin Altman and Dalmus Taylor (1973) further suggest that relationships begin, develop, grow, and deteriorate based on this exchange.

**Rewards** are the elements of a relationship that you feel good about—things about the person or your relationship that benefit you in some way. There are *extrinsic rewards,* which are those you gain from association with another person (such as social status or professional connections); *instrumental rewards,* which are the resources and favors that partners give to one another (for example, living together to save on rent and utilities); and *intrinsic rewards,* which result from an exchange of intimacy (for instance, intellectual stimulation or feelings of safety) (Rempel, Holmes, & Zanna, 1985). **Costs**, by contrast, are the things that upset or annoy you, cause you stress, or damage your own self-image or lifestyle. For example, let's return to Carrie from *Sex and the City.* When she finds out that Aidan, a man she's very interested in, can't date a smoker, she needs to weigh her feelings for him against her addiction to cigarettes. Quitting smoking is a difficult prospect, but because she sees potential for a worthwhile relationship with a man who is handsome, charming, and kind, she tosses her cigarettes and dons a nicotine patch. For Carrie, the reward (dating Aidan) outweighs the costs (quitting smoking).

**CONNECT**

Most of us don't ponder the costs and rewards of our relationships on a daily basis. But when we feel that a relationship involves too many costs, conflict often ensues. As you learn in Chapter 7, we like to feel that we are both giving and receiving in a relationship. So if your roommate Tamara is always leaving her chores for you, you might need to engage in conflict management to balance the relationship.

# what about you?

## Determining Your Own Costs and Rewards

Consider the following list of traits and behaviors, and decide which you consider rewards and which you consider costs in a romantic relationship. Write R1 next to rewards that you feel you must have from your partner and R2 next to those you see as less important. Write C1 next to costs that you simply couldn't tolerate from your partner and C2 next to costs that you could live with.

———— Laughs at my jokes

———— Is affectionate

———— Is physically attractive

———— Fits in with my friends

———— Fits in with my family

———— Makes inappropriate jokes or comments

———— Dislikes sharing emotions

———— Ignores my feelings

———— Is career-oriented

———— Wears clothes I dislike

———— Has views about religion different from mine

———— Has views about children similar to mine

———— Has an exciting personality

———— Overlooks my shortcomings

———— Has annoying friends

———— Shares similar dreams for the future

———— Is likely to be financially successful

———— Enjoys very different hobbies and activities

———— Comes from a close-knit family

———— Is of a different race or from a different culture

There is no official scale to help you grade this self-assessment; its purpose is to help you clarify your goals and desires for a relationship. Now think of a romantic relationship that you have been in or are currently in. How well does your partner meet your expectations regarding costs and rewards? Just for fun, retake the quiz with friendship rather than romance in mind, and see whether or not your evaluation of rewards and costs changes.

## Reducing Uncertainty

We begin to weigh the costs and rewards involved in a relationship at its beginning stages. Early in a relationship, uncertainty creates excitement at the prospect of a new friendship to enjoy or romance to explore. But frustration can occur when the person fails to meet your expectations or hurts your feelings. According to the **uncertainty reduction theory** developed by Charles Berger and Richard Calabrese (1975), when two people meet, their main focus is on decreasing the uncertainty that lies between them. The level of uncertainty relates to the number of ways that a person could potentially behave: the less sure you are of what will happen, the higher the degree of uncertainty. As two people reduce uncertainty between them, they become better at predicting what the other will do or say.

The best way to reduce uncertainty is to obtain information about your new relational partner. Doing so places you both on a more intimate level, which helps you make more accurate predictions and feel more comfortable about developing the relationship further. But how do you go about gaining more information about a partner and reducing uncertainty? Depending on the situation, three types of strategies may work well: monitoring, proactive strategies, and indirect strategies.

### Monitoring

In the movie *10 Things I Hate About You*, bad boy Patrick Verona (Heath Ledger) is roped into seducing the school rebel, Kat Stratford (Julia Stiles), so that Cameron (Joseph Gordon-Levitt) can ask out Kat's younger sister, Bianca (Larisa Oleynik). Why all the drama? Kat and Bianca's father declared that Bianca cannot date until her sister does. So in the hopes of getting to know Kat better and getting on her good side, Patrick observes her in her natural habitat: playing soccer, dancing at a concert, and strumming a guitar in a music store. Patrick is employing a useful strategy called **monitoring**. Monitoring allows you to observe and evaluate people as they go about their business and communicate with others.

### Proactive Strategies

**Proactive strategies** let you obtain information about a person more directly. Cameron asks Bianca (on Patrick's behalf) for the scoop on her sister: What music does she listen to? What types of men is she interested in? Cameron is hoping that with this new insight, he'll be better able to tell Patrick how to get the girl.

Once Patrick and Kat have spent some time together and he becomes genuinely interested in her, he is able to be more forthright and ask her questions directly. *Direct questioning* increases Patrick's chances of learning what he really wants to know about Kat (like why she acts like such a rebel) and also shows her that he's interested in her. Although direct questioning is helpful in reducing uncertainty, it also entails risks. If Patrick asks questions that Kat finds too forward or inappropriate, he might do more harm than good.

It's important to reduce uncertainty in all communication contexts. For example, in Chapter 11 we discuss audience analysis, which allows you to learn about the people who will listen to your speech. By understanding your audience's expectations, learning about their general opinions of your topic, and carefully considering their demographics, you can reduce uncertainty and determine the most effective way to reach them.

● **AT FIRST, PATRICK** gets to know Kat through his and Cameron's sleuthing. Once he is able to get closer to her and spend more time with her, he learns more about her through direct questioning.

## Indirect Strategies

When monitoring cannot provide specific information and proactive strategies are deemed too direct or risky, a third alternative is available. **Indirect strategies** can help you obtain information from a relational partner without specifically asking for it. Indirect strategies are especially useful when issues are too sensitive to bring into the open or when the relationship may not be ready for a full-blown discussion of some topics. For example, in the "Double Date" episode of *Gilmore Girls* (season one, episode 12), Lane asks Rory to set her up with Dean's best friend, Todd. She thinks Todd might just be the love of her life, even though she knows nothing about him. While they're waiting in line for a movie, she babbles on and on about her favorite singer, Nico, in the hopes of eliciting a reaction from Todd that would indicate whether or not they shared the same musical interests. Her actions are motivated by her desire to know what topics of conversation are of interest to him without putting herself out there too much.

# Dialectical Tensions

Weighing costs against benefits and reducing uncertainty are not the only challenges we face in developing relationships. In any relationship, it is common to experience contradictions or opposing feelings about your relational partner and about the relationship itself (Baxter & Erbert, 1999; Pawlowski, 1998). When a love relationship becomes serious, for example, one or both partners might find themselves mourning their old, single lifestyle, despite the benefits of commitment.

Researchers call this phenomenon **relational dialectics theory**, which holds that **dialectical tensions** arise when opposing or conflicting goals exist in a relationship. These tensions can be external (between the partners and the people they interact with) or internal (within their relationship). Many types of dialectical tensions are possible, but we will focus on three internal tensions that dominate research: *autonomy* versus *connection, openness* versus *closedness,* and *predictability* versus *novelty* (Baxter & Simon, 1993). Note that dialectics exist along a continuum; they are not all-or-nothing trade-offs or alternatives but rather ranges of options that need to be continually negotiated and adjusted (Baxter, Braithwaite, Bryant, & Wagner, 2004). Also, these tensions are natural and normal—experiencing them does not indicate that your relationship or your communication is falling apart!

## Autonomy Versus Connection

In all close personal relationships—family connections, romantic relationships, and friendships—individuals may struggle to strike a balance between independence (autonomy) and dependence (connection). Take Debbie and Pete (Leslie Mann and Paul Rudd) from the 2007 film *Knocked Up.* If you've seen the movie, you know that Debbie's nature is a bit, let's say, controlling. She's constantly harping on her husband, Pete, to settle down and spend more time at home with her and with the kids, even though she likes to go out dancing.

● IN *KNOCKED UP,* Debbie and Pete constantly struggle to find a balance between pursuing their own interests and spending time together.

When Pete begins to "work" late at night, she becomes worried that he is having an affair. The truth is that Pete just wants to escape Debbie's clutches for a few hours by playing fantasy baseball with some friends. Pete's lying is the last straw for them, and they spend some time apart due to the lack of balance between autonomy and connection. They eventually reconcile, recognizing the importance of their relationship and time spent together *and* the importance of their own individual space.

### *Openness Versus Closedness*

Every superhero from Batman to Superman knows about this tension! To become close, individuals must share information with their relational partners. However, by disclosing information, they reveal a part of their private self. The tension comes as partners strive to find a balance between sharing information (openness) and a desire to keep some things private (closedness). Look at poor Peter Parker (Tobey Maguire) in *Spider-Man 2*. He loves Mary Jane (Kirsten Dunst) and wants to have what he sees as a normal romantic relationship—going out on dates, sharing private thoughts, and having someone know him intimately. But for her own safety and to keep his identity protected, Peter fears telling Mary Jane that he is Spider-Man. He cannot tell her why he disappears when she needs him or why he couldn't make it to the opening of her show. Clearly, the animated TV series *Justice League* had the right idea by bringing the superheroes together to work on a team where they can be entirely open and honest about their true identities!

But for us powerless folks, each partner in a relationship needs to disclose private information to the other in order to facilitate a perception of involvement and deep understanding. This is not to say that you're going to share the same depth of information at the same time in all of your relationships. So you might tell your best friend, Brad, about how you're holding up after your parents' divorce, but you're probably not going to tell your soccer coach or your manager about it.

● **POOR PETER PARKER.** His top-secret profession as Spider-Man means he is always on call and must often leave his very bewildered and hurt girlfriend, Mary Jane, behind without any explanation.

### *Predictability Versus Novelty*

Which is more important to you, safety and security or excitement and novelty? This third dialectic tension assumes that most people have a simultaneous need for stability through predictable relational interaction as well as a need for new and exciting experiences in personal relationships. On the one hand, partners seek daily routines and stable patterns of interaction: Colin and Casey, for example, enjoy the comfort of their evening routine of dinner and television, as well as their usual Friday night at their favorite diner. At the same time, every relationship needs some degree of spontaneity and novelty. This is why Colin and Casey have made plans to travel to Japan next summer and why they find enjoyment in working together on odd projects—such as building their own computer or learning to cook Thai food—that shake up their routine.

**AND YOU?**

Consider your relationship with your oldest friend or with a close family member. Evaluate the ways in which dialectical tensions have manifested themselves in that relationship over the years. Have these tensions shifted over time? Is there one particular tension that continues to crop up?

● **IN MOST** budding relationships, the goal is to increase intimacy. Unfortunately for Henry in *50 First Dates*, his love interest, Lucy, has short-term memory loss and can't remember who he is the next day!

# Self-Disclosure and Interpersonal Relationships

Do you remember Angelica from Chapter 2? In case you've forgotten her, she's in debt over her head because of the lifestyle she leads (expensive vacations, a new car, a nice apartment, and so on). When she divulges her personal financial mishaps to a friend, she is self-disclosing, revealing very personal information. As you've likely experienced in your own life, self-disclosure has a powerful impact on the development of interpersonal relationships (Samter, 2003). The process of choosing what information to disclose to others and when has long fascinated communication researchers and scholars. So in the sections that follow, we'll look at the ways in which we choose to divulge or withhold personal information and how those decisions affect relationships.

## Social Penetration Theory

For many relationships, a primary goal is to increase intimacy, or relational closeness. So your goal for your new love might be to develop a deep sense of intimacy rather than awkwardly staring at each other across a booth at your favorite pizza joint for the next twenty years. Altman and Taylor (1973) proposed the **social penetration theory** (SPT) to explain how partners move their relationships from superficial levels to levels of intimacy. SPT (and our favorite ogre, Shrek) uses an onion as a metaphor to describe how relationships move through various stages: just as you might peel off layer after layer of an onion in an attempt to reach the core or center, a relational partner attempts to reach the most intimate thoughts and feelings at the other partner's "core" (see Figure 6.1).

According to SPT, each layer contains information that is increasingly more private and therefore more risky to divulge to someone else. The outer layer represents aspects of the self that are obvious and observable, such as appearance and nonverbal behavior. When we form a new acquaintance, these outer layers are explored first. Successive layers become more private and less obvious to others: at each layer, partners assess the costs and benefits of the relationship and of disclosing information to each other. If costs exceed rewards, it is unlikely that the partners will move inward toward the more deeply concealed layers. So upon getting to know Grace, for example, you might find that beneath her boisterous, funny exterior she is somewhat insecure and uncomfortable with her appearance. But Grace must choose to reveal this information: it is a part of her that only her closest, most trusted friends know, and it's something that she's likely to reveal only as a relationship becomes closer and more intimate.

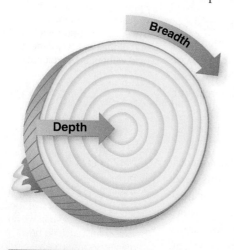

**FIGURE 6.1**

**SOCIAL PENETRATION THEORY (SPT) MODEL** According to the SPT model, relational partners peel away layers of intimacy to reach each other's core.

# COMMUNICATIONACROSSCULTURES

## Socializing Around the World over Drinks

Alcohol has long been used to grease the wheels of interpersonal communication. Greeks cut loose with shots of ouzo, Czechs argue about football in beer halls, Japanese businessmen close deals over cups of sake, and urban American women trade stories while sipping cosmopolitans. Alcohol is used to forge and strengthen social bonds all over the world. And according to Tom Standage's book *A History of the World in Six Glasses,* this isn't a recent phenomenon: in one form or another, alcohol has been a social lubricant for roughly twelve thousand years.

Between 10,000 and 4000 B.C.E., inhabitants of the Fertile Crescent discovered that grain could be fermented into beer, an alcoholic beverage that was far safer to drink than the potentially disease-ridden water of Mesopotamia. The rise of beer occurred at a pivotal time when humans were switching from a nomadic, hunting and gathering lifestyle to a more settled farming existence. As people settled down, cities formed, and neighbors became permanent, beer took on significant importance as a social drink. Sumerian pictograms from 3000 B.C.E. show two people drinking beer through straws from the same vessel.

Standage (2005) observes:

> The most likely explanation . . . is that, unlike food, beverages can be shared. When several people drink beer from the same vessel, they are all consuming the same liquid; when cutting up a piece of meat, in contrast, some parts are usually deemed to be more desirable than others. As a result, sharing a drink with someone is a universal symbol of hospitality and friendship. It signals that the person offering the drink can be trusted, by demonstrating that it is not poisoned or otherwise unsuitable for consumption. (p. 18).

Our tradition of clinking glasses can be traced back to this ancient Middle Eastern practice; imbibers are symbolically reuniting their glasses into a single vessel of shared liquid.

The use of alcohol as a centerpiece for interpersonal interaction dates back a long way—ancient Egyptians would greet each other with the phrase "Beer and bread," which meant "Have a good day." But despite this common original starting point, modern rituals and practices vary widely from one culture to the next. In Spain, home entertaining isn't very common, so friends and neighbors get together at local bars. In the nineteenth century, Andalusian bartenders began putting a slice of sausage or ham on top of their customers' wineglasses to keep insects out. And suddenly Spain had *tapas* (the verb *tapar* means "to cover"). Korean rituals emphasize the social aspect of drinking—you fill your companion's glass, not your own—and encourage the "keep 'em coming" philosophy—it's considered disrespectful to allow your drinking companion's glass to get empty.

**THINK ABOUT THIS**

❶ The Qur'an forbids the consumption of alcohol. Does the absence affect communication between non-Muslim drinkers and Muslim nondrinkers?

❷ Drinking on the job is frowned on in corporate America. But at work-related lunches and dinners, businesspeople often run up considerable bar tabs. Why might alcohol be encouraged in one setting but discouraged in the other?

❸ Do you think there are topics that people feel more comfortable talking about when sharing a glass of wine with a family member or meeting a friend at a pub? How might your answers be influenced by the culture you come from?

## Communication Privacy Management

If social penetration theory holds that we categorize our personal information into varying levels of privacy, then how do we determine what information is private and what we are willing to share? Why is it that Celeste, for example, can boldly share her faith while for Eddie, matters of faith and religion are intensely private?

Sandra Petronio (2000, 2002) draws on the social penetration theory in formulating her **communication privacy management** (CPM) **theory**. CPM helps in understanding how people perceive the information they hold about themselves and how they disclose or protect it. As Petronio (2004) states:

> The CPM theory presumes that people believe they own their private information. Individuals need to control that information because it has the potential to make them vulnerable. In addition, control is also important because people feel they have the right to determine what happens to their private information. Consequently, ownership and control are rudimentary to understanding the way people define and handle their private information. (p. 202).

Central to the notion of privacy management are two key features of relationships. First, privacy management is susceptible to dialectical tensions similar to those we have already discussed. The dialectical tension of openness versus closedness, discussed earlier in the chapter, would be an example: you want to share information in order to increase intimacy with your partner, but it is risky to do so, and maintaining private information is a worthy goal in its own right. The dialectical tension brings needs for privacy management into sharp focus. Second, privacy management requires cultural rules or expectations by which people must be willing to abide. For example, it would likely be considered impolite for you to ask your boss about his medical condition because that topic is far too private for a work context.

### AND YOU?

Do you post any personal information on a social networking site, such as Facebook or MySpace? What kind of information are you willing to reveal? What kind of information do you consider private?

## Strategic Topic Avoidance

Certain topics are simply too sensitive for some people to confront openly. **Strategic topic avoidance** is used by one or both relational partners to maneuver the conversation away from undesirable topics (Dailey & Palomares, 2004) because of the potential for embarrassment, vulnerability, or relational decline. As we touched on in our discussion on communication privacy management, there are also topics we avoid because we are culturally trained to do so. For example, researchers have learned that prior relationships, negative information, dating experiences, money issues, and sexual experiences are largely considered inappropriate for public communication (Baxter & Wilmot, 1985; Dailey & Palomares, 2004; Guerrero & Afifi, 1995). So if you're hanging out in the office lunchroom and your colleague asks you how big your bonus was this year, you might well proclaim that it's none of his business, but research shows that you'd likely use a less direct avoidance tactic, such as keeping silent, deflecting, giving an unrelated response, lying, or simply ending the conversation (Dailey & Palomares, 2004).

Like other issues related to self-disclosure, there are some ethical considerations regarding pursuing and avoiding topics. Is it appropriate for Crystal to push her brother Nathan to talk about the events leading up to his recent divorce, even if the issue is something that Nathan would rather not discuss? In return, is it acceptable for Nathan to use topic avoidance techniques with his sister? Every relationship is unique, and as we have discussed, relational partners may experience different degrees of comfort with self-disclosure at various points in the relationship.

Research in this area is just beginning to draw some supportable conclusions about the benefits and detriments of strategic topic avoidance. Most people in healthy relationships, for example, report that topic avoidance seems to work best when partners are sensitive to each other's concerns and when polite and accommodating strategies are used (Dailey & Palomares, 2004). In other words, Crystal and Nathan's relationship might grow stronger if she allows Nathan to bring up his divorce in his own time and in a way that makes him feel comfortable. You may find that some of your relational partners are more comfortable disclosing personal history at a slow rate, especially sensitive issues such as childhood abuse, financial problems, medical diagnoses, substance abuse, or complications experienced in prior relationships.

## Stages of a Relationship

Although every relationship is unique, research by Knapp and Vangelisti (2000) and other scholars reveals that most relationships go through somewhat predictable stages (see Figure 6.2). Communication differs during each stage as relational partners select messages that are individualized for the stage they perceive themselves to be in (Avtgis, West, & Anderson, 1998). Not every relationship will experience every stage—our assessments of costs and rewards will determine how the relationship will change. So if you feel like you're not getting something out of your relationship with a new friend early on, you're probably going to move to end the relationship rather than take it deeper. Let's look at the stages in detail.

> **AND YOU?**
> What topics do you consider strictly off limits? Are there some topics you are willing to discuss with some people but not with others? How do you inform others of your unwillingness to discuss these topics?

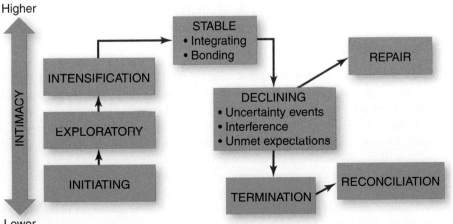

**FIGURE 6.2**

**TYPICAL STAGES OF A RELATIONSHIP** Most of us will move between these eight stages over time in our interpersonal relationships.

It can be awkward to verbally indicate that you want a relationship to end or to move beyond the initiating stage. You wouldn't tell a new classmate, "I don't like you. Stop talking to me." Luckily, nonverbal communication helps you address this issue. You can indicate like or dislike with facial expressions, posture, use of space, or touch, as we discuss in Chapter 4. Then you must hope that this individual properly decodes your message! (See Chapter 1.)

## Initiating Stage

The **initiating stage** of a relationship is one in which you make contact with another person. For Knapp and Vangelisti (2000), this stage has to do with how we use communication to meet people. So you might say hello to the person sitting next to you in class and ask his or her name. Now, if you think about the number of new people you initiate with on a given day, you won't be surprised to learn that many, if not most, relationships don't move beyond this stage. Just because you say "Good morning" to the woman who sold you a bagel doesn't mean the two of you will be chatting on the phone later today. But according to Sunnafrank and Ramirez (as cited in Canary, Cody, & Manusov, 2008), you will likely use your first impression of a person to gauge whether or not you're interested in moving forward with the relationship.

## Exploratory Stage

In the **exploratory stage**, you are seeking relatively superficial information from your partner. You make small talk, asking things like "Do you watch *Lost*?" or "How many brothers and sisters do you have?" In this stage, you're not likely to reveal anything too deep or personal; you're still testing the waters, so to speak. This stage is also where we find a great deal of monitoring strategies at work in order to reduce uncertainty. In addition to the small-talk questioning we mentioned, you're likely to observe your partner closely in order to learn more about his or her attitudes and behaviors. As in the initiating stage, you'll want to invest further in the relationship if the rewards seem high.

## Intensification Stage

The **intensification stage** occurs when relational partners become increasingly intimate and move their communication toward more personal self-disclosures. Knapp and Vangelisti (2000), for example, note that this stage includes the use of informal address or pet names ("honey," "darling") as well as "we" talk ("We're going to the concert on Friday night, right?" "Where are we going for your birthday next week?"). Relational partners in this stage also understand each other's nonverbal communication to a greater degree and often share their affection with one another ("What would I do without you!").

## Stable Stage

By the time partners reach the **stable stage**, their relationship is no longer volatile or temporary. They now have a great deal of knowledge about one another, their expectations are accurate and realistic, and they feel comfortable with their motives for being in the relationship. According to Goss and O'Hair (1988), relationships reach the stable stage when uncertainty about each other (and the relationship) reduces to the point where partners feel comfortable understanding their preferences and goals for each other. That doesn't mean, however, that stable relationships are set in stone, as the partners and their goals can still change.

Knapp and Vangelisti (2000) note two processes that occur during the stable stage. First, we see relational partners **integrating** or "becoming one." You and your friend Dana have grown closer, and you become friends with several of her friends; you and your romantic partner begin to sound more alike. In addition, **bonding** takes place when two partners share symbolic messages with the world that their relationship is important and cherished. Before concerns about HIV,

## WIREDFORCOMMUNICATION

### Cell Phonies

As cell phones continue to rise in popularity, more and more people are having private conversations in public spaces—on buses, in restaurants, and worst of all, on crowded elevators. But how many of these conversations are real?

According to James E. Katz, a professor of communication at Rutgers University, quite a few people talking on the phone around you are actually faking it. Odds are, you're faking your fair share of cell phone conversations too. "People are turning the technology on its head," Katz said. "They are taking a device that was designed to talk to people who are far away and using it to communicate with people who are directly around them." People are faking conversations for a variety of reasons and purposes. There's more than one kind of "cell phony."

Many individuals are staging calls to avoid contact with other people. They whip out their phone and begin an intense conversation with absolutely no one just so that they don't have to talk to the people who are actually around them—neighbors, coworkers, flirts, casual acquaintances, encyclopedia salesmen, whoever. The cell phone pressed firmly to the ear sends a clear message to those around them: "I'm busy; leave me alone." One woman confessed to us that she regularly walks into her apartment with her phone against her ear, conversing with nobody. "If I don't do it, my roommate's boyfriend will trap me in a painful fifteen-minute conversation," she said. "Fortunately, he respects the cell phone buffer."

Other people, when walking home late or finding themselves suddenly alone in a sketchy area, will fake a conversation to feel safer and more protected. The reasoning goes that if criminals see somebody communicating with the outside world—someone who could potentially call 911 on the victim's behalf—they will be less inclined to do something malicious. Thirty-year-old Liza Karleen recently found herself being followed by a group of men in Washington, D.C. So she called her nonexistent ex–football player friend. "OK," she said loudly, "I'll see you in five minutes. Are you bringing your dog?"

Some cell phonies are essentially performing for others' benefit in order to communicate information about themselves. Imagine a fellow student bragging about his grades over the phone in the library during finals week. A cell phony who is insecure about dining alone in a restaurant might make phantom calls to imply that a friend or companion exists somewhere, even if it's not true. The fake conversation lets others know that the speaker is a valued partner in a relationship, even if he or she is physically alone at the time.

**THINK ABOUT THIS**

❶ In what ways have cell phones revolutionized interpersonal communication? How have your personal relationships (with parents, friends, siblings, and others) changed as a result of the cell phone?

❷ Have you ever faked a cell phone conversation? Why? Did your fake conversation fulfill its purpose?

❸ Consider the example about using the cell phone to communicate information about yourself. In what ways is this tactic useful in the early stages of a relationship (particularly the initial and exploratory stages)? Do you see any ethical issues with communicating this way?

Source: Harmon (2005). Adapted with permission.

The differences among communication climates are often related to language and nonverbal communication (Chapters 3 and 4). In addressing conflict with a friend, you might use few words and avoid eye contact (uncertain climate), raise your voice or speak sarcastically (defensive climate), or offer reassuring touch and speak openly with a firm but understanding tone (supportive climate).

## Communication Climate

Conflicts have a tendency to produce an atmosphere, or certain feelings, about them. This is known as a **communication climate**. According to Folger, Poole, and Stutman (1997), climates represent the dominant temper, attitudes, and outlook of a group and provide continuity and coherence in mutual activities.

How might you determine what type of climate you may face when engaging in conflict with others? We suggest three likely possibilities: uncertain, defensive, and supportive (Gibb, 1961). Many science fiction shows, such as SciFi Network's *Battlestar Galactica,* illustrate the ways different climates affect conflict management.

▶ **Uncertain climates** are those in which at least one of the people involved is unclear, vague, tentative, and awkward about the goals, expectations, and potential outcomes of the conflict situation. Many conditions can create uncertain climates, including unfamiliarity with the people, the surroundings, or the topic at hand. In uncertain climates, communicators are hesitant to take action, and conflict management can bog down. On *Battlestar Galactica,* characters trying to create a colony called New Caprica on a barely hospitable planet find themselves under the ruthless rule of the Cylon. As an underground rebellion emerges, characters become paranoid, uncertain of who their allies really are. Their experience leads to conflict between rebels, ultimately dooming many relationships.

▶ **Defensive climates** are those in which the people involved feel threatened. It is an atmosphere of mistrust, suspicion, and apprehension. On *Battlestar,* the suspicions and resentments that arose on New Caprica continue to fester back in the starship convoy. Veterans of the rebellion hold one another responsible for the losses incurred on the planet and are unforgiving of those who benefited from the rebellion but did not make the same sacrifices. The climate among survivors becomes extremely defensive.

▶ **Supportive climates** are ideal because they offer communicators a chance to honestly and considerately explore the issues involved in the conflict

● *BATTLESTAR GALACTICA* is a good example of how one environment can have all three communication climates: uncertain, defensive, and supportive.

situation. Communicators are open to one another's ideas and feelings and together construct a reality that induces productive resolution of the problems that instigated the conflict in the first place. On *Battlestar,* supportive climates are hard to find. But small groups—military units, couples, families, and even some Cylon groups—manage problems among themselves by exploring issues and being sensitive to one another's feelings.

How do you move from a defensive or uncertain climate to a supportive one? Your first task is to make sure you know which climate you are experiencing. Your gut instincts are helpful with this task; how you feel is a credible guide. Beyond feelings, however, you can make some formal assessment of the climate situation. What are your past experiences with this topic, this person or group, these conditions? How do you feel things turned out? Once you know the climate you are in, you can take steps to move toward a supportive climate. Figure 7.1 offers several communication steps to help you find your way to supportive conflict climates.

## Culture and Conflict

Culture and conflict are clearly linked. If we consider how important culture is to our identities and how pervasive conflict is in our lives, we can begin to understand how culture influences and guides our conflict experiences. Differences in cultural values, beliefs, and attitudes can lead to conflict directly, and they can also affect how individuals perceive conflict, what their goals are for conflict, and how conflict is handled.

Research in the area of race, ethnicity, and conflict often examines differences between individualistic, low-context cultures and collectivistic, high-context cultures. **Individualistic cultures** emphasize personal needs, rights, and identity over those of the collective or group. **Collectivistic cultures** emphasize group identity and needs. You can think of collectivistic cultures as

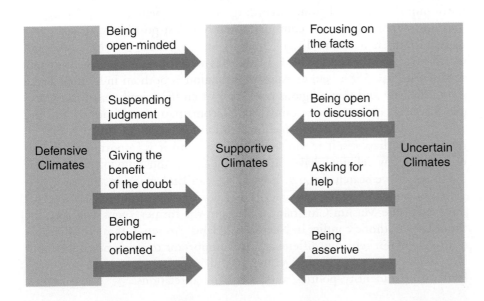

**FIGURE 7.1**

**STEPS TO REACHING A SUPPORTIVE CLIMATE**

having a "we" attitude and individualistic cultures as having an "I" attitude. Furthermore, as you learned in Chapter 3, in high-context cultures, people rely more on social norms and nonverbal communication than on what is actually said. In low-context cultures, people are expected to say what they mean. Simply put, in high-context cultures, things are often "understood," whereas in low-context cultures, things are often "spelled out."

According to Stella Ting-Toomey and her colleagues (2000), European Americans are individualistic and low-context, while Latinos and Asians are collectivistic and high-context. People in individualistic, low-context cultures tend to view conflict as a necessary way to work out problems and feel that specific conflict issues should be worked out separately from relational issues. In collectivistic, high-context cultures, conflict is perceived as having a negative effect on relational harmony, and conflict issues cannot be divorced from relationships. Because conflict is viewed as damaging to relationships, Asians tend to avoid conflict (Trubisky, Ting-Toomey, & Lin, 1991).

When it comes to power in relationships, individualistic, low-context cultures rely on and compete for tangible power resources. For example, people with power can reward and punish others; power is often asserted through threats and direct requests. In collectivistic, high-context cultures, however, power is about gains or losses in reputation and is displayed subtly through indirect requests. Communication during conflict in individualistic, low-context cultures is expected to be clear and direct, whereas in collectivistic, high-context cultures, people are supposed to pick up on subtle cues and vague verbal messages. So whereas a Canadian parent might assert, "I'm angry with you because you used my car without asking," a Vietnamese parent may stare at his son or daughter, wait for an acknowledgment of wrongdoing, and then ask, "Why did you take the car without asking?" Understanding these very influential differences between cultures can help us understand how confusion, frustration, and miscommunication can happen when communicating across cultures.

Another cultural influence on conflict that is often overlooked but of great importance is religion. According to Jeffrey Seul (1999), "Religious meaning systems define the contours of the broadest possible relationships— to self; to others near and distant, friendly and unfriendly; to the nonhuman world; to the universe; and to God, or that which one considers ultimately real or true" (p. 558). Seul explains that religion is both an individual and a group identity and that religious conflict is often historically based on struggles for social and material resources that become part of a religion's tradition. Sometimes these struggles become justification for the use of violence. Not all religious conflicts result in violence, however, and it is important to recognize that many religions have principles of peace and nonviolence in their doctrines. If we search through history, we can find many instances of religious conflict: among the most recent, the persecution of the Jews during the Holocaust, the Muslim-Christian conflicts in the former Yugoslavia, and the Protestant-Catholic conflict in Northern Ireland. Although these conflicts are not solely about religious differences, it is important to think not only about how religion affects individual values and identity but also about how it affects national identity, politics, and international relations.

Finally, there is a wealth of research concerning how sex and gender affect conflict situations. For example, John Gottman (1994) is known for studying marital conflict and the differences in conflict behaviors between men and women. He believes that four destructive behaviors are predictors of relationship dissolution: criticism and complaints, contempt, defensiveness, and stonewalling. He calls these behaviors the "four horsemen of the apocalypse." Criticism is attacking your partner's character, especially when the criticism is weaved into the complaint; contempt is attacking your partner's sense of self-worth; defensiveness is making yourself the victim; stonewalling is refusing to engage in conflict and withdrawing from the interaction. Gottman (1994) found that women tend to criticize more than men and that men tend to stonewall more than women. A great example of the differences in conflict behavior between men and women are Ben and Allison's big blowout fight in the 2007 movie *Knocked Up*. When Allison accidentally becomes pregnant by Ben and decides to keep the baby, they decide to give romance a shot as well. This is easier said than done, due to their polar opposite lives and personalities. She is a driven person and has a good job as an interviewer for E!, while he spends most days hanging out with his friends and living off the few hundred dollars he has left in his bank account. Their differences come to a head when Ben suggests that he'll miss the male camaraderie he has now when the baby comes. She retorts angrily that he hasn't sacrificed anything or changed in any way to prove that he's ready to be a dad while she's sacrificed everything—her job, her youth, her figure. She berates him for being lazy and poor and demands that he give in to her because he should always support her even when she's wrong. When he calls her a lunatic, she unceremoniously kicks him out of her car.

● IF *KNOCKED UP*'S Allison and Ben had refrained from criticism and complaints, they could have resolved conflict productively.

**AND YOU?**
Do you see yourself as more of a feminine or masculine individual? In what ways have gender differences influenced the conflicts you've experienced with people whose gender is different from yours?

However, the outcome of such behavioral patterns does not mean inevitable doom for relationships. According to Gottman's Web site, gottman.com, one way of improving conflict is to focus on the bright side of the relationship and give five positive statements for every one negative. If *Knocked Up*'s Allison could resist the urge to list all of Ben's shortcomings and if Ben could refrain from further provoking her by calling her names, their conflicts would take a more productive turn.

When we think about conflict and culture, it is important to remember that cultural values are not either-or. Assuming that cultures are at one extreme or the other is dangerous because it can lead people to believe that differences in culture mean irreconcilable differences in conflict. It may be difficult to understand others' cultural values, and we may feel compelled to persuade others to see things the way we do, but competent communication in conflict means understanding and respecting cultural differences while working to "expand the pie" for both parties. Even in the most uncomfortable and frustrating conflict situations, we can learn a great deal about others and ourselves through culture.

● **THE COFOUNDER** of Wikipedia, Jimmy Wales, allegedly broke up with his girlfriend on his Wikipedia page. Perhaps this wasn't the best choice!

## CONNECT

A lack of nonverbal communication can pose problems when handling conflict via electronic channels (Chapter 4). If you text an apology to your friend, he can't see your facial expressions to appreciate how sorry you are. Emoticons do help display feelings (☺!), but competent communicators must consider if nonverbal communication is needed for a particular message. When dealing with conflict, it might be better to speak face-to-face or by phone so that nonverbal behaviors such as tone of voice can be decoded.

## Communication Channel

In many communication situations, we don't think much about which available channel to choose in order to deliver a message. Not so when it comes to conflict. If you've ever sent flowers as a way of apologizing or delivered bad news via voice mail, e-mail, or text message, chances are you chose that channel as a way of avoiding engaging in conflict face to face. But conflict and communication channels are often intertwined: conflict can arise from poor channel choices, as we perceive things differently depending on the channel used (see Chapter 2). But even more interesting is the powerful way that channel choice influences conflict management.

Of course, some practical considerations can influence which channel we select to communicate with someone else about a disagreement. For example, if you live far away from your sister, and you and she need to address an issue that has come up between you, you may decide to talk about it by phone rather than make the long journey to have a face-to-face conversation. However, our reasons for choosing one channel over another are often rooted in emotions. For example, if you're intimidated by someone you're in a conflict with, you may feel safer communicating with them by e-mail or letter rather than over the phone or face to face. But beware: managing conflict with close friends or romantic partners through electronic channels can come across as insensitive and even cowardly. Just ask anyone who found out that a relationship was over via a changed "relationship status" on his or her significant other's Facebook page!

On another front, the relative anonymity of electronic communication has opened the door to a new kind of conflict: heated and often unproductive electronic exchanges in Internet forums, in e-mails, and through social networking sites. Of course, people have long been able to provoke conflict anonymously—prank phone calls were common in the days before caller ID, and people can still send unsigned letters to others (including newspaper editors). But the Internet has provided a vast arena for something called **flaming**—the posting of online messages that are deliberately hostile or insulting and usually intended only to provoke anger. Flame wars erupt online when friendly, productive discussions give way to insults and aggression. In many cases, the root cause of these conflicts is not even a disagreement but one person's misinterpretation of another's message. Technological channels create an arena for even more aggressive conflict behaviors, such as **cyberbullying**—abusive attacks conducted through electronic channels. Social networking sites like MySpace and Facebook offer an open forum for bullies, who demean or threaten individuals without risk of retaliation. Sociologists and educators point out that traditional bullying, while highly unpleasant, is also extremely intimate; cyberbullying, by contrast, makes use of e-mails, instant messages, and text messages to deliver cruelty to its victims, anonymously and with limited threat of retaliation (Maag, 2007b). Among teens and preteens, the problem has serious consequences, as evidenced by the suicide of a thirteen-year-old Missouri girl, Megan Meier. Moments after receiving a message that "the world would be a better place without you" from a boy she'd connected with through MySpace, Megan ran to her closet and hanged herself with a belt. Megan had been corresponding and flirting with this boy, Josh Evans, for months before he viciously turned on her. He told her that he had heard she was terrible to her friends and that he was no longer interested in being friends with her. A few other teens who were linked to Josh's profile also joined in on the attack, sending her hate-filled messages. In the aftermath of her suicide, it was revealed that the boy didn't really exist and was in fact a creation of the mother of a former friend of Megan's (Maag, 2007a).

## Strategies for Managing Conflict

A number of strategies might be employed to manage any conflict. To get an initial sense of these strategies, let's consider a common, simplified scenario: Leslie is sitting with her twin sister, Kathy, at the dinner table after a family meal. There's one last piece of key lime pie (or whatever kind of pie you like best), and both sisters want it.

> **AND YOU?**
>
> Consider a recent conflict. What channel did you select to communicate with the other person? How did the communication channel affect the quality of the exchange? Did the channel you chose lead to a productive conflict or an unproductive one? Why?

---

## WIREDFORCOMMUNICATION

### Pouring Water on the Flames: How Forum Moderators Keep Conflict Under Control

Internet forums are, in a sense, a grand experiment in free speech. A trip to an open forum on just about any topic—from *Desperate Housewives* to the war in Iraq—is likely to yield astute critiques, interesting perspectives, and lots of irrelevant, incoherent, offensive, and inflammatory banter. That's because for the most part, Internet forums are both interactive and uncensored: users are able to post whatever they want. It's up to the network of users to self-police the interaction, keep it on topic, and eliminate any rude or irrelevant chat. Forum members may reprimand or ignore a flamer, but voluntary cooperation doesn't always work.

Moderated forums, by contrast, trade complete openness for order. Forum moderators—commonly known as mods—set strict rules for posts, often review all posts before making them public, and have the power to censor or ban specific posts. At the fiercely moderated television commentary site *Television Without Pity,* for example, moderators set clear and strict rules and regularly review discussion threads to eliminate posts that fall off topic or are repetitive. While some critics claim that the moderators do so to rid the site of bad language or positions at odds with the moderators', most critics see a clear advantage to the site's authoritarian moderation of its boards: the discourse is civil and literate, and conflicts between posters are respectful and productive (Stevens, 2007).

### THINK ABOUT THIS

❶ Do you participate in Internet forums? Do you prefer moderated or open forums? What makes you prefer one over the other?

❷ Which is more important, a free-speech open forum or a managed, productive conflict? Do you think it's necessary to trade off one for the other?

❸ Does self-policing work on the Internet? What circumstances might inhibit a user group's ability to self-police?

● SOMETIMES THE competition for a lone piece of pie can mask larger emotional issues.

In certain conflict situations, such as a competition for a piece of pie, the people involved can resolve the conflict—that is, bring it to an end—in just seconds. But when the conflict is more complex or when a seemingly simple disagreement is a symptom of a larger problem between people, resolving the situation will require more time and thought. If Leslie is growing resentful of always having to share everything with Kathy—her room, her friends, her computer, her clothes—their conflict is bigger than a piece of pie. Resolving it may require a more involved approach, such as honest, lengthy dialogue about Leslie's resentments and possible ways for her to have more things she can call her own. Nonetheless, the strategies we use for managing conflict, be they simple or complicated, generally fall into one of three basic categories: escapist, challenging, or cooperative (see Table 7.1).

## Escapist Strategies

One way for Leslie to manage the conflict is to make a decision to avoid it, and let Kathy have the pie, even though she really wants it for herself. Through such **escapist strategies**, people try to prevent or avoid direct conflict. Perhaps they want to steer clear of a confrontation because they're afraid a direct conflict would hurt the other person or the relationship. Or maybe they wish to postpone dealing with the conflict until a more convenient time, when they can talk at length about it with the other person. Another reason for selecting this type of strategy might be to force the other person to raise the issue instead of having to do so themselves.

In certain situations, escapist strategies can be harmless and practical, offering a quick resolution to issues that are relatively unimportant (like pie), and can help maintain relationships that might be damaged if conflict erupted

**TABLE 7.1**

**CONFLICT STRATEGIES: THE KEY LIME PIE INCIDENT**

| Type | Description | Examples |
|------|-------------|----------|
| Escapist | Conflict is avoided or prevented; goals may not be important; conflict is not seen as a viable alternative | • Relinquish the pie ("You can have the pie") |
| Challenging | Individual goals are pursued; relationship is threatened | • Take the pie ("That's my piece of pie")<br>• Fight for the pie ("Oh, no, it's not") |
| Cooperative | Pursuit of mutual interests; problem-solving approach emphasized; relationship is preserved | • Share the pie<br>• Flip a coin for the pie<br>• Broker a deal for the pie ("I'll do the dishes if you let me have the pie") |

over every little thing. But such strategies may be unproductive if they continually prevent people from dealing with issues that need addressing: if Leslie always defers to Kathy, for example, resentment is likely to brew between the sisters. The pie could become a tipping point for a larger issue, prompting Leslie to take a different approach.

# real communicator

**NAME:** Anonymous
**HOMETOWN:** Chicago, Illinois
**OCCUPATION:** Police officer
**FUN FACT:** Due to security reasons, officer must remain anonymous

I'm a police officer in Chicago. Cops on TV are always running around with their guns drawn or tossing bad guys against brick walls, and while I do some of that, of course, I'd say that over 90 percent of my job is spent communicating with people. And most of that time is about managing conflict.

In my first few years out of the academy, I responded to a lot of domestic disputes. Neighbors call in about other neighbors making too much noise; spouses and parents call in about fighting in the home. These are unproductive conflicts: screaming, destruction of property, and all too often violence. And few things have the potential to escalate unproductive conflict like uniformed men and women coming into your home with guns, right?

The first thing I do is use my eyes to see if physical injuries are apparent or if a crime has been committed. If so, it's a domestic violence situation, and I arrest the perpetrator, taking him or her to jail. The conflict is temporarily resolved. Most of the time, however, these calls are incidents of domestic *disputes*. A crime hasn't been committed. I can't make an arrest. And my job becomes much more difficult. Now I have to manage conflict—through mediation.

First off, I don't use any challenging strategies as I might with a drug dealer on the street.

I stay nonaggressive (I am, after all, in someone else's home). I try not to lean forward, I stay out of people's faces, and I speak in a monotone. I try to exude calmness, because everyone else in the place is freaking out.

One time, I had a man who simply wouldn't stop screaming at and about his wife: *I hate her! I hate her guts!* As calmly as possible, I asked, "You hate who?" He said, *I hate my wife!* I looked shocked and said, "Sir, you hate your *wife*?" I kept the questions coming. In the academy they call this verbal judo, the sword of insertion. In communication classes, it's called probing. I asked the man simple questions, getting him down to facts, getting him to think about things reasonably, as opposed to thinking about them emotionally.

Sometimes, I'll turn to one party and say, as respectfully as possible, "Listen, I know I don't have a right to ask you to leave your own house, but maybe there's a cousin's place you can go crash at for the night, or maybe you can go take a long walk and cool down." It's not a win-win or lose-lose resolution; it's a separation, a temporary one. It's an escapist strategy, a prevention of further unproductive conflict, a rain check on the situation until a better time, when heads are cooler. Often that's the best I can do. I've got other homes to go to, other conflicts to manage.

## Challenging Strategies

If Leslie decides that she wants the pie more than she wants to preserve the quality of her relationship with Kathy, she might demand the entire piece for herself, at her sister's expense. Such **challenging strategies** promote the objectives of the individual who uses them, rather than the interests of the other person or the relationship. Challenging strategies are often referred to as assertiveness. Assertive people are generally good at getting what they want and also effective at handling conflicts because they don't let negative emotions like anxiety, guilt, or embarrassment get in the way.

Clearly, challenging strategies don't do much to strengthen the relationship of the people involved. However, there are some situations in which people seem to be driven to use them. One study found that people tend to employ challenging strategies when they feel the need to defend themselves from a perceived threat (Canary, Cunningham, & Cody, 1988). For instance, if Leslie believes that Kathy "always gets her way" and that "it's my turn to get *my* way," she may take a challenging approach.

In some relationships, challenging strategies may not cause harm to the partners' bond, even though these strategies are intended to put one of the partners' priorities first. To illustrate, perhaps Leslie and Kathy are so close and feel so confident of their love for one another that Leslie knows a moment of selfish behavior on her part will be overlooked or forgiven by Kathy. Conversely, if the relationship is not really valued, challenging strategies can enable individuals to get what they want without any consequential losses, since maintaining the relationship is not a priority. For example, Leslie might adopt a challenging strategy if she were in competition with a stranger for the last piece of pie while on the lunch line at school.

## Cooperative Strategies

Of course, the most practical and fairest way for Leslie to manage this conflict is to propose a compromise, offering to split the last piece of pie with Kathy. If Leslie decides to share the pie, she is attempting to arrive at the best outcome for both partners in this relationship. Strategies that benefit the relationship, serve mutual rather than individual goals, and strive to produce solutions that benefit both parties are called **cooperative strategies**.

Whether the issue is pie or child custody decisions, several tactics are useful in cooperative conflict management. For example, let's consider a larger issue that is causing conflict within a family: nineteen-year-old Kieran wants to drop out of college to join the Army. His mother is very upset and wants him to continue his education. A number of strategies can help them manage the conflict cooperatively.

### Focus on Issues

With any issue, it's very important that the discussion remain centered on the matter at hand and steer clear of any personal attacks. In our simplified example, if Leslie says to Kathy, "You're overweight, and you know this pie won't

**AND YOU?**

Are there certain people with whom you engage in more challenging strategies than others? Do you engage in conflict with strangers more or less than you do with people who are important to you?

help," she's making the argument personal, making it about Kathy when it's really about pie. Such **verbal aggressiveness**—attacks on individuals rather than issues—are common, especially in the media (witness the personal assaults that characterize political campaigns and celebrity gossip), but they are also unproductive. One study found that people who lack argumentative skills often resort to verbal aggressiveness, perhaps because personal attacks may be the only way they feel they can deal with another person in a conflict situation (Infante & Wigely, 1986).

Such personal attacks do little to foster cooperation and usually succeed only in putting the other person on the defensive and making the interaction more heated. So Kieran's mother would do better to keep the focus on Kieran's decision ("I really don't like the idea of your dropping out of school when you're

## COMMUNICATIONACROSSCULTURES

**THINK ABOUT THIS**

### Culture of Nonviolence

On April 16, 2007, a gunman brutally shot and killed thirty-two individuals in one of the deadliest mass-shooting rampages in United States history (Hauser & O'Connor, 2007). The murders at Virginia Technical University seemed to stem from the gunman's anger at wealthy students (CNN.com, 2007). After the shootings, many people were understandably angry themselves—at the gunman, at the school, and at the system for failing to prevent this tragedy (Johnson, Williams, Jansing, & Stewart, 2007). According to attribution theory (also termed the self-serving bias), blaming others, whether in one-on-one conflicts or large groups, is a natural reaction (Landau, 2003).

Consider, then, another shooting that occurred at an American school less than a year before the massacre at Virginia Tech. On October 2, 2006, an armed gunman entered a small one-room schoolhouse in the Amish community of Nickel Mines, Pennsylvania. The gunman, who was not Amish, took hostages and eventually lined up all the girls and began firing. Seven children were shot—five of them fatally—before the gunman, knowing that state troopers were closing in, turned his weapons on himself and committed suicide (Dewan, 2006).

Like the shootings at Virginia Tech—and those that have occurred at various schools around the United States in recent years—the murders at Nickel Mines shook the nation. But while members of the mainstream American culture reacted with anger, shock, and a need to assess blame, the pacifist Amish were fervent in their desire to forgive and actually embraced the gunman's family in the aftermath of the tragedy (Goodstein, 2006). When asked how the Amish community was dealing with the loss of these young girls, one grandfather told the press, "We must not think evil of this man" (CNN.com, 2006). Another member of the community noted, "He had a mother and a wife and a soul and now he's standing before a just God."

**1** Is forgiving those who do harm an acceptable outcome for a conflict of this magnitude? Did the reaction of the Amish to their children's killer and to his family effectively resolve the conflict, or was it rather a way of managing it?

**2** How do the reactions of these Amish survivors differ from those expressed by Americans after the Virginia Tech shootings? What about after 9/11?

**3** The Amish forgive those involved in conflict with them because of their deeply held religious beliefs. Are there other reasons for forgiveness that can be useful in a conflict?

**4** What is your reaction to the information on Amish forgiveness in light of what we learned about Amish shunning earlier in the chapter?

halfway finished with your degree") than to focus her criticisms on Kieran himself ("What kind of idiot drops out of college with only three semesters to go?").

## Debate and Argue

As noted earlier in this chapter, when we engage in conflict by debating the issue at hand, we exchange more ideas, reach better decisions, and foster stronger,

## what about you?

### Hitting Above and Below the Belt

The concepts of argumentativeness and verbal aggressiveness are important to the study of conflict management because the first is more likely to produce positive outcomes than the second. Examine the items below, and mark each one according to how you feel about most conflicts (1 = true, 2 = undecided, 3 = false).

_____ 1. Arguing over controversial issues improves my intelligence.

_____ 2. I really come down hard on people if they don't see things my way.

_____ 3. I am good about not losing my temper during conflict situations.

_____ 4. Some people need to be insulted if they are to see reason.

_____ 5. I prefer being with people who disagree with me.

_____ 6. It is exhilarating to get into a good conflict.

_____ 7. I have the ability to do well in conflict situations.

_____ 8. It is not hard for me to go for the throat if a person really deserves it.

_____ 9. I know how to construct effective arguments that can change people's minds.

_____ 10. I avoid getting into conflicts with people who know how to argue well.

_____ 11. I know how to find other people's personal weaknesses.

_Scoring:_ Add your scores for items 1, 3, 5, 6, 7, and 9. Reverse your scores for items 2, 4, 8, 10, and 11 (1 = 3, 3 = 1); after converting the numbers, add all of these scores to your previous total. If you scored between 11 and 18, you are prone to argumentativeness. If you scored between 26 and 33, you are likely to be verbally aggressive when you are in conflict situations. If you scored between 19 and 25, you are probably neither very argumentative nor very aggressive.

Source: From Infante, D. A. (1988). Adapted with permission of the publisher.

healthier relationships. Healthy debate is therefore a cornerstone of cooperative conflict management. A number of tactics can help foster debate.

One is **probing**—asking questions that encourage specific and precise answers. If Kieran's mother asks probing questions ("Why do you want to join the Army now when you're so close to graduating?"), she'll get a better understanding of why and how he's come to this decision. Likewise, Kieran will get a better sense of his mother's feelings if he asks similar questions of her ("Why is it so important to you that I finish my degree now?").

Probing can help parties explore the pros and cons of an issue, encouraging either side to consider both the positive and the negative aspects of it. This allows one individual to clarify his or her argument to the other and the other to critique it. Kieran, for example, might note that he's been looking at the job market for college graduates in his major, and it's in a downturn, and so he sees the Army as a solid employment opportunity. His mother might point out that he'll still have to pay back all his college loans, with or without his degree, and that all that expenditure will have amounted to little if he doesn't finish. Kieran's mother might also play the role of **devil's advocate**—pointing out the worst-case scenarios ("There's a war going on. What if you get hurt or killed?")—to make sure her son has considered all the possible outcomes of his decision (and revealing her own fears in the process).

### Consider Options and Alternatives

Offering—and potentially negotiating—alternatives is a useful tactic for cooperative conflict management. Kieran's mother might suggest, for example, that he join the Army Reserve instead, which would allow him to finish school while also serving his country and ensuring a career if he wants to go on active duty after graduation.

### Consider the Importance of the Outcome

Obviously, a disagreement over a serious issue like quitting school to join the Army clearly warrants serious debate. But many of the conflicts in which we find ourselves embroiled (like disputes over pie) don't seem all that important. Nevertheless, it's important to clarify that the issue will have consequences. Kieran's mother might emphasize that the Army is not a job he can simply quit if he doesn't like it; Leslie might remind Kathy that their father told them that whoever gets the pie has to do the dishes.

### Reassure Your Partner

To resolve a conflict cooperatively, a straightforward explanation of your good intentions might be in order. When Kieran's mother tells him, "Please, I just want to talk about this to make sure I understand your

In Chapter 6, we discuss the relational repair tactics that help partners shift the focus from the problems to the benefits of their relationship. By separating the issues from the person, partners can remember why they value each other in the first place. Instead of telling your roommate that she is inconsiderate and messy, remember that she makes you laugh and prepares your meals when you're sick. *Then* approach her to work out your issues.

● **WHILE KIERAN** might be sure he wants to join the Army, negotiating alternatives with his mother might allow him to explore his choices and uncover other options.

**AND YOU?**

Think of a person with whom you have recently had a disagreement who isn't willing to discuss the situation with you. What might be causing this reluctance? And which technique might best help you draw the person into discussion about your conflict?

● *SEX AND THE CITY'S* Big and Carrie reach a compromise through trading.

reasons before you make a rash decision," she's stating her desire to resolve the disagreement, showing him that she respects his feelings and intelligence, and reassuring him that she wants to engage in a discussion with him, not simply tell him what to do.

## Conflict Outcomes

As we noted earlier, conflict cannot always be resolved. But every conflict does, eventually, have some outcome. Regardless of how they engage in it, the conflict between twins Leslie and Kathy will produce some outcome: one or the other sister may get the pie, the two might share the pie, or neither might get any pie at all. Conflict outcomes fall into several categories (see Table 7.2 on p. 218).

### Compromise

In most cases, compromise presents a simple way to resolve a conflict. Sometimes compromise might be a matter of sharing a piece of pie; other times, it might involve setting up a schedule for using a jointly owned computer or splitting the cost of some shared item. With most **compromises,** both sides give up a little to gain a little.

Compromises can be arrived at through **trading**, whereby one partner offers something of equal value in return for something he or she wants. For example, on the TV series *Sex and the City,* when Carrie and Big argue over why it feels as though there is no place for her in his apartment and why he never visits her place instead, they each give a little and take a little in order to reach a compromise. He starts spending more time at her place, and she stops eating oranges in his bed. Other options might include **random selection** (such as if Big and Carrie were to decide where to spend time by flipping a coin) or, when appropriate and practical, taking a vote.

The advantage of compromise is that it lets you and the other person quickly resolve or avert a conflict by agreeing on a decision-making method. However, important relationships can suffer if the people involved are *always* making compromises. That's because compromising means giving up *some* of what you want, even though you're getting a little of something else in return. After a while, that can get tiresome. With romantic partners, close friends, and family members, it's better to come up with more creative, thoughtful approaches to ongoing conflicts that lead to "win-win" resolutions.

### Win-Win

When both participants in a conflict discuss the situation and arrive at a solution that fully satisfies each of them, the conflict has been resolved productively. Thinking back to the key lime pie incident, if sisters Leslie and Kathy use that conflict to work through their issue of having to share everything, they may be able to arrive at a variety of solutions to the problem and strengthen their relationship in the process. They might agree to pool their money for a second computer or come up with a system for sharing certain items of clothing while placing others off limits. Through such "win-win" solutions, both parties can meet their own goals (unlimited computer access, a bigger wardrobe), help the other with her goals, and improve their relationship.

## Lose-Lose

Of course, there are times when a conflict is resolved without either side getting what it wants. If Leslie decides that if she can't have the pie, nobody can, and tosses it in the trash, she's resolved the conflict at hand, even though she didn't get what she wanted. While such outcomes seem childish, they are in fact relatively common. Individuals often stay in jobs that they hate and do them poorly because they don't see the possibility for other outcomes; in such cases, both the individual and the employer lose, along with any customers or clients who depend on them.

● **MANY PEOPLE STAY** in jobs they hate because they fear the unknown. But this way, nobody wins: you're unhappy and do your job poorly, which affects those who depend on you.

## Separation

By contrast, individuals who quit jobs opt for a different outcome: **separation**. Removing oneself from a situation or relationship is a clear way to end a conflict without necessarily creating clear wins or losses for either party. For example, suppose you're renting an apartment from a friend who, as the landlord, never repairs burst pipes or fixes the fridge when it breaks, even though you pay your rent on time every month. You've tried to reason with him; you've even tried to guilt him into reimbursing you for the money you've spent on repairs he should have paid for. But nothing has worked. In this case, the best resolution to this conflict may be to simply pack up your things and move.

## Allocation of Power

Yet another way to resolve conflict is to decide, with the other person, which of you will have the power to make certain decisions in the relationship. For example, in a couple, one individual may be dominant on one issue (such as finances) while the other makes the decisions on others (such as child rearing); in a work environment, several employees may split the responsibilities of a given project, with one member making financial decisions, another in charge of creative ones, and a third in charge of communicating all those decisions to others outside the group.

TABLE 7.2

**CONFLICT OUTCOMES: THE GOOD, THE BAD, AND THE UGLY**

| Incident | Dispute | Outcome |
|---|---|---|
| The Great Compromise, 1787 | In forging the United States Constitution, disagreement emerges between small states, who want equal representation in the legislature, and large states, who want representation to be apportioned according to population. | Win-Win (via Win-Lose): The framers create a bicameral Congress, consisting of the Senate, which offers equal representation (small states win, large states lose), and the House of Representatives, which gives larger states a bigger voice (large states win, small states lose). In the long run, the bicameral Congress serves the interests of both large and small states (win-win). |
| Montgomery Bus Boycott, 1955–1956 | Following the lead of Rosa Parks, African Americans in Montgomery, Alabama, begin walking to work and school rather than riding on segregated buses. | Win-Lose: African Americans in Montgomery rely heavily on public transportation, so the decision to boycott the buses presents some serious hardships for them. But since they constitute three-fourths of the ridership on city buses, their actions translate into a major loss of revenue. Their hardships pay off: in June 1956, a federal court rules that Alabama's law requiring segregated buses is unconstitutional. |
| Don't Ask, Don't Tell, 1993 | President Bill Clinton, seeking to fulfill a campaign promise, tries to eliminate restrictions on homosexuals' serving in the military; he is met with opposition from conservatives, as well as from some members of the armed forces. | Lose-Lose: Neither side is entirely satisfied with Clinton's compromise, which prohibits the military from investigating individuals' sexuality but still allows dismissal of gay and lesbian military personnel if their homosexuality becomes known. |
| The 2007–2008 Writers Guild of America strike | Writers for television and film put down their pencils for more than three months when they are unable to negotiate a contract with producers. What do they want? A bigger share of revenues from DVD sales and a portion of revenues generated from content posted online. | Win-Win (via Lose-Lose): The strike itself has negative effects not only on union members who sit out and the producers whose shows they have halted but also on members of other unions put out of work for the duration of the strike. But the resolution offers a compromise as producers give in to some demands and everyone gets back to work. The other unions benefit, too, as the WGA contract sets a precedent for future negotiations for related organizations. |

BACK TO ▷ *30 Rock*

At the beginning of this chapter, we talked about Liz Lemon and Jack Donaghy, characters on the TV sitcom *30 Rock*. Let's revisit these two fictional characters' conflict management strategies in light of what we've discussed in this chapter.

▶ Liz would like to think of her approach to conflict management as cooperative, but in fact, her avoidance of conflict is quite unproductive. In many instances, Jack's assertive conflict management strategies are more effective than Liz's, which are aimed at avoiding unpleasantness and often involve unethical behaviors such as lying.

▶ Context plays a role here as well. While Jack relishes the opportunity to renegotiate an actor's contract or fight with his ex-wife, he's quite the opposite when dealing with his mother, taking great pains to avoid talking to her at all; he even goes so far as to enlist one of the actors to impersonate Jack on the phone when his mother calls. So when the situation requires it, he's willing to adopt Liz's avoidant strategies.

▶ The reasons for Jack's and Liz's differing styles are many. Personality plays a role, as does gender. But perhaps most important is the fact that Liz is focused on a different goal than Jack. His job is to focus on profits and to make decisions that others will be charged with carrying out; he doesn't have to worry about minor conflicts between staff. On the other hand, Liz's main responsibility is to get a fairly large group of people to write and perform a live show each week. What seem like minor conflicts to Jack can cause major difficulties for Liz, so she does anything she can to avoid them.

## THINGS TO TRY

1. The engagement in and resolution of interpersonal conflict are often key factors in romantic comedies (like *10 Things I Hate About You* or *When Harry Met Sally*), as well as in buddy-driven action films (such as *Shanghai Noon* or *Lethal Weapon*). Try watching such a film, and pay attention to the way in which the principal characters engage in conflict with one another. How does their conflict management lead to relationship growth?

2. For an interesting look at conflict and debate, you need not search further than the U.S. Congress. Debates on the floor of the Senate and House of Representatives are broadcast on C-SPAN and provide an interesting glimpse into the way that conflict and argument shape new laws and policy. In addition to observing how this process works, pay attention to

# Group and Organizational Communication

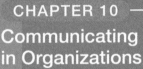

**Individuals** work together to achieve a shared goal: keeping people informed through Wikipedia.

# 8

# Communicating in Groups

**How many major league pitchers have pitched a perfect game?** Who was Mother Jones? How did the band Arcade Fire come up with that name? And when will Halley's comet next pass the earth? If you've ever found yourself curious about such obscure facts, chances are you've wound up on Wikipedia. Launched in 2001, the online "open content" encyclopedia boasted more than ten million articles in 253 languages just seven years later.

The nonprofit organization behind the project has fewer than twenty employees, but the encyclopedia itself is the result of a larger volunteer group effort (Cohen, 2008). Wikipedia isn't just a project or a destination—it's a community where writers from around the world contribute, edit, and critique articles, flag questionable items, and link articles throughout the site to each other and other Web sources. There is no advertising, and contributors are not paid to provide content.

Of course, the collaborative nature of Wikipedia does present some problems. While commercial encyclopedias are overseen by editors and publishers who take responsibility for ensuring quality and consistency, Wikipedia is largely self-policed: the community weeds out bias and errors. Nobody's really held accountable for mistakes, and articles can languish without being edited or fact-checked. Contributors' motivations can also present some problems, as when the Sea World entry was edited to eliminate critiques of the park's treatment of orcas. The edit was traced back to Anheuser-Busch, the parent company of Sea World—shedding light on the ability of corporations, and individuals, to use the site for public relations purposes (Hafner, 2007).

The site is also vulnerable to fraud. In 2007, a prolific contributor known as EssJay, who described himself as a tenured professor of religion at a private university, was revealed to be a twenty-four-year-old college dropout who used his falsified credentials as leverage in resolving disputes on the site (Cohen, 2007). In the aftermath, it was once again the community that got to work, examining all of EssJay's contributions and repairing the site's content and its reputation.

After you have finished reading this chapter, you will be able to

- List the characteristics and types of groups and explain how groups develop

- Understand how group size affects communication

- Identify the influence of networks in groups

- Analyze aspects that determine a group's effectiveness

- Define the roles individuals play in a group

- Identify other issues affecting group communication

As you will recall from Chapter 1, communication between two individuals (a dyad) is far more complicated than many of us assume. In a dyad, both participants simultaneously deliver, receive, and interpret messages presented through verbal and nonverbal means—and these messages can be misunderstood in light of perceptual differences or faulty listening. So consider how much more complex things can get when you add more people to the communication scenario. When three or more people come together, their interactions and relationships—and their communication—take on whole new characteristics, as you can see in our discussion of Wikipedia. In this chapter, we'll learn more about group communication, how groups operate, and the factors that influence their communication.

## Understanding Groups

Your family sitting down to dinner. Ten adults on a bus to Cleveland, Ohio. Your fraternity or sorority at an event. Your buddies at work grabbing lunch before a meeting. Six exasperated parents sitting in a doctor's office with sick kids. Each of these examples involves multiple people (sometimes crowds of people) engaged in some activity—and most of us would probably say that these are examples of "groups of people." But are they *really* groups? We'll explore what it actually means to be in a group, in addition to understanding what types of groups exist and how those groups develop in the first place.

### Characteristics of Groups

For our purposes, a **group** is a collection of more than two people who share some kind of relationship, communicate in an interdependent fashion, and collaborate toward some shared purpose. When we break that definition down, we can identify three key characteristics that make a group something other than just a collection of individuals:

▶ *A shared identity.* Members of a group perceive themselves as a group. That is, they share a sense of identity with other members of the group: they recognize other members of the group, have specific feelings toward those individuals, and experience a sense of belonging in the group. Thus a huge array of people who identify themselves as part of a group (political parties, for example, or fan organizations) are as much a group as a baseball team or a string quartet.

▶ *Common goals.* Members of a group usually identify with one another because they have one or more goals in common. Goals may be very specific—coming up with an ad campaign for a new project or organizing a mission trip for a congregation—or they might be quite general, such as socializing or discussing books or films. In either case, a shared sense of purpose helps define a group, even when there is some disagreement about specific goals or ways of achieving them.

▶ *Interdependent relationships.* Members of a group are connected to one another and communicate in an interdependent way. Simply put, the behavior of each member affects the behavior of every other member. This interdependence is fostered by the way that group members adopt specific roles and collaborate to accomplish goals. These goals might be very specific (completing a specific task) or very general (socializing).

● **THE MEMBERS OF** *The Jane Austen Book Club* share a common goal: to read all of Jane Austen's novels and find guidance for their own lives in her stories.

Looking back at the examples that we opened this section with, you can probably guess that your family, your sorority or fraternity, and your pals at work constitute a group. You share an identity with the other members and have feelings about them (for better or worse!); you likely have common goals, and you are interdependent—that is, you rely on them, and they on you, for love, friendship, or professional growth. This is not the case with the strangers on a bus to Cleveland. They might share a goal (getting to their destination), but they are not interdependent, and they do not share an identity. The same point can be made for the parents waiting in the office of the pediatrician.

Size and proximity were once major factors in group creation, but the ease with which modern technology allows individuals to communicate with others means that these factors are no longer as relevant to group formation as they once were. Four friends chatting over coffee at your local Starbucks constitute a group; so do twenty individual photographers who've never met but contribute to a group photo pool on Flickr.com. In both cases, the individuals are joined by shared goals, shared identity, and interdependence; it is these three key factors—not size or proximity—that determines group status. Of course, not all groups are alike. Let's take a look at different types of groups.

**AND YOU?**

In Chapter 6, we talked about family as an example of interpersonal relationships. Now think about your family as a group. What are the family's common goals? What do the members of your family see as the family's defining traits? How can a change in behavior by one family member affect other members?

## Group Types

Groups can take many forms. The most common among them are called **primary groups**—long-lasting groups that form around the relationships that mean the most to their members. Your family constitutes one primary group to which you belong; your friends are another.

In addition to primary groups, there are groups defined by their specific functions (for instance, support groups, study groups, and social groups). However, any one of these groups can perform multiple functions. Alcoholics Anonymous (AA), for example, is primarily a **support group**—a set of individuals who come together to address personal problems while benefiting from the support of others with similar issues. But AA is also a **social group**, as membership in the group offers opportunities to form relationships with others. And finally, as a group with a specific mission—to help members manage their struggles with alcohol and addiction—AA is also a **problem-solving group**.

While all groups are to some degree social, some groups are more task-oriented than others. **Study groups**, for example, are formed for the specific purpose of helping students prepare for exams. A **focus group** is a set of individuals asked to come together to give their opinions on a specific issue (Frantz, 2007; Sinickas, 2000). For example, when a new TV pilot is getting ready to air, a network will assemble a focus group to gauge how the public might respond to the pilot.

Perhaps the most task-oriented and goal-driven type of group is the **team**— a group that works together to carry out a project or a specific endeavor or to compete against other teams. Sports teams are an obvious example, but teams are

## WIREDFORCOMMUNICATION

### Social Networking Grows Up

For most students today, social networking on sites like MySpace or Facebook has become common enough not to merit comment or explanation. Virtual groups are de facto networks, connecting scores of individuals, creating new relationships, and fostering a new kind of group communication. Surprisingly, it has taken some time for the benefits of social networking to trickle up to the business and professional world. Part of the reason is, of course, that posting videos or confessing company secrets would be considered unprofessional in most business environments: chatting about information that might be confidential or badmouthing one's company or colleagues could have serious repercussions for one's career. Also at issue is the fact that successful professionals spend their lives putting together their social networks— so they tend to be protective of them.

Nonetheless, a few sites have begun to take hold, including LinkedIn, a networking tool that connects business professionals, allowing individuals to view connections among their various contacts, to reconnect with former colleagues and classmates, and to offer (and receive) recommendations for their work. While not as big as MySpace or Facebook, LinkedIn has created an online community of more than twenty million members, about half of them outside the United States.

For recruitment and job hunting, social networking seems like a logical but basic use of technology. But as professionals become more comfortable with the idea of social networking, new models are beginning to emerge. Take Sermo.com, a social networking site for physicians, where doctors can consult with more than 25,000 colleagues to form more accurate diagnoses or gain insights into critical treatments. Or INmobile.org, a community site for executives in wireless technology. Unlike Facebook, MySpace, or LinkedIn, which are open to anyone who wants to join, these professional networking sites are open only to credentialed professionals whose identities are verified, even if their names are kept private. New registrations at Sermo, for example, are authenticated individually, and prospective members must provide confidential information such as phone numbers and the schools from which they received their medical degrees in order to join (Vascellaro, 2007).

THINK ABOUT THIS

❶ Would you prefer to be a part of a more narrowly focused group than of a large, open social network? What benefits would a more strictly controlled membership offer?

❷ Why is it important that doctors at Sermo, whose names may not be made public on the site, provide credentials and proof of identity? How do the insistence on authentication of identity and the providing of private information shape the nature of the group?

❸ In what ways do you think social networking could benefit business professionals? In what ways could you envision it hurting them or their careers?

● **GROUPS COME** in all shapes and sizes. While the design team from *Extreme Makeover: Home Edition* and a hip-hop dance crew might vary in size and purpose, they are both considered groups.

also common in large organizations or as subsets of other groups: an Army unit might select a few members to form a reconnaissance team; a community group might nominate a team of individuals to take charge of its annual fundraiser.

One of the more noteworthy types of groups in today's organizations is the **self-directed work team**, a group of skilled workers who take responsibility for producing high-quality finished work (Douglas, 2002). In self-directed work teams, members bring complementary skills and experiences that enable the team to accomplish more than any individual member could achieve independently (Katzenbach & Smith, 1993). Self-directed work teams have proliferated in the last few decades in a variety of organizations and industries (Beyerlein, 2001; Yandrick, 2001).

In self-directed work teams, many typical management functions are completely controlled by the team members. For example, members arrange their own schedules, buy their own equipment, and set their own standards for productivity, quality, and costs. They conduct their own peer evaluations, bring in new members, and coordinate future plans with management. The theory is that when people have more control over their work, they have a more positive attitude and are more committed to the group. Perhaps the most dramatic impact of self-directed teams is the improved performance and behavior of employees throughout the organization. In enterprises characterized by self-directed teams, the environment is marked by cooperation rather than competition. (See Table 8.1 on p. 232 for tips on working in a self-directed work team.)

Of course, the lessons of self-directed work teams extend far beyond work situations. Collaborative software programs (most commonly known as *open-source pages* or *wikis*) allow many individuals to collaborate on a written project, creating, editing, and linking content and reviewing the work of others.

**AND YOU?**

In your first job out of college, do you think you would prefer to work as part of a self-directed work team or in a more traditionally arranged team where a manager takes control? What would be the advantages of each?

| Action | Considerations |
|---|---|
| Define a clear purpose for the team | What are the team's goals—short term *and* long term? |
| Foster team spirit | Build a sense of energy, excitement, and commitment in your team by engaging in team-building activities and events, rewarding members who demonstrate commitment, and identifying new challenges for the team to take on. |
| Train | Working on a self-directed team may be a new experience for some members. See if your organization can provide training to help members understand and implement the defining practices of self-directed teams. |
| Clarify expectations | Make sure all members of the team understand what's expected of them in terms of their roles and performance. For example, what functions will each member serve? How, specifically, will the team define "success"? |
| Set boundaries | Articulate where the team's responsibilities begin and end. If necessary, remind members that they are working in the service of the organization and that they need to stay focused on their specific purpose. |

Sources: Capozzoli (2002); Nelson (2002); Rosenthal (2001).

## Group Development

If you've ever become wrapped up in a reality TV show such as *Survivor, The Apprentice,* or *Top Chef,* you know how fascinating and dramatic group interactions can be. In each of these shows, a season typically opens with the forming of a group: cast members always start off as strangers but are quickly thrust into a group situation—sharing a living space and working together to accomplish certain tasks. As the season progresses, the group members bond, conflicts erupt, and alliances are forged and reforged. In fact, much of the drama in reality television stems from the tensions that arise between cast members as they struggle to work with—or against—one another. Contestants on Bravo's *Top Chef,* for example, must team up to work on certain projects (such as running a restaurant or catering a big event). The network stirs things up by having chefs who may have different culinary styles or dislike each other work together. For example, in season two, Marcel's perceived arrogance and love for "molecular gastronomy" quickly made him the target of others' wrath. It came to a boiling point in the episode where the "cheftestants" were asked to create a seven-course meal based on the seven deadly sins (pride, envy, wrath, greed, sloth, gluttony, and lust). While each chef was responsible for one course, they all helped with plating and serving the dishes, except when it came to Marcel's dish: no one except Elia assisted him; the others lounged around on the patio and yelled insults at him. Nonetheless, when reality show contestants are brought together at the season's end, most describe the experience as positive. They note that they felt privileged to work with so many talented chefs and learned a great deal from one another.

Of course, these "reality" shows are to some degree manipulated—contestants are selected at least in part for their TV "presence," and scenes are edited to heighten the drama. But the shows do reflect some basic truths about how groups develop (Wheelan, 1994). Research shows that a group becomes a group through five specific stages, memorably called forming, storming, norming, performing, and adjourning (Tuckman, 1965). Using *Top Chef* as an extended example, let's take a look at each stage.

● ON BRAVO'S *TOP CHEF*, teams examine their group's strengths and weaknesses and use them to decide on a team leader and what dishes they will cook.

### Forming

When a group first comes together, its members are unsure how to act around one another, are nervous about how others perceive them, and aren't clear on what roles they'll be playing within the group. In this **forming** stage, group members try to negotiate who will be in charge and what the group's goals will be. The primary purpose of this stage is for group members to make friends, come to a point where they feel that they "fit in," and learn more about one another and the group's objectives. Once individuals feel accepted, they can begin to identify with the group (Moreland & Levine, 1994). The first few episodes of *Top Chef* generally depict the forming stage, as cast members meet for the first time and begin establishing relationships and forming opinions about the other contestants.

### Storming

After forming, group members move into the **storming** stage, in which they inevitably begin experiencing conflicts over issues such as who will lead the group and what roles members will play. When tasked with a group challenge, teammates on *Top Chef* will toss around ideas and consider what strengths each member brings to the team before deciding on a menu. For example, season one's sommelier-turned-chef, Stephen, was often responsible for putting together the wine pairings for his team.

### Norming

During the **norming** stage, members establish agreed norms governing expected behavior. **Norms** are recurring patterns of behavior or thinking that come to be accepted in a group as the "usual" way of doing things (Scheerhorn & Geist, 1997). During this stage, group roles also solidify, and a leader emerges. In addition, group identity grows stronger as members begin to realize the importance of their roles within the group and the need to cooperate to accomplish goals.

Beginning a relationship with a group isn't so different from starting a new interpersonal relationship. In both contexts, we reduce uncertainty about our relational partners so that we feel secure and confident about roles, interactions, objectives, and so on. So whether you're beginning a new romance or forging a study group, it might be helpful to try the monitoring, proactive, and indirect strategies we discuss in Chapter 6 (see pp. 177–178).

Typically in *Top Chef* group challenges, the leader of the group is viewed as the head chef, responsible for overseeing the entire menu, and the rest of the team act as sous-chefs, each person responsible for creating one or two components of the meal.

## real communicator

**NAME:** Stephanie Lam
**HOMETOWN:** Hong Kong, China
**OCCUPATION:** Youth trainer
**FUN FACT:** My dream is to watch my favorite soccer team, Chelsea, play at their headquarters in Stamford Bridge, England.

I work at the Hong Kong Federation of Youth Groups (HKFYG), an organization dedicated to developing a pool of young leadership talent for the future of Hong Kong. Specifically, I am a professional trainer in youth team building. We use experiential learning at the HKFYG. I don't teach students in a traditional, lecture-style delivery. Instead, the students gain experience on their own, in groups. We are trained to help these groups teach themselves, to develop their own perceptions about a concept. For example, a couple of years ago, we sent twenty kids to South Africa for the Cathay Pacific International Wilderness Experience. The overriding aim was to have students learn about the environment, which is important for them as future decision makers.

My first job was to get these twenty students to think of themselves as more than just a collection of individuals. They needed to think of themselves as a team, a group that must work together to solve problems and accomplish goals. To do that, I concentrated a lot of my energy on the formation stage of group development. Building initial rapport and fostering team spirit are vital to a group's future success. In South Africa, the kids were encouraged to have a giant mud fight with one another (not that they needed much encouragement!). It brought them closer to nature and to one another. It got the students enthusiastic, and an enthusiastic group is a more cohesive group. And a cohesive group is better at achieving goals.

Next, I helped the group build self-confidence, giving the students incrementally more difficult tasks to accomplish. First, they went snorkeling in the Indian Ocean, with the aim of exploring a reef ecosystem and learning the importance of its conservation. Then they participated in a sociocultural exchange: as a group, they had to learn how to fish and prepare food in the traditional way of the local Tsonga culture.

Next—and here's where it got tough—they had to build a Tsonga boat and race it down the river, competing against other teams. It was important that I phrase the goal as a problem to be solved: build a boat. I established clear standards for success: floating. And with the help of the Tsonga people, I identified the resources the group would need to accomplish that goal: the tools and materials necessary to build a boat.

With a clearly defined common goal, the students were forced to communicate more effectively. Members of the group started to feel—if they hadn't already—that they were connected; their communication became interdependent.

When it was all over, students discussed and debated environmental problems and opportunities. I think that because they became better at group communication, they became better individual communicators as well.

### Performing

Once the group has established norms, the action shifts to accomplishing tasks. During the **performing** stage, members combine their skills and knowledge to work toward the group's goals and overcome hurdles. For example, in the episode "The Elements" in season four, Ryan becomes frazzled when he realizes that he used all the pomegranate juice for a salad dressing, forgetting that he would need some to make the "pomerini" cocktail as well. Nikki quickly thinks of a solution, coming to his rescue and helping their team achieve its goal.

### Adjourning

Many groups—though clearly not all—eventually disband. During the **adjourning** stage, group members reflect on their accomplishments and failures as well as determine whether the group will disassemble or take on another project. To mark this stage, some groups hold a celebratory dinner or simply say thank you and good-bye. Alternatively, some groups may decide to continue to work together on new tasks. Members may also opt to maintain friendships even if they will no longer be working together. In reality shows, some or all of the contestants will often return for a reunion episode of the season and may form friendships that endure long past the end of the show. Many *Top Chef* contestants continue to keep in touch and often support and eat at each other's restaurants.

> **AND YOU?**
>
> Think about your experience as part of a group to which you no longer belong—an old job, your high school class, or a club that you're not a part of anymore. Did the group go through all five phases described here?

## Group Size and Communication

When you chat with an instructor in her office, you probably speak freely and informally. The two of you may exchange questions and comments rapidly, interrupt one another, and prompt each other for more information. But when you sit in a classroom with that same professor and a roomful of other students, the nature of your communication changes—you would be out of line if you interrupted when she was speaking; you might be expected to raise your hand, defer to other students who are already speaking, or not ask questions at all.

● **WHEN YOU'RE** chatting with a professor during office hours, you are the focus of your professor's attention. However, in the classroom, you have to respect that other students want to speak as well!

What has changed? Why is the nature of your communication so different in the classroom from the way you converse in her office? When a situation changes from a dyad to a group, communication becomes more complex. In this section, we'll take a look at how group communication grows more complex as the number of individuals increases.

## Size and Complexity

The basic logistics of communication—the need to take turns speaking and listening, for example—grow more complex the larger a group gets. You might find it fairly easy to keep up an IM conversation with one friend online, but when a third person starts IM-ing, the communication becomes muddied and complicated. And this complexity creates the need for increasingly structured exchanges among members. Specifically, the bigger the group, the more its communication takes on the following characteristics:

▶ *Interaction is more formal.* Group communication simply cannot work in the same kind of informal way that dyadic communication occurs, due to the need to include more communicators in the discourse. Individuals participating in a group may feel the need to obtain permission to speak, and they may also be reluctant to interrupt a speaker.

▶ *Each member has limited opportunities to contribute.* Participants may want or be required by a leader to share "floor time" with other group members. Such time constraints can inhibit the quality and quantity of their contributions.

▶ *The communication becomes less intimate.* The greater the number of participants, the less comfortable participants feel self-disclosing or voicing controversial opinions.

▶ *The interaction consumes more time.* As more participants are invited to contribute or debate, the interaction takes longer to complete.

▶ *Relationships become more complex.* Another factor that separates dyads from groups concerns the complexity of the relationships that are present and must be maintained. As more participants are added, the relationships become more complex. In the dyad, of course, there is only one relationship—that between person 1 and person 2.

As indicated by Figure 8.1, adding just one person to a dyad means that each of the three members of the new group must now deal with four potential relationships—one between persons 1 and 2; another between persons 1 and 3; a third between persons 2 and 3; and finally, the group relationship among all three participants. The number of relationships at play multiplies with each additional participant that joins a group: in a group of four, there are 11 potential relationships; in a group of five, there are 90; a six-member group involves 301 relationships; and so on.

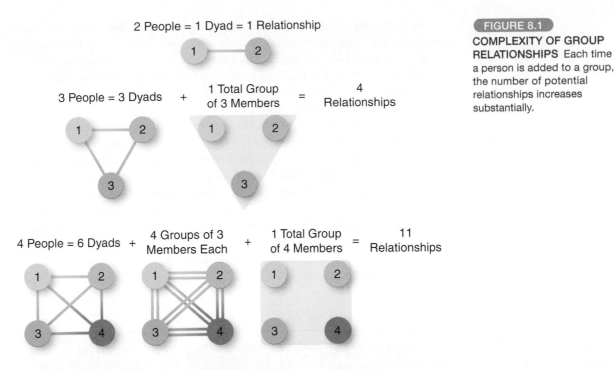

**FIGURE 8.1**
**COMPLEXITY OF GROUP RELATIONSHIPS** Each time a person is added to a group, the number of potential relationships increases substantially.

## Size and the Formation of Cliques and Coalitions

In an episode from the fourth season of *That '70s Show,* the guys (Eric, Fez, Kelso, and Hyde) decide to have a "guys' night out" at a bowling alley. Hyde ruins that plan when he's excited to have his friend Jill show up. Kelso and Fez decide to meet new women as well. Eric, however, is stuck feeling left out. The episode is appropriately titled "The Third Wheel." Perhaps you've felt like Eric—you love hanging out with your best friend, but whenever she invites you to hang out with her and her boyfriend, you feel like you might as well be invisible. That's because your presence has changed the nature of the communication from dyadic to group communication, but the other two people haven't adjusted their communication behavior. They've remained a dyad, forming a subgroup that leaves you the lone outsider.

● **THE GUYS** on *That '70s Show* are a tight-knit clique and they do almost everything together. Needless to say, Eric was probably quite disgruntled to find their "guys' night out" ruined by a bunch of girls!

As a group's size increases, similar problems arise. **Cliques** (or coalitions) emerge—small subgroups of individuals who have bonded together within a group (Wilmot, 1987). Cliques and coalitions are a common part of group life—they're a fixture in middle and high schools. You have your marching band kids, your football players, the "in" crowd, the art students, and so on. The 2004 film *Mean Girls* is a classic example of the power of high school cliques as the young women who form "the Plastics" set social agendas, influence dress and fashion, and control the rumor mill. Many people think that they will escape cliques like the Plastics once high school ends, but this is usually not the case. In college, you might be tempted to form cliques with others in your major, your dorm, or a particular organization. In office settings, members of cliques or coalitions typically sit next to each other in meetings, eat lunch together, share the same opinions about what's going on in their organization, and support one another's positions.

When cliques or coalitions take shape in a group, communication becomes more challenging because members are no longer dealing only with other individual

# EVALUATINGCOMMUNICATIONETHICS

THINK ABOUT THIS

## Sketchy Behavior

You have recently formed a comedy troupe with four other friends: Calvin, Eddie, Meredith, and Sylvia. Your first live show with the group is in just a few weeks, and your group has written and rehearsed five sketches. But you and Calvin have had doubts about one sketch, written by Eddie and Sylvia, since day one. Rather than voice your concerns, you and Calvin have been trying to come up with an alternative sketch. During a late-night session, the two of you come up with an idea for a sketch that in your opinion outclasses the one you've been having problems with.

It is now a few days before the show, and the two of you have decided, independent of the other members, that the weaker sketch needs to be changed in favor of the one you've written. You are concerned about how this will look and have a nagging feeling the other members are going to perceive your writing of this sketch as a selfish way to push your work over that of your teammates, but you feel strongly that the new sketch will make the show a greater success. Calvin suggests that you present your sketch to Meredith, since she was not involved in writing either sketch. "If we convince Meredith that our sketch is the stronger one," Calvin reasons, "we'll be able to point to her opinion as a truly objective opinion—she's got no agenda."

You're pretty certain that Meredith will prefer your sketch, not only because you feel it is better but also because it features a role that Meredith would love to play. And you know that if you talk to Meredith beforehand, you'll have a clear majority in favor of your sketch should the decision be put to a vote. But is this ethical?

❶ What role did group communication play in this scenario? Might cliques have been involved? What were other communication options?

❷ Is it unethical to attempt to gain Meredith's vote even if you honestly believe that it's in the best interest of the group?

❸ What ethical implications arise from approaching Meredith with the new sketch? Should the sketch be presented to the entire team at the same time? Is it fair to tempt Meredith with a juicy role in exchange for her vote?

members. Rather, they must navigate relationships and figure out how to communicate with entire subgroups. In addition, **countercoalitions**, in which one subgroup positions itself against another on an issue, can leave anyone who isn't affiliated with a subgroup in a very awkward position.

## Group Size and Social Loafing

On many education and learning blogs, you can find students and instructors complaining about one of the most dreaded assignments of all time: the grueling group project! Consider the following post from an angry group member: "In the 21 courses that composed my MBA program, I had to do a total of seven group projects. I won't bore you with all the gory details, but there were people who didn't do their work, control freaks who wouldn't allow anyone else's input, you name it. Group projects should be abolished." At first glance, doesn't it seem that group projects should be easier than working solo? There are more minds to share in the work and more people to try out ideas with. But what we all dread is having group members who don't pull their own weight. The fact is, the larger a group, the more prone members may become to **social loafing**—failing to invest the same level of effort in the group that they'd put in if they were working alone or with one other person. Social loafing affects all kinds of group activities, from sports competitions to professional work assignments.

Clearly, social loafing affects both participation and communication in groups (Comer, 1998; Shultz, 1999). When a person fails to speak up because he or she feels shy around a lot of people, the person is engaging in social loafing. Social loafing also results from the feelings of anonymity that occur in large groups. The larger the group, the more difficult it is for an individual member's contributions to the group's efforts to be evaluated and measured. Thus a member may put in less effort, believing that nobody will notice that he or she is slacking off or, conversely, that he or she is working hard. Social loafing even occurs in large electronic networks: some members of an online discussion group, for example, may actively engage in the discourse by posting regular messages, while others—known as lurkers—may just read others' posts and contribute very little.

> ### AND YOU?
> Is social loafing really about shyness or anonymity? Can you identify any of your own experiences in a group that you now recognize as social loafing?

## Group Networks

Just as a group's size strongly influences communication within the group, so do networks. **Networks** are patterns of interaction governing who speaks with whom in a group and about what. To understand the nature of networks, you must first consider two main positions within them. The first is *centrality*, or the degree to which an individual sends and receives messages from others in the group. The most central person in the group receives and sends the highest number of messages in a given time period. At the other end of the spectrum is *isolation*—a position from which a group member sends and receives fewer messages than other members.

A team leader or manager typically has the highest level of centrality in a formal group, but centrality is not necessarily related to status or power. The

CEO of a company, for example, may be the end recipient of all information generated by teams below her, but in fact only a limited number of individuals within the organization are able to communicate directly with her. Her secretary, in fact, may have a higher degree of centrality in the network. As you might imagine, networks play a powerful role in any group's communication, whether the group is a family, a sports team, a civic organization, or a large corporation.

### Types of Networks

In some groups, all members speak with all others regularly about a wide range of topics. In others, perhaps only a few members are "allowed" to speak directly with the group's leader or longest-standing member about serious issues. In still other groups, some members may work alongside one another without communicating at all. There are several types of networks (as indicated by Figure 8.2) (Bavelous, 1950). In a **chain network**, information is passed from one member to the next rather than shared among members. Such networks can be practical for sharing written information. But this form of group communication can lead to frustration and miscommunication when information is conveyed through other codes, such as spoken words. It can be like a game of telephone, where the message gets distorted as it progresses down the chain. Person A tells person B that their boss, Luis, had a fender bender on the way to work and will miss the 10:00 A.M. meeting. Person B tells person C that Luis was in an accident and will not be in the office today. Person C tells person D that Luis was injured in an accident; no one knows when he'll be in. You can imagine that Luis will be in a full-body cast by the time the message reaches person G!

In an **all-channel network**, all members are an equal distance from one another, and all members interact with each other. When people talk about round-table discussions, they're talking about all-channel groups: there is no leader, and all members operate at equal levels of centrality. Such networks can be useful for collaborative projects and for brainstorming ideas, but the lack of order can make it difficult for such groups to complete tasks.

Wheel networks are a sensible solution for situations in which individual members' activities and contributions must be culled and tracked in order to avoid duplicating efforts and to ensure that all tasks are being completed. In a **wheel network**, one individual acts as a touchstone for all the others in the

**AND YOU?**

What group are you spending most of your time in these days? What type of communication network exists in the group? Is that network helping the group achieve its goals? If not, what changes might the group make to operate more effectively?

**FIGURE 8.2**
GROUP COMMUNICATION
NETWORKS

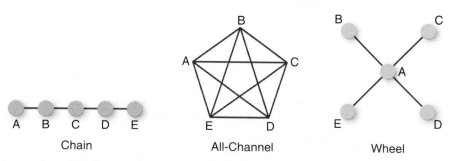

Chain    All-Channel    Wheel

Source: Scott (1981), p. 8. Adapted with permission.

group; all group members share their information with that one individual, who then shares the information with the rest of the group. In a newsroom, for example, a team of copyeditors works under a copy chief, who must ensure that all news items are edited, that articles are not redundant, and that the copyediting style is consistent. Such groups have the lowest shared centrality but are very efficient (Leavitt, 1951).

### Changing the Shape of a Network

In some groups, the network produces communication that's ineffective or problematic. In such cases, you will want to think about ways to change the shape of the network to improve communication within the group.

● **THE COPYEDITING TEAM** in a newsroom works as a wheel network. All the copy-editors report to one copy chief, who regulates the copyediting style.

For example, suppose you're part of a group whose members seem to be engaging in a lot of activity, interacting constantly, and getting along well. But the group's not really being productive; it's not achieving its goals. When you examine the patterns of communication within the group, you see that an all-channel network exists in the group. You realize that the group would be far more productive if someone took on a leadership role and became more central in the group's network. You encourage Diane, a member of the group, to take on this role. She agrees and begins asking the other members of the group to report regularly to her on their activities. This simple change has altered the network shape from all-channel to a wheel. Important information has begun flowing to the leader, who needs it to make key decisions.

## Additional Factors Affecting Group Communication

In addition to size and networks, numerous other factors affect communication within groups—most notably interdependence, cohesion, group climate, norms, roles, clarity of goals, groupthink and conflict, and individual differences. In the sections that follow, we explore each of these additional factors in more detail.

## Interdependence

As you've seen, interdependence is one defining characteristic of a group. In a true group, members need one another to accomplish the group's goals, and each member's actions and decisions affect the other members. This interdependence can foster a feeling of responsibility and a commitment to the group's efforts. Members gain a sense of ownership over the tasks they're carrying out for the group and the decisions they're making. Thus the result of the group's efforts—be it a product, a service, or an idea—belongs to the group and not to any one member. Likewise, failures are seen as shared

● THE *MYTHBUSTERS* team is an interdependent one. They rely on one another and share ideas, like trying to lift a sunken boat by pumping it full of Ping-Pong balls.

In Chapter 3, we discuss *jargon,* vocabulary unique to a specific hobby or profession. Jargon helps build group cohesiveness as it connects members to one another and distinguishes them from outsiders. A group of police officers might speak about perps (perpetrators), vics (victims), collars (arrests), and brass (supervisors)—terms that their mechanic or physician friends would not use. This use of language helps officers bond as a group.

by the group, not as the fault of a particular member. Interdependence thus strengthens group identity and strongly affects communication. Indeed, the more interdependent a group is, the more its members will use words such as *we, us,* and *our* during meetings and conversations.

Interestingly, the use of such language further reinforces feelings of interdependence. Thus interdependence both affects *and* is affected by communication in the group. On a baseball team, for example, if a big hitter doesn't come through in the clutch and the team loses the game, all the members of the team (fielders, pitchers, catchers, managers) acknowledge their role in the loss, just as they would all have shared in a victory.

## Cohesion

**Cohesion** is the degree to which group members have bonded and consider themselves to be one entity. A cohesive group identifies itself as a single unit rather than a collection of individuals, which helps hold the group together in the face of adversity. Much research has focused on how cohesion affects a group's effectiveness and communication. In general, cohesive groups perform much better than noncohesive groups on decision-making tasks (for example, selecting a course of action more quickly and making more informed choices) (Carless & DePaola, 2000).

You can determine group cohesion in two ways. First, take a look at how the participants feel about their own membership in the group. Members of a cohesive group are enthusiastic, identify with the purposes of the group, and tell outsiders about its activities. Even positive, constructive argumentation (as opposed to verbal aggressiveness) can be a sign of group cohesiveness (Anderson & Martin, 1999).

Second, consider how well the group retains members. A cohesive group will retain more members than a noncohesive group. That's why employers are often concerned with employee turnover—the number of people leaving and joining the staff. Not only do the arrival and departure of staff cost time and money for retraining and such, but they also affect—and reflect—group cohesion. The more that members receive satisfaction and fulfill their needs through their group participation, the more cohesive the group. Shaw (1988) provides numerous ideas about cohesiveness:

▶ Member satisfaction is greater in high-cohesion groups than in low-cohesion groups.

▶ High-cohesion groups exert greater influence over their members than low-cohesion groups.

▶ Communication is more extensive and more positive in high-cohesion groups than in low-cohesion groups.

▶ High-cohesion groups are more effective than low-cohesion groups in achieving goals.

Clearly, cohesion can make or break an individual group.

# COMMUNICATIONACROSSCULTURES

## The Multilingual Locker Room: Communicating in the Modern NHL

Sharing a common code seems like it would be imperative in any group. But what do you do when a group is so diverse that its members don't even speak the same language?

Historically, National Hockey League teams have always been multilingual, composed primarily of English-speaking Americans and Canadians and French-speaking Quebecois, with some players from western Europe. But when the Iron Curtain came down in the late 1980s, players from eastern Europe headed for North America. Although fluent in the language of hockey, many were less skilled in English.

How do English-speaking coaches and teammates build team cohesiveness, discuss plays, and provide training and assistance when individual players might speak only Czech or Russian?

When it comes to getting the job done, most players and coaches simply use alternative communication codes—tools other than language—to get meaning across. When Pavel Bure, the "Russian Rocket," entered the NHL in 1991, he didn't speak any English. "The coach told me where to go and what to do on the chalkboard," Bure explained years later ("He Said What?" 1999). It worked: Bure was named rookie of the year. Hockey players also rely on nonverbal behavior—movements of the face, eyes, and arms—to communicate with each other. NHL players develop shared nonverbal meanings so they can communicate effectively on the ice. As French Canadian Hall of Famer Denis Potvin noted, "I could play with a guy and look at his eyes and see his movement and tell where he was going. It was never an issue of, 'OK, pass me the puck NOW!'" ("He Said What?" 1999).

However, hockey players' nonverbal communication skills are probably most effective when hockey is the focus. Professional players, as well as coaches and game officials, share an intricate understanding of the game that can make communicating about plays and strategy using symbols and gestures easier. However, they might have a harder time using the same tools to communicate about other things, such as baking a cake!

Lacking a shared language also makes it harder for teammates to build group cohesion. Consequently, many teams instigated English-only rules for players and coaches to smooth communication and discourage the development of cliques within the teams. "What happens here sometimes is if three Czech players are sitting together and talking Czech between periods, other guys don't understand what they're talking about," Florida Panthers general manager Bryan Murray said. "We're asking our guys to be a team, and to respect that if you're going to be a team, you have to have a common way to communicate" ("He Said What?" 1999). To discourage clubhouse cliques, the Washington Capitals fine players $100 for not speaking English. Most players are willing to go along with this, as they feel that learning a common language fosters team unity and makes foreign-born players feel less isolated.

**THINK ABOUT THIS**

❶ How might instituting an English-only policy help increase group cohesion? What might the downsides of such a policy be?

❷ Who is responsible for developing a shared code when coaches and players speak different languages? How might the rules of communication be worked out between individuals who speak different languages?

❸ What other cultural differences might inhibit communication on a professional sports team? How does multiculturalism and globalization affect other sports?

Nonverbal behaviors (Chapter 4) offer insights into a group's climate. The climate is positive in groups where members show involvement and interest by allowing others to speak, nodding to show active listening, and speaking with an upbeat tone of voice. Negative climates, by contrast, are characterized by group members with downcast expressions who interrupt each other or roll their eyes while someone is speaking.

## Group Climate

Just as we find with interpersonal relationships, over time a group will develop a unique temperament called a *climate* (Folger, Poole, & Stutman, 2001). A group's climate influences what it feels like to be a member, as well as how members behave and communicate with one another. Not surprisingly, groups with a positive climate, where members take pride in the group, treat each other with respect, feel confident about their abilities, and so forth, have better success in accomplishing their goals. And after achieving one goal, members often feel motivated to "go for more." A positive climate can also foster optimism and confidence in the face of obstacles. A self-confident group tends to minimize problems, eliminate barriers, and cope well with crises. Its members believe they cannot be defeated.

How can you cultivate a positive climate in the groups you belong to? You can remind yourself and your fellow group members to adopt the following communication practices (Gouran, 2003):

▶ Avoid dominating other members.

▶ Stay focused on the tasks the group must accomplish.

▶ Be friendly.

▶ Show sensitivity to and respect for other members.

▶ Demonstrate that you value others' opinions.

▶ Cooperate with other members rather than competing with them.

The responsibility for promoting a positive climate rests with all group members. However, you can do your part by applying these practices. Behave in these ways yourself, and you just might inspire your fellow group members to follow suit!

## Norms

As you saw earlier in the chapter, over time a group will develop norms. Norms are determined by the group itself and are imposed by members on themselves and each other. Norms direct the behavior of the group as a whole and affect the conduct of individual members. In a business environment, norms might dictate the kinds of topics that can be expressed in a meeting (Should non-task-related conversation be interjected? Are jokes appropriate?). In an online group, norms might evolve to govern the use of foul language or the submission of spoilers that give away endings to books or films. In either setting, norms might also set the ground rules for how long someone speaks, who should speak first, and whether negative comments and criticism are acceptable.

Some norms have a negative impact on communication. For example, suppose a group permits one member to dominate the conversation or allows members to dismiss an idea before discussing its pros and cons. A group with these norms will have difficulty generating enough diverse ideas to make informed decisions. If you find yourself in a group with unproductive norms like these, consider modifying them—this is possible if you approach the task diplomatically (Brilhart & Galanes, 1992). The following three-step process can help:

1. *Express your loyalty and dedication to the group, to show that you have the group's best interests at heart.* For instance, "I've been a member of this school committee for two years now and have hung in there during the tough times as well as the good times. I want to see us be the best we can be."

2. *Cite specific examples of the behavior you find harmful to the group's effectiveness.* To illustrate, "When we didn't take time to explore the pros and cons of the special-ed funding strategy that came up last month, we ended up making a decision that we regretted later."

3. *Ask other members for their opinions about the problem norm you've identified.* If others feel that the norm is still warranted, they may advocate keeping it ("Well, there are some situations where we don't have as much time as we'd like to consider the merits of an idea. During those moments, we need to be able to move ahead with a decision quickly"). With respectful, productive discussion, the group may decide to maintain the norm, change it under specific conditions ("We'll have someone play devil's advocate when time allows"), or abandon it entirely.

## Roles

Individuals often play specific roles in the group, and these roles influence members' behavior and group communication. There are three types of roles—task, social, and antigroup. Let's look at each of them in turn.

### Task Roles

In some cases, a role is defined by a task that needs doing, and a person is asked or appointed to fill it (or he or she volunteers). Such **task roles** are concerned with the accomplishment of the group's goals—specifically, the activities that need to be carried out for the group to achieve its objectives. For example, your role on a committee charged with organizing a sorority rush party might be to post advertisements for the event in key locations around campus and in the campus newspaper.

Task roles can also be specifically related to the group's communication; for instance:

▶ An *information giver* offers facts, beliefs, personal experience, or other input during group discussions ("When the sisters of Chi Omega posted their ad in the student lounge, they had good attendance at their rush party").

▶ An *information seeker* asks for additional input or clarification of ideas or opinions that members have presented ("Jane, are you saying you're not comfortable with the party theme we're proposing?").

▶ An *elaborator* provides further clarification of points, often adding to what others have said ("I agree with Ellie about selecting Currier & Chives as our caterer; my friend works there, and she's a great cook").

▶ An *initiator* helps the group move toward its objective by proposing solutions, presenting new ideas, or suggesting new ways of looking at an issue the group is discussing ("How essential is it that we schedule the rush party for the last Friday of the month? If we moved it a week later, we'd have more time to find the right band").

▶ An *administrator* keeps the conversation on track ("OK, let's get back to the subject of when to schedule the party") and ensures that meetings begin and end on time ("We've got five minutes left; should we wind up?").

### Social Roles

Some group roles evolve to reflect individual members' personality traits and interests; such roles are called **social roles**. For example, a nurturing housemate might unofficially fill the role of "house parent"—baking cookies for everyone, listening compassionately to people's problems, and making everyone feel taken care of. Consider these additional examples of social roles (Anderson, Riddle, & Martin, 1999; Benne & Sheats, 1948; Salazar, 1996):

▶ A *harmonizer* seeks to smooth over tension in the group by settling differences among members ("OK, you both want the party to succeed; you just have different ideas about how to get there").

▶ A *gatekeeper* works to ensure that each member of the group contributes to discussions ("Tonya, we haven't heard from you yet on this question of when to schedule the party. What are your thoughts?").

▶ A *sensor* expresses group feelings, moods, or relationships in an effort to recognize the climate and capitalize on it or modify it for the better ("I'm registering a lot of frustration in the committee right now. Let's take a break and reconnect in half an hour").

● **THE THEME SONG** of *Arrested Development* establishes Michael Bluth's role as a harmonizer: "Now the story of a wealthy family who lost everything and the one son who had no choice but to keep them all together."

Each member in a group can play task *and* social roles. For example, though Evelyn was appointed chairperson of the rush party committee, she also serves as the group's unofficial harmonizer because she has a knack for mitigating tensions between people. Members can also adopt a personal or task role if they believe the role is needed but no one else seems to be willing to fill it. To illustrate, by the end of the rush party committee's first meeting, Candace noticed an air of excitement infusing the gathering as ideas for the party theme began flying back and forth. Wanting to build on that excitement and channel it into commitment to the group's cause, she took on the role of sensor. As the meeting came to a close, each member took a moment to explain what tasks she would be responsible for that week. When Candace's turn came, she told the other members, "I'm really excited about all the progress we made today. I think that with this kind of enthusiasm, we're going to throw the best rush party in our history!" The meeting ended on a high note, and members adjourned eager to dig into their tasks.

### Antigroup Roles

Unlike task and social roles, **antigroup roles** create problems because they serve individual members' priorities at the expense of group needs. You've probably seen evidence of these antigroup roles in the groups you belong to:

> ▶ A *blocker* indulges in destructive communication, including opposing all ideas and stubbornly reintroducing an idea after the group has already rejected or bypassed it ("None of the dates any of you proposed will work for the party. It really needs to be five weeks from today, as I said earlier").

> ▶ An *avoider* refuses to engage in the group's proceedings by expressing cynicism or nonchalance toward ideas presented or by joking or changing the subject ("Well, whatever, I'm guessing it's not a big deal if this party doesn't even happen, right?").

> ▶ A *recognition seeker* calls attention to himself or herself by boasting or by going on and on about his or her qualifications or personal achievements ("I planned a gathering for a women's studies group last year, and it went really well. People still talk about it! So trust me on this one").

> ▶ A *distractor* goes off on tangents or tells irrelevant stories ("Does anyone know what happened on *Grey's Anatomy* last night? I missed it").

To mitigate the impact of these antigroup roles, members can revisit the norms the group has established and make the changes needed to improve group communication (for example, "All ideas get a fair hearing"). People fulfilling certain task or social roles can also help. For instance, if you're a gatekeeper, you can prompt an avoider to contribute her opinion on a proposal that the group has been considering.

### Role Conflict

Imagine that you work at a local stationery store and you've been promoted to store manager. As part of your new role, you will have to manage staff members who are working as individual contributors at the store. Several of them are also your close friends, and you all used to be at the same level in the store.

**Role conflict** arises in a group whenever expectations for a member's behavior are incompatible. The roles of manager and friend are inherently in conflict. After all, as a manager, you'll have to evaluate staff members' performance. And how can you give a good friend a poor performance review and still remain friends?

As you might imagine, role conflict can make group communication profoundly challenging, and there are no easy answers to this kind of dilemma. In the case of the stationery store, you might decide not to give your friend a negative review in the interest of saving the friendship. Or perhaps you'll decide to give candid constructive feedback to your friend on his performance. But you'll try to constrain the damage to your friendship by saying something like "I hope you know I'm offering this feedback as a way to help you improve. As your friend and manager, I want to see you do well here."

**CONNECT**

Competent leadership can address problematic antigroup roles. As you learn in Chapter 9, a *directive leader* might lay out tasks to thwart a distractor; a *supportive leader* might thank each member for his or her contributions, preventing a recognition seeker from claiming all the glory. Leaders have the power to affect norms and roles, encouraging group members to make productive contributions.

**AND YOU?**

Have you ever been in a leadership role among a group of friends? Have you ever been subordinate to a friend in a group situation? Did any conflict arise, and if so, how did you resolve it?

## Clarity of Goals

Think of the worst group meeting you've ever attended. How would you describe that meeting? Was the conversation disorganized? Unproductive? Confusing? Did all the talking seem like just a lot of hot air and a huge waste of time? Did you leave the meeting with a bad feeling about working with the group again in the future? When people have these kinds of reactions to a group's communication, the culprit is very likely the lack of a clear goal. To communicate productively in any group, members need goal clarity: that is, they must understand what the group's purpose is, what goals will help the group achieve its purpose, how close the group is to achieving its goals, and whether the activities members are engaging in are helping the group move toward its goals.

Goals vary considerably from one group to another. For example, a team in one of your classes may have the simple goal of completing a fifteen-minute in-class exercise and reporting the results to the rest of the class. Your volunteer group at a rape crisis center may have the goal of helping victims recover from their ordeal. An urban beautification fund-raising committee may have the goal of collecting $4,000 for new landscaping at a neighborhood park.

How can you make sure your group has clear goals? You might suggest the goals yourself. However, you'll get even better results by encouraging the rest of the members to define the group's goals. When members take part in establishing goals, they feel more committed to and excited about achieving those objectives. Research has also shown that a group is more likely to reach its goals when those goals are communicated in terms that are specific ("Raise $4,000 by the end of March"), inspiring ("Imagine our neighborhood becoming a community of choice for young families"), and prioritized ("We'll need to focus on this goal first and then this other one next") (O'Hair, Friedrich, & Dixon, 2002).

Groups are also more likely to reach their goals if members have some autonomy in deciding how to achieve them. For example, everyone on the urban beautification committee has agreed that the group wants to raise $4,000 by the end of March. But the committee chair decides not to dictate how the group should approach this task. Instead, he invites members to brainstorm ideas for reaching the goal. By encouraging people to come up with ways to achieve the goal, a group leader ensures that members produce a wide range of ideas. And the more ideas the group explores, the more likely its members will ultimately make an informed choice about how to move forward.

Here are some additional communication strategies for setting group goals effectively (O'Hair et al., 2002):

▶ *Define goals in terms of problems to be solved* (for example, "Our goal is to raise $4,000 to beautify Dixon Park"), *not values to be embodied* ("Our goal is to be good citizens of this community"). Value-based goals are vague, so it's difficult to know if and when you've achieved them. (What does "being a good citizen" mean in practice, anyway?)

▶ *Establish clear performance standards.* How will your group know when it has succeeded in reaching its goal? For example, "We will have $4,000 in our checking account by the last day of March."

▶ *Identify the resources your group will need to accomplish its goals.* Include such things as members' time, office space, funds, and equipment. By anticipating resources, you avoid getting into a situation where your worthy goal shrivels and dies because it never received sufficient funding or attention.

▶ *Recognize contingencies that may arise.* For instance, "Our goal is to have $4,000 in our account by the end of March, on the assumption that we have good weather for the fund-raising campaign we're planning to hold on the town common."

▶ *Determine how you will monitor and report progress toward your group's goals.* Will the group hold a weekly status meeting? Will members circulate daily e-mails to update one another?

Once your group begins working toward its goals, encourage yourself and your fellow members to talk regularly about the decisions you're making and the actions you're taking, to ensure that these all support progress toward the goals.

## Groupthink and Conflict

As you learned in Chapter 7, engaging in productive conflict fosters healthy debate and leads to better decision making. Unity and cohesion are important for groups to operate effectively, but if these qualities are taken to an extreme—that is, if they become more powerful than members' desire to evaluate alternative courses of action—the group can't generate enough diverse ideas to make smart decisions.

Consider the tragic explosion of the U.S. space shuttle *Challenger* in 1986. Prior to launch, there had been some concern among many engineers that certain fittings (called O-rings) might fail, but the shuttle launched in spite of these concerns. Eventually, those fittings were indeed found to be related to the explosion, but a large part of the blame for the disaster was laid on communications failures within NASA. Engineers later testified that the climate at NASA made them reluctant to voice their concerns if they couldn't back them up with a full set of data (McConnell, 1987). Indeed, the Rogers Commission (1986),

● **SOMETIMES VOICING** dissent is more important than group unity. If the engineers at NASA had shared their concerns, the *Challenger* disaster might not have happened.

which investigated the disaster, noted that had safety concerns been more clearly articulated—and had NASA management been more receptive to concerns raised by engineers from various departments—it is unlikely that *Challenger* would have launched that day.

The *Challenger* explosion is often pointed to as a classic example of **groupthink**—a situation in which group members strive to minimize conflict by refusing to critically examine ideas, analyze proposals, or test solutions (Janis, 1982). Groupthink results from overly strong feelings of loyalty and unity within a group and from too much cohesion (Park, 2000). In a more receptive group climate, a productive conflict over the O-rings might have revealed the problems that the engineers sensed but couldn't quite put their fingers on. The following are some symptoms of groupthink:

► Participants reach outward consensus and avoid expressing disagreement so as not to hurt each other's feelings or appear disloyal.

► Members who do express disagreement with the majority are pressured to conform to the majority view.

► Tough questions are ignored or discouraged.

► Members spend more effort justifying their decisions than testing them.

The best way to prevent groupthink is to encourage dissent among members *and* manage it productively (Klocke, 2007). Some of the same practices for handling interpersonal conflict discussed in Chapter 7 can help you deal constructively with disagreements in a group. For example, frame conflicts as disagreements over issues or ideas, not as evidence of a weak character or some other personal shortcoming in particular members. To illustrate, when someone in the group expresses a dissenting viewpoint, don't say, "It's clear that you aren't as dedicated to our cause as I had hoped" or "Jim here obviously doesn't know what he's talking about." Instead, you might say something like "It looks like we have some different ideas circulating about how to handle this new problem that has come up. Let's list these ideas and talk about the possible benefits and risks of each of them."

## Individual Differences

Members of a particular group may share goals and an identity, but they each bring personal differences to the group as well. And these differences can strongly affect communication. Let's examine how cultural factors and comfort levels—which vary by individual—affect our ability to communicate in groups.

### Cultural Factors

As you've learned throughout this book, culture has a big impact on how we communicate. And when a group has culturally diverse members, that diversity can have benefits (such as enabling the group to produce a wide array of viewpoints) as well as challenges (including misunderstandings between members).

As we noted earlier, cultures in nations such as the United States, Great Britain, and Canada are largely *individualist*. Their members value personal accomplishment and competition and strive to differentiate themselves from one another. In an individualist culture, people place a high value on leadership and view "followers" as supporting figures. People from an individualist culture tend to want to control group discussions and to see their ideas "win" in any debate within the group. In a *collectivist* culture (such as that in Japan, China, and Pakistan), people value cooperation and group harmony. They allow group norms (rather than their own personal goals) to have the largest influence on their behaviors and thoughts (Triandis, Brislin, & Hul, 1988). They are more drawn to consensus than to dissent.

Not surprisingly, consensus seeking does not come as easily for most individualists as it does for collectivists (Cathcart & Cathcart, 1997). People from individualist cultures tend to vocalize their disagreement with others, while collectivists prefer to take stock of other group members' feelings and opinions without expressing their own objections or doubts. Obviously, these differences can create communication challenges in a culturally diverse group.

Gender and sex differences can also affect group communication largely due to the social expectations of masculine and feminine individuals. For example, research shows that women are socially encouraged to focus on establishing relationships within a group, while men—who are socialized to focus on autonomy and success—tend to pay more attention to completing the task at hand (Baird, 1986). Moreover, some men seek to display signs of their power while communicating in groups (for example, pointing out their credentials or their achievements). Meanwhile, women are more likely to show signs of affection toward each other. Men tend to perceive power as something to be claimed and used to increase personal status. Women often perceive power as something to be shared, a resource for empowering oneself and others (Helgesen, 1990). In addition, women tend to use complaining as an indirect request for action in a group setting, while men use complaining as an explanation for their behavior or as a way to make themselves appear superior (Alicke et al., 1992).

An exaggerated example of these types of differences can be seen in the "Girls Just Want to Have Sums" episode of *The Simpsons* (from season seventeen). After Principal Skinner has a nervous breakdown following a sexist comment about women's ability to achieve in mathematics, a new female principal takes over and separates Springfield Elementary into boys' and girls' schools. The new group setting and dynamics at first appeal to Lisa, who enjoys the camaraderie of the other girls in the absence of boys, but things turn ugly when she enters math class for the first time. Instead of the task-focused nature of the classroom in the mixed or all boys' school, the girls' school focuses on *feeling* math, self-esteem, and group sing-alongs. Lisa misses the hard number-crunching and problem-solving focus of her old class. So she dons some boys' clothes and crosses the sex barriers to attend the all boys' school where she can learn without anyone worrying about hurting people's feelings! Lisa rejected her gender socialization in order to find a more appropriate group setting in which to further her study of her favorite subject.

● **POOR LISA.** She enjoys the camaraderie of other girls at school, but she wants to learn how to *do* math, not feel it!

MATT GROENING

If you suffer from communication apprehension in groups, you're probably aware of the negative effects it can have on your social and professional life. Luckily, there are many strategies for dealing with apprehension, as we discuss in Chapter 13. Check out our tips on *systematic desensitization, deep muscle relaxation, cognitive restructuring,* and *self-talk* to conquer your fears and improve your competency in groups.

## Communication Apprehension

The next time you're sitting in your communication classroom or logging on to a discussion forum in your online course, take a peek around. Is there someone who never speaks up or raises a hand? Is there someone who rarely posts thoughts on a discussion board? Perhaps you're assuming that this person has nothing to say or that he or she is a social loafer. Maybe you're right. But it's also possible that this individual feels uncomfortable participating in group conversation even when his or her contribution would clearly help the group. What explains this communication apprehension? Scholars have identified several causes (Schullery & Gibson, 2001):

▶ *Lack of self-esteem.* When an individual doubts the worth of his contributions, he may decline to speak up in a group. Fear of being wrong, of being mocked, or of creating a bad impression can further lead to communication apprehension.

▶ *Status differences.* Group members who hold a relatively low position in the group's social or political hierarchy may avoid disagreeing with their superiors in the group because they fear retribution from the more powerful persons.

▶ *Unbalanced participation.* When a group member—or a small number of group members—dominates the conversation in a group, the less aggressive members may retreat from communicating. This strongly influences how decisions get made in the group. One classic study found that groups tend to adopt ideas that receive the largest number of favorable comments (Hoffman & Maier, 1964). If most of those comments come from a single member *and* that person has inaccurate or incomplete information to back up his or her argument, the group risks making a faulty decision.

Some simple techniques can help a group address communication apprehension among members. For example, to ease self-esteem problems, consider starting a group meeting by having each member tell the member to their left what he or she appreciates about that person. To neutralize status differences, have members sit in a circle and invite lower-status members to speak before higher-status ones. To rebalance participation, suggest a norm that calls for *everyone* to weigh in on ideas presented in the group. Or look for members who are holding back and invite them specifically to contribute their views.

● **PARIS GELLER** of the *Gilmore Girls* has strong opinions. When working on group projects, she gets bossy and aggressive; other group members simply defer to her.

## what about you?

○ **How Well Do You Interact in a Group Setting?**

In order to test how apprehensive you might be in a group setting, complete the following six items, which are based on the Personal Report of Communication Apprehension (PRCA-24). Use the following scale: 1 = strongly agree; 2 = agree; 3 = undecided; 4 = disagree; and 5 = strongly disagree.

_____ 1. I do not like to participate in group discussions.

_____ 2. Generally, I feel comfortable participating in group discussions.

_____ 3. I am tense and nervous while participating in group discussions.

_____ 4. I like to get involved in group discussions.

_____ 5. I get tense and nervous when I engage in a group discussion with new people.

_____ 6. I am calm and relaxed while participating in group discussions.

*Scoring:* Use the following formula, in which the numbers in parentheses represent your answers to the six items. (For example, if you answered "4" for item 1, then replace the "1" in the formula with a 4.)

$$18 - (1) + (2) - (3) + (4) - (5) + (6)$$

A score of 24 or above indicates a high level of communication apprehension for participation in group discussions; a score of 12 or below indicates a low level of communication apprehension for this situation.

Source: McCroskey (1982). Adapted with permission.

## BACK TO ▷ Wikipedia

At the beginning of this chapter, we talked about Wikipedia, the most successful open-source site on the Web today. Consider the nature of the Wikipedia community in light of what you've learned in this chapter.

▶ The communication network at Wikipedia is essentially a circle network, where all contributors carry relatively equal weight in arguments. A traditional encyclopedia, on the other hand, works more like a wheel network, with contributions from many sources that are filtered through a main editor or publisher who takes responsibility for what is printed. As one librarian noted, "The main problem [with Wikipedia] is the lack of authority. With printed publications, the publishers have to ensure that their data is reliable, as their livelihood depends on it. But with something like this, all that goes out the window" (Waldman, 2004, para. 8).

▶ Why do people contribute to a site like Wikipedia? According to founder Jimmy Wales, it's not altruism or a desire for rewards; it's because "doing intellectual things socially is a lot of fun" ("10 Questions," 2007, para. 9). But in fact, many contributors' goals are in fact reward-driven: Wikipedia offers an open invitation for interest groups, corporations, or anyone else to edit entries to suit their own needs. Users of the site need to think about contributors' goals when they read articles.

▶ It's up to the community to deal with content issues, meaning that conflicts can and do erupt between contributors. Existing rules allow the community to ban fraudulent posters, and the organization is currently developing tools that will enable the community to quarantine edits from new contributors ("10 Questions," 2007).

▶ The EssJay fraud case is an example of a violation of norms in the group, which is largely built on trust. EssJay's use of fraudulent credentials, which he leaned on to support his edits and gain power in arbitrating disputes, was unacceptable to the community at large (Cohen, 2007).

▶ And in case you were wondering, according to Wikipedia, as of April 2008, there have only been seventeen perfect games in more than 130 years of major league baseball; Mary Harris "Mother" Jones was a nineteenth-century labor activist; the name Arcade Fire refers to a story about a fire in a New Hampshire arcade—most likely untrue—that the group's leader, Win Butler, heard as a child; and Halley's comet, last seen from the earth in 1986, will return in 2061.

## THINGS TO TRY

1. Consider a group to which you belong—your communication class, your family, your religious community, etc. Draw a chart that depicts members of the group and the patterns of communication among them. What kind of network does the group most closely resemble?

2. Read up on the history of some influential but now defunct music group (such as the Beatles, Nirvana, or Public Enemy). Did the group go through all the stages of group development outlined in this chapter? How did the group determine roles and establish norms? How did members deal with conflict? How did the eventual disbanding of the group play out?

3. Consider the adjourning phase of group development for a group you were part of that disbanded—Scouts, a sports team, the school newspaper staff—and think about what aspects of the group made for the hardest good-bye from the

group. Are high-performing groups hardest to leave? Groups with the clearest established norms? What sorts of closing rituals have you experienced?

4. The telephone game, passing a message from person to person, is fun simply because of the inevitable message distortion that gets revealed at the end. Can you think of a time when a message was passed to you from an indirect source that you discovered to be blatantly wrong? Maybe it was bungled homework instructions or a wrong meeting time or place. Given these sorts of problems, what type of workplace might function best with a chain network?

5. Analyze the group dynamics from five of your favorite television shows. See if you can identify the various social and antigroup role types in each of the groups.

6. The *Challenger* disaster is a classic example of groupthink. Run an Internet search on "groupthink," and find other historical examples. Have any of these occurred in your lifetime? How are they similar to or different from the *Challenger* incident?

## IF YOU'RE INTERESTED

*Team of Rivals: The Political Genius of Abraham Lincoln,* by Doris Kearns Goodwin (New York: Simon & Schuster, 2005)

Noted historian Goodwin examines President Lincoln's unique cabinet, which he staffed with three of his fiercest political rivals. An intriguing look at the ways in which successfully engaging in productive group conflict leads to better decision making.

*Band of Brothers,* by Stephen E. Ambrose (New York: Simon & Schuster, 1992) and the HBO series by the same name

Ambrose follows the men of E Company, 506th Regiment, 101st Airborne throughout their trials in World War II. The experience was so powerful that the surviving men remained friends for the rest of their lives.

*The Breakfast Club* (A&M Films, 1985)

In this classic coming-of-age film, a group of teenagers who seem to have nothing in common are forced to spend a day of detention in the high school library as punishment for various indiscretions. The students—each representing a specific high school stereotype (athlete, criminal, brain, princess, outcast)—meet, fight, and eventually bond. The group's progression from a random collection of strangers to a cohesive group follows a clear pattern common in group dynamics.

*Mean Girls* (Paramount Pictures, 2004)

Based largely on the nonfiction book *Queen Bees and Wannabes: Helping Your Daughter Survive Cliques, Gossip, Boyfriends, and Other Realities of Adolescence,* by Rosalind Wiseman, *Mean Girls* deftly examines the ways in which cliques shape and are shaped by teenage girls.

*The Wire* (HBO television series, 2002–2008; available on DVD)

Each season of this highly acclaimed series examines group communication related to a specific reality of urban life, from public safety and education to labor and politics. Throughout the series, a group of detectives must work within—and sometimes around—a crushing bureaucracy to bring down drug dealers who work in a similarly ordered group. As you watch, note the degree to which particular characters are isolated or centralized within group networks and how these positions affect events and relationships in the story.

*The Commitments* (United Artists, 1991)

Goals, roles, networks, and leadership all play a role in the short rise and fall of a group of down-and-out young Dubliners who form a soul band in the early 1990s. Based on the novel by Roddy Doyle, *The Commitments* touches on many nuances of group behavior and offers insights into stages of group development.

**Now that you have finished reading this chapter, you can**

List the characteristics and types of groups and explain how groups develop:

▶ A **group** is a collection of more than two people who have a shared identity, have common goals, and are interdependent (p. 228).

▶ **Primary groups** are long-standing and meaningful groups, such as family groups (p. 229).

▶ Specific function groups include **support groups**, **social groups**, **problem-solving groups**, **study groups**, and **focus groups** (pp. 229–230).

▶ A **team** is a task-oriented group, and a **self-directed work team** is a group with responsibility for producing high-quality finished work (pp. 230–231).

▶ Groups develop through five specific stages: **forming**, **storming**, **norming** (**norms** are recurring patterns of thought or behavior), **performing**, and **adjourning** (pp. 233–235).

Understand how group size affects communication:

▶ The bigger the group, the more interaction becomes formal, less intimate, more time-consuming, and complex and the less opportunity members have to contribute (p. 236).

▶ The bigger the group, the more likely **cliques** (coalitions)—small subgroups—will emerge, making communication more challenging (p. 238).

▶ A **countercoalition**—a subgroup positioned against another subgroup—may leave unaffiliated members in an awkward position (p. 239).

▶ The larger the group, the more members are prone to **social loafing**, giving less effort (p. 239).

Identify the influence of networks in groups:

▶ **Networks** are patterns of interaction governing who speaks with whom in a group (p. 239).

▶ The member who sends and receives the most messages has the highest degree of centrality; the other end of the spectrum is isolation (p. 239).

▶ In a **chain network**, information is passed from one member to the next rather than shared among members (p. 240).

▶ In an **all-channel network**, all members are equidistant and all interact with each other (p. 240).

▶ In a **wheel network**, one individual is the touchstone for the others (p. 240).

Analyze aspects that determine a group's effectiveness:

▶ Interdependence strengthens group identity and shared commitment (p. 241).

▶ **Cohesion**, how tightly group members have bonded, helps hold the group together in the face of adversity (p. 242).

▶ A positive climate fosters optimism and confidence (p. 244).

▶ Norms direct the behavior of the group, sometimes negatively, requiring modification (p. 244).

Define the roles individuals play in a group:

▶ **Task roles** involve accomplishment of goals and include information giver, information seeker, elaborator, initiator, and administrator (pp. 245–246).

▶ **Social roles** evolve based on personality traits and members' interests and include harmonizer, gatekeeper, and sensor (p. 246).

▶ **Antigroup roles** put individual needs above group needs and include blocker, avoider, recognition seeker, and distractor (p. 247).

▶ **Role conflict** arises when expectations for behavior are incompatible (p. 247).

Identify other issues affecting group communication:

▶ Goals should be specific, arrived at by group decision, clearly defined, supported with the necessary resources, and able to be monitored (pp. 248–249).

▶ **Groupthink** occurs when members minimize conflict by refusing to critically examine ideas and test solutions (p. 250).

▶ Cultural factors can create challenges (p. 250).

▶ Men and women work differently in groups because of their socialization (p. 251).

▶ Lack of self-esteem, status differences, or unbalanced participation by more aggressive members may provoke communication apprehension in some members (p. 252).

**Jack's assertiveness** and calm personality make him a natural leader in the eyes of the other *Lost* survivors.

# 9

# Leadership and Decision Making in Groups

**We see what he sees:** carnage, broken bodies, screaming strangers—the wreckage of Oceanic Flight 815, on which the man was a passenger. Dr. Jack Shephard is a spinal surgeon thrust into a new life on ABC's *Lost*, and he immediately assumes a leadership role in the group of forty-eight surviving strangers on an uncharted island. Jack uses his skills to care for the wounded and to organize the survivors into smaller groups to search for food and water.

Though Jack is a leader, he realizes that he needs help. When he is injured, he enlists fellow survivor Kate Austen to help him close his wounds. Although Kate doesn't seem up to the task, Jack is able to coach her into completing the simple surgery. In this moment, Jack finds his closest confidant on the island. Kate swiftly steps into the role and assumes leadership duties of her own.

As the group adapts to its new environment, others start to take on different leadership positions. When food becomes scarce, the mysterious John Lock steps up to hunt wild boar. When people need some TLC or a laugh, they go to the lovable Hugo "Hurley" Reyes. And when Jack needs answers from someone who doesn't want to give them, he enlists the help of a different sort of leader, one whose code of ethics is quite different from his own: former Iraqi Republican Guard torturer Sayid Jarrah.

Like its literary predecessor *Lord of the Flies*, *Lost* offers a compelling vision of leadership in groups that forms out of chaos. Leaders emerge to impose order, foster cohesion, and encourage cooperation. And as new situations arise, leadership adapts, changes, and is challenged. The stakes are high, and if they don't work together, it could mean the end for the survivors of Oceanic Flight 815.

## chapter objectives

After you have finished reading this chapter, you will be able to

○ Understand what makes an effective leader

○ Describe leadership styles

○ Identify how culture affects leadership

○ List the forces that shape a group's decisions

○ Explain the six-step group decision process

○ Show how effective leadership is crucial for good communication in meetings

○ Know the three aspects of assessing group performance

What makes a leader? Skills? Character? Power? An ability to make decisions? And is it possible for groups to exist, if not thrive, without someone like Jack Shephard taking a leadership role? In this chapter, we continue our discussion of group communication by examining two additional processes that often emerge in groups: leadership and decision making. These two processes are tightly interrelated: a group's leader affects how the group makes decisions, and the decisions a group makes affect how the leader operates. When leadership and decision making work together in a constructive way, a group stands the best possible chance of achieving its goals. To understand how these processes influence a group's effectiveness, let's begin by taking a closer look at group leadership.

## Understanding Group Leadership

It's a word that's constantly tossed about in political campaigns, highlighted on résumés, and used in book titles and biographies. But just what is *leadership*? Scholars have grappled with the task of defining leadership for many years. Consider these definitions:

▶ "The behavior of an individual when he [or she] is directing the activities of a group toward a shared goal" (Hemphill & Coons, 1957, p. 7)

▶ "Interpersonal influence, exercised in a situation, and directed, through the communication process, toward the attainment of a specified goal or goals" (Tannenbaum, Weschler, & Massarik, 1961, p. 24)

▶ "An interaction between persons in which one presents information of a sort and in such a manner that the other becomes convinced that his [or her] outcomes . . . will be improved if he [or she] behaves in the manner suggested or desired" (Jacobs, 1970, p. 232)

Notice that two key terms—*direction* and *influence*—show up or are hinted at in these definitions. That's because in its most essential form, **leadership** is the ability to direct or influence others' behaviors and thoughts toward a productive end. This capacity for influence may stem from a person's power or simply from group members' admiration or respect for the individual. Because influence is essentially power over others, let's take a look at power—what it is and where it comes from.

## Five Sources of Power

If you've ever seen the classic Steven Spielberg film *Jaws,* you know that it is, on the surface, the tale of a small coastal town being terrorized by a nasty, man-eating shark. But at the heart of the tale is the interaction among a group of men, each of whom bears or takes some responsibility for ridding the waters of the treacherous animal. First, there's the town's mayor, whose main priority is protecting the local economy. Second, there's the town's new chief of police, who's thrust into

 **QUINT, CHIEF BRODY,** and Matt Hooper each bring something different to the shark-hunting mission, and derive their power from different sources.

the story when the first body washes ashore soon after his arrival. Also playing a role are Matt Hooper, a young marine biologist who studies sharks, and the local shark hunter, a war-scarred fisherman who goes only by the name of Quint. Over the course of the film, each man demonstrates leadership that is firmly rooted in the nature of the power he possesses.

Researchers have identified five types of power—legitimate, coercive, reward, expert, and referent (French & Raven, 1959).

► **Legitimate power** comes from an individual's role or title. The president, your supervisor at work, and the coach of a team all possess legitimate power as elected or appointed leaders. In *Jaws,* the elected mayor of Amity Island, Larry Vaughn, has some degree of legitimate power, as does Martin Brody, the chief of police, though his power is subordinate to the mayor's.

► **Coercive power** stems from a person's ability to threaten or harm others. A harsh dictator who keeps his people under threat of violence or economic hardship holds such power, but so does a boss who threatens to dock or demote employees if they step out of line. In *Jaws,* the mayor—whose primary concern is protecting the town's economy, which is dependent on the summer tourist season—uses this kind of power to influence or override decisions made by the police chief. He hired Chief Brody, and he can fire him.

► **Reward power** derives from an individual's capacity to provide rewards. For example, your boss might offer all the people in your department a paid day off if they work late three nights in a row on an important project. In the film, the mayor uses reward power to motivate the local fishermen, offering a monetary reward to the team that catches the shark.

▶ **Expert power** comes from the information or knowledge that a leader possesses. Faced with any other kind of homicide, Brody's credentials as a former New York City police officer might have given him a fair amount of expert power. But as a newcomer, he gets little respect from the islanders, especially the fishermen, who think of him as a city slicker without sea legs. The scientist, Matt Hooper, who studies sharks, fares a little bit better. But Quint, who has decades of shark-hunting experience, quickly emerges as the true expert, garnering the respect of his crewmates.

▶ **Referent power** stems from the admiration, respect, or affection that followers have for a leader. Such is the source of Oprah Winfrey's power—every

## COMMUNICATIONACROSSCULTURES

### Trying to Change a Culture of Violence

Is violence a virus? Can it be contained and controlled—like the spread of HIV or tuberculosis? Gary Slutkin thinks it can. He's the founder of CeaseFire, a Chicago-based group that focuses on stopping gang-related violence in the city's most troubled neighborhoods. The group works by identifying violent situations that have the potential to snowball into more violence. By keeping an ear to the street (and the local emergency rooms), group members are able to intercede with gang members, for example, who would normally seek retribution.

Crucial to CeaseFire's operations is its credibility. Most of the men and women employed by the group to intercede are former felons—and often former gang members—who have strong ties to the community and the gang culture. Many of them were identified and recruited while serving time in jail and were hired upon their release from prison to serve as CeaseFire's "conflict interrupters." And that is their role: when a situation arises that the group feels is likely to erupt into violence (a shooting, a turf war, even an insult hurled), conflict interrupters seek out the individuals involved and try to pressure them not to seek revenge, to keep their guns at home, and to let the matter go.

The reasoning behind the group's practices links with Slutkin's background as an epidemiologist, someone who studies factors affecting health and illness in a population. Years earlier, while trying to contain an outbreak of cholera in a Somalian refugee camp, he learned that the best way to change the behavior of a group was to have members of the group take the lead. In that instance, he found that training Somali birth attendants to identify, treat, and prevent the disease was the most effective way of stopping it from spreading, because members of the group were more likely to take the advice of someone from within their own culture. "Copying and modeling the social expectations of your peers is what drives your behavior," Slutkin notes. The idea for using former felons and gang members as leaders to prevent violent escalations in inner cities is based on the same principle (Kotlowitz, 2008).

**THINK ABOUT THIS**

❶ Why is it important that CeaseFire's violence interrupters come from the gang culture? Does their history as felons who've served time truly empower them?

❷ What practical and logistical benefits does hiring members of the community offer CeaseFire? Would Slutkin himself be able to identify and track down individuals who might seek retribution?

❸ What kinds of leadership skills are needed to change the culture of violence in these communities? Should the conflict interrupters employ the same kinds of leadership skills in dealing with the community that the project's founder might use in managing them?

book recommendation or activity she suggests ripples through American popular culture. In *Jaws,* Quint demonstrates this kind of power: when he relays his story as a survivor of the USS *Indianapolis* during World War II, Brody and Hooper gain a new sense of understanding and admiration for his obsession with killing sharks.

It's important to note that these types of power are not exclusive of one another; indeed, most leaders wield several, if not all, of these types of power. Quint, for example, demonstrates legitimate power as captain of his own vessel as well as expert and referent power. Note also that individuals gain power only if others grant it to them. That's true to some degree even of coercive power: for example, Brody could have chosen to quit his job early on rather than to acquiesce to the mayor. Thus group members often decide to allow a particular individual to lead them.

## Shared Leadership

With so many sources of power, it's not surprising that in some groups, several individuals take on leadership roles, each drawing from different sources of power. Thus leadership is shared by a few members of the group who divvy up the power and take control of specific tasks. For example, imagine that your sorority is planning a trip to Jazz Fest in New Orleans. As chair of the social committee, you take care of organizing the group for the event—publicizing the trip and recording the names of individuals who are interested in going. Another sorority sister, Eva, takes care of booking a block of hotel rooms in the French Quarter and negotiating a group rate. Lily, the chapter president, gets in touch with the sister chapter at Louisiana State University to arrange a meet-up. Meanwhile, Tina, your chapter's community outreach chair, organizes a fund-raiser on campus in the hope of raising money to donate toward rebuilding efforts in New Orleans that your sorority will present to Habitat for Humanity during your visit.

When the talents and powers of each group member are leveraged through shared leadership, members feel more satisfied with the group process (Foels, Driskell, Mullen, & Salas, 2000) and more motivated to perform. As a result, the group is more likely to achieve its goals. Probably for these reasons, many businesses and professional organizations in the United States are moving toward a shared-leadership model, whereby they give people at lower levels of the organization decision-making and leadership responsibilities.

## Leadership Styles

The best group leaders, whether they're leading alone or sharing power with someone else in the group, adapt their leadership styles to the situation at hand. They can choose from four styles—directive, participative, supportive, and achievement-oriented—each of which works best under specific conditions (Gouran, 2003; Pavitt, 1999).

**AND YOU?**

Consider three groups to which you belong. Is there a clearly established leader for each group? If so, what type of power does this leader have? Do you find certain types of power more ethical or appropriate than others? Explain your answer.

Shared leadership is at the heart of the *self-directed work teams* that we describe in Chapter 8, where sharing leadership goes beyond improving group member motivation to allow members to set standards for the group, conduct peer evaluations, bring in new members, and coordinate plans with management. The end result is often goal achievement and a sense of cooperation rather than divisive competition among members.

● *LAW AND ORDER'S*
Lieutenant Van Buren never
leaves her detectives hanging; she gives them specific
and thorough directions for
every step of a case.

### Directive

A **directive leader** controls the group's communication by conveying specific instructions to members.
This style works best when members are unsure of
what's expected of them or how to carry out the
group's tasks. Directive leaders can move their group
in the right direction by charting next steps in the
group's tasks and clarifying the group's goals, plans,
and desired outcomes. For example, Lieutenant Anita
Van Buren on NBC's *Law and Order* takes a directive
approach in guiding how her detectives handle specific cases: she offers guidance in determining which
leads to follow, whom to bring in for questioning, and
what information to follow up on. She also has the final say on when to approach the district attorney for
warrants, oversees the questioning of witnesses and suspects, and disciplines her
detectives when they overstep their bounds.

### Participative

A **participative leader** views group members as equals, welcomes their opinions,
summarizes points that have been raised, and identifies problems that need discussion rather than announcing solutions. This style works best when group
members are competent and motivated to take on the task at hand. Such leaders
typically guide and facilitate rather than dictating orders to group members. To
follow up on our *Law and Order* example, consider another crime drama, CBS's
*CSI*. In the fictional Las Vegas crime lab, Gil Grissom oversees his team of foren-
sic scientists with a more participative style, allowing them to follow leads and
conduct experiments as they see fit.

### Supportive

A **supportive leader** attends to group members' emotional needs. This style is
especially helpful when members feel frustrated with a task or discouraged with
the group's progress. Supportive leaders can best apply this style by stressing the
importance of positive relationships in the group, reminding members of the
group's importance, and expressing appreciation for members' talents and work
ethic. Consider Tim Gunn of *Project Runway*. He acts as a leader and mentor
figure to the aspiring designers, helping them visualize their designs and talk
through their frustrations and encouraging team members to communicate
with each other, listen to each other, and "make it work." He is always profuse
in his praise, and even when a particular design doesn't impress him, he is encouraging and positive in his criticism.

### Achievement-Oriented

An **achievement-oriented leader** sets challenging goals and communicates high
expectations and standards to members. This style works best when group members
see themselves as competent and are motivated to excel at their tasks. In addition
to setting lofty goals, such leaders encourage outside-the-box thinking, compare
the group with other high-performing groups, and keep members focused on

**AND YOU?**

Consider a leadership
position that you currently
hold or held in the past.
Did you favor a particular
leadership style? Was it effective and appropriate for
the group and situation at
hand? If not, can you look
back and say that another
leadership style would
have been more effective?
Which one and why?

# what about you?

## What Type of Leader Are You?

Choose the answer that best describes what you might do in each situation.

1. Your chemistry professor assigned a full-semester group project and has asked you to take the lead in your group because chemistry is your best subject. When it comes down to assigning your tasks to the other group members and getting the project done, what do you do?
   A. Ask a lot of questions. Who knows, someone else may know just as much as you, but is too shy to act on it.
   B. Get down to business! You know the facts, so you immediately delegate work to each member of the group.
   C. Assume you're working with very smart people and allow everyone a chance to say what direction the group should take.
   D. Don't want to hurt anyone's feelings, so you ask for input and watch everyone's emotional reactions to ensure that everyone is happy.

2. You organized a study group to prepare for your history final exam and invited a handful of other hardworking students from class. Another classmate, Scott, shows up. Scott is rarely prepared for class and isn't contributing to the group. What do you do?
   A. Start asking Scott questions in areas you think he might be knowledgeable. You hope that by inviting him to participate, he will begin contributing to the group.
   B. Don't really notice if Scott is contributing or not because you're too busy organizing the group's class notes.
   C. Try to get Scott to participate but don't go out of your way too much. If he is to be an equal member of the group, he has to reach out too.
   D. Become concerned with Scott's feelings. You move your chair next to his and ask how he's doing. This may slow the group's progress, but at least it includes Scott.

3. Managing a local, casual restaurant has its ups and downs, and today is one of the downs. Customers have been complaining that the waiters and waitresses have not been friendly, so you've decided to call a "worker meeting" to address the problem. What do you do at the meeting?
   A. Tell the workers what the customers said and then sit back and listen to everyone's responses.
   B. Explain the problem and offer possible solutions while delegating particular tasks (such as checking in on customers) to specific individuals.
   C. Tell your workers about the complaints and explain that you're shocked—you could never have imagined that this scenario would happen.
   D. Open the group meeting by having each member state what's been on his or her mind lately; you figure personal problems may affect the working environment.

**If your answers are mostly A's:** You are a participative leader.
**If your answers are mostly B's:** You are a directive leader.
**If your answers are mostly C's:** You are an achievement-oriented leader.
**If your answers are mostly D's:** You are a supportive leader.
(A mix of answers indicates a diverse leadership style.)

● *BRING IT ON'S* Torrance Shipman is her team's "cheertator." She commands them to focus on the prize and never give up.

tangible outcomes. In the movie *Bring It On,* Torrance Shipman, the captain of the Toros, is a great example of an achievement-oriented leader. Although she finds out that their previous captain had been stealing their winning routines from another squad, the Clovers, she is determined not to let this ruin their chances of winning the national championships. Torrance keeps her squad focused on getting to the nationals and competing against the Clovers. Even with initial setbacks, she leads them in putting together a routine that borrows moves from genres other than cheer- leading, such as martial arts and even mime.

## EVALUATING COMMUNICATION ETHICS

### Leading the Interns

You are currently working as an assistant to an editor at a reputable music magazine, and among your responsibilities is leading a group of young, aspir- ing summer interns. You find this task especially rewarding because as a col- lege student, you suffered through a number of magazine internships in order to get your foot in the door, so you hope that you can make this internship rewarding for the students in your department.

Back when you were an intern, you worked with an assistant named Bradley, who was in a position similar to the one you're in now. Bradley al- ways seemed to pass off his boring, menial tasks—such as filing, answering his boss's e-mail, and setting up appointments—to the interns so that he could sit and listen to new records in an attempt to further his career in rock criticism. You and the other interns were willing to take on just about any task in order to get a good recommendation, but you always slightly resented Bradley, feeling that he had used you and others in your group.

Since you started working long hours at your assistant job, however, you've wondered if Bradley actually had the right idea. Like Bradley, you as- pire to be a music critic, and the mundane tasks of your job are beginning to frustrate you. Such tasks are, however, part of your job description—they are what every assistant does.

You want to have time to talk to writers, to write or edit copy, and to be able to sit in on pitch meetings. Bradley kept you from such experiences as an intern because you were too busy fetching lattes for his boss. The problem is, now you need to get lattes for your own boss, and this is keeping you from gussying up your own portfolio. Yet here are new, young interns willing and eager to do anything to get ahead, perhaps even taking over those menial tasks. What should you do?

### THINK ABOUT THIS

❶ Was Bradley wrong, or was he just doing what any aspiring journalist would do to free up his time? Do you have a greater understand- ing for his struggle in light of your own position?

❷ Is it OK to pawn your work off on unpaid college students, even if they're willing to do it?

❸ As the group's leader, do you have a responsibility to these interns to ensure that they get the most from their internship experience?

## Competence and Ethics

An ability to mix and match leadership styles to suit your group's needs is an essential skill for a leader. But to be a truly competent leader requires other skills as well. The most effective leaders remain focused on their group's goals, and they hold both themselves *and* the group accountable for achieving those results. They treat all group members in an ethical manner. They also have credibility with their group. That is, members see them as knowledgeable, experienced, believable, and respectable—even if they don't like their leader personally. Finally, competent leaders use skilled communication techniques, such as describing a compelling vision of success and acknowledging the group's valuable talents, to inspire members to contribute their best.

But not all leaders demonstrate these qualities. Some use unethical tactics to try to acquire and keep control over an entire group or individual members within a group. These tactics can include **bullying** or behaviors such as harsh criticism, name-calling, gossip, slander, personal attacks, or threats to safety or job security (Smith, 2005). It can also include offensive gestures, ignoring, withering looks, or a sarcastic tone of voice. Bullies may also try to manipulate group members by withholding needed information, excluding them from meetings, or insisting on unrealistic deadlines or expectations. Unfortunately, such unethical tactics can prove successful for some leaders to some degree. Take chef Gordon Ramsay on the reality TV series *Hell's Kitchen*. Aspiring chefs are split into two teams that are pitted against each other in challenges while also preparing and serving dinner to a roomful of diners. Ramsay is very particular about how he wants the food to taste and look. If something is not up to par, he often screams profanities at the contestant responsible for the mistake and tosses the offending food on the ground. Ramsay has no qualms about insulting any of the contestants or getting personal; in fact, he repeatedly referred to a blonde contestant as a "dumb blonde" and a "Barbie." While his insults and derogatory statements are usually met by a grim "Yes, chef," and while he may gain the respect of some of the contestants, some do tire of being abused on a regular basis and break down or walk out.

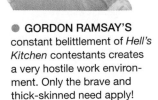

● **GORDON RAMSAY'S** constant belittlement of *Hell's Kitchen* contestants creates a very hostile work environment. Only the brave and thick-skinned need apply!

**CONNECT**

In many organizational contexts, bullying behaviors can escalate to illegal *harassment,* communication that hurts or offends, creating a hostile environment. Victims of bullying may find our tips in Chapter 10 (p. 310) helpful for dealing with such unethical behavior in a group, in an organization, or even in an interpersonal relationship.

## Culture and Group Leadership

As in any other human endeavor, culture can strongly shape the way people approach leading a group and the way members respond to a leader. Let's look at three particular factors—gender, high versus low context, and power difference—that prove to be particularly powerful when leading a group.

## Masculine and Feminine Leadership

Hillary Clinton's historic bid for the presidency in 2008 had the nation buzzing over age-old and blatantly sexist concerns about whether a woman would make a strong leader. Despite the history of strong female heads of state elsewhere in the world—Queen Elizabeth I built the British Empire back in the sixteenth century, and Margaret Thatcher led it with unmistakable toughness four hundred years later—the notion of a female in command still seemed novel. Yet there is some indication that the media debate over gender and politics may have been overblown: a February 2007 Gallup poll found that 88 percent of Americans said they would vote for a well-qualified woman for president (Kohut, 2007).

When it comes down to it, is there really a difference between men and women as leaders? Interestingly, consensus among researchers is growing that the traditional masculine approach to leadership, which emphasizes command and control over others, is not as effective in today's world as it may have been in previous times. In the business arena, for example, competition has heated up as business has become more global. To stay ahead of rivals, many companies have adopted strategies such as forming cross-functional teams to sell a wider range of products and services. Such teams function best when they're led by people who know how to build and maintain a network of relationships and manage diverse and often competing stakeholders (such as personnel from different divisions in a large company) (Mumby, 2000). Under these complex conditions, ordering people around simply doesn't work.

What does seem to work are the attitudes and behaviors exhibited in more feminine leadership styles. Indeed, some research has suggested that women tend to think of organizations as webs of relationships, with leaders at the center of the web, in contrast to the more traditionally masculine view of organizations as pyramids with a leader at the top. Many women also view the boundaries between work and personal life as more fluid than men do. Female leaders who hold this viewpoint are more likely to communicate their understanding of employees' need to balance professional and personal obligations and to win these employees' loyalty. In addition, many women see work as a means of developing personal identity (Grossman & Chester, 1990; Helgeson, 1990; Lunneborg, 1990; Mumby, 2000; Rosener, 1990). Female leaders with this perspective tend to ask their followers what skills they want to acquire or strengthen and then give them opportunities to achieve these goals. This approach to leadership can further earn women leaders loyalty from their followers as well as sharpen their organizations' competitive edge.

These findings about women's leadership qualities raise some intriguing questions. For example, can power be defined as something that is shared rather than concentrated only in one person within a group (Reuther & Fairhurst, 2000)? Can viewing groups as networks of relationships rather than pyramids with one leader at the top lead to better group performance (Ferguson, 1984)? As women continue to occupy more leadership positions in organizations, we'll have more empirical data with which to answer these questions.

> ## AND YOU?
>
> What is your opinion on the research on masculine and feminine leadership styles? Are there different contexts in which each would be appropriate? Do you ever notice yourself favoring a gendered style, regardless of your biological sex?

## Context and Power Distance

In addition to gender differences, other cultural differences can affect the way a person might lead a group and how the group members respond. For example, as we've discussed in earlier chapters, people from high-context cultures tend to communicate in indirect ways, while those from low-context cultures communicate more directly (Hall, 1976). Thus a leader who grew up in a high-context

● IN A LOW–POWER DISTANCE culture, meetings might feel like roundtable discussions, where everyone gets a chance to speak. In a high–power distance culture, meetings are usually more hierarchical.

culture might make suggestions to members of his or her group ("One possibility we could consider is moving the deadline for this project earlier by two weeks; what do you all think?") rather than dictating orders or imposing solutions to problems ("I'm moving the deadline earlier by two weeks; that means you'll need to accelerate your work accordingly"). If the members of this group also came from a high-context culture, they might communicate in a similarly indirect way with their leader ("We have some concerns about the new deadline") rather than through direct means ("Sorry, we can't make the new deadline").

In addition to high- and low-context cultures, power distance is another cultural difference that affects the ways that groups communicate. **Power distance** is the extent to which less powerful members of a group, be it a business organization or a family, expect that power is distributed unequally. In cultures with high power distance, the power structure is more hierarchical, and people often automatically defer to those with higher status or authority. In cultures with low power distance, people view power as more democratic, exerted only when it is legitimate (Hofstede, 1984). This means that a person who is leading a group in a high–power distance culture and wants all members to offer their ideas in a meeting might need to make a special effort to encourage everyone to participate in the discussion, whereas in a group with low power distance, members are likely to offer their opinions without much prodding. For example, a manager in a software development company in Hong Kong (a region with high power distance) says that she often needs to reassure her employees that she does want to hear what they think and does want them to take the initiative in developing new ideas and products.

## Decision Making in Groups

As you learned in Chapter 8, the communication between group leaders and members strongly influences how a group makes decisions. And because of the large numbers of exchanges and people involved, decision making in a group differs markedly from decision making by one individual or between just two people. For one thing, in a group, a complex set of forces influences decision making.

These forces also influence how a group progresses through the decision-making process. In the following sections, we examine each of these topics in detail.

## Forces That Shape a Group's Decisions

Experts have identified three forces—cognitive, psychological, and social—that strongly affect how groups and their leaders discuss and arrive at decisions (Hirokawa, Gouran, & Martz, 1988). Going back to the devastating *Challenger* example from Chapter 8, let's take a deeper look at these forces.

### Cognitive Forces

**Cognitive forces** consist of group members' thoughts, beliefs, and emotions. These affect how everyone in a particular group perceives, interprets, evaluates, stores, and retrieves information, which in turn influences the group's decisions.

Cognitive forces influenced the NASA officials who made the fateful decision to launch the *Challenger* shuttle, a subject you read about in Chapter 8. The officials discounted the credibility of key information available to them at the time, and they drew incorrect conclusions from the data. They also wrongly believed that the shuttle system was sound, which made them overly confident in their ability to have a successful launch.

### Psychological Forces

**Psychological forces** refer to group members' personal motives, goals, attitudes, and values. In the *Challenger* disaster, lower-level NASA decision makers had initially recommended postponing the launch until the day had warmed up. But when higher-ups pressured them to reverse their recommendation, they caved in—perhaps because they were worried about losing their jobs if they didn't go along.

The decision makers also changed their attitudes about which criteria to use for postponing a shuttle launch. Previously, NASA rules dictated that a launch wouldn't take place if anyone doubted its safety. But with *Challenger,* the rule had changed: the launch would proceed unless someone presented conclusive evidence that it was unsafe. Engineers' qualms about the launch didn't constitute conclusive evidence, so they hesitated to express their concerns. And the launch proceeded.

### Social Forces

**Social forces** are group standards for behavior that influence decision making. In the *Challenger* disaster, engineers were unable to persuade their own managers and higher NASA officials to postpone the launch. They tried to prove that it was *unsafe* to launch rather than take the opposite (and possibly more effective) tactic: showing that no data existed to prove that the launch was *safe*.

## The Problem-Solving Process

To make decisions, groups and their leaders typically go through a six-step process (Dewey, 1933). To illustrate these steps, consider the EcoCrew, a group

**AND YOU?**

How do cognitive, psychological, and social forces affect decision making in groups you're currently involved in? Have these forces ever caused your group to make a poor decision? If so, how?

of sixteen environmentally active students at a West Coast community college who wish to resolve environmental problems in their community.

## Identifying the Problem

The EcoCrew has scheduled its first meeting in the student union lounge. Susan, who initially had the idea of forming the EcoCrew, is the group's designated leader. Deciding to adopt a participative leadership style, Susan invites each person to give his or her perception of the problem the group will set out to address. "No debate or questions until we have all voiced our perceptions," Susan says. Members pipe up with a number of issues and activities they'd like the group to address. "The campus bookshops and food courts need to eliminate plastic bags," says one; "the beaches are covered with litter during the winter months," says another.

By inviting members to voice their concerns one at a time, Susan is providing an opportunity for the group to identify and define several problems. Once all the members have presented their views, Susan encourages the group to discuss the various proposed definitions of the problem and agree on one that the EcoCrew can productively address. The group decides that litter, both on campus and on the nearby beach, is the most immediately troubling environmental issue.

Having defined the problem it wants to address, the EcoCrew has gotten off to an effective start. According to researchers, many groups don't spend enough time identifying the problem they want to tackle (Gouran, 2003). Without a clear, agreed-on problem, a group can't work through the rest of the decision-making process in a focused way.

## Analyzing the Problem

Having decided to tackle litter cleanup as its primary mission, the EcoCrew begins to analyze the problem. Susan suggests that each member carry a diary for one week as they travel around campus and the surrounding area and note where the litter is most concentrated and how much litter they see. When the group meets again the following week, all members agree that the two biggest litter problems in the area are on the beaches and in the wooded areas surrounding the campus parking lots. Several members note that the trash cans on the beaches are not being emptied often enough by city sanitation workers; they appeared to be overflowing with trash, which was being blown out of the cans by the gusting ocean wind.

● **WRITING DOWN** any ideas your team has on a whiteboard can be a great way to get the creative juices flowing.

## Generating Solutions

Once the EcoCrew has identified and analyzed the problem, the next step is to come up with a solution. Susan starts asking for ideas from the group and writes them down on a whiteboard. "Just give me any ideas you've got," Susan says. "We'll evaluate them later."

This technique, called *brainstorming*, encourages members of a group to come up with as many ideas as possible without judging the merits of those ideas yet. The intent is

**FIGURE 9.1**
**SUSAN'S WHITEBOARD**

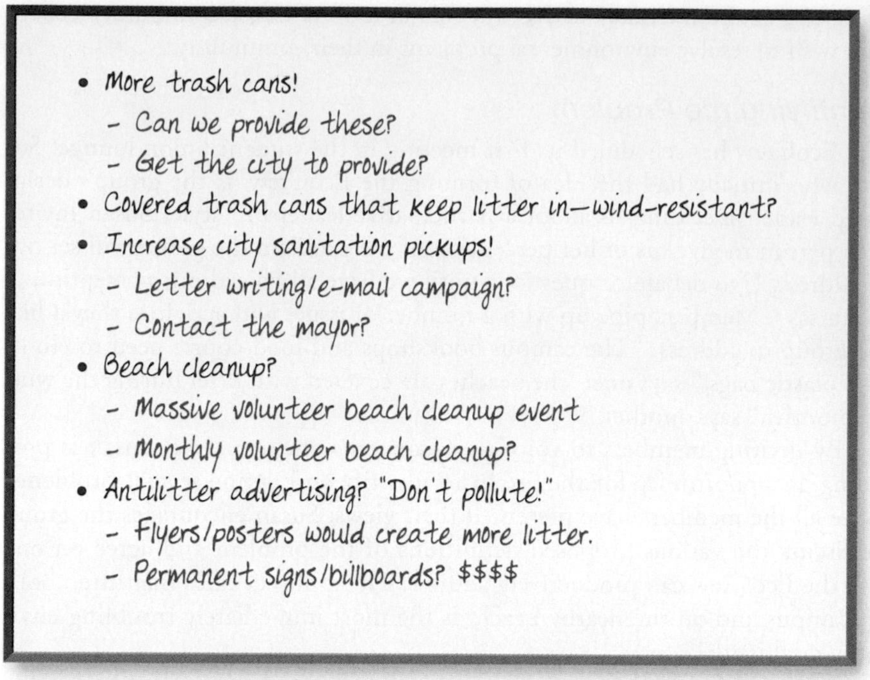

- More trash cans!
  - Can we provide these?
  - Get the city to provide?
- Covered trash cans that keep litter in—wind-resistant?
- Increase city sanitation pickups!
  - Letter writing/e-mail campaign?
  - Contact the mayor?
- Beach cleanup?
  - Massive volunteer beach cleanup event
  - Monthly volunteer beach cleanup?
- Antilitter advertising? "Don't pollute!"
  - Flyers/posters would create more litter.
  - Permanent signs/billboards? $$$$

**CONNECT**

*Brainstorming* and *clustering* can help you in both public speaking and small group settings. When choosing a topic, both strategies allow you to generate ideas based on your interests, your audience's interests, and your time constraints (Chapter 11). In a group, brainstorming and clustering allow you to identify and discuss solutions from a variety of perspectives to ensure that the solution meets the needs of the group.

to prompt fresh thinking and to generate a larger number of potential solutions than a group might arrive at if members evaluated each idea as it came up. As the EcoCrew members throw out idea after idea, the whiteboard grows dense and colorful with possibilities (see Figure 9.1).

Once the members have run out of new ideas, they'll need to narrow down the list. To help them focus on the one or two strongest ideas, Susan invites them to define the criteria that eventual solutions will have to meet. First, Susan reminds them that the primary goal would be to reduce litter on the beach. Another member, Wade, then points out that at this point, the group has no budget, so it needs to limit its initial efforts to tasks that have little or no cost. Another member, Larissa, notes that because the group has a relatively small membership, it should focus on things either that the group can manage on its own or in which the group could encourage nonmembers to participate. The group concludes that an acceptable solution must meet these key criteria.

### Evaluating and Choosing Solutions

Once the EcoCrew has generated its list of possible solutions, group members have to evaluate the pros and cons of each idea to consider how well it meets the criteria the members have defined. For example, one member, Kathryn, points out that the lack of funding makes replacing the garbage cans out of the question and would make an antilitter advertising campaign difficult, if not impossible. Wade notes that organizing a beach cleanup would cost next to nothing: they could all volunteer to get together to pick up garbage and clean up the beach. Larissa adds that if they get the word out, they'd also be able to attract additional volunteers—and potential new members—from outside the group to participate. Thus the group decides to launch a monthly beach cleanup; this would be a regular social event that could raise awareness of the group, encourage nonmembers to participate and new members to join, and involve little to nothing in terms of cost.

## Implementing the Solution

Implementing a solution means putting into action the decision that the group has made. For the EcoCrew, this means making plans for the regular beach cleanup. The group focuses first on logistics, setting dates and times. One member, Allison, volunteers to act as a liaison with the county sanitation department to see if it can provide trash bags and picks for the volunteers and to arrange for the sanitation trucks to pick up the trash once it's been bagged.

Larissa adds that with a bit of legwork, the group could turn the cleanup into a large community event; she volunteers to arrange for an end-of-day gathering and to see if she can get her mother's sandwich shop to donate food. Wade notes that he can probably get his roommate's band to entertain free of charge as well.

## Assessing the Results

Once a group has implemented a solution it has decided on, members should evaluate the results. Evaluation can shed light on how effective the solution was and whether the group needs to make further decisions about the problem at hand. For the EcoCrew, it will be helpful to assess the first event in terms of how well it met the three key criteria:

▶ Was the beach cleaner at the end of the day as a result of the group's efforts? Before-and-after photos of the beach reveal a very successful cleanup.

▶ Did the event wind up costing the members any money? Thanks to the donations of local restaurants and supplies provided by the county sanitation department, the event cost the group absolutely nothing.

▶ Did the event attract volunteers from outside the group? Fifteen nonmembers participated in the cleanup, among them several schoolchildren who attended with their parents.

By revisiting these criteria, the group is able to tweak its plan for the following month's cleanup event. Larissa suggests that the members pitch in a few dollars to place an ad in the local paper thanking the volunteers and donors and announcing the date of the next cleanup. Wade follows up by suggesting that the group make a pitch at the local elementary school to get more kids and their families involved. Kathryn volunteers to submit a brief story about the cleanup, along with photos of the event and the results, to the campus newspaper. And Susan suggests holding a raffle at the next event, with half the proceeds paid out in prizes and half retained by the group, to get a small budget started to cover future ads and expenses.

**AND YOU?**

Consider the six steps to problem solving we've just discussed. If Susan, the leader of the EcoCrew, had chosen a different leadership style, would this have affected how the problem-solving steps were carried out? If so, how? What has your experience been in solving problems in groups with different types of leaders?

● **AFTER THEIR BEACH** cleanup, the EcoCrew needs to assess the results. The first question should be: "Was the beach cleaner after our event?"

## Leadership in Meetings

The EcoCrew was able to identify a problem, create a solution, and implement it very successfully. Much of the planning and implementation took place in meetings. Group leader Susan was able to direct the discussion and manage the deliberations in ways that kept the group focused and invited input from all participants. Indeed, meetings—be they face to face, over the phone, online, or through a combination of media—are an integral part of many group activities. But they are not always successful, and the failure of a meeting often rests on the shoulders of the group leader.

Consider Julia, a freelance Web designer who works from a home office. On Friday, Julia received an e-mail from her biggest client, Jacob, asking her to phone in to a meeting with the sales team to discuss marketing materials related to the launch of the new Web site she's designing for his skateboard manufacturing company. Struggling with several competing deadlines, Julia dreaded spending an hour or two listening to a group of people she'd never met discuss parts of the project with which she had little to do. But she reluctantly confirmed that she could take part in the meeting the following Monday.

After spending the better part of Monday morning reviewing her design for the project and outlining a few ideas for ways it could be teased into the marketing campaign, Julia dutifully dialed in to the conference room at the designated time, only to find herself placed on hold—complete with irritating piped-in music—for twenty minutes before the team picked up. The meeting that followed was equally frustrating: Jacob spent the better part of an hour describing the content of the site, how it would work, and the potential for revenues it would generate for the team of salespeople, who were entirely unfamiliar with the project. Julia—who was responsible only for creating the look and functionality of the site and had nothing to do with content or sales—sat miserably watching the clock, grateful that at least the team couldn't see her as she scribbled angry doodles and notes to herself.

Meetings can be integral to group decision making, but they can often be unproductive and frustrating. Ineffective meetings are one of the top time wasters cited by workers: a 2004 survey of more than thirty-eight thousand workers worldwide found that people spend more than five working hours per week in meetings, and about 70 percent of the respondents felt that most meetings weren't productive (Microsoft, 2005). In this section, we'll analyze meetings from a communication perspective and consider how they can be best used to arrive at better decisions and solutions. We'll discuss how technology has changed meetings—and how it hasn't. Most important, we'll show that effective leadership is crucial to conducting effective and productive meetings.

## Planning Meetings Effectively

Let's consider all the reasons why Julia found the meeting we've just described so frustrating. First, it was a bad time: she was struggling to meet deadlines and really didn't want to stop working to sit in on a meeting. What's worse, she probably didn't really have to be there either—the client was using the meeting to inform

**CONNECT**

Planning a meeting can be similar to planning a speech, particularly regarding audience analysis (Chapter 11). In both contexts, you must be aware of the expectations and goals of others involved (your audience or attendees): Why are they present? Why should they listen to you? How is the meeting or speech relevant to them? In addition, you need to consider the situational context for the event (location, room setup, and so on) in both contexts to ensure that it won't inhibit communication.

the sales team about the site as a whole, not to discuss anything that dealt with Julia's design. Further complicating the issue were the facts that the meeting didn't start on time, Julia had not met anyone on the sales force before, and the medium used—speakerphone—limited Julia's communication with the team in concrete ways. Put simply, the meeting was poorly planned.

Proper planning is crucial for successful meetings. Making a few decisions beforehand and taking steps to clarify goals and logistics for the team can lead to more effective decision making during the meeting itself. Yet research has shown that as many as 30 percent of groups do not plan meetings effectively (or at all), even though planning can improve decision-making quality by as much as 35 percent (Gouran, 2003). There are several steps that group leaders can take to plan meetings more effectively.

● **EVERYONE PRESENT** at the Dumbledore's Army gatherings are well aware of the goal of these meetings: to learn how to fight and defend themselves against the evil Voldemort.

### Justify the Meeting

Before calling a meeting, a group leader should consider what he or she wants to accomplish and assess whether a meeting is even necessary to meet that goal. If there are no clear goals for a meeting, it's impossible for any goals to be met as a result of it. What's more, the leader needs to ensure that only those whose presence is necessary in order to meet the goals or who would truly benefit from attending are included. While not a typical meeting, a good example of this is when Harry Potter first begins to assemble Dumbledore's Army in *Harry Potter and the Order of the Phoenix.* He determines the goals of the meetings (to teach other students how to defend themselves in the face of Voldemort's return to power) and invites only students that he knows will use the training and won't derail the meeting.

In many cases, meetings can be avoided altogether or made smaller and more efficient by asking team members to contribute information ahead of time or simply picking up the phone to ask someone a question when one arises (Conlin, 2006).

### Clarify the Purpose and the Participants

If a meeting is necessary, it is the responsibility of the leader to clearly articulate the goals of the meeting and the roles of everyone who is to attend. Think back to Julia's situation. Her client, Jacob, wants to get his sales force interested and excited about the launch of the Web site. Getting the sales force together to view the beta version and get feedback on it might seem like a good way to brainstorm ideas for marketing. But Jacob failed to clarify what he wanted to accomplish at the meeting and what Julia's role would be. Jacob might have made a more efficient use of Julia's time if he'd simply discussed elements of the design with her prior to the meeting or asked her to outline a few key features for him and then used her information in his meeting with the sales force without any need for Julia to attend.

**AND YOU?**

How do you feel about group meetings? Do you find them energizing, boring, a waste of time? Consider an effective meeting and an ineffective meeting that you've attended. To what degree did the leaders plan appropriately, justify each meeting, and clarify the purpose?

## Set an Agenda

President Dwight D. Eisenhower noted, "I have often found that plans are useless, but planning is indispensable." Creating a plan is a valuable phase in decision making, even if the plan itself isn't followed to the letter in the end. Setting an agenda is crucial.

An **agenda** for a meeting should detail the subject and goal of the meeting and logistics like time, place, or log-in or conference call information. It should set a schedule for the meeting as well so that participants will know how much time to block out for the meeting and so that the group leader can manage time effectively during the meeting itself. It should list or include any materials that participants would need to have read or reviewed in advance of the meeting so that everyone arrives with the appropriate background on the issue. A sample agenda for Jacob's meeting is provided in Figure 9.2.

**FIGURE 9.2**

**JACOB'S AGENDA**
Although Jacob's meeting agenda is very well organized, there is no indication that Julia needs to be present for or plays a role in this meeting.

---

**Meeting with sales team to discuss marketing strategies for new SlickBoards Web site.**

Date: March 24, 2009
Time: 10:00 A.M.–12:00 P.M. (EST)
Location: Conference Room 2. Call-in number 555-555-0823.

AGENDA

I.   Welcome
   A. Quick introduction of core team working on Web site
   B. Introduce purpose of meeting—to discuss the marketing strategies for the new SlickBoards Web site
II.  Why do we need a new SlickBoards Web site?
   A. Overview of our current Web site and its deficiencies
   B. Present the concept of the new Web site, why we needed a revamp, and how it improves on the old site
III. What will be on the new SlickBoards Web site?
   A. Outline all the new information about the products that will be on the Web site and how it will increase sales
   B. Explain how clients will be able to customize their SlickBoard directly on the new Web site
IV.  How should we market this new Web site?
   A. Discuss the focus of the marketing campaign: What's the message?
   B. Brainstorm how to get the message out
   C. Distill list of ideas; assign roles
V.   Conclusion and follow-up
   A. Take any questions or concerns
   B. Establish next meeting time and what should be accomplished by then

## Managing Meetings Effectively

So you now see that meetings can go well—or they can go horribly off track. During a meeting, it is the responsibility of the leader to manage the discussion in ways that help the group communicate while remaining focused on the meeting's goal. The following steps can help.

### Arrive Prepared

The veteran businessman and writer Simon Ramo estimates that he's attended forty thousand meetings during his career, so he has a strong sense of what works and what doesn't. When running a meeting, the most important thing for a leader to do, Ramo advises, is to be prepared. If you've planned properly, you are fully aware of your goals for the meeting and familiar with all the background information you'll need.

### Keep the Group Focused

It's also important to know who the participants are. You should have a sense beforehand of which participants are likely to be the biggest contributors, as well as who will likely need to be kept on track or prevented from going off on tangents. One member might bring up a topic that's not on the agenda, and others might be unnecessarily long-winded. When these things occur, Ramo advises, "as tactfully as possible, interrupt to move the discussion along" ("Why Most Meetings Stink," 2005). This might be as simple as saying, "We're getting off the subject here," and bringing the group back to the main topic of the meeting.

Of course, as the meeting progresses, it is likely that the goal may be redefined or new goals may emerge. "Keep the objective of the meeting constantly in your mind so you'll keep moving toward the goal," Ramo advises. "But if the goal changes during or because of the meeting, be prepared to invent Plan B."

### Summarize Periodically

As a group explores and settles on decisions, it's important that someone (a leader or any member) regularly summarize what has happened. Summaries provide members with opportunities to confirm, correct, or clarify what has occurred so far during the conversation. Summaries thus help ensure that everyone in the group is in agreement about what the group has decided, what steps it will be taking next, and how members are to carry out their designated tasks.

### Keep an Eye on the Time

Nobody likes to waste time, and nobody likes sitting through a long meeting when a short one would do. Group leaders need to be aware of time constraints to keep their meetings running efficiently and to respect the time pressures on the other members. When large groups are involved or when the agenda includes many topics or issues, it can be helpful to impose *time limits* on certain components of the discussion. When a decision must be made, taking an informal vote on a decision—a tactic called a **nonbinding straw poll**—can help you move the group forward.

CONNECT

To keep a group focused and productive, you must employ effective listening skills (Chapter 5). You might think that leaders should talk more than listen, but without informational, critical, and empathic listening skills, they miss opportunities to learn new information from others or to analyze ideas that might help the group achieve goals. In addition, *paraphrasing*—restating a message—helps keep group members focused and provides the important summary we discuss here.

### Manage Conflict

As you saw in Chapter 7, the best decisions are usually those that have come from productive conflict (Kuhn & Poole, 2000; Nicotera, 1997). When group members deal with conflict productively, they ask clarifying questions, challenge

## real communicator

**NAME:** Jim Simons
**HOMETOWN:** Marietta, GA
**OCCUPATION:** Project manager at an architecture firm
**FUN FACT:** I've worked on projects all over the world, from Thailand to the United Arab Emirates.

I'm a project manager at an architecture firm. Clients come to us and say, "We own this building site, and we want to use it productively, but we don't exactly know what form that should take." Maybe they know they want an office building with retail at the street level and parking underground, and they want us to get the maximum square footage for the property—or maybe they know much less. Once the client's request gets to me, I can put together a team.

For this task, it's important for a team to consist of varied professionals: me (the project manager), senior architects, creative designers, junior architects, and consultants (structural engineers, for example). We will need to work together to produce the product that the client has asked for.

I go into the first team meeting highly prepared and I try to keep the atmosphere loose and informal. I dress professionally, but not in a manner that may intimidate others. I provide food to give even the most disinterested team member a reason to become interested. Once the bagels have been passed around, I go to work outlining the goals of the meeting. I identify the problem and I make explicit what the group must accomplish. I tell the team *everything* I know about the client's request—the problem at hand needs to become everyone's problem. Open and honest communication is vital at this stage.

In a diverse group, people hear things differently. One way to clarify the message is to invite questions—misunderstandings will become exposed and can be cleared up. At this point, the meeting becomes a dialogue among equals with me serving more as a moderator. I keep an eye on the clock, but I'm careful not to cut people off *too* early. Architects are creative, and creative people need the opportunity to express their ideas. It's all about respecting and getting to know the individuals on your team and learning their strengths and weaknesses.

Once our task has been explicitly identified, I adopt an achievement-oriented leadership style. I delegate responsibilities. I give everyone on the team ownership over some component of the project, so that each individual can be his or her own supervisor on that particular component—whether it's the building's core, the exterior enclosure, the form, the numbers, or the mechanical system. Thus clear goals are established for each participant and interaction between team members will begin.

That's the first meeting. In the next meeting, each team member makes a brief presentation. This meeting is about reconciling solutions. My job here is twofold: (1) to bring group members' creative ideas back to the original task, the client's request, and (2) to summarize, summarize, summarize. Through explicit summaries, I hope to facilitate dialogue and cooperation and create order and cohesion out of a number of different ideas. I need to walk out of this meeting with a particular solution, a story to sell. Next, I will make an informational and persuasive presentation to the client. But that's a different story. I've got to wear a suit and tie in *that* meeting.

one another's ideas (in a respectful way), consider worst-case scenarios, and revise proposals as needed to reflect new information and insights. This process leads to sound decisions, because it enables group members to generate the widest possible range of ideas as well as test each idea's pros and cons. Any idea that survives this rigorous process has a fighting chance of delivering the hoped-for results when it's put into action. For example, in one challenge on season three of *Project Runway*, the contestants were put in groups to create a three-piece outfit for Macy's. On one of the teams, members disagreed on embellishment for their outfit. Angela, a contestant who considered rosettes her signature, wanted to put them all over the outfit. Both Michael and Laura felt that having rosettes everywhere would detract from the elegance and sophistication of the outfit. Instead of arguing unproductively about the rosettes, they discussed possible ways to incorporate rosettes without making the outfit look gaudy. They ended up using the rosettes as buttons, not only satisfying all members of the group but also winning the challenge.

The other advantage of productive conflict is that the group members who engage in it feel a sense of ownership of the group's final decision. That's because they've had a hand in exploring and arriving at the decision. And when people share ownership of a decision, they're more likely to feel committed to carrying it out. Thus decisions made through productive conflict have a greater chance of being implemented. That's a good thing, since even the most brilliant decision is useless unless a group puts it into action.

For this reason, making decisions by consensus is often a better approach than making decisions by majority vote. According to the consensus approach, everyone must agree on the final decision before it can be implemented. Consensus enhances members' feeling of ownership and commitment to carrying out the decision. But as you might imagine, it takes more time than deciding by majority vote. Still, because of its power to enhance commitment from group members, consensus should be used whenever time allows.

### Follow Up

After the meeting has concluded, group members should implement their decisions and take stock of the results as well as the experience of working together. A simple follow-up e-mail that details the decisions reached at the meeting can ensure that everyone came away with the same perceptions and is aware of what each person must do to keep the group moving toward its goal.

## Using Technology in Meetings

Technology has changed the nature of meetings in both positive and negative ways. Obviously, the ability to set up virtual meetings through teleconferencing and videoconferencing makes it possible for groups to collaborate over long distances. That's how Julia, the freelance designer, is able to "attend" a meeting with her client and his sales staff without actually having to leave home. Such virtual links can be beneficial for a team that needs to actively communicate about some issue or problem. But it also can be abused; the fact that everyone *can* be included doesn't necessarily mean that everyone *must* be included. Julia, for example, did not need to sit in on the meeting with the

**AND YOU?**

Do you have experience with group conflict, as either a group member or leader? If so, how was this conflict handled? Did conflict strengthen or weaken the communication between group members?

● **ALTHOUGH SOME** *Project Runway* contestants considered Angela's rosettes to be eyesores, they decided to work productively with her rather than pick a fight with her.

sales team; she had little to add and gained nothing by being there. Further, the ability to share information with team members quickly and efficiently via e-mail and file sharing has enabled teams to avoid some meetings altogether (Conlin, 2006). Julia and Jacob, for example, might have done well to e-mail a link to the beta version of the site to the entire sales team rather than having a meeting to discuss it in the abstract.

But is there a difference between face-to-face meetings and virtual meetings? Research indicates that face-to-face teams perform better initially but that

## WIREDFORCOMMUNICATION

### Bridging Space and Time

Outsourcing, combined with time zone differences between members of a virtual team, means that groups can literally work around the clock. Sharyn, an account manager in Seattle, can spend all day on her accounts and send them to Indira in Bangalore at day's end, to be processed overnight and returned to Sharyn before her day begins the next morning.

Even as technology makes building virtual teams easier and more common, in far-flung, virtual environments, seemingly mundane tasks (such as scheduling or conducting a meeting) can become logistically difficult and personally taxing. Indeed, having workers in another time zone work while folks at the home office sleep can save an entire business day, which can be very beneficial when working on time-sensitive projects. But it can also cause frustrating delays if one member of the team has a question for another team member who is on a different continent. If Sharyn neglects to include some vital piece of information in the files she forwards to Indira, the project can be delayed for an entire day because of something that Sharyn could have provided in a matter of minutes if she were working at the same time as Indira.

Leaders of virtual teams must also grapple with unique challenges when trying to build team cohesion among coworkers who will most likely never meet face to face. Sharyn and Indira, for example, never talk but are in constant contact via e-mail. If either one of them has a question or complaint about the other's work, it's unlikely that they'll ever be able to resolve the conflict productively by talking to each other. It's up to their supervisor or group leader to handle the problem between them.

Managing meetings between virtual groups—even groups in the same time zone—can also be a challenge. Telephone conference calls, for example, typically involve members of one group on a speakerphone with other team members, either individuals or other groups, connected at the other end. In such situations, the larger group tends to dominate the discussion, and smaller groups or individuals find themselves left out. It is up to the group leader to manage such situations. One easy way to do it, notes one expert, is to "send people to their rooms"—that is, to have each team member sit at his or her own desk (rather than in groups) and dial in to the same conference call (Snyder, 2003). This way, the team consists of a group of individuals rather than a collection of small, competing groups.

**THINK ABOUT THIS**

❶ What can a group leader do to foster communication among team members in different locations and time zones?

❷ Should team members be expected to make themselves available via e-mail, text message, or telephone during non-working hours to attend to questions or problems that might arise? What problems might this kind of communication cause?

❸ Can virtual teams ever build group relationships if they can never communicate in real time?

once the group is established, virtual teams actually do better at brainstorming, while face-to-face teams perform better on tasks that require negotiation or compromise (Alge, Wiethoff, & Klein, 2003; Salkever, 2003). Savvy team leaders, then, will bring their teams together for face time early in the process, if possible, so that team members can get to know one another and get a sense of the others' styles and personalities. But as the teams develop, electronically mediated communication—especially e-mail—can often take the place of face-to-face group meetings.

# Evaluating Group Performance

Groups that intend to work together and meet on a regular basis should evaluate their decision-making performance periodically. By assessing how well the group makes decisions, achieves its goals, and solves problems, a group can identify and address areas needing improvement. Think of your group as an automobile: to make sure your car keeps running smoothly, you have to take stock of how it's operating and adjust a few things as needed (such as giving it a tune-up or replacing the tires). When evaluating your group's performance, it's helpful to assess the group's overall effectiveness as well as the performance of individual members and leaders.

   Albert Kowitz and Thomas Knutson (1980) have done extensive research evaluating groups as a whole. They recommend assessing three aspects of a group's performance: the informational, the procedural, and the interpersonal.

## Informational Considerations

Ask yourself whether your group is working on a task that requires everyone's expertise and insights. If not, the group doesn't actually need to be a group! In this case, it should select a different task or assign just one or two members to deal with the current task.

● **THINK ABOUT** whether each group member's expertise is necessary to achieve a goal. If not, they don't need to be present.

If the task does require contributions from all members, how well is the group doing on this front? For example, are members conducting needed research and inviting one another to share information during group gatherings? Does the group know when it needs to get more data before making a decision? Does the group analyze problems well? Come up with creative solutions? Offer opinions respectfully? Elaborate on problems, concerns, and solutions?

By regularly assessing these aspects of information management in your group, you can identify where the group is falling short and address the problem promptly. For instance, if you notice that the group rushes to make decisions without getting all the facts first, you could say something like "I think we need to find out more about the problem before we take action."

## Procedural Effectiveness

How well does your group coordinate its activities and communication? Key things to evaluate on this front are how the group elicits contributions, delegates and directs action, summarizes decisions, handles conflict, and manages processes.

For example, do some members talk too much while others give too little input? If so, the group needs someone to improve the balance of contributions. Simply saying something like "Allie, I think we should hear from some other people on this subject" can be very effective.

Or does your group tend to revisit issues it has already decided on? If so, you can expect many members to express frustration with this time-wasting habit. A leader or another member can steer the group back toward its current task by saying something like "OK, what we've been talking about is . . ." or "I'm not sure revisiting this previous decision is helping us deal with our current problem."

Finally, what does your group do when things become tense during a meeting? Another sign of procedural effectiveness is a group's ability to release tension. For example, someone cracks a joke or tells a funny story. Or a member says, "Well, the temperature in this room just dropped a few degrees!"—prompting everyone to acknowledge the tension and then resume the discussion.

## Interpersonal Performance

How would you describe the relationships among the members of your group while everyone is working together to accomplish a task? If these relationships are strained, awkward, or prickly, the group probably won't function effectively. Observe how group members behave on the following four fronts:

▶ Do they provide *positive reinforcement* for one another—for instance, by showing appreciation for each other's contributions and hard work?

▶ Do members seem to feel a sense of *solidarity* with one another—for example, by sharing responsibility for both successes and failures?

▶ Do members *cooperate freely* with one another, fulfilling the responsibilities they've agreed to shoulder and pitching in when needed?

▶ Do members demonstrate *respect* for one another—for example, by keeping disagreements focused on the issues or positions at hand rather than on personal character?

If you can answer yes to these four questions, your group scores high on interpersonal performance.

## BACK TO ▶ *Lost*

At the beginning of this chapter, we talked about the television show *Lost,* which tells the tale of a group of plane crash survivors on a mysterious island and the ways in which individual characters employ their leadership skills to manage the group. Let's take another look at the role of leadership in the story and how it relates to what you've learned in the chapter.

▶ In the aftermath of the crash, Jack's skills as a doctor prompt him to take a leadership role: his medical experience and decision-making capabilities allow him to present himself as a competent leader. Further, he quickly gains the group's trust as a man concerned primarily with the well-being of others, with a moral compass that simply will not allow him to let these people down. Although he has no legitimate power, he becomes a leader as a result of his expert and referent power.

▶ At the beginning of the series, Jack adopts a directive style of leadership as he takes control of the situation, organizes the survivors, and gives them directions on what they should do. But as he begins to recognize the strengths of members of the group, he takes a more participative approach.

▶ Jack soon learns that aside from the wounded survivors, he's got supernatural forces to deal with, not to mention the ghostly "others" on the island and an acerbic and unpredictable rival by the name of Sawyer. Adapting to the changing demands of this leadership role presents a constant challenge for Jack.

## THINGS TO TRY

1. Arrange an interview with the chair, president, or director of an organization to determine how the various groups within the organization operate. How closely do these groups conform to the decision-making process discussed in this chapter? Report what you have learned to the class.

2. Create a chart that lists the four leadership styles described in this chapter (directive, participative, supportive, and achievement-oriented). Evaluate the leaders of each of the different groups in which you participate—your boss at work, your professors, the resident assistant of your dorm—in terms of their leadership style. Where do they fall on your chart? Do some fit more than one category? Do some fit none?

3. Select a city, state, or campus problem that is relevant to the members of your class. Form a group to solve the problem using the six-step decision-making process described in this chapter.

## IF YOU'RE INTERESTED

*Katherine Graham: Personal History,* by Katherine Graham (New York: Knopf, 1997)

> Katherine Graham's autobiography tells of her rise to head the *Washington Post* and of the personal trials behind her success.

*No Ordinary Time: Franklin and Eleanor Roosevelt: The Home Front in World War II,* by Doris Kearns Goodwin (New York: Touchstone Books, 1994)

> Goodwin chronicles the Roosevelt White House during World War II, focusing on the domestic leadership roles of both the president and Mrs. Roosevelt.

*Apollo 13* (Universal, 1995)

> The world held its collective breath when in April 1970, three American astronauts headed for what was becoming a routine moon landing found themselves stranded on a broken ship with no clear way of landing either on the moon or back on earth. Ron Howard's film examines the nature of teamwork and leadership under unbelievable pressure as the crew of three and an army of engineers back in Houston struggle to bring the team safely back home.

*Iron Jawed Angels* (Home Box Office, 2004)

> This vibrant film tells the story of Alice Paul and Lucy Burns, two leaders of the early-twentieth-century women's suffrage movement in the United States. Taking a bold leadership style unprecedented and unexpected from "the weaker sex" in those days, these two brave women led a movement resulting in the successful passage of the Nineteenth Amendment in 1920.

*Hoosiers* (Orion, 1986)

> In this classic sports story, Gene Hackman's character, Coach Norman Dale, overcomes personal adversity to lead a small-town Indiana high school basketball team to the state championship. Coach Dale runs the team with ironclad rules but still helps each player develop to his utmost potential. At the heart of the story is how the boys come to trust their coach, and each other, and go out and beat the odds.

# REAL REFERENCE → A Study Tool

**Now that you have finished reading this chapter, you can**

Understand what makes an effective leader:

- ► **Leadership** is the ability to influences others' behaviors and thoughts toward a productive end (p. 260).
- ► **Legitimate power** comes from an individual's role or title (p. 261).
- ► **Coercive power** stems from the ability to threaten or harm others (p. 261).
- ► **Reward power** is derived from the ability to bestow rewards (p. 261).
- ► **Expert power** comes from the information or knowledge an individual possesses (p. 262).
- ► **Referent power** stems from the respect and affection that followers have for a leader (p. 262).
- ► Most leaders will use more than one type of power, and often leadership is shared by more than one individual (p. 263).

Describe leadership styles:

- ► The best leaders adapt their leadership styles to the situation (p. 263).
- ► A **directive leader** gives specific instructions; this is a good choice when members are unsure of expectations (p. 264).
- ► A **participative leader** views members as equals, inviting collaboration; this is effective when members are competent and motivated (p. 264).
- ► A **supportive leader** attends to members' emotional needs; this is helpful when members are frustrated or discouraged (p. 264).
- ► An **achievement-oriented leader** sets challenging goals and has high expectations; this is useful when members are motivated to excel (p. 264).
- ► The best leaders behave ethically and avoid **bullying** (p. 267).

Identify how culture affects leadership:

- ► Traditional leadership, identified as masculine, emphasizing command and control, may not be as effective in today's competitive arena as it once was (p. 267).
- ► Research suggests that women tend to think of organizations as webs of relationships (p. 268).
- ► Leaders from high-context cultures tend to make suggestions rather than dictating orders or imposing solutions (p. 268).

- ► **Power distance** is the extent to which members expect that power is distributed unequally; members in a high–power distance culture automatically defer to those with higher status (p. 269).

List the forces that shape a group's decisions:

- ► **Cognitive forces** are members' thoughts, beliefs, and emotions (p. 270).
- ► **Psychological forces** refer to members' personal motives, goals, attitudes, and values (p. 270).
- ► **Social forces** are group standards for behavior that influence decision making (p. 270).

Explain the six-step group decision process:

- ► Identify and define the problem (p. 271).
- ► Analyze the problem (p. 271).
- ► Generate solutions, identifying the criteria that eventual solutions will have to meet (p. 271).
- ► Evaluate and choose a solution (p. 272).
- ► Implement the solution (p. 273).
- ► Assess the results (p. 273).

Show how effective leadership is crucial for good communication in meetings:

- ► To ensure a well-planned meeting, you should assess whether the meeting is necessary, ensure that those present are necessary, ask for information in advance, articulate the goals, and set an **agenda** (p. 276).
- ► To manage the meeting, you should arrive prepared; keep the group focused; summarize periodically; keep an eye on the time, perhaps using a **nonbinding straw poll** to help move things along; manage conflict; foster productive conflict; and follow up after the meeting (p. 277).
- ► Use technology effectively, arranging a face-to-face meeting for the start-up, but as the team develops, allowing mediated communication (p. 279).

Know the three aspects of assessing group performance:

- ► Informational considerations: Does the group require all its members? Does it need more data? Does it come up with creative solutions? (p. 281)
- ► Procedural effectiveness: Does it coordinate activities and communication? Manage problems? (p. 282)
- ► Interpersonal performance: Do the members reinforce one another? Feel a sense of solidarity? Cooperate freely? Respect one another? (p. 282)

**It's much easier** to get up and go to work when you can whiz around on a bike at your office!

# chapter

## 10

# Communicating in Organizations

**Would you work harder or more efficiently** if your employer provided you with free gourmet meals whenever you were hungry? Would a midday massage increase your creativity? Wouldn't life be easier if you could just get your laundry done while you're at work? And might a midafternoon nap on a big, comfy sofa help prevent that energy dive you experience after lunch?

Folks at Google, one of the fastest-growing companies in the world, think it might. With a belief that happy employees are productive and creative employees, they built their sprawling campus in Mountain View, California, with a focus on fun. Most employees have meals at Charlie's Place, a company café, where they can hash over ideas they're working on or thinking about. "Meetings that would take hours elsewhere are frequently little more than a conversation in line for lunch," the company notes, "and few walls separate those who write the code from those who write the checks" (Google, 2008a). Workers literally scoot—or bike—from office to office, take breaks for midday volleyball games, and linger in lounges stocked with refreshments and furnished with pool tables. Walls are covered with whiteboards where workers scrawl graffiti and cartoons that turn random thoughts into innovative ideas (Google, 2008b).

But is a colorful and fun place to work enough to fuel the kind of innovation that makes companies like Google work? Probably not. That's why the company does more than just let its people play: it gives them room—and time—to think. Google's famous policy requiring engineers to spend 20 percent of their time on personal pet projects has yielded a few major innovations, including Google Suggest, AdSense for Content, and Orkut (Google, 2008c). It may be somewhat unclear whether it's the happy employees that are making this organization so successful or whether it's Google's success that offers plenty of money to spend on its employees. But in any case, it's a fun place to be—just ask the people at *Fortune* magazine, who rated Google number one on its 2007 list of the hundred best companies to work for ("100 Best," 2007).

After you have finished
reading this chapter,
you will be able to

- Recognize the various
approaches to managing
an organization

- Describe how
organizational culture is
communicated

- Explain the various
contexts in organizations

- Identify the challenges
facing today's organiza-
tions

The management at Google takes a particular interest in communication. The company cares about how employees communicate with one another, how management communicates with employees, and even what the office setting communicates about the company. And while not every workplace lets its employees take afternoon naps, these larger points about Google's communication hold for most **organizations**, groups with a formal governance and structure. You see this in action every day: your college or university, student groups, fraternity, religious community, volunteer organizations, and town, county, and state governments are all actively involved in the process of communicating messages about themselves and their members. This is why we stress that **organizational communication**, the interaction necessary to direct a group toward a set of common goals, is about more than meeting agendas and skills or getting along with moody bosses. It is at work in your life *right now* (Eisenberg, Goodall, & Trethewey, 2007). So it's important that we understand these organizations and how we communicate in them. In this chapter, we'll look at several approaches to managing organizations, issues related to organizational culture, important contexts for communicating in organizations, and common issues facing organizations today.

## Approaches to Managing Organizations

For as long as we humans have been working together toward shared common goals, we've been trying to figure out how to organize ourselves to achieve success. Whether we're talking about effective ways to build a castle, establish a town in the wilderness, or run a factory, preschool, or student government, it's useful to learn the various approaches to managing organizations. Over the centuries, these approaches have changed quite dramatically, and the changes have had important implications for how people in organizations work together and communicate. In the following sections, we'll take a quick trip through time to see how this evolution has played out, beginning with the classical management approach and moving on to the human relations, human resources, and systems approaches.

### Classical Management Approach

In Tim Burton's 2005 film *Charlie and the Chocolate Factory,* Charlie, an impoverished youngster, wins a tour through the most magnificent chocolate factory in the world, run by the highly unusual candymaker Willy Wonka (played by Johnny Depp). As Charlie tours the factory with a small group of other children, he sees strange creatures, each performing specific tasks. Some do nothing but pour mysterious ingredients into giant, clanking candymaking machines. Others focus on guiding the tour boats that ferry the children along rivers of sweet liquid. Still others work only on packing finished candies into boxes as the candies come off the assembly lines. You could almost compare the chocolate factory to a car and each worker to a specific part with a specific job—seat belt, brakes, steering wheel, and so on.

To Charlie, the factory might be a novelty or a curiosity, but to organizational communication scholars, it's a pretty clear example of the **classical management**

● **WHETHER YOU'RE** part of a fraternity trying to rush new members or part of Greenpeace's efforts to save the oceans, your organization communicates its beliefs and goals to the outside world.

**approach**—an approach that likens organizations to machines, with a focus on maximizing efficiency. Not surprisingly, classical management reached its peak during the Industrial Revolution in the nineteenth century—a time when factories and machinery were proliferating rapidly in various parts of the world, particularly Europe, North America, and Japan.

Classical management depends on two central ideas, both of which have strong implications for communication. The first is a **division of labor**, or the assumption that each part of an organization (and each person involved) must carry out a specialized task in order for the organization to run smoothly. This is exactly what you see in *Charlie and the Chocolate Factory:* each creature has a very specific job, and there is little reason for individual workers—or groups of workers on different tasks—to communicate with one another. Classical management approaches also favor **hierarchy**, which refers to the layers of power and authority in an organization. To illustrate, in Willy Wonka's chocolate factory, Willy has the most power to control the working conditions, rewards, and other aspects of life for all the creatures who work in the factory. His team of lower-level "managers" (such as the head of the Oompa Loompas) have somewhat less power. And the workers themselves have almost no power at all. As illustrated, communication in such situations is often top-down. It's unlikely that a creature pouring chocolate would contact Willie Wonka to make suggestions for improving the factory.

## Human Relations Approach

If reading about the classical management approach makes you want to protest that you're a person, not a machine,

**AND YOU?**

Are you involved with or familiar with any organizations that favor hierarchy and a division of labor? What are the pros and cons for communication in such organizations?

● **THE OOMPA LOOMPAS** in *Charlie and the Chocolate Factory* are responsible for rowing a boat down this chocolate-filled river, and not much else!

you're not alone. Critics of such organizational practices became more vocal during the Great Depression and World War II, times characterized by massive social and economic changes in the United States. For example, scholars Eric Eisenberg, Bud Goodall, and Angela Trethewey (2007) discuss the work of Mary Parker Follett (1868–1933), a Boston social worker who developed new and seemingly radical ideas about leadership, community, and communication. She believed that "only cooperation among people working together in groups under a visionary leadership produced excellence in the workplace, the neighborhood and the community" (p. 82). That's a far cry from the classical management approach. Follett and others set the stage for the **human relations approach** to management, which considers the human needs of organizational members (enjoying inter-personal relationships, sharing ideas with others, and so forth).

The benefits of this approach came into sharper focus in the 1930s when Harvard professors Elton Mayo and F. J. Roethlisberger conducted an experiment at Western Electric's Hawthorne plant in Cicero, Illinois, in order to discover why employees were dissatisfied and unproductive. The researchers conducted an experiment in which they separated workers into two different rooms. In one room, the researchers slowly increased the amount of light; in the other, the amount of light was held constant. Much to the researchers' surprise, both groups of workers showed an increase in productivity, regardless of the amount of light they were exposed to. Why? It turns out that the employees were motivated by the increased attention they were receiving from management rather than the in-creased amount of light (Eisenberg et al., 2007).

In organizations managed with the human relations approach, communica-tion takes on a different flavor than in companies managed through the classical approach. Managers express more interest in employees (for example, encourag-ing them to give their best on the job), and they emphasize the notion that "we're all in this together," so employees have a greater sense of belonging to a larger cause or purpose. Similarly, organizational members are encouraged to interact on a more personal level, allowing for satisfying exchanges of thoughts and ideas.

## Human Resources Approach

The human relations approach was an improvement over the classical one in terms of bettering workforce productivity. But it didn't take into account em-ployees' own goals and motivations for success. While incorporating the basics of human relations, the **human resources approach** takes things one step further by considering organizational productivity from the workers' perspectives.

In Chapter 15, we will introduce you to Abraham Maslow and his hierarchy of needs, which asserts that people must fulfill basic needs (such as obtaining food and shelter) before they can achieve higher needs (such as finding friend-ship, love, and enjoyable work). As you will discover, Maslow's work is particu-larly useful when discussing persuasive speaking, but it also had a powerful impact on communication in organizations. For example, in consideration of Maslow's work, managers learned to focus on employees' higher-level needs, such as self-esteem and self-fulfillment, rather than lower-level needs, like food and safety. After all, the fact that your organization has a security guard and a cafeteria isn't what's going to compel people to want to work there!

Maslow's ideas also play out in other organizational situations. Imagine that you're a new member of a synagogue and you're not quite sure how to get involved. Your rabbi might find that you have a knack for working with kids; he or she might motivate you to become a more productive member of the community by telling

## real communicator

**NAME:** Pat Driscoll
**HOMETOWN:** Belle Harbor, NY
**OCCUPATION:** Online producer
**FUN FACT:** While working as an NBC page, I was "fired" live on the *Today* show by Donald Trump.

When I was in college, majoring in communication, I remember hoping that I'd one day work for a company that takes a human resources approach to organizational communication. I didn't want to end up like the Charlie Chaplin character in *Modern Times,* the guy who works on an assembly line and then gets sucked into the machine, his body pulverized by giant wheels, cogs, and levers.

Today I work as a writer-producer for black20.com, a comedy network on the Internet. Thankfully, black20—like all organizations with an HR approach—stresses interpersonal relationships and the sharing of ideas. It's how we make comedy.

Black20 was founded by three friends who worked together at a major television network, and many people who have joined the company have a personal relationship with one of the original three. In other words, we're all friends—which makes for a unique organizational culture. There are supervisors, but we share responsibilities. Producers work with writers who work with the on-air talent who are themselves writers and producers. We get to work at 10:00 A.M., and everyone stays until that day's work is done.

Because of the human relations approach, quirky ideas can quickly snowball into a polished comic video. For instance, a black20 employee was—for no discernible reason—singing the Feist song "1-2-3-4" in a vampire accent. Because every office door in the company is always open, I overheard him. I came into his office and said,

"What if Dracula loved pop hits?" From there we started singing different songs in Dracula's accent. We figured he'd probably be a fan of Puff Daddy's "Bad Boys for Life" and Kid Rock's "Bawitdaba." A video was taking shape.

I went to one of my bosses—he's more like a mentor, actually—and he laughed. With most jobs that's probably a bad sign, but not here. We held a meeting, which is an informational presentation in which the audience is made up of heckling class clowns. Everyone's ideas were mapped out on a whiteboard. Instead of one music video, we decided it would be funnier to do a fake commercial selling a CD called (in a takeoff of those *NOW! That's What I Call Music* compilations) *NOW! That's What Dracula Calls Music*. We spent hours debating how the video should be approached, how particular lines should be spoken, whether to film Dracula at a cemetery or popping out of a coffin (we went with both). We took all ideas, and—as always—majority ruled.

Since we're all friends, I have the utmost trust in the people I work with. No one is trying to outdo the other. And because we're young comedians working at a start-up Web site, each of us realizes that our career is riding on the person next to us. There's a sense of common goals and interdependence. I just happen to work at a place in which the common goal is pretending to sell a CD that doesn't exist sung by a fictional neck-biting vampire. That's my job. Somebody's got to do it.

● **THE HUMAN RESOURCES** approach takes into consideration your likes and dislikes as an employee.

you that you have a gift for teaching and encouraging you to fulfill your potential by volunteering with the Hebrew school class each week. Similarly, your manager at the tutoring center where you work ten hours a week might take the time to find out what you really value about your job. If you particularly enjoy tutoring Spanish, he or she might be interested in setting you up with students struggling in this subject: you'll be more engaged with your job, and the students will receive high-quality help, which can lead to improved grades and increased interest in tutoring services. Everyone wins.

## The Systems Approach

You can see that human relations and human resources had a huge impact on the plight of organizational members. No longer is an employee a "cog in the machine" of the classical approach; an employee is now a person with feelings and ambitions who is a valuable member of an organization. But note that neither approach considers the importance of *both* the individual *and* the organization as a whole. This realization led to the **systems approach**, which views an organization as a unique whole made up of important members who have interdependent relationships in their particular environment (Monge, 1977). This means that no individual can work in isolation; no company, group, or team can insulate itself from the interactions of its members; and outside forces can change the communication processes of organizations.

Figure 10.1 shows how a college or university works as a system. Its members include faculty, students, office staff, financial aid staff, and the bursar, all of whom have relationships with one another. The college exists within an environment, which includes other systems that directly affect it. These other systems might be the city and state where the college is located, the legislature that sets tuition, local employers who offer students full-time or part-time jobs, the families that the students come from or live with, and the high schools that supply many of the students.

Two of the most important components of organizations as systems are openness and adaptability. **Openness** in a system refers to an organization's awareness of its own imbalances and problems. For example, in our university example, let's say that our college begins receiving messages from local elementary schools that the university's student teachers seem ill prepared for the classroom. The university has two choices: it can ignore this feedback about the health of its program, or it can look to correct the problem, perhaps restructuring its elementary education program with feedback from local educators, professors, students, and government and policy representatives. The latter choice clearly helps the organization move forward by allowing for change and growth in light of changing times and circumstances. This ability to adjust is known as **adaptability**. And at the heart of it all is communication. If everyone involved in the system, from students to professors to principals, keeps to themselves and never voices concerns or ideas, the system can become closed and collapse under the weight of its own problems.

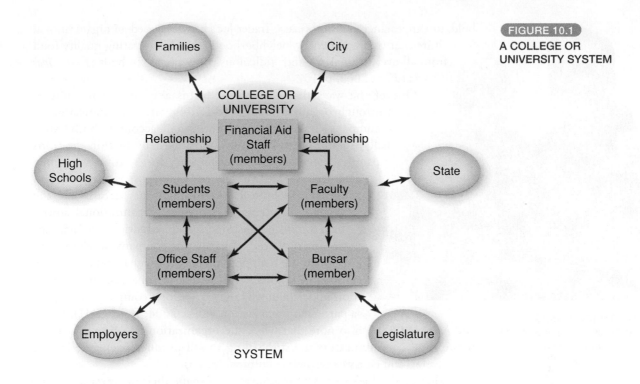

FIGURE 10.1
A COLLEGE OR
UNIVERSITY SYSTEM

## Communicating Organizational Culture

The management approaches you learned about in the preceding section can cause one organization to feel quite different from another. If you were working in a nineteenth-century factory that valued classical management, you probably wouldn't have team birthday parties or picnics the way you might under the management of the human resources approach, which values individuals. Yet understanding how different organizations come to give off different vibes is more complex than simply understanding their management styles. We must come to understand **organizational culture**, an organization's unique set of beliefs, values, norms, and ways of doing things (Harris, 2002). What's particularly fascinating to scholars in our discipline is the pivotal role that *communication* has in both the shaping and the expression of organizational culture. We'll elaborate on this topic in the sections that follow, looking at the popular Trader Joe's grocery store chain.

## Organizational Storytelling

Do you enjoy food shopping? We don't. The lines are long, the store lighting is never flattering, and there's always someone who leaves a cart in the middle of the aisle so that you can't pass. But if you're lucky enough to live near a Trader Joe's, you might have a very different experience when purchasing groceries: employees smile and recommend their favorite salsa, food prices remain reasonable despite nationwide increases, and the colorful South Seas décor gives the place a

● **AT TRADER JOE'S,** employees always have bright smiles—and plenty of tasty food recommendations!

bold, fun appearance. This is because Trader Joe's has developed an organizational culture that values a friendly, neighborhood feel while offering quality food from all over the world—and "ridiculously low prices" to boot (*Trader Joe's Fearless Flyer,* 2008, p. 10).

One of the ways that Trader Joe's forms and ensures its cultural values is through **organizational storytelling**, the communication of the company's values through stories and accounts, both externally (to an outside audience) and internally (within the company). An organization telling a story isn't so different from a parent telling a story to a young child. Just as fairy tales and children's books teach kids important lessons, like the dangers of talking to strangers, organizational stories help would-be customers and potential members answer the question "What is this company all about?" or "Why should I support or join this organization?" They also help employees and current members of an organization understand why they work for a company or support a particular organization (Aust, 2004; Boje, 1991). James and Minnis (2004) also note that when the organization is a for-profit business, "good communicators use storytelling to sell products, generate buy-in and develop and cultivate corporate culture" (p. 26).

What Trader Joe's stories communicate and shape their organizational culture? We'll look at several examples. First, consider the stories that the store itself tells us. As we noted earlier, it looks different from other grocery stores. Employees wear sneakers and Hawaiian shirts, hand-lettered signs tout low prices, and someone with really nice penmanship takes the time to write puns on a giant chalkboard ("Leaf it to us to give you your favorite bagged salads"). The message is clear: we're fun, we've got cool stuff, and we're cheap. Trader Joe's Web site and newsletter (*Trader Joe's Fearless Flyer*) also present fun drawings, facts about the company, and cleverly written highlights of featured products (anyone up for some Spanish gazpacho soup or lemon raspberry Zinger bundt cake?).

In addition, like many successful organizations, Trader Joe's makes use of metaphors in its storytelling. A *metaphor,* you may recall, is a figure of speech that likens one thing to something else in a literal way, although there is no literal connection between the two (see Jacobs & Heracleous, 2006). You probably use metaphors often: "This classroom is a freezer" or "This assignment is a nightmare." Trader Joe's metaphor is, essentially, "We are a ship." Ships are associated with travel, perhaps even vacation, which highlights the company's commitment to provide quality products from all over the world. The employees at Trader Joe's are all crew members, including the captain (store manager) and the first mate (assistant store manager) (Lewis, 2005). Each member is essential to keeping the ship running; no one is expendable. These titles communicate Trader Joe's commitment to being employee-friendly, which in turn leads to friendly employees and happy customers.

Trader Joe's also makes use of stories about **organizational heroes**, individuals who have achieved great things for the organization through persistence and commitment, often in the face of great risk (James & Minnis, 2004; Schulman,

**AND YOU?**

Think about a store that you shop at frequently. What messages do the store layout and décor send customers? Does the store offer any literature or brochures about itself? Does it have a Web site? If so, what do these media communicate about the organization?

1996). Trader Joe's employees and would-be customers alike all learn about "Trader Joe" himself, a Stanford University M.B.A. graduate named Joe Coulombe who opened a chain of Pronto Market convenience stores in the Los Angeles area during the 1950s. In the 1960s, 7-Eleven stores invaded southern California, threatening to crush Joe's business. Rather than admit defeat, Coulombe changed his tactics: trusting that the burgeoning airline industry would entice more Americans to travel—and that those Americans would want to find the foods they enjoyed abroad once they were back home—Coulombe began stocking imported foods other convenience stores didn't carry. Thus began the first Trader Joe's in 1967 (Hoover, 2006).

## Learning About Organizational Culture

Could someone who dislikes people, low prices, Hawaiian shirts, and bean dips find a successful career at Trader Joe's? Well, that would depend on how well the individual is able to adapt to the organization's culture. According to Van Maanen and Schein (as cited in Mignerey, Rubin, & Gorden, 1995), the process by which someone "learns the ropes" of participating in a particular organization is known as **organizational assimilation**. A study by Lester (as cited in Mignerey et al., 1995) notes that successful assimilation is often based on a newcomer's ability to figure out and make use of behaviors that will be appropriate and effective in a given organization. Typically, new organizational members are quite motivated to get these behaviors figured out because the uncertainty of not knowing what to do or say can be a bit scary. Organizations understand this as well and generally seek to help. That's why fraternities and sororities have rush parties, so that prospective members can see if they'll fit in. Similarly, religious organizations often have new-member meetings or classes, and employers often have an orientation program to acquaint newcomers with the organization.

At Trader Joe's, for example, new employees are subject to the group "huddle," when all staff members at the store come together in a circle to share information and introduce themselves, perhaps noting where they're from or how long they've been with Trader Joe's. The idea is to make each new employee feel like part of the team (or in this case, crew) and to get to know everyone. You can imagine a new employee walking away from the huddle thinking, "OK, these people value friendliness and team building," which in turn reflects what Trader Joe's values and communicates to customers. A new employee at a different organization who eats lunch alone in a corner would likely experience a very different set of values.

Similarly, an additional perk of working for Trader Joe's is the free samples. Employees are always encouraged to try new products and even make up recipes for everyone to try (Lewis, 2005). The benefit of this is that employees become actively engaged with the products: they feel personally connected to the products and can make heartfelt recommendations to customers, thereby furthering Trader Joe's value of a friendly, interactive shopping experience.

Organizational stories can also help new individuals assimilate. For example, stories illustrate praiseworthy and unacceptable behaviors, reflecting the values of an organization (Meyer, 1995). Imagine you're new at a part-time job at your

**CONNECT**

Strategies that help reduce uncertainty in interpersonal relationships (Chapter 6) can also help in new organizational settings. At a new job, you might use *monitoring strategies* to learn whether joking with peers during work hours is acceptable, *proactive strategies,* like asking where to find office supplies, or *indirect strategies,* like asking a colleague how your new boss reacts to difficult situations. Such strategies help you assimilate faster and more comfortably.

local library. The environment seems really laid back and casual, but not about everything. The children's librarian, Faith, approaches you and says, "Did you hear that the boss screamed at Shira this morning for being five minutes late? Her car wouldn't start, but he didn't care. She's in the bathroom crying right now." Your boss could tell you two hundred times that being on time matters in this organization; he could post memos around the library stating the same thing. But neither is as effective or as powerful as the message that your colleague is weeping in a bathroom stall after getting yelled at for violating the boss's rules.

## Relational Contexts in Organizations

● *THE OFFICE*'S MICHAEL SCOTT wants his employees to view him as a friend first and a boss second, but that only leads to awkward and inappropriate encounters in the Dunder Mifflin office.

Different cultures clearly affect communication in an organization. But no matter how laid back or formal an organization is, the relationships between organizational members will have an impact on the way communication happens. Consider *The Office*'s Michael Scott, who is, frankly, a pretty awkward guy. While we may get a good laugh out of his antics, we can't help but admit that we feel a little embarrassed for him when he makes an entirely inappropriate comment about his personal life to one of his employees or addresses his manager with the salutation "Yo, wazzup." We laugh and we groan because Michael is utterly unaware that there are special considerations when sharing messages with different people in an organization, such as supervisors, mentors, and peers. Let's consider each of these relationships in turn.

### Supervisor-Supervisee Relationships

Few relationships are parodied as often as the relationship between supervisors and the people they manage. Think of Homer Simpson reporting to Mr. Burns, Dr. Cox reporting to Dr. Kelso on *Scrubs,* or the aforementioned employees from *The Office* reporting to Michael Scott. We often enjoy portrayals of the "bad" boss or the "crazy" boss who causes employees to sit around the lunch table complaining, even though in real life, most bosses are fairly reasonable people. Perhaps we find pleasure in these portrayals because supervisors, inherently, have power over us. Bosses negotiate our salaries and approve our vacation time; they might determine our hours or whether or not we get promoted. There are supervisory roles in nonworkplace situations as well. Your priest may require you to attend premarital counseling sessions before he will agree to marry you and your fiancé; you have to get your student government president to approve your idea for this year's budget before you can actually makes plans to do anything with that money. And to achieve anything worthwhile with your supervisor, the two of you must be communicating regularly.

If you're involved in a professional, community, or student organization where people are reporting to you, don't be a Mr. Burns! You should know how to get the most out of your conversations with the people you supervise. Often you can improve communication by following just a few simple steps:

▶ Schedule adequate time for important conversations. For example, if you are the president of a student organization and you need to speak to the treasurer about his messy bookkeeping, don't do it in the ten minutes you have between classes. Set up an appointment, and allow adequate time to discuss the problem and generate solutions.

▶ Minimize distractions or interruptions in order to give your full attention to your supervisee or employee.

▶ Ask supervisees for suggestions and ideas. For example, if you're working as a manager in a bank, you might ask the tellers for suggestions to make the work schedule more equitable.

▶ Demonstrate that you're listening when a supervisee is speaking to you, giving appropriate verbal and nonverbal responses, such as paraphrasing what you're hearing and nodding.

Even if you manage several people, you almost certainly report to a supervisor yourself—and it's important that you be able to communicate competently in this context as well. You can certainly follow the guidelines regarding listening and avoiding distractions that we mentioned earlier, but there are a few additional points to consider when you're the person with less power:

▶ Spend some time thinking about what you'd like to say to your boss. What are the main points you want to make? What do you hope to achieve through this discussion? It's embarrassing to start talking with a supervisor only to realize that you forgot what you wanted to say.

▶ Then spend some time *rehearsing* what you want to say to your manager. You might even ask a friend or family member to rehearse the conversation with you so that you can hear yourself speak.

▶ When you speak with your manager, try to avoid being emotional or hurling accusations such as "You always . . ." or "You never . . ." It's typically more productive to be specific and logical and to ask for clarification: "When you removed me from the Edwards project, I took that to mean that you didn't think I was capable of handling it. Am I misunderstanding something?"

▶ Remember to be open-minded in discussions (whether with your boss or with other members of your organization). In the example above, for instance, you boss may have taken away a particular project because he or she has something else in store for you. Be an active listener.

▶ Keep the lines of communication open. Misunderstandings or unfocused goals are often the result of a lack of clear communication.

CONNECT

In addition to the tips we list here, competent communication with your boss will also include effective and appropriate use of nonverbal communication (Chapter 4). Be sure to make appropriate eye contact, avoid fidgeting, and use an appropriate tone of voice. Shifty eyes, rapid movements, or a sarcastic tone can make you come across as guilty, hostile, or anxious—not desireable when discussing a difficult or intense situation with your manager.

● **BIG BROTHERS** and Big Sisters of America is a good example of how mentor and protégé relationships work. The "Bigs" spend time with their "Littles" and act as a positive influence and support system for them.

**CONNECT**

For competent communication in the evolving relationship between mentor and protégé, you need to understand key aspects of the relational context—history, goals, and expectations—discussed in Chapter 1. As a protégé, you might be uncomfortable if your company mentor asked *you* for professional advice; it might be equally awkward to ask your mentor for advice on searching for a new job when you first meet. Such communication would likely defy expectations.

## Mentor-Protégé Relationships

Somewhat related to the supervisor-supervisee relationship is the mentor-protégé relationship. A **mentor** is a seasoned, respected member of an organization who serves as a role model for a less experienced individual, his or her **protégé** (Russell & Adams, 1997).

If a new employee or member of an organization has a supervisor or access to some other person in a position of authority, does he or she really need a mentor? Doesn't that just muddy the waters and create confusion for the newcomer? Research shows that mentoring actually provides a number of key benefits for everyone involved (Jablin, 2001). For one thing, it accelerates the protégé's assimilation into the organization and its culture, which helps the newcomer become productive faster and thus helps the organization meet its goals. Protégés win, too, by receiving career guidance, sharpening their skills quickly, learning about the organization's challenges, and gaining access to other influential people in the organization (Russell & Adams, 1997). And the mentors themselves benefit by receiving recognition as their protégés begin to achieve in the organization. Plus there's always the personal sense of accomplishment of teaching and supporting another person (Kalbfleisch, 2002).

Many colleges and universities set up mentorship relationships for incoming students in order to help them adjust to life at the college or perhaps even life away from home. In many cases, second-, third-, or fourth-year students agree to be "big brothers" or "big sisters" to help the newcomers figure out campus parking, where to get a decent sandwich between classes, or which professors to take or avoid. First-year students may then become mentors themselves in future years. As you can imagine, the communication between mentor and protégé changes over time in this example. At first, the protégé may rely quite heavily on the mentor, since everything in the college environment is new and perhaps somewhat frightening. However, as the first-year student adjusts and begins to feel comfortable and self-assured, he or she will rely less and less on the mentor. By the next fall, the protégé may well be on an equal par with the mentor, and the relationship may have turned into a friendship or may have dissolved entirely. Understanding that mentor-protégé relationships go through four distinct stages—initiation, cultivation, separation, and redefinition—can help both parties adjust to these natural changes. See Table 10.1 for more on these stages and the communication that takes place during each.

If you are new to an organization—be it a community college, a house of worship, or a job—and a mentorship relationship interests you, you can see if the organization has a formal program. If such a program does not exist, you can still find a mentor, albeit in a more informal way. Consider the following tips (Kram, 1983):

► Ask your peers (colleagues, members of a congregation, and so on) to recommend individuals who might be interested in serving as a mentor.

► Identify people who have progressed in the organization in ways that interest you, and determine whether one of them would make a good mentor.

**TABLE 10.1**

**STAGES IN MENTOR-PROTÉGÉ RELATIONSHIPS**

| Stage | Communication Goal | Mentor Responsibilities | Protégé Responsibilities |
|---|---|---|---|
| Initiation | Get to know one another | • Show support through counseling and coaching<br>• Help protégé set goals | • Demonstrate openness to suggestions and loyalty to the mentor |
| Cultivation | Form a mutually beneficial bond | • Promote the protégé throughout the organization (for example, by introducing him or her to influential people)<br>• Communicate knowledge about how to work best with key people and what the organization's culture is | • Put new learning to use (for example, by forging relationships with influential people)<br>• Share personal perspective and insights with mentor |
| Separation | Drift apart as protégé gains skill | • Spend less time with protégé | • Take more initiative in the organization<br>• Strive for development or promotion |
| Redefinition | Become peers | • Occasionally provide advice or support as needed | • Stay in touch with mentor at times if additional advice is required |

▶ Build rapport with someone you think would be an effective mentor. Ask if he or she would like to sponsor you in a mentor-protégé relationship. Explain why you think he or she would be a good mentor, and describe your qualifications as a protégé—such as your ability to learn or to cultivate networks quickly.

## Peer Relationships

One of the most fun aspects of watching the television show *Scrubs* is keeping track of the web of relationships among the staff at Sacred Heart Hospital. Workplace friendships, secret crushes, full-fledged romances, and bitter resentments could definitely keep your night interesting! Yet these interactions also interest us as scholars, because such **peer relationships** reveal the importance of **peer communication**, communication between individuals at the same level of authority in an organization. Researchers, management coaches, and popular magazines warn that Americans are spending more and more time in the workplace, leaving less and less time for outside personal relationships. Yet we all need friends and confidants. So where do we find them? You guessed it—in the organizations we devote time to, particularly the organizations we work for. Research, however, seems to say some contradictory things about whether or not this phenomenon is healthy.

According to *USA Today* (Jones, 2004), 29 percent of employees say that they have a "best friend" at work. And a Gallup Poll survey of five million workers

● **HAVING WORKPLACE FRIENDS** has its ups (you have someone to take a coffee break with) and its downs (they might accidentally blab your personal information at work).

When communicating with peers in organizations, remember *communication privacy management* (Chapter 6), which helps you understand how people perceive and manage personal information. You may decide that certain topics, such as your romantic life or your interest in graduate studies, are off limits at work. You must determine for yourself what is private in different relationships—and it's also wise to consider the cultural expectations of your organization before sharing.

tells us why this statistic matters. Out of the approximately three in ten people who state that they have a best friend at work, 56 percent are engaged with, or enjoy, their work, while 33 percent are not engaged. Only 11 percent are actively disengaged and negative about their work experience. On the other hand, of the seven in ten workers who do not have a best friend at work, only 8 percent are engaged while 63 percent are not. The remaining third of employees without a workplace best friend are actively disengaged from their work. These findings have powerful implications for employers: having a workplace best friend makes workers seven times more likely to enjoy their work and consequently be more productive. Perhaps this is the thinking behind organizational initiatives to help employees get to know one another—office picnics, hospital softball teams, and school Frisbee and golf tournaments.

But there's also a downside to these workplace intimacies. One is that the relationships may not actually be so intimate after all. *Management Today* warns that professional friendships are often based on what is done together in the workplace. When the mutual experience of work is taken away, the friendship can easily wither and die ("Office Friends," 2005). Privacy and power also come into play, since sharing personal details about your life can influence how others see you in a professional setting. For example, Pamela, an insurance broker from Chicago, did not want her colleagues or boss to know that she was heading into the hospital to have a double mastectomy in order to avoid breast cancer. But she did tell her close friend and colleague, Lisa. When Pamela returned to the office, there was a "get well soon" bouquet of flowers from her boss waiting on her desk. Lisa had blabbed; Pamela felt betrayed and had the additional burden of her colleagues' knowing this private, intimate detail about her life (Rosen, 2004). It's also important to remember that friendships in the workplace—and all organizations—are going to face trials when loyalty and professional obligations are at odds. For example, in the *Scrubs* episode "My Way or the Highway," medical intern J.D. asks his friend, surgical intern Turk, to help persuade his patient that the man does not need surgery. In Turk's professional opinion, however, he feels that surgery is the patient's best option—and he says so. This leaves J.D. embarrassed and annoyed and leaves Turk feeling defensive.

Please don't take this to be a warning against making friends in the organizations you belong to. Relationships with colleagues and other members of organizations can be both career-enhancing and personally satisfying. But it's important to be mindful as you cultivate such relationships. The following tips can help (Rosen, 2004):

▶ *Take it slow.* When you meet someone new in your organization (be it your job or your residence hall association), don't blurt out all of your personal details right away. Take time to get to know this potential friend.

▶ *Know your territory.* Organizations have different cultures, as you've learned. Keep that in mind before you post pictures of your romantic partner all over your gym locker for the rest of the soccer team to see.

▶ *Learn to handle conflict.* If your friend Alisha from a particular student organization wants to run for president despite the fact that you plan to run as well, talk it out. Manage the conflict or awkwardness before it becomes problematic.

▶ *Don't limit yourself.* It's OK to take the time to make friends outside of your fraternity or sorority or outside of your job!

▶ *Accept an expiration date.* Sometimes friendships simply don't last outside of the context they grew in. You may have found that you lost some of your high school friends when you started college; this point is also particularly true for friendships on the job. Accept that life sometimes works out like this and that no one is to blame.

## Challenges Facing Today's Organizations

*Diversity* is a word you likely hear a lot nowadays. We use it throughout this book to highlight the importance of understanding and respecting people from various co-cultures with experiences different from our own. But you also hear about companies needing to "diversify" and the importance of tailoring messages

> ### AND YOU?
> Who are your three closest friends? Are they members of any organizations that you belong to? If so, has your joint membership affected the friendship in any particularly positive or negative ways? Explain your answer.

---

# EVALUATINGCOMMUNICATIONETHICS

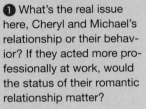

### More Than Friends at Work

You've begun to notice that two colleagues at work, Cheryl and Michael, are spending an inordinate amount of time together, and you suspect that they may be romantically involved—or at least engaged in a very strong flirtation. They work together on the same self-directed work team, and so it's natural that they spend a lot of time together, but you—along with a few of your colleagues—are beginning to be annoyed by the amount of time the two spend in one or the other's office, chatting about personal and other non-work issues and generally goofing off during working hours. Both of them are beginning to fall behind on their work, and their slacking off is affecting the performance of your entire department. You've approached Michael about it, noting that "people are beginning to notice" how much time he spends with Cheryl. They cooled it for a few days after that, but gradually, they returned to their old behavior.

Personally, you don't have a problem with the two of them having a relationship outside the office. However, you know that the company has a policy requiring employees to disclose any romantic relationships between coworkers—a policy that you see as an invasion of privacy and with which you don't agree. But the constant chatter and goofing off that they do at work is beginning to affect your own work, not to mention feeding the gossip mill around the watercooler, thus distracting other members of your team from getting their work done.

You've considered speaking to your boss, who works on a different floor and isn't aware of Cheryl and Michael's day-to-day behavior, or even talking to human resources about it. But you're reluctant to "rat them out," especially because you're not even sure that the two are actually romantically involved. What should you do?

### THINK ABOUT THIS

❶ What's the real issue here, Cheryl and Michael's relationship or their behavior? If they acted more professionally at work, would the status of their romantic relationship matter?

❷ How does your opinion of the company policy on dating at work factor into your decision? Does the impact of your coworkers' flirtation change your opinion of the policy?

❸ What other approaches could you take to get Cheryl and Michael to change their behavior? Is going over their heads your only option?

to a "diverse" audience. What does it all mean? It means that today's organizations need to branch out and be open to new ideas and experiences. They must make use of new communication technology and address colleagues and other organizations worldwide. Organizational members must find ways to balance the multitude of pressures for their time and must also learn to be tolerant of each other's differences and behave competently and respectfully at all times. We examine these important issues in the sections that follow.

## Communication Technology

Advances in communication technology—including instant messaging, professional and social networking sites, and videoconferencing—enable members of organizations to communicate more easily, particularly with clients and colleagues who work offsite or in home offices. But they've also introduced new challenges for organizations.

First, there's the question of figuring out which channel is most appropriate for a particular message in an organizational setting. We've discussed this point in earlier chapters—you might, for example, text a friend an apology if you're too embarrassed to call her. But there are additional ethical and legal considerations when choosing channels in organizations. If you're a manager, you simply cannot fire someone in an e-mail with the entire department copied. Rather, you would need to have a private face-to-face meeting—or perhaps a phone call if the employee works elsewhere in the country or the world. This is an illustration of **media richness** (Daft & Lengel, 1984, 1986), the degree to which a particular channel is communicative. Media richness theory suggests that people must consider the number of contact points a particular channel offers for a message. Face-to-face communication is the richest, because it allows for verbal and nonverbal contact. Speaking on the phone is slightly less rich, as it allows for verbal contact and some limited nonverbal contact (tone of voice, rate of speaking, and so on) but removes the opportunity to communicate with body movements. E-mails and text messages are even less rich, for they lack most nonverbal cues and need not be responded to immediately. The level of richness people expect in their communication vehicles depends on their goals. So if you need to tell the treasurer of your student organization that your meeting has been moved to a

● **IF YOU HAVE** something sensitive to discuss with a colleague, it's better to do so in a face-to-face situation rather than with a text message.

different room, you can just text her. It's fast and easy, and the message is unlikely to be misunderstood. However, if you needed to discuss the fact that you noticed a $250 discrepancy on the books, you'd have better luck with a face-to-face conversation.

Research shows that most people do make conscious decisions about which communication vehicle to use, based on the situational and relational context. Table 10.2 offers a look at various organizational goals and people's perceptions about the most competent channel for achieving those goals.

With such a variety of communication technologies available to organizational members to keep in close contact with one another, it should come as no surprise that people wind up using technology to achieve personal goals as well. This is particularly important in professional work environments. Twenty years ago, employees might get in trouble if they spent too much time making personal phone calls on the job. So consider how much more distracting it can be to have the ability to bank online, text message friends, chat on your cell phone, purchase groceries to be delivered to your home, e-mail your romantic partner, and read your brother's blog while the boss thinks that you are taking care of your work. Sixty-nine percent of workers admit that they access the Internet at work for non-work-related purposes (Schweitzer, 2007), and many of them are quite busy on the social networking site Facebook. Richard Cullen of the Internet filtering company SurfControl, for example, states that Facebook alone may be costing Australian businesses $5 billion a year due to decreased worker productivity (West, 2007). After all, it's hard to get anything meaningful accomplished while you're busy writing on your sister's wall or playing Oregon Trail and Scrabble!

These statistics have led many organizations to an increase in **surveillance**, or monitoring of employees, to see how they're using technologies such as e-mail, the Internet, and instant messaging (Williams, 1993). On some levels, monitoring seems to make sense, particularly when employees are spending time on questionable non-work-related activities. Yet it still raises several important ethical questions.

Does monitoring constitute an invasion of employees' privacy? Should workers accept monitoring as a fact of organizational life? These questions are stimulating important research and lively debates in legal circles, but no one seems to have a clear answer. One thing seems obvious, however: in any organization, you'll be

| Task | By E-Mail | By Phone | In Person |
|---|---|---|---|
| Edit or review documents | 67% | 4% | 26% |
| Arrange meetings or appointments | 63% | 23% | 12% |
| Ask questions about work issues | 36% | 17% | 44% |
| Bring up a problem with one's supervisor | 6% | 6% | 85% |
| Deal with sensitive issues | 4% | 9% | 85% |

**TABLE 10.2**

**EMPLOYEE SURVEY OF APPROPRIATE COMMUNICATION CHANNELS FOR ORGANIZATIONAL TASKS**

Source: Pew Internet & American Life Project Email at Work Survey, April-May 2002; *N* = 1003; margin of error = ± 3%.

much more productive if you limit the amount of time you spend using communication technologies for personal matters.

## Globalization

Daily direct flights to locations around the world, instant messaging and videoconferencing, international wire transfers—we're living in an age where the other side of the world is an e-mail away. Globalization is the buzzword in today's society—

## WIREDFORCOMMUNICATION

### Back to the Future

Back in the 1980s, when the Internet emerged and the prices of personal computers began to fall, there were countless predictions regarding the effects of an Internet-connected populace on communities, cities, and workplaces. In 1984, *Time* magazine estimated that by 1999, as many as ten million corporate employees would be working from home, electronically connected to coworkers and supervisors via the World Wide Web, fax, and phone. The prevailing wisdom was that as telecommuting became cheaper and easier, the importance of the office as a work environment would lessen: fewer people would commute to work, traffic jams would become a thing of the past, and cities would become obsolete (Grieves, 1984).

In the years since these predictions took hold, the Web has indeed become pervasive. It is estimated that today, some thirteen million corporate employees are working from home more than eight hours each week. Online learning programs allow students to enroll in colleges and universities hundreds or even thousands of miles away and take classes from home. Telecommuting is indeed becoming a part of the nature of work, education, and play in the twenty-first century. Logic would suggest that such ease of communication would make distance a nonissue in the postindustrial world, and employers would be happy to do away with expensive corporate offices in pricey cities in favor of cost-saving electronic offices for their employees. Yet despite 1980s notions about the future of the workplace, telecommuting hasn't replaced corporate offices or university centers or even lessened their importance. Consider, for example, that in recent years, Hewlett-Packard—once a trailblazer in telecommuting—has focused on bringing more workers back into the office to facilitate brainstorming and teamwork (Holland, 2006). Why do location and distance still matter?

It turns out that although the Internet is great for sharing and exchanging information, it is less useful when it comes to completing other functions of communication, such as expressing affiliation and influencing others. That's why electronic communication simply cannot replace the value of "face time," especially between employers and employees: we rely heavily on face-to-face communication in order to build trust (Harford, 2007). It turns out that even telecommuters need to have some face time with their bosses and colleagues in order to communicate well.

**THINK ABOUT THIS**

❶ Do you think that organizations benefit more from having employees work face to face or from having employees work from home? Does it have to be one way or the other?

❷ What communication benefits does telecommuting offer employees? What does it offer the organization?

❸ How can organizations ensure that telecommuting staffers are able to develop strong working relationships? How can they build "face time" into a virtual team?

you hear it on the evening news, read about it in magazines and newspapers, and see the evidence of it in your everyday life. If you've bought something with a "Made in China" sticker or if you've recently seen a foreign film at your local theater, you've experienced the effects of globalization. **Globalization** is the growing interdependence and connectivity of societies and economies around the world.

● **HAVE YOU EVER** bought something in the United States with a "Made in China" label? That's globalization at work!

Globalization is especially evident in the business world. Increases in communication technology and the convenience of travel have allowed companies to expand their labor force beyond geographical boundaries. More often than not, when you call customer service for help on the DVD player you bought in the United States, the person who picks up the phone is in India. More and more services are being outsourced to developing countries, where wages and operating costs are lower. Take Kenneth Tham, a high school sophomore in California. Most afternoons, he signs on to an online tutoring service, TutorVista. His tutor is Ramya Tadikonda, a twenty-six-year-old mother in Chennai (formerly Madras), India. TutorVista's president, John J. Stuppy, thinks that in this day and age, global tutoring makes the most sense because it makes "high-quality, one-on-one tutoring affordable and accessible to the masses" (Lohr, 2007). This example highlights a few of the benefits of globalization. U.S. companies benefit from the lower costs of operating in developing countries, and people in those countries benefit from better-paying jobs and a higher quality of life.

While globalization has torn down some of the barriers to legitimate commerce between countries, it has also made unethical labor practices easier. **Human trafficking**, the recruitment of people for exploitative purposes, is an example of the darker side of globalization. As wages rise in countries that have grown past the early stages of development, there is a need for even cheaper labor to be shipped in from even poorer countries, such as Cambodia and Bangladesh. Workers are lured in by shady labor brokers with false promises of high wages. The workers pay their brokers huge sums of money for this opportunity, only to work for paltry sums of money and often in unsavory working conditions. The story at Local Technic, a Malaysian company that makes cast aluminum bodies for hard disk drives, is a typical example of the forced labor that has increased with globalization. An unnamed executive at Local Technic admits that most of the company's guest workers have been duped into working there. He insists it's not the company's fault: sleazy brokers promise more than the company can afford. However, once the workers arrive and find out they've been taken for a ride, they can't quit, because under Malaysian law, they have had to sign multiyear contracts and surrender their passports to their employer. The parts made at Local Technic are used in virtually every name-brand machine on the market, thus implicating companies like Western Digital that have used components made by Local Technic. Although Western Digital is a member of the Electronics Industry Citizenship Coalition (EICC), which aims to improve industry working conditions, its relationship with Local Technic sends a conflicting message (Wherfritz, Kinetz, & Kent, 2008).

Globalization is a powerful force, and its impact on organizations is undeniable. However, without clear global labor laws, unethical practices such as human trafficking are difficult to control and police.

## COMMUNICATIONACROSSCULTURES

### Organizations in a Flat World

The next time you call a customer service line, check your credit card balance, or order something over the phone, take a moment to ask the person on the other end of the line where he or she is. The airline agent booking your ticket home for spring break might very well be working from her own kitchen; the technician talking you through a computer problem might be at an office park in India.

In 2004, *New York Times* columnist Thomas Friedman was traveling in India, working on a documentary about the emerging economy of Bangalore for the Discovery Channel. As he encountered corporation after corporation making its name—and its fortune—on services outsourced from the United States and elsewhere, Friedman felt his perceptions shift. The Internet, global telecommunications, and the increasing ease with which they allowed information to be shot around the globe meant that Americans were working with—and often competing with—coworkers and colleagues half a world away. The economic landscape, which once favored wealthy nations like the United States, was rapidly flattening (Friedman, 2007).

Just as "the office" no longer refers exclusively to a brick-and-mortar workplace, it's quite likely that any large American company will have some presence—perhaps even its main headquarters—outside of the United States. IBM, for example, has employees located in more than seventy countries (Glover, n.d.). In order to operate in the new world marketplace—as an employee or as a customer—an understanding of different cultures can be a valuable asset. Some jobs require international travel, for example, and in many cases, you might find that you yourself are the cultural minority—that many people with whom you would potentially be working are not American (Kohls, 2001). And even as an everyday consumer, you will no doubt find yourself on the phone at some point with somebody who was born, raised, and employed within a culture very different from yours.

Cultural differences can affect behavior during meetings and interviews. For example, when greeting an American employer, client, or colleague, career consultants suggest a firm handshake while looking directly at your greeter (Chaplin, Phillips, Brown, Clanton, & Stain, 2000). But in Australia, women often kiss other women on the cheek in business situations, and in Mexico, you might receive a hug (Morrison, Conaway, & Borden, 1996). You should also be prepared for questions that may seem inappropriate to you. In the United States, questions focusing on family, such as "How is your family adjusting to the area?" are usually considered illegal (or at least in bad taste) during an interview. But such banter is common in Italy, as Italians often engage in small talk, especially about family, before business meetings begin (Morrison et al., 1996).

**THINK ABOUT THIS**

❶ How does the "flattening" of the world affect communication within organizations? Does an international organization in effect create a new, diverse culture of its own?

❷ How does the international nature of modern organizations affect communication with outsiders? For example, should consumers have to adapt to a service provider from a different culture, or vice versa?

❸ What experiences have you had with international communication in your student life? Have these experiences presented challenges, opportunities, or both?

## Work-Life Balance

Diane is a single mom with a seven-year-old son. She works forty hours a week as a receptionist in a medical office and is currently completing classwork to become a dental hygienist. She is also the "room parent" for her son's second-grade class and is frequently called on to help bake for classroom celebrations and to chaperone class trips. Inez is a nineteen-year-old sophomore at a state university. She is working two part-time jobs to help meet the cost of tuition and is also taking six classes with the hopes of graduating one semester early. She dreams of studying in France next year and would love to live in foreign-language housing in order to improve her French, but she's not sure how she could add the mandatory conversation hours to her already overbooked schedule.

Both of these individuals have different lives, different goals, and different constraints. Yet they have one thing in common: they are sinking under intense pressures from the organizations in their lives. We've already indicated that Americans are spending more and more time on the job, making it increasingly difficult to enjoy outside relationships. But other types of organizations make huge demands on our time as well. If you are a parent, you may, like Diane, find that your child's school or the PTA simply expects you to be available for events. As a college student, you may discover that taking on too many classes and academic responsibilities prevents you from enjoying other aspects of the college experience, such as joining a particular club, volunteering, or just hanging out with friends. In any of these examples, the end result is often **burnout**—a sense of apathy or exhaustion that results from long-term stress or frustration. Burnout hurts its victims as well as the organizations and communities they belong to. Many researchers maintain that burnout leads to negative self-evaluations and emotional exhaustion (Maslach, 1982), and no wonder: television shows and movies flaunt glamorous people who manage to work hard, play hard, meet the partner of their dreams, raise adorable kids, and look great doing it all. So we ask, "Why can't I do it all too?" Yet the more we try, the more we burn out.

Many workplaces are aware of the dangers of burnout and implement programs to assist employees with **work-life balance**, which involves achieving success in one's personal and professional life. Such programs include flexible work arrangements, paid vacation, and onsite child care. In addition, more and more companies are recognizing that they must top their competitors in offering new and creative work-life options in order to recruit the best job candidates. According to a survey by the Association of Executive Search Consultants, 85 percent of recruiters have seen outstanding candidates reject a job offer because the position didn't provide enough work-life balance (Ridge, 2007).

Yet even in seemingly supportive work environments, many employees are still unable to balance their work and their personal life. For some, this is a choice: "I never go on vacation," says New York City real estate agent Ellen Kapit. "And when I do, I have my computer, my Palm, my e-mail, and my phone with me at all times" (Rosenbloom, 2006).

● **COMPANIES ARE** increasingly aware that their employees need to maintain a work-life balance, which has resulted in more onsite child-care centers.

For employees like Kapit, choosing the organization over other areas of life may be a sign of ambition, pride, guilt, a sense of overimportance, or simply a love of work, according to Ellen Galinsky, president of the Families and Work Institute (as cited in Rosenbloom, 2006). Yet it can also be a sign of fear. In 1977, 45 percent of people felt secure in their jobs. Today, only 36 percent feel that way (Rosenbloom, 2006). The sad truth remains that in far too many workplaces, there is an unspoken rule that if you take a vacation, put your family first, or have outside interests that take up a lot of time, you are not committed to the organization.

So if you're feeling burned out or on the verge of collapsing from organizational pressure, what should you do? This question is at the forefront of a great deal of research in sociology, psychology, business, and communication. Here are a few tips that various scholars, medical doctors, and other professionals find helpful (Mayo Clinic, 2006):

## AND YOU?

Consider the suggestions we've offered to help you balance your life commitments. Do you practice any of these currently? Are they realistic for your life and the organizations you belong to? If not, what impediments prevent you from making such changes?

▶ *Keep a log.* Track everything you do for one week, including school- and work-related activities. Note which activities are nonnegotiable (such as taking a mandatory math class), and decide which other commitments matter the most to you. Consider cutting commitments that are not fulfilling or necessary.

▶ *Manage your time.* Organizing your life can help you feel more in control of your circumstances. Set up specific times to study, work, and have fun—and try your hardest to stick to your schedule.

▶ *Communicate clearly.* Limit time-consuming misunderstandings by communicating clearly and listening carefully to the important people in your life.

▶ *Nurture yourself.* Set aside time each day for an activity that you enjoy, such as watching a particular TV show, working out, or listening to music.

▶ *Get enough sleep.* Enough said!

## CONNECT

Cultural differences, like those discussed in Chapter 3 and Chapter 4, can lead to perceptions of harassment when communicators fail to remember the cultural context. Gestures that are entirely appropriate in one area of the world might be considered offensive elsewhere. The same can be said for verbal messages such as commenting on an individual's appearance. Companies and communicators should take time to clarify perceptions and adapt messages in order to avoid miscommunication.

## Sexual Harassment

There are days when none of us like being at work or at school, particularly when the weather is nice or there's some other fun activity to take part in. Imagine, however, if your main reason for not wanting to head to class or to your job is fear. For many women and men around the world, a fear of being bullied or harassed in the workplace, on campus, or in other settings is far too common. **Harassment** is any communication that hurts, offends, or embarrasses another person, creating a hostile environment. It can take many forms, such as antagonizing people about their sex, race, religion, national origin, sexual orientation, age, or abilities (Federal Communications Commission, 2008).

One particularly offensive type of harassment is **sexual harassment,** which the Equal Employment Opportunity Commission (EEOC, 2008) defines as follows: "Unwelcome sexual advances, requests for sexual favors, and other verbal or physical conduct of a sexual nature [that] explicitly or implicitly affects an individual's employment, unreasonably interferes with an individual's work performance, or creates an intimidating, hostile, or offensive work environment." Specific conduct that can create such an environment may include sexist remarks, embarrassing jokes, taunting, displays of pornographic photographs, and unwanted physical contact such as touching, kissing, or grabbing.

How big a problem is sexual harassment? Well, over 90 percent of *Fortune* 500 companies have reported cases of sexual harassment (Keyton, Ferguson, & Rhodes, 2001), and in fiscal year 2007, the EEOC (2008) received 12,510 complaints of sexual harassment. In addition, the American Association of University Women

## what about you?

### Are You Off Balance?

1. Which statement best describes you after you leave work for the day?
   A. I don't think about work again until I arrive the next morning.
   B. I usually check my work e-mail before bed.
   C. I check my work e-mail or make calls three or four times during the evening.

2. A big project requires you to stay late to meet a deadline. You think to yourself:
   A. "This is happening way too much. I'll have to talk to my supervisor about it."
   B. "Oh, well, I'll take off a little early next week to make up for it."
   C. "I wonder if Bud, the night watchman, will bring me a sandwich like he always does."

3. Which statement best describes what you usually do on vacation?
   A. I kick back, relax, and savor the time off.
   B. I check in with my organization at least once so that people know I'm available.
   C. I continue to check my e-mail because you never know when an emergency might arise.

4. It's Tuesday, and you arrive home at 5:30 p.m. How do your family or housemates react?
   A. They say hello and discuss dinner plans.
   B. They act surprised—they never know if you'll be on time or not.
   C. They wonder if you've been fired because you're home so very early.

5. What are you most likely to do to manage your time at home?
   A. Organize chores and write to-do lists
   B. Try to run errands on days off from work or school
   C. Tackle chores and errands one at a time as needed

**If your answers are mostly A's:** You're leading a fairly well-balanced life—congratulations! You may, however, need to give your organization more priority now and then, particularly during time-sensitive projects.

**If your answers are mostly B's:** You're striking a great balance! Keep up the good work.

**If your answers are mostly C's:** You're likely headed toward burnout. Consider some of the strategies we discuss to find more balance.

Source: CNN.com/living (2008). Adapted with permission.

Educational Foundation notes that nearly two-thirds (62 percent) of two thousand college students surveyed in 2005 said that they had been subject to sexual harassment in college (National Organization for Women [NOW], 2006). Women are most commonly the victims of sexual harassment, but men can also experience its negative effects. In fact, 16 percent of the charges filed with the EEOC in 2007 were complaints from men (2008). In addition, three-quarters of lesbian, gay, bisexual, and transgendered (LGBT) students report that they have experienced incidents of sexual harassment on campus (NOW, 2006). These statistics are clearly problematic, but what is even more challenging is that victims often feel shame and embarrassment, preventing many of them from filing official complaints. For example, only 7 percent of students say that they reported sexual harassment to a member of their college or university; LGBT students in particular report that they are extremely angry and embarrassed by their experience (NOW, 2006). Still other victims fear that they will lose their jobs if they speak out—particularly if they are harassed by a boss or other individual with power (Witteman, 1993).

Sexual harassment costs organizations millions of dollars ever year and robs individuals of their dignity and sense of self-worth. For this reason, organizations have instituted official codes of conduct and clear definitions and penalties for sexual harassment. Many even offer training to educate organizational members. For example, some programs discuss gendered communication, noting that women socialized in feminine nurturing are more likely than men to disclose personal information in the workplace. Men, who tend to be more private about personal information at work, may interpret that behavior as flirting and may respond with a sexual advance. Similarly, men may use smiling, extensive eye contact, and touch as signals that they are sexually attracted to someone, while many women use these same nonverbal behaviors to demonstrate their interest in a conversation topic and their support of the person who is speaking (see Berryman-Fink, 1993). By understanding and being aware of such communication differences, incidents can be prevented before they happen. Nonetheless, when incidents do occur, victims should recognize that the law is on their side; they should feel empowered to take action against an illegal act. If you are a victim of sexual harassment—or even if you think you might be—consider the following communication strategies:

▶ Clearly and firmly tell the harasser that his or her advances are not welcome.

▶ Immediately report the incident to someone who can assist you: a trusted professor, a counselor, or your boss. If the harasser is your boss, you can contact a representative in your organization's human resources department.

▶ Document each incident in writing. Include a description of the incident, the date, the person or persons involved, and any action you took.

▶ If anyone else in the organization witnessed the harassing behavior, have each witness verify the details of the incident and add that information to your documentation.

Likewise, be careful not to inadvertently behave in a harassing manner yourself. For example, if a friend e-mails a dirty joke or pornographic photo to you at work, *don't forward it to anyone else in the organization*. It's not appropriate under any circumstances. And if your organization is like many, it may well fire you on the spot.

# BACK TO ▶ Google

At the beginning of the chapter, we explored life at Google's Mountain View, California, headquarters. Life there seems like a techie paradise, a place where the best and the brightest minds in computer engineering work and play around the clock. Let's revisit the Googleplex and consider how and why the people at Google structured their organization—and organized their offices— in this particular way.

▶ The organizational structure at Google shows little in the way of corporate hierarchy. There is, however, a strong emphasis on creating networks of individuals who share ideas and work together (reflecting a human relations approach), and the company's interest in keeping employees challenged and happy (reflected most clearly in the policy of allowing engineers time to pursue non-work-related projects) shows the influence of the human resources approach.

▶ Google takes pride in its story as a company focused on the goal of building the perfect search engine, of creating fast, easy, and practical tools for accessing the ever-growing amount of information on the Web. The company founders have often said that they "are not serious about anything but search" (Google, 2008a). They take pride in the company's reputation as one where work represents a challenge rather than a chore.

▶ Google is in many respects the face of technology and innovation today. It is interesting to note, however, that the company also sees the value in old-fashioned, face-to-face communication. The café, sofas, and layout of offices encourage employees to meet and mingle, bounce ideas off of one another, and work out problems together. Decidedly low-tech whiteboards abound to capture ideas and inspiration as they occur.

## THINGS TO TRY

1. Compare two organizations that you belong to or have regular contact with (a social organization, a volunteer organization, or a company). What type of management approach does each of these two organizations have? Also think about how these two organizations differ in their organizational culture. Be specific about how their values, artifacts, slogans, or assimilation practices vary.

2. *The Office* plays off many of the silly and ludicrous things that can go wrong in an organizational setting. However, the show does accurately portray organizational life beneath the hijinks. Watch a few episodes of *The Office,* and reflect on the different organizational contexts shown. What are the supervisor-supervisee relationships like? Are there any mentor-protégé relationships? What about peer relationships? How do these various relationships affect the way their organization functions?

3. In the chapter, we talk about some of the challenges that today's organizations face, including work-life balance, harassment, and communication technology. Does your organization also tussle with some of these challenges? What challenges are specific to your organization? How might your organization minimize or adapt to some of these challenges?

## IF YOU'RE INTERESTED

*The New Handbook of Organizational Communication: Advances in Theory, Research, and Methods,* edited by Frederic M. Jablin and Linda L. Putnam (Thousand Oaks, CA: Sage, 2001)

> This is one of the best resources for organizational communication research that is available in one place. The book has twenty chapters that cover almost all of the topics discussed in this chapter and offers a broad perspective on organizational communication.

*Organizational Communication: Balancing Creativity and Constraint,* by Eric M. Eisenberg, H. L. Goodall Jr., and Angela Tretheway (New York: Bedford/St. Martin's, 2007)

> This reader-friendly textbook covers most organizational communication issues in a relevant manner. The authors are experts in conducting this type of research and consult with many organizations in solving communication problems.

*Office Space* (20th Century-Fox, 1999)

> This cult classic sharply lampoons organizational culture. It takes on the mind-numbing cubicle culture at a generic software company, where employees are coerced into working weekends on reports that nobody will read, the fax machine is a source of constant frustration, and consultants are brought in to interview each staffer to determine whether his or her position can be outsourced or eliminated.

*The Turnaround: How America's Top Cop Reversed the Crime Epidemic,* by William Bratton with Peter Knobler (New York: Random House, 1998)

> This biography details how one police commissioner reorganized and refocused the nation's largest police force and contributed to an unprecedented drop in crime in New York City in the 1990s.

*The 9/11 Commission Report: Final Report of the National Commission on Terrorist Attacks upon the United States* (authorized ed.), by the National Commission on Terrorist Attacks (New York: Norton, 2004); also available online at http://www.9-11commission.gov

> The seminal event of our age is examined in careful detail in this government report by the commission created to investigate the September 11, 2001, attacks on New York and Washington, D.C. The bipartisan committee found that, among other problems, communication failures within and between intelligence-gathering organizations contributed to the tragedy.

**Now that you have finished reading this chapter, you can**

Recognize the various approaches to managing an organization:

▶ **Organizations** are groups with a formal governance and structure (p. 288).

▶ **Organizational communication** is the interaction necessary to direct a group toward a set of common goals (p. 288).

▶ The **classical management approach** focuses on how to make an organization run efficiently. This approach is dependent on two main ideas: the **division of labor**, the assumption that each part of the organization has a specific function, and **hierarchy**, the layers of power in an organization (pp. 288–289).

▶ The **human relations approach** considers the human needs of organizational members (p. 290).

▶ The **human resources approach** also considers organizational productivity from the workers' perspective (p. 290).

▶ The **systems approach** views an organization as a whole in which all members have interdependent relationships. Two key components of this approach are **openness**, an organization's awareness of its problems, and **adaptability**, an organization's allowance for change and growth (p. 292).

Describe how **organizational culture**, an organization's unique set of beliefs, values, norms, and ways of doing things, is communicated:

▶ Through **organizational storytelling**, the communication of the organization's values through stories to the organization's members and to the outside world (p. 294).

▶ Using **organizational heroes**, the people who achieve great things for the organization (p. 294).

▶ Through **organizational assimilation**, the process by which people "learn the ropes" of the organization (p. 295).

Explain the different contexts in organizations:

▶ In supervisor-supervisee relationships, the supervisor has power over the supervisee (p. 296).

▶ In mentor-protégé relationships, the **mentor** is a respected member of the organization and serves as a role model for a less experienced individual, the **protégé** (p. 298).

▶ **Peer relationships** are the friendships that form between colleagues at an organization as a result of **peer communication**, communication between individuals at the same level of authority (p. 299).

Identify the challenges facing today's organizations:

▶ The wealth of new communication technology has enabled easier communication, but there is the added challenge of figuring out which channel to use, taking into consideration **media richness**, the degree to which a particular channel is communicative (p. 302).

▶ The proliferation of communication technology has increased organizations' use of **surveillance**, or the monitoring of employees, to see how they're using e-mail, the Internet, and instant messaging (p. 303).

▶ **Globalization**, the growing interdependence and connectivity of societies and economies around the world, reduces barriers between countries for business. However, unethical practices such as **human trafficking**, the coercion of people into exploitative situations, are also a result of globalization (p. 305).

▶ Employees struggle with **work-life balance**, finding a balance between their work and their personal life. Many take on too many responsibilities or work long hours, often resulting in **burnout**, a destructive form of stress (p. 307).

▶ **Harassment** is any communication that hurts, offends, or embarrasses an individual, creating a hostile environment. One common type is **sexual harassment**, unwanted verbal or physical conduct of a sexual nature that affects an individual's employment, interferes with work performance, or creates an intimidating, hostile, or offensive work environment (p. 308).

**His passionate presentations** on saving the earth transformed Al Gore from a boring politician to Hollywood's hottest property.

# chapter 11

# Preparing and Researching Presentations

**Al Gore was never considered a dynamic speechmaker.** Throughout his tenure as a U.S. senator, two terms as vice president, and his bid for the presidency in 2000, he was widely lampooned as a bore. The image of Gore as dull, stiff, and "wooden" was common material for late-night comics and cable news pundits—after Gore attended a rally in New York's Central Park, for example, David Letterman joked, "Halfway through his speech, squirrels were climbing on him." The image of Gore in the media and popular culture was that of a dull but dedicated college professor, the one who is committed and knowledgeable but just can't keep his students awake in the lecture hall.

But the perception of being a bore never stopped Gore from speaking out about the things he was passionate about, and for more than three decades, he has been vocal on the subject of global warming. During the 1970s, Gore helped organize the first congressional hearings on climate change, and his 1992 book *Earth in the Balance* was a bestseller. In 2001, Gore toured the country with a PowerPoint presentation focusing on the threat of climate change and global warming.

Despite his reputation as a less than dynamic speaker, audiences filled lecture halls around the country to hear him talk about the environment and global warming. In May 2004, the film producer Laurie David saw a short version of his presentation and was moved to make it into a documentary (Booth, 2006). The resulting film, *An Inconvenient Truth*, quickly became the rage of the 2006 Cannes and Sundance film festivals. By the end of that year, Gore's name and the subject of global climate change were on everyone's lips. The film won the Academy Award for Best Documentary and became one of the highest-grossing documentaries in U.S. movie history (Minkel & Stix, 2006).

After you have finished
reading this chapter,
you will be able to

○ Understand the power
of public speaking and
how preparation eases
natural nervousness

○ Identify the purpose of
your speech

○ Analyze your audience

○ Choose an appropriate
topic and develop it

○ Support and enliven
your speech with
effective research

○ Cull from among your
sources the material that
will be most convincing

○ Give proper credit
to sources and take
responsibility for your
speech

A public figure is naturally expected to speak well. Presidents Kennedy, Reagan, and Clinton, for example, were all known for their natural ease in front of audiences and television cameras. Others in the public eye, like Al Gore, manage to speak and communicate well in public even though they might lack the charismatic flair of these three presidents. As you will learn in this chapter, the groundwork of becoming a confident, competent speaker and developing strong presentations lies in planning, development, and research. Yet you might still be asking, "Why does public speaking matter so much?" Let's take a look at why it is so important.

## The Power of Public Speaking

Jack has what his Irish mother called the gift of blarney. He is an eloquent conversationalist who dominates the discourse in business meetings and at cocktail parties. But put him in front of an audience, and he'll panic. Jack's ability to charm friends and colleagues, impress potential dates, and talk his way out of parking tickets disappears completely once the atmosphere changes from informal to formal and his conversational partners are reduced to a more passive audience.

**Public speaking** always includes a speaker who has a reason for speaking, an audience that gives the speaker attention, and a message that is meant to accomplish a specific purpose ("Public speaking," n.d.). It is an incredibly powerful form of communication that has, in fact, changed the world. From the ancient philosophers, who taught debate skills for use in the courts of ancient Greece, to nineteenth-century American abolitionists, who argued to end slavery in the United States, public speakers continue to chart the course of civilization. Think about what Jack could do if he used his powers of persuasion on a larger and more formal scale. Rather than complaining about local politicians, he might consider running for office. Rather than pitching ideas to his supervisor at work, he might be developing them himself and pitching them directly to clients. Learning how to speak publicly can also play a powerful role in *your* personal and professional life, giving you an edge over less skilled communicators and putting you in a leadership role (O'Hair & Stewart, 1998). Companies and personnel managers all over the United States have stated that public speaking is one of the most important skills a potential employee can possess (O'Hair, Stewart, & Rubenstein, 2007).

But what if you feel anxious about public speaking? First of all, realize that you are not alone: 75 percent of people experience pounding hearts and sweaty palms when they think about getting up in front of an audience (Richmond & McCroskey, 1998). Look around the next classroom you enter: that's three out of every four people! (And we suspect that even the one in four who doesn't experience anxiety at least feels some nervousness. Anyone who denies that is probably lying.) Second, recognize that through patience and practice, you can counter some of this anxiety, if not conquer it altogether. This chapter and the chapters that follow show you how to approach public speaking calmly and pragmatically. The first step lies with preparation, the focus of this chapter. The next step focuses on organization, which we'll talk about in Chapter 12. Then in Chapter 13, we will discuss the causes of speech anxiety and offer techniques that you can use to manage any concerns you may have. For now, know that being concerned with giving a speech is natural, but preparation and solid effort can make you a successful speaker, for this sort of skill building will enable you to conquer your nervousness (Schroeder, 2002).

## Clarifying the Purpose of Your Speech

In the real world, choosing a topic and purpose for a speech is seldom a difficult task. You speak because you volunteered—or were forced—to speak on a topic for which your expertise is relevant to the situation. For example, you are a public health nurse giving a community presentation on the benefits of a high-fiber

**AND YOU?**

Have you ever experienced the power of a speech? Think about a specific presentation that you've seen—be it a watershed event like President Bush's statements on 9/11 or a more personal experience such as a eulogy at a loved one's funeral. What about the speech stirred your emotions?

---

# COMMUNICATIONACROSSCULTURES

## Private Pain and Public Speaking

There are people who will do just about anything to avoid public speaking. In the minds of many people, the fear of public speaking is worse than the fear of death, disease, or serious illness (Wallace, Wallace, & Wallechinsky, 2004). And then there are those who cannot *not* speak out—people whose lives have been forever altered by events, illness, crime, and even death. For many victims, patients, and survivors, speaking publicly about their ordeals has proved to be a valuable tool for personal healing and public change.

Consider Carolyn McCarthy, a New York nurse, wife, and mother whose life was anything but public until her husband was murdered and her son injured in a gun massacre on the Long Island Rail Road in 1993. McCarthy suddenly emerged as a public figure, a spokeswoman for the victims and families of victims injured and killed by assault weapons. Unhappy with her congressional representative's record on gun control laws, she ran for Congress in 1996—and won. "All I wanted to do was make something come out of a horrible situation," said the freshman congresswoman in 1996 (Barry, 1996).

Others find that adversity simply takes their public life in a different direction. The actor Christopher Reeve first became a household name in the early 1980s when he starred in the *Superman* series of films. Offscreen, he was an active public speaker—for example, he testified before Congress in March 1995 to prevent cuts to funding for the arts (Wines, 1995). But only a few months later, a horse-riding accident left him a quadriplegic, unable to move any of his limbs or breathe without a respirator. Although he said he contemplated suicide at first, Reeve instead was moved to fight for his life, taking his battle to regain his strength and mobility very public. With his wife, Dana, he founded the Christopher Reeve Paralysis Foundation and testified before Congress many times on issues related to spinal cord research. Through public appearances and a continued presence in Hollywood, he managed to inspire and promote change until his death in October 2004 (Martin, 2004).

**THINK ABOUT THIS**

❶ In what ways were the public lives of Reeve and McCarthy similar? How were they different?

❷ How does adversity inspire public speaking and, indeed, public life? In American culture, what defines a public figure?

❸ How does celebrity culture relate to public speaking? Is a movie star more capable of drawing support for a cause than an ordinary citizen?

❹ Is a shooting victim or the family of a victim more credible on the issue of gun control than someone whose life has not been touched by gun violence?

diet; your candidate for student government president wants you, as campaign manager, to make the nominating speech; or you are presenting a group gift at a farewell party for a colleague who is off to join the Peace Corps. Often the parameters for a speech are quite general: a high school valedictorian or keynote speaker, for example, has to write a speech that both honors and inspires a large group. The possibilities for such speeches are endless. This communication class may provide a similar challenge—finding a speech topic and purpose that fit within your instructor's guidelines, which may range from very specific ("give a five-minute speech defending the constitutional right to free speech") to quite vague ("give a persuasive speech").

## Identifying the General Purpose of Your Speech

Speaking assignments usually fit within one of three general purposes: informative, persuasive, and special-occasion.

### Informative Speeches

● **PRESIDENT FRANKLIN D. ROOSEVELT** was able to inform a wide audience about events around the country through his radio broadcasts.

In our information society, managing and communicating information is a key to success (Berrisford, 2006). *Informative speeches* aim to increase your audience's understanding or knowledge by presenting new, relevant, and useful information. Such speeches can take a variety of forms. They might explain a process or plan, describe particular objects or places, or characterize a particular state of affairs. Some speeches accomplish many tasks at once. Apple Computer chairman Steve Jobs, for example, addresses conventions of software developers with speeches that describe the company's growth and success while explaining and demonstrating features of new products.

Informative speeches also attempt to answer questions that we have about the world around us, addressing emergencies or making statements on current events. Take the storied Fireside Chats that President Franklin D. Roosevelt delivered during the 1930s. Through the then-emerging medium of radio, Roosevelt was able to reach, inform, and reassure a vast number of Americans suffering through the depths of the Great Depression. An excerpt from his first such address, delivered shortly after he took office and in the immediate aftermath of widespread bank failures, is offered as Sample Speech 11.1. Note how Roosevelt first describes what happened with the banks, follows up with how the government has dealt with the crisis, and finally details his plans for getting banks back up and running.

> **SAMPLE SPEECH 11.1** ——————————————————
>
> ### Fireside Chat on the Bank Crisis
>
> FRANKLIN D. ROOSEVELT
>
> I want to talk for a few minutes with the people of the United States about banking—with the comparatively few who understand the mechanics of banking but more particularly with the overwhelming majority who use banks for the making of deposits and the drawing of checks. I

want to tell you what has been done in the last few days, why it was done, and what the next steps are going to be. I recognize that the many proclamations from State Capitols and from Washington, the legislation, the Treasury regulations, etc., couched for the most part in banking and legal terms should be explained for the benefit of the average citizen. . . .

First of all let me state the simple fact that when you deposit money in a bank the bank does not put the money into a safe deposit vault. It invests your money in many different forms of credit-bonds, commercial paper, mortgages and many other kinds of loans. . . . In other words the total amount of all the currency in the country is only a small fraction of the total deposits in all of the banks. •

What, then, happened during the last few days of February and the first few days of March? Because of undermined confidence on the part of the public, there was a general rush by a large portion of our population to turn bank deposits into currency or gold—a rush so great that the soundest banks could not get enough currency to meet the demand. The reason for this was that on the spur of the moment it was, of course, impossible to sell perfectly sound assets of a bank and convert them into cash except at panic prices far below their real value.

By the afternoon of March 3 scarcely a bank in the country was open to do business. Proclamations temporarily closing them in whole or in part had been issued by the Governors in almost all the states.

It was then that I issued the proclamation providing for the nationwide bank holiday, and this was the first step in the Government's reconstruction of our financial and economic fabric. •

The second step was the legislation promptly and patriotically passed by the Congress confirming my proclamation and broadening my powers so that it became possible in view of the requirement of time to extend the holiday and lift the ban of that holiday gradually. This law also gave authority to develop a program of rehabilitation of our banking facilities. I want to tell our citizens in every part of the Nation that the national Congress—Republicans and Democrats alike—showed by this action a devotion to public welfare and a realization of the emergency and the necessity for speed that it is difficult to match in our history.

The third stage has been the series of regulations permitting the banks to continue their functions to take care of the distribution of food and household necessities and the payment of payrolls.

This bank holiday, while resulting in many cases in great inconvenience, is affording us the opportunity to supply the currency necessary to meet the situation. No sound bank is a dollar worse off than it was when it closed its doors last Monday. Neither is any bank which may turn out not to be in a position for immediate opening. The new law allows the twelve Federal Reserve banks to issue additional currency on good assets and thus the banks which reopen will be able to meet every legitimate call. . . .

• Note how Roosevelt explains how banking works in very simple terms for those listeners who might not be familiar with the process.

• Here Roosevelt begins to lay out and explain his plan for addressing the crisis so that listeners feel more comfortable about what's going on.

As a result we start tomorrow, Monday, with the opening of banks in the twelve Federal Reserve bank cities—those banks which on first examination by the Treasury have already been found to be all right. This will be followed on Tuesday by the resumption of all their functions by banks already found to be sound in cities where there are recognized clearing houses. . . .

I do not promise you that every bank will be reopened or that individual losses will not be suffered, but there will be no losses that possibly could be avoided; and there would have been more and greater losses had we continued to drift. . . .

Confidence and courage are the essentials of success in carrying out our plan. You people must have faith; you must not be stampeded by rumors or guesses. Let us unite in banishing fear. We have provided the machinery to restore our financial system; it is up to you to support and make it work.

It is your problem no less than it is mine. Together we cannot fail.

Source: From "On the Bank Crisis," radio address by Franklin Delano Roosevelt delivered March 12, 1933. Retrieved from "Fireside Chats by Franklin D. Roosevelt" at the Franklin D. Roosevelt Presidential Library and Museum, http://www.fdrlibrary.marist.edu/031233.html

## Persuasive Speeches

Persuasive speeches are very common in daily life and are a major focus of public speaking classes (R. Smith, 2004). You may think that persuasion is a dishonest tactic used to coerce someone into doing or believing something, but that is not the case. Rather, *persuasive speeches* are intended to influence the attitudes, beliefs, and behaviors of your audience. Although they often ask for a *change* from your audience, persuasive speeches can also reaffirm existing attitudes, beliefs, and behaviors.

Consider Sample Speech 11.2, a persuasive and powerful speech by Sojourner Truth, an American abolitionist and women's rights activist. She was born into slavery in the late eighteenth century in New York State and escaped in 1826 (though the state technically abolished slavery in 1799). She felt a strong desire to persuade others to see the evils of slavery and the mistreatment of women, as you will note in her speech, "Ain't I a Woman?"

### SAMPLE SPEECH 11.2

### Ain't I a Woman?

SOJOURNER TRUTH

Well, children, where there is so much racket there must be something out of kilter. I think that 'twixt the negroes of the South and the women at the North, all talking about rights, the white men will be in a fix pretty soon. But what's all this here talking about?

That man over there says the women need to be helped into carriages, and lifted over ditches, and to have the best place everywhere. Nobody ever helps me into carriages, or over mud-puddles, or gives me any best place! And ain't I a woman? Look at me! Look at my arm! I have ploughed and planted, and gathered into barns, and no man could head me! And ain't I a woman? I could work as much and eat as much as a man—when I could get it—and bear the lash as well! And ain't I a woman? I have borne thirteen children, and seen most all sold off to slavery, and when I cried out with my mother's grief, none but Jesus heard me! And ain't I a woman? •

Then they talk about this thing in the head; what's this they call it? [member of the audience whispers "intellect"] That's it, honey. What's that got to do with women's rights or negroes' rights? If my cup won't hold but a pint, and yours holds a quart, wouldn't you be mean not to let me have my little half measure full?

Then that little man in black there, he says women can't have as much rights as men, 'cause Christ wasn't a woman! Where did your Christ come from? Where did your Christ come from? From God and a woman! Man had nothing to do with Him.

If the first woman God ever made was strong enough to turn the world upside down all alone, these women together ought to be able to turn it back, and get it right side up again. And now they is asking to do it, the men better let them. •

Obliged to you for hearing me, and now old Sojourner ain't got nothing more to say.

Source: From Sojourner Truth, "Ain't I a Woman?" speech delivered at the Women's Convention in Akron, Ohio, May 1851. Retrieved from http://www.feminist.com/resources/artspeech/genwom/sojour.htm

> • Notice how Truth encourages the audience to extend this existing belief about women to her as she too is a woman.

> • Truth invokes religious stories that are familiar to the audience members in her effort to persuade them.

## Special-Occasion Speeches

*Special-occasion speeches* use the principles of both informative and persuasive speaking for special occasions, such as introducing a speaker, accepting an honor or award, presenting a memorial, or celebrating an achievement. Almost certainly at some point in your life you will be called on to deliver a speech at a wedding, a toast at a retirement party, or a eulogy at a funeral. Special-occasion speeches are frequently delivered on the world stage as well. In 2005, for example, Bruce Springsteen inducted fellow rockers U2 into the Rock and Roll Hall of Fame. An excerpt of his speech is presented in Sample Speech 11.3 (see p. 324). Note how he focuses on the band's history, the uniqueness of its sound, and the special bond that has kept the band together for so long. The speech is intended to bring everyone listening to the same conclusion: that this band is a true icon of rock and roll that changed the sound and scope of popular music.

> • **JENNIFER HUDSON** might have imagined giving a toast at a friend's wedding, but until her Oscar nomination, she probably hadn't considered preparing for such a public and important acceptance speech.

## U2 Rock and Roll Hall of Fame Induction

### BRUCE SPRINGSTEEN

*Uno, dos, tres, catorce.* That translates as *one, two, three, fourteen.* That is the correct math for a rock and roll band. For in art and love and rock and roll, the whole had better equal much more than the sum of its parts, or else you're just rubbing two sticks together searching for fire. A great rock band searches for the same kind of combustible force that fueled the expansion of the universe after the big bang. You want the earth to shake and spit fire. You want the sky to split apart and for God to pour out.

It's embarrassing to want so much, and to expect so much from music, except sometimes it happens—the Sun Sessions, Highway 61, Sgt. Pepper, the Band, Robert Johnson, *Exile on Main Street, Born to Run*—whoops, I meant to leave that one out (laughter)—the Sex Pistols, Aretha Franklin, the Clash, James Brown . . . the proud and public enemies it takes a nation of millions to hold back. This is music meant to take on not only the powers that be, but on a good day, the universe and God himself—if he was listening. It's man's accountability, and U2 belongs on this list. . . . •

● Springsteen compares U2 to other accomplished, well-known artists in order to show the level of their success.

They are both a step forward and direct descendants of the great bands who believed rock music could shake things up in the world, who dared to have faith in their audience, who believed if they played their best it would bring out the best in you. They believed in pop stardom and the big time. Now this requires foolishness and a calculating mind. It also requires a deeply held faith in the work you're doing and in its powers to transform. U2 hungered for it all, and built a sound, and they wrote the songs that demanded it. They're keepers of some of the most beautiful sonic architecture in rock and roll. . . .

Now the band's beautiful songwriting—"Pride (In the Name of Love)," "Sunday Bloody Sunday," "I Still Haven't Found What I'm Looking For," "One," "Where the Streets Have No Name," "Beautiful Day"—reminds us of the stakes that the band always plays for. It's an incredible songbook. In their music you hear the spirituality as home and as quest. How do you find God unless he's in your heart? In your desire? In your feet? I believe this is a big part of what's kept their band together all of these years. •

● Here Springsteen lists U2's impressive accomplishments.

See, bands get formed by accident, but they don't survive by accident. It takes will, intent, a sense of shared purpose, and a tolerance for your friends' fallibilities . . . and they of yours. And that only evens the odds. U2 has not only evened the odds but they've beaten them by continuing to do their finest work and remaining at the top of their game and the charts for 25 years. I feel a great affinity for these guys as people as well as musicians. . . .

This band . . . has carried their faith in the great inspirational and resurrective power of rock and roll. It never faltered, only a little bit.

They believed in themselves, but more importantly, they believed in "you, too." Thank you Bono, the Edge, Adam, and Larry. Please welcome U2 into the Rock and Roll Hall of Fame.

Source: From "Bruce Springsteen Inducts U2 into the Rock and Roll Hall of Fame, March 17, 2005." Copyright © 2005 by Bruce Springsteen. Retrieved from http://www.u2station.com/news/archives/2005/03/transcript_bruc.php

## Determining the Specific Purpose of Your Speech

Once you've determined the general goals of a speech, you'll need to zero in on a more specific purpose. You might begin by asking yourself, "Precisely what is it about my topic that I want my audience to learn, do, consider, or agree with?" A **specific purpose statement** expresses both the topic and the general speech purpose in action form and in terms of the specific objectives you hope to achieve with your presentation.

For example, let's return to the transcript of FDR's Fireside Chat in Sample Speech 11.1. The general purpose of the address was, obviously, to inform Americans (about the recent bank failures). Its more specific purpose was to explain, in everyday terms, how and why the bank failures occurred and to help Americans feel reassured that the federal government was acting to rectify the situation. But let's also consider another example (since you might not be giving a radio speech to calm the entire nation anytime soon!). Imagine you are giving a persuasive speech on volunteerism, a topic you feel very strongly about. Your general purpose and specific purpose might look like this:

**Topic:** Volunteer reading programs

**General purpose:** To persuade

**Specific purpose:** To have audience members realize the importance of reading with local elementary school children so that they sign up for a volunteer reading program such as Everybody Wins

There is an additional level of specificity to consider when preparing your speech. It is called the *thesis statement*—you're probably familiar with this term from high school or your college composition course. We will help you understand and develop your own thesis statement a little bit later in this chapter, but first let's understand a factor that will help you write the strongest possible thesis statement: audience analysis.

## Analyzing Your Audience

For FDR, the audience was obvious: the bank failures had caused such widespread panic and fear that just about every American was going to listen to or at least read his speech. But most speeches are delivered to more specific audiences.

As you will quickly discover, audience analysis is a critical step in the speech preparation process (Yook, 2004). Because you are asking the audience members to accept your message—to learn new information; to change their attitudes, beliefs, or actions; or to recommit themselves to a cause or organization—it is important for you to know where they are starting from in terms of both previous knowledge of your topic and their perceptions of you as a speaker. Gaining an understanding of your audience will also be crucial to choosing a topic that will resonate with them.

## Determining Your Audience's Expectations

People naturally bring different sets of expectations and emotions to a speech event (O'Hair et al., 2007). And as with other forms of communication discussed in this book, competent public speaking involves understanding and acknowledging the expectations of your communication partners—in this case, your audience.

Audiences are likely to have expectations about your speech based on the speaking situation, the topic, the information their culture provides about public speaking, and even their knowledge about you as an individual or as a speaker. For example, think about the types of expectations you bring to a wedding toast or a valedictorian's speech. Would you expect a best man to use his microphone time to talk about the fact that the bride is untrustworthy because she cheated on her taxes last year? How would you have felt if your valedictorian spent twenty minutes of your graduation talking about what a horror high school had been? These types of speeches would clearly defy expectations. Similarly, as we learned from some Russian colleagues, an American businessperson giving a speech in Moscow might defy audience expectations by coming right to the point when informing them about a particular technology. In Russia, audiences expect speeches to favor storytelling rather than direct fact sharing.

Audiences can also be influenced by a variety of factors that you cannot plan for. Be aware of issues such as the time of day of your speech, events happening in the outside world, or the comfort and attractiveness of the room—because these issues do matter. Our publishing colleagues at Bedford/St. Martin's (Karen, Sally, and Erika) will be presenting our book to the company's sales representatives at a sales convention. They always pray, "Please, anything but the 3:00 P.M. Friday speech slot"—the last time slot of the meeting. Karen, Sally, and Erika know that they'll have to be even more enthusiastic and on top of their speech when they're giving it to an audience exhausted after days of meetings and eager to return home to friends and family (and they're pretty tired at that point too!).

## Types of Audiences

To make an educated guess about your audience's expectations, you will want to consider characteristics of the audience members and draw conclusions about them based on those characteristics. Specifically, how do you make use of their beliefs, attitudes, values, experiences, and needs? A good place to start is to classify the total audience in terms of cohesiveness or togetherness. H. L. Hollingsworth (1935) uses this variable to group audiences into five types, which are presented in Figure 11.1 (see p. 328).

**AND YOU?**

Have you ever attended a speaking event where the speaker did not behave appropriately for the occasion? How did it make you feel as a listener?

**CONNECT**

Analyzing expectations in a speaking situation may seem difficult, but you actually do this work in other communication contexts all the time. As we learn in Chapter 6, relational partners must address each other's expectations in order for the relationship to grow. Similarly, the speaker must remember the audience's expectations for the speaking occasion (level of formality or appropriate language, for example) in order to be competent and successful.

The least cohesive group is the **pedestrian audience**—an audience of people who have no obvious connection with either the speaker or one another. A preacher standing on a busy street corner attempts to attract an audience by

# real communicator

**NAME:** Amy Talluto
**HOMETOWN:** New Orleans, Louisiana
**OCCUPATION:** Freelance Web designer and fine artist
**FUN FACT:** I like to gobble at flocks of wild turkeys to see if I can get a gobble back. So far I enjoy about a 90 percent return.

I'm a visual artist. I do some photography, some ink and pencil drawings, but mostly I paint landscapes. Thickets, cascading rivers, Silver Pond in Montana. Not too long ago, I was asked to go out to Eastern Illinois University and speak to about fifty graduate students getting their master's in the visual arts. I was asked to talk about my work.

My work? What do you want me to say?

So first things first. This was an informational presentation on my work. But what specifically did I want my audience to learn? What, as my undergraduate public speaking professor might ask, was my purpose?

I didn't know exactly. So I started thinking about who would be in my audience and what they might want to hear about. Well, they're artists—photographers, painters, sculptors, graphic designers. They think visually, and they probably learn visually too. Also, and just as important, they're students, many of them young, many of them putting together a body of work for the first time.

So I knew my presentation would have to be visual (pretty obvious, since I was asked to speak about my visual work). And I decided, based on this understanding of my audience, to focus my presentation on the creative process: how a finished landscape painting gets finished. Traditionally, visiting artist lectures are done using a projector and slides and consist of a straightforward march of single images projected on a large screen. Click. Click. Click. Dust coming off the top of the carousel. I wanted to do something different. I wanted to juxtapose (and enhance) the images of my finished landscapes with the source photos I used as references, in-progress painting sequences, and images of New York and the Chelsea gallery district. I wanted to visually show my creative process. To do that, I went to PowerPoint.

Uploading my digital photos onto PowerPoint, I was able to zoom in and out, show exactly what I wanted to show. And knowing my audience, I kept text to an absolute minimum. I avoided those long bulleted lists. (With one exception: I had noticed, while attending traditional slide-based artist lectures, that the audience often repeatedly asked about basic details of the works—like the size, year completed, or medium—disrupting the flow of the discussion. So I used PowerPoint to add that brief information next to each image during my slide show.)

I didn't just let the images speak for themselves, however. I had to present them. I elaborated on each image verbally, and I didn't work off the cuff. Before the presentation, I used the "Notes" feature in PowerPoint to type my own text references for the verbal discussion. These notes were for my eyes only and would not appear onscreen. I was able to save my slide show to Microsoft Word, which automatically arranged all of my hidden text notes and paired them with thumbnails of my art images, creating the perfect reference document as I went through my presentation. The audience was then free to visually enjoy the large images while listening to me speak.

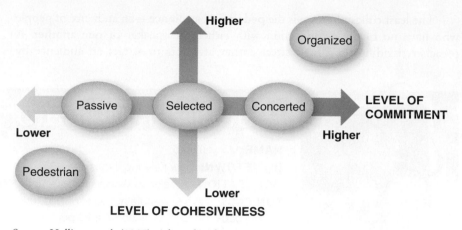

Source: Hollingsworth (1935). Adapted with permission.

**FIGURE 11.1**

**TYPES OF AUDIENCES**
Understanding your audience's levels of cohesiveness and commitment will help you as you plan your speech.

vividly describing people's sins. The speaker's first task in this and similar situations is to capture the attention of individuals who are likely to have other things on their minds.

The **passive audience** is a group that is already gathered to hear the speaker, but its motivation level is not high. When you speak in class, for example, an attendance requirement guarantees you the presence of an audience; it does not, however, guarantee that your audience will be interested in everything (or anything) you have to say. Because you are addressing a passive audience whose attention you have already claimed, your first task is to sustain and direct listeners' interest.

In a **selected audience**, the speaker and audience share a common and known purpose, but they do not necessarily agree on the best way to achieve their mutual goals. As Republicans gather at their convention, for example, they agree, in general, on the goal of getting their party's candidates elected. Nevertheless, different wings of the party are likely to have different concerns about what should be included in the platform or different opinions on the best approach to such issues as the economy or defense. The **concerted audience** is similar to the selected audience in that its members share a need to achieve some end and are usually positively disposed toward the speaker and the topic. When former President George W. Bush addresses the conservative wing of his party, for example, the audience is likely to be predisposed to do what he suggests. Thus your task when addressing a concerted audience is to capitalize on the audience's predisposition to accept your ideas.

Hollingsworth's final audience type is the **organized audience**. Such audiences are completely devoted to the speaker and to the speaker's purpose. Some religious and political groups fall into this category, as do audiences who have committed themselves to a noncontroversial cause (for example, honoring a well-known and respected actor for receiving

● **THE BANE** of a school presenter's existence? Fidgety kids who would much rather poke their neighbors than pay attention.

the American Film Institute Achievement Award). Informing and persuading organized audiences is therefore typically less important than celebrating with them. Your main job in this instance is to specify an action and give the audience direction to carry it out.

## Audience Demographics

Although identifying the type of audience you will face is an important component of audience analysis, it is only the first step. You should also examine your audience's demographics. **Demographics** is the systematic study of the quantifiable

---

## WIREDFORCOMMUNICATION

### THINK ABOUT THIS

### In a Click, Lectures Become Interactive

One of the challenges of public speaking has always been that the communication is, for the most part, one-way. And while some audiences might provide lots of feedback (in the form of applause, boos, silence, hysteria, and so on), others might not even want to pay attention. When dealing with a passive audience, speakers generally have little chance for real dialogue and interaction. But teachers are finding new technology that allows their once passive student audience to actively engage in their lectures.

Through the use of remote controls commonly referred to as "clickers," lecturers at hundreds of colleges and universities (and even some elementary and secondary schools) are able to pose questions to large groups of students and, within a minute or two, tally up all the answers and display the results. The technology is changing the nature of lectures. "It's not like an hour-long lecture where the professor is droning on and everybody goes to sleep because they don't know what's important," explained one physics professor. "It lets the lecture turn into a two-way conversation" ("Classroom Clickers," 2005).

The clickers supply both lecturers and audiences with instant feedback. "I've found that in [the lecture] setting, you find yourself thinking, 'Well, what are they thinking?'" noted one instructor. "I use it to take their pulse" ("No Wrong Answers," 2005). Students answering questions get instant feedback as well. "You don't have to wait for someone to sit back and grade them by hand," one student said of classroom assignments. "Right away you're able to get your answers back" ("Classroom Clickers," 2005).

Students have responded positively, with many instructors noting improvements in class participation and attendance; some instructors even note a marked improvement in grades ("Classroom Clickers," 2005; "No Wrong Answers," 2005). Originally used primarily in science classes, the clickers are proving extremely useful in the humanities and social sciences as the technology becomes more widespread. One key advantage of the clicker is its anonymity. Students who might have been hesitant to raise their hand for fear of giving a wrong answer or expressing an unpopular opinion can now have their answers logged electronically—and anonymously—with the click of a button.

**1** What other advantages does the clicker give the speaker? What kinds of new challenges might it pose?

**2** How does the clicker change the nature of the lecture? Does it change the relationship between speaker and audience? Or does it simply change the interaction between them?

**3** If you were giving a speech to an audience armed with clickers, what kinds of questions would you ask? How might the audience's responses change the nature or style of your speech? Could you make those changes on the fly?

As you consider the demographics of your audience, remember the powerful impact of stereotyping and schemas, discussed in Chapter 2. While it is helpful to know that your audience has many commuter students or students from a particular city, don't fall into the trap of believing that all of these people are alike. Tips for removing perceptual barriers (Chapter 2, see pp. 50–51) can help you use demographic information appropriately and effectively.

characteristics of a large group. An audience analysis might focus on such statistics as gender, socioeconomic status (including income, occupation, and education), religious and political affiliation, family status (married, single, divorced, partnered, with children, without children), age, and ethnic or cultural background. Other statistics that might be relevant to you in your speech class are student enrollment status (full time or part time), student residential status (living on campus or off campus), major area of study, or even what cities, states, regions, or countries your fellow students hail from.

Understanding such statistics can lead speakers to topics that will be of interest and will carry meaning for specific audiences. For example, one of the most easily quantifiable and useful demographic statistics to consider is age range of your audience. If you have a good sense of how old most of your audience members are, you'll be able to choose a topic that is relevant to concerns of their generation and ensure that the examples and anecdotes you use in your speech will resonate with the age groups you are addressing. For example, note how in his Hall of Fame induction for the band U2, Bruce Springsteen chose to reference other influential artists and albums (James Brown, *Exile on Main Street*) with little or no explanation. That's because he concluded that the audience—consisting primarily of rock musicians and rock enthusiasts, most of a certain age—would connect with such references. Similarly, should your own analysis reveal, for example, that much of your audience is composed of twenty-something part-time students working full-time jobs outside of school, you might choose a topic for your speech, as well as examples and references, that are relevant to them.

In addition, it is important to note that some audience characteristics will be more *salient*—or significant—in some speaking situations than in others. For example, if your audience members are mostly Latin American women in their fifties who have survived breast cancer, their status as survivors is not likely to

● **JOHN EDWARDS** has clearly thought about his audience. At the MySpace/MTV debates, he is wearing jeans and a sportier blazer, projecting a younger and hipper vibe. At the more formal Council on Foreign Relations event, he is dressed in a full suit and tie.

be salient if you are informing them about the importance of maximizing their annual contributions to their 401(k) plans before retiring in the next ten years. But if you are persuading a group to contribute money to the American Cancer Society in order to support new research campaigns, their experience fighting cancer should be firmly in your mind as you develop and deliver your speech.

Now, we know what you're thinking: "Right, Dan and Mary. How can I possibly know all of the demographics of my audience members or how their characteristics will affect their reaction to my speech?" You're right, of course. You can't necessarily know that the guy who sits three rows back on the left side of the classroom is a heterosexual Libertarian genetics major from a working-class family in Philadelphia and a Christian who works thirty hours a week at the deli around the corner from his off-campus apartment. But you can look for some general traits and trends. If a significant percentage of students at your university commute from off campus, a persuasive speech about the importance of getting off-campus students involved in the life of the school might be of interest to your audience—if commuting is salient at your institution, this topic is likely to be relevant to students who reside on campus and those who commute.

As we'll discuss elsewhere in this chapter and the chapters ahead, having this kind of sense of who your audience is will be useful in helping you select language and examples that are relevant to them and avoid language and examples that are inappropriate or offensive.

## Choosing Your Topic

Choosing a topic can seem like a daunting task, but it doesn't have to be. As we have just noted, you'll want to consider the audience's expectations for the speech and topics that will interest them, taking their demographics into account. In this course, you may have some guidance, in that your instructor—arguably your most important audience member—will likely have given you a specific assignment. Read the speech assignment carefully. What is it you are expected to do? Inform? Persuade? And has your professor given parameters for the topic? Be certain of your instructor's expectations for your speech, asking questions if necessary, to ensure that your topic and speech are appropriate. Once you've got a strong sense of what's expected, it's time to start thinking about your topic. In searching for a good topic, you might try two proven strategies for generating ideas: considering personal interests and brainstorming.

### Finding a Topic That Intrigues You

It's hard to give an inspiring speech about something you don't find particularly inspiring or an informative speech on a topic you know nothing about. Finding a speech topic that is truly interesting to you will serve you well as you prepare your speech, making you more motivated to research and refine the topic and generating an enthusiasm in you as a speaker that will impress your audience.

But when you have a variety of interests, it can be hard to pinpoint one to speak about. One way to get started is to write up a list of topics that interest

**AND YOU?**

Have you ever found yourself feeling disconnected from a speaker, be it a course instructor or a politician, because he or she failed to consider your age, gender, sexual orientation, or cultural background? Conversely, have you ever found a speaker very effective because he or she did consider such factors?

**TABLE 11.1**

## PERSONAL INTEREST TOPICS

| Personal Experiences | Controversial Issues | Current Events | Hobbies | Beliefs and Values |
|---|---|---|---|---|
| • Camping trips<br>• Vacations<br>• Life-threatening event<br>• Awards<br>• Education<br>• Organizations<br>• Friends<br>• Accomplishments<br>• Parenthood | • Intelligent design versus evolution<br>• Smoking bans<br>• Nature versus nurture<br>• Driving age<br>• Drinking age<br>• Same-sex marriage | • Global warming<br>• Political campaigns<br>• Budget deficits<br>• Space flights<br>• Sporting events<br>• Musical performances | • Skiing<br>• Golf<br>• Travel<br>• Cooking<br>• Camping<br>• Automobile restoration<br>• Gardening<br>• Shopping<br>• Surfing (waves or Internet) | • Spirituality<br>• Social justice<br>• Environmentalism<br>• Humanitarianism<br>• Political beliefs<br>• Mysticism<br>• Supernatural events<br>• Retribution |

Source: O'Hair, Stewart, & Rubenstein (2007), tab. 7.4, p. 98. Adapted with permission.

you. For example, take a look at the variety of interests listed in Table 11.1. Creating a thorough and detailed list of topics that interest you—or even looking at topics that interest other people—can be a great tool for stimulating ideas for your speech.

## Brainstorming Your Topic

Once you've determined a very general topic—by focusing either on an area of interest to you or on a general topic assigned by your instructor—you'll need to start amassing information, thinking creatively, and considering problems and solutions related to your topic. This is a process known as **brainstorming**. You might begin by considering what you already know about your subject. For example, assume that the assignment requires you to give a two- to three-minute speech describing a place. Consider some places you know, from very specific (the corner table by the window at your favorite coffeehouse) to the very general (the Midwest).

You might also consider using a technique called clustering (R. E. Smith, 1993). **Clustering** is a creative technique for identifying potential speech topics. It begins with a core idea, from which the writer branches out into a web of related thoughts and ideas in a stream-of-consciousness manner. The process is somewhat similar to brainstorming; however, instead of resulting in a list of possibilities, clustering "spills" its ideas onto paper. To begin, simply write a main or "nucleus" word or phrase in the center of a piece of paper and circle it. The word can be whatever strikes you—it need not seem to fit with the assigned topic. For example, you might start with the word *baseball*. From the nucleus word, create a web or a collection of ideas inspired by the nucleus word or phrase. Baseball might make you think of Babe Ruth. Babe Ruth might bring to mind the Babe Ruth museum in Baltimore, which might in turn elicit thoughts of other tourist

**AND YOU?**

Do topics for speeches, papers, or conversation come easily to you? Have you ever come upon a useful topic by accident—starting off with a clear idea about a particular topic, for example, and winding up with a better one as the result of going off on some tangent or reading some seemingly unrelated article?

attractions in that city, and each of those thoughts might lead to other ideas. As the ideas come, write each one, circle it, and connect it to the word or phrase that inspired it. A sample of such a cluster appears in Figure 11.2. As the process continues, you'll be struck by some concepts that strike you as potential topics for your speech. In a sense, it's like you're Googling your own brain, starting out with a word or concept and branching to form a web of links to related thoughts.

Remember that you can always turn to friends, classmates, professors, family, and others to talk about topics for speeches. Not only can they help you generate topics that you may not have thought of, but they can also help you evaluate the topics you find appealing. It always helps to bounce ideas off other people.

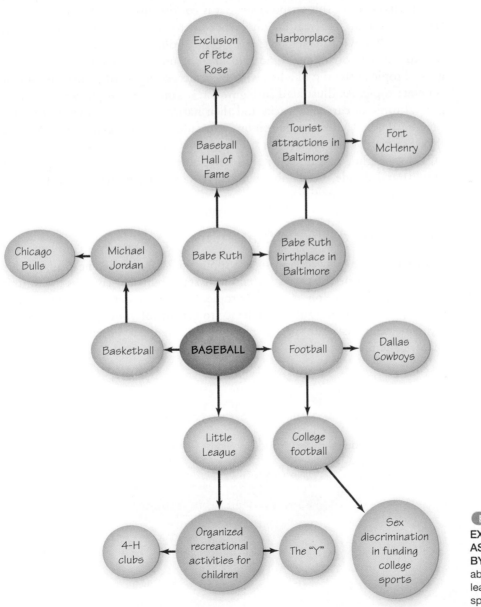

**FIGURE 11.2**

**EXAMPLE OF A WEB OF ASSOCIATIONS PRODUCED BY CLUSTERING** Thinking about the word *baseball* can lead to numerous possible speech topics.

## Narrowing Your Topic

Once you have searched for potential topics, it's time to make a choice. Your goal is to select the topic that best meets the following three criteria:

1. Is it a topic you are interested in and know something about?
2. Does the topic meet the criteria specified in the assignment?
3. Is it a topic that your audience will find worthwhile?

Once you are satisfied that your topic meets these criteria, you can begin to consider how to break down your topic further so that it is more specific and manageable. This will aid you a great deal in your research (a topic we will discuss later in this chapter) since it is considerably easier—and less frustrating—to find information on a specific topic (traditional Jewish foods served for Passover) than an extremely general one (the Jewish religion). One way to narrow down your topic is to break it up into categories. Write your general topic at the top of a list, with each succeeding word a more specific or concrete topic. As illustrated in Figure 11.3, you might begin with the very general topic of cars and trucks and then narrow the topic down a step at a time until you decide to focus on one particular type of truck (hybrid SUVs). If you discover that this topic is still too broad to cover in less than five minutes, you might focus on one specific hybrid model (the Toyota Highlander hybrid) and decide to talk about the advantages of owning a hybrid vehicle with all the SUV amenities.

## Developing a Thesis Statement

Once you have narrowed your speech topic, you can start to encapsulate your speech in the form of a **thesis statement**, a statement that conveys the central idea or core assumption about your topic. The thesis statement must clearly summarize what you want the audience to get out of your speech, but is not the same thing as your specific purpose statement; as noted earlier in this chapter, the thesis statement is more specific. Let's go back to our example of

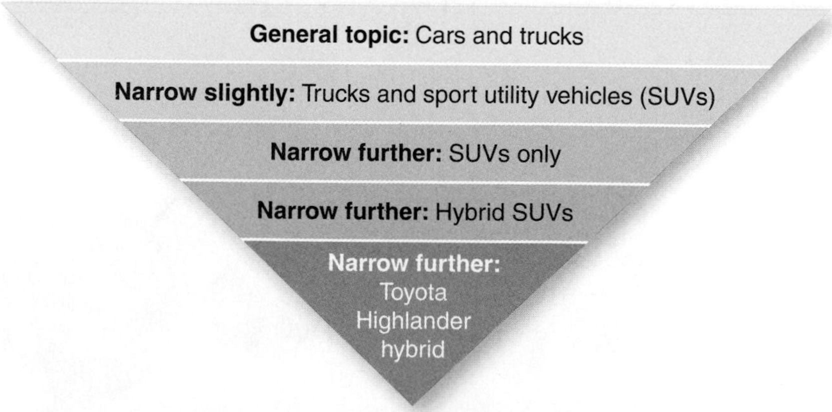

**General topic:** Cars and trucks

**Narrow slightly:** Trucks and sport utility vehicles (SUVs)

**Narrow further:** SUVs only

**Narrow further:** Hybrid SUVs

**Narrow further:**
Toyota
Highlander
hybrid

**FIGURE 11.3**

**NARROWING YOUR TOPIC**
Start with a general idea and become increasingly specific until you have a manageable topic for your speech.

volunteer reading programs. Our topic, general purpose, and specific purpose were as follows:

> **Topic:** Volunteer reading programs
>
> **General purpose:** To persuade
>
> **Specific purpose:** To have audience members realize the importance of reading with local elementary school children so that they sign up for a volunteer reading program such as Everybody Wins

Your thesis statement, then, should express the core idea that you want your listeners to walk away with.

> **Thesis statement:** Volunteers who read with local elementary school children through programs such as Everybody Wins improve young lives by enhancing children's self-esteem and expanding their possibilities for academic success.

Can you see how the thesis statement works? Offering a solid thesis statement your audience will remember long after your visual aids have faded from their minds will help you achieve your general purpose and your specific purpose: to persuade your listeners to get out there and read with local kids. For additional examples of thesis statements, see Table 11.2.

Your thesis statement helps you stay focused on your goals for communicating with others in a public speaking situation. But staying focused on goals also matters in communication contexts such as running a meeting. As we discuss in Chapter 9, clearly stating the purpose of your meeting and organizing your agenda around it helps everyone stay focused and makes you more likely to achieve your goals.

## TABLE 11.2
## GENERATING A THESIS STATEMENT

| Topic | General Purpose | Specific Purpose | Thesis Statement |
|---|---|---|---|
| Low-carbohydrate diets | To inform | To inform listeners about low-carbohydrate diets so that they can make good decisions about their own eating habits | Before choosing to start a low-carbohydrate diet, it is important to have a thorough understanding of how carbohydrates affect your body and what the possible benefits and risks of the diet are so that you can make an informed decision about your health. |
| Study-abroad programs | To persuade | To have listeners realize that studying abroad is an exciting opportunity and encourage them to consider spending a semester taking classes in another country | Studying abroad is an amazing opportunity to learn about another culture, to enhance your educational experience, and to make yourself more appealing to prospective graduate schools and employers. |
| My grandparents | To honor an amazing couple on their fiftieth wedding anniversary (special occasion) | To celebrate with my family and my grandparents' friends in light of this happy milestone in their lives | In big and small ways, my grandparents have shared their fifty years of love and commitment with their family, their congregation, and their students, having been dedicated teachers for three decades. |

## Researching the Topic

Anyone can make a speech—to stand on a stump or at a podium and speak on one matter or another is a birthright in the United States, regardless of whether or not what you are saying is useful, interesting, meaningful, or even truthful. But a good speech must offer listeners something new, some information, insight, perspective, or idea that they didn't have before. Such original thoughts are usually the product of both deep reflection and careful research.

In a speech, research is information that helps support the points that you make, strengthening your message and credibility. For many students, the prospect of researching for a speech or presentation might seem boring, overwhelming, or both—and it can be. But if you are working with a topic that truly intrigues you and you approach your research in a methodical and practical way, the research process can be better than you think.

### Types of Information to Consider

A wealth of material is available to enliven your speech and make it more effective. It is important not only to choose the appropriate type of supporting material but also to use it well. Listeners respond best to a range of information, so try to include a variety of types of support materials in your speech.

When you need to prove a point about which you are not an authority, incorporating the voice of an expert into your speech can lend it some validity. **Expert testimony** is the opinion or judgment of an expert, a professional in his or her field. Opinions from doctors, coaches, engineers, and other qualified, licensed professionals serve as expert testimony. In a speech about knee surgery, for example, you might cite an orthopedic surgeon when explaining the difference between arthroscopy and knee replacement surgery. **Lay testimony** is the opinion of a nonexpert who has personal experience or witnessed an event related to your topic. In a speech on weather disasters, you could provide the testimony from a witness who survived a tornado.

Numbers can often impress an audience more than mere words. **Statistics**—information provided in numerical form—can provide powerful support for a speech. Statistics reveal trends, explain the size of something, or illustrate relationships. Statistics can be made more meaningful when paired with or made part of *factual statements*—truthful, realistic accounts based on actual people, places, events, or dates. For example, in testimony before a congressional subcommittee in 2006, New York Mayor Michael Bloomberg used a combination of statistics and factual statements to back up his position that more needed to be done to stem the flow of illegal guns into New York City: "The harsh reality is that far too many people continue to be killed with illegal guns—and nearly all of those guns are purchased outside of New York State." Bloomberg backed up this factual statement with statistics: "Last year, illegal guns were used to take the lives of more than 300 people in our city. . . . 82% of the guns used in crimes in New York City were purchased outside of New York State."

While facts and statistics are useful for gaining credibility, they can also be boring, abstract, and easily forgotten. An effective way to breathe life into

**AND YOU?**
What type of supporting information do you find most compelling in speeches? Expert testimony? Statistics? Anecdotes? Why? Do you find that your preference depends on the topic of the speech? Why or why not?

them—and into your speech in general—is to flesh it out with background information and personal details that give faces to statistics and facts and make them part of a memorable and cohesive story. **Anecdotes** are brief, personal stories that have a point or punch line. For example, in a similar speech on illegal guns, Mayor Bloomberg might provide an anecdote about police detectives killed in the line of duty while trying to shut down gun traffickers. Anecdotes can be pointed, humorous, or emotionally moving; in all cases, they add a personal element to your speech.

Calling on the words of others can lend your speech a sense of history, perspective, and timeless eloquence. *Quotations,* repeating the exact words of another person, are usually most effective when they are brief, to the point, and clearly related to your topic. You might quote a historical figure, a celebrity, a poet, or a playwright. For example, in a speech about motivation, you could quote Michelangelo: "The greatest danger for most of us is not that our aim is too high and we miss it but that it is too low and we reach it." Your sources do not need to be famous—in accepting an award, you may be motivated to quote a friend or family member: "My grandfather always told me, 'An education is never a burden.'" Be sure to point out the source of your quote and, if appropriate, explain who the person is or was.

Each of these tools has the potential to liven up your speech and make it more memorable for your audience. You might also consider playing these tools off of each other to make an even bigger impression. *Comparisons* measure the similarity of two things. In a comparison, the likeness or resemblance of two ideas or concepts are pointed out. Recall how in Sample Speech 11.3, Bruce Springsteen compared U2 to such rock icons as James Brown, Robert Johnson, and the Clash. *Contrasts* show dissimilarities among two or more things. By illustrating differences, speakers can make distinctions among ideas they are discussing. A speech on school funding, for example, might call attention to disparities between schools by providing contrasting descriptions of the equipment in their science labs or gyms. You could follow that up by contrasting statistics on their students' average test scores or graduation rates.

## Researching Supporting Material

Of course, the facts, statistics, anecdotes, and other supporting material that you want for your speech won't come out of thin air. Now that you've got your list of ingredients for your speech, you'll need to do some shopping—that is, you'll need to go out and find the material. Here's how.

### Talk to People

If you're looking for testimony, narratives, real-world examples, and anecdotes, you'll need to start talking to people. You may be looking for experts in a particular field or people who have had firsthand experience with an event or occurrence, which can be a challenge. You can start by networking—making connections with people you don't know through people you do know. Searching through literature and Internet resources is another way to track down people who may be able to provide support for your speech.

**CONNECT**

The type of information you choose for your speech should be influenced by its general purpose. If you are persuading your audience (Chapter 15) or giving a speech for a special occasion, try using personal anecdotes to touch your audience emotionally. When informing your audience (Chapter 14), make sure that your use of anecdotes illuminates your topic and doesn't persuade the audience to think a certain way about it.

Another useful reason to talk to people is to conduct a survey. **Surveys** involve soliciting answers to a question or series of questions related to your topic from a broad range of individuals. Conducting a survey can give you a sense of how a group of people view a particular event, idea, or phenomena. For example, if you are giving an informative speech on fear of terrorism in the United States, you might randomly select students on campus and ask them how safe they feel from terrorist attacks. Results from surveys can be discussed to back up your points ("Of the forty students with whom I spoke, only twelve felt that a terrorist attack is likely in this region of the United States").

● **SURVEYING LOCAL FARMERS** about the effects of factory farming and mass-produced food on their livelihood will likely give you some interesting insights and quotations to use in your speech.

## Search the Literature

Published literature lets you reach beyond your own knowledge and experience and can be a valuable resource for supporting material for your speech. If you're giving a speech on hip-hop music, for example, you're likely to find some great material in the pages of magazines like *Vibe* or *Rolling Stone*. If you're looking for studies on mental health issues affecting rescue workers after Hurricane Katrina, you might search through newspaper archives or scholarly journals such as the *New England Journal of Medicine*.

Most current publications are available in searchable databases in libraries; some are even searchable from home computers (though you may have to pay a fee to download complete articles). Such databases give you access to a wealth of stored information. The Internet Movie Database (www.imdb.com) is a great example of a commonly used database that is accessible online and growing daily.

Another type of secondary resource is a **directory**. Directories are created and maintained by people rather than automatically by computers. Because human editors compile them, directories often return fewer links but higher-quality results. Directories guide you to the main page of a Web site organized within a wider subject category. If you type the keywords "public speaking skills" in Galaxy.com (a popular directory), you will be given links to the main pages of thirty-seven sites, all in the category of "Social Sciences: Communication." You can access useful literature through **library gateways**— collections of databases and information sites arranged by subject, generally reviewed and recommended by experts (usually librarians). These gateway collections assist in your research and reference needs because they identify suitable academic pages on the Web. In addition to scholastic resources, many library gateways include links to specialty search engines for biographies, quotations, atlases, maps, encyclopedias, and trivia. There are also a number of "virtual libraries" that exist only on the Internet. Some well-known library gateways, as well as other Internet search resources, are identified in Table 11.3 (see p. 340).

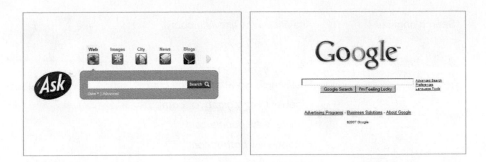

## Make the Internet Work for You

Twenty years ago, the first stop on any research mission would have been the library. Today, the Internet puts a multitude of information at your fingertips, accessible at any hour. Navigating the vast sea of information (and misinformation) available on the Internet can be daunting, and if you don't search wisely, it can be a waste of time. A solid knowledge of search tools can therefore make your searches more fruitful and efficient.

**Tools for navigation.**   An Internet **search engine** is a program that indexes Web content. Search engines such as Google, AltaVista, and Excite search all over the Web for documents containing specific keywords that you've chosen. Typically, a search engine functions by fetching as many documents as possible that retrieve meaningful results based on location and frequency of keywords. Search engines have some key advantages—they offer access to a huge portion of publicly available Web pages and give you the ability to search through large databases. But they frequently return irrelevant links, and they don't index the "invisible Web"—databases maintained by universities, businesses, the government, or libraries that cannot always be accessed by standard search engines.

If a search engine fails to produce useful results, try a **metasearch engine**—a search engine that scans multiple search engines simultaneously. Metasearch technology delivers more relevant and comprehensive results than a search engine. However, the results from metasearch engines include commercial as well as noncommercial sites. For example, the metasearch engine Dogpile accesses and compiles information from several search engines, including About, Ask, FindWhat, Google, LookSmart, Overture, Teoma, and Yahoo. Table 11.3 lists some of the best search engines and metasearch engines, along with their URLs.

**Finding the right words.**   Choosing an appropriate form of the word or words you're looking for is also important. *Word stemming,* a procedure used by some search engines, will return results for words based on a particular stem. For example, a search for "fish" might return pages containing the words *fisher* or *fishing.* By reducing a word to its "stem," the process of word stemming often produces results beyond what you are looking for.

TABLE 11.3

**USEFUL INTERNET SEARCH SITES**

| | |
|---|---|
| **Search engines** | AltaVista *www.altavista.com* |
| | Ask *www.ask.com* |
| | Excite *www.excite.com* |
| | FastSearch *www.fastsearch.com* |
| | Gigablast *www.gigablast.com* |
| | Google *www.google.com* |
| | Hotbot *www.hotbot.com* |
| | InfoSeek *infoseek.go.com* |
| | WebCrawler *www.webcrawler.com* |
| | Yahoo! *www.yahoo.com* |
| **Metasearch engines** | Dogpile *www.dogpile.com* |
| | SavvySearch *www.savvysearch.com* |
| | The Big Hub *www.thebighub.com* |
| **Library gateways** | Digital Librarian *www.digital~librarian.com* |
| | Internet Public Library *www.ipl.org* |
| | Living Web Library *www.livingweb.com/library/search.htm* |
| | New Canaan Library *www.newcanaanlibrary.org* |
| **Directories** | Academic Info *www.academicinfo.net* |
| | LookSmart *www.looksmart.com* |
| | Open Directory Project or DMOZ *www.dmoz.org* |

## Evaluating Supporting Material

Once you've gathered a variety of sources, you must critically evaluate the material and determine which sources you should use. After all, your credibility as a speaker depends largely on the accuracy and credibility of the sources that you cite in your speech as well as the appropriateness of the sources for your topic and your audience.

### Credible Sources

In today's media, anyone can put up a blog or a Web page, self-publish a book, or post a video to YouTube. What's more, a large and growing number of opinion-based publications, broadcasting networks, and Web sites provide an outlet for research that is heavily biased one way or the other. Consequently, it is always worth spending a little time evaluating **credibility**—the quality, authority, and reliability—of each source you use. One simple way to approach this is to look at the author of the material and evaluate his or her credentials. This means that you should note if the author is a medical doctor, Ph.D., attorney, CPA, or other licensed professional and whether he or she is affiliated with a reputable organization or institution. For example, if you are seeking statistics on the health effects of cigarette smoke, an article written by an M.D. affiliated with the American Lung Association would be more credible than an editorial written by your Uncle Albert, who's an accountant.

### Up-to-Date Sources

In most cases, you'll want to use the most recent information available to keep your speech timely and relevant. Isaiah, for example, is speaking to a group of potential clients about his company's graphic design services. If, during his speech, he makes reference to testimonials from satisfied clients in 2003 and earlier, the audience may wonder if the company has gone downhill since then. For this reason, always determine when your source was written or last updated; sources without dates may indicate that the information is not as timely or relevant as it could be.

### Accurate Sources

When compiling support for your speech, it is important to find accurate sources—sources that are true, correct, and exact. A speaker who presents inaccurate information may very well lose the respect and attention of the audience. There are several ways to help ensure that you are studying accurate sources. Considering the credibility of the source and whether it is up-to-date, as just mentioned, is a start. In addition, accurate sources are "exact" sources, meaning that they offer detailed and precise information. A source that notes that more than 42,000 people died as a result of automobile accidents in the United States last year is less accurate than a source that notes that 42,636 people died in such accidents. The more precise your sources, the more credibility you will gain with your audience.

### Relevant Sources

Audiences are impressed with speakers who support their speeches with information that is relevant to the topic. If you are speaking to persuade an audience to donate time and money to the American Cancer Society, you might cite statistics, testimonials from doctors, or personal anecdotes from cancer survivors—but you probably would not need to talk about the biological process of cancer growth in the human body. Although such information may be accurate and interesting, it is not necessarily relevant to your topic or the purpose of your speech.

One way of demonstrating the relevance of your supporting material is through its *timeliness,* its connection to its time and the subject under discussion. Timely information is not the same as new or up-to-date information: in fact, examples, research, and studies that are quite old can be timely if recent events have rendered them relevant. For example, if Lea decides to inform her audience about high gas prices in 2008, she might use examples and statistics from the oil crisis of 1973 in her speech, because the 2008 situation makes discussions of historical oil shortages and price hikes relevant. Such a discussion, however, would have been less interesting and relevant to audiences in 2000, when gas prices were quite low.

### Compelling Sources

Support material that is strong, influential, interesting, and believable is considered to be *compelling* information. Information that is convincing and persuasive helps your audience understand, process, and retain your message. When Mike Bloomberg refers to police statistics that show that 82 percent of the guns used in crimes in his city are purchased outside of New York State—a state with very strict gun laws—that's a compelling statistic.

To be compelling, your supporting material should also be *vivid*. Vivid material is clear and vibrant, never vague. For example, in a speech about the 2004 cicada invasion of the Washington, D.C., area, Ana might reference a source describing these bugs as large insects, about one and a half inches long, with red eyes, black bodies, and fragile wings; she might also use a direct quotation from a D.C. resident who notes that "there were so many cicadas that the ground, trees, and streets looked like they were covered by an oil slick." Such vivid (and gross!) descriptions of information interest listeners. Look for clear, concrete supporting details that encourage the audience to form visual representations of the object or event you are describing.

### Reliable Sources

A reliable source will show a trail of research by supplying details about where the information came from. A reputable publication will supply a thorough list of references, either as endnotes or footnotes. Examining this list—and perhaps even investigating a few of the sources—will help you determine the validity of the material. Similarly, in news writing, source information is integrated into the text. A newspaper or magazine article, for example, will credit information to named sources ("Baseball Commissioner Bud Selig said . . .") or credentialed but unnamed sources ("One high-ranking State Department official said, on condition of anonymity . . .").

The Internet poses special problems when it comes to reliability due to the ease with which material can be posted online. Check for balanced, impartial information that is not biased. The source should mention the background or credentials of the authors. Be sure the information is accurate and recent. If references are listed, verify them to confirm their authenticity. Web sites can be quickly assessed for reliability by looking at the domain, or the suffix of the Web site address. Credible Web sites often end with *.edu* (educational institution), *.org* (nonprofit organization), *.mil* (military site), or *.gov* (government). Most people are familiar with *.com* (commercial business). Be aware of addresses that contain a tilde (~) because this usually indicates a personal Web page and may not necessarily contain dependable information.

## Ethical Speaking: Taking Responsibility for Your Speech

As a responsible public speaker, you must let ethics guide every phase of planning and researching your speech. But what does it mean to be an ethical speaker? The short answer is that it means being responsible: responsible for ensuring that

**CONNECT**

The sources you cite in your speech are part of your *self-presentation* to your audience (Chapter 2). If your sources are outdated or from your cousin's blog, you will present a self that says, "I am unprepared and I didn't research my topic thoroughly." Conversely, if you offer statistics, facts, and stories from a variety of current, reliable, and compelling sources, you present yourself as trustworthy, prepared, and competent—and your audience is more likely to consider what you're saying.

proper credit is given to other people's ideas, data, and research that you have incorporated into your presentation, as well as being responsible for what you say (and how you say it) to your audience. Let's review, starting with what happens when you fail to cite your sources properly: plagiarism.

## Recognizing Plagiarism

**Plagiarism** is the crime of presenting someone else's words, ideas, or intellectual property as your own, intentionally or unintentionally. It is a growing problem (Park, 2003) and is not limited to the written word—or to students. In the fall of 2002, for example, Eugene Tobin, a historian and the president of Hamilton College, stepped down after admitting that he failed to credit his sources in his speeches (Debraggio, 2002). Most universities and colleges have clear definitions of plagiarism and enforce strict penalties regarding the issue. In fact, we wouldn't be surprised if your professor included information about your school's plagiarism policy in your syllabus. If so, *read this document carefully.* The syllabus is like your contract with your professor; by reading it and staying in the course, you have agreed to follow it.

Despite the problems associated with plagiarism, many students, writers, and speakers remain unsure of how, when, or why they must credit their sources. In fact, many people are shocked to find that they can be guilty of plagiarism with a small, seemingly unimportant error, like simply failing to include one little footnote that slipped their mind at 2:00 A.M. when they were finishing their paper or speech. To avoid making this mistake, it is extremely important that you keep careful track of where all your material comes from and document it properly. In the next chapter, we will explain how to document your sources in your speech; for now, we will focus on the important role of taking accurate and thorough notes during the research phase.

## Taking Accurate Notes

You need to keep track of every single one of your references to avoid unintentionally plagiarizing. The first step in doing so is to compile a comprehensive record of all your research. Every time you make use of information from an outside source, it's important that you copy it correctly and write down for your own reference whether the material is copied *verbatim* (word for word) or *paraphrased* (put into your own words).

Keeping track of all your outside material and its sources can be one of the most challenging aspects of conducting research. Note cards can be useful for documenting references separately. Each note card should contain the quote or material you want to use, along with pertinent information such as author names, title, volume, publisher, location, date, and page numbers. Use one note card for each source so that you can maintain a complete entry for individual references. When your research is complete (or nearly complete), you'll be able to shuffle these individual thoughts and references around as you develop your speech without losing track of their sources. Two sample note cards are shown in Figure 11.4 (see p. 345).

**AND YOU?**

How do you feel about the fact that even unintentionally using someone else's words, ideas, or intellectual property is still plagiarism? Does it seem unfair that you might suffer severe consequences (such as being expelled) even if you do something without intent? Why or why not?

You'll also need to keep a **running bibliography**—a list of resources you've consulted, to which you can refer on your note cards. For each source to which you refer, take down all the pertinent information you'll need to cite in the final speech. This information includes the following details:

# EVALUATING**COMMUNICATION**ETHICS

## Plagiarism: Intentional or Unintentional?

You and Tivya have been studying together for your speech communication course. You are both working on speeches about looking into the past—Tivya is researching the 1990s while you research the '70s. You are using an organizational style based on remembering the past and have titled your speech "Back in the '70s." Tivya thought that sounded like a good idea and decided to begin her speech with an attention getter that asked listeners if they remembered watching certain television cartoons or playing with certain toys that were popular in the 1990s.

When Tivya gives her speech, the class enjoys it, but you notice that the speech seems very similar to an e-mail that had gone around that year titled "Remember the '90s." You're a bit startled. Is it possible that Tivya has intentionally copied the entire e-mail and presented it as her own? Or might she have read the e-mail long ago and internalized it to the point that she thinks it's her own original material?

In some respects, all work is derivative: it carries the influence of all the things we've read, seen, and heard throughout our lives. But even though it's a given that any piece of writing will have been influenced by the work of others, it is the writer's responsibility to ensure that the work one produces is truly one's own. Borrowing words from another source, even unintentionally, is plagiarism. In 2006, a young novelist was accused of doing just that. Kaavya Viswanathan, a sophomore at Harvard University, had just published her first book, *How Opal Mehta Got Kissed, Got Wild, and Got a Life,* when reporters from the *Harvard Crimson* accused her of having taken numerous passages from another writer's work. Viswanathan's novel was pulled from bookstores and revised for a second printing. The author issued an apology, claiming that as a high school student, she had read both *Sloppy Firsts* and *Second Helpings,* the two Meghan McCafferty novels from which she was accused of stealing. "I wasn't aware of how much I may have internalized Ms. McCafferty's words," Viswanathan said in a statement. "I am a huge fan of her work and can honestly say that any phrasing similarities between her work and mine were completely unintentional and unconscious" (Memmot, 2006).

Intentional or not, plagiarism is extremely problematic. It's a common enough mistake among writers and speakers, but what of your friend Tivya? Intentionally or unintentionally, she had plagiarized that e-mail quite extensively. Her grade, her status in school, and her reputation are at stake. What should you do?

**THINK ABOUT THIS**

❶ How is Tivya's mistake plagiarism? How about Kaavya Viswanathan's? How are these cases similar, and how are they different? In either case, does it matter if the plagiarism is intentional or unintentional?

❷ Was Viswanathan's apology statement appropriate? What kinds of steps could Tivya take to address her mistake? Should she tell her instructor? Should you?

❸ Imagine that as the instructor or publisher, it is your responsibility to respond to an instance of plagiarism. How would you handle the situation?

- The type of source (magazine, book, interview, and so on)

- The complete name of each author, or origin of the source if no author is named ("National Science Foundation Web site," or "*New York Times* editorial")

- The title and subtitle of the source (article, book chapter, Web page) and of the larger work in which it appears (magazine, newspaper, journal, book, Web site)

- The publication date of the source; for Web sources, date of publication and date of access; for journals, volume and issue numbers

- For books, publisher and city of publication; for Web resources, the complete URL

- Page numbers for the material used and for the entire work being cited

FIGURE 11.4
**SAMPLE NOTE CARDS**

---

*SMOKING/Teenagers/Statistics*

SOURCE: Chan, Sewell. "Study says..." *NY Times*, p. B1. 3/10/2006
Paraphrased:

NYC study shows sharp decline in teen smoking over past four years,
only 11% of public HS students smoking, compared to 23% in 1997.
National average per 2003 National Risk Behavior Survey was 21.9%.
Mayor Bloomberg attributes decline to high tax on cigarettes (bringing
prices up to around $8 per pack), to bans on smoking in the workplace.

---

*SMOKING/Teenagers/Addiction*

SOURCE: Arday, D. R., et al. "Cigarette smoking..." *American Journal of
Health Promotion*, 10, 111–116.
Verbatim:

"The younger people start smoking cigarettes, the more likely they are to
become strongly addicted to nicotine." (p. 112)

Your running bibliography may be a handwritten list, depicted in Figure 11.5; or you may prefer to make an individual note card for each entry, which will allow you to alphabetize the cards after writing your speech. Alternatively, you may choose to create a running bibliography on your computer or PDA, which will allow you to edit and add sources electronically. Regardless of the format you choose, keeping a running bibliography will free you from having to write the same information over and over on your note cards if you are using multiple details or quotes from a given source. Instead, you can simply refer to the article used by author or article name, with a page number reference for each detail or quote.

Although note cards remain a valuable tool, it's impossible to talk about modern research without addressing the ease with which most research material can be taken from the Internet. Printing out entire Web pages can save researchers a great deal of time when gathering information; going through the printouts with a highlighter or pen can help you emphasize useful passages for your speech. But remember to treat those pages just like note cards: make sure each one includes the source for the material so that you can clearly identify where the page came from, who wrote it, when it was published, and the complete URL for the page. You'll need all that material to prepare a proper citation. We'll discuss how to incorporate such references into your finished work—both in the speech and in a separate bibliography—in Chapter 12.

**FIGURE 11.5**

**SAMPLE RUNNING
BIBLIOGRAPHY**

*References*

Arday, D. R., Giovino, G. A., Schulman, J., Nelson, D. E., Mowery, P., & Samet, J. M. (1995). Cigarette smoking and self-reported health problems among U.S. high school seniors, 1982–1989. *American Journal of Health Promotion, 10,* 111–116.

Chan, S. (2006, March 10). Study says teenagers are avidly shunning cigarettes. *The New York Times,* p. B1.

Fisher, E. B. (1998). *American Lung Association: Seven steps to a smoke-free life.* New York: Wiley.

Zickler, P. (2006). Combination treatment for one year doubles smokers' quit rate. Retrieved October 4, 2007, from http://www.drugabuse.gov/NIDA_notes/NNvol20N4/Combination.html

## Speaking Ethically and Responsibly

Your responsibility as a speaker goes beyond simply giving credit to others' work; you need to take responsibility for what *you* say.[1] If you use inflammatory, hurtful, or hateful language—even if it is language that is quoted from another source—it is you who will bear the brunt of the audience's reactions. Providing a footnote or endnote can reinforce your points, but it cannot excuse you from taking responsibility for them.

The First Amendment to the United States Constitution guarantees every citizen the right to free speech, but not all speech is ethical. As a public speaker, you are responsible for providing your audience with all of the necessary information for them to make accurate, appropriate decisions about you and your message. The speeches by Chinese leader Deng Xiaoping, who tried to intimidate Chinese citizens into revealing the whereabouts of leaders of the unsuccessful 1989 student uprising in Tiananmen Square in Beijing, were unethical and coercive. In addition, it's important to recognize that the right to free speech in this country is not without limits. As Supreme Justice Oliver Wendell Holmes wrote in 1919, the Constitution "would not protect a man falsely shouting fire in a theater and causing a panic" (*Schenck* v. *United States,* 1919). Speech that endangers people—for example, speech that incites riots or causes unnecessary panic—would not only be ethically questionable but might be illegal as well.

Although everyone has different standards for ethical communication, the qualities of dignity and integrity are universally seen as core to the idea of ethics. *Dignity* is feeling worthy, honored, or respected as a person (Gudykunst, Ting-Toomey, Suweeks, & Stewart, 1995, p. 92). *Integrity* is incorruptibility—the ability to avoid compromise for the sake of personal gain (p. 92). Basic rules for ethical speaking require that we adhere to four principles: we should strive to be trustworthy, respectful, responsible, and fair in our speeches (Day, 1997, p. 3).

▶ *Trustworthiness* refers to being honest with your audience about the goal of your message and providing accurate information.

▶ By treating people right, you are showing *respect*. In public speaking, respect is shown by focusing on issues rather than on personalities, allowing the audience the power of choice, and avoiding excluding the audience in discussions.

▶ As a *responsible* public speaker, it is your job to consider the topic and purpose of the speech, evidence and reasoning of the arguments, accuracy of your message, and honest use of emotional appeals.

▶ Ethical public speakers must be *fair* by presenting alternative and opposing views to the audience. A fair speaker will not deny the audience the right to make informed decisions.

---

[1]Much of this discussion was inspired by the work of Michael Josephson, founder and president of the Joseph and Edna Josephson Institute of Ethics in Marina del Rey, California.

**AND YOU?**

Consider your own personal opinions about ethical speaking. Would you add anything to the four principles noted here? If so, what characteristics would you cite?

● **WHILE THE** First Amendment allows anyone to step up on a soapbox and say whatever he or she wants to say, it's still important to refrain from unethical or derogatory speech.

# what about you?

**Assessing Your Speech**

As you work through the early stages of putting together your speech, consider the following points. Give yourself an honest assessment on each one.

1. The purpose of my speech:
   A. Is clear: My opening lets the audience know what I'm going to talk about.
   B. I make several main points, but I'm not sure if I'm getting the big picture across.
   C. This speech was supposed to have a purpose?

2. My topic:
   A. Is interesting and fun to research and will be of interest or use to my audience.
   B. Is interesting to me, but I'm not entirely sure my audience will care.
   C. Who cares about my audience? It's not even interesting to me.

3. My thesis statement:
   A. Is clear and is well supported by main points and subpoints.
   B. Is implied.
   C. Isn't the thesis the same thing as the purpose of my speech?

4. My sources:
   A. Are reliable: I've used only respected written material and interviews with experts.
   B. I've used some material that is questionable, like unverified Internet sources.
   C. My only source is my imagination!

5. Keeping track of my sources:
   A. I'm using a working bibliography and/or note cards.
   B. I'm printing relevant pages from the Internet and photocopying material.
   C. I'm sticking Post-it Notes on a few pages of books that, now that I think of it, may have already been returned to the library.

6. Avoiding plagiarism:
   A. I'm indicating whether each piece of information is quoted or paraphrased.
   B. I'm making mental notes to remind myself to use air quotes when necessary.
   C. I'm changing a few words in material I copied from other sources.

7. Taking responsibility for my speech:
   A. I'm confident that I've created an appropriate and ethical presentation.
   B. Well, I'm feeling a little sheepish about some of my facts, and I may have exaggerated details in some of my examples.
   C. Hey, if someone is foolish enough to follow my instructions, that's not my fault!

**If your responses were mostly A's:** You've done a thorough job researching and outlining your speech.

**If your responses were mostly B's:** You might need to reassess your topic, refine your thesis statement, or check your sources.

**If your responses were mostly C's:** Sorry, but you just might need to start over! You can't build a good presentation without solid research and a firm grip on your topic.

## BACK TO ▶ Al Gore

At the beginning of this chapter, we talked about the success of Al Gore's documentary *An Inconvenient Truth,* a film that is essentially a movie of his slide show presentation on global warming. Why were audiences willing to flock to movie theaters to see a presentation by a speaker with a reputation for being boring? As we've learned in this chapter, despite the popular notion that Gore is a bore, his presentation benefits from good planning and research.

▶ Gore knows his audience. For the most part, the people flocking to see his presentations and his films are already in his camp. They're concerned, or at least curious, about global warming and the environment; many were supporters of his 2000 run for president and were hoping he'd run again.

▶ When it comes to the environment, Gore has credibility. He's been talking about global warming for decades, wrote a popular book on the subject, and pushed for environmental issues throughout his tenures as senator and vice president. He's also passionate about the subject, and the enthusiasm he brings to it influences his speech and his audience's perceptions of it.

▶ Gore backs up his presentation with solid and verifiable sources. He calls on experts to make the point that there is almost universal acceptance of the reality of global warming in the scientific community.

▶ The presentation and the film make use of compelling examples and visual aids, including video footage of glaciers falling into the ocean and snow melting on the peak of Africa's storied Mount Kilimanjaro.

## THINGS TO TRY

1. Think back to a memorable speech you've witnessed, either in person or through the media. What kind of speech was it? Was the speaker trying to inform, persuade, or celebrate? Was he or she successful in that endeavor? Did the speech change the way you felt?

2. Tune in to a few news pundits—for example, Bill O'Reilly, Al Franken, or Keith Olberman—on radio or television. Listen carefully to what they say, and consider how they back up their statements. Do they provide source material as they speak? Can you link to their sources from their online blogs? How does the way they back up their points or fail to back them up influence your perceptions of what they say?

3. Take a look at your school's policy on plagiarism. Does your school clearly define what acts constitute plagiarism? How harsh are the punishments? Who is responsible for reporting plagiarism? How is the policy enforced?

4. The next time you read something—a magazine article, a work of nonfiction, a chapter in a textbook—take time to think about the research presented in it. What kinds of research did the authors do? How do they back up their statements? What kinds of research materials do they include?

## IF YOU'RE INTERESTED

*A Speaker's Guidebook* (3rd ed.), by Dan O' Hair, Rob Stewart, and Hannah Rubenstein (New York: Bedford/St. Martin's, 2007)

*A Pocket Guide to Public Speaking* (2nd ed.), by Dan O'Hair, Hannah Rubenstein, and Rob Stewart (New York: Bedford/St. Martin's, 2007)

These handbooks walk readers through every step of public speaking, from researching and developing speeches to delivering them.

*Doing Honest Work in College: How to Prepare Citations, Avoid Plagiarism, and Achieve Real Academic Success,* by Charles Lipson (Chicago: University of Chicago Press, 2004)

This handy guide provides clear guidance on when and how to cite sources for any paper or speech. It includes basic rules and advice for avoiding plagiarism as well as comprehensive guidelines for writing proper citations in any discipline.

*FDR's Fireside Chats,* by Russell D. Buhite and David W. Levy, eds. (New York: Penguin, 1993)

The editors of this text offer faithful transcripts from all thirty-one of Franklin Delano Roosevelt's "fireside chats" to the American people on topics ranging from the banking crisis to the New Deal to the United States' entry into World War II. The text also provides insightful introductions and discussions on a variety of topics related to FDR and American politics during his presidency, including commentary on the careful crafting of the fireside chats with a team of advisers and speechwriters.

*An Inconvenient Truth* (Paramount Classics, 2006)

As noted at the beginning and end of this chapter, this Academy Award–winning documentary shows how former Vice President Al Gore developed his signature slide presentation on global warming and took it on the road. It's a fascinating look not only at the subject of climate change but also at the connections among research, activism, and public speaking.

# REAL REFERENCE ► A Study Tool

**Now that you have finished reading this chapter, you can**

Understand the power of **public speaking** and how preparation eases natural nervousness.

Identify the purpose of your speech:

▶ *Informative speeches* aim to increase the audience's understanding and knowledge of a topic (p. 320).

▶ *Persuasive speeches* are intended to influence the beliefs, attitudes, and behaviors of your audience (p. 322).

▶ *Special-occasion speeches* are given at common events (like weddings and funerals), and many of us will deliver them at some point in time (p. 323).

▶ A **specific purpose statement** expresses the topic and the general speech purpose in action form and in terms of the specific objectives you hope to achieve with your presentation (p. 325).

Analyze your audience:

▶ It is important to understand and appreciate your audience's expectations for the speech (p. 326).

▶ The **pedestrian audience** has no obvious connection with the speaker (p. 327).

▶ The **passive audience** is gathered intentionally to hear the speaker but is not highly motivated (p. 328).

▶ A **selected audience** shares a common purpose with the speaker but may not have shared goals (p. 328).

▶ The **concerted audience** shares a need to achieve some end with the speaker and is positively disposed toward him or her (p. 328).

▶ The **organized audience** is devoted to the speaker and the speaker's purpose (p. 328).

▶ Knowing **demographics**, the quantifiable characteristics of your audience, will help you identify topics that the audience would be interested in learning about (p. 329).

Choose an appropriate topic and develop it:

▶ Speak about something that inspires you (p. 331).

▶ Use **brainstorming** to amass information, think creatively, and consider problems and solutions related to your topic (p. 332).

▶ Hone your topic by **clustering**, creating a web of thoughts and ideas about your topic on paper (p. 332).

▶ Narrow your topic, and write a **thesis statement**, a summary of your central idea (p. 334).

Support and enliven your speech with effective research:

▶ Include **expert testimony**, the opinion of an authority, or **lay testimony**, opinion based on personal experience (p. 336).

▶ **Statistics**, information in numerical form, can clarify your presentation (p. 336).

▶ **Anecdotes**, relevant personal stories, bring the human experience to the speech (p. 337).

▶ **Surveys** will add the point of view of a larger range of people (p. 338).

▶ Use databases to find material, such as **directories**, **library gateways**, **search engines**, and **metasearch engines** (pp. 338–339).

Cull from among your sources the material that will be most convincing:

▶ Take time to evaluate the **credibility**—the quality, authority, and reliability—of each source you use (p. 340).

▶ Up-to-date information convinces the audience of its timeliness (p. 341).

▶ Citing accurate and exact sources gains audience respect (p. 341).

▶ Relevant information supports the core topic (p. 341).

▶ Compelling information is influential and interesting (p. 342).

▶ Reliable sources provide reputable information (p. 342).

Give proper credit to sources and take responsibility for your speech:

▶ Avoid **plagiarism**, presenting someone else's intellectual property as your own (p. 343).

▶ Keep accurate track of all your references to avoid unintentional errors (p. 343).

▶ Keeping a **running bibliography**, the list of resources you've consulted, will free you from having to write the same information over and over (p. 344).

▶ Honor the basic rules for ethical speaking (p. 347).

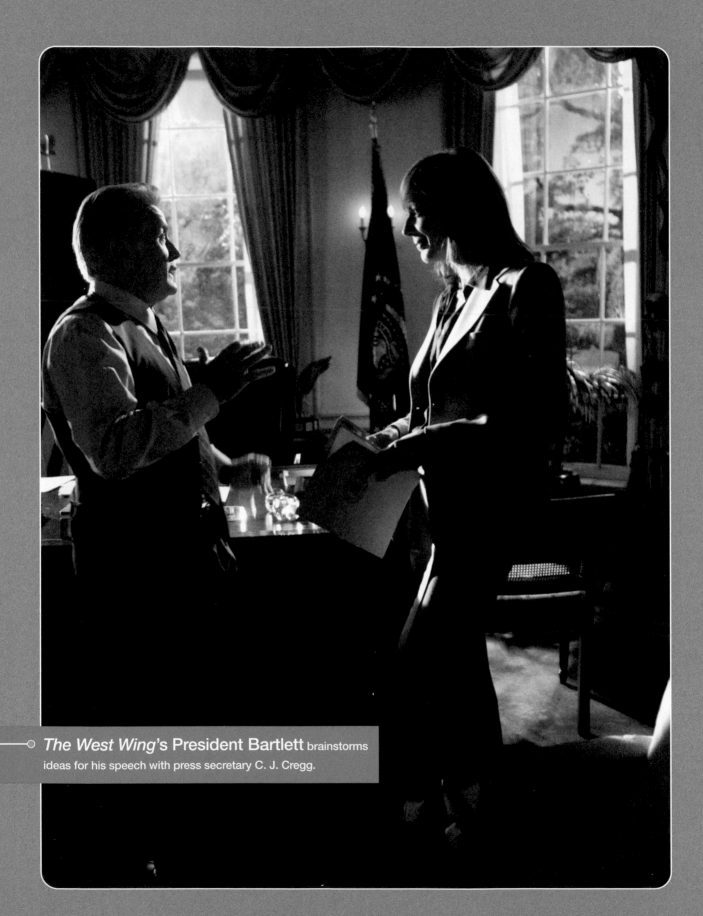

*The West Wing*'s **President Bartlett** brainstorms ideas for his speech with press secretary C. J. Cregg.

# chapter 12

# Organizing, Outlining, and Writing Presentations

**The Constitution of the United States of America** makes a simple demand of the president. "He shall from time to time give to the Congress Information of the State of the Union, and recommend to their Consideration such Measures as he shall judge necessary and expedient" (art 2, sec. 3).

For much of our nation's history, the State of the Union address was a lengthy letter to Congress read to members of the Senate and House by a congressional clerk. But over time it has evolved into an elaborate and highly politicized annual affair that allows the president to present major ideas and issues directly to the public: the Monroe Doctrine (James Monroe, 1823), the Four Freedoms (Franklin D. Roosevelt, 1941), and the War on Terror (George W. Bush, 2002) were all detailed for the American people during State of the Union addresses (Longley, 2007).

And so each January, White House speechwriters face the daunting task of addressing both Congress and the nation with a speech that outlines what is going on in foreign and domestic policy in a way that flatters the president and garners support for his agenda for the following year. As if that weren't a sufficiently difficult task, speechwriters must also navigate a deluge of requests from lobbyists, political consultants, and everyday citizens eager to get their pet project, policy, or idea into the president's speech. "Everybody wants [a] piece of the action," lamented former White House speechwriter Chriss Winston in 2002. "The speechwriter's job is to keep [the speech] on broad themes so it doesn't sink of its own weight." Matthew Scully (2005), one of President George W. Bush's speechwriters, concurred: "The entire thing can easily turn into a tedious grab bag of policy proposals."

Imagine that you are building a bridge, a skyscraper, or even a humble little house. You might start with a picture of it in your head, but before you can build it, you need to form a solid foundation and develop a framework that is structurally sound. Any architect will tell you that even the most exciting and lofty designs are useless without these two crucial components. Skimp on either one, and your structure will crack, shift, or collapse.

Building a speech follows a similar process. Whether you are writing a national address for the president of the United States or a three-minute presentation for a communication class, you will be unable to make your point if your speech is not structurally sound. As we discussed in Chapter 11, you begin with your idea and then build your foundation with research and a clear thesis statement. The next step is to develop your framework—the overall structure of your presentation. In this chapter, we'll focus on organizing all of your ideas and information into a clear and practical framework and integrating them into a well-written speech.

## Organizing Your Main Points

You've got your purpose, your research, and your thesis. But before you jump into the deep end of the pool and begin writing, it's best to organize your ideas—to set out the points you want to make, examples you plan to use to support them, and the basic order in which you want to present them. In this section, we'll focus on identifying your main and supporting points and introduce you to a few useful approaches to organizing them in your presentation.

### Identifying Your Main Points

First and foremost, you must determine the **main points** of your speech, which are the central claims that support your specific speech purpose and your thesis statement (which you learned about in Chapter 11). That is, you need to identify and organize key ideas that will lead the audience members to accept or consider what you are asking them to do, believe, or consider. If, for example, you want to persuade an audience to vote yes on removing candy and soda vending machines from your local high school in order to help combat the obesity epidemic in your community, what key points do you think will influence your listeners to vote this way? Perhaps they would be motivated to do so if they knew the scope of the problem: 15 percent of children and teens in the United States are overweight, and another 15 percent are considered at risk of becoming overweight (Palo Alto Medical Foundation, 2005) (*main point 1*). You'd likely further your argument by connecting the types of food and beverages in vending machines to the obesity problem: a 2004 study showed that 75 percent of beverages and 85 percent of snacks from vending machines were of poor nutritional value (Center for Science in the Public Interest, 2004) (*main point 2*). Finally, they might want to hear about some success stories: if several major school districts, such as in New York City and Los Angeles, have successfully pulled soda pop machines out of their schools, so can we (Keen, 2004) (*main point 3*).

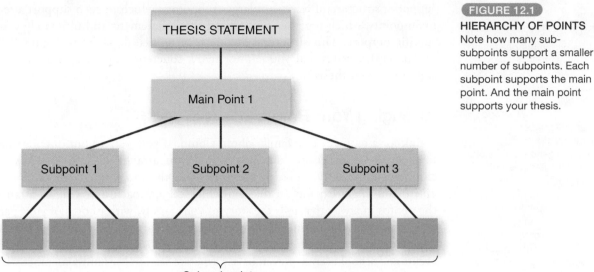

**FIGURE 12.1**
**HIERARCHY OF POINTS**
Note how many sub-subpoints support a smaller number of subpoints. Each subpoint supports the main point. And the main point supports your thesis.

Remember that each main point should include only one major idea—you do not want to overwhelm yourself or your audience with too much information. If each of your main points covers only one main idea, it is much easier for you to supply evidence to support each point in the form of examples, testimony, statistics, facts, or quotations. When in doubt about developing a main point, always ask yourself, "Does this point prove my thesis? Does it help me achieve my specific purpose?" If you can confidently answer yes, you are on the right track.

## Utilizing Your Main Points and Subpoints

Each main point—as well as your speech as a whole—is fully fleshed out with the use of **subpoints** that provide support for the main points. Subpoints must back up your main points in the same way that your main points back up your thesis statement; you can use a similar test to check their usefulness, asking yourself, "Does this bit of information back up my main point?" For example, two subpoints under our main point about vending machines offering food of poor nutritional value might expand on what this means: "Vending machines typically offer cookies and cakes, which are high in trans fats and lack useful vitamins and nutrients" and "Vending machines in our high school offer five varieties of sugary sodas, which are packed with nutritionless calories." Like main points, subpoints may—and often should—be backed up with more information, referred to as *sub-subpoints*.

Well-chosen supporting points will naturally fall under your main point in a clear hierarchy of ideas that will form the basic outline of your speech. Each main point should be supported by a number of coordinating subpoints, each carrying equal weight, as well as sub-subpoints that carry less weight. The resulting structure reflects a pyramidlike hierarchy of ideas: a foundation of many sub-subpoints

● **THINK OF YOUR MAIN POINTS** and subpoints as Russian *matryoshka* dolls—each sub-subpoint should nest inside a subpoint, which should nest inside your main point.

support a structure of fewer but larger subpoints, which in turn support a few main points, which together support the thesis statement and ultimately your specific purpose. This structural hierarchy of points, depicted in Figure 12.1 (see p. 355), ensures that you've presented a coherent and sturdy argument in support of your thesis.

## Arranging Your Points

Think for a moment of a family photo album. If you were to put one together that covered your entire life, how would you arrange it? You could work chronologically, simply placing the photos in the order in which they were taken. You might expand on that chronological approach by trying to arrange the photos in a way that tells the story of your family, with photos of your parents before you were born and family milestones like weddings and new babies. Alternatively, you might arrange it by topic, with separate sections for family events and school events or even have a separate section for family member with pages dedicated to each one's sporting events, birthday parties, proms, and graduations.

You have similar options when preparing a speech. During the process of sorting out your main points and subpoints, you may have taken the initial step of arranging your ideas in some sequence. Here are some common patterns to consider.

### Chronological Pattern

Often it makes sense to organize your points according to time: what happened first, second, and so on. A **chronological pattern** presents the main points of a message forward (or backward) in a systematic, time-related fashion. For example, you might use a chronological presentation when speaking about the development of Picasso's style over the course of his life or in describing the events leading up to the Cuban Missile Crisis. A chronological organization can be especially useful when analyzing a step-by-step process, such as a presentation on how to use a new computer program.

● **DECIDING HOW** to organize your speech, like deciding how to arrange your photos on a wall, can be tricky, as you have many options to consider: you can do it chronologically, topically, or even spatially.

### Topical Pattern

Also known as a *categorical pattern,* the **topical pattern** is based on organization into categories, such as persons, places, things, or processes. Thus you might use it to describe the various departments in an organization, the characteristics of a successful employment interview, or the reasons for giving a charitable contribution to a specific organization. One key concern when selecting this approach is the sequencing of topics—which topic to offer first, second, and so on. Depending on the circumstances, the best approach is often ascending or descending order—that is, according to the relative importance, familiarity, or complexity of the topics.

## Spatial Pattern

The geographical or **spatial pattern** arranges main points in terms of their physical proximity to or position in relation to each other (north to south, east to west, bottom to top, left to right, outside to inside, and so on). As an organizational pattern, it is most useful when describing objects, places, or scenes in terms of their component parts. Thus you might describe the physical layout of a media-enhanced classroom or the Mall in Washington, D.C., using a spatial pattern of organization.

## Problem-Solution Pattern

If you're trying to call an audience to action to address a particular problem, the **problem-solution pattern** of organization can be especially effective. This pattern involves dramatizing an obstacle and then narrowing alternative remedies down to the one that you recommend. The message is organized to focus on three key points:

1. There is a problem that requires a change in attitude, belief, or behavior.
2. A number of possible solutions might solve this problem.
3. Your solution is the one that will provide the most effective and efficient remedy.

Topics that lend themselves to this pattern include business, social, economic, and political problems for which you can propose a workable solution. For example, you might use it when proposing a new course evaluation system for your college or suggesting a plan for reducing college loan debt.

## Cause-Effect Pattern

With the **cause-effect pattern**, you attempt to organize the message around cause-to-effect or effect-to-cause relationships. That is, you might move from a discussion of the origins or causes of a phenomenon (for example, rising fuel costs) to the eventual results or effects (increases in the cost of airplane tickets). You can also work in reverse, starting with a description of present conditions and then examining apparent or possible causes. The choice of strategy is often based on which element—cause or effect—is more familiar to the intended audience: if you're talking about fuel prices, for example, it might be best to start with the cost of gasoline—a very familiar expense—and work backward from there. The cause-effect pattern of organization is especially useful when your purpose is to get your audience to agree with or understand your point, rather than to call people to action.

## Narrative Pattern

Speakers often tie their points together in a way that presents a vivid story, complete with characters, settings, plot, and imagery. This is called a **narrative pattern**. However, most speeches built largely on a story (or a series of stories) are likely to incorporate elements of other organizational arrangements. For example, you might present a story in a cause-effect design, in which you first reveal why something happened (such as a small aircraft crash) and then describe the events that led up to the accident (the causes).

● **IF YOU** were to give a presentation about London, wearing this shirt as a visual aid might help you point out places and streets of note.

● **WHEN ORGANIZING** your speech in a narrative pattern, put your feet in a Pixar storyboard artist's shoes. Visualize your outline as a storyboard, and think of your speech points as scenes.

### Motivated Sequence Pattern

Created more than seventy years ago by the noted public speaking scholar Alan Monroe, the **motivated sequence pattern** is a plan for organizing a speech that can be useful in a variety of contexts. Based on the psychological elements of advertising, the motivated sequence pattern includes five phases, which may be modified to suit the desired outcome of your speech:

1. *Attention:* the speaker gains the interest of the audience.
2. *Need:* the speaker addresses an unmet need apparent to the audience.
3. *Satisfaction:* the speaker proposes a solution that satisfies the need.
4. *Visualization:* The speaker illustrates how the solution meets the need.
5. *Action:* The speaker demonstrates how the solution may be implemented.

Monroe argued that when constructed effectively, speeches incorporating the five-step plan motivate listeners. Presentations that lend themselves to the motivated sequence include persuasive presentations, inspirational speeches, graduation addresses, and motivational talks. We will elaborate on this pattern in Chapter 15.

## Using Your Research

Clare is preparing to give a speech for her introductory communication class. She's got her topic—the rising rate of poverty in her city. She has nailed down her general purpose, her specific purpose, her thesis statement, and her main points (see Figure 12.2). Clare has also amassed a wealth of supporting material, having spent hours combing through U.S. Census Bureau statistics and newspaper articles and talking to people at local soup kitchens. Her research has yielded lots of statistics, quotes, anecdotes, stories, and facts—details we discussed in Chapter 11. Now let's take a look at how to actually *use* this material to build up a speech.

When deciding which types of supporting material to use in your speech, keep the cultural context (Chapter 1) in mind. Cultural variables affect the type of research audience members respond to. For example, if Clare's audience is made up largely of students who work full-time to pay for school, they will likely be responsive to statistics and facts about cost of living and stories of those struggling to make ends meet.

## Clear Definitions

Clare won't get too far with her speech on poverty if she isn't careful to define her terms. Even familiar words like *poverty* can be unclear: for some people, poverty might mean being unable to afford food or pay rent; for others, it might mean being unable to afford to purchase one's own home. Clare needs to establish a definition for poverty for the purposes of her speech and clarify that meaning to the audience. She might note the federal government's definition of the poverty line: "The U.S. federal government sets the poverty threshold at $19,350 per year for a family of four" (U.S. Department of Health and Human Services, 2005; see also U.S. Census Bureau, 2005).

## Facts and Statistics

Clare is armed with plenty of statistics to back up her points about poverty. If she wants to make a connection between poverty and petty crime, she might pair her Census Bureau data with crime statistics from local police departments. Such statistics will capture her audience's attention, and if she is careful to cite her sources, she'll reinforce the validity of those sources and establish her own credibility at the same time.

Clare can also make use of facts. She might look into the cost of living in her city by combing through real estate ads to get a sense of what it would cost to rent an apartment there. She might compare the costs of milk, bread, or gasoline around the country. She might state the local and federal minimum wage and ask a number of local employers how much they pay starting employees per hour. Armed with such facts, Clare will be able to back up her points, as noted in Figure 12.2.

**FIGURE 12.2**

**CLARE'S SPEECH POINTS**

**TOPIC:** The rising rates of poverty in Oakland, California

**GENERAL PURPOSE:** To persuade

**SPECIFIC PURPOSE:** To persuade my audience that poverty should not be defined nationally but rather locally

**THESIS:** Federal statistics on poverty do not accurately reflect the number of Americans whose standard of living is at the poverty level due to the high cost of living in specific areas of the country.

**MAIN POINT 1: The real cost of living varies greatly in different cities around the United States.**

  *Subpoint A:* The average cost of rent for a two-bedroom, 700-square-foot apartment in U.S. cities (Oakland, CA; Newark, NJ; Austin, TX; Iowa City, IA; Tacoma, WA; and Colorado Springs, CO)

  *Subpoint B:* The cost of a gallon of milk, same six U.S. cities

  *Subpoint C:* The average cost of transportation, same six U.S. cities

**MAIN POINT 2: The Census Bureau statistics on poverty are misleading.**

  *Subpoint A:* Proof that the national threshold, being an average, underserves people living in more expensive areas

    Sub-subpoint 1: How the national thresholds work

    Sub-subpoint 2: Census data for the nation as a whole

    Sub-subpoint 3: Census data for the six U.S. cities

  *Subpoint B:* Comparison of the standard of living at the poverty threshold in the six U.S. cities

  *Subpoint C:* Suggested real poverty thresholds for the six U.S. cities

## Meaningful Examples

Speeches work best when audiences are able to relate what a speaker says to the world in general and to their own experiences specifically. One of the easiest and most effective ways to show audiences the relevance of what you are saying or to illustrate unfamiliar concepts is to pepper your speech with useful examples—specific cases that clarify the ideas or experiences of real people in the real world. An example can be brief or extended, actual or hypothetical.

Clare has many choices for examples that will liven up her speech, clarify her points, and back up her statistics. When she defines the poverty threshold for a family of four, for example, she might wish to point out that the government's thresholds are actually very low. She could do this by posing a hypothetical example based on real statistics:

> It's important to bear in mind that these thresholds are calculated nationally and do not take into consideration the varying costs of living in different parts of the country. Here in the San Francisco Bay Area, it is nearly impossible to find a studio apartment, much less a space suitable for a family of four, in a decent, safe neighborhood for less than $1,000 a month. That means that after paying the rent, a family that earns $20,000 a year would be left with a mere $8,000 annually—before taxes—to spend on food, clothing, utilities, transportation, child care, and medical expenses. And they're living in one room! Yet the federal government does not consider such families to be living below the poverty line.

Clare might back up this example with an even more vivid real-world anecdote:

> I met Vicky, a single mother of two, at a soup kitchen in Oakland. She earns $10 per hour—well above the federal minimum wage—working at a local warehouse store. But even though she works full time, she finds that once she's paid the rent and utilities and for after-school care for her kids, she's got very little to live on. Vicky relies on free school breakfasts and lunches and the local soup kitchens and food pantries to keep her family fed.

● **IT MIGHT** be tempting to compare the price of a Bel Air mansion to a modest condo in Wisconsin to emphasize the exorbitant real estate prices in Bel Air, but the comparison would be skewed and inaccurate.

Such examples are usually representative cases that highlight one story among many (Consigny, 1976). Such vivid, concrete examples have a strong impact on listeners' beliefs and actions (O'Keefe, 2002).

## Comparisons

If Clare wishes to persuade her audience that poverty should be defined locally, she might make use of comparisons to prove that point. She might compare the cost of living in California with that of several states around the country.

A *literal* comparison examines two things that are similar. For example, Clare might compare the average cost of a two-bedroom house in California with the cost of a similar home in Alaska, Mississippi, or Wisconsin; she might compare the poverty rates of those states as well. When using a literal comparison, it is important to make sure the things you are comparing are indeed very similar. As the saying goes, you can't compare apples to oranges: Clare should not compare the cost of a mansion in California to the cost of a one-bedroom condominium in Mississippi. However, if she compares similar homes in similar communities with similar school districts and similar employment opportunities, she can make a more accurate comparison.

## COMMUNICATIONACROSSCULTURES

### Does Culture Define Evidence?

Creating a speech always involves finding evidence to support your points. But what, exactly, constitutes evidence? In the scientific community, the term *evidence* refers to factual statements that can be consistently proved through the scientific method. But can other cultures define *evidence* differently? Can they define *science* differently?

Over the past century, debate has continued over the teaching of evolution and creationism in American schools. While evolution, a widely accepted scientific theory introduced by Charles Darwin in 1859, has been taught in schools for decades, creationism—based on the Bible—has been banned from most public schools as a violation of the constitutional separation of church and state. In response to such bans, religious groups began looking for a more scientific refutation of Darwin's theory and began talking about "intelligent design" (ID) (*Edwards* v. *Aguillard,* 1987). The basis for ID theory is that there is an order to the universe and to life on earth that cannot have arisen at random and hence must have been created by a higher power. Proponents of intelligent design claim that ID is a scientific theory, different from religion-based creationism, because whereby creationism asserts that God created the world, ID does not specify who or what designed the universe. Some ID supporters even believe that ID is compatible with Darwin's theory of evolution (Engber, 2005). Supporters of ID contend that Darwin's theory is just that—a theory—and so is intelligent design, and therefore both should be taught in schools.

Detractors of ID assert that it is religion (creationism) in sciencelike clothing and does not stand up to scientific scrutiny. Their main argument is that there is no way to prove or disprove the ID theory using experiments. According to the scientific method, a theory that is not subject to experimentation and does not yield measurable results is not a scientific one.

**THINK ABOUT THIS**

❶ If you were giving a speech in support of evolution, what kinds of evidence would you require? Would you look for the same type of evidence if you were speaking in support of intelligent design?

❷ What additional evidence would ID need to supply to qualify as a scientific theory? Why isn't this a significant debate in schools?

❸ How fair is it to judge an argument of any kind based on one type of supporting evidence?

## Outlining Your Speech

In preparation for your speech, you will usually create two outlines: one that you'll use to pull your speech together and a second, more final version that you'll use as a reference when you actually deliver your speech. The **working outline** is a type of rough draft that you will use (and probably revisit and revise continually) throughout the preparation for your speech. The function of a working outline is to firm up your thesis statement, establish and organize your main points, and develop your supporting points. The **speaking outline**, or *delivery outline,* is your final speech plan, complete with details, delivery

---

# EVALUATINGCOMMUNICATIONETHICS

### The Ethics of Using Research

Your condo association has asked you to give an informative presentation about the dangers of certain breeds of dogs as pets at the next association meeting. The board intends to use your speech as a springboard for passing a resolution to ban these animals from the community. Several residents have raised particular concerns about your elderly neighbor's large dog, a chow–German shepherd mix.

You research the issue carefully and find conflicting information. You find powerful examples in some widely publicized mauling cases, including the death of a San Francisco woman who was attacked by her neighbors' Presa Canarios outside of her apartment in January 2001 and the June 2005 case of a twelve-year-old boy killed by his family's own pet pit bulls. You have also read that some homeowners' insurance companies deny coverage to individuals who own certain dog breeds, such as Rottweilers, Dobermans, pit bulls, Presa Canarios, chows, and wolf hybrids because of risks associated with these breeds (Treaster, 2002). At the same time, however, a veterinarian friend reminds you that any individual dog, regardless of breed, is unlikely to pose a threat to the community. Indeed, some veterinarians warn that small, seemingly docile dog breeds can pose more of a threat to safety than large dogs (Treaster, 2002).

On a personal level, you would love to see these "dangerous" dog breeds banned from the complex—you were bitten by a Doberman when you were a child and have been terrified of most dogs ever since. But you also empathize with your neighbor who lives alone and got his dog after his home was burglarized. And you know that while his dog is very protective of the home, barking loudly whenever someone comes near the property, he's well trained and has never shown signs of being vicious.

You know that your job is to inform your listeners, not to persuade them toward one side or the other. But as you prepare to use your supporting material for your presentation, you wonder what sort of ethical obligations you face as you inform the condo association members.

**① Consider** what you've learned from your research. Is it more important to be honest and truthful with your audience, to honor the wishes of the condo association board who asked you to speak, or to prevent your neighbor from possibly losing his pet?

**② Think** about some of the potential ethical dangers of crossing the line between an informative and a persuasive speech in this case. Where might you be tempted to persuade your audience? How can you keep your speech strictly informative?

**③ Might** there be some middle ground? Could you adjust the topic to focus on verifiable facts? For example, you could investigate whether banning dogs would lower the insurance premiums paid by the association as well as premiums on individual homeowners' insurance policies. Would this be ethical?

tips, and important notes about presentational aids (which we will discuss in Chapter 13). You will be able to pull together your speech on note cards using the speaking outline.

## Outlining Essentials

In every phase of outlining, basic guidelines will help you structure and prepare your speech. A solid outline will clearly reveal the structure of your arguments, the hierarchy of your points.

▶ *Use standard symbols.* What an outline does, essentially, is put the hierarchy of points visualized in Figures 12.1 and 12.2 into a text format. To do this, outlines generally use roman numerals, letters, and standard numbers to indicate different levels of importance in the hierarchy:

    I.  Main Point
       A.  Subpoint
          1.  Sub-subpoint
          2.  Sub-subpoint

If you need to break down the sub-subpoints even further, you may use lowercase letters (a, b, etc.) to create sub-sub-subpoints.

▶ *Use subdivisions properly.* It is basic logic that a whole of anything—a sandwich, a doughnut, or an outline heading—can never be split into fewer than two pieces. Therefore, as you divide your ideas from main points to subpoints, remember that each numbered or lettered entry must come in a series of at least two points: if you have a I, you must have a II; if you have an A, you must have a B; and so on.

▶ *Separate the parts of your speech.* We will study introductions, conclusions, and transitions later in this chapter, but it is typically helpful to label these speech parts to distinguish them from the body of your speech (your main points and support).

▶ *Cite your sources.* As discussed in Chapter 11, it is extremely important to give proper credit to sources that you cite in your speech. As you work on the outline, you should always mark where a specific point requires credit. Directly after the point, either insert a footnote or a reference in parentheses; once you complete the outline, arrange the references in order on a separate sheet headed "Notes" or "References." Citations can be presented in a variety of formats, including styles dictated by such organizations as the Modern Language Association (MLA) and the American Psychological Association (APA). Figure 12.3 (see p. 364) shows how you might handle references in APA format. Your instructor may have his or her own preferences about how to handle citations, so when in doubt, ask.

▶ *Give your speech a title.* Once all of your ideas and points are organized on paper, you can give your speech a catchy title that captures its essence. You

The ability to outline complex information into manageable steps is useful beyond public speaking. Chapter 8 covers *task roles* in groups, which involve people organizing the activities that help achieve a group's goals. If you and your siblings want to plan a huge celebration for your parents' twenty-fifth wedding anniversary, you should outline all of the steps needed to make it happen: creating a guest list, contacting and comparing venues, sending out invitations, and so on.

● **ALTHOUGH HOMER SIMPSON** typically eats a whole doughnut in one big bite, he does, on occasion, split it up. Even he knows you can't split it into less than two bites!

might also consider using a provocative question as the title or part of a memorable quotation that you will use in the body of the speech.

When you review your outline, you should see a clear hierarchy of points reflected in each tier of your structure. A weak link in the outline—an unsupported argument, an unrelated point—reveals an overall weakness in the way you've presented and defended your thesis. A solid outline shows not only how well you've organized your material but also how each point is supported by two or more subpoints, making a stronger case for your thesis statement. It also shows the scope and validity of your research by detailing your evidence with complete citations.

## Styles of Outlines

There are three basic approaches you can take to outlining your speech, which vary according to the level of detail. All three formats—sentence outlines, phrase outlines, and keyword outlines—can be valuable tools in developing and eventually delivering your speech. In most cases, you'll move from one format to another as you progress from your working outline to your speaking outline.

**FIGURE 12.3**
**CLARE'S REFERENCES
IN APA STYLE**

### References

Fox, L. (2007, January 31). *Economic snapshots: Minimum wage increasingly lags poverty line.* Retrieved December 19, 2007, from
http://www.epi.org/content.cfm/webfeatures_snapshots_20070131

Greenhouse, S. (2007, May 9). Maryland is first state to require living wage. *The New York Times.* Retrieved December 17, 2007, from http://www.nytimes.com

Northeast Midwest Institute. (2007, August 29). Poverty rate by state, 2002–2006. Retrieved December 18, 2007, from http://www.nemw.org/poverty.htm

Porter, E. (2006, August 19). Rents are rising rapidly after long lull. *The New York Times.* Retrieved December 16, 2007, from http://www.nytimes.com

Steffans, S. (2007, December 7). Hand up for the homeless. *Contra Costa Times.* Retrieved December 17, 2007, from http://www.contracostatimes.com

U.S. Census Bureau. (2005). *Poverty thresholds, 2005.* Retrieved December 12, 2007, from http://www.census.gov/hhes/www/poverty/threshld/thresh05.html

U.S. Department of Health and Human Services. (2005). *The 2005 HHS poverty guidelines.* Retrieved December 14, 2007, from
http://www.aspe.hhs.gov/poverty/05poverty.shtml

## Sentence Outline

The first type of outline is the **sentence outline**, which offers the full text of your speech, often the exact words that you want to say to your audience. Sentence outlines are typically best suited for working outlines, as they help you become more comfortable with all aspects of your speech; they are typically not ideal for speaking outlines, as many speakers wind up reading directly from the outline, missing out on valuable eye contact with the audience. Consider the following example from Sample Speech Outline 12.1 (see pp. 367–369) regarding sleep deprivation:

**II.** **[Main Point 1]** There are many causes of sleep deprivation, according to the Centers for Disease Control and Prevention.
   A. Emotional stress and excitement are important causes of sleep deprivation.
   B. Prescription medications and other drugs can also cause sleep deprivation.
      1. Medications for depression and anxiety, like MAO inhibitors, can cause a person to have difficulty sleeping.
      2. Caffeine increases your heart rate, making it difficult to fall asleep.

## Phrase Outline

A **phrase outline** takes parts of sentences and uses those phrases as instant reminders of what the point or subpoint means. Consider the following example:

**II.** **[Main Point 1]** Many causes of SD (CDC)
   A. Emotional stress and excitement
   B. Prescription medications and other drugs
      1. Depression meds (MAO inhibitors)
      2. Caffeine increases heart rate

The phrase outline is often the preferred format as it offers speakers a clear road map of their presentation, with reminders of key points and phrases. Yet it also keeps speakers on their toes, allowing them to deliver a speech rather than simply read it.

## Key-Word Outline

A **key-word outline** is the briefest possible outline, consisting of specific "key words" from the sentence outline to jog the speaker's memory. This type of outline allows the speaker to maintain maximum eye contact with the audience, though the speaker must be *extremely* familiar with the content of the speech to be comfortable using this type of outline. An example of a key-word outline is as follows:

**II.** **[Main Point 1]** Causes (CDC)
   A. Emotional stress and excitement
   B. Medications and drugs
      1. Depression meds
      2. Caffeine

# From Working Outline to Speaking Outline

As noted, the working outline is, as you would expect, a work in progress. You will typically find that you have to rearrange main points or choose different supporting points or even refine your thesis statement. Don't worry—this is a natural part of taking your ideas and your research and boiling them down to the parameters of your speech. In most cases, it will be entirely acceptable for you to use a sentence outline at this point (though, as always, check with your instructor if you will be submitting your outline before presenting your speech).

The working outline becomes the raw material for your speaking outline. As you move toward a final speaking outline, it's best to switch from a sentence format to a phrase or key-word approach (or a combination of the two). To do this, look at your full sentences, and pull out key words or phrases that will jog your memory as you speak; boil down longer passages into quick headers that will serve as guideposts for your more extemporaneous delivery. Sample Speech Outline 12.1 shows the full progression from working outline to speaking outline.

Your speaking outline should also include **delivery cues**, brief reminders about important information related to the delivery of your speech that are for your eyes alone. We'll talk in greater depth about your delivery in the next chapter, but for now, be aware that you'll likely want to remind yourself to show a presentation aid or speak slowly at the beginning of the speech, when you are the most nervous. These points should be noted in your outline. Table 12.1 offers additional delivery cues that may be helpful to you.

**TABLE 12.1**

## USEFUL DELIVERY CUES

| Delivery Cue | Purpose | Example as It Might Appear in Your Outline |
|---|---|---|
| Transition | A segue from one topic or idea to another; might be a simple reminder that you're changing tone here or a specific example or story that takes the speech from one topic to another | • [TRANSITION]<br>• [TRANSITION: Use dog story!] |
| Timing and speaking rate | A reminder to use a specific speaking rate, either for emphasis or to quell anxiety | • [Slow down here]<br>• [Speed up here]<br>• [Repeat for emphasis] |
| Volume and nonverbal behavior | A reminder to raise or lower your voice at particular points in your speech or to use particular gestures or body movements for emphasis | • [Louder]<br>• [Softly]<br>• [Thump on podium]<br>• [Count out on fingers] |
| Sources | Sources for cited material | • [Dowd, M. (2007, May 23). Pass the clam dip. *The New York Times*.] |
| Statistics | Statistics for reference, with source | • [U.S. Census Bureau: 64% of voting-age citizens voted in 2004, 60% in 2000] |
| Quotations | Exact wording of a quotation you plan to use | • [Dwight D. Eisenhower: "I've always found that plans are useless, but planning is indispensable."] |
| Pronunciations | Phonetic reminders for difficult-to-pronounce names or words | • [Hermione (her-MY-uh-nee)]<br>• [Kiribati (kee-ree-BAHSS)] |
| Visual aids | Reminder for when to incorporate particular visual aids | • [Census chart]<br>• [Show model] |

Source: O'Hair, Stewart, & Rubenstein (2007), tab. 13.2, p. 201. Adapted with permission.

## SAMPLE SPEECH OUTLINE 12.1

## From Working Outline to Speaking Outline

**Title:** Sleep It Off: Understanding the Dangers of Sleep Deprivation

**General Purpose:** To inform

**Specific Speech Purpose:** To inform my audience about the causes and effects of sleep deprivation as well as how to prevent it. With this information, my listeners can learn to take care of their health and avoid problems related to sleep deprivation.

**Thesis:** Understanding the causes and the effects of sleep deprivation, as well as simple ways to prevent it, will allow us to tackle this massive problem.

**Working Outline (as a sentence outline)**

I. **[Introduction]** Sleep deprivation is a continuously growing problem in society with real implications.

  A. Dr. Arkeenah Jones, a family physician, told me that "sleep deprivation can be equivalent to being legally drunk with respect to reaction time and mental stability."

  B. The National Sleep Foundation's 2005 survey notes that 70% of adults sleep less than 8 hours per night, and 40% sleep less than the minimum recommended 7 hours per night.

  C. **[Thesis]** Understanding the causes and the effects of sleep deprivation, as well as simple ways to prevent it, will allow us to tackle this massive problem.

II. **[Main Point 1]** There are many causes of sleep deprivation, according to the Centers for Disease Control and Prevention.

  A. Emotional stress and excitement are important causes of sleep deprivation.

  B. Prescription medications and other drugs can also cause sleep deprivation.

   1. Medications for depression and anxiety, like MAO inhibitors, can cause a person to have difficulty sleeping.

   2. Caffeine increases your heart rate, making it difficult to fall asleep.

  C. **[Transition]** Stress, excitement, medical conditions, and drug use all cause sleep deprivation, which can affect a person's ability to perform everyday tasks.

III. **[Main Point 2]** The effects of sleep deprivation can greatly affect society, as noted by Dulce Zamora, Miranda Hitti, and Jennifer Warner, physicians and writers for WebMD.

  A. The physical effects include the following:

   1. Sleep deprivation makes us less able to perform fine motor functions efficiently.

   2. Sleep deprivation compromises the immune system, making us less effective at fighting off harmful bacteria and viruses.

B. The mental effects include the following:

   1. Sleep deprivation causes loss of concentration and impairs memory.

   2. Extreme cases of sleep deprivation can cause hallucinations and emotional instability.

C. [Transition] As you can see, the effects of sleep deprivation can be severe, but they are easily controlled by good sleep practices.

IV. [Main Point 3] Preventing sleep deprivation requires but a few simple steps.

A. Dr. Jones advocates having a consistent bed time and wake-up time.

B. You should not watch TV or read in bed. Try to reserve your bed for sleeping.

C. [Transition] Regulating your schedule and developing good habits are essential for preventing sleep deprivation.

V. [Conclusion] Sleep deprivation is a big concern in today's society. Luckily, it is preventable.

A. The effects of sleep deprivation are scary. The U.S. Department of Transportation estimates that 100,000 traffic accidents per year are caused by drowsiness or fatigue. That equals 1,550 deaths annually!

B. Preventing sleep deprivation is as easy as adjusting your schedule and adopting good sleep habits.

C. Hopefully, you will reconsider before pulling all-nighters during finals.

**Speaking Outline (as a key-word or phrase outline)**

I. [Introduction—speak slowly and look at audience] Sleep deprivation (SD) = growing problem with real implications.

A. Dr. Arkeenah Jones: "SD can be equivalent to being legally drunk with respect to reaction time and mental stability."

B. National Sleep Foundation 2005 survey: 70% of adults sleep less than 8 hours per night; 40% sleep less than 7 hours per night.

C. [Thesis] Understanding the causes and the effects of SD and ways to prevent it= allow us to tackle it.

II. [Main Point 1] Many causes of SD (CDC)

A. Emotional stress and excitement

B. Medications and other drugs

   1. Depression meds (MAO inhibitors)

   2. Caffeine

C. **[Transition—eye contact]** Causes → SD → problems with everyday tasks.

III. **[Main Point 2]** Great effect on society (Dulce Zamora, Miranda Hitti, & Jennifer Warner, physicians/writers for WebMD)

    A. Physical effects **[speak slowly ; don't read as list]**

        1. Impaired fine motor skills

        2. Compromised immune system (bacteria/viruses)

    B. Mental Effects

        1. Loss of concentration and memory

        2. Sometimes hallucinations and emotional instability

    C. **[Transition]** Effects of SD can be incredibly severe but can be controlled by good sleep practices.

IV. **[Main Point 3]** Preventing SD

    A. Consistent schedule (Dr. Jones)

    B. Bed for sleeping only!

    C. **[Transition]** Regulating schedule and developing good habits = less SD

V. **[Conclusion]** SD is a big concern. Luckily, it is preventable.

    A. SD is Scary = 100,000 traffic accidents per year = 1,550 deaths annually due to SD (U.S. Dept. of Transportation). **[Show crash scene image for effect here]**

    B. Prevention = adjusting schedule and adopting good sleep habits.

    C. No more all-nighters!

Another important aspect of your speaking outline is that it should contain notes for your **oral citations**, the references to source materials that are worked into the narrative of your speech. After a sentence or phrase in your outline, you might simply place the source in parentheses so that you remember to give credit. For example, the key words "SD = legally drunk (Dr. Jones)" should prompt you to say: "In a personal interview, Dr. Arkeenah Jones, a family physician, noted that sleep deprivation can be equivalent to being legally drunk with respect to reaction time and mental stability." For material quoted word for word from the source, the oral citation must clarify that the material is in fact quoted rather than your own expression ("As Dr. Arkeenah Jones stated during our interview, 'Sleep deprivation can be equivalent to being legally drunk with respect to reaction time and mental stability'"). In such instances, you will likely want to use full sentences in your outline, rather than key words or phrases, to ensure that you do not misquote or misrepresent your source.

Finally, you should choose a comfortable format for using your speaking outline in front of your audience. You may transfer the outline to note cards, or

**AND YOU?**

How do you outline? Do you think of an outline as a hard-and-fast map, written before you begin writing and strictly adhered to throughout the process? Or do you start with a rough outline, revising and refining the organization as you move through the writing process?

Your speech introduction is the first impression you give your audience. But introductions are important in other contexts as well. The Appendix shows how your résumé and cover letter give a potential employer an introduction to you and your abilities. If your résumé has typos or other errors, your first impression will be less than stellar—just as a disorganized or inappropriate speech introduction can leave a negative first impression with your audience.

you may use a standard-size sheet of paper. It's entirely up to you, unless your instructor gives you specific instructions.

## Tying It All Together

Throughout this unit, we've talked about the architecture of putting together a speech, from choosing a topic to outlining your points. But the true art of crafting a speech lies in weaving all of these elements together and walking the audience through all of your points and evidence in a smooth and interesting way. In this section, we'll take a look at the parts of your final speech and offer advice on various tools and techniques you might use in crafting them.

## Writing Introductions

Any journalist knows that the single most important part of a news story is the lead: without an effective lead paragraph, nobody will proceed to paragraph two. Like a lead paragraph, the introduction to your speech must accomplish three crucial tasks: it must offer a preview of your main points; it must establish the tone of your speech, giving your listeners a sense of who you are and why they should want to hear what you have to say; and it must grab your audience's attention.

### Preview Your Main Points

A key goal for your introduction is to provide a preview of the main points that will be covered in the body of the speech. Tell the audience the points that you will discuss in the order that you will talk about them. For example, if you are giving a speech about why students should enroll in an art course, you might say:

● INTRODUCTIONS can be hard to write! Even Abraham Lincoln probably had trouble starting what is now known as one of the most famous and most frequently quoted speeches in U.S. history.

"There are two reasons why every college student should enroll in an art course. First, it provides students with a creative outlet, and second it teaches students useful and creative ways of thinking about their own subject of study." Audiences prefer to listen to speakers who are prepared and have a plan the audience can follow; by previewing, you offer a mental outline that your listeners can follow as they attend to your speech.

### Connect with Your Audience

A second goal for your introduction is to establish a relationship with your listeners, providing them with a sense of who you are and why they should listen to what you have to say. Like participants in an interview, the members of your audience will come to your speech with three points in mind. They will be curious about the nature of your speech: will it be boring, interesting, or inspiring? They'll also be wondering what they will get from it: will the speech be worth their time and attention? Finally, they will be curious about you as a speaker: will they like you? Should they trust you? Your introduction should provide enough information to allow the audience to make accurate assumptions about your speech and about you.

One way that a speaker can establish a relationship with the audience is to demonstrate why listeners should care about the topic. First, make sure that you verbally link the topic to the audience's interests. One way to do this is to show the topic's relevance. As discussed in Chapter 11, consider timeliness to show how your topic is related to current events or local interests. You should also try to appeal to your listeners' personal needs—let them know what's in it for them. For example, a college recruiter speaking at a high school might talk about what his school offers prospective students. He might also touch on recent local or national events to show the relevance of the school's curriculum: "I've been told that many students in this room participated in the Mock United Nations program last summer. If that experience has piqued your interest in international diplomacy, you might want to consider Sterling College. Our outstanding international relations program offers internships with the United Nations in New York and the State Department in Washington, D.C."

## Capture Your Audience's Attention

Finding a creative, attention-grabbing opening can be a struggle, but in the end it will be well worth the effort, for your first words can and do make a big impression on your audience (Hockenbury & Hockenbury, 2002). If you open with something as boring as "Hi, my name is . . ." or "Today I'm going to talk about . . . ," your audience may conclude that there's nothing more interesting to follow. In many cases, you'll write—or at least finalize—your introduction after the bulk of your speech is complete. This is an advantage because you will approach your introduction armed with your main points and your supporting material—and probably a few ideas on how to make it lively! Consider the following suggestions.

**Use surprise.**    It is likely that during research on your topic, you came across a fact, statistic, quote, or story that truly surprised you. Chances are that such information will likewise come as a surprise to your audience. A startling statement uses unusual or unexpected information to get an audience's attention. For example, our sleep deprivation outline author might have chosen to begin her speech as follows:

> Did you know that every semester, university students are legally drunk for one week straight? Yet despite feeling drunk, they never drink a drop of alcohol. During finals week, students at the University of Oklahoma sleep an average of five hours per night. Sleep deprivation—characterized by getting five hours or less sleep per night—can affect reaction time and mental sharpness. After being awake for seventeen hours straight, a sleep-deprived person has the reaction time and mental sharpness of someone with a blood alcohol concentration of 0.05, which is considered legally drunk throughout most of Europe.

**AND YOU?**
Take a look at your research. Of all the evidence you have gathered for your speech, what jumps out at you? Did you come across any statistics that shocked you? Did you encounter any individuals whose stories touched you—with humor, sadness, or surprise? Think about how any of the statistics, facts, anecdotes, and quotes you've gathered might be worked into an effective introduction.

Opening statements might be funny, surprising, shocking, or simply intriguing. You might open with a startling fact: "Take a look around this room. Each of the women you see here has a one in seven chance of developing breast cancer in her lifetime." Or you might pose an intriguing question: "Do your friends have beady, red eyes, or are they always ending up headless? If so, you could use instruction in photography" (Angela Ratkowski, cited in "Principles of Public Speaking," 2004). Both of these openings will surprise listeners and likely pique their interest.

**Tell a story.** As discussed in Chapter 11, anecdotes can be useful illustrations for your speech. Audiences of all ages react to relevant stories that are told expressively. Avoid stories that are too long, don't read them verbatim, and be sure to tie the story in to your speech. Stories used in introductions may be personal or derived from someone else's experience. Real-world stories can be particularly effective when worked into your opening:

> Johnny walked into the cold, white room on April 23, 1992. The beeping of the machines echoed immensely in his head, and he knew that the noise would haunt him for the rest of his life. He walked in farther to join the group that stood beside a solitary bed. He hung his head in grief and through misty tears got one last look. Johnny bent over and gently whispered, "Good-bye, Grandma. I love you." It was then the nurse made the machines make a more painful sound—silence. This is the act of euthanasia, which is the hardest decision for a family to make when the choice is a life of suffering or death. (adapted from Heather Vasilopulos, cited in "Principles of Public Speaking," 2004)

**Start with a quote.** Leading with a quotation is a convenient and interesting speech opening. Quotes can connect you as a speaker to real people and real situations. Consider the way the following opening makes the AIDS epidemic very personal:

> "I came here today to ask that this nation, with all its resources and compassion, not let my epitaph read, 'He died of red tape.'" That is what Roger Gail Lyon said to a congressional committee in August 1983. Roger died of acquired immune deficiency syndrome (AIDS) while Congress was discussing whether or not the virus actually existed. (adapted from Karen Williams, cited in "Principles of Public Speaking," 2004)

Quotations can also come from familiar sources. Well-known quotations, even ones from fictional or unknown sources, can also be useful, as they establish a connection between the speaker and the audience. Quoting common or anonymous proverbs can also be an effective way to open a speech. As with any research, it's important to acknowledge a known source: "Ben Franklin once said, 'By failing to prepare, you are preparing to fail.' This is nowhere more true than in the public education system." Table 12.2 offers tips for using quotes wisely.

**Ask a question.** Posing a question is a great way to get the audience's attention and to make people think. Rather than simply presenting some bit of information, posing a question invites listeners to react, in effect making them participants

| | | TABLE 12.2 |
|---|---|---|
| Use quotes worth using. | Don't quote something that you could say or explain more effectively in your own words; paraphrase instead, with an attribution to the original source. | **USING QUOTES WISELY** |
| Use relevant quotes. | Even the prettiest bit of prose is useless if it doesn't support your points. | |
| Include a clear attribution. | Whether you're quoting Shakespeare or your six-year-old nephew, it's important that audiences know who said what. | |
| Is the quote from a notable source? | Cite not only the author in your speech but also the date and the work in which the quote appeared, if relevant. | |
| Double-check for accuracy. | You do not want to misquote anyone in your speech, so it's important that you proofread your copy against the original. If you've used an online quote source, it is wise to double-check the quote against additional sources known to be reliable, as many online quotes fail to provide accurate source information. | |

in the speech.[1] For example, "Would you put your mouth on the end of a car's muffler and inhale? Then why would you continue to smoke?" (Regina Testa, cited in "Principles of Public Speaking," 2004). Here again, saying something startling can add to the effect: not only have you gotten your listeners' attention by saying something provocative, but you've also asked them to internalize what you've said and to react to it. As a result, they're likely to be more interested in and open to what you're about to say.

**Make them laugh.**   Humor is another effective way to begin your speech. Usually, humor that is brief, relevant to your topic, and makes a point is most effective. For example, consider this opening, which makes the audience laugh but is clearly tied to the main topic of the speech on the benefits of brevity: "A banquet speaker had just finished his presentation and was looking for confirmation of his performance from his wife. He whispered to her, 'Honey, how do you think I did?' 'Very well,' she replied, 'except you missed several good opportunities to sit down'" (adapted from Braude, 1965, p. 52).

## Using Transitions

When you look at your outline, you should have a solid list of points, subpoints, and sub-subpoints that you want to make to prove your thesis. But moving from one point to another in a numbered outline is different from presenting them in front of your audience. How do you move from one point to another without sounding as though you are simply reading a list or an outline?

---

[1]Asking questions is an effective way of gaining participation in many communication contexts; see O'Hair, O'Rourke, & O'Hair (2000).

The key to connecting these dots is **transitions**—words, phrases, and observations that connect different thoughts, points, and details in a way that allows them to flow naturally from one to the next. Clear transitions cue the audience in on where you're headed with the speech and how your ideas, points, and supporting material are connected. Transitions also alert your audience that you will be making a point.

### Signposts

Full-sentence transitions are often written out in your working speech outline. However, once you are familiar enough with your speech during rehearsals, you may shorten your transitions to key words or phrases, such as *next, first,* or *however*. Key words or phrases that signify transitions between points are called **signposts**. Think of signposts as links or pivot points at which you either connect one point to another ("similarly," "next," "once again,") or move from one point to a related but perhaps opposing or alternative point ("however," "on the other hand"). Table 12.3 provides a list of useful signposts.

When you're presenting a great deal of information, your transitions need to be straightforward, clear, and frequent. You have at your disposal a number of useful tools and techniques for making transitions in your speech that we'll take a look at in the sections that follow.

### Internal Previews and Internal Summaries

Like a good map that shows travelers points along the way to their destination, verbal previews alert listeners to the speaker's map of ideas. As mentioned earlier, the introduction should preview the essential points of the speech. But previewing is also an important part of the *body* of the speech, where **internal previews** serve as extended transitions that prime the audience for the content immediately ahead. They often work best in conjunction with **internal summaries** that allow the speaker to crystallize the points made in one section of a speech before moving to the next section. For example, "So far, I have presented two reasons why you should enroll your puppy in obedience school. First, it benefits your dog. Second, it benefits your family. Now I will address my third point: that taking your dog to obedience school benefits your neighborhood." By first summarizing and then previewing, the speaker has created a useful transition that gracefully moves the speech forward while offering audiences an opportunity to synthesize the information already received.

● **ONE OF THE MOST** crucial moments in a trial is the closing statement. It's the lawyer's last chance to make his or her case to the jury.

## Writing Your Conclusion

There's a reason why courtroom dramas like TV's *Law and Order* almost always include footage of the hero lawyer's closing statements. When a wealth of evidence, testimony, and facts have been presented, it's easy for juries (and television audiences) to get bogged down in the details and lose track of the bigger, more dramatic picture. For any speaker—be it a college sophomore in front of a communication class or a fictional lawyer in

| Function | Example |
|---|---|
| To show comparison | Similarly<br>In the same way<br>In comparison |
| To contrast ideas, facts, or data | On the other hand<br>Alternatively<br>In spite of |
| To illustrate cause and effect | It follows, then, that<br>Consequently<br>Therefore<br>Thus |
| To indicate explanation | For example<br>In other words<br>To clarify |
| To introduce additional examples | Another way in which<br>Just as<br>Likewise<br>In a similar fashion |
| To emphasize significance | It's important to remember that<br>Above all<br>Bear in mind |
| To indicate sequence of time or events | First, Second, Third<br>Finally<br>First and foremost<br>Once<br>Now, Then<br>Until now<br>Before, After<br>Earlier, Later<br>Primarily |
| To summarize | As we've seen<br>Altogether<br>Finally<br>In conclusion |

**TABLE 12.3**
**USEFUL SIGNPOSTS**

Source: O'Hair, Stewart, & Rubenstein (2007), p. 181. Adapted with permission.

front of a mock courtroom—it is important to end a presentation with a compelling and pointed conclusion. In a speech, the conclusion must address a number of functions.

## Signal the End

Your conclusion should alert the audience that the speech is coming to a close. You might do that by using a transitional phrase such as "In conclusion," "Finally," or "Let me close by saying . . ." Such phrases serve as signposts, telling audiences that you're about to conclude and asking for their full attention one last time. Remember to keep it brief. Audiences do not like to be overwhelmed with a lot of new information at the end.

**AND YOU?**
What kind of impression would you want to leave your audience with? What is the one thing you'd like people to remember about you and your speech?

# real communicator

**NAME:** Jon Clarke
**HOMETOWN:** Rockaway Beach, New York
**OCCUPATION:** Stand-up comic and freelance writer
**FUN FACT:** My first screenplay, *Idiots in the Atlantic,* was featured at the New York Film and Video Festival.

I wasn't a huge fan of my mandatory college public speaking course. But as much as I hate to admit it, it has helped me out quite a bit in my profession as a comedian. For example, in order to make connections with the people in my audience, I have to pick up on physical cues—are they bored, are they entertained, should I keep going with this bit? I have to make equal amounts of eye contact—particularly hard when the lights on stage are so bright that you physically can't see anyone (in those cases, I just fake it and act as if I can see them). But probably the most helpful thing I learned was how to outline a presentation, or in my case, a routine.

You hear this all the time: start with a joke. But in stand-up comedy, everything's got to be a joke. The first joke has to be a particular kind—it has to be my "persona setter." It has to indicate the type of person I am, what ideas I'm concerned with. Lately I've been starting out with "I'm nerdy but not a *complete* nerd. I used to hang out with the cool kids in school, but I was always waiting for them to beat me up." Now everything I say after that first joke gets filtered through that persona: nerdy but not too nerdy.

After that first joke, I go into my bits. Comedy routines are made up of bits. Bits are about a minute long apiece, and they've got four or five jokes in them. But which bits should go next to one another? This is a big challenge for me when I'm putting together a routine. I do this one about *Sesame Street* on how Cookie Monster can't eat cookies. After that, I can either go into more pop culture stuff (I've got a bit on Spike TV), or go into family stuff (my mother always told me never to talk to strangers; that first day of school was tough). It all depends on the

audience that night. Is it college kids who might appreciate Spike TV references? If not, I've got to drop that particular bit.

Even after I know which bit goes where, it's very difficult to actually get there. I used to spend about twenty seconds making the transition from *Sesame Street* to Spike TV, saying things like "Well, I watched a lot of TV as a kid, and I still do. I love TV. The other day, I was sitting on my couch, flipping channels, and I see this Spike TV . . ." But in comedy, those kinds of segues might as well just be dead air. I want to do them because I have this writerly impulse to flesh things out and have people know me, but the audience is only there for the jokes, and details that don't contribute to the jokes have got to go. Instead of wasting time trying to labor a transition from one bit to the other, I allow my audiences to make thematic connections. I'm talking about *Sesame Street,* and now I'm talking about Spike TV. They can put it together in their heads.

When there's a minute left to go, a light will go on at the back of the club. That's how I know that it's time for me to go into wrap-up mode. I try to end with fast jokes. And as soon as I get a big laugh, I'm out of there. I thank the audience, reintroduce the emcee, and get off the stage before the audience's energy can flag.

A routine usually takes six to eight minutes. The better it is organized—if the persona-setting opening joke is nice and quick and the subsequent material fits that persona well; if bits follow one another logically, allowing transitions to be implicit rather than laboriously explicit—the better the routine goes. Sometimes it feels like it's over in a flash, like a dream, and I'm feeling great all week. Sometimes those six to eight minutes take an eternity. But it's always exciting.

### Summarize Your Points

A competent speaker realizes that a valuable conclusion reinforces the information contained in the speech. In other words, the speaker should reiterate the main points of the speech so that listeners are able to mentally check off what they have heard and what they should remember.

### Make an Impact

All your efforts developing your points and sharing your research will have been in vain if your audience doesn't care to keep anything you've said in mind! Several techniques discussed in the section on introductions can be useful for memorable conclusions as well.

**Quotes and questions.**   To wrap up a speech, speakers often use quotes from historical figures, writers, philosophers, or celebrities. Take care in choosing a quote so that you leave the audience with something to think about. For example, if you are concluding a speech that illustrates the importance of friendships, you might quote the writer Edna Buchanan: "Friends are the family you choose for yourself" (www.ednabuchanan.com). A strong quotation helps make an unforgettable impression.

**A final story.**   Stories are also as effective for conclusions as they are for introductions. Stories should always tie in to your speech topic, be relatively short, and make a related point. For example, if you are advocating a college-level foreign-language requirement for your university, you might tell this well-known tale: "Mother Mouse was crossing the street with her three children. She got about halfway across when she saw a cat, crouched and ready to pounce upon them. The cat and Mother Mouse eyeballed each other for two to three minutes. Finally, Mother Mouse let out an enormous 'WOOF!' The cat ran away. Mother Mouse turned to her children and said, 'NOW do you see the advantage of a second language?'"

## Using Language That Works

Before we move on to Chapter 13, where we will address speech delivery, we want to reinforce the importance of language. The words that you choose for your speech are extremely powerful, so it's important to think about them *now,* while you're preparing and writing your speech, so that you can incorporate them into your working and speaking outlines.

## Respect Your Audience

As noted earlier, communication involves not only what we say but how others perceive what we say. Most audiences are composed of both men and women from many different cultures, races, religious backgrounds, lifestyles, and educational levels. Therefore, it is important to use unbiased and appropriate language that makes the entire audience feel included and respected.

Part of using language your audience understands involves a careful consideration of *jargon*—technical language specific to a particular industry, organization, or group (see Chapter 3). Jargon might be useful among a very homogenous group, but it can alienate audience members in other settings. A doctor explaining the need to immunize children might speak in medical jargon when addressing colleagues but would need to use layperson's terms when addressing a group of new parents.

## Keep It Simple

Albert Einstein once advised, "Make everything as simple as possible, but no simpler." The physicist's wisdom applies to language as well. Speakers and writers who use unfamiliar or inappropriate language are not as effective as those who speak directly and in terms that their audience can readily understand and interpret. This is not to say that you should "dumb down" your thesis or your points, only that you need to make your points in a language that is clear, simple, and unambiguous so that your audience can follow what you are saying. In addition, there is no speaker quite as dreaded as the long-winded speaker. (Admit it—you've been to a wedding or sports award banquet where the best man or honoree droned on seemingly forever. We've all been there!) A speaker who repeats the same points or uses six examples when one would suffice will quickly lose audience interest. If you keep your speech short and to the point, you'll have a better chance of reaching your audience with your intended message.

## Use Vivid Language

Language paints a picture for an audience. The more vivid your terms, the more the audience members can use their imaginations and their senses. For example, if you say you have a car, your listeners get a vague impression of a forgettable fact. If you tell them that your father drove a faded orange 1972 Volkswagen Beetle with a dent in the left fender and a broken taillight, you'll give them a very clear and memorable picture of this vehicle. Over our years of teaching human communication, we've had many students become frustrated with us about our

**AND YOU?**

Have you ever tried to sit through a speech when the speaker failed to use language the audience easily understood? Do you remember anything important from this speech—or even its main point? How did you feel during the speech? If you can't think of a specific public speaking event, consider an interaction in a medical or academic context.

● **SOMETIMES YOU** don't need to be long-winded to get your point across. The KISS principle says it best: "Keep it simple, stupid!"

*"My concession speech will be brief. You win."*

insistence on "painting a picture with words"; too many times we've heard, "But I have these great eye-catching slides and props!" We'll elaborate more on the use of presentation aids in the next chapter, but for now, remember that your words count—often even more than your PowerPoint slides.

## Use Language to Make a Lasting Impression

In August 1963, Martin Luther King Jr. delivered one of the most powerful, effective, and memorable speeches of the twentieth century from the steps of the Lincoln Memorial in Washington, D.C. Anyone who has seen or heard footage of King's "I Have a Dream" speech can recite at least some of the lines he spoke. His speech was effective not only because of his message but also because his masterful use of language helped make a profound impression on his listeners. (See Sample Speech 12.1 on p. 380.)

## WIREDFORCOMMUNICATION

### Bullets to the Brain

There is something sinister in the world of technology. You've undoubtedly been exposed to it, at work or at school. It's probably in your home computer. But it's not a virus. You probably paid to have it there. And according to one of the nation's leading experts, it's making all of us stupid.

Edward Tufte is a professor of political science, computer science and statistics, and graphic design at Yale University and has been academia's most influential voice on the subject of the visual display of information for over two decades. He is an expert on the use of graphs and visual aids to explain any number of types of information, from train schedules to empirical data. He uses computers all the time to crunch numbers and present quantitative information. But Tufte is no fan of slideware. And slideware—specifically, Microsoft's PowerPoint—is everywhere.

The problem, Tufte (2003) explains, is that programs like PowerPoint force presentations into an outline format, with little development beyond a series of bulleted lists. Because a typical slide contains a mere forty words—about eight seconds of reading—presentations become a succession of short, boring lists of facts, presented out of context and with little room for evaluation. In schools, where PowerPoint has become a common teaching tool, Tufte finds the problem even more alarming. By forcing information into short, bulleted lists and colorful graphics, such tools teach students to create infomercials rather than reports and to write ad copy rather than sentences.

Visual aids can indeed be a valuable asset for a presentation, and Microsoft's program is, Tufte concedes, a useful tool for managing and presenting slides. But often presenters rely on the program to design the content of their speeches rather than to enhance it, and Tufte finds that a program's format "routinely disrupts, dominates, and trivializes content." The best remedy? Focus on content. "If your numbers are boring, then you've got the wrong numbers," Tufte writes. "If your words or images are not on point, making them dance in color won't make them relevant."

**THINK ABOUT THIS**

❶ The use of bulleted lists predates Microsoft Power-Point—instructors and presenters have made use of overhead projectors and slide shows for decades. Why is Tufte being so hard on Microsoft?

❷ We've spent much of this chapter talking about the importance of outlining and of communicating your final outline clearly to your audience. How is that different from presenting your outline in slide form?

❸ Are there some subjects or types of speeches that lend themselves to PowerPoint presentations? Are there others that don't?

## SAMPLE SPEECH 12.1

### From "I Have a Dream"

#### REVEREND DR. MARTIN LUTHER KING JR.

I say to you today, my friends, so even though we face the difficulties of today and tomorrow, I still have a dream. It is a dream deeply rooted in the American dream. •

I have a dream that one day this nation will rise up and live out the true meaning of its creed: "We hold these truths to be self-evident: that all men are created equal." •

I have a dream that one day on the red hills of Georgia, the sons of former slaves and the sons of former slave owners will be able to sit down together at the table of brotherhood.

I have a dream that one day even the state of Mississippi, a state sweltering with the heat of injustice, sweltering with the heat of oppression, will be transformed into an oasis of freedom and justice.

I have a dream that my four little children will one day live in a nation where they will not be judged by the color of their skin but by the content of their character.

I have a dream today.

I have a dream that one day down in Alabama, with its vicious racists, with its governor having his lips dripping with the words of interposition and nullification, one day right there in Alabama, little black boys and black girls will be able to join hands with little white boys and white girls as sisters and brothers.

I have a dream today. . . . •

And if America is to be a great nation, this must become true.

So let freedom ring from the prodigious hilltops of New Hampshire!

Let freedom ring from the mighty mountains of New York!

Let freedom ring from the heightening Alleghenies of Pennsylvania!

Let freedom ring from the snowcapped Rockies of Colorado!

Let freedom ring from the curvaceous slopes of California!

But not only that; let freedom ring from Stone Mountain of Georgia!

Let freedom ring from Lookout Mountain of Tennessee!

Let freedom ring from every hill and molehill of Mississippi!

From every mountainside, let freedom ring.

And when this happens, when we allow freedom [to] ring, when we let it ring from every village and every hamlet, from every state and every city, we will be able to speed up that day when all of God's children, black men and white men, Jews and Gentiles, Protestants and Catholics, will be able to join hands and sing in the words of the old Negro spiritual, "Free at last! free at last! Thank God Almighty, we are free at last!" •

• Note the repetition of the title phrase.

• Here King alludes to the Declaration of Independence; although he doesn't name the document, he trusts his audience to recognize the line.

• Note King's use of parallel construction here. He begins by repeating the phrase "I have a dream" and then uses parallels to define different aspects of that dream.

• In the closing line of his speech, King alludes to a less well-known source, an old Negro spiritual. Whereas he trusted listeners to recognize the source for the Declaration of Independence, here he chose to incorporate the source into the speech.

● MARTIN LUTHER KING'S "I Have a Dream" speech was one of the most memorable speeches of the twentieth century and a major event in the civil rights movement.

# what about you?

## Assessing Your Speech

As you are organizing, outlining, and writing your speech, consider the following questions. Indicate which answer best matches your own.

1. Do all of my subpoints support my main points? Do my main points support my thesis statement and my specific speech purpose?

   YES:  There is a clear hierarchy of points in my outline.

   NO:  But I really wanted to include all these tangential points too!

2. Did I select the organizational arrangement that works best for my topic and purpose?

   YES:  I considered different approaches but settled on one.

   NO:  I've gone with kind of a stream-of-consciousness arrangement. It's edgy!

3. Have I made use of my research by incorporating definitions, facts and statistics, examples, etc. where they best support my speech?

   YES:  I've incorporated a variety of appropriate evidence for my audience.

   NO:  I have a few personal stories. That should be enough.

4. Does my introduction capture my audience's attention, preview my main points, and establish a relationship with my audience?

   YES:  I've got a really compelling opening. I think it will really grab them!

   NO:  I'm not sure. Maybe I can just open with my thesis statement.

5. Have I chosen language that is respectful, clear, and vivid?

   YES:  I've tailored the language to suit all members of the audience and chosen key phrases to grab their attention.

   NO:  I've used a few curse words. That should make an impression!

6. Do I transition successfully throughout my speech?

   YES:  I've used signposts and previews both to help audiences absorb the material and as delivery cues for myself.

   NO:  I've got one really long paragraph. Should I change it to a bulleted list?

7. Does my conclusion signal the end of my speech, summarize my main points, and leave an impact that will help the audience remember my speech?

   YES:  My closing sums up my points and reiterates my thesis. And I've worked in signposts to let my listeners know that this is the end of the speech.

   NO:  I think I should let the audience come to its own conclusions. Like in the final episode of *The Sopranos*. People loved that!

If you can't honestly answer each of these questions with a heartfelt yes, you need to go back and determine why so that you can make revisions.

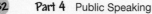

In Chapters 4 and 13, you learn about nonverbal aspects of speech such as speaking rate, pauses, tone, volume, and pitch. In many cases, such factors can help you use repetition effectively. For example, throughout Dr. King's speech, his repeated phrase is accompanied by an upward inflection of voice followed by a pause. This allows the audience to anticipate the next line and enhances their retention of his main points.

### Repetition

The repetition of certain terms, phrases, or even entire sentences at appropriate times in your speech can help increase the likelihood that the audience will remember them. Throughout King's speech, he repeats the phrase "I have a dream" several times. These four words will forever be associated with King's quest for equal rights because they are simple, powerful, and memorable.

### Allusion

An allusion is making vague or indirect reference to people, historical events, or concepts to give deeper meaning to the message. Allusions can be useful in evoking emotions or responses without making direct statements. They can also ground your speech, providing context that goes beyond what you are saying. In King's "I Have a Dream" speech, for example, he alludes to the Declaration of Independence with the words "We hold these truths to be self-evident: that all men are created equal." King does not name the source; he trusts his audience to recognize the most famous line from one of the nation's founding documents.

### Comparisons: Similes and Metaphors

One of the most common and useful tools in public speaking is the figure of speech known as the simile. A *simile* uses *like* or *as* to compare two things. King uses simile to conjure up the image of little black children and white children walking together "as sisters and brothers." A simile from an anecdote you are using might be "Fog enveloped the city like a heavy blanket."

Like similes, *metaphors* liken one thing to another in a literal way, even though there may be no literal connection between the two. A metaphor presents a comparison as a statement of fact—it does not contain the word *like* or *as*—but it is not expected to be taken as a fact. King employs a metaphor when he speaks of "the heat of injustice." A metaphor you might use in your anecdote would be "The fog was a heavy blanket over the city."

## BACK TO The State of the Union Address

As this chapter shows, outlining and organizing your speech are crucial steps in writing—and eventually delivering—an effective presentation. Recall our discussion of White House speechwriters preparing the State of the Union address from the beginning of the chapter. What considerations and challenges will affect their organization and outline? How will their organization influence their audiences' perceptions of the speech?

▶ Ideas will come in from every direction, so planning and organization are key. As a former White House speechwriter, David Frum, observed, "The planning for the next State of the Union really begins the day after the last State of the Union" (quoted in Jackson, 2006).

▶ Speechwriters need to bear in mind that they are writing for two different—albeit not mutually exclusive—audiences. Chriss Winston (2002) points out that members of Congress and Washington insiders judge the speech primarily on its policy content, while everyday Americans tend to look for leadership qualities in the president, as well as evidence that he shares their values. The challenge lies in choosing content and language that speak to both groups.

▶ The key to avoiding what Matthew Scully (2005) refers to as a "tedious grab bag of policy proposals" lies in the skillful and artful use of transitions. Instead of jumping from point to point, speechwriters need to find and build unifying themes among the many policies under discussion. Thus George W. Bush's speechwriters were able to draw connections between such issues as cloning and war by focusing on the overall theme of human dignity and human rights. These connections allowed for natural transitions from one issue to the next (Scully, 2005).

▶ Creating unified themes is also crucial to keeping the content (and length) of the speech from spiraling out of control. President Clinton was known for long State of the Union speeches that detailed many policy proposals. President Bush preferred to stick to big ideas. "He's not going to talk about everything under the sun," said one deputy director in advance of Bush's 2006 address; "he's going to be talking about a handful of very big themes" (Jackson, 2006).

## THINGS TO TRY

1. Take a look at the outline of this chapter in the Detailed Table of Contents. Do you see a clear hierarchy of points, subpoints, and evidence? Within the chapter, how are transitions used to move from point to point? How might the techniques used in this chapter work in your speech?

2. Read a famous or familiar speech (such as Martin Luther King's "I Have a Dream" speech), and create an outline for it. Can you follow a clear sequence of points? Do the points support the speaker's main points?

3. When creating the outline for your speech, write each main point on a separate index card. Spread the cards out on a table, and then pick them up in the most logical order. Does this order match the order of your outline? How did you choose to arrange the topics—spatially, chronologically, or topically?

4. Establishing a relationship with the audience is important when giving a speech. Make a list of all of the possible members of your audience. How do you plan to connect with all members of the audience? Pretend you are giving a speech at your old high school. Will your introduction affect the seniors the same way it affects the principal?

5. Pick a general topic, and try to come up with several different attention getters for that topic. Here's an example for the topic "dogs":

   ▶ Tell a funny story about your dog.
   ▶ "Did you know that the human mouth contains more germs than a dog's mouth?"

▶ "In my hometown, there is a dog that walks upright like a human because he does not have any front legs."

▶ "Did you know that approximately 10 million unwanted dogs are euthanized annually in the United States?"

Try this with a topic such as your favorite food, favorite vacation spot, or some other appealing topic.

## IF YOU'RE INTERESTED

*On Speaking Well: How to Give a Speech with Style, Substance, and Clarity,* by Peggy Noonan (New York: Regan Books/Harper Perennial, 1999)

Ronald Reagan's most noted speechwriter—and later a consultant on *The West Wing*—Noonan offers basic guidelines for writing and delivering speeches, insights from her own career, and commentary on modern and historical political speeches.

*The Dream: Martin Luther King Jr. and the Speech That Inspired a Nation,* by Drew Hansen (New York: Harper Perennial, 2005)

An in-depth examination of King's most famous speech, the most important speech of the civil rights era and among the most powerful speeches of the twentieth century. Hansen reveals the events leading up to King's 1963 delivery from the steps of the Lincoln Memorial, as well as the speech's enduring impact on the American psyche and cultural landscape, with valuable insights into King's rhetorical style.

*The Language of Speech and Writing,* by Ronald Carter (New York: Routledge, 2001)

This brief, introductory book geared toward undergraduates analyzes the processes involved in writing and speaking. It looks at a variety of written and spoken texts (from literary works to e-mail to advertisements) and also asks the reader to consider the relationship between writing and speaking.

*The West Wing,* television series available on DVD (Warner Home Video, 2007)

Few television programs, films, or plays have captured the workings of the American presidency like this ensemble drama. In its six seasons on the air (1999–2006), numerous episodes dealt with the subtle art of speechwriting, notably "He Shall, from Time to Time" (season one) and "Bartlet's Third State of the Union" (season two).

**Now that you have finished reading this chapter, you can**

Organize your main points:

▶ Identify your **main points**, the central claims that support your specific speech purpose and your thesis statement (p. 354).

▶ **Subpoints** support your main points (p. 355).

▶ A **chronological pattern** presents main points in a systematic, time-related fashion (p. 356).

▶ A **topical pattern** is based on categories such as person, place, thing, or process (p. 356).

▶ A **spatial pattern** arranges points according to physical proximity or direction from one to the next (p. 357).

▶ The **problem-solution pattern** presents an obstacle and then suggestions for overcoming it (p. 357).

▶ The **cause-effect pattern** moves from the cause of a phenomenon to the results or vice versa (p. 357).

▶ The **narrative pattern** uses a story line to tie points together (p. 357).

▶ The **motivated sequence pattern** uses a five-step plan to motivate listeners: attention, need, satisfaction, visualization, action (p. 358).

Use your research:

▶ Consider your audience when you choose support material (p. 358).

▶ Clearly define the terms you use (p. 358).

▶ Capture attention and establish credibility with relevant sources (p. 358).

▶ Use examples that resonate with listeners (p. 360).

▶ Literal and similar comparisons help give context to a point (p. 361).

Outline your speech:

▶ Write a **working outline** to organize and develop your speech (p. 362).

▶ The **speaking outline**, or delivery outline, is your final speech plan (p. 362).

▶ The outline puts the hierarchy of points into a text format (p. 363).

▶ The hierarchy of points for a strong outline will show each point supported by two or more subpoints (p. 363).

▶ As you progress from your working outline to your speaking outline, move through the three styles of outlines, from most detailed to sparest: **sentence outline**, **phrase outline**, **key-word outline** (p. 365).

▶ Add **delivery cues**, brief reminders about important information, to your speaking outline (p. 366).

▶ **Oral citations**, references to source materials to be included in your narrative, should also be in your speaking outline (p. 369).

Develop a strong introduction, a crucial part of all speeches:

▶ Preview your main points to provide a mental outline for your audience (p. 370).

▶ Establish a relationship with the audience (p. 370).

▶ Grab listeners' attention with surprise, a good story, a quote, a question, or humor (p. 371).

Move smoothly from point to point:

▶ Build strong **transitions**, words, phrases, and observations that connect the points so that topics flow naturally (p. 374).

▶ Use **signposts**, key words or phrases that signify transitions (p. 374).

▶ **Internal previews** serve as extended transitions that prime the audience for the content immediately ahead (p. 374).

▶ **Internal summaries** crystallize points in one section before moving on (p. 374).

Conclude with the same strength as in the introduction:

▶ Signal the end to ask for listeners' full attention, and wrap up quickly (p. 375).

▶ Summarize your points (p. 377).

▶ Make a final impact with a memorable closing quote, question, or story (p. 377).

Harness the power of language:

▶ Consider your audience when you choose your words (p. 377).

▶ Use simple, unambiguous words (p. 378).

▶ Use jargon—technical language specific to a particular group—only when appropriate (p. 378).

▶ Be concise (p. 378).

▶ Use vivid language (p. 378).

▶ Use repetition, allusion, similes, and metaphors to make a lasting impression (p. 379).

If only *Avatar: The Last Airbender*'s Sokka had read this chapter before he gave his speech . . .

# chapter

## 13

# Delivering
# Presentations

Nickelodeon's popular cartoon *Avatar: The Last Airbender* delights audiences of all ages as Aang, the Avatar (master of water, earth, fire, and air), and his friends travel around the globe figuring out how to defeat the brutal Fire Nation in a world war that has been raging for over one hundred years. After learning that the Fire Nation will be powerless during an upcoming solar eclipse, it is up to Aang's friend Sokka, a warrior from the Southern Water Tribe, to present an invasion plan to a small army of friends from his own tribe and the Earth kingdom.

But Sokka has a problem: shortly before his speech, he panics. He knows this invasion plan by heart, having dedicated a significant amount of time to studying the layout of the Fire Nation royal palace and plotting each advance, minute by minute, during the eclipse. But his anxiety gets the better of him. With a look of horror on his animated face, he ascends the stage and immediately falls down, dropping all of his presentation aids, getting them hopelessly mixed up. As he scrambles to recover, he begins to ramble nonsensically and to laugh nervously, leading him to drop his presentation aids again.

From this point, poor Sokka seems unable to get back on track. He shrieks in a high-pitched voice, talking so rapidly that no one can understand him—and what we can understand has nothing to do with his presentation topic! His audience members, who feel passionately about his cause, stare at him confused, yawning, and scratching their heads. Luckily, Sokka is saved by his father, a strong warrior and public speaker, who presents the invasion plan clearly and confidently, citing main points that support his thesis and speech purpose and even making appropriate use of those pesky presentation aids.

Later, Sokka confesses to Aang that he feels like a failure for having flubbed the speech, but Aang reassures him, "That speech wasn't your moment of truth. That was just public speaking. And nobody is really good at that" (DiMartino & Volpe, 2007).

## chapter objectives

**After you have finished reading this chapter, you will be able to**

- Control your nervousness

- Choose a delivery style best suited to you and your speaking situation

- Employ effective nonverbal cues

- Employ effective visual cues

- Connect with your audience

- Enhance your words with effective presentation aids

- Make efficient use of your practice time

What Aang, in all his avatar wisdom, likely meant to tell his friend Sokka is that few people are *naturally* good at public speaking—and many people experience a great deal of anxiety when they think about standing up in front of a roomful of people. That's why that scene from this cartoon resonates with viewers: we're all afraid of being Sokka, of falling flat on our faces and then tripping over our words, resulting in an ineffectual visual and vocal performance. But conquering those fears is not impossible; with the right tools and plenty of practice, even the most nervous individuals can become accomplished and engaging speakers. In this chapter, you'll learn the basics of effective speech delivery, as well as a few confidence-building strategies that will help you connect with your audience and deliver a vocally and verbally effective presentation.

## Controlling Your Nervousness

Jerry Seinfeld once joked, "According to most studies, people's number one fear is public speaking. Number two is death. . . . This means to the average person, if you go to a funeral, you're better off in the casket than doing the eulogy" (Peck, 2007). Whether Seinfeld's statistics are accurate or not, it's true that a great many people suffer from speaking anxiety. In fact, a 2001 Gallup poll revealed that 40 percent of Americans are terrified to speak in front of an audience; the only thing they feared more was snakes (Ligos, 2001). For some individuals, however, this nervousness goes far beyond giving a speech and extends to such essential speaking tasks as answering a question in class or voicing an opinion on a subject that will affect their own well-being. Fear of speaking up or speaking out can cripple their career prospects, opportunities, and lifestyle. "Being a poor speaker is the principal reason people don't make it into the executive ranks," noted one professional career adviser (Ligos, 2001).

### Understanding Communication Apprehension

Before you can conquer your nervousness, you need to identify it. Just what has you so frightened? A common barrier to effective delivery is what is known as **communication apprehension (CA)**. The communication scholar James McCroskey (1977) defines communication apprehension as "an individual's level of fear or anxiety associated with either real or anticipated communication with another person or persons" (p. 78). Communication situations typically produce **anxiety**, a feeling of dread that comes from internal doubts about our ability to perform effectively. Rarely do we really believe that speaking publicly will put us in any physical danger, but we do worry that we will embarrass ourselves or that others will think less of us based on our performance or on what we have to say. What many people don't realize is that audiences do not notice the nervousness that speakers often think is as obvious as an extra head (Sawyer & Behnke, 1990, 1996, 2002).

Most people experience **state communication apprehension**—a situational anxiety attack the intensity of which depends on such factors as the size of your audience, how well you know the people in your audience, how well you know your subject, and the status of the individuals in your audience (McCullough, Russell, Behnke, Sawyer, & Will, 2006; Witt et al., 2006). For other people, however, communication apprehension operates as a *trait*. Persons with high levels of **trait communication apprehension** have an enduring tendency to be apprehensive about communication in all contexts; they do everything they can to avoid communication situations. For such individuals, the level of fear or anxiety is high whether talking with friends or strangers, interacting in small groups, or giving a public speech.

But don't despair! Whether you suffer from trait (enduring) CA or state (situational) CA, the good news is that you can learn to control both forms. If you suspect that CA is a problem for you, ask your instructor or someone in your campus counseling center whether there are any programs on campus to help students reduce CA. Such programs are generally based on the two most common approaches for reducing high levels of CA: systematic desensitization and cognitive restructuring.

### Systematic Desensitization

Introduced in 1966, **systematic desensitization** is a method for reducing anxiety that involves countering stress by gradually retraining individuals to react differently to stress-inducing stimuli (Friedrich & Goss, 1984). Systematic desensitization is used for many anxiety disorders and has proved especially useful in treating communication apprehension (Ayres, Hopf, & Will, 2000). It involves three phases or components.

In the first phase, individuals learn to counter the physiological symptoms of the stress reaction through *deep muscle relaxation*. In this phase, the trainer may instruct the client, "Tense your fist; now relax it." The exercise proceeds to cover basically every part of the body, from the feet all the way to the face. The key to this approach is to concentrate on the differences you feel when muscles are in a tense state and when those same muscles are in a relaxed state.

Second is the construction of hierarchies of CA-eliciting stimuli. The individual thinks of a range of activities, from those that produce low anxiety (such as hanging out on a comfy couch watching a favorite movie) to those that cause high anxiety (such as asking someone out on a first date). As with deep muscle relaxation, these exercises help patients sense the difference between various levels of stress.

The third component involves the graduated pairing, through imagery, of anxiety-eliciting situations with the relaxed state. Upon naming an apprehension-producing condition ("you are approaching the podium for your speech, and you drop your note cards"), the trainer says, "Please raise your hand if this situation produces apprehension for you. Identify the part of the body where you feel tension, and bring it to a relaxed condition. Relax it completely."

Within each phase, many variations are possible. For example, the timing of the tension and relaxation phases of training in deep muscle relaxation is highly variable. Research leaves little doubt that systematic desensitization is an effective approach for treating CA.

**CONNECT**

Since many people are apprehensive about speaking publicly, we might assume that communication anxiety (CA) is limited to this context. However, throughout this book you learn that anxiety can occur in many contexts. Some people experience high levels of CA in interpersonal relationships with friends, romantic partners, or others (Chapter 6). Others get anxious working in groups (Chapter 8). And still others find that interviews (Appendix) trigger CA. The techniques in this chapter are useful in all situations where CA occurs.

**AND YOU?**

Have you ever had an embarrassing public speaking moment? What did you do? Did it affect your confidence level or your perception of your own competence? Now compare this to how you reacted to someone else's embarrassing speaking moment. Do you think less of a fellow student who flubs a few words or drops his or her note cards?

Chapter 2 discusses *self-efficacy*, or your ability to predict your likelihood of success in a given situation. If you believe that you cannot succeed at giving a speech, asking someone for a date, or interviewing for a job, you're more likely to avoid such communication. In any of these examples, cognitive restructuring can help you manage your negative self-talk so that you can interact competently and achieve your goals.

● **MEDITATING OR PRACTICING** yoga can help you learn to relax your muscles and focus your attention.

*Cognitive Restructuring*

A second common approach is **cognitive restructuring** (Fremouw & Scott, 1979). In cognitive restructuring, anxious students are first taught to identify a series of anxiety-producing negative statements (for example, "I'll say something stupid" or "I will fall flat on my face on my way up to speak") that create and enhance their CA. These statements are **self-talk**, internal dialogues or statements that influence behavior. You might generate them the night before you speak, or while sitting in courses that precede your speech class. The negative self-statements have three characteristics: they are without evidence, future- rather than present-oriented, and unrealistic. Repeating these statements is not a productive use of your time.

Once you have mastered this task, you are asked to replace these negative statements with coping statements of three types: task statements that represent skills that are under your control ("Speak slowly—it prevents me from stumbling over my words"), context statements ("No one will remember this thirty minutes after class"), and self-evaluation statements ("This was easier than last time"). As with systematic desensitization, cognitive restructuring's effectiveness in reducing high levels of CA has been demonstrated by substantial experimental research (Ayres & Heuett, 1997; Ayres & Hopf, 1993).

## Building Your Confidence

Although systematic desensitization and cognitive restructuring both reduce high levels of trait CA, neither treatment is generally necessary for persons suffering from milder and more common forms of state CA. Most people can cope effectively with periodic bouts of anxiety by applying the following advice:

▶ Develop a constructive attitude toward fear and anxiety.

▶ Grab every opportunity to prepare and practice for each public presentation.

▶ Remind yourself that your listeners want you to succeed.

▶ Consider a worst-case scenario, and prepare a plan of action on how to avoid it.

▶ Modify your thoughts and attitudes in a positive way.

▶ Visualize your success.

▶ Use relaxation techniques such as stretching, deep breathing, and positive visualization.

▶ Depersonalize the situation, and realize people are judging your speech and not you.

Research demonstrates that confidence does come through preparation and skill building (Schroeder, 2002). If you're confident that you've done adequate research on your topic and know the material you are to present, you're far more likely to feel confident at the front of the room. So now let's move on to preparing you for the final aspect of your speech: the actual delivery of it!

## Methods of Delivery

When you think of a great speaker, you might envision someone who speaks eloquently yet sounds as though he or she is speaking without having prepared a written speech. Although that's possible in certain situations, most speakers spend time preparing in the ways we've already discussed—they might write out a full speech and then prepare a speaking outline as a phrase or key-word outline. Deciding just how to prepare for your speech affects, and is affected by, your choice of delivery style. We'll examine four specific delivery options and the potential benefits and pitfalls of each.

## Speaking from Manuscript

If you have watched the president of the United States deliver the annual State of the Union address, you may have noticed that he alternates between two teleprompter screens as he reads his speech. That's because he's delivering a speech from manuscript. When you speak from manuscript, you write your entire speech out and then read it word for word from the written text because your allegiance is to the words that you have prepared.

## WIREDFORCOMMUNICATION

### Facing Your Public Speaking Fears in Virtual Reality

Picture yourself at a podium in front of a huge audience. The people in the audience look bored, even sleepy. As you stand before them, every yawn, cough, and shuffle of their feet echoes in the vast auditorium. You struggle to make eye contact with one person or another, but their responses seem far off, their expressions disconnected from everything you are doing and saying.

This may sound like a very real situation—or a very realistic nightmare. In fact, it's a virtual reality simulation designed to help individuals suffering from public speaking anxiety overcome their fear. Companies specializing in virtual reality therapy (VRT) use 3-D imaging software, video footage, and sometimes mechanized props that simulate movement to create artificial representations of stress-inducing environments. Clients wear helmets, and motion sensors allow them to interact with the virtual reality environment. "It's a therapist's dream," notes one psychologist who has used the simulations to treat certain social anxieties. "To help people deal with their problems, you must get them exposed to what they fear most" (Lubell, 2004).

The effectiveness of VRT on public speaking anxiety is unclear. The technology is not yet widely used. And although some individual therapists using the technology claim success rates as high as 90 percent, there have been no large-scale, scientific studies of the programs (Lubell, 2004). Nonetheless, it does offer individuals a chance to test their skills in front of an audience in a very private and constructive way.

**THINK ABOUT THIS**

❶ Do you think virtual reality simulations would be helpful aids in preparing for public speaking? Whom might they help more, individuals with moderate speech anxiety or severe speech anxiety?

❷ What are the benefits of practicing in front of a virtual audience? How would it compare to a real one?

❸ What aspects of the public speaking situation do you think a VRT simulation could effectively simulate? What aspects would it be impossible to capture?

● **GREAT NEWS ANCHORS**
like Dan Rather deliver the
news from a teleprompter
without sounding robotic or
unnatural.

Speaking from manuscript is common for presidential speeches like the State of the Union. That's because such speeches are by nature quite long and will likely be quoted and interpreted throughout the world the following day. A mistake in the delivery of such a speech might not merely embarrass the president but affect world events! Manuscript delivery is useful in any situation where accuracy, time constraints, or worries about misinterpretation outweigh the need for a casual and natural delivery style.

However, manuscript delivery also has a number of downsides. First, it's time-consuming, involving countless rewrites to get the written message exactly right. That's one reason why, although it works for the president (who has a team of speechwriters at his disposal), this is not a form of delivery that students typically use in class. Second, the static nature of reading from a written speech—be it from a typed manuscript in your hand or a teleprompter in front of you—restricts your body movement and limits your ability to communicate nonverbally. Chained to the written word, you are less able to move around the stage, use facial expressions or hand gestures, or make eye contact with members of your audience. As you'll learn later in this chapter, planning and rehearsal are crucial for overcoming these tendencies when delivering a speech from manuscript.

## Speaking from Memory

Speaking from memory is an ancient public speaking tradition referred to as **oratory**. In this style of speaking, you prepare the speech in the manuscript form as just described but then commit the words to memory.

Oratory delivery is fairly uncommon today as a form of public speaking, as it is both time-consuming and risky. A speaker who forgets a word or phrase can easily lose his or her place in the speech, panic, and never recover. But even if every line is delivered perfectly, the very nature of memorization can create a barrier between speaker and audience. Having memorized the speech and rehearsed without an audience, the speaker tends to deliver it as if the audience wasn't there. Such a speech can therefore end up feeling more like a performance, a one-man or one-woman show, rather than a communication situation in which the speaker is engaging with the audience.

## Speaking Spontaneously

**Impromptu speaking** refers to situations where you speak to an audience without any warning or preparation. (Talk about public speaking fears!) When you are unexpectedly called on to speak in class or suddenly motivated to give a toast at a party, you must speak impromptu. The secret to excelling at impromptu speaking is understanding that it's never *entirely* spontaneous; if you are always prepared to give a speech unexpectedly, no speech is entirely unexpected! The following steps can help you be prepared.

● **DURING PRESIDENTIAL** debates, candidates need to think on their feet to answer curveball questions and challenge their opponent's viewpoint.

### Think on Your Feet

When called on to speak unexpectedly, begin by first acknowledging the person who introduced or called on you, and then repeat or rephrase the question or issue. This will give you a moment to focus on the topic and quickly construct a game plan. Usually you'll want to choose a simple format for responding, such as noting advantages and disadvantages, cause and effect, issues or problems, agreement or disagreement, and then apply it to the topic. For example, let's say you're a high school teacher attending a board of education meeting. Your principal is speaking on how to maximize the funds allocated toward art and music at your school when he suddenly turns to you and asks you to respond to the proposal. After initially wanting to crawl under a table, you'd likely want to restate your principal's points about the importance of art and music in the lives of many teens and then discuss what you agree with regarding the proposal and what you think could be changed. Or you might talk about the advantages of the proposal, following up with a few disadvantages.

### Listen to Others

One of the best ways that you can prepare to speak when you are unprepared to do so is by reflecting on the event you are attending to see if there is something that has been emotionally moving to you. Determine if you have some personal application of a point or an example that a speaker has made that either substantiates or refutes another speaker. Most audiences enjoy hearing speakers tell a brief story that illustrates a point that a speaker made or a theme that an event uses. At a "roast" for a retired quarterback, for example, various teammates shared stories of old times with the audience. When the emcee asked for others to contribute on an informal basis, one participant reflected on an occurrence that a previous speaker had described and added several humorous insights of his own.

## Speaking Extemporaneously

Remember the type of speaker we mentioned at the beginning of this section? The calm, cool, collected kind that speaks as though making it up as he or she goes along in a surprisingly organized manner? This is called **extemporaneous speaking**.

In an impromptu speaking situation you should be aware of the relational, situational, and cultural context in which you're communicating (Chapter 1). This knowledge will help you tailor your speech to be appropriate and effective, whether you're giving a toast at a friend's wedding surrounded by her religious family members, or at an international meeting of a professional association surrounded by colleagues and potential employers.

When you speak extemporaneously, you plan the content, organization, and delivery well in advance, but instead of writing the entire speech out word for word, you speak from an outline of key points, words and phrases, or speaking aids such as computerized slideware programs (such as Microsoft PowerPoint). Extemporaneous speaking involves delivering your speech in an impromptu style, even though the speech is neither spontaneous nor unrehearsed. Most speakers favor extemporaneous delivery because they can fully prepare and rehearse their presentations while economizing on time because they need not determine in advance the exact words that they want to use.

What's the secret to succeeding at extemporaneous speaking? You can achieve success and confidence through practice and preparation. Consider the following points:

▶ *Prepare well in advance.* You can begin preparing for an extemporaneous speech as soon as you decide on a topic. Think about some possible points you want to make and how you might support them.

▶ *Don't forget the outline!* You studied outlining in Chapter 12, so we won't repeat that information here except to remind you that your key-word or phrase outline keeps you focused but gives you lots of flexibility with your word choice.

▶ *Practice truly makes perfect.* Do actors and jazz musicians give the exact same performance every single time they perform? Certainly not! But they do practice a whole lot. When you get really familiar with a script or a musical composition (or a speech), you may indeed memorize parts of it, but a little bit of it will change each and every time, allowing for a more natural delivery.

● **WILL FERRELL** and his costars ad-libbed much of *Anchorman,* not unlike what you will do when speaking extemporaneously.

# Guidelines for Effective Delivery

Everything that you have done up to this point, from selecting a topic to researching information to outlining your presentation, is a prerequisite to the big moment: actually delivering your speech. In this section, we'll take a fresh look at a point that we've emphasized throughout this book: *how* you say something is as important as *what* you say. That is, audiences receive information not only from the actual words that you speak but also through two channels of nonverbal communication: the vocal and the visual. Let's see how these nonverbal channels play out in your speech.

## Effective Vocal Delivery

Ben Stein is a lawyer, an economist, a law professor, and a former White House speechwriter, but he is perhaps best known for his acting and voice-over roles in films, commercials, and animated television. It may be funny to hear his flat, unchanging voice coming from an animated pixie on *The Fairly Odd Parents,* but listening to him deliver a long speech in the same style would likely lull you to sleep (or perhaps cause you to fantasize about throwing things at the podium).

Obviously, your voice and the language you choose are extremely important components of your speech. But your voice is also a powerful *nonverbal* factor that affects delivery. By using varying aspects of your voice, you can engage your audience as well as convey confidence and trustworthiness. Through practice, you can learn to control the elements of vocal delivery, which include pitch, volume, rate, pauses, pronunciation, and articulation.

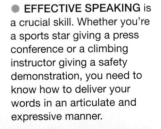

● **EFFECTIVE SPEAKING** is a crucial skill. Whether you're a sports star giving a press conference or a climbing instructor giving a safety demonstration, you need to know how to deliver your words in an articulate and expressive manner.

## Varying Your Pitch

To be an effective public speaker, you must make use of the range of vocal sounds that the human voice is capable of producing. These variations of sound range from high to low—like musical notes—and are known as **pitch**. Your pitch conveys anger, sincerity, sarcasm, and enthusiasm. If you end a sentence with a low pitch, it signals finality ("We are leaving"). If you end a sentence with a high pitch, it signals possibility or even disbelief ("We are leaving?"). You speak in a **monotone** (like Ben Stein) when you do not vary your pitch at all. And as we indicated, it can be painful to listen to a monotonous speaker. So how do you ensure that you are using your pitch effectively? One way to practice is to record yourself speaking ahead of time to determine if there are places where you need to use more energy and extend your pitch levels.

## Adjusting Your Volume and Speaking Rate

Speakers can use vocal cues to signal to the audience what is important to pay attention to. Just as we use boldfaced and italic type in the pages of this book to emphasize certain words and phrases, as a speaker you can use audible cues to emphasize certain points.

How fast or slow you speak is known as your **speaking rate**, and it can also be a key factor in effective speaking. You want to speak slowly enough that your audience is able to hear and absorb what you say but quickly enough to capture the urgency and importance of what you are saying. Changes in rate are significant indicators of your enthusiasm while you speak, and they generate enthusiasm from your listeners as well. Typically, if you speak faster, compared with surrounding material, you signal your enthusiasm for the content, and the audience's interest will follow. When you slow down, your rate signals a degree of seriousness and concern. You would deliver a persuasive call-to-action speech at a faster pace in order to show and elicit enthusiasm. You would deliver a tribute or dedication, such as a eulogy, at a slower pace to demonstrate sincerity and seriousness.

Changes in **volume**—how loudly or quietly you speak—can also be used to emphasize certain points. What do you want to stand out from your speech for the audience to remember? Is it a statistic, a name, or a product? Think about giving one word or phrase in every few sentences some "punch." This differentiates the word or phrase from its context.

## Using Pauses for Effect

A well-placed pause is one of the most powerful tools available to speakers. Because many speakers believe that their entire goal is to talk, they pause too infrequently. But taking a moment between statements, words, or phrases and not saying anything at all can add drama to your speech by offering the audience a moment to reflect on what you have said and building anticipation for what will follow. For example, consider how President Barack Obama made use of pauses for emphasis and reflection in Sample Speech 13.1, delivered during his 2008 presidential campaign.

## SAMPLE SPEECH 13.1

## Iowa Victory Speech

BARACK OBAMA

They said this day would never come. [*Pause*]

They said our sights were set too high. [*Pause*]

They said this country was too divided, too disillusioned to ever come together around a common purpose. [*Pause*]

But on this January night, at this defining moment in history, you have done what the cynics said we couldn't do. [*Pause*] •

You have done what the state of New Hampshire can do in five days. [*Pause*]

You have done what America can do in this new year, 2008. [*Pause*] •

In lines that stretched around schools and churches, in small towns and in big cities, you came together as Democrats, Republicans, and independents, to stand up and say that we are one nation. We are one people. And our time for change has come. [*Pause*]

You said the time has come to move beyond the bitterness and pettiness and anger that's consumed Washington. [*Pause*]

To end the political strategy that's been all about division, and instead make it about addition. To build a coalition for change that stretches through red states and blue states. [*Pause*]

Because that's how we'll win in November, and that's how we'll finally meet the challenges that we face as a nation. [*Pause*] •

I'll be a president who finally makes health care affordable and available to every single American, the same way I expanded health care in Illinois by bringing Democrats and Republicans together to get the job done. [*Pause*]

I'll be a president who ends the tax breaks for companies that ship our jobs overseas and put a middle-class tax cut into the pockets of working Americans who deserve it. [*Pause*]

I'll be a president who harnesses the ingenuity of farmers and scientists and entrepreneurs to free this nation from the tyranny of oil once and for all. [*Pause*]

And I'll be a president who ends this war in Iraq and finally brings our troops home . . . who restores our moral standing . . . who understands that 9/11 is not a way to scare up votes but a challenge that should unite America and the world against the common threats of the twenty-first century. [*Pause*] . . . •

Tonight, we are one step closer to that vision of America because of what you did here in Iowa. . . .

• Early in the speech, Obama's pauses allow his listeners to reflect on the magnitude of what Obama feels has been achieved in his victory in Iowa.

• Here Obama's pauses highlight the involvement of the audience and the Iowa voters. And they also underscore his hope for victory in New Hampshire and in the presidential election.

• Here we see Obama pausing to note that change is coming. He offers several ideas (Democrats and Republicans working together, ending the bitterness in Washington) and allows the audience to reflect on each idea.

• Finally, we see Obama pausing to drive home each point regarding something he hopes to achieve in Washington should he be elected president.

## Speaking Clearly and Precisely

One of the quickest ways to lose credibility with your audience is to mispronounce a word—especially a word that is specifically related to the subject of your presentation. **Pronunciation** is the correct formation of word sounds. Many words in the English language are frequently mispronounced, to the point that individuals are not even aware that they are saying these words incorrectly. For example, many Americans say "supposably" when the correct word is *supposedly* and say "liberry" instead of *library*.

Throughout his presidency, George W. Bush was the butt of countless jokes—often even self-deprecating ones—for his frequent mistakes in pronunciation. So why did anyone listen to him speak (aside from the fact that he was the president, of course!)? Even though Bush sometimes made mistakes in pronunciation, he *articulated* well. **Articulation** is the clarity and forcefulness with which the sounds are made, regardless of whether they are pronounced correctly. To speak clearly, even if incorrectly, is to be articulate. All speakers strive to be articulate, but there are several ways in which we routinely sabotage our efforts (O'Hair, Stewart, & Rubenstein, 2007).

When a speaker omits certain sounds in a word, runs words together, and speaks so softly that a listener can hardly hear, the speaker is guilty of **mumbling**. Unless they have a speech impediment, most people mumble either because they are in a hurry or because they are not prepared to speak clearly. And like mispronunciation, mumbling can also be simply a matter of habit.

Audience perceptions about a speaker's skills can be tainted by **accents**—patterns of pronunciation that are specific to a certain upbringing, geographical region, or culture. Speakers who hail from different countries, or even different regions or cultures within the United States, typically speak with distinctive accents. While the word choices that they make may differ from time to time, the greatest difference that you hear is in their emphasis on syllables and cadence or rhythm while speaking. British and Australian speakers tend to emphasize syllables differently than Americans and speak with different cadences as well. Southern speakers tend to drawl (use a slower pace) and elongate vowel sounds. Speakers from the Northeast tend to omit sounds from the middle of words such as *park* and *word*. Midwestern speakers tend to insert an "r" sound into words such as *wash*.

Some accents are associated with stereotypes that can be harmful or beneficial for the speaker. For example, in the reality television show *Supernanny,* a British nanny travels to the United States to tame misbehaving kids. An interesting aspect of this show is the effect her accent has on both children and parents when she gives guidance and advice to the family as a whole. Somehow, being British makes her seem more intelligent or more sophisticated. In turn, knowing that her accent gives her greater authority helps her gain compliance with her commands.

● **NANNY JO FROST'S** British accent enhances her authority and helps her gain control of the kids in a disastrous situation.

## Effective Visual Delivery

In the same way that a monotone can lull an audience to sleep, so can a stale, dull physical presence. This doesn't mean that you need to be doing cartwheels throughout your speech, but it does mean that you should avoid keeping your hands glued to the podium and that you should look up from your note cards once in a while. Otherwise, you'll be little more than a talking head, and your audience will quickly lose interest. What's more, effective visual cues can enhance a presentation, helping you clarify and emphasize your points in an interesting and compelling way.

### *Using Effective Eye Behavior*

As we noted in Chapter 4, eye behavior is a crucial aspect of nonverbal communication that can be both effective and appropriate when you consider the cultural context in which you are communicating. In Vietnamese culture, for example, it

## COMMUNICATIONACROSSCULTURES

THINK ABOUT THIS

### Speaking American: A Wealth of Dialects

In a country as large and expansive as the United States, diversity means more than a mere ethnic, cultural, or racial mosaic. Regional dialects—local speech patterns, including unique pronunciations and vocabulary—create a special challenge for competent communication. English may be our common language, but even if we all technically speak the same language, each of us actually speaks it somewhat differently.

Evidence suggests that we perceive people's intelligence levels through their dialects, even though the two are in fact unrelated. Linguistically speaking, there is no inherent difference between dialects: everyone speaks with some accent, and no accent is superior or inferior. But that is not to say that we do not all attach stereotypes to accents. In the United States, for example, the midwestern accent is often perceived as being the "most correct," while strong southern and New York City accents are perceived as signs of lower intelligence (Preston, 1998).

There are also strong regional patterns related to the speed with which we speak. While evidence suggests that the ideal rate of speech is around 180 words per minute, in the northeastern areas, such as New Jersey and Massachusetts, native speakers of English are clocked at over 240 words a minute (Humpherys, 1996). Other regions and cultures speak more slowly and expressively: southern Baptists, for example, have a rich tradition of eloquence, emotion, and animated body language. This difference could be attributed to the rural nature of congregants during earlier times (Trachtenberg, 1982/2000). However, established Baptist churches in many northern areas, like Chicago, tend to be more reserved and deliberate (Kenyon, 1999).

❶ What does your accent sound like? How would it be perceived by people in your own region? How about an audience from a different region?

❷ What perceptual challenges would a southern Baptist preacher face in front of an audience in New York City? How might a southern congregation perceive a fast-talking New Yorker?

❸ Why do most newscasters tend to speak with a midwestern accent? Why is that accent considered the most neutral?

❹ If a speaker has a strong regional accent, should he or she try to lessen it when speaking publicly? What about changing the speed with which he or she speaks?

is considered inappropriate and rude to make prolonged, direct eye contact with someone, particularly if that person is of a higher rank or social status. In the many Western cultures, conversely, a lack of eye contact can make a speaker seem suspicious or untrustworthy; in the United States in particular, direct eye contact is one of the most important nonverbal actions in public speaking, essential to signaling respect and interest to the audience (Axtell, 1991). But how can a speaker make and maintain eye contact with a large group of individuals?

One way is to move your eyes from one person to another (in a small group) or one section of people to another (in a large group), a technique called **scanning**. Scanning allows you to make brief eye contact with almost everyone in an audience, no matter how large. To use it, picture yourself standing in front of the audience, and then divide the room into four imaginary sections. As you move from idea to idea in your speech, move your eye contact into a new section. Select a friendly-looking person in the quadrant, and focus your eye contact directly on that person while completing the idea (just make sure you don't pick a friend who will try to make you laugh!). Then change quadrants, and select a person from the new group. Tips for using the scanning technique are offered in Table 13.1.

## Incorporating Facial Expressions and Gestures

Have you ever seen an anime cartoon in which a character's face contorts, the jaw dropping unnaturally (sometimes to the floor) and the eyes becoming small white dots, and a large question mark appears in the background? The animator certainly gets the point across—this character is either entirely surprised or seriously confused! Your facial expressions, while not as exaggerated

<table>
<tr><td colspan="2">TABLE 13.1<br><br>TIPS FOR SCANNING YOUR AUDIENCE</td></tr>
<tr><td>Work in sections</td><td>Do not scan from left to right or right to left. Always work in sections and move randomly from one section to another.</td></tr>
<tr><td>Avoid the "lighthouse" effect</td><td>You'll look like a human lighthouse (or a lawn sprinkler) if you simply rotate your upper torso from left to right while you talk, looking at no one person in particular.</td></tr>
<tr><td>Look people in the eye</td><td>Avoid looking at people's foreheads or over their heads; look them in the eye, even if they are not looking back at you.</td></tr>
<tr><td>Focus for a moment</td><td>Remember to pause long enough on an individual so that the person can recognize that you are looking directly at him or her.</td></tr>
<tr><td>Don't jump away</td><td>If someone is not looking at you, stay with the person anyway until you've finished your thought. Then move on to another; you can always return to that person the next time your eyes move to that quadrant of the room.</td></tr>
<tr><td>Divide large groups</td><td>If the audience is too large for you to get to everyone, look at small groups of two or three people sitting together.</td></tr>
</table>

as those of an anime character, serve a similar purpose: they let your audience know when your words arouse fear, anger, happiness, joy, frustration, or other emotions. The critical factor is that your expressions *must* match the verbal message that you are sending in your speech. As a competent communicator, you are unlikely to smile when delivering a eulogy—unless you are recounting a particularly funny or endearing memory about the deceased.

Like facial expressions, gestures amplify the meaning of your speech. Clenching your fist, counting with your fingers, and spreading your hands far apart to indicate distance or size all reinforce or clarify your message. What is most important about using gestures is that they should be appropriate and natural. So if you want to indicate your deeply held emotional sentiments when persuading your audience about the benefits of becoming a foster parent, but you feel awkward putting your hand over your heart, don't do it! Your audience will be able to tell that you feel uncomfortable and unnatural. Focus instead on what you do feel comfortable with. You might indicate the giant bear hug your foster child greets you with every morning if that feels like a better fit for your personality (Buckley, 1999, p. 209).

● **YOU CAN** clearly tell that Astroboy is angry from his aggressively slanted eyebrows and wide-open mouth.

## Controlling Body Movements

In October 2006, the actor Michael J. Fox found himself in a controversy over this very issue: body movements. Fox suffers from Parkinson's disease, a condition of the nervous system that causes trembling of the arms and legs, stiffness of muscles, and slowness of movement that becomes less controllable as time goes on. A strong advocate of stem cell research to treat chronic illnesses, Fox appeared in several televised ads to support political candidates who back this particular cause. In one ad supporting now-senator Clare McCaskill of Missouri, Fox clearly displays the effects of his condition: he appears rigid, unable to control his arms, and unable to sit straight. On October 23, the radio personality Rush Limbaugh declared, "He is exaggerating the effects of the disease. He's moving all around and shaking and it's purely an act. . . . This is really shameless of Michael J. Fox. Either he didn't take his medication or he's acting" (Montgomery, 2006).

In response to Limbaugh, Fox claims that he did take his medication—that in fact he was overmedicated, since treatments for Parkinson's can cause symptoms similar to the disease itself (CBS News, 2006). But the point that we want to make with this example is that medication or no medication, Fox's body movements unwittingly highlight and underscore the cause that he is addressing: the devastating effects of chronic illness. Your body movements will also have a powerful effect on your audience—though likely in a different way from Fox. In most speaking situations you encounter, the best way to highlight your speech content is to restrict your body movements so that the audience can focus on your words. Consider, for

● **ACTOR MICHAEL J. FOX** found himself at the center of a controversy over body movements when speaking about and displaying the effects of Parkinson's disease.

example, your **posture**, or the position of your arms and legs and how you carry your body. Generally, when a speaker slumps forward or leans on a podium, rocks back and forth, sways left and right, paces forward and backward, or appears to dance behind a lectern, the audience perceives the speaker as unpolished and lacking control, and listeners' attention shifts from the message to the speaker's body movements.

How do you prevent such movements from happening, particularly if you're someone who fidgets when you're nervous? One useful technique is called **planting**. Stand with your legs apart at a distance that is equal to your shoulders. Bend your knees slightly so that they do not lock. From this position, you are able to gesture freely, and when you are ready to move, you can take a few steps, replant, and continue speaking. The key is always to plant following every movement that you make.

# EVALUATINGCOMMUNICATIONETHICS

THINK ABOUT THIS

## Judging Speeches

Later in this chapter, you will read about Anna Capps (our Real Communicator), and we've talked about the struggles that people with physical challenges (such as Michael J. Fox) face when delivering speeches. But how do culture and ethics collide when it comes time actually to judge or assign a grade to a presentation?

Imagine that your speech class is engaging in peer evaluation. In groups of six, you practice delivering your speech before the final presentation to the entire class. You will evaluate your group members' speeches twice—and a portion of your grades will be determined by the improvement they make between the first two practice speeches and then between the final rehearsal and the delivery before the entire class.

One woman in your group, Evelyn, has cerebral palsy, a neurological disorder that permanently affects body movements and muscle coordination. It can have a diverse number of symptoms, but Evelyn struggles most with slurred speech, balance, and exaggerated reflexes. Evelyn is quite comfortable talking about her disability and appears to be a confident speaker. Yet as she talks, you find it somewhat difficult to understand her speech. Because many of her words are slurred, you feel like you're missing a few main points. And as much as you try not to, you find the fact that she sways when she speaks and that she must grip the back of her chair for balance somewhat distracting.

You feel bad making these comments to Evelyn on her first evaluation, and so you focus your remarks on improvements she can make on the outline. But you're worried about how the rest of the class will react to Evelyn and even what sort of grade she might get from your professor (who has a reputation for being a difficult speech grader). You're now facing your second round of evaluations for Evelyn.

❶ Is it ethical to share your concerns with Evelyn? Or is it more appropriate to keep quiet in this situation?

❷ You may have been reading this scenario under the assumption that you do not have any physical challenges. Now imagine that you have speech challenges, that you are unable to walk, or that you suffer from a chronic illness. Does this influence your critique of Evelyn's speech? Does it make you more or less comfortable addressing her?

❸ The situation need not be restricted to someone with a health condition. What if Evelyn is not a native speaker of English? What if she is from a different region of the United States and you find her accent difficult to understand? Is it ethical to address these concerns when judging her speech?

## Connecting with Your Audience

It is through vocal and visual delivery that speakers are able to interact with their audiences—that's what makes public speaking different from just writing a good presentation. When you compose an essay, you write it and it goes off to the reader; it's a linear model of communication (as discussed in Chapter 1). But speaking before an audience is more than just providing information through words; it's an interaction between speaker and audience.

The most talented public speakers are always keenly aware of this. Gifted speakers like Ronald Reagan and Bill Clinton were known for their ability to connect with members of any audience on a very personal level and for their knack for delivering even the most formal speeches in a style that felt conversational, personal, and familiar. That's because both were able to use their words, voices, and gestures to convey the way they felt about a subject. They also spoke directly to their audiences in a way that felt unrehearsed and sincere. Let's now take a look at the way our words converge with our vocal and visual delivery to establish such a connection with the audience. We'll also consider the ways we can adapt our delivery to suit the audience's needs and expectations.

### Expressing Emotion

If you do not feel passion for what you are talking about, you can be sure that your audience will not feel it either. One of your responsibilities is to ensure that throughout your speech, the audience feels the same emotions that you do for your subject matter, such as enthusiasm, anger, compassion, or grief. Many Americans, for example, felt an intimate connection to New York Mayor Rudy Giuliani when he addressed the media in the immediate aftermath of the terrorist attacks on the city on September 11, 2001. Although he remained authoritative and in control, he was also able to express his grief and devastation in a way that rang true to everyone watching or listening. When an audience feels that a speaker is acting, that he or she is staging some emotional response rather than generating it spontaneously, they may question the sincerity of the message.

It may seem strange for a speaker to "listen" to the audience, but this is a crucial step. In Chapter 5, you learn that listening involves selecting, attending, understanding, remembering, and responding to communication partners. The same points are helpful in public speaking. By *attending* to your audience's nonverbal behavior (slouching, head nodding, etc.) you can appropriately *respond:* if they seem confused, speak more slowly; if they seem to agree with you, reveal more passion through emphasis.

● AMERICANS WATCHING Rudy Giuliani's September 11 televised address sensed that he was deeply upset by the tragedy even though he kept his emotions in check.

### Interacting with Your Audience

One common mistake speakers make is to speak to—or even *at*—the audience. Competent public speakers always think of their presentations as speaking *with* the audience. As discussed earlier, in Western cultures, this generally means making and maintaining eye contact. But it also means listening to audience reactions, paying attention to listeners' body movements, and continually gauging their responses to what you say and do so that you can make adjustments to your speech as you go along. For example, if you observe audience members frowning or

# real communicator

**NAME:** Anna Capps
**HOMETOWN:** Cleveland, Georgia
**OCCUPATION:** Student at Gainesville State College
**FUN FACT:** I have a cocker spaniel named Lady who always lets me know when someone's at the door.

At Gainesville State College, I took a course called Introduction to Human Communication. On the first day of class, I saw on the syllabus that I would have to deliver two speeches: one informative, one persuasive. You know Jerry Seinfeld's comment about Americans preferring to be in the casket rather than delivering the eulogy? That's me. I had never given a speech in my life. And to make things harder, I'm deaf. Oral communication does not come as easy to me as it does to people who've grown up learning language by hearing language. But I wasn't going to let that stop me. I was going to ace that first speech.

I didn't ace that first speech. It was an informational presentation on gemstones, and I was *so* nervous. I held the lectern in a death grasp. According to my professor, I talked way too fast and didn't establish direct eye contact with my audience. What's worse is that as I was speaking, I could tell things were not going well. My particular disability leaves me visually hyperaware, so I saw confused, puzzled, what-is-she-talking-about looks on my listeners' faces. The hardest part was that it seemed as if the other students were becoming increasingly embarrassed for me. They were not used to hearing my voice and couldn't understand what I was saying. I started to get really frustrated, and that only made me more nervous. I finished my speech (forgetting about half of it) and sat back down in my chair, my face burning.

I learn well from my mistakes, however. For my second presentation, I didn't need to consider a hypothetical worst-case scenario in order to manage my communication apprehension; I'd already lived it! I evaluated what went wrong. One of the problems in my first speech was that my audience didn't understand me. I wasn't speaking clearly. I decided that in the second speech, I'd have to maximize my strengths and play down my weaknesses. I went to disability services and got a sign language interpreter. I also wrote a speech I was more interested in: Addressing the smog problem for allergy sufferers. And I practiced and practiced. Was I still nervous when it came time to deliver the speech? Of course. But now I had an attack plan. I would concentrate on my visual delivery, particularly eye contact, as I had to make sure to look at my audience and not at the interpreter. I scanned the room, looking people in the eye—and not only did direct eye contact establish credibility for me as a speaker, but looking at all those people responding positively also made me more confident in myself. Then too—and here is where my hearing disability helped—I have very animated facial expressions. I was able to communicate through gestures, and the audience members who are visually oriented responded to that. By the end of the speech, feeling more assured, I was smiling and standing up straight.

I know that I will have to deliver speeches and face other challenging communication situations in the future (as we all will!). But this experience has given me a huge boost of confidence in many areas of my life, so I know that I can face what's ahead. And the next time I speak in front of a group, I know that I will do a good job. I've already done it once. Who's going to tell me I can't do it again?

squinting, it may be a sign of misunderstanding. You can take this as a cue to slow down or emphasize key points more explicitly. Alternatively, if you notice your audience members responding with smiles, focused eye contact, or even laughter, you probably want to maintain the style of speaking that produced such a positive reaction.

## Effective Presentation Aids

Are you ready for Apple's newest and coolest gadget? Steve Jobs, co-founder and CEO of Apple Computers, is—and he can't wait to tell you and millions of other audience members about it. That's why he's preparing an informative presentation on the what, when, where, how, and why of Apple's next invention for broadcast on YouTube and the evening news. But how do you speak clearly and informatively on a piece of technology that software enthusiasts, employees, and the general public are not yet familiar with? You show it, that's how! Steve Jobs will once again don his favorite speaking outfit—a pair of blue jeans, a black shirt, and some beat-up sneakers—and pull out his trusty presentation aid, a digital projector attached to his iPod or iPhone. If you visit YouTube, you can pull up Jobs's 2007 presentation introducing the iPhone and see for yourself how he clearly and masterfully uses the device and the screen to bring the audience in on the fun of moving between music, your phone book, and your voice mail. Would the speech be the same—or as effective—without his presentation aids? Certainly not. Part of getting people excited about a new product is letting them try it out—or at least feel like they're trying it out.

Like Jobs and like Al Gore, who traveled the country with his PowerPoint presentation on the environment (see Chapter 11's opening vignette), today's speakers have many tools at their disposal that can allow them to create dramatic visual presentations that enhance their words and deepen the audience's understanding of the topic. We'll explore how presentation aids work in the sections that follow.

● **STEVE JOBS** has his presentations of Apple products down pat. His casual outfit makes him instantly relatable, and his product demonstration allows the audience to feel connected and excited.

## The Function of Presentation Aids

You already know that presentation aids can be a valuable asset to a speech, heightening an audience's interest and helping you convey technical information. But it's important to remember that a presentation aid should *supplement* your speech, not substitute for the speech. Sure, you may indeed have a moving video, a hilarious reenactment, or shocking images to share with the audience. But if you haven't researched your topic thoroughly, assembled a useful speaking outline, or even looked up from the podium while speaking, who will care? To be truly useful, presentation aids must *enhance* your speech, accomplishing three goals:

> ▶ *Help listeners process and retain information.* Your goal while speaking with a presentation aid is to ensure that the audience sees relationships among

concepts, variables, or items. Always make a point, refer to the presentation aid, direct the listeners' attention to where you want them to focus, and then restate, reiterate, or rephrase what you have said.

▶ *Promote interest and motivation.* If you show terms, photographs, statistics, tables, and other items that truly reinforce your spoken message, the audience will be more likely to go along with you. This is true whether your purpose is to inform, entertain, or persuade the audience.

▶ *Convey information clearly and concisely.* There is no comparison between the amount of time it would take you to read a series of figures versus showing them on a table, graph, or chart. A good visual can present a lot of information in a clear, concise, and simple matter, saving the speaker's time for interpretation and elaboration.

## When to Use Presentation Aids

Determining when a presentation aid will be effective and appropriate is an important part of the planning process. There are several circumstances in which a visual aid can enhance a speech.

### Enhancing or Substituting Words

Some things, people, places, or processes are difficult to describe with only words and gestures. When it is more practical to show something than it is to explain or describe it, as in Steve Jobs's introduction of the iPhone, visual aids can be both effective and appropriate. An object, or *prop,* removes the burden from the audience of having to imagine what something looks like as you speak. For instance, if you are giving an informative speech on the way to tune a guitar, you might find it difficult to explain the process with only words and gestures. Demonstrating the process on an actual guitar would be an effective visual (and in this case, audio) aid. When it is not feasible to bring a full-size object or prop for your speech, you can rely on a scale model instead to show how something works or what something consists of. Architects, for example, routinely use scale models of their designs when they present plans to developers and clients.

● **AN INTERESTING PROP** can be a helpful visual aid. This speaker might have trouble illustrating certain muscles and nerves in the human body without his model.

Visual material can also enhance your speech by complementing your words and points. Pictures—illustrations or photographs—can help clarify an image or process that you are describing. A speaker talking about birth defects, for example, might show a photograph of a child born with a cleft palate rather than trying to describe the defect in words. Photographs also have the advantage of being objective when words can sound harsh or insensitive. Similarly, audio and video *clips* can add authenticity and drama to a speech. For example, a clip of the riots that ensued in Iraq after the U.S. invasion in 2003 demonstrates the ugliness in a way that simple words cannot.

Graphics can be useful for describing a more complex process or arrangement. For example, if you wanted to explain what an employee in a company must do to qualify under the Family and Medical Leave Act (FMLA), you could produce a diagram showing each step of the process, from start to finish, pointing to the aid as you address each step verbally.

### Displaying Data and Facts

When you're delivering a speech rich in statistics, data, and facts, visual aids can be an indispensable presentation tool. You can cut your presentation time drastically and increase your listeners' interest by pointing to some figures on a graph rather than reading them number by number. And distilling one's facts and data into a few clear and dramatic graphics can allow the speaker to speak extemporaneously about facts and figures that they present visually without risking a misrepresentation of the data.

Let's say you are giving a speech on entry requirements for your college or university. You have compiled statistics on class standing and SAT or ACT scores for incoming freshmen. If you were to read off the breakdown of the scores, it would be hard to follow and boring; it would also mean that you would have to stick closely to a manuscript lest you chance making a mistake on the numbers. But if you present your figures in a simple table, your audience can read them as you speak. Even better, creating a bar graph or pie chart that illustrates the breakdown of scores in a visual way would have a stronger impact, and it would allow you to talk about what the numbers mean rather than simply reading them off. Various graphs that can be used to show data and statistics are detailed in Figure 13.1.

### The Pitfalls of Presentation Software

Sitting through hours of slides from your Aunt Sonja's trip to Phoenix is boring enough (no offense, Arizona readers!). Sitting through a slide show that essentially repeats your speech outline can be unbearable.

**FIGURE 13.1**

**SAMPLES OF EFFECTIVE GRAPHS** Bar graphs use bars of varying lengths to make comparisons. Pie charts depict the division of a whole.

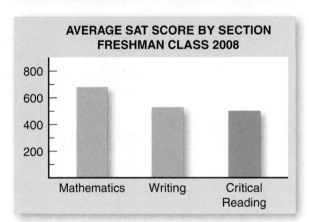

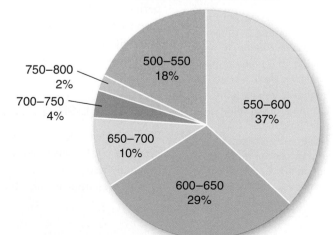

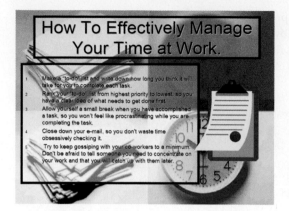

● **BEWARE THE TERRIBLE** PowerPoint slide! A long bulleted list of all your speaking points on a distracting background is a surefire way to detract from your speech and lose your audience's attention.

A great many presentations today depend on slide show software, and indeed, programs like Microsoft PowerPoint are exceptionally useful for speeches where visual information is a must. Slide shows are excellent for sharing really useful visual aids, such as graphs, charts, tables, and photographs, with an audience. But too many speakers use slide show programs to present written information, such as outlines and bulleted lists of points.

Always remember that you are giving a speech, not a slide show. The major focus of the audience and the presentation should be on you and what you have to say. If this is not true, then you might as well send your entire speech to your audience via e-mail and ask the recipients to download it and play it while you are off doing something else. Never forget that *you* are the star of the show; your presentation aids are not.

## Practicing Your Speech

If there's one key to developing skill as a public speaker, it's practice. Practice transforms nervous public speakers into confident ones and good public speakers into great ones, particularly when speakers pay attention to four important points: remembering the speaking outline, practicing with presentation aids, simulating the speaking situation, and practicing the actual delivery.

The words in your speaking outline must prompt you to remember your ideas. During your rehearsal, you'll discover whether you've chosen key words that are at an appropriate level of *abstraction*, or vagueness vs. concreteness (Chapter 3). If the word is too vague, it may not jog your memory under pressure. But if it's too concrete, you may be tempted to read directly from your notes. Like Clare, you will need to practice under realistic conditions to discover the right level of abstraction.

## Remember Your Speaking Outline

You've heard quite a bit from us about writing your outline and using it for speaking, and you know the benefits of creating a speaking outline consisting of key words and phrases. Now it's time to practice from it. Our friend Clare from Chapter 12, for example, would need to make sure that the key words "living costs" actually prompt her to discuss the difference in cost of living in various parts of the United States in her speech on poverty. If Clare gets to this point in her speech and suddenly forgets what she wanted to talk about, perhaps her key words are too vague. She'll need to revise her outline to ensure that they are clear for her presentation. Practicing from her outline will also help her gauge her time limits: if she's falling short or running long, she'll need to adjust her outline as well.

## Practice Using Presentation Aids

We both give speeches in front of committees and colleagues at national communication conferences. And even though we've been doing this professionally for many years, we always experience at least a twinge of anxiety at the thought of our presentation aids having some sort of breakdown. Even if this hasn't

# what about you?

## Assessing Your Speech Delivery

After you've practiced your speech a few times, record it on video, and use the following questions to determine how well you performed.

1. Did your expression seem deadpan?

   A. No, never. You seem animated and lively.

   B. A little stiff at times, but for the most part lively.

   C. You look like your face has become paralyzed after a badly botched Botox injection.

2. Your use of gestures seems . . .

   A. Natural and spontaneous.

   B. Preplanned, perhaps, but still effective.

   C. Inappropriate or confusing.

3. Your body language seems . . .

   A. Easygoing and casual, yet authoritative.

   B. Stiff at times, but not distractingly so.

   C. Panicked—you look like you would rather be suffering from a severe case of the flu than delivering this speech.

4. Your voice sounds . . .

   A. Animated and lively, with lots of changes in pitch and speed.

   B. A little too fast-paced, but you're not losing the audience.

   C. So monotonous that it seems exciting when you cough.

5. Your presentation aids seem . . .

   A. Useful and complementary to what you are saying.

   B. Interesting, if a little tangential to your key points.

   C. Annoying. Please, not another bulleted list!

**If your responses were mostly A's:** You've got a good handle on delivery; go out there and speak!

**If your responses were mostly B's:** You're getting there, but you need to keep practicing and refining your technique.

**If your responses were mostly C's:** You've got some work to do, but don't worry—as you practice more, you'll be able to build your confidence and your technique.

Source: O'Hair, Stewart, & Rubenstein (2007), pp. 260, 270. Adapted with permission.

happened to you before, you probably remember the nervous laugh of your third-grade teacher when he or she tried to put on a DVD (or a videocassette, for those of us born before 1990) and couldn't get the television to work. (Shudder.) Happily, this doesn't have to happen if you prepare and rehearse. Consider the following points.

▶ *Eliminate surprises.* To the best of your ability, make sure that your aids function. If you're using any kind of technology, practice with it long before your deliver your speech. Show up with a DVD that skips or an MP3 clip that didn't download properly, and you'll start nervously laughing like that third-grade teacher.

▶ *Write notes to yourself.* In your outline, make sure that you provide cues to let yourself know when to move to the next item or slide or when to show an image or play a clip. This will help you avoid rushing ahead to get to a particular aid, as well as ensure that you don't forget any.

▶ *Rehearse your demonstrations with a partner.* When your presentation aid is actually a live prop (for example, a student in your own class), you'll need to practice with this person in advance of the presentation. For example, if you want to demonstrate how to administer CPR to your audience, you can do so either with a mannequin or with another student.

## Simulate the Situation

You already know that few people can simply walk up to a podium for the first time in their life and deliver a perfect speech. Seasoned public speakers often look and sound great in large part because they've done it before and done it often. Exposing yourself to some of the more unnerving aspects of public speaking—for example, an audience—can help you become more comfortable. You can do this by simulating some aspects of your speech delivery during your rehearsals. For example:

▶ *Create similar conditions.* Think about the room you'll deliver your speech in: what is its size, space, layout? Keep these things in mind as you rehearse— or even better, arrange to rehearse in the room where you will be speaking. Awareness of these conditions will help you practice eye contact, movement, gestures, and your use of notes and presentation aids.

▶ *Practice in front of someone.* Try practicing in front of someone or, preferably, a few people. One method for getting over anxiety about speaking in front of an audience is to "practice upward": practice first in front of one friend, then two, then three, and so on, until you are comfortable speaking before a fairly large group.

▶ *Keep an eye on your time.* Use a stopwatch or a kitchen timer to stay on target with your allotted speech time. You might even keep track of how much time you spend on each point, particularly if you have a tendency to go into a lot of detail early on or to rush at the end.

## Practice Your Delivery

In any speech, your objective should be to communicate a message to an audience. If your message is clear, the audience will connect with it; if it's buried in a sea of mumbling or stammering or if it's forced to compete with distracting body language or fumbling with visual aids, the audience will miss your point. As you practice, you can improve the aspects of delivery you studied in this chapter and concentrate on your message.

▶ *Focus on your message.* Concentrate on the way that you express an argument, paraphrase a quotation, or explain a statistic. Emphasize the quality of your expression of ideas rather than how you look, move, gesture, or stand. If you focus on your message, the right delivery will usually follow naturally.

▶ *Use mirrors cautiously.* Conventional wisdom has advocated rehearsing in front of a mirror in order to practice eye contact, maximize facial expressions, and assess gestures and movement. But we have mixed thoughts on this because there won't be any mirrors when you deliver the speech; their presence adds an artificial element to your rehearsal. They can make you feel even more self-conscious about your appearance, distracting you from the message you want to communicate.

▶ *Record a practice session.* Before you gasp at the horror and skip to the next bullet point, please trust us: this really does help. Many teachers and professors even record themselves to get a sense of their presence in the classroom ("Do I favor one side of the room?" "Do I tend to interact with only the front row?"). Recording your performance will allow you to get a sense of how well you project your voice, articulate your points, and use body movements, facial expressions, and gestures.

▶ *Ask for feedback.* See if you can find a person or two to listen to your speech who will give you an honest and constructive critique of your performance. Ask what they remember most about your presentation. Did they focus mostly on your content, or were they distracted by your postures, gestures, or stammering? Were your presentation aids helpful, or were they distracting or confusing?

**AND YOU?**

After you have practiced in front of one or more friends, family members, or classmates, consider their feedback. Was anything about the feedback surprising? Did they note the strengths and weaknesses that you expected them to pick up on, based on your own self-assessment? If not, how might you incorporate their feedback into your next practice session?

## BACK TO ▶ Sokka's Speech

At the beginning of the chapter, we reviewed Sokka's attempt to present his plan to invade the Fire Nation and end the world war. Unfortunately, Sokka let his anxiety get the best of him, and his delivery fell apart. Like Sokka, we can all use a few tips on controlling our anxiety and improving our speech delivery through the skills and techniques discussed in this chapter.

▶ In the scene before he takes the stage, we see Sokka looking positively terrified. He, like most of us, probably just needed to relax and imagine himself succeeding in front of the crowd while practicing some deep breathing exercises. Moreover, Sokka should have kept in mind that his audience is passionately committed to his speech topic and therefore wants him to make a successful presentation.

▶ It seems like Sokka tried to speak from memory. In a way, that makes sense here—after all, he has been studying the Fire Nation and the eclipse and planning for this invasion for a great many months. Nonetheless, he likely would have benefited from a key-word or phrase outline to remind him of the points he needed to make to inform his audience about the plan.

▶ Sokka, like the rest of us, clearly could have benefited from some practice! Had he asked his friends Aang, Katara, and Toph to listen to his presentation and offer feedback, he might have learned an important lesson on being aware of volume, speaking rate, enunciation, facial expressions, and gestures.

▶ Finally, Sokka should have kept in mind that public speaking is an opportunity to interact *with* the audience rather than speak *at* the audience. When audience members began to yawn and scratch their heads, he should have taken that as a sign to take a deep breath, control his nervousness, and try to make his points clearly.

## THINGS TO TRY

1. While in class, select a partner and give a one- to two-minute impromptu speech on a topic of your choice. Your partner will write down both negative and positive feedback to share with you, and you will do the same in return. Then team up with another pair of partners. You and your original partner will take turns giving the same speeches again, incorporating improvements suggested by your partner the first time around. The new partners in your group will likely give both negative and positive feedback. Listen carefully, and apply their advice. Now add another pair of partners to your group, for a total of six people, and give your speech one last time. Think of the feedback from all three sessions. If you received the same negative feedback more than once, you know where further improvement is needed. Did you feel more confident giving your speech the third time than you did the first time?

2. The next time you are in a theater or a crowded room, practice scanning. Think about your speech in your head as you scan the faces in the room. Practice varying the time you spend on each face and in various locations in the room. Be sure to look at people in the back of the room just as often as you make eye contact with those in the front.

3. Pay attention to how you meet people and the general first impression you receive from them. Ask yourself what it was that made you feel the way you do about the person. Did the person make you feel comfortable by smiling at you? Did he or she look you in the eye? Come across as sincere? If you can pinpoint the reasons for your own first impressions, you can better understand what an audience expects from a speaker (and adjust your own behaviors in order to make a good impression).

4. When practicing a speech you will give, pay attention to your gestures and body movements. Practice once using movements that you feel are appropriate and comfortable; then practice in front of a friend, and ask how appropriate they actually look. Are you using too many gestures? Too few?

## IF YOU'RE INTERESTED

*The Greatest Speeches of All Time* [DVD], published by the Nostalgia Company (Soundworks International, 1998)

> This two-volume collection offers footage of some of the greatest speeches of the modern era from a diverse group of influential, inspiring, and controversial figures, including Presidents John F. Kennedy, Ronald Reagan, Richard Nixon, and Bill Clinton, as well as Martin Luther King Jr., Barry Goldwater, and General Douglas MacArthur.

*Thank You for Smoking* (Fox Searchlight Pictures, 2006)

> This is the film version of Christopher Buckley's 1994 novel satirizing the lobbying industry. Nick Naylor "talks for a living" on behalf of the cigarette industry. A talented speaker with a gift for turning arguments around on people, Naylor is so proud of what he does and how well he does it that he takes his twelve-year-old son with him on business trips to teach him the craft. The film is a scathing yet lighthearted parody of spin doctors and the power of public speaking.

"An American Girl in Paris, Part Une," episode of *Sex and the City* (HBO, 2004)

> Chosen to speak at a breast cancer awareness event, outspoken Samantha struggles to come up with an inspiring speech. Midway through her prepared speech—sweating through a chemotherapy-induced hot flash—she tosses her notes, yanks off her wig, and speaks bluntly and honestly about the everyday challenges patients face while fighting the disease. Her exasperated gesture prompts the many cancer survivors in the audience to stand up, wigs removed, in a moment of sincere and heartfelt solidarity. A great illustration of the value of sincerity and authenticity in an inspirational speech.

*An Inconvenient Truth* (Paramount Classics, 2006)

> We described this documentary in Chapter 11, but it is worth a look in this chapter as well. See how Al Gore effectively uses his PowerPoint presentation without making his slide show the center of attention.

"The Day of Black Sun, Part 1: The Invasion," episode of *Avatar: The Last Airbender* (Nickelodeon, 2007)

If you take a look at Sokka's speech that we've described in the opening and closing of this chapter, you'll be able to critique it with a new understanding of anxiety and delivery techniques. Keep watching to see Sokka's father rescue him and salvage the invasion speech. It is interesting to see him speak in a calm but passionate manner, using main points and a clear organization.

# REAL REFERENCE ▸ A Study Tool

**Now that you have finished reading this chapter, you can**

Control your nervousness:

- ▸ **Communication apprehension (CA)**, fear or anxiety associated with communication, is a common barrier to effective delivery (p. 388).
- ▸ **Anxiety** is the feeling of dread that comes from our internal doubts about our ability to perform effectively (p. 388).
- ▸ An attack of anxiety about a specific communication situation is **state communication apprehension**, while enduring anxiety about communication in all contexts is categorized as **trait communication apprehension** (pp. 388–389).
- ▸ Anxiety can be controlled using **systematic desensitization**, designed to help you identify the feelings of tension and relaxation so that you can bring yourself into a relaxed state using a three-step process of deep muscle relaxation, construction of hierarchies of CA-eliciting stimuli, and graduated pairing of anxiety-producing and relaxing situations (p. 389).
- ▸ **Cognitive restructuring** is a second approach to reducing CA focusing on replacing negative **self-talk** with positive coping statements (p. 390).
- ▸ Confidence comes from preparation and skill building (p. 390).

Choose a delivery style best suited to you and your speaking situation:

- ▸ Speaking from manuscript is good when you need to get the details 100 percent right but can be static and dull (p. 391).
- ▸ Speaking from memory, referred to as **oratory**, doesn't invite rapport with the audience and is rare today (p. 392).
- ▸ Speaking spontaneously—when you're asked to speak with no warning beforehand—is known as **impromptu speaking** (p. 392).
- ▸ **Extemporaneous speaking** makes the speech look easy and impromptu, but it's actually based on an outline of key points and practice, practice, practice (p. 393).

Employ effective nonverbal cues:

- ▸ Use **pitch** to vary your sound range and avoid a **monotone** (p. 396).
- ▸ Cue the audience as to what's important by adjusting your **speaking rate** and **volume** (p. 396).
- ▸ Add drama to the speech by pausing for effect (p. 396).
- ▸ Speak clearly and precisely: Use proper **pronunciation**, practice careful **articulation**, and avoid **mumbling** (p. 398).
- ▸ If you have an **accent**, be aware of how it might influence your audience (p. 398).

Employ effective visual cues:

- ▸ Make brief eye contact with almost everyone, using the technique known as **scanning** (p. 400).
- ▸ Facial expressions and gestures must match the verbal message of your speech (p. 400).
- ▸ Maintain a steady, confident **posture** by positioning your legs at a distance equal to your shoulders, with slightly bent knees, in the stance known as **planting** (p. 402).

Connect with your audience:

- ▸ Share your passion for the topic with your audience (p. 403).
- ▸ Gauge the audience response, and adapt to it (p. 403).

Enhance your words with effective presentation aids:

- ▸ Sometimes an object or prop is better than words (p. 405).
- ▸ Explain what data mean, and let visuals display the numbers (p. 407).

Make efficient use of your practice time:

- ▸ Make sure the key words in your speaking outline are meaningful prompts (p. 408).
- ▸ Do a run-through with your presentation aids (particularly the electronic ones), and try to simulate the actual speaking conditions (p. 410).
- ▸ Focus on the message (p. 411).

**Erin Gruwell** makes learning relevant to her students' lives.

**Do you remember your favorite teacher** from elementary, middle, or high school? What was it about this teacher that made him or her so memorable? Most likely that teacher made you feel cared for and important; but he or she also probably captivated your attention with innovative and creative lessons that made you desire to learn more about a subject, be it math, English literature, or art. Teachers, from kindergarten instructors to college professors, face an important and daunting task every day: to inform a group of students at various levels of preparedness and interest about a topic so that the students can grow in knowledge and understanding of new material.

Dedicated teachers will go to great lengths to inspire students with their informative presentations. Hollywood has caught on to this truth in key scenes from famous "teacher movies." For example, the classic film *Stand and Deliver* (1988) features a scene in which teacher Jaime Escalante (played by Edward James Olmos) attempts to inform his uninterested students about fractions and percentages. He opens his lesson with a great attention getter by standing in front of the class dressed as a chef. He then proceeds to explain halves and quarters by using a tasty visual aid—an apple, knowing that food is typically of interest to high school students.

Similarly, in the film *Freedom Writers* (2007), Hilary Swank portrays real-life ninth-grade English teacher Erin Gruwell, who passionately wants to teach her students about literature, history, and writing—subjects that seem irrelevant to her racially divided students, who deal with gang violence on a daily basis. But Gruwell proves to be a master of audience analysis. She learns what matters to her students and finds opportunities to hear their voices, allowing her to develop creative and hands-on lessons to inform them about grammar, the Holocaust, classic literature—and even about the worlds and shared experiences of other racial groups in the class.

After you have finished
reading this chapter,
you will be able to

○ Understand the goals of
informative speaking

○ Describe each of the
eight categories of informative speeches

○ Outline the four major
approaches to informa-
tive speeches

○ Make your audience
hungry for information

○ Make your speech easy
to listen to

Few occupations require as much public speaking as teaching. Every day, educators must stand before an audience and deliver what are, essentially, informative speeches. The best teachers know how to analyze their audience and tailor their lectures to engage students quickly and completely. They organize their information clearly and efficiently, so students can learn it with ease. And they present information in an honest and ethical manner—they offer information, not opinions. We use the same type of informative speaking whenever we share information, teach something new, or help others understand an idea. In this chapter, we'll take a look at how you can use these same techniques to deliver competent informative speeches in any situation.

## The Goals of Informative Speaking

As you'll recall from Chapter 11, the purpose of **informative speaking** is to increase the audience's understanding or knowledge; put more simply, the objective is for your audience to *learn* something. But to be a truly effective informative speaker, your presentation must not only fill your listeners' informational needs but do so with respect for their opinions, backgrounds, and experiences. You also want to be an *objective* speaker, focusing on informing (not persuading) your audience, and you want to be an *ethical* speaker. In this section, we take a closer look at these goals and investigate ways that you can ensure that your speech remains true to them at every phase of development and delivery.

### Meeting the Audience's Informational Needs

Effective speakers engage their listeners because they have made the effort to understand the needs of their audience members. This is especially important in informative speaking. You want to avoid delivering a long list of facts that are already common knowledge because the object is for your audience to learn something new, something novel. But understanding your listeners' needs goes beyond knowing what they know. It also involves choosing an appropriate topic and making that topic relevant to your listeners. Let's take a look at these points using *Freedom Writers*'s Erin Gruwell as an example.

▶ *Gauge what the audience already knows.* Estimating the knowledge level of the audience helps determine where to begin, how much information to share, and at what level of difficulty the audience can understand and still maintain interest. When Erin Gruwell mentions the Holocaust in class, she realizes that most of her students have never even heard about the tragic and horrific events that took place in Nazi Germany. She introduces the topic in light of a very familiar topic, gang violence, stressing that the Nazis were one of the most dangerous gangs in history: "You think your gangs are tough? This gang took over countries!"

▶ *Decide on an appropriate approach to the topic.* Involving the listeners through the appropriate use of language and presentation aids gives the impression that the speaker has fine-tuned the speech for this particular group of people. Gruwell further engages her students by having them hear from Holocaust survivors, read *The Diary of Anne Frank,* and visit the Los Angeles Museum of Tolerance, where they passed through the simulated entrance to a concentration camp gas chamber. Now, you're probably thinking that Gruwell's tactics would be impossible in a three-to-five-minute speech in front of your classmates, and you would be right! But consider the types of sources that she uses: firsthand expert testimony, quotations from literature, haunting visual images, and personal experience. These sorts of things will captivate your audience and help them remember the new information you are teaching them.

▶ *Make it relevant to each member of the audience.* Always specifically connect the subject to the audience by pointing out how it is pertinent and useful to your listeners' lives. Certainly this was Gruwell's main objective in informing her students about the Holocaust. She wanted them to see that they were not alone in fearing violence and death on a daily basis—history speaks volumes about groups of people suffering from intolerance, injustice, and hatred. Whether the students were part of or affected by Hispanic, Cambodian, or African American gangs, they could all see themselves as Anne Frank; they could all see themselves as victims of a Holocaust.

**CONNECT**

Meeting your audience's information needs is important in various contexts. When you're running a meeting in a group (Chapter 9), gauge what your audience already knows and make the content of the meeting relevant. No one wants to sit through a two-hour meeting on details of a situation that the group members already understand. And don't make your topic—the reason you're gathered in the first place—seem confusing or irrelevant!

## Informing, Not Persuading

As you learned in Chapter 11, informative speaking serves as the base for persuasive speaking: in many cases, speakers inform audiences in hopes of persuading them to act or behave in a certain way. In a similar vein, persuasive speakers must first inform their audiences about certain facts and information before they can attempt to influence them. But while these two types of speaking are naturally related, it's important to recognize that informative and persuasive speeches differ in one very important way: an informative speech is intended to be **objective**—it presents facts and information in a straightforward and evenhanded way, free of influence from the speaker's personal thoughts or opinions. A persuasive speech, by contrast, is expected to be **subjective**—it presents facts and information from a particular point of view.

This means, essentially, that when delivering an informative speech, you must always remain objective; if you find yourself expressing an opinion or choosing only facts, information, or other material that supports your personal view, you are in fact delivering a persuasive speech. So when delivering an informative speech, it's important to examine your process at every step in the development of the speech to ensure that you are being truly objective. Some of the issues you'll need to evaluate are examined in Table 14.1 (see p. 420).

● **WHEN YOU'RE** speaking to an audience that is knowledgeable about your topic, you don't want to bore them with a long list of facts they already know. Tell them something new!

TABLE 14.1

INFORMATIVE VERSUS
PERSUASIVE SPEAKING

|  | Informative Speeches | Persuasive Speeches |
| --- | --- | --- |
| Approach | From a perspective of inquiry or discovery; the speaker researches a topic to find out what information exists and shares that information with an audience. | From a perspective of advocating a position or desired outcome; the speaker researches a topic to find information that supports a particular point of view and then tries to convince an audience to change an attitude or take some action based on that point of view. |
| Objectivity | The speaker reports information objectively, in the role of a messenger. | The speaker argues a case subjectively and speaks from a particular point of view. |
| Use of facts and information | The speaker sets out the current facts or state of affairs concerning the topic. | The speaker builds a case that he or she is passionate about and includes information that supports his or her favored position. |
| Expression of opinions | The speaker may provide others' opinions but refrains from giving his or her own. | The speaker provides others' opinions that support his or her own position or viewpoint; the speaker may mention differing opinions only to rebut or discredit them. |

## Speaking Appropriately and Ethically

Objectivity is not the only ethical consideration you must bear in mind when delivering an informative speech. Because communication is a powerful instrument for influencing people's attitudes, beliefs, and behaviors, we must consider the implications of our actions (Sides, 2000). As we've discussed throughout this book, an ethical speaker has a responsibility to an audience to provide information that is relevant and reliable in a way that is respectful of both the audience and the subject. The types of supporting material you offer (or do not offer) and the motives for why you are speaking on a particular subject reveal quite a bit about you as an ethical speaker. Remember, an ethical speaker provides information in an honest and truthful way and chooses appropriate topics for discussion. A fellow communication professor, who provided helpful feedback on this book, told us that one of her students gave an informative presentation on how to grow marijuana! No matter what your opinion is on the legalization of marijuana, its use is still illegal in the United States, so informing your audience about how to grow it is simply unethical.

Ethical speakers also always remember to avoid plagiarism by orally citing sources and providing a complete list of references at the end of a speech outline. If your speech misinforms your audience in any way, you are not offering an appropriate or ethical informative speech.

## Topics for Informative Presentations

When it comes to choosing a topic for an informative speech, there are countless options. You can speak, for example, about something very concrete, such as a person, place, thing, process, or event. In many cases, your topic will fit into more than one category: for example, a speech on emo music might include descriptions of the genre (thing) as well as of particular bands (people) and performances (events). You might also talk about the way the music developed over time (process). We'll take a look at eight categories for informative speech topics identified by the communication researchers Ron Allen and Ray McKerrow (1985).

---

### EVALUATING COMMUNICATION ETHICS

#### Ulterior Motives

As captain of the school swim team, you've been asked to deliver an informative speech to the school's alumni during homecoming week detailing the team's past three seasons and hopes for the future. You've outlined a short, simple speech that notes individual members' personal bests, team achievements, and the coach's laudable efforts to recruit promising high school athletes. When your coach reviews your speech outline, she asks you to include more about the many scholarships that the school makes available to athletes.

You know that the coach has many motives for asking you to include more information about scholarship money. She's hoping, first and foremost, to convince alumni to support the team financially, in order to entice more financially strapped but talented swimmers to choose your school. But you're feeling torn: you know that most of the money that goes to your school's sports programs is devoted to the larger and more popular basketball program. You're also feeling annoyed because four years ago, the coach recruited you as a high school scholar-athlete with a partial scholarship that she promised would grow to a full scholarship the following year. The full scholarship never materialized, and now you're about to graduate with huge student loans that you had thought you'd be able to avoid when you chose to attend this school over others that courted you.

As team captain, you're proud of your team's record and eager to inform the alumni about it. But you also don't want to give them information that you feel is somewhat misleading. What should you do?

**THINK ABOUT THIS**

❶ What are the ethical obligations of a speaker in preparing informative presentations? Can you ignore the coach's request and just say what you want to say?

❷ Is the coach's request really an attempt to inform alumni of what the swim program needs in order to persuade them to donate money?

❸ Are your motivations really ethical? Do you want to avoid talking about scholarship money because you think it will never materialize or because you're angry that the coach misled you?

● **THERE ARE** countless topics for an informative speech. Stonehenge, Eve Ensler, volcanic eruptions, and the Special Olympics are just a few of the possibilities.

Your audience is an important variable to consider as you choose your topic. Your goal in an informative presentation is to meet the audience's information needs, so you must understand their knowledge and interests. Before you decide to inform your audience about backyard gardening, solicit information about your listeners using the strategies in Chapter 11 (pp. 325–331). If you learn that most of your audience members live in apartments, they probably won't care about gardening in a backyard they don't have.

## People

If there's one subject that fascinates most people, it's other people. That's why shows like A&E television's *Biography* and E! Entertainment Television's *E! True Hollywood Story* enjoy such success; it's why we might sneak a peek at *In Touch Weekly* or the *National Enquirer* when we're stuck on line at the grocery store (even though we know very well that the cover story on Elvis's reincarnation and the woman giving birth to a watermelon cannot possibly be true.). And it's why you don't hang up the phone when your mother or father says, "Did you hear what happened to your cousin Leah?" The life of another person certainly makes for an interesting informative speech topic. You might lean toward giving a speech about someone who is famous (or infamous)—indeed, audiences are usually receptive to learning about someone who is famous simply because they revere or worship celebrity (Atkinson & Dougherty, 2006). Yet an obscure but interesting person can often be a great topic for a speech as well.

The key to giving a successful speech about another person is to focus on the person's human qualities as well as his or her achievements. Bear in mind also that you need not limit your speech to one person. For example, if you are talking about Mother Teresa, who devoted her entire life to helping India's poor, you might draw parallels between her life's work and that of 1999 Nobel Peace Prize nominee Dr. Catherine Hamlin. Known as the "Angel of Ethiopia," Hamlin has provided free medical care to young women suffering from the devastating effects of difficult childbirths. You might go on to talk about similar efforts by other women who have worked on humanitarian efforts in Third World countries, including some who are quite well known (Angelina Jolie) and others who are completely unknown (your aunt Eloise, who joined the Peace Corps at age sixty). In any case, the key is to show not merely what these people did but why and how they did it. You need to give your audience a real sense of who these people are. To meet this goal, your speech should include anecdotes, quotes, and stories that show the motivations behind their actions. Chapter 11 offers help in adding these speech supports.

## Places

Like people, places can be interesting and compelling topics for an informative speech. You might focus on an inspired description of a real but perhaps unfamiliar place (the surface of Mars, the Arctic tundra) or even a fictional one (the fires of Mount Doom in *The Lord of the Rings*). Even a very familiar place offers opportunities to provide audiences with some new information. For example, you might investigate the oldest building on your campus or in your town and detail some of its history in your speech. This will allow you not only to describe the place but also to talk about the people who designed and built it and how the building has been changed over the years.

## Objects and Phenomena

A third source of ideas for informative speeches consists of objects or phenomena. These speeches explore anything that isn't human, such as living things (like animals, plants, even entire ecosystems), as well as inanimate objects, such as your first car, an iPhone, or the *Mona Lisa*. Objects can also be imaginary things (unicorns) or hypothetical ones (a perpetual motion machine) or even entire phenomena (the history of break dancing, the competition between Apple and Microsoft).

## Events

Noteworthy occurrences (past and present) are good topics for informative speeches. Our understanding of history is shaped by events—the Civil War, the assassination of Martin Luther King Jr., the breakup of the former Soviet Union, the terrorist attacks of 9/11. At a more intimate level, events of personal significance can also make interesting and compelling topics for speeches.

You might build an informative speech around important, tragic, funny, or instructive events in your personal life—the day you went skydiving, your bar mitzvah, the death of a close friend, or the birth of your first child. Just remember that these stories of personal events must be ethical and truthful!

At this point, you may have many good topics for an informative speech. But if you need more ideas, remember the advice we offer in Chapter 11 on searching for a topic. Try brainstorming or clustering, soliciting ideas from others, or using the library and the Internet to identify possible topics. Always ask yourself: Is this topic interesting to me? Do I know enough about it? Is it a good topic for an informative speech?

## Plans and Policies

Allen and McKerrow's final category for informative speeches concerns plans and policies. In such speeches, the speaker tries to help an audience understand the important dimensions of potential courses of action (for example, privatizing Social Security or reinstating the military draft). In such speeches, the speaker does not argue for a particular plan or policy; he or she simply lays out the facts. Like issue speeches, plan and policy speeches can easily evolve into persuasive addresses, so you must be very careful to focus on objective facts; if you find yourself unable to keep your opinion from influencing your speech, consider a different topic.

## Approaches to Conveying Information

Once you have selected a topic for an informative speech, you can develop it in a variety of ways. Here we will briefly describe the four major approaches to informative speeches: description, demonstration, definition, and explanation.

### Description

Description is a way of verbally expressing things you have experienced with your senses. While most speeches use some type of description to add drama or clarity, some focus on this task more closely than others. The primary task of a **descriptive presentation** is to paint a mental picture for your audience; this type of speech allows the speaker to portray places, events, persons, objects, or processes clearly and vividly.

An effective descriptive speech begins with a well-structured idea of what you want to describe and why. As you move through the development process, you emphasize important details and eliminate unimportant ones, all the while carefully considering your audience as you think of ways to make your details more vivid. Descriptive speeches are most effective when the topic is personally connected to the speaker. Consider the following excerpt from a speech by Prince Harry of the United Kingdom. Delivered on the tenth anniversary of the death of his mother, Princess Diana, the speech focuses on offering a poignant snapshot of Diana as a mother rather than the Diana of the popular media.

> When she was alive we completely took for granted her unrivalled love of life, laughter, fun and folly. She was our guardian, friend and protector. She never once allowed her unfaltering love for us to go unspoken or un-demonstrated. She will always be remembered for her amazing public work. But behind the media glare, to us, just two loving children, she was quite simply the best mother in the world. We would say that, wouldn't we. But we miss her. She kissed us last thing at night. Her beaming smile greeted us from school. She laughed hysterically and uncontrollably when sharing something silly she might have said or done that day. She encouraged us when we were nervous or unsure. . . . But what is far more important to us now, and into the future, is that we remember our mother as she

would have wished to be remembered—as she was: fun-loving, generous, down-to-earth, entirely genuine. We both think of her every day. We speak about her and laugh together at all the memories. Put simply, she made us, and so many other people, happy. May this be the way that she is remembered. (Steel, 2007)

## Demonstration

On July 5, 2007, New York City resident Peggy Paul appeared on *The Rachael Ray Show* after telling the celebrity host that she could prepare a four-course gourmet dinner in her tiny apartment with no appliances except a microwave and a hot plate. Sound impossible? But what if she showed you? Rachael Ray (and Peggy Paul) have caught on to an important truth: often the best way to explain how something works is to demonstrate it. **Demonstration speeches** answer "how" questions—how to use an iPhone, how to bake a perfect pie crust, how to salsa dance, how to buy a used car—by show-

● **PEGGY PAUL** demonstrates her resourceful culinary abilities.

ing an audience the way something works. In this case, Peggy used a combination of explanatory narration and physical demonstration to show how she whips up baked apple pork chops, pear and gorgonzola salad, and chocolate hazelnut quesadillas as easily as we make peanut butter and jelly sandwiches, all the while making use of props, models, and other visual aids.

The key to delivering an effective demonstration speech is to begin with a clear statement of purpose and to follow a very straightforward organizational pattern. In most cases, a chronological pattern works best for a demonstration, with the process broken down into a number of steps that are presented in order of completion. Even with a strict chronological format, however, it can be helpful to introduce the completed end product first before going through the process of creating or completing it from the first step. The following outline of the steps in the process of decorative painting techniques illustrates a demonstration speech in chronological order. You can imagine the speaker showing each of the three methods.

> To demonstrate how to liven up a room with faux paint, you can use three popular types of decorative wall painting: color washing, sponging on, and ragging off.
> Color washing hides flaws in the wall and gives it a textured look. First, paint your wall a base color. Next, with short strokes, brush one or more glaze colors loosely over the contrasting base color (show photographs).
> The sponging-on technique gives the wall depth and texture with a variable pattern. Apply two or more coats of paint—satin, flat, semigloss, or

gloss—on your wall. After the base coat dries, apply a glaze coat using a sea sponge (show sea sponge and photograph).

Ragging off gives the wall a delicate, evenly textured appearance. Apply two base coats of two colors. While the second color is still wet, use a clean, dry rag (such as an old T-shirt) wrapped around a paint roller, and roll it across the wall (demonstrate this technique). Replace the rag after it becomes soaked with glaze mix.[1]

## Definition

Informative speaking often involves defining information; when you define something, you identify its essential qualities and meaning. Most informative speeches require that the speaker define a term or an idea. For example, in a speech about the work of a training and development consultant, you would define the term *benchmarking* for your listeners. By answering the question "What is benchmarking?" (the process of comparing your technique, program, or organization against the best in the field in order to aspire to their standards), you elevate your entire audience to a certain level of knowledge that enables them to understand your presentation.

Although we typically think of definitions as short entries in a dictionary, in fact a great many speeches (as well as books, journal articles, and Supreme Court decisions) are focused entirely on definitions. The main goal of **definitional speeches** is to provide answers to "what" questions. Such questions as "What is torture?" and "What is marriage?" have prompted heated debate in the halls of Congress (and elsewhere) in recent years, making it clear that defining terms is neither simple nor unimportant. As a speaker, you can approach a definitional speech in a variety of ways. A definition in a speech might use one of these approaches; a definitional speech might incorporate more or even all of them.

▶ An **operational definition** defines something by explaining what it is or what it does. For example, a *salsa* can be defined by what it is: "A *salsa* is a condiment, usually made of tomatoes, onions, and peppers, common in Spanish and Latin American cuisine." Alternatively, it can be defined by what it does: "*Salsas* are most commonly used as dipping sauces for fried tortilla chips, but they also work well alongside grilled fish."

▶ **Definition by negation** defines something by telling what it is not. For example, "A *salsa* is not the same as taco or piquante sauce."

▶ **Definition by example** defines something by offering concrete examples of what it is. For example, "*Salsas* include the basic tomato version you get at your local Mexican restaurant, as well as variants made from mangoes, pineapples, or tomatillos."

**CONNECT**

When offering definitions, competent speakers remember that words have *connotative meanings*—emotional meanings—for people (Chapter 3). Consider the words "marriage" and "torture." Even if you offer clear dictionary definitions of these terms, your audience may have strong attitudes about them that are influenced by their cultural background. As an informative speaker, you should be aware of the power of connotative meanings while not trying to persuade people to feel differently about terms.

---

[1]We thank Daniel Bernard and Cory Cunningham and their students for contributing the examples featured in this discussion.

▶ **Definition by synonym** defines something by using words that closely mean the same thing. For example, "a *salsa* is basically just a chunky sauce, similar to a chutney in Indian cuisine."

▶ **Definition by etymology** defines something by using the origin of a word or phrase. For example, "*Salsa* is the Spanish and Italian word for sauce, derived from the Latin word for 'salty.'"

As noted, definitional speeches can take one or more of these approaches to defining a specific term. In the following speech excerpt, for example, the speaker's goal is to define the concept of "nanotechnology." Note that the speaker's explanation is primarily operational.

*Nanotechnology* is a term often used but seldom described. According to Merriam-Webster's online dictionary, *nanotechnology* is "the art of manipulating materials on an atomic or molecular scale, especially to build microscopic devices." The main unifying theme is the control of matter on a scale, smaller than 1 micrometer, normally between 1 and 100 nanometers, as well as the fabrication of devices on this same length scale. The most difficult part of understanding nanotechnology is its size in relation to things we can see. Just take comfort in the fact that you will never have to visually observe nanotechnology.

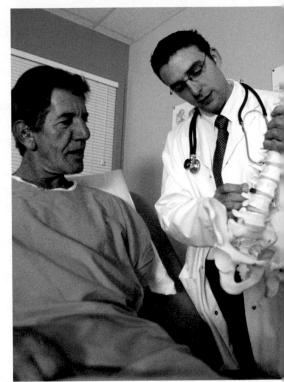

● **DOCTORS OFTEN** give explanatory speeches to their patients, explaining to them why they need a procedure done and how it will help them.

## Explanation

The basic purpose of most informative speeches is to create awareness or understanding; **explanatory speeches** answer the questions "Why?" or "What does that mean?" For example, a speech demonstrating how to upload a video to YouTube creates awareness of the process, whereas a speech explaining how YouTube works deepens understanding. Explanatory presentations delve into more complexity by providing reasons or causes and demonstrating relationships. To make your points in an explanatory speech, you must use interpretation and analysis. To this end, you should keep three main goals in mind.

### Clarifying Concepts

If an audience's chief difficulty rests with understanding the meaning and use of a certain term, the speaker should provide **elucidating explanations**—details that illuminate the concept's meaning and use. Good elucidating explanations do three things. First, they define a concept by listing each of its critical features. For example, notice in the following sentence how the speaker provides succinct illustrations for the concept of rhetoric: "Aristotle described the canons of rhetoric as consisting of *pathos* (appeal to emotions), *logos* (appeal to logic), and *ethos* (appeal to character)."

Second, elucidating explanations contrast examples of the concept. For instance, a speaker might suggest that the difference between gun control and partial gun control is as distinct as night and day. Finally, elucidating examples present opportunities for audiences to distinguish examples from contrasting examples by looking for a concept's critical features—for example, demonstrating that the most important features of a golf swing are keeping the left arm straight and keeping the head still.

One of our students opened an informative speech with an effective elucidating example that explained what "science" means. The student began:

> We all know what science is. It's what Carl Sagan and Mr. Wizard do, right? Since we know, we should agree on some basic ideas. How many people think biology is a science? [Nearly all hands rise.] How many think psychology is? [A few hands rise.] How about astrology? [A few hands rise.]

This speech was effective because after establishing that science is hard to explain, the speaker offered a definitional listing of the concept's critical features, gave an array of examples and nonexamples of science, and offered the audience opportunities to distinguish examples from contrasting examples with a short oral quiz.

## Explaining the Big Picture

If an idea is difficult chiefly because its complexity makes its main points—the "big picture"—hard to grasp, speakers should use a *quasi-scientific explanation*. Just as scientists try to develop models of the world, **quasi-scientific explanations** model or picture the key dimensions of some phenomenon for a typical audience. Speakers presenting complex topics to laypeople—topics such as how microchips work, the similarities and differences between levees and dams, or how DNA molecules pass along genetic information—should try to use quasi-scientific explanations. For example, we heard a particularly good quasi-scientific speech explanation for how radar works. The speaker made use of a simple comparison, noting that radar works essentially the way an echo does, except that it involves radio waves rather than sound waves. The presentation was effective because consistent references to this analogy clarified the speaker's main points.

Effective quasi-scientific explanations highlight the main points with such features as titles, organizing analogies, visual aids, and signposts ("The first key point is . . ."). Good quasi-scientific explanations also connect key points by using transitional phrases such as "for example," connectives ("because"), and diagrams depicting relationships among parts.

## Challenging Intuition

Sometimes the chief source of difficulty is that the idea is contrary to what intuition tells us. Let's say you're giving a speech on Newton's third law of motion, which states that for every action there is an equal and opposite reaction—that if, for example, one pushes a concrete wall, the wall exerts an equal and opposite force on the pusher. The law contains no difficult terms and little detail, but if you ask the average guy on the street, it just seems hard to believe. So how can you explain it to your audience?

When this is the case, speakers should design their talks as *transformative explanations*. **Transformative explanations** help people understand ideas that are counterintuitive. They are designed to help speakers transform "theories" about phenomena into more accepted notions. Speakers frequently use "why" questions if an audience is predisposed to skepticism or hostility. Thus an important function of transformative explanations is to calm the audience by telling why a condition exists or why an action is being taken. For example, if members of a city's board of education are fully informed about the factors that led the mayor to reduce the school budget, they are likely to be more disposed to work with the new budget than if they had not been told about the conditions that led to the cuts. Transformative explanations are most effective when they (1) state the audience's "implicit" or "typical" theory about a phenomenon, (2) acknowledge that this theory is reasonable, (3) demonstrate its inadequacy, (4) state the speaker's explanation, and (5) demonstrate that this explanation is in some way better than the other one.

## COMMUNICATIONACROSSCULTURES

### Let's Talk About Sex

Few subjects can make an audience as uncomfortable as sex. Religious beliefs, age, experience, and even politics inform not only people's views about sex but also the degree to which they are willing to discuss sexual matters publicly. In many cases, for example, it is unthinkable for Muslims to discuss sexual practices, especially with strangers or in public (El Ahl & Steinvorth, 2006). And in many villages in South Africa, sex is a taboo many women do not—or are told they should not—discuss (le Roux, 2006). And even in cultures without such restrictions, talking about sex is often considered impolite and can make listeners feel embarrassed or uneasy. In diverse populations like the United States, speakers—including health care providers, educators, social workers, and policymakers—must be responsive to the sensitive nature of sexual openness when they speak to audiences.

Some people are already learning how. One of these individuals is Heba Kotb (El-Magd, 2005), whose weekly television program offers information on sex to women throughout the Middle East. Kotb remains respectful of her audience's—and her own—religious beliefs by framing her discussion in a religious context, accompanying scientific information about the body with explanations of how Islamic texts address the subject at hand. Indeed, both medical experts and Islamic clerics participate in her show. She also pays careful attention to nonverbal communication: she wears the traditional Muslim headscarf and speaks in a serious tone and uses serious facial expressions. Kotb's sensitive approach, taking cultural taboos, norms, and beliefs into account, seems to allow her to talk more freely about this once forbidden topic.

**THINK ABOUT THIS**

❶ Kotb's approach to informing women about sex is a far cry from the often lighthearted and humorous approaches used by talk show hosts in the United States. How might her approach to informative speaking be perceived in the United States?

❷ Imagine that you have to give an informative speech about a sexual topic in front of your nursing class. How would you approach the subject? Would you handle it differently if you were speaking in front of your parents? Your religious community?

❸ Does gender play a role in public speaking as well? Would Kotb's message be as well received by her audience if she were a man?

# Guidelines for Informative Speeches

In Chapters 11 through 13, we provided the basics for developing, preparing, writing, and delivering effective presentations. In this section, we'll take a look at how you can tailor those basic strategies to the needs of an informative speech. Your first goal as a speaker is to get your audience interested in your topic. After all, if you can't demonstrate to your listeners that the subject is important or relevant, they are unlikely to give you their attention. But you'll also want to make sure that your speech is easy to listen to. It's hard to inform people who are struggling to keep up with you—or wishing they were somewhere else!

## Create Information Hunger

You want to make your audience hungry for the information you are going to present—get them excited about, or at least interested in, your topic. As you consider a topic for your informative speech, ask yourself, "How will this audience benefit from this information?" If you can't come up with a compelling reason for each person to pay attention to what you say, you need to rethink your topic.

● **KIMONOS** are beautiful, but you'll still need to make them relevant to your audience if you really want to draw them in.

### *Arouse People's Curiosity*

A few years ago, we watched a student inform the audience about kimonos. A kimono is a long, loose Japanese robe with wide sleeves traditionally worn with a broad sash as an outer garment. The speaker defined a kimono, contrasted different types of kimonos, and then demonstrated how to get into one and wear it properly. Although her speech was interesting and her demonstration was effective, in the end we had no idea why we had listened to it! The problem was that although she competently explained the historical and cultural significance of the kimono and gave a detailed demonstration of the process of designing and wearing one, she did little to make the audience interested in the subject as a whole. She might have fared better had she offered some sort of connection between the kimono and the daily lives of the audience. For example:

> Think of your favorite article or ensemble of clothing—that one perfect item or outfit that you just hope you have the occasion to wear. Would you have worn it ten years ago? Will it still be stylish ten years from now? Magazine editors and clothing designers like to throw the word *timeless* around, claiming that some things—the Armani suit, the little black dress—will never go out of fashion. But the truth is that style is a fickle thing, and lapels, hemlines, colors, and waistbands change with the tides. Today, I'm going to talk about an article of clothing that truly is timeless, one that is worn by both men and women and has remained largely unchanged in shape and form for over one thousand years. I'm speaking, of course, about the traditional garment of Japan, the kimono.

Here we've piqued people's interest by asking them first to think about themselves—something they own or wish to own. We then draw them into our subject, the kimono, by contrasting it with what Westerners tend to consider "classic" fashion. Such comparisons and personalization of the subject can help keep the audience interested. We might, for example, go on to show ways in which the kimono has influenced Western fashion or compare the time involved in getting into a kimono to that of modern Western clothing.

## *Work Your Topic*

But what if you can't change the topic? Sometimes, as in a speech class or at a convention, you may have the luxury of choosing a topic that you find interesting and engaging. But in many real-world situations, you may be asked to explain, define, describe, or demonstrate something that strikes you as boring or irrelevant. A CEO will frequently need to address shareholders with reports of profits and losses, for example, and spokespersons for government agencies are often required to make statements about public policies or current events.

In every one of these cases, the speaker must find the relevance of the subject and establish it for the audience quickly and assertively. If your topic seems somehow disconnected from your audience, it's your job to find the relevance. For example, can you save the audience money or time? Can you help people do something better (such as make higher grades) or improve quality (such as increasing the worth of a stamp collection)? Even if the benefit is not for the short term, will listening to your speech help them in some way in the future, once they become parents or graduate students or homeowners? Unless you present a clear benefit that people can derive from listening to you, you will not get or keep their attention.

● **PEOPLE USUALLY** groan at the thought of sitting through a boring software presentation, but if the speaker makes it relevant to their needs, they might change their minds.

For example, imagine that you are an office manager and need to deliver a presentation to your colleagues explaining how to fill out the company's new expense reports. Your first job, then, is to get them interested in what they might initially perceive as an unnecessary and time-consuming presentation about a boring and mundane task. One way to do this is to show them that learning how to do this task will benefit them in some way:

> I know it's hard to get excited about something as mundane as filing expense reports. But the good news is that our new electronic transmittal system will get your reimbursements to you faster and more reliably. As you know, it typically takes four to six weeks for an expense report to be routed, approved, and transmitted to accounts payable and another two weeks for accounts payable to cut the check. With this new system, we'll be able to have funds deposited directly to your bank account in as little as ten business days. So with that in mind, let's take a look at how the new system works.

**AND YOU?**
What techniques can you use to look at a subject and find its relevance to you or to your audience? How can these tactics help you create more interesting informative speeches?

By clearly connecting the subject with the lives and needs of your listeners, you're more likely to have their attention as you demonstrate the less interesting aspects of the process. If you find that you cannot find the subject's relevance, you may need to refine or revise the topic.

# real communicator

**NAME:** Nick Hengen
**HOMETOWN:** Rapid City, South Dakota
**OCCUPATION:** Graduate instructor at the University of Minnesota
**FUN FACT:** I played in punk rock bands in high school.

I'm a teaching assistant at the University of Minnesota. I've been doing this for a couple of years now, but I still remember—with perfect clarity—the first time I led a discussion section. I was standing at the front of the classroom, wearing the one tie I own.

"So what did everyone think about the Robert Frost poems?" I asked.

Silence.

"Were they good?"

Silence.

"Bad?"

Silence. Only forty-eight minutes left in the class period. I loosened my tie, getting chalk all over it. Forty-seven minutes to go.

I thought we'd all just sit around in a circle and discuss poetry. But before we could get to that point, I needed—as the teacher—to provide my students with some information; in other words, I needed to deliver an informational presentation. OK, not too scary. I took a class on public speaking in college. Step one is creating information hunger. Why do my students want to hear about Robert Frost's poems? I decided I'd start with Robert Frost the person.

People love hearing about people. In creating information hunger, I've found that biography is a good starting point. I like to balance the big accomplishments (Frost's four Pulitzer Prizes) with the wackier, more human facts. For instance, Frost married his high school sweetheart, was consistently late to his college classes (I advise against this), joined a fraternity, dropped out of college (I also advise against this), was a failure as a chicken farmer, read his work at John F. Kennedy's presidential inauguration, visited the USSR as a goodwill ambassador, and was born in California and not New England as one might expect. I also bring supplementary material into class when going over Frost's biography. I play audio of him reading his work. I show the episode of *The Simpsons* in which Krusty the Clown dumps a bucket of snow on Frost's head. My intent with all this is to get my students curious and to create some information hunger about Frost and his work.

However, I still need to make the information *relevant* to each student's life. The easiest way for me to do this is to get my audience involved. I have the class members write poems of their own. In order to think about creative works, it helps to write creative works. I let my students know that these poems won't be graded; therefore, the stakes are low, and no one has anything to lose. And I tie this assignment specifically to Frost's work, asking students to write poems that tackle some of his more frequent themes: love, loss, war, death, destructive relationships, violent emotions. Everyone has some kind of experience with these things. Articulating these ideas through writing allows students to access Frost's poems on a more personal level.

Suddenly, the silence is gone. People are talking. The informational presentation becomes interactive. Just as I'd hoped, we are sitting around in a circle and discussing poetry.

## Make It Easy

Creating a good informative speech is hard work; listening to one should not be! Your job as speaker is to find and distill a lot of information in a way that is easy for your audience to listen to, absorb, and learn. In short, you need to do your listeners' work for them. To this end, there are a number of objectives to bear in mind as you prepare your speech.

### *Choose a Clear Organization and Structure*

People have orderly minds. When they are presented with new information, they need to organize it in a way that makes sense to them. You can help them in this endeavor by organizing your speech around a clear and logical structure. Recall from Chapter 12 that there are a number of arrangements for presentations, including chronological, topical, and spatial organizations; problem-solution, cause-effect, and narrative patterns; and arrangements based on motivated sequences. Your choice of organizational pattern will depend on your topic, and every speech will have several organizational options.

For example, if you're planning to deliver a speech on the history of punk rock, you might choose a chronological organization, beginning with mid-1960s garage bands and following through the 1970s peak with bands like the Sex Pistols and the Ramones, through the post-punk era, and ending with modern punk-influenced bands like Green Day or the Libertines. But you might find it more interesting to approach the topic spatially, noting differences between American and British punk, or even causally, demonstrating how the form arose as a reaction to the popular music that preceded it as well as to the economic and political climate of the times. Table 14.2 (see p. 436) offers some ideas for using organizational approaches to different informative topics, in addition to considering the approaches we discussed earlier (definition, description, demonstration, and explanation).

### *Emphasize Important Points*

Another way to make it easier for your audience to follow and absorb your speech is to clarify what the important parts are. As you learned in Chapter 12, one of the best means to achieve this is by using a preview device and a concluding

**CONNECT**

As you learn in Chapter 5, there are many challenges to competent listening. Your audience members have an obligation to overcome these barriers, but you (as the speaker) must help them. If you've analyzed your audience (Chapter 11), you've likely chosen a topic and support material that your audience will care about. And don't forget that your nonverbal and verbal communication should also be appropriate when speaking (Chapter 13).

● **IF YOUR SPEECH** is on punk rock, you might organize it spatially, moving from the British band the Clash to the American band the Ramones.

**TABLE 14.2**

## TYPES OF INFORMATIVE SPEECHES, SAMPLE TOPICS, INFORMATIONAL STRATEGIES, AND ORGANIZATIONAL PATTERNS

| Subject Matter | Sample Topics | Informational Strategy (*definition, description, demonstration, explanation*) | Suggested Organizational Patterns |
|---|---|---|---|
| Speeches about objects or phenomena | • Personal digital assistants<br>• Dialects<br>• Comparison of weight-loss diets<br>• El Niño wind patterns in the western United States | *Define* and *describe* the object or phenomenon in question. Depending on your specific speech purpose, either conclude at that point or continue with an in-depth *explanation* or a *demonstration* of the object or phenomenon. | You might use a *spatial* pattern if you are explaining how a geographic positioning system (GPS) works in cars. Other patterns that could be used for speeches about objects include *topical, problem-solution,* and *cause-effect.* |
| Speeches about people | • Authors<br>• Humanitarians<br>• Inventors<br>• Political leaders<br>• Athletes<br>• Unsung heroes | Paint a vivid picture of your subject using *description*. Use *explanation* to address the person's or group's significance. | *Narrative* patterns could be useful for speeches about people since stories can include rich details about a person's life. Other patterns that could be used for speeches about people include *motivated sequence* and *chronological*. |
| Speeches about events | • MTV Awards<br>• Democratic or Republican national conventions<br>• Battle of the Bulge<br>• Iraq War<br>• Olympic Games | Use *description* to paint a vivid picture. Use *explanation* to analyze the meaning of the event. | You might use a *chronological* pattern for a topic focusing on events if time or sequence is relevant to your purpose. Other patterns that could be used for speeches about events include *motivated sequence, problem-solution,* and *spatial*. |
| Speeches about processes | • How Tsunamis form<br>• How the thyroid regulates metabolism<br>• How to practice "power yoga"<br>• Using visualization in sports | If physically showing a process, rely on *demonstration*. If explaining a process, vary strategies as needed. | *Cause-effect* patterns of speech organization are helpful in explaining processes of various kinds. Additional patterns of organization could include *spatial, problem-solution,* or *chronological*. |
| Speeches about issues | • Police brutality<br>• Alternative theories to evolution<br>• Political issues in the Middle East<br>• Trade deficits<br>• Climate change<br>• No Child Left Behind Act | Focus on *description* and *explanation*. | *Problem-solution* is a strong choice for organizing speeches about issues. Other helpful patterns for issues include *topical, spatial,* and *cause-effect*. |

| Speeches about concepts | • Global warming<br>• Artificial intelligence<br>• Chaos theory<br>• Nanotechnology<br>• Free speech | Focus on clear *definitions* and *explanations*; the more difficult a concept is, the more ways you will want to define and explain it. Vivid *description* can also be useful. | Consider *topical* organizational patterns for speeches about concepts, as well as the *narrative* pattern. Other patterns that might work well include *spatial* and *problem-solution*. |

Source: O'Hair, Stewart, & Rubenstein (2007), p. 23. Adapted with permission.

summary. The preview device tells the audience what you are going to cover ("First, I will discuss X, second, Y, and third, Z"). A concluding summary reviews what the audience heard during the speech ("Today, I talked about X, then showed you Y, and finally, discussed Z").

Careful and deliberate use of phrases like "The key issue here is . . ." and "I have three main points regarding this piece of legislation" can also signal to your audience that you're about to say something important. In some cases, you might actually highlight what is important by saying so. You may choose to be even more direct, saying, "This is what I really want you to remember," or "The most important thing I want you to take away from this presentation is this." When you use phrases like these, you're not only supporting the organization of your speech but also giving people useful tools for organizing the information as they listen. It's important to make certain, however, that you don't contradict yourself. If you say, "I have one key point to make," and you then list four points of equal importance, you will likely confuse (and annoy) your audience.

## Don't Overwhelm Your Audience

Have you ever sat through a lecture or a presentation where the speaker seemed to give far too much information? Sitting through an endless stream of subtopics, subpoints, examples, facts, and statistics can wear an audience out. Ironically, too many points can make a speech seem pointless, and an overabundance of facts and statistics can make it difficult to follow and impossible to retain. Research shows that message receivers' attention and interest levels drop significantly due to information overload. Simply put, too much information overwhelms the audience (Van Zandt, 2004).

Your goal, then, is to keep your presentation as simple as possible so that audiences will find it easy to follow. As you review and rehearse your speech, critically evaluate each and every fact, point, example—indeed, every word—to make certain that it makes a real contribution to your speech. Eliminate anything that is redundant or goes off on a tangent. You want to strike a perfect balance by telling your listeners just what they need to know to understand your topic—nothing more, nothing less.

## Build on Prior Knowledge

Another way to make your speech easier to listen to and retain is to relate old ideas to new ones. In other words, introduce concepts that are new by relating them to familiar ideas. People are more open to new ideas when they understand how they relate to things they already know about. In an informative speech about successful Internet fashion businesses, you might discuss the concept of the "virtual model image." Instead of trying on clothes in a store (a familiar idea), shoppers can see how certain garments would look on their particular body types. By supplying your measurements online, you can visualize what you would look like in outfits by using the virtual model image (new idea).

## Define Your Terms

Defining your terms is not just for definitional speeches. As we've emphasized throughout this book, words are symbols that carry meaning, and it's important to use terms in a way that all parties understand if communication is to be competent. When delivering a speech, that means choosing terms that your audience will know and understand—and providing clear definitions for any words they might not. If at any point in your speech, audience members find themselves wondering what or who you are talking about, you will begin to lose their attention. When a term comes up that requires definition, you must explain it clearly and succinctly before moving on; for example, "For those of you who are unfamiliar with the term, *rhinoplasty* is the technical name for cosmetic or reconstructive surgery on a person's nose." If you think an audience is familiar with a word but just want to be sure, you can simply allude to a more common synonym: "People tend to think of rhinoplasties—commonly referred to as 'nose jobs'—as cosmetic in nature, but in fact many are performed to help improve nasal functioning."

Note that definitions are often necessary for proper nouns as well. Audiences may not have a strong background in geography, politics, or world events, so it can be useful to identify organizations and individuals in the same way that you would define a term: "People for the Ethical Treatment of Animals, or PETA, is the largest animal rights organization in the world," or "Colin Powell, a former U.S. Army general and secretary of state under President George W. Bush, noted that . . ." If you can define words and identify people, places, and things in a way that is smooth and diplomatic, you will enable audience members who are unfamiliar with them to continue to participate in your presentation. At the same time, you'll gain the confidence of audience members who do know the terms when you explain them accurately.

## Use Interesting and Appropriate Supporting Material

Select examples that are interesting, exciting, and clear, and use them to reinforce your main ideas. Examples not only support your key points but also provide interesting ways for your audience to visualize what you are talking about. If you are giving a speech about the movie career of Clint Eastwood, you would provide examples of some of his most popular films (*Dirty Harry, In the Line of Fire*), his classic films (*Fistful of Dollars, Hang 'Em High*), his lesser-known films (*The First Traveling Saleslady, Honkytonk Man*), and his directorial efforts (*Unforgiven, Mystic River*). You might also provide quotes from reviews of his films to show the way Eastwood has been perceived at different points in his career.

When you are offering examples to explain a concept, it's important to choose examples that your audience will understand. Some examples may be

● REFERENCING *COLUMBO* in your speech about cop shows might work well for an audience of baby boomers, but it will probably go right over the heads of today's teenagers—*The Wire* will be more familiar to them.

familiar enough to your audience that you can make quick references to them with little explanation. If you are giving a speech on city planning and rebuilding after disasters today, you could probably mention Lower Manhattan after 9/11 or New Orleans after Hurricane Katrina, and almost any adult member of your audience will get it. But other examples or audiences might require more detail and explanation. For example, if you are giving a speech about conformity, you might wish to use as an example the incident in Jonestown, Guyana, in 1978, when more than nine hundred members of a religious cult committed mass suicide by drinking cyanide-laced punch. As with many aspects of delivering a speech, audience analysis is crucial: if you are speaking to an audience of people in their late teens and early twenties, you'll need to offer a good deal of explanation to make this example work. However, an audience consisting mainly of baby boomers, historians, or social psychologists would require little more than a brief reference to "Jonestown" to get the point of the example.

## Use Appropriate Presentation Aids

Presentation aids help audiences follow and understand the information you present in your speech. As you will recall from Chapter 13, the value that effective presentation aids add to your speech can be immense (Mayer, 2001). Such aids can be especially helpful in informative speeches. For example, in an informative speech about the importance of a person's credit score, the speaker might show (via slides, slideware, or handouts) sample credit reports from the three main credit bureaus: TransUnion, Experian, and Equifax. Seeing this information in addition to hearing about it will underscore the importance of your message: everyone has a credit report and a credit score. By viewing the information while hearing the oral message, audience members will understand what to look for in their own credit reports and how to go about correcting any mistakes.

Informative speeches also benefit greatly from the use of graphic presentation aids. In a speech describing a process, for example, a flowchart outlining the steps you describe in your speech can help audiences visualize how the process works. Since many informative speeches include a wealth of numerical or statistical information, graphs can be very helpful presentation aids. If you take time to think of the best ways to enhance your speech and put forth the effort to create professional, imaginative presentation aids, your speech will be a success. Furthermore, the combination of hearing your message (the speech content) and seeing your message (through visual or audio presentation aids) helps the audience retain the information in your informative speech.

## WIREDFORCOMMUNICATION

### Learning via Podcast

In 2004, Duke University made news by giving each first-year student an iPod. Students may have been happy to have an additional tool for carrying portable music, but the university's intention was academic. Instructors at the university would be recording their lectures, as well as additional supplementary material, and making them available as podcasts, which students could easily download and play back on their computers, iPods, or other MP3 players. And while students and instructors are not entirely in agreement over the experiment—some have argued that it is more marketing than education—the program has continued, and other schools are following suit (Read, 2005).

Of course, audio recordings of lectures and presentations are nothing new. For decades, speakers have made their presentations available on audiocassette or, more recently, CD. And corporations and consultants have long offered audio training seminars on cassette so that employees could learn on the road. Podcasting makes producing and distributing audio files cheaper and more convenient than ever before. So what's all the fuss about?

In fact, recordings of informative presentations have proved valuable in a number of ways. For auditory learners—learners who prefer to take in information through the aural channel—listening to a playback of a presentation is an effective strategy for retaining information. Any student who may have missed something while taking notes or may not have understood something in the lecture can play back the troublesome parts; this is an especially helpful tool for nonnative speakers of English. And podcasts allow all students to compare their notes to the speech to see if they missed anything or to make up a missed class (Kaplan-Leiserson, 2005).

**THINK ABOUT THIS**

❶ What are the benefits of having an audio file available? Why is podcasting more effective than old-fashioned analog recordings?

❷ Are downloaded presentations as effective as live ones? Can they replace live presentations, or should they just supplement them?

❸ What kinds of presentations do you think would work best as podcasts? What kinds would not work well? Are podcasts useful outside academia?

# what about you?

○ **Assessing Your Speech**

1. When it comes to your audience's informational needs, you
   A. Really want your listeners to learn something new, so you've considered how much they know, how to approach the topic, and how to make it relevant.
   B. Know how much your audience knows about the topic, but you feel pretty clueless about how to make it relevant to each audience member.
   C. Hey, the topic was new to you—isn't that enough?

2. Your speech topic is informative rather than persuasive because
   A. You feel confident that you can be objective when presenting important information.
   B. You know that you have a strong opinion on the topic, and you feel pretty sure that you might be able to prevent that from influencing your speech.
   C. When you present the information, your audience will be persuaded to agree with your opinion, even if you don't state it outright.

3. As far as your speech topic and approach go,
   A. You're confident you've selected appropriately for an informative speech. For example, you're giving a speech on making ice cream (a process) using a demonstration (an approach).
   B. You want to speak about a person, Corrie ten Boom, but aren't sure what approach to take—should you *describe* how she helped hide Jews during World War II? Should you *explain* the religious beliefs that caused her to do so?
   C. You just can't get that persuasive speech topic and approach out of your head, can you? It's unforgettable!

4. When it comes to making your informative speech easy to listen to,
   A. You are working with a strong organization and clearly defined terms, and you know how and when to emphasize important points.
   B. You have some pretty cool supporting material and nifty visual aids, but when it comes to the whole speaking part, well . . .
   C. We talked about organization two chapters ago. Surely that doesn't apply here!

**If your responses were mostly A's:** Congratulations! You're ready to give an informative speech.

**If your responses were mostly B's:** You might benefit from a chat with your instructor or a friend to help you grasp what's most exciting about your topic and how to best inform your audience about it.

**If your responses were mostly C's:** Time to reread this chapter!

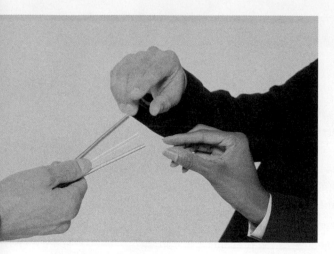

Let's take a look at a speech Dan Bernard gave when he was an undergrad at California State University, Fresno. Dan has chosen to inform his audience (fellow students) about an important health issue: asthma. Dan's speaking outline is presented following his speech.

## Sample Student Speech

### Daniel Bernard
*California State University, Fresno*

### Asthma: Breathe Easy

● **A FUN PROP** that your audience can interact with is a great way to grab their attention at the start of your speech.

*(Dan begins by passing out straws to everyone in the room.)* I would like you to take the straws I have passed out and put them up to your mouth. Now take a deep breath through the straw. Only inhale and exhale through the straw. *(Dan pauses for a few seconds.)* OK, stop. Was it hard for many of you to breathe that way? The difficulty you all had breathing is very similar to what an asthma attack feels like. ●

● This is a great way to get everybody's attention and get the audience involved in the speech early on.

Today I will speak about types of asthma, avoiding asthma attacks, and what to do if an attack happens, as you will likely encounter someone with this common condition. ●

● Dan clearly outlines his thesis and previews his main points.

Let me begin by explaining what asthma is. According to the Asthma and Allergy Foundation of America, the AAFA, in 2006, asthma is a disease of the lungs that blocks or narrows the airway, making it hard for the person to breathe. An asthma attack, according to *Help Your Child Gain Control over Asthma,* published in 2004 by the United States Environmental Protection Agency, the EPA, occurs when the airway is so constricted that the lungs do not get enough air to breathe. ●

● Dan offers a clear definition (specifically, an operational definition) to help his audience understand his topic.

There are two main types of asthma: allergic and nonallergic. According to the Asthma and Allergy Foundation of America in 2006, allergic asthma is caused by an external factor, often triggered by dust, mite allergens, pollen, mold, or pet dander. Nonallergic asthma, the AAFA explains, is caused by internal factors, such as anxiety, stress, exercise, hyperventilation, or exposure to smoke or to cold or dry air. ●

● Dan offers oral citations throughout his speech.

Now that I have explained what asthma is and the two main types of asthma, allergic and nonallergic, I will discuss what you can do to avoid an asthma attack. ●

● Dan transitions into his second main point.

To prevent an asthma attack, one must be familiar with what can potentially trigger an attack. According to a pamphlet obtained from the University Health Center titled *Asthma,* the biggest factor in avoiding an asthma attack is to find out what triggers an attack and then reduce the amount of exposure to elements that might cause an attack.

For example, the Centers for Disease Control and Prevention, the CDC, suggest, in a 2006 article titled "Asthma Speaker's Kit for Health Care Professionals" that I consulted online, that to reduce exposure to dust mites, one might wash bed linens frequently, wash stuffed animals in hot water, and remove curtains and replace them with shades or blinds. •

• Inclusion of credible and recognizable sources lends support to Dan's assertions.

There are several other external and internal factors to consider, and numerous medications and inhalers are available to prevent and treat asthma attacks. For those of you who would like more information on how to avoid an asthma attack, I'll be handing out some pamphlets that you can take home at the conclusion of this speech.

Now that I have spoken to you about how to avoid a possible asthma attack, I will tell you what you should do if someone is having an asthma attack. •

• Dan transitions into his third main point.

If someone is having an asthma attack, there are several things you can do to help. •

• Here Dan makes the speech information very personal and very relevant to each audience member.

If the person having the attack is you, remember to slow your breathing and take your time getting your medicine or inhaler. You want to make sure you take the medicine that reduces the attack and not your regular prevention medicine. In addition, let the people around you know what to do if you have an asthma attack. According to the Environmental Protection Agency, you should create an "asthma action plan" and let others know what it consists of. This way, if you have an attack, you and those around you will be well prepared to reduce the attack quickly.

The CDC has identified asthma as the leading chronic illness in children and youth in the United States. This means that you are very likely to witness an attack at some point. Familiarize yourself with the warning signs of an attack. According to the AAFA, symptoms might include coughing, wheezing, shortness of breath, and a feeling of tightness in the chest. Ask if you can help the person. Perhaps you can assist in locating the medicine the person needs or remind the person to breathe slowly and relax. These are only a few of the ways in which you can help someone struggling with an asthma attack.

So now you know what asthma is and what types exist. You know how to avoid an asthma attack. And you know what to do if you or someone you know has an asthma attack. •

• The speaker reminds the audience of his main points and thus provides a transition into the conclusion.

I hope that this presentation will be of use to you in the future; after all, asthma is a serious lung disease affecting over seventeen million Americans, according to the EPA in a 1999 brochure titled *Your Children Will Breathe Easier.* Thank you. •

• Dan closes with some impressive facts and statistics backed up by a reliable source.

Speaking Outline

Asthma: Breathe Easy

Daniel Bernard, California State University, Fresno

**TOPIC:** The lung disease asthma

**GENERAL PURPOSE:** To inform

**SPECIFIC PURPOSE:** To inform my audience about asthma, a common condition affecting 17 million Americans.

**THESIS STATEMENT:** Today I will speak about types of asthma, avoiding asthma attacks, and what to do if an attack happens, as you will likely encounter someone with this common condition.

**Attention Getter:** Pass out straws and have everyone breathe through them. Hard to breathe? Like asthma attack. [EYE CONTACT]

**Thesis/Preview of Main Points:** Inform about asthma: what it is and types, avoiding asthma attack, what to do if someone around you has attack. [PAUSE]

I.  What is asthma?

   A. Disease of the lungs, narrow airways, hard to breathe.

   B. Asthma attack = airways so constricted that lungs don't get breath
      (*Help Your Child Gain Control over Asthma*, 2004, EPA).

   C. Two types (Asthma and Allergy Foundation of America, 2006)

      1.  allergic (dust, mite, pollen, mold, pet)

      2. nonallergic (anxiety, stress, exercise, hyperventilation, smoke, cold/dry air)

**Transition:** I explained asthma, now discuss how to avoid attack.

II.  Preventing attack = understanding triggers.

   A. Reduce exposure to triggers (University Health Center pamphlet *Asthma*)

   B. CDC: avoid dust mites by washing sheets and stuffed animals and replacing
      curtains with blinds (online article, "Asthma Speaker's Kit for Health Care
      Professionals," 2006)

   C. Medication and inhalers (Note: mention pamphlets but don't pass out now)

**Transition:** [Don't speed up] You know how to avoid attack but what to do if someone has one?

III. You can help someone with asthma attack
    A. If you have attack
        1. Slow breathing
        2. Get your inhaler
        3. Let people know (have "action plan" according to EPA)
    B. Be familiar with symptoms: coughing, wheezing, shortness of breath, tightness in chest
    C. If someone else has attack
        1. Ask if you can help
        2. Remind person to breathe slowly

**Transition:** I informed you about asthma: what it is and types, avoiding asthma attack, what to do if someone around you has attack. [PAUSE]

**Conclusion:** I hope my speech will help you because 17 million Americans have asthma
(EPA brochure, *Your Children Will Breathe Easier*, 1999). Might happen to you or someone you know. [NOTE: Pass out brochures]

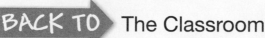

# BACK TO    The Classroom

At the beginning of this chapter, we talked about teachers as public speakers entrusted with an incredibly difficult yet important job: informing students about various topics and engaging their interest in order to inspire them to learn more. We've seen examples from two famous Hollywood films about various ways that teachers can achieve their informative aims: Jaime Escalante mastered the captivating opening and the use of effective visual aids. And Erin Gruwell learned to analyze her audience, figured out what mattered to her listeners, and related content to the very heart of her students' lives. But what about your beloved middle school history teacher? How did he or she use the suggestions and tips we've offered in this chapter? Let's say you're learning about World War II:

▶ Your teacher is planning an informative lesson on an event. You may spend a later class period learning about some of the key people involved in the war, and you will likely learn about many of the places affected by battle, but the focus is still on the war as a global event. This is an entirely appropriate plan for an informative speech, assuming that your teacher is not seeking to persuade you to change your thoughts about the war or adopt a particular point of view.

▶ Your teacher will build on prior knowledge by showing how this unit on World War II relates to material the class has studied before. For example, if you have just learned about the Great Depression, he or she might make the point that the emerging wartime economy was largely responsible for ending the Great Depression.

▶ Your teacher can also make clear connections to students' lives by linking the events of World War II in general to things with which students are more familiar. He or she might reference war films like *Saving Private Ryan* (1998) or *Pearl Harbor* (2001) or the miniseries *Band of Brothers* (2001). The teacher could effectively describe the shock the nation felt after the Pearl Harbor attack, for example, by comparing it to the terrorist attacks of September 11, 2001, which occurred during the students' lifetime.

## THINGS TO TRY

1. Review the speech on asthma reprinted in this chapter. What category does the topic of this speech fall into? Which approaches (description, demonstration, definition, explanation) did the speaker use, and was he successful in using those approaches? Did the speaker prove himself to be reliable and well informed? In what ways did he attempt to create information hunger and make the speech easy to listen to? Was he successful?

2. Informative speeches are everywhere—in your classroom, on the news, and in your community. Watch an informative speech (or read a transcript, available online from many government agencies' and officials' Web sites). Look to apply the concepts you have learned in this chapter to these informative presentations. For example, is the presentation well organized and well delivered? Does the speaker or author present information objectively? At any point in the speech, do you feel as though the speaker is trying to persuade you to do or believe something? It's important to be a critical listener in order to catch the often subtle differences between informing and persuading.

3. Think of a topic that you find excruciatingly dull (for example, balancing your checkbook, studying for a required course you don't like, or taking a summer or part-time job doing something utterly mind-numbing). What would you do if you had to give an informative presentation on such a subject? Based on the information presented in this chapter, can you think of ways to build a presentation on the topic that is informative and interesting? As strange as this task may sound, it is likely that you will have to do something like this at times in your career. (Recall the example from this chapter on informing employees about the new electronic reimbursement system.)

4. Imagine a process you do every day, such as driving a car. Think about how you would explain the process to someone who's never done it or even seen it done before. Consider different ways you could make the level of the presentation appropriate for different audiences. Talking to a child, for example, you might simply say that pressing on the gas pedal makes the car go; you might offer more detail when speaking to adults, explaining how the car works.

## IF YOU'RE INTERESTED

*The Visual Display of Quantitative Information* (2nd ed.), by Edward R. Tufte (Cheshire, CT: Graphics Press, 2001)

This classic of graphic design provides a direct and thorough evaluation of the best ways in which to present statistics and other numerical data in clear and interesting graphic displays. A useful guide for speakers wishing to include visual aids in presentations, as well as anyone concerned with making data more accessible.

*Jimmy Carter and the Energy Crisis of the 1970s: The "Crisis of Confidence" Speech of July 15, 1979: A Brief History with Documents,* edited by Daniel Horowitz (New York: Bedford/St. Martin's, 2005)

This reader offers an in-depth analysis of Carter's speech, explaining the ramifications of the Arab oil embargo of 1978–1979 to the American public. In it, Carter drew connections between the immediate problem of the United States' growing reliance on foreign oil and what he considered larger, more spiritual problems plaguing the nation.

*Freedom Writers* (Paramount Pictures, 2007)

As noted in the chapter opener, this film follows the early teaching experiences of Erin Gruwell and her students in Long Beach, California. Gruwell's informative lessons fail to capture her students' interest until she learns how to make history and literature applicable to their lives by relating the history of Nazi Germany to their everyday experiences with gangs, violence, and racism.

*Stand and Deliver* (Warner Brothers, 1988)

This timeless film chronicles the dedication of high school teacher Jaime Escalante, who employs effective informative strategies to teach his students about mathematics and inspires them to achieve more than they thought possible.

*Anthony Bourdain: No Reservations,* television series (Travel Channel, 2005)

In this "off the beaten path" documentary, the chef and author Anthony Bourdain travels to familiar destinations like Las Vegas and more obscure places like Namibia in search of authentic experiences of the local food, people, and culture. His frank and informative commentary highlights for viewers the genuine nature of these locales, allowing viewers to see these places as more than tourist destinations.

# REAL REFERENCE ▶ A Study Tool

**Now that you have finished reading this chapter, you can**

Understand the goals of informative speaking:

▶ Use **informative speaking** to teach the audience something new (p. 418).

▶ Gauge what the audience already knows to determine where to begin (p. 418).

▶ Find an approach that will engage the audience (p. 418).

▶ Explain the subject's relevance to the audience (p. 419).

▶ Present facts and information in an **objective**, even-handed way, unlike in a persuasive speech, which is **subjective**, presenting a point of view (p. 419).

▶ Speak ethically (p. 420).

Describe each of the eight categories of informative speeches:

▶ People: focus on human qualities as well as achievements (p. 422).

▶ Places: find new aspects of known places, or describe the unfamiliar (p. 423).

▶ Objects and phenomena: focus on any nonhuman topic (p. 423).

▶ Events: describe noteworthy events in history, or relate a personal experience (p. 423).

▶ Processes: show how something works, or teach how to do something (p. 424).

▶ Concepts: explain an abstract idea (p. 424).

▶ Issues: remain objective to report on a social or personal problem (p. 425).

▶ Plans and policies: describe the important dimensions of potential courses of action (p. 426).

Outline the four major approaches to informative speeches:

▶ The **descriptive presentation** paints a mental picture, portraying places, events, persons, objects, or processes (p. 426).

▶ **Demonstration speeches** combine explanatory narration and physical demonstration (p. 427).

▶ There are five categories of **definitional speeches**: an **operational definition** defines something by explaining what it is or what it does; **definition by negation** defines something by telling what it is not; **definition by example** offers concrete examples; **definition by synonym** defines something with closely related words; **definition by etymology** explains the origin of a word or phrase (pp. 428–429).

▶ **Explanatory speeches** answer the question "Why?" with **elucidating explanations**; with **quasi-scientific explanations**, or models; or with **transformative explanations** that change preconceptions (pp. 429–431).

Make your audience hungry for information:

▶ Make listeners curious by personalizing the topic and contrasting it to what they know (p. 432).

▶ Present a clear benefit to learning about the topic (p. 433).

▶ Stress the topic's relevance (p. 433).

Make your speech easy to listen to:

▶ Devise a clear, logical structure (p. 435).

▶ Signal your audience when you're about to say something important (p. 435).

▶ Keep it simple (p. 437).

▶ Relate new ideas to familiar ideas (p. 437).

▶ Define terms your audience may not know (p. 438).

▶ Select interesting examples (p. 438).

▶ Use strong presentation aids (p. 439).

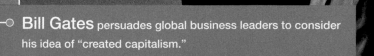

**Bill Gates** persuades global business leaders to consider his idea of "created capitalism."

# chapter 15

# Persuasive Speaking

**"As I see it,"** Bill Gates told the World Economic Forum in early 2008, "there are two great forces of human nature: self-interest and caring for others." Gates knows a thing or two about both. One of the founders of Microsoft, Gates quickly learned the business opportunities that emerging technology creates. By the turn of the millennium, Microsoft's Windows operating system was the dominant computer system in the world, and Gates was one of the richest individuals alive. Following in the footsteps of Andrew Carnegie, John D. Rockefeller, and Warren Buffett, Gates also became a trailblazing philanthropist. He and his wife established and funded the Bill and Melinda Gates Foundation, a global organization dedicated to the lofty goals of improving education in the United States and eradicating poverty and disease the world over.

In July 2008, Gates stepped down as chairman of the company he built and dedicated himself to speaking about sharing technological wealth to close the gap between the world's richest people and its poorest. But he wasn't asking for simple charity in the form of monetary donations. Instead, Gates described his vision for a system of "created capitalism," a kind of business model that challenged established companies and entrepreneurs to recognize and embrace the importance of helping others not only to the betterment of mankind but also to their own bottom line. "Such a system must have a twin mission: making profits and also improving the lives of those who don't fully benefit from today's market forces."

Gates urged the standing-room-only crowd of global business leaders to consider a free market "where governments, business, and nonprofits work together to stretch the reach of market forces so that more people can make a profit, or gain recognition, doing work that erases the world's inequities."

What do you think of when you hear the word *persuasion*? We often ask our students this question before beginning a lesson on persuasive speaking. Their answers are telling. They think of sneaky used-car salesmen and dishonest politicians. They also point to a terrorist group's attempt to have *24*'s Jack Bauer assist in a political assassination in order to save his kidnapped wife and daughter, as well as James Bond being tortured to give away a secret code in the 2006 film *Casino Royale*. The first two examples might involve people attempting to be persuasive, but they certainly involve unethical communication. The final two examples are clear-cut descriptions of **coercion**, the act of using threats, intimidation, or violence to gain compliance.

**Persuasion** is none of these things. It is, quite simply, the process of influencing attitudes, beliefs, and behaviors. And done properly, it is also an ethical practice. Think of all of the important accomplishments that can come from a competent use of persuasion, such as petitioning for money to support victims of natural disasters or, like Bill Gates, making the case that charity and profitability can go hand in hand. What's more, persuasion is not just a tool for people driven by a particular vision for society. It's a tool that you probably use every day, whether you are touting the merits of a high-speed cable line in the hopes of getting your roommates to replace their paaaiiiinnnfully slow dial-up connection or even convincing your four-year-old to eat his peas. In this chapter, we will examine the nature and goals of persuasive speaking while helping you consider your audience, the support for your speech, and helpful organizational patterns.

## The Goals of Persuasive Speaking

**Persuasive speaking** is speech that is intended to influence the attitudes, beliefs, and behavior of your audience. Although these three terms may be familiar to you, let's take a moment to examine them in light of how we will think about them in this chapter.

- ▶ **Attitudes** are our general evaluations of people, ideas, objects, or events (Stiff & Mongeau, 2003). When you evaluate something, you judge it as good or bad, important or unimportant, boring or interesting, and so on. For example, you might have a positive attitude toward sports and exercise: "Exercising regularly is good."

- ▶ **Beliefs** are the ways in which people perceive reality (Stiff & Mongeau, 2003). They are our feelings about what is true and real and refer to how confident we are about the existence or validity of something: "I believe that exercise is an important component of a healthy lifestyle."

- ▶ **Behavior** is the manner in which we act or function. It refers to what we *do* in response to our attitudes and beliefs (Homer, 2006). For example, if your attitude about exercise is really positive and you believe that it is an important component of a healthy lifestyle, you'll probably be motivated to get out there and walk or jog or lift weights.

In many ways, speaking to persuade your listeners is similar to speaking for informative purposes. Just look at any presidential campaign. The candidates all want to inform you about their plans and goals for the nation, but they also use organized and well-developed presentations to influence their audience's *attitudes* and *beliefs* about their suitability for the presidency (for example, "I really like Candidate X—what a nice person!" or "I believe that Candidate Y is the most competent person for the job"). And of course, they want to influence your *behavior* by getting you to vote for them.

Influencing your audience's attitudes, beliefs, or behavior does not necessarily mean changing them. It can also mean reinforcing attitudes, beliefs, or behavior that already exists. For example, when a political party attempts to rally its base, it will usually focus its candidates' speeches on issues on which the party faithful already agree. To do this, they must first correctly identify an existing attitude or belief among listeners. The key to determining your audience's attitudes—as well as whether your goal is to change or reinforce those attitudes—lies with audience analysis (discussed in Chapter 11).

**CONNECT**

As you consider your audience's attitudes, beliefs, and behavior, don't forget the cultural context (Chapter 1). Your listeners' gender, religious beliefs, socioeconomic status, ethnicity, and political beliefs—as well as their personal experiences—inform their attitudes, beliefs, and behavior. If you fail to respect these factors, you will likely fail to persuade your audience.

## Developing a Persuasive Topic and Thesis

An effective topic for a persuasive speech must share characteristics with an informative one: it should be something that you're interested in, that you know something about, and that is specific enough that you can find a variety of appropriate sources on the topic but not so specific that you can't possibly develop your thoughts on it. When your general purpose is to persuade, however, you must keep a few other points in mind.

First, your topic should be somewhat controversial—that is, a topic that people could have reasonable disagreement about. Issues such as stem cell research, campaign finance reform, and mandatory year-round schooling lend themselves to a persuasive purpose because people hold strongly differing opinions about them. Second, the topic must allow the speaker to develop a message intended to cause some degree of change in the audience. For example, the topic of mandatory smoking bans could seek changes from different audiences who hold very different views: encouraging action (a change in behavior) from people who already agree that smoking should be banned in public or seeking a change in the attitudes of smokers who currently see no problem with smoking in public places.

Once you have determined that a particular topic interests you and can be persuasive, it's time to think about developing your thesis statement. In a persuasive speech, thesis statements are often given as a **proposition**, or a statement about your viewpoint or position on an issue. There are three types of propositions that we will examine: propositions of fact, propositions of value, and propositions of policy.

### Propositions of Fact

If you've ever argued on behalf of something you believed to be true, you've made a **proposition of fact**—a claim of what is or what is not. Persuasive speeches built on propositions of fact commonly involve issues that are open to some interpretation and on which there is some conflicting evidence or beliefs. The truth of the statement may be debatable, but the goal of the speech is clear: you want to align the audience's perception or opinion of the fact with your own. Now, it may seem simple to give a speech on a proposition of fact: state your belief, back up your points with research that persuades your audience, and you're done! However, it can actually be quite challenging. Propositions of fact get at the heart of how you view the world, and your viewpoints may be quite different from how members of your audience perceive reality (beliefs about religion, family, marriage, friendship, education, money, and so on). Consider the following proposition-of-fact thesis statements:

▶ "Single people are as capable of raising happy, healthy, well-adjusted children as married couples."

▶ "Your auto dealership will lose money on its sales of compact cars if your inventory is too small."

▶ "HMOs are a sensible choice for less expensive health care coverage."

Each statement is presented as a fact, yet audiences realize that they are really the beliefs of the speaker, presented for the listeners' consideration.

Take a closer look at the sample thesis regarding single people raising children. At the heart of this proposition is your definition of *family*—that a family need not contain two parents. However, members of your audience may very well believe—and feel strongly—that *family* refers to a married couple and children. It's important to be tolerant and understanding of people's deeply held beliefs, especially if you hope to get others to see your point of view.

## Propositions of Value

Some speeches go beyond discussing what is or what is not and make claims about something's worth. Such evaluative claims are called **propositions of value**. In speeches of this type, you seek to convince an audience that something meets or does not meet a specific standard of goodness or quality or right or wrong. For example:

▶ "Torturing prisoners of war is immoral."

▶ "The Olympics are becoming less relevant as a sporting event."

▶ "Organized religion has done a great deal of good for the world."

Each statement offers a judgment about the overall value of the person, event, object, way of life, condition, or action discussed. Like propositions of fact, it's clear to the audience that these statements of value are not absolute truths but rather the opinion of the speaker. And as with propositions of fact, the speaker must present arguments and evidence that will persuade listeners to align their beliefs and attitudes with the speaker's.

## Propositions of Policy

The third type of proposition is concerned with what *should* happen. In **propositions of policy**, the speaker makes claims about what goal, policy, or course of action should be pursued. For example:

▶ "Gays and lesbians should have the same rights as all other Americans."

▶ "Colleges and universities should not consider race when making admission decisions."

▶ "Any vehicle that gets poor gas mileage (say, less than 25 miles per gallon) should be banned in the United States."

● **FROM PROPOSING** to increase the quality of campus dining to championing for more money for student events, propositions of policy are common in student government elections.

In advocating for any of these statements, your task as the speaker would be to persuade the audience that a current policy is not working or that a new policy is needed. Propositions of policy are common during election campaigns as candidates—especially challengers—offer their ideas and plans for what the government should do and how they would do it.

No matter what your topic, and no matter which type of proposition you are advocating, you'll need to know as much as possible about your listeners in order to persuade them effectively. This is the topic of the next section.

## Persuading Your Audience

A student once told us an interesting story about audience analysis. At a church service the Sunday after Thanksgiving, her pastor preached on the religious meaning of Christmas (likely in response to the shopping binges known to take place the weekend after many of us eat a little too much turkey, stuffing, and pie). He was hoping to persuade his audience to remember the religious meaning of the holiday and to avoid getting caught up in commercialism, present swapping, and credit card debt. "He was passionate about the topic, and his points were right on," the student said, "but the congregation already agreed with him. It almost felt like he was angry with us or something. It was . . . strange."

As this story shows, it is crucial to know your audience before developing your speech, as this knowledge will help you tailor your organization, research, and supporting points. It will even help you determine your specific purpose—whether to try to change or to reaffirm the audience's attitudes, beliefs, and behavior. This was the mistake of our student's pastor. He would have been better off affirming his parishioners' beliefs than trying to convince them of something they already agreed with.

**AND YOU?**
During a campaign season, pay attention to the candidates' speeches and debates, or visit presidentialrhetoric.com to view current and past presidential speeches. How often does the speaker put forth propositions of fact? Of value? Of policy? Does one type of proposition seem to cause more debate or controversy than others?

## Understanding Your Audience's Disposition

It is often helpful to think about your audience members as belonging to one of three different categories, depending on their attitude toward your speech topic: the receptive audience, the neutral audience, or the hostile audience.

● CORETTA SCOTT KING found a receptive audience when she spoke to other like-minded individuals at a press conference on ending the Vietnam War.

▶ A **receptive audience** is an audience that already agrees with your viewpoints and your message and is likely to respond favorably to your speech.

▶ A **hostile audience** is one that opposes your message (and perhaps you personally); this is the hardest type of audience to persuade, particularly if you are trying to change people's behavior.

▶ A **neutral audience** falls between the receptive audience and the hostile audience: its members neither support you nor oppose you. Their neutrality can be based on several causes: perhaps they are simply uninterested in your topic, or they don't see how the topic affects them personally. Or they may know very little about the topic and are therefore unable to take a stance until they learn more.

Consider the importance of your audience's disposition in light of the following example. Imagine that you are the student government president at a residential school in a small state where it is easy for students to get home on weekends to visit with family and friends. While this may be a benefit for some students, your school has gained a reputation of being a "suitcase" school, making for dull weekends for those students who do remain on campus. To address this problem, you want to propose that the school ban first- and second-year students from having cars on campus, making it more likely that they would remain on campus during the weekend and invest more in creating a life at the school. To garner support for your position, you speak to three different groups of first- and second-year students:

▶ Residential students who wish that there was more to do on campus every weekend and that there were more people to hang out with (the receptive audience)

▶ Nonresidential commuting students who are typically off campus on the weekends anyway (the neutral audience)

▶ Residential students who regularly leave campus on weekends (the hostile audience)

When you address the receptive audience, you probably don't need to do too much to get your listeners to like what you're saying—they already agree with you. You're reaffirming what they believe and strengthening your case.

Your neutral audience may need some more information about the issue: What percentage of students leave campus each weekend? How exactly does that affect campus life? Most important, you'll need to tell your listeners why they should care. Perhaps, for example, if there were more to do on campus on the weekends (and more students to interact with), commuting students would be more interested in getting involved in weekend cultural and social events, helping them feel more connected to the community.

Your hostile audience will, of course, need some very special consideration. You will want the members of this audience to find you trustworthy and full of goodwill—in other words, you don't want them to think that you're out to rob them of their transportation or prevent them from interacting with friends at home. You also want to avoid making them feel as though you are trying to force them to accept your viewpoint; research shows that such behavior will backfire and make your audience less likely to engage with you (Brehm, 1966). Instead, you would want to acknowledge their point of view, look for ways to bridge the gap between your beliefs and their beliefs—perhaps encouraging them to get friends and family involved in the life of the school (rather than going home as frequently) or even making allowances for students who need cars for medical reasons or to get to off-campus jobs.

You must also consider what you want your audience to *do* at the end of your speech. A lot of what listeners will be willing to do is related to their **latitude of acceptance and rejection** (Sherif & Sherif, 1967), which is the range of positions on a topic that are acceptable or unacceptable to them. In the case of our example, you can probably get members of your receptive audience to do quite a bit, including change their behavior. They might, for example, be very willing to help you collect names for a petition or pass out flyers. Members of your neutral audience might be willing to sign a petition or to discuss the topic with friends, but they're not going to go out of their way to help you. When it comes to your hostile audience, it's unlikely that you'll see much behavior change. These people aren't going to help you achieve your goals! But you might be able to affect some level of belief and attitude change, helping them at least see your point of view and thus not actively oppose your plan.

## Understanding Your Audience's Needs

If you feel that your child isn't getting sufficient or proper instruction in mathematics, you probably aren't going to be too interested in hearing a speech on the importance of raising money for new school football uniforms. And if you're working two jobs to pay for college, you probably aren't going to want to hear anyone speak on the great value of buying a particular $40,000 luxury car. That's because these speech topics don't address your personal *needs,* or deficits that create tension. Helpful in understanding audience needs is the work of Abraham Maslow (1954). Maslow argues that an individual's motivations, priorities, and behavior are influenced primarily by that person's needs. He identifies needs in a hierarchical structure of five categories (see Figure 15.1 on p. 458), from low (immature) to high (mature), known as the **hierarchy of needs**.

**AND YOU?**

When a speaker ignores your needs, do you find yourself ignoring the speaker? Think of an instance when you encountered such a speaker—a professor, a political figure, or a medical professional, perhaps. What exactly was the speaker's mistake? How might he or she have been able to understand your needs and those of the other audience members?

**FIGURE 15.1**
**MASLOW'S HIERARCHY OF NEEDS**

Maslow's famous *hierarchy of needs* matters in organizations as well. As you learn in Chapter 10, the *human relations approach* to management helps managers better understand the higher-level needs of their employees—things like self-esteem and personal development. This helps employees feel more *self-actualized* in their communication (see Chapter 2) and motivated to achieve on the job.

The theory is that the most basic needs must be met before an individual can become concerned with needs farther up in the hierarchy.

1. *Physiological/survival needs:* These are the things you need for basic survival, such as air, water, food, shelter, sleep, clothing, and so on. Even in the short term, if you listen to a speech while you are very hungry, your mind is likely not on the message but rather on getting food.

2. *Safety needs:* These are needs for security, orderliness, protective rules, and avoidance of risk. They include not only actual physical safety but safety from emotional injury as well. When people in a community are concerned with violence and crime, for example, they are less likely to listen to persuasive appeals to increase local arts funding.

3. *Belongingness/social needs:* These needs center around your interactions with others. They include the desire to be accepted and liked by other people and the need for love, affection, and affiliation. These needs are normally met by family ties, friendships, and membership in work and social groups.

4. *Esteem/ego-status needs:* These needs involve validation—being accepted by some group and being recognized for achievement, mastery, competence, and so on. They can be satisfied by special recognition, social and professional rewards, promotions, power, and achievement. Unlike the previous three categories, esteem needs are not satisfied internally; they require praise and acknowledgment from others.

5. *Self-actualizing needs:* Needs at the highest level focus on personal development and self-fulfillment—becoming what you can become. Instead of looking for recognition of your worth from others, you seek to measure up to your own criteria for personal success.

The implications of Maslow's hierarchy for persuasive speaking are straightforward: understanding your audience's needs will help you determine your strategy for persuading your listeners. As a persuasive speaker, you must consider the level of the hierarchy that characterizes the majority of the audience and adapt the message appropriately. The message must target the *unfulfilled* need of the audience. A need that is already met will not move an audience, nor

● **MASLOW'S HIERARCHY** of needs is helpful in understanding your audience's needs. For example, it might be hard to convince a group of low-income single mothers to enroll their kids in various costly extracurricular activities.

will one that seems too far out of reach in the hierarchy. A speech persuading audience members to plant more flowers on an already beautiful college campus is unlikely to have much effect, as they perceive that the need for an attractive place to live or study has already been fulfilled; however, the same appeal to plant flowers on a campus where buildings are in serious disrepair is also unlikely to get a response, as the audience may be more concerned with those basic infrastructure issues.

## Understanding What Is Relevant to Your Audience

Along with appealing to audience needs, you can also work to persuade listeners—especially neutral listeners—by anticipating their question "How is this relevant to me?" The **Elaboration Likelihood Model (ELM)**, developed by Richard Petty, John Cacioppo, and their associates, highlights the importance of relevance to persuasion. ELM is based on the belief that listeners process persuasive messages by one of two routes, depending on how important the message is to them (Petty & Cacioppo, 1986; Petty & Wegener, 1998; see also Kruglanski et al., 2006). When they are motivated and able to think critically about the content of a message, they engage in **central processing**—that is, they think deeply about the speaker's message and may seriously consider acting on it. When listeners lack motivation to listen critically or are unable to do so, they engage in **peripheral processing** of information, giving little thought to the message or even dismissing it as irrelevant, too complex to follow, or simply unimportant.

Whenever possible, you want your audience to engage in central processing, as it produces deeper, more long-lasting changes in audience perspective than peripheral processing does. Audience members who engage peripherally can certainly be influenced, but they tend to pay attention to things other

## WIREDFORCOMMUNICATION

### Interactive Advertising: Persuasion for a Millennial Audience

If you were born between 1980 and 2000, advertisers want you, even if they aren't quite sure what to do with you. They call you the Millennials or the Bridgers or a variety of generational initials: Generation Y (because you follow Generation X), Generation D (for Digital), Generation M (for Multitaskers). Your Generation X predecessors (born between 1964 and 1979) were challenging enough, with their tendency to videotape television programs and speed through commercials. But you're even trickier with your TV and video downloads and customized, commercial-free programming. This presents a challenge for advertisers, as well as a wealth of opportunities. They want to reach you, they want to persuade you, and they're just starting to figure out how.

One strategy they are employing is viral marketing—marketing that takes advantage of preexisting social networks. While viral marketing exists offline (where it is better known as a word-of-mouth campaign), it really blossoms online. Advertisers can produce an advertisement and get it in front of millions of potential customers, provided that you find it funny or compelling enough to forward a link to your friends.

Marketers have also tapped into your generation's unprecedented technological know-how to get you involved in the advertising process. User-generated content is persuasive on several levels. Contests for user-generated advertisements can boost interest in a product or service, and the ads themselves can potentially go viral. They also lend an edgy, young image to the product being advertised. Converse sneakers, for example, posted user-generated videos on its Web site, which became an online hit, and MasterCard solicits users to create copy for its ongoing "Priceless" campaign (Bosman, 2006).

Marketers are also trying to make the ads themselves interactive, a challenge for an industry that has been focused for decades on producing linear, thirty-second television spots. One tactic has been to create games that invite users to engage with their product. In 2007, Toyota launched *The Book of Deviants,* an online game in which "little deviants" murder dull, conformist "Sheeple," creating a hot new Scion xD in the process (Beam, 2007). Bayer Healthcare went a step further, creating an interactive game that invited users to follow a fictional storyline that had a real payoff: for each user who clicked through the entire game (which takes over a minute), the company would make a donation of $5 or $10 to an environmental conservation fund (Lauro, 2007). Whether these new tricks of the advertising trade will lure in your Millennial dollars is yet to be determined. But until Generation Z comes along, they'll keep trying.

**THINK ABOUT THIS**

❶ How many advertisements do you think you encounter in a day? How persuasive do you think they are?

❷ Do you think user-generated content is more persuasive to people in their twenties than traditional advertisements? Do you think it is more persuasive to people in other age groups as well?

❸ When advertisements appear on a Web page, are you annoyed? What kind of Web ad would prompt you to click it?

❹ Would a donation to a cause you support be enough to keep you clicking through a game, regardless of content? Would it be enough to persuade you to send a link to all your friends?

than the central message, such as the speaker's appearance or reputation or any slogans or emotional manipulation used in the speech. Such shallow acceptance of a speaker's message is unlikely to lead to meaningful long-term changes in attitudes or behavior.

To put the principles of the ELM model of persuasion into practice, consider the following points:

▶ Make certain that your message is relevant to your listeners.

▶ Be sure to present it at an appropriate level of understanding.

▶ Establish credibility with the audience.

▶ Establish a common bond with your listeners and ensure that they see you as trustworthy.

These steps will increase the odds that your persuasive appeal will produce lasting, rather than fleeting, changes in their attitudes and behavior. (O'Hair, Stewart, & Rubenstein, 2007).

## Strategies for Persuasive Speaking

> When the conduct of men is designed to be influenced, persuasion, kind unassuming persuasion, should ever be adopted. It is an old and true maxim that "a drop of honey catches more flies than a gallon of gall." So with men, if you would win a man to your cause, first convince him that you are his sincere friend. Therein is a drop of honey that catches his heart, which, say what he will, is the great highroad to his reason, and which, once gained, you will find but little trouble in convincing him of the justice of your cause. . . . (Lincoln, 1842, para. 6)

This quote from President Abraham Lincoln truly touches on the important strategies you will need to keep in mind as you persuade your audience: your own sincerity and goodwill in presenting your message; your audience's reasoning (and your own ethical use of solid logic and honest reasoning); and your audience's heart or emotions. Let's take a closer look at each of these points.

### Forms of Rhetorical Proof

In his classical treatise on rhetoric, Aristotle explained that persuasion could be brought about through three means or **forms of rhetorical proof**. The first, appeals to ethos, concerns the qualifications and personality of the speaker; the second, appeals to logos, concerns the nature of the message in a speech; the third, appeals to pathos, concerns the nature of the audience's feelings. According to Aristotle—and generations of theorists and practitioners who followed him—you can build an effective persuasive speech by incorporating a combination of these factors.

**CONNECT**

It will be hard to get your audience to engage in *central processing* if you can't get them to listen to your speech. As you learn in Chapter 5, you need to encourage thoughtful *active listening*. While your audience certainly bears some of the responsibility for that, you can help by making sure that you offer relevant, effective supporting material (Chapter 11), present an organized speech (Chapter 12), and ensure that your delivery is easy to listen to (Chapter 13).

**CONNECT**

Part of revealing *ethos* to your audience is offering an accurate, ethical presentation of yourself. As you learn in Chapter 2, *self-presentation* is often strategic—you reveal or hide particular things about yourself to achieve a goal. But if you're giving a speech on the importance of safe driving and you fail to mention that you've been issued five tickets for speeding, you aren't being ethical. Your ethos would be increased if you shared your story and the lesson you've learned from it.

### Ethos

If audience members have little or no regard for the speaker, they will not respond positively to his or her persuasive appeals. In fact, attitude change in your audience is related to the extent to which you, as the speaker, are perceived to be credible (Priester & Petty, 1995). Aristotle believed that speechmaking should emphasize the quality and impact of ideas, but he recognized that the speaker's character and personality also play an important role in how well the audience listens to and accepts the message. He referred to this effect of the speaker as **ethos**, or moral character.

Exactly which elements of a persuasive appeal are based on ethos? The first element is good sense, also known as *credibility* or the speaker's knowledge and experience with the subject matter. You can evoke this quality by skillfully preparing the speech at all stages (from research to delivery), by demonstrating personal acquaintance with the topic, by revealing familiarity with the work of experts on your topic, and by ensuring that your speech is well organized.

Another element of an ethos-based appeal is the speaker's *character;* the speaker's own ethical standards are central to this element. Research suggests, for example, that a brief disclosure of personal moral standards relevant to the speech or the occasion made in the introduction of a speech will boost audience regard for the speaker (Stewart, 1994). Indeed, you should prepare and present every aspect of your speech with the utmost integrity so that your audience will regard you as *trustworthy*.

A third element of ethos is showing *goodwill* toward the audience. To show goodwill, you must remember that one of your responsibilities is to help your audience make informed choices. By giving listeners all the information they need to make a decision, you show that you have their best interests at heart. Furthermore, you can show your goodwill by demonstrating an interest in and a concern for the welfare of your listeners and by addressing their needs and expectations relative to the speech.

● **IN PERSUADING** the affected residents of Hinkley, CA, to cooperate on the PG&E lawsuit, Erin Brockovich employed elements of ethos, like getting to know each person's story and gaining each resident's trust.

### Logos

Many persuasive speeches focus on issues that require considerable thought. Should the United States adopt a national health care plan? Are certain television programs too violent for children? When an audience needs to make an important decision or reach a conclusion regarding a complicated issue, appeals to reason and logic are necessary. Aristotle used the term **logos** to refer to persuasive appeals directed at the audience's reasoning on a topic.

**Reasoning** is the line of thought we use to make judgments based on facts and inferences from the world around us. This basic human capability lies at the heart of logical proof: when we offer our evidence to our audience in hopes that our listeners will reach the same logical conclusions as we have, we are appealing to their reason. There are two types of reasoning: inductive and deductive.

**Inductive reasoning** occurs when you draw general conclusions based on specific evidence. When you reason inductively, you find specific examples, incidents, cases, or statistics from your research and then produce a general argument that uses your findings as support. For example, if you work at an animal shelter and have been bitten or snapped at several times by small dogs but never by a large dog, you might conclude inductively that small dogs are more vicious than large dogs. This argument may or may not be persuasive to your listeners; if you produce only a few anecdotal examples from your own experience, the audience might dismiss your evidence as inconclusive. But if your listeners know that you are very experienced with dogs—that is, if they find you credible—they may accept your conclusion even if they feel that your evidence is somewhat lacking.

**Deductive reasoning**, by contrast, proceeds from the general to the specific. You begin with a general argument and then apply it to specific cases, incidents, and locations. The most popular way to argue deductively is with a **syllogism**, a three-line deductive argument that draws a specific conclusion from two general premises (a major and a minor premise). Consider this classic syllogism:

*Major premise:* All humans are mortal.

*Minor premise:* Socrates is a human.

*Conclusion:* Therefore, Socrates is mortal.

Applied to a speech, you might use a syllogism in the following ways:

*Major premise:* Laws to prohibit smoking in all restaurants should be enacted.

*Minor premise:* Granny's Chicken Palace in Lake Junaluska, North Carolina, is a restaurant.

*Conclusion:* Therefore, smoking should be prohibited at Granny's Chicken Palace.

The extent to which your syllogism is persuasive depends on how well the audience accepts the major premise of your case. If the people in your audience do not accept your major premise that smoking should be prohibited in all public places, they may believe either that smoking should never be prohibited in any public place or that smoking should be prohibited in some, but not necessarily all, public places. In either case, your conclusion may not be completely acceptable to them.

Another way to reason deductively is with an **enthymeme**. Enthymematic reasoning is essentially a syllogism, except that one of the premises is so widely known and accepted that it is not specifically included (Crick, 2004). Taking an enthymematic approach to the syllogism featuring Socrates, the argument would sound like this: "Socrates is mortal because he is human." This enthymeme assumes that the audience knows that all humans are mortal. One of the most notable uses of the enthymeme was in the murder trial of former NFL superstar O. J. Simpson in 1995. As his lead attorney, Johnnie Cochran, displayed the bloodied gloves allegedly found at the murder scene, he asked his client to put them on and stated, "If it [the glove] doesn't fit, you must acquit." In full syllogistic form, the jury would have heard, "If the glove doesn't fit the defendant, you must acquit the defendant. The glove doesn't fit the defendant. Therefore, you must acquit the defendant" (DeClamecy, Wilson, & Philips, 2005).

## Pathos

Another means of persuasion is appealing to the listeners' emotions. The term Aristotle used for this is **pathos**. It requires "creating a certain disposition in the audience." Aristotle taught that successful public speakers identify and appeal to four sets of emotions in their listeners. He presented these sets in opposing pairs: anger and meekness, love and hatred, fear and boldness, shame and shamelessness. Speakers often evoke such emotions through vivid description and emotionally charged words. For example, consider this statement: "The vivid picture of cold, emotionless fishermen slashing and slicing baby seals should send chills through even the numbest and most stoic capitalists on earth." Makes your skin crawl, doesn't it?

Although emotion is a powerful means of moving an audience, relying solely on emotion to persuade will often fail unless you can offer your audience practical ways of dealing with the emotion and personal responsibility

---

# EVALUATINGCOMMUNICATIONETHICS

## THINK ABOUT THIS

### Pathos and Persuasive Accounts

Adding personal accounts to your speech can appeal to your audience's emotions and also lend you credibility as a speaker. But what if you don't have any firsthand experiences to share? Some of the most persuasive pieces of writing—Upton Sinclair's book *The Jungle,* Harriet Beecher Stowe's *Uncle Tom's Cabin,* and John Steinbeck's *The Grapes of Wrath,* to name just a few—are works of fiction. The stories are not real, even if the experiences and the people described in them were inspired by real people and events.

But is it ethical to fabricate details in order to persuade an audience about an issue? Imagine this scenario. You are an anti–death penalty activist, and your organization successfully delivered a series of speeches that persuaded your city council to sign a resolution condemning the state government for reinstating the death penalty.

You were particularly impressed with your group's leader, Anthony, who delivered a powerful speech in front of the council in which he detailed his experience watching the execution of a young convict in a Texas prison. At dinner with other group members that night, you say to Anthony: "That must have been just terrible for you, as a young reporter, to watch a man die such a horrible death!" He replies with a funny smile on his face, "Not really. You see, I kind of took a few liberties there. I never witnessed any executions. But I had read a really moving firsthand account in a book while I was researching. It was such a good illustration, so much better than any thirdhand description I could have prepared. I think," he grins and continues, "that might have been the very thing that won them over! There's nothing like a 'personal account' to get your audience in your corner!"

You and your other group members sit in an uncomfortable silence that your leader doesn't appear to notice. What do you think you should do?

① Is it ethical for Anthony to make up a "personal account" to use as an illustration in his persuasive appeal, even if it's based on a true story? Is there a difference between lying "for a good cause" and lying for any other reason?

② How do Anthony's actions differ from those of the three writers mentioned? Does it matter that Tom Joad, the hero of *The Grapes of Wrath,* never existed?

③ If you were a member of the city council, would you have reacted to the story differently if the speaker had presented it as a thirdhand account? Why or why not?

④ How will your group react to this revelation? What will you do or say to Anthony about this issue?

for it. This is particularly true if the emotion you arouse is fear (Rothman, Salovey, Turvey, & Fishkin, 1993; Sutton, 1982). Though emotion can grab the audience's attention and stimulate a desire to act, reason should then be presented as justification for the action while ethos builds up the speaker's credibility and competence. For an example of an appeal to pathos that also includes effective logos, consider the Montana Meth Project, a research-based marketing campaign that "realistically and graphically communicates the risks of methamphetamine to the youth of Montana" devised to address that state's growing meth use problem. The ads and commercials are indeed graphic and frightening, playing into viewers' love of family and friends, fear of poor health and degenerating appearance, and sense of shame and horror. A particularly moving print ad depicts a mother crumpled in front of a kitchen sink, bloodied and bruised by her meth-addicted son or daughter. It reads, "My mom knows I'd never hurt her. Then she got in the way" (Montana Meth Project, 2007). The logical appeal is sound—teenagers who become addicted to methamphetamines will destroy themselves, their futures, and their loved ones—and the ring of truth enhances the persuasiveness of the emotional appeal. The project's follow-up research reveals that the ads have had a significant effect on teens' attitudes toward meth, showing that their credibility is solid as well. The campaign tagline leaves viewers and readers with a practical suggestion to avoid the fearful images of meth addiction: "Meth, not even once." The message is clear: don't try meth even once, and this won't happen to you.

## Avoiding Logical Fallacies

In a predictable scene from just about any coming-of-age television drama or film—or perhaps real-life situation—a teenager argues with her parents: "Why can't I go to the party? All of my friends are going!" she cries. The exasperated parents roll their eyes and counter, "If your friends were all jumping off a bridge, would you jump too?" In their attempts to persuade the other, both the parents and the child fail miserably. In the eyes of the parents, "All of my friends are going" is simply not a valid reason why the child should go to the party as well, and comparing

CONNECT

Your word choices have a powerful impact on your audience, as words have different meanings for different people (Chapter 3). Let's say you're persuading your audience to adopt a healthy diet. Some people define healthy as low fat and high fiber, whereas others perceive healthy as an organic, vegan diet. To make sure your audience is on the same page, define how *you* are using the term.

### AND YOU?

Think about the last major purchase you made. Now consider the information you had prior to the purchase (advertisements, reviews in the media, advice from others). Did you rely primarily on emotional appeals, ethical appeals, or logical appeals?

● THE MONTANA METH Project persuades with appeals to reason, emotion, and credibility.

attending a party to jumping off a bridge makes absolutely no sense to the teenager (and perhaps anyone reading this example!).

**Logical fallacies** are invalid or deceptive forms of reasoning. When audience members recognize such a fallacy in your speech, they will reject it, and the speech will not be persuasive. So be on the lookout for several types of logical fallacies.

---

# real communicator

**NAME:** Bryan Au
**HOMETOWN:** Los Angeles, California
**OCCUPATION:** Raw organic chef, cookbook author, and spokesperson
**FUN FACT:** I honestly believe that raw organic desserts are the best desserts you will ever try, and they're a great way to get into raw and organic eating.

Cheeseburger combo meals. Frozen pizzas. Drive-thru fried chicken and microwaveable fried chicken. Get a burrito at the convenience store. Tear off the plastic wrapper. Throw the burrito in the microwave. Press 3. This isn't how college students eat. This is how many people eat. It's SAD—the Standard American Diet.

I advocate the benefits of raw organic food. I recently published a cookbook, *Raw in Ten Minutes,* and I pitch my ideas to agents, publishers, businesses, and TV executives. I deliver persuasive presentations over the Internet, on television shows, in conference rooms, one on one, and in front of thousands of people. I talk about vegan food, and I promote wheat-, gluten-, and dairy-free food. And as you may have already guessed—*what? no cheese? no burgers? no cheeseburgers?*—I run into some very hostile audiences.

Fortunately, I have a background in communication. As an undergraduate, I took a number of communication classes, and the principles and concepts I learned in those classes have been especially valuable to me as a persuasive speaker. For example, as a persuasive speaker, I seek to influence my audience's preexisting attitudes and beliefs toward raw organic food. Those attitudes and beliefs include, but are not limited to, raw food = gross. I try to counteract those beliefs and attitudes, and by doing so, I hope to influence my audience's *behavior*. In other words, I hope to change people's eating habits.

The proposition-of-fact part is easy. Through stories, slides, examples, and statistics, I can persuade my audience that organic food is healthier than overprocessed food. There is, for example, a great bonus feature on the *Super Size Me* DVD that shows a plate of french fries from a certain fast-food restaurant. Those fries have been left out on a counter, unrefrigerated, for a number of months. At the end of those months, the fries look exactly the same. Images like that bolster my propositions of fact.

Because I deal with hostile audiences, it's particularly important that I make appeals to ethos. I need to come across as trustworthy and full of goodwill. I start my presentation with an informal question-and-answer session. People ask me questions, and I ask them questions. *Has anyone eaten any raw food this week? What about a salad?* Through this informal Q&A, I try to demonstrate to my listeners that I'm not trying to force a particular diet on them. I acknowledge their point of view (*hey, I like fast food too!*), and I look for ways to bridge the gap between us. I also appeal to their senses. My raw organic food recipes don't look like lumpy white tofu on a bed of wheatgrass. My recipes look and taste like comfort food.

Finally, with a bridge established between me and my audience, I make a quick little pathos appeal. I dare everyone to give raw organic food a try. Just as I'm daring you.

### Bandwagoning

When our teenager uses "All of my friends are going" as an argument, she's guilty of what the Greeks called *argumentum ad populum* and we call the **bandwagon fallacy**—accepting a statement as true because it is popular. Speakers must be careful not to confuse consensus with fact. A large number of people believing in ghosts is not proof that ghosts exist; the enormous popularity of Microsoft Windows–based computers is not evidence of the system's superiority over that of Apple's less popular Macintosh.

### Reduction to the Absurd

When parents counter their daughter's request to go to a party with her friends by comparing it to following them off a bridge, they are doing little to persuade their daughter. That's because they have extended their argument to the level of absurdity, a fallacy the Greeks referred to as *reductio ad absurdum* and we know as **reduction to the absurd**. Pushing an argument beyond its logical limits in this manner can cause it to unravel: the teenager sees no connection between going to a party and committing suicide.

### Red Herring

In the **red herring fallacy**, the speaker relies on irrelevant information for his or her argument, thereby diverting the direction of the argument. If you say, for example, "I can't believe that police officer gave me a ticket for going 70 in a 55-mile-per-hour zone! On my way to work yesterday, I saw a crazy driver cut across three lanes of traffic without signaling while going at least 80. Why are the cops bugging people like me instead of chasing down these dangerous drivers?" you would be using a red herring. There may well be worse drivers than you, but that doesn't change the fact that you broke the law.

### Personal Attacks

A speaker who criticizes a person rather than the issue at hand is guilty of the *ad hominem* **fallacy**—an attack on the person instead of on the person's arguments. Political campaigners often resort to such fallacies. For example, if a speaker says, "Terry Malone is the better candidate for district court judge because she is happily married, whereas her opponent just kicked his wife out of their house," the argument is focused on the individual and not the person's particular qualifications for the job.

### Begging the Question

Speakers who use the fallacy of **begging the question** present arguments that no one can verify because they are not accompanied by valid evidence. If you heard someone say, "Students who complete high school have more job options open to them," you would probably agree, but where are the studies, statistics, or examples that prove this?

● IN *10 THINGS I Hate About You,* Bianca tries valiantly (but often unsuccessfully) to persuade her father to let her date with the "But all my friends are doing it!" line.

● IN THE 2008 election season, both Barack Obama and John McCain vowed to put an end to the kinds of personal attacks that typically occur during political campaigns.

### Either-Or Fallacy

Speakers might try to persuade by using the **either-or fallacy**, presenting only two alternatives on a subject and failing to acknowledge other alternatives. For example, imagine someone making the following statement about diet choices: "You either love animals and follow a strict vegan diet or you care little for them and continue to eat meat."

### Appeal to Tradition

When speakers **appeal to tradition**, they are suggesting that listeners should agree with their point because "that's the way it has always been." An example of an appeal to tradition would be: "My family has been happily eating red meat and white bread for generations; I'm not going to stop now just because some doctor tells me it's not healthy."

### The Slippery Slope

The **slippery slope** fallacy is employed when a speaker attests that some event must clearly occur as a result of another event without showing any proof that the second event is caused by the first. For example, "Video surveillance cameras should not be installed in major metropolitan areas. The next thing you know, the government will be listening in on our cell phone conversations and reading our personal e-mail!"

Avoiding these logical fallacies goes a long way toward building ethos with your audience—particularly if the audience is hostile toward your speech topic. You want to rely on facts, research, honest emotion, and your own well-rehearsed presentation to persuade your audience. If you're finding yourself slipping into any logical fallacy to persuade your listeners, you are lacking solid, compelling evidence in that area of your speech.

**AND YOU?**
What kinds of logical fallacies do you regularly see used in the media? What is your reaction when advertisers, political campaigns, or pundits try to persuade you using faulty logic?

## Organizing Patterns in Persuasive Speaking

You've got everything you need to get going on your persuasive speech. You've picked a topic that you're excited about, you've done some research on your audience, and you've thought about how to deal with logic, emotion, and competence in your presentation. Now what? Time to organize all of the information you've compiled. As you will recall from Chapter 12, there are a number of organizational strategies available for your speech; the choice you make depends on your objective, your audience, and your available time. When it comes to persuasive speeches, certain organizational strategies can be particularly helpful.

## Problem-Solution Pattern

As discussed in Chapter 12, when you use a *problem-solution pattern* for your speech, you establish and prove the existence of a problem and then present a solution. When your objective is to affect the attitudes, beliefs, or behavior of the audience, you also need to add a set of arguments for your proposed

## Sample Student Speech

LISA ROTH
*Illinois Central College*

### Emergency in the Emergency Room

In 2006, forty-nine-year-old Beatrice Vance began experiencing some alarming symptoms—nausea, shortness of breath, and chest pain. She called her daughter, Monique, and asked to be driven to the emergency room at Vista Medical Center in Lake County, Illinois. Upon Beatrice's arrival, a nurse met with her briefly. She asked Beatrice to wait until she could be seen by a doctor, as patients are treated in order of severity.

Fully two hours later, when her name was finally called, Beatrice didn't respond. In fact, hospital officials found her slumped over in her chair, ten feet or so from the admitting station, unconscious and without a pulse. According to an ABC News report on September 18, 2006, Beatrice Vance had died of a massive heart attack while waiting to be seen by a doctor. •

Sadly, Beatrice is not the only one who suffers at the hands of an overwhelmed, sometimes inconsistent, and sometimes incompetent emergency room staff. Hospitals across the country are wrought with discord. According to experts on the front line, such as Dr. Brent Eastman, chief medical adviser at Scripps Health Hospital in San Diego, America's emergency rooms are in a crisis that could jeopardize everyone in this room and all our loved ones. •

Today, we'll examine the catastrophic conditions that exist in America's emergency rooms, discover what is causing these conditions, and look at how to restore our faith in a system that has—to quote from an editorial in the June 21, 2006, edition of the *New York Times*—"reached a breaking point." •

To begin, emergency rooms are desperately overcrowded. According to a landmark series of three reports conducted by the Institute of Medicine, the need for emergency rooms has increased by 26 percent since 1993; during the same period, 425 emergency departments closed their doors. The average emergency room wait is now almost four hours, according to a report broadcast on *Good Morning America* on

• Lisa uses an effective real-life story as an attention-grabbing opener. She also invokes pathos to make her audience feel sad and angry about Beatrice's unfortunate death.

• Lisa states her thesis (a proposition of policy) using expert testimony.

• Here Lisa previews her main points. Note her use of the problem-cause-solution pattern of organization.

● **A GOOD WAY** to grab your audience's attention in your speech on the state of emergency rooms is to paint a picture of how overcrowded and understaffed ERs are.

solution. This format is valuable for persuasion because it allows you to establish common ground with your audience about the existence of a problem before moving to more delicate parts (your solution). Although audience members may disagree with the evidence and reasoning you use to build your case, your presentation allows for the possibility that they will find the information interesting, exciting, and plausible. In some cases, an audience may reject a solution that you present but at least leave convinced that "something has to be done."

For example, note in the following outline that the first two main points probe the problem and the third main point offers a solution:

> *Thesis:* Present methods for recycling in our community are inadequate.
>
> *Main point 1:* The current system for recycling generates low participation by citizens.
>
> *Main point 2:* Each community in our area has its own recycling plan and system.
>
> *Main point 3:* Recycling should be a regional, not local, responsibility.

● **WHEN SPEAKING ABOUT** recycling, you might utilize the problem-solution pattern to clearly establish the problem before persuading your audience with a solution.

Some speakers like to use a *problem-cause-solution format*, making the second point the cause of the problem. This format is often useful because getting your listeners to understand the cause helps them reflect on the problem—and makes your solution seem plausible or even inevitable. In the following example, the first main point proves the problem, the second main point proves the cause, and the third main point offers a solution:

> *Thesis:* United States presidents should be able to serve more than two terms.
>
> *Main point 1:* Acceptance of foreign and domestic politics is harmed by changes in administrations.
>
> *Main point 2:* Historically, our country's greatest periods of weakness have occurred with changes in the presidency.
>
> *Main point 3:* The American people should choose whether a president is worthy of serving up to four consecutive terms.

This type of format tends to work particularly well when you are presenting a proposition of policy, as it often proposes a course of action or a series of steps to achieve resolution.

## Refutational Organizational Pattern

If people in your audience have strong objections to a position you are promoting, you will be wise to present, and then refute, their arguments against your

## what about you?

### Assessing Your Persuasive Speech

1. Which best describes your topic?
   A. You've chosen a topic that is controversial, with the intent to influence your audience's attitudes, beliefs, or behavior.
   B. You're not sure if your listeners will even be *interested* in your topic.
   C. You picked a topic that is so controversial and emotional that it will be hard for your audience not to form some opinion on it.

2. Regarding the audience for your persuasive speech, you
   A. Have a good sense of how to get the receptive audience to act, have considered how to make the neutral audience feel that the topic matters, and have thought about bridging the gap between you and the hostile audience.
   B. Feel that you have a pretty good handle on the receptive and neutral audience . . . but the hostile audience? That's just scary.
   C. Aren't even sure who is going to be *in* the audience.

3. How will you consider the audience's needs in your speech?
   A. Everything, from your topic to your research, takes into account how you can use your audience's unmet needs to be persuasive.
   B. You think your topic addresses a need most of the audience members have, but what does your speech development have to do with their needs?
   C. The topic addresses a need that you think is important—and if people don't agree, they'll still have to listen, right?

4. Have you effectively worked ethos into your presentation?
   A. You are secure that you will demonstrate credibility, character, trustworthiness, and goodwill.
   B. You don't know how your audience will feel about you, but you think your sources are credible enough to carry the load.
   C. Ethos? You're more of the logos sort.

5. How can you be sure that the logic in your speech is sound?
   A. You've checked your speech against the logical fallacies section and even asked a friend to make sure you didn't fall into any of those traps.
   B. OK, you found a red herring. But it's a cool example, and you really want to keep it, even if it is a little off topic.
   C. Who needs logic when you can appeal to emotion?

**If your answers are mostly A's:** Congratulations! You've applied everything in the chapter and created a solid persuasive speech.

**If your answers are mostly B's:** You're getting there, but you still have some work to do. Review tips for dealing with different types of audiences, and make sure you've presented your points in a logical manner.

**If your answers are mostly C's:** Consider how ethical you've been in selecting your topic, examples, and evidence. And reassess your goals for the speech.

---

Emergency in the Emergency Room

Lisa Roth, Illinois Central College

**TOPIC:** The crisis of care in the U.S. emergency room system

**GENERAL PURPOSE:** To persuade

**SPECIFIC PURPOSE:** To persuade members of my audience that a crisi[s]
the U.S. system of emergency rooms and to enlist them in working towa[rd]

**THESIS STATEMENT:** The U.S. system of emergency room care is failing
understaffing, and underfunding and requires reorganization to restore

**Attention Getter:** Story of Beatrice Vance (Details: daughter = Moni[ca]
Center, Lake County, IL. 2-hr wait. ABC News 9/18/06) [PAUSE]

**Thesis/Preview of Main Points:** America's ERs are in crisis, and we are
Today: Uncover problems in U.S. ERs, examine causes and solutions to
system that has reached "real breaking point" (NYT 6/21/06)

I. Problems
   A. Overcrowding
      1. Institute of Medicine stats
         a. Need for ER up 26% from 1993
         b. 425 closed ERs
      2. Avg. wait = 4 hrs. Can be 48 hrs for bed. (*Good Morning, Am*[erica]
   B. Understaffed w/ specialists, unprepared employees [Make Eye (
      1. NYT: specialists avoid ER calls
      2. No $ for specialists
      3. Malpractice
      4. *Columbus Dispatch* 7/6/06: EMTs get 1 hr of disaster prep
      5. *Fort Worth Star-Telegram* 6/15/06: major disaster could br[
   C. Not enough $
      1. NYT: ER = $ losers
      2. ER receives fraction of budget allotted
      3. *Pittsburgh-Tribune Review:* No $ = 200,000 fewer beds tha[n]

---

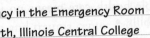

## BACK T[O]

about entre
successful e
ity and tru
profit—be
medicines i

▶ Gates unde
able talking
where in t
nomic theo
relate to th
lishes his a

▶ Gates's bas
consider a 
value: note
rations. He
also his evi

▶ Gates's argu
experience 
also presen
appeal to l
real human

## THINGS

1. Check out
   the Web si
   watch the 
   Did the sp
   ment? Wh
   attitudes, 
   of rhetoric
   (character)

2. On your n
   magazine a

search.) Page through the magazines, paying special attention to the advertisements, and look for examples of appeals to ethos, logos, and pathos. Consider the following questions.

- ▶ What magazine and ads did you choose to examine?

- ▶ Which form of proof do you find most persuasive? Why?

- ▶ Which form of proof do you find least persuasive? Why?

- ▶ Is there a form of proof used consistently in the ads in the magazine you looked at? Why do you think that is?

3. At one point in this chapter, we asked you to think of a time when an instructor presented a viewpoint that went against one of your own deeply held beliefs. Now it's time for you to be the speaker.

- ▶ Choose a topic that you feel very passionate about (a controversial topic would work best here).

- ▶ Now imagine that you are presenting the topic to a receptive audience, a neutral audience, and a hostile audience. What do you as a speaker need to do in order to prepare to present your topic to each type of audience? What do you know about your listeners' beliefs, attitudes, and behavior? What do you know about their needs? What is most relevant to them?

- ▶ Particularly when dealing with your neutral and hostile audiences, what are some ways that you can bridge the gap between your beliefs and those of your audience members? How can you generate goodwill and understanding?

- ▶ Is there a particular organizational pattern that would best suit you, your topic, or your audience? For example, are you comfortable with and knowledgeable enough about your hostile audience's counterpoints that you are comfortable refuting them using the refutational organizational pattern?

## IF YOU'RE INTERESTED

*The Persuasion Handbook: Developments in Theory and Practice,* edited by James Price Dillard and Michael Pfau (Thousand Oaks, CA: Sage, 2002)

This excellent book is full of research on how we convince others of our ideas. It is very readable and is often used as a textbook in persuasion classes. The contributors are experts at persuasion and offer readers many practical tips on using language and nonverbal cues to become more effective communicators.

*Common Sense,* by Thomas Paine (1776)

One of the most influential tracts in American history, Paine's 1776 pamphlet laid out a clear and persuasive argument for the colonial rebellion against the British crown. It was wildly popular, selling hundreds of thousands of copies during Paine's lifetime, and is widely credited for building popular sentiment in favor of the American Revolution. In it, Paine clearly lays out his key points, elaborating on each one with appeals to logic, emotion, and character.

*To Kill a Mockingbird,* by Harper Lee (1960)

This classic American novel tells the story of a southern lawyer's crusade to acquit an African American unjustly accused of rape in the Jim Crow–era South. Narrated by the lawyer's precocious young daughter, the story revolves around the difficult task of persuading an audience (in the form of a jury and an entire town) that is for the most part hostile to the message.

*What Women Want* (Paramount Pictures, 2000)

In this innocuous comedy, a male chauvinist advertising executive gets a glimpse into women's minds and finds ways to use his new insights to cleverly market products to a female audience. A fantasy version of audience analysis.

*Sicko* (Michael Moore, 2007)

Documentarian Michael Moore takes on the American health care system with a scathing indictment of the health insurance industry. While his informative case on the failings of the current system are compelling and for the most part hard to find fault with, his argument for creating a national health care system falls into some logistical traps due to various logical fallacies he employs.

*Big Love,* "Pilot" (2006)

This HBO drama revolves around the life of Bill Henrickson, a Mormon polygamist; his three wives (Barbara, Nicki, and Margene); and their three households with seven combined children. The show avoids judgment on the moral or legal implications of polygamy, leaving viewers to come to their own conclusions; nonetheless, it is interesting to watch the first episode, looking for examples of ethos, pathos, and logos used as subtle means of persuading the viewer to reaffirm or reconsider stereotypes about polygamy and the people who practice it.

*Mind Control with Darren Brown* (2007)

This Sci-Fi Network original series focuses on the British television phenomenon of "con artist" Darren Brown. Brown uses manipulation techniques, persuasion, misdirection, and psychological processes to amaze everyday people with his skills. You can watch the show on the Sci-Fi channel or go to the Web site, www.scifi.com.

**Now that you have finished reading this chapter, you can**

Define the goals of persuasive speaking:

▶ **Coercion** involves threats, intimidation, or violence (p. 452).

▶ **Persuasive speaking** uses the process of **persuasion** to influence **attitudes**, **beliefs**, and **behavior** (p. 452).

Know how to develop a persuasive topic and thesis:

▶ Choose a topic that is controversial, and aim to create change in the audience (p. 453).

▶ Thesis statements are often given as a **proposition**, a statement of your viewpoint on an issue (p. 453).

▶ A **proposition of fact** is a claim of what is or what is not and addresses how people perceive reality (p. 453).

▶ A **proposition of value** makes claims about something's worth (p. 454).

▶ A **proposition of policy** concerns what *should* happen and makes claims about what goal, policy, or course of action should be pursued (p. 455).

Understand your listeners and tailor your speech to them:

▶ A **receptive audience** agrees with you (p. 456).

▶ A **hostile audience** opposes your message (p. 456).

▶ A **neutral audience** neither supports nor opposes you (p. 456).

▶ The **latitude of acceptance and rejection** refers to the range of positions on a topic that are acceptable or unacceptable to your audience (p. 457).

▶ Maslow's **hierarchy of needs** holds that our most basic needs must be met before we can worry about needs farther up the hierarchy (p. 457).

▶ The **Elaboration Likelihood Model (ELM)** highlights the importance of relevance to persuasion and holds that people will process the message by one of two routes: **central processing** (deep, motivated thinking) or **peripheral processing** (unmotivated, less critical thought) (p. 459).

Explain three **forms of rhetorical proof**:

▶ The speaker's moral character, or **ethos**, influences the audience's reaction to the message (p. 462).

▶ **Logos** refers to appeals to the audience's **reasoning**, judgments based on facts and inferences (p. 462).

▶ **Inductive reasoning** involves drawing general conclusions from specific evidence; **deductive reasoning** applies general arguments to specific cases (pp. 462–463).

▶ A **syllogism** is a three-line deductive argument, drawing a conclusion from two general premises (p. 463).

▶ An **enthymeme** is similar to a syllogism, except it omits one of the premises, which you assume your audience already understands (p. 463).

▶ **Pathos** appeals to the listeners' emotions (p. 464).

Recognize the **logical fallacies**, deceptive forms of reasoning:

▶ The **bandwagon fallacy**: a statement is considered true because it is popular (p. 467).

▶ **Reduction to the absurd**: an argument is pushed beyond its logical limits (p. 467).

▶ The **red herring fallacy**: irrelevant information is used to divert the direction of the argument (p. 467).

▶ Personal attacks, the ***ad hominem* fallacy**: focus is on a person rather than on the issue (p. 467).

▶ **Begging the question**: advancing an argument that cannot be proved because there is no valid evidence (p. 467).

▶ **Either-or fallacy**: only two alternatives are presented, omitting other alternatives (p. 468).

▶ **Appeal to tradition**: "that's the way it has always been" is the only reason given (p. 468).

▶ The **slippery slope**: one event is presented as the result of another, without showing proof (p. 468).

Choose an appropriate organizational strategy for your speech:

▶ The *problem-solution pattern* proves the existence of a problem and then presents a solution (p. 468).

▶ The **refutational organizational pattern** presents the main points of the opposition to your argument and then refutes them. This works well when the opposing argument is weak (p. 470).

▶ The **comparative advantage pattern** tells why your viewpoint is superior to other viewpoints on an issue (p. 470).

▶ Monroe's motivated sequence is a five-step process that begins with arousing listeners' attention and ends with calling for action (p. 472).

Stephen Colbert: master of the satirical interview.

# Competent Interviewing

**Stephen Colbert sits across the desk** from Congressman Barney Frank in the congressman's Washington office. He raises an eyebrow over his signature rimless eyeglasses and poses a question: "President Bush: great president or our greatest president?" The Massachusetts Democrat, looking perplexed, tells Colbert that he doesn't agree with either evaluation: "I think he's been a disaster." Colbert replies, simply, "I'll put you down for great, then" (Colbert, 2005). It's a regular question—and a common answer (or lack of an answer) on *The Colbert Report*'s 434-part series "Better Know a District," in which Colbert corners congressional representatives and forces them to play straight to a series of loaded and often inane questions.

Since his days as a fake news analyst on *The Daily Show*, Stephen Colbert has perfected the art of the satirical interview. Casting himself as a hard-right-leaning commentator who "feels" the truth rather than concerning himself with facts, Colbert has interviewed representatives from more than fifty districts for his series. Colbert stays in character for the length of the interview and, as one critic explains, "poses either ridiculous questions on serious topics or earnest questions on ludicrous ones" (Patterson, 2006). Each interview is then edited down to a three- to five-minute comedy segment. Through clever editing, sight gags, and a deadpan performance from Colbert, each representative is made to look somewhat ridiculous.

While the interviews are clearly parody, with Colbert coming off as the biggest fool of all, many politicians refuse the interviews. In fact, in 2007, Democratic caucus chairman Rahm Emanuel (D-Ill.) warned freshman lawmakers to turn down offers to be interviewed for the series (Kaplan, 2007). Yet many representatives still accept. As Phil Hare (D-Ill.) notes, "This job is terrifically important, and I take it seriously. But I don't take myself too seriously" (Ross, 2007). Hare says he told reporters that he laughed through the entire ninety-minute interview, during which Colbert asked the congressman (who had once considered becoming a funeral director), "If you could embalm anyone in Congress, who would it be?"

Although Stephen Colbert's discussions with members of Congress are not serious, they do follow many important rules for interviews. From Colbert and company, for example, we can learn about the roles of the interviewer and interviewee and the effects of questions and answers. In this appendix, we'll examine interviews from a communication standpoint—how they relate to other forms of communication, what kinds of factors are at work in an interview situation, and how all people, from recent college graduates to congressional representatives to newscasters, can improve their interviewing skills.

## The Nature of Interviews

Although interviewing is not exactly like grabbing a Big Mac with one of your friends, the same principles that apply to all forms of communication are also at work in an interview, with some important differences.

An **interview** is an interaction between two parties that is deliberate and purposeful for at least one of the parties involved. By nature, interviews are more structured and goal-driven than other forms of communication, and they are a form of discourse that is planned, dyadic, and interactive (O'Hair, Friedrich, & Dixon, 2007).

▶ *Interviews are planned.* Interviews have a purpose that goes beyond the establishment and development of a relationship. At least one of the parties (sometimes both) has a predetermined reason for initiating the interview (for example, to gather information).

▶ *Interviews are goal-driven.* Because a goal exists in advance of the interaction, it is beneficial for at least one of the participants to plan a strategy for initiating, conducting, and concluding the interview. For example, if you want to obtain a family history from a relative, you plan a series of questions that will help you get the information you want and still give your interviewee the freedom to add things you may not have thought about.

▶ *Interviews are structured.* The primary goal of an interview is almost always defined at the beginning of the meeting, something that's rarely true of a conversation with a friend. Relationships are more formally structured, and clear status differences often exist. One party usually expects to exert more control than the other.

▶ *Interviews are dyadic.* Like other forms of interpersonal communication, the interview is dyadic, meaning that it involves two parties. In some instances, a "party" consists of more than one person, as when survey researchers conduct group interviews or when job applicants appear before a panel of interviewers. In such situations, even though a number of individuals are involved, there are only two parties (interviewers and interviewees), each with a role to play.

▶ *Interviews are interactive.* Interviews involve two-way interactions in which both parties take turns in speaking and listening roles, with a heavy dependence on questions and answers. Although most interviews occur face to face, interactions over the phone or via a videoconference are also considered interactive discourse.

● **ALL INTERVIEWS,** whether an E! red carpet interview or a serious job interview, are goal-driven, as well as dyadic and interactive in nature.

Think back to Stephen Colbert. His interviews are not only dyadic and interactive but also highly planned. He writes questions ahead of time, based on the politician's views and background, and structures his interviews in a way that helps him achieve his goal: a hilarious spoof on American politics.

## Types of Interviews

What type of scene plays out in your mind when you think of the word *interview*? Maybe you start sweating thinking about an upcoming job interview for a position that you really want. Or maybe you even laugh, thinking about movies like *The Nanny Diaries,* where highly agitated parents worry about perfecting the interview to get their toddlers and young children into the right preschool or elementary school. But interviewing encompasses much more than just getting a job or getting into the right school. In this section, we look at the different types of interviews that play a role in most of our lives (Stewart & Cash, 2006).

### The Information-Gathering Interview

In the 2007 film *Juno,* sixteen-year-old Juno MacGuff sits in the expensively furnished living room of Mark and Vanessa Loring, a couple interested in adopting Juno's unborn child. Vanessa and her adoption lawyer, Gerta Rauss, pepper Juno with questions like "How far along are you?" and "You really think you're going to go ahead with this?" What they're really getting at is obtaining *information* from Juno by collecting attitudes, opinions, facts, data, and experiences through an **information-gathering interview**. We take part in, or are exposed to, the results of such interviews every day; we might complete telephone surveys on political or cultural topics or read interviews with

**AND YOU?**

Have you ever imagined interviewing a particular celebrity, political leader, or historical figure? If you were given such an opportunity, what would your goals be for the interview? What kinds of questions would you ask?

● **VANESSA LORING WANTS** to learn as much information as she can about Juno at their first meeting. Her goal is to determine if Juno will back out of their adoption agreement.

musicians in *Rolling Stone.* Perhaps you've compiled a survey about experiences with campus parking, or maybe you've initiated information gathering when you asked your communication professor about career possibilities. In all these instances, the information-gathering interview serves to transfer knowledge from one party to the other.

## The Appraisal Interview

In just about every career—including your academic career—**performance appraisals** are a regular part of reviewing your accomplishments and developing goals for the future. In most corporate environments, a performance appraisal is a highly structured routine dictated by company policies, involving a written appraisal and a one-on-one interview between a supervisor and an employee. But in other situations, we also take part in less structured performance appraisals. For example, you might meet with your professor to discuss a project or paper or to lobby for a change in your grade. Although being evaluated can be stressful, the appraisal can offer insight into strengths as well as weaknesses. In other words, the appraisal interview can offer reassurance about what you're doing well and give some guidance for improvement or growth (Arvey & Murphy, 1998).

## The Problem-Solving Interview

Of course, not every appraisal interview is positive. Sometimes a **problem-solving interview** is needed to deal with problems, tensions, or conflicts. If you've ever seen an episode of A&E Television's *Intervention,* you've seen this type of interview in action. Typically, friends and family contact an interventionist (a counselor) to help them deal with a loved one's addictive behavior, whether it's drug abuse, gambling, or video game addiction. The interventionist works with the family, asking questions, gathering information, and formulating a plan or solution before the official intervention, when the counselor, friends, and family all confront their loved one.

Problem-solving interviews can also occur in the workplace (typically when there are performance issues) and even in medical situations. For example, your primary care physician listens to problems or concerns in your life that may affect your physical health and tries to resolve the health problem; in the interview, you should also feel free to ask questions and volunteer information to help solve the problem (Coulehan & Block, 2006; Kreps & Kunimoto, 1994).

**AND YOU?**

Do you think of a problem-solving interview as a reprimand or as an opportunity to create needed changes? How can you change the nature of a negative-toned interview into a more positive experience?

## EVALUATINGCOMMUNICATIONETHICS

**THINK ABOUT THIS**

### Surveys: Interviewing at Large

Imagine that you are an officer in your college's alumni association, and you have been asked to interview other alumni in order to produce marketing materials that will help increase the number and quality of students applying to your school. Your association wants to show how much graduates enjoyed their school experience and how well they have succeeded in their careers.

You produce a simple one-page survey that asks alumni to rate their school and their postgraduate experience from poor to excellent, which you plan to mail to everyone listed in the alumni register. You are hoping that once all the responses have been tallied, you'll be able to make declarative statements in your marketing materials noting the high percentage of graduates who rate their experience as "excellent." But when you submit your plan and a draft of the survey to the alumni association, you are shot down. "We don't want to hear from everyone," says the alumni president. "We only want to hear from successful graduates who are working at *Fortune* 500 companies or who have made big names for themselves in the sciences."

You are asked instead to create an in-depth survey and conduct it by phone with graduates who have donated more than $1,000 to the school in the past five years. You know that this will skew the results of your survey toward former students who love the school and who have been financially successful since graduating. The association is asking you to present this information as though these students are representative of all students. But you know that although the alumni association depends on successful and wealthy graduates for support, such graduates represent a minority of the students who have attended your school. You know that many students have gone on to successful and fulfilling, if less lucrative, careers in education and the arts. You are concerned that the skewed survey you are being asked to conduct will not paint an accurate picture of the school for prospective students. What are the ethical implications here?

**1** Does your plan for a survey of graduates present a more accurate picture of the school than a telephone survey with only the wealthiest graduates?

**2** What about students who attended the school but did not graduate or who are not in the alumni rolls? Would leaving them out skew the results of your survey as well?

**3** Does it really matter? Remember, this survey is for material to be used in marketing. Do you think students will infer that quotes from very successful graduates mean that every student at the school goes on to a high-profile, six-figure-salary career?

**CONNECT**

Ethical considerations are important when planning a persuasive interview. As you learn in Chapter 15, there is a difference between persuading people and *coercing* them with threats. If you're going door-to-door to support a political candidate, remember that your job is to give people information—not to intimidate or belittle them into supporting your candidate. That is clearly unethical communication!

● **PARODYING THE FORMAT** of shows like *The Bachelor,* Cartman and the gang question and screen various secondary characters on the show, hoping to uncover the new Kenny.

## The Exit Interview

Hiring and training new people is an expensive process in terms of both time and money, so most organizations want to keep good employees. By conducting **exit interviews** with employees who opt to leave the company, employers can identify organizational problems—such as poor management style, noncompetitive salary, or weak employee benefits—that might affect employee retention. College professors—including us—often conduct similar exit interviews with students who are moving on in their education or embarking on a career. We use the information to help them clarify their goals and help us build a stronger program.

## The Persuasive Interview

At times the goal of an interview is not merely to inform or gather information. In a **persuasive interview**, questions are designed to elicit some change in the interviewee's behavior or opinions. Some political surveys, for example, are aimed at securing your support for (or against) a particular candidate or cause. After you graduate, your alma mater may call to ask you questions about your college experience (hoping to remind you of sunny walks across campus, interesting classes, and the good times you had) and then ask you to contribute to a scholarship fund or an annual financial drive. You might also do some persuasive interviewing to convince others to give blood during a campus campaign or to vote for your candidate in a campus, local, or national election.

## The Service-Oriented Interview

Did your computer freak out and delete all of your programs? Do you have a roach problem? Have you ever found unauthorized charges on your credit card bill? If any of these things have ever happened to you, you are probably intimately familiar with "help desk" or customer service lines. Representatives contacted at these organizations will conduct **service-oriented interviews** or helping interviews designed to cull information and provide advice, service, or support based on that information. Such interviews are crucial in many contexts—consider what kind of work you'd get from a lawyer, a health care provider, or a landscaper if the person didn't talk to you about your case, ideas, or desires first.

## The Selection Interview

If you're a fan of *South Park,* you might remember the "Professor Chaos" episode (season six) in which Stan, Kyle, and Cartman hold a series of interviews and competitions to fill the open slot (left void by Kenny's demise) in their group of four. Silly as it may be, it's an example of a **selection interview**, the primary goal of which is to secure or fill a position within an organization. Selection interviews usually involve recruiting, screening, hiring, and placing new candidates

(Baker & Spier, 1990). Members of an organization (such as a company, sorority, fraternity, volunteer organization, or university) and candidates evaluate one another by exchanging information to determine if they'd make a good match. Usually both parties want to make a good impression: the interviewer wants to persuade the interviewee about the value of the position or organization, while the interviewee wants to sell his or her unique qualities and abilities.

The **job interview** is one of the most common types of selection interviews in business, government, and military organizations, with the end goal of filling a position of employment (DiSanza & Legge, 2002). Since job interviewing is usually very important to college students, we devote much of this chapter to helping you become more competent in this context.

● **AFTER EVERY CHALLENGE** on *The Apprentice,* the losing team is subjected to a lengthy questioning by "The Donald" and his advisers to try to figure out what went awry.

## The Format of an Interview

For the premiere season of Donald Trump's reality TV show *The Apprentice,* more than two hundred thousand people applied for sixteen slots (Naughton & Peyser, 2004); sixteen lucky winners were thrown into a lengthy employment interview in front of approximately eighteen million weekly fans. Drama, tears, yelling, and backstabbing naturally ensued. This is certainly not a typical interview format (and doesn't sound like much fun to us), but *The Apprentice* illustrates the goal orientation of all interviews. Whether you are interviewing for a job or answering questions for a news reporter, you will note the same basic pattern: an opening, the questions, and a conclusion.

### The Opening

Regis and Kelly and David Letterman's interviewees are always welcomed with a grand entrance and audience clapping and cheering. Even Jerry Springer's guests are ushered in with some fanfare (unfortunately, most of it involves cursing, booing, and attempts at violence). But if you're not planning to star in an Oscar-nominated film or find out the paternity of a child on national television, you probably won't have to worry about this. Your interviews will begin in a calmer manner, setting the tone for the discourse to follow. Before or just as the interview begins, you should always think about three interrelated issues:

▸ The *task:* the nature of this interview and how it will proceed

▸ The *relationship:* whether you like or trust the other party

▸ *Motivation:* what you hope to gain by participating in the interview

For example, Eva is doing a telephone survey on student attitudes about parking on campus. The students she calls want to know about the topic of the interview

**CONNECT**

The opening of an interview is much like the introduction to a speech. As we discuss in Chapter 12, speech introductions help you achieve three goals: capturing your audience's attention, previewing your main points, and establishing a relationship with your audience. Openings in both contexts establish the interaction that follows, so your success in engaging your listeners depends on your competency right from the start.

and how long it will take (the task). They want to know something about her and how the information she gathers will be used (the relationship). They want to know how they (or someone else) will benefit from participating in the interview (the motivation). Eva needs to plan what she can say or do at the *start* of the interview that is responsive to these needs. As she considers the unique requirements of each interview, she might use one or more of the opening behaviors in Table A.1 to help her address task, relationship, or motivational issues.

## TABLE A.1

### INTERVIEW OPENING TECHNIQUES

| Behavior | Definition | Example |
|---|---|---|
| Make a brief statement about a problem or need. | This type of statement orients an interviewee who is vaguely aware of the problem but is not well informed about its details. | "As you know, we're looking for individuals to join our sales staff. Our new sales associates will have some exciting opportunities that may not have been mentioned." |
| Give a brief explanation of how you happened to learn that a problem existed, coupled with the suggestion that the interviewee will want to discuss it. | This avoids the appearance of lecturing or talking down to a person and encourages a spirit of cooperative, objective discussion of a shared problem. | "In speaking with Lynette, I learned that the two of you are having some trouble working together on this project. I'd really like to hear your thoughts and your ideas for making this situation work for everyone." |
| State an incentive (goal or outcome) that may be expected if the problem or need is fulfilled. | Potentially the most powerful of all, this incentive can be easily abused; avoid what sounds like a high-pressure "sales pitch." | "Our graduate program offers smaller classes and more direct learning than a larger university, and we have a scholarship program that you may qualify for." |
| Request the interviewee's advice or assistance with regard to a problem. | This approach is effective when sincere; don't use it as a slick gimmick. | "I'm hoping that you can help me learn more about why there seems to be a strain between marketing and production in this division." |
| Refer to the known position of the interviewee regarding a situation. | This common-ground approach is excellent to use when the interviewee has taken a public position or has already asked you to bring in proposals or the like. | "You've expressed a desire to take our brand national. I want to hear your ideas about how we can branch out into a larger market." |
| Identify the person who directed you to the interviewee. | This is appropriate when the interviewee doesn't know you and may be wondering why you have sought out him or her; it is especially effective when the third party is respected by the interviewee. | "I was referred to you by Tamar Stein, who told me that you've done great work for her in the past." |
| Identify the company, organization, or group you represent. | This is appropriate when you need to explain your presence or when added prestige is needed. | "I'm calling from Amnesty International, and I'm hoping you'll take a few minutes to let me know your opinions on the current situation in Darfur." |
| Request a specified, brief period of time. | This strategy can be useful when dealing with an impatient, irritable, or very busy interviewee. | "I'm hoping that you can spare ten minutes of your time to discuss the Nelson project." |

Source: Goyer & Rickey (1968), p. 10. Adapted with permission.

## The Questions

Once you have set the stage for the interview with an appropriate opening, you need to develop the organizational plan for the body of the interview. Questions and answers are the core of the interview. They accomplish the goals of the interview through structuring, soliciting, responding, and reacting. The interviewer sets up the structure of the interview (identifying the purpose of the interview) and then solicits a response from the interviewee. This response then prompts reactions from the interviewer, and it just keeps building from there. To have the most effective and most successful interview possible, whether you're the interviewer or interviewee, you need to consider question type, impact, and sequence.

### Types of Questions

The path of the interview is largely determined by the types of questions asked. Questions vary in two distinct ways: the amount of freedom the respondent has and how the questions relate to what has happened in the course of the interview.

First, questions vary in terms of how much leeway the interviewee has in generating responses. An **open question** gives the interviewee great freedom in terms of how to respond. Questions like "Tell me about yourself," "What's it like being a student here?" or "What issues will influence your decision to vote for one of the presidential candidates?" allow the interviewee to determine the amount and depth of information provided. Interviewers often ask open questions when the interviewee knows more about a topic than the interviewer does or to help the interviewee relax (there is no "correct" answer, so no answer is wrong).

In other situations, the interviewer will want a more direct answer. **Closed questions** give less freedom to the interviewee by restricting answer choices. For example, an interviewer conducting a survey of student attitudes toward parking on campus might ask more closed questions ("When do you arrive on campus?" "Where do you park?" "How long do you stay?"). The most closed

● PROSPECTIVE STUDENTS on a campus tour should ask their student guides open questions ("What's the social scene like?") and closed questions ("Is the dining hall open on the weekends?") to figure out what student life is *really* like.

form of a question is the **bipolar question**, for which there are only two possible responses, "yes" and "no" ("Do you normally eat breakfast?" "Do you own a car?" "Did you vote in the last election?"). Another possibility is to ask interviewees to respond to a scale, as with the question "How would you rate parking availability on campus?"

| 1 | 2 | 3 | 4 | 5 |
|---|---|---|---|---|
| Very poor | Poor | Adequate | Good | Excellent |

Questions also vary in terms of how they relate to what has happened so far in the interview. **Primary questions** introduce new topics; **secondary questions** seek clarification or elaboration of responses to primary questions. Thus an interviewer might open an area of questioning by asking, "What can you tell me about my family history?" This primary question might then be followed by a number of secondary questions, such as "How did my grandparents meet?" and "How did they deal with the fact that their parents disapproved of their marriage?" Secondary questions can take a variety of forms. Some of the more common forms are illustrated in Table A.2.

### Question Impact

In addition to considering question type, interviewers must also consider the likely impact of a question on the interviewee. The way in which a question is constructed can directly influence the information received in response. A good question is clear, relevant, and unbiased. To create clear questions, consider the following criteria:

▶ Make questions understandable. Ask the classic and simple news reporters' questions of who, what, when, where, why, and how (Payne, 1951) before you proceed to more complex ones.

▶ Ensure that the wording of the question is as direct and simple as possible. For example, asking, "For whom did you vote in the last presidential election?" will get you a more precise answer than asking "How do you vote?"

▶ Keep the question short and to the point.

▶ Phrase questions positively. For example, asking, "Have you ever voted in campus student government elections?" is clear and objective; using negative phrasing ("You haven't ever voted in the campus student government elections, have you?") can be confusing (not to mention unethical and biased) (Doris, 1991).

Speaking of ethics, a question that suggests or implies the answer that is expected is called a **directed question**. Some such questions are subtle in the direction they provide ("Wouldn't it be so much fun if we all got together to paint my apartment this weekend?"). These subtle directed questions are **leading questions**. Other directed questions are bolder in their biasing effect and are called **loaded questions** ("When was the last time you cheated on an exam?" This question, of course, assumes that you *have* cheated.) Questions that

| Behavior | Definition | Example |
|---|---|---|
| Clarification | Directly requests more information about a response | "Could you tell me a little more about the reasons you chose to join the military after high school?" |
| Elaboration | Directly requests an extension of a response | "Are there any other specific features that you consider important in your search for a new house?" |
| Paraphrasing | Puts the response in the questioner's language in an attempt to establish understanding | "So, you're saying that the type of people you work with is more important to you than location?" |
| Mirroring | Similar to paraphrasing but simply repeats the response, using the language used by the respondent | "Hmm, it is important to be located near a university." |
| Silence | Waits without speaking for the respondent to begin or resume speaking | Look at the other person with an appropriate facial expression. |
| Encouragement | Uses brief sounds and phrases that indicate attentiveness to and interest in what the respondent is saying | "Uh-huh," "I see," "That's interesting," "Good," "Yes, I understand." |
| Summarizing | Summarizes several previous responses and seeks confirmation of the correctness of the summary | "Let's see if I've got it: your ideal job involves an appreciative boss, supportive colleagues, interesting work, and living in a large metropolitan area?" |
| Clearinghouse | Asks if you have elicited all the important or available information | "Have I asked everything that I should have asked?" |

**TABLE A.2**

**SECONDARY QUESTIONS**

Source: Labels and definitions from O'Hair, Friedrich, & Dixon (2007).

provide no hint to the interviewee concerning the expected response are **neutral questions**. For example, "What, if anything, is your attitude toward the fraternities and sororities on this campus?" Additional examples are given in Table A.3 (see p. 496).

## Question Sequence

The order in which the interviewer asks questions can have a big impact on the interview; it can affect both the accomplishment of goals and the comfort level of the interviewee. There are three main "shapes" that guide the ordering of questions: the funnel, inverted funnel, and tunnel sequences.

In the **funnel sequence**, the interviewer starts with broad, open-ended questions (picture the big end of a funnel) and moves to narrower, more closed

CONNECT

Even neutral questions can become leading questions if you fail to consider nonverbal communication (Chapter 4). If you grimace, roll your eyes, or change your tone of voice when you ask the neutral question "What, if anything, is your attitude toward fraternities and sororities on this campus?" you are actually asking a leading question (and letting others know your attitude toward the Greek system on campus).

| Question Behavior | Definition | Example |
|---|---|---|
| Leading | Questions that subtlely direct interviewees to the correct or desired answer | "Do you take home office supplies like most employees?" |
| Loaded | Extremely leading questions that almost dictate the correct answer; to be avoided in most cases | "When was the last time you took home supplies from the office?" |
| Neutral | Questions that allow respondents to choose their answers without pressure from the interviewer's wording | "Do you think the office should provide you with supplies to work at home?" |

questions. The questions become more personal or more tightly focused as the interview progresses, giving the interviewee a chance to get comfortable with the topic and open up. The funnel sequence works best with respondents who feel comfortable with the topic and the interviewer.

► "What do you think about children playing competitive sports?" (general)

► "So what disadvantages have you witnessed?" (specific)

► "What constraints would you then advocate for young players?" (very specific)

The **inverted funnel sequence** starts with narrow, closed questions and moves to more open-ended questions. The inverted funnel works best with interviewees who are emotional, are reticent, or need help "warming up."

**FIGURE A.1**
FUNNEL, INVERTED
FUNNEL, AND TUNNEL
SEQUENCES

► "Did you perform a Mozart piece for your piano recital in junior high school?" (very specific)

► "What other classical compositions are you comfortable playing?" (specific)

► "How did you feel about taking piano lessons as a child?" (general)

In the **tunnel sequence**, all of the questions are at one level. The tunnel sequence works particularly well in polls and surveys. A large tunnel would involve a series of broad, open-ended questions. A small tunnel (the more common form) would ask a series of narrow, closed questions, as in the following example:

► "Have you attended any multicultural events on campus?" (specific)

► "Have you attended sports games or matches?" (specific)

► "Have you attended any guest lecturer series on campus?" (specific)

The three sequences are depicted visually in Figure A.1.

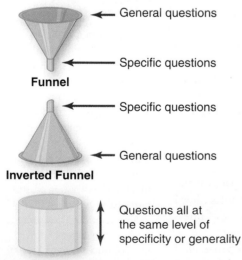

General questions

Specific questions

**Funnel**

Specific questions

General questions

**Inverted Funnel**

Questions all at the same level of specificity or generality

**Tunnel**

Interviewers can put together the three sequences in various combinations over the course of an interview, based on the goals for the interview, the direction the interview takes, and the comfort level of both parties involved.

## real communicator

**NAME:** Richard McWhorter
**HOMETOWN:** Atlanta, Georgia
**OCCUPATION:** Independent journalist, marketing specialist
**FUN FACT:** I'm addicted to peanut butter–covered pretzels.

You're eating in a restaurant. All of a sudden, you look up and you see a *celebrity:* a film actor or a basketball player or a contestant on one of those reality shows. You might approach this celebrity and say, "Hi, nice to meet you, big fan, really love your work, I think you're top-notch." The celebrity says, "Thanks." You and the celebrity stare at each other awkwardly. Then you go back to your table. Based on these kinds of interpersonal interactions, you might think celebrities are reserved and direct, men and women of few words.

If only it were so.

As a freelance journalist, I get to interview celebrities, both on the phone and in person. Far and away the hardest part of my job is getting these celebrities to *stop* talking. Talking is great, obviously, but my job is to conduct information-gathering interviews—in other words, to obtain solid information relating to the specific article I'm working on. That can be tough, however, when celebrities start gabbing.

For example, I had to put together an article on the relationship between hip-hop and the development of mobile technology. So I interviewed a prominent entertainer with the goal of obtaining his opinions on this particular issue. It was a telephone interview, and I had a hard time keeping my celebrity on track. He wanted to talk about his career and his experiences in the industry; he wanted to talk about the economy, the great divide between the wealthy and the poor—interesting stuff, but it didn't really relate to the topic at hand: mobile technology and hip-hop. To achieve my goals and write my article, I needed to get the interview (and my interviewee) back on track.

Because I'm a communication major, I've acquired the skill sets to get what I needed. I had a plan—a list of clear and concise questions structured around my central goal. But the further my interviewee got from those questions, the harder it was for me to stick to my list and ask the next question. It would have been too abrupt, too rude. So I improvised broad questions that then became increasingly focused. When my celebrity started talking about Wall Street, I asked, "How might this weakened economy play a role in the elections?" And then, "What effect, if any, do you think hip-hop will have on politics, or vice versa?" And finally, "Do you think technology and the hip-hop industry will improve the economic situation as more and more entertainers try to make a living?" *Voilà!* By asking increasingly relevant questions, I got the interview back on track.

By having a clearly defined goal, by preparing a list of questions organized around that goal, and by listening carefully, I was able to gather the information I needed. The interview felt less like an interview and more like a conversation. Eventually, I even got to hang up the phone.

## The Conclusion

When *CSI: Miami*'s Horatio Caine is finished interviewing a suspect or gathering information at the scene of the crime, he often delivers a killer punch line (frequently pausing somewhere in the middle to put on his trademark sunglasses). While Caine's tactics are quite amusing—inspiring countless YouTube tributes and even a Jim Carrey spoof—we can promise that most interviews will end on a far less dramatic note. Once the purpose of the interview has been achieved, the interaction should come to a comfortable and satisfying close. This closing phase of the interview is especially important because it is likely to determine the impression the interviewee retains of the interview as a whole.

Mark Knapp and his colleagues studied the functions and norms involved when individuals take leave of each other (Knapp, Hart, Friedrich, & Shulman, 1973). They conclude that in closing the interview, the interviewer needs to employ both verbal and nonverbal strategies to serve three important functions (Von Raffler-Engel, 1983):

▶ To *conclude,* or signal the end of the interview

▶ To *summarize,* or review the substantive conclusions produced by the interview

▶ To *support,* or express satisfaction with the interaction and project what will happen next

Table A.4 illustrates closing strategies that may help you conclude, summarize, and support. As these sample statements indicate, bringing the interview to a close is largely the responsibility of the interviewer. In the next section, look at how this and other responsibilities and roles are filled in a variety of interviewing situations.

● **HORATIO CAINE'S** suave move indicates that he's done interviewing a suspect or surveying the crime scene. Your job interview will have a simple, comfortable conclusion.

# Understanding Roles and Responsibilities in Interviews

Jan, a thirty-five-year-old high school biology teacher, is on the hunt for a new career. She can approach this job hunt in two ways. First, she could simply answer advertisements for open positions and hope to be called in for an interview. Alternatively, she can identify people or organizations that she thinks she'd like to work for and arrange for information-gathering interviews with them. In the first approach, Jan, the job hunter, fills the role of *interviewee*—she answers questions posed by the interviewer. In the second example, Jan acts as the *interviewer,* asking people in various positions for information about potential career paths in their industry. So how are these roles different? How are they similar? Let's find out.

## Roles and Responsibilities of the Interviewer

In any interview situation, there are specific behaviors that competent interviewers share. Specifically, they must identify potential barriers, make the interviewee

**TABLE A.4**

## CLOSING STRATEGIES

| Behavior | Definition | Example |
|---|---|---|
| Declare the completion of the purpose or task. | The word *well* probably signals a close more than any other phrase; people automatically assume the end is near and prepare to take their leave. | "Well, I think we've covered a lot of territory today." |
| Signal that time for the meeting is up. | This is most effective when a time limit has been announced or agreed on in the opening of the interview. Be tactful; avoid being too abrupt or giving the impression that you're moving the interviewee along an assembly line. | "We have just a few minutes left, so . . ." |
| Explain the reason for the closing. | Be sure the reasons are real; if an interviewee thinks you're giving phony excuses, future interactions will be strained. | "Unfortunately, I've got another meeting in twenty minutes, so we'll have to start wrapping things up." |
| Express appreciation or satisfaction. | This is a common closing because interviewers have usually received something from the interview (information, help, a sale, a story, a new employee). | "Thank you for your interest in our cause." |
| Plan for the next meeting. | This reveals what will happen next (date, time, place, topic, content, purpose) or arranges for the next interview. | "I think we should follow up on this next week; my assistant will call you to arrange a time." |
| Summarize the interview. | This common closing for informational, appraisal, counseling, and sales interviews may repeat important information, stages, or agreements or verify accuracy or agreement. | "We've come to three major agreements here today." |

Source: Labels from Stewart & Cash (2006).

comfortable, ask ethical and appropriate questions, and effectively listen and respond to the interviewee. In addition, interviewers must be culturally sensitive. (You'll read more about this issue in the "Communication Across Cultures" box on page 501.)

### Identify Potential Barriers

Before heading into an interview situation, interviewers should take some time to reflect on potential barriers that might disrupt the interview. For example, is the space where the interview will take place quiet, private, and fairly neat and organized? True story: Val is an academic counselor at a prestigious university who is unfortunate enough to have an office next door to the copy room. The old Xerox machine causes her wall to shake whenever one of her colleagues makes a photocopy; on top of this, her university recently installed "see-through" blinds that don't actually keep the sunlight out. Every afternoon, she must take students to a private conference room when interviewing them about their coursework or their career plans in order to avoid distractions.

### Make the Interviewee Comfortable

Interviewees, particularly job applicants and medical patients, are often very nervous in interview situations—and understandably so. A good interviewer should adapt to the situational and relational contexts to help the interviewee feel at ease. It would be effective and appropriate, for example, for an interviewer to smile, make eye contact, and offer a handshake. But imagine if your doctor entered the examining room and gave you a big hug or if a job interviewer told you about his problems with his partner's parents. Be sure to keep verbal and nonverbal behaviors appropriate to the context.

### Ask Ethical and Appropriate Questions

We've already discussed types of questions and question sequences that you can use to guide productive, competent interviews that achieve your goals. But beyond knowing how to use open and closed questions or funnel or inverted funnel sequences, it's important to remember that good questions are also ethical and appropriate questions. For example, if Erik is a representative from his school newspaper interviewing a biology professor about her recent grant from the National Institutes of Health (NIH), his questions should stick to her research and her plans to implement a new lab on campus. It would be inappropriate and unethical for him to ask how much money she will be receiving from the NIH or whether or not she expects to receive a promotion and salary increase from the university after receiving the award.

On a job interview, certain unethical and inappropriate questions are also illegal. We will talk about these later in this chapter.

### Listen and Respond Effectively

The role of the interviewer is not limited to structuring an interview and asking questions. After all, an effective interviewer needs to listen, respond, and evaluate the information that those questions reveal. Throughout the interview, the interviewer should keep both immediate and future goals in mind by making notes (written or mental) during the interview. A medical doctor might take notes about your family history and ask follow-up questions or order tests regarding your health based on this discussion.

**AND YOU?**

Have you ever been in an interview where you felt that the interviewer neglected his or her responsibilities? In what ways did the interviewer fail? How would you have handled things differently?

## Roles and Responsibilities of the Interviewee

True, the interviewer is responsible for quite a bit of work in an interview situation, but that doesn't mean that the interviewee is off the hook! If you are the interviewee, you will benefit greatly by clarifying your personal goals, being prepared, listening and responding effectively, and adapting to the interviewer and the situation.

### Clarify and Fulfill Personal Goals

One of the most important things that an interviewee can bring to the interview is a clear sense of personal goals. That is, you should have a clear idea of what *you* want to achieve in the interview. This insight allows you to look for and seek out opportunities to advance your aims, such as looking for specific openings in the conversation (Waldron & Applegate, 1998). A job interviewee—whose goal it might be to impress a hiring manager—can seek out appropriate places to give examples of his or her energy, drive, and willingness to be a team player. An informational interviewee may advance the public relations goals of her organization by selecting information to be shared with the press ("Our office has always been supportive of student groups; last year alone, we gave over $5,000 to the Intercultural Student Union at XYZ Community College").

---

# COMMUNICATIONACROSSCULTURES

## Doctors, Patients, and Cultural Considerations

The ways we perceive others, our expectations of certain communication events, and how we express ourselves always carry some cultural component. For medical professionals, who must interview patients every day, cultural differences can have major consequences.

Consider Su. Su has suffered from allergies and asthma for most of her life, but her attacks have recently become more frequent and severe. Her doctor is busy with other patients and is frustrated to see Su in his office yet again with the same complaints. He has already advised her to remove her carpeting and replace her old drapes, invest in a top-quality air filter for her bedroom, and take her medication regularly. In the doctor's estimation, Su is back in the office because she has not followed orders because she is either lazy or noncompliant.

But the doctor is overlooking several important cultural clues that offer tremendous insight into Su's health situation. First, Su is seventy-two years old. Like many older individuals, she wants her doctor to sit down and explain factors that trigger her condition; she wants to understand what the medication will do and why she needs to take pills that cost her $60 a month. But her doctor rarely has the opportunity to give Su such attention because he is slotted to see two other patients at the same time. In addition, Su is a widow who lives on a very small fixed income, her deceased husband's pension. It is entirely impractical for her to replace all the drapes in her home, have her carpet replaced with hardwood floors, or spend $300 on an air filter for her room.

Would it make a difference to know that Su and her family immigrated to the United States from China fifty years ago? According to research, yes, it would. Direct questions requiring yes or no answers are often seen as invasive and pushy by people from high-context cultures like China, so the physician should avoid putting Su on the spot. Questions like "Did you purchase that air filter I mentioned?" might be more disconcerting to Su than asking, "What questions might you have about the cleaning suggestions we discussed at your last visit?" (Stewart & Cash, 2006). Su's gender plays a role as well. Women are more likely to use questions ("Do you really think this regimen will help?") that may seem hesitant to men, and women's hedges ("I guess I could try this medication") may be their way of maintaining relational harmony even if they are unsure or unconvinced (Mulac, 1998).

**THINK ABOUT THIS**

❶ Is it really possible for Su's doctor to pay attention to all of the cultural factors that play into her health care simultaneously? Is it enough for him to consider her financial constraints but not her needs as an older woman?

❷ How might Su's doctor be able to improve his competence in these health interviews?

❸ Would your assessment of Su's doctor's competence be different if you knew that, for instance, most of his patients shared Su's cultural and socioeconomic background? Would you feel differently about his reactions to her if he worked at a large public clinic or if she were visiting him at a small, private practice specializing in geriatric health care?

❹ Should Su be responsible for making any changes in her communication with her doctor?

● **THE KIND** of job you're interviewing for dictates your dress. For an interview in the typically more conservative finance industry, you will need a suit. For an interview at an art gallery, you *might* wear a more casual outfit.

## Prepare Yourself Responsibly

Your school's career services office and your previous employment situations have likely prepared you for the fact that you'll need to draft a résumé and a cover letter in advance of a job interview. But all interviews, from job interviews to legal interviews, benefit from some advance planning.

For one thing, you'll want to be well rested and physically and mentally alert for the interview. From personal experience, we urge you not to skip meals—more than a few of our students have had growling stomachs during interviews! You'll also want to be dressed appropriately for the occasion. Now, this can mean different things to different people—the key is to think about the context. If you are having an information-gathering interview with your neighbor in your backyard because he's interested in learning about your vegetable and herb garden, you can certainly wear jeans and a favorite football team T-shirt. But if you are having an official job interview at a large financial firm that has a conservative dress policy, it would be best to wear a dark-colored professional suit or dress.

Another point to keep in mind is to plan what you should bring with you to the interview. If you're going to a medical interview with a new doctor, you should bring your medical history (perhaps your file from your previous physician) and a list of the medications you take (include dosage and frequency). Also provide your family medical history and a list of any symptoms you are experiencing (Gosselin, 2007).

## Listen and Respond Effectively

Just as interviewers must listen and respond effectively, so must the interviewee. For example, you should listen carefully to your doctor's specific questions about your sprained, swollen knee and offer clear and concise responses—don't go off on tangents about the hiking trip where you hurt yourself because the doctor might find this distracting. At your performance appraisal, carefully consider your answers to your boss's questions. For example, if she asks you to assess what you have accomplished and excelled at, an effective answer would be an honest one that highlights your achievements or the accomplishments of the team you work with but one that is not false, exaggerated, or unethical.

## Adapt to the Interviewer and the Situation

It is the interviewee's responsibility to adapt to the interviewer and the interview appropriately—particularly with your verbal and nonverbal communication. If a professor in your department is interviewing you to see if you would be a good fit for your college's honors program, you should plan on looking at the interview quite formally. For example, you would use professional, formal address when speaking to the professor ("Professor Arisetty" or "Dr. Edmunds"). But if you have known this professor for three years, you babysit her children, and she insists that you call her Emilia, you can adapt, feeling free to use her first name and a less strict, more personal style of conversation.

As we've mentioned, culture plays a profound role in interviewing situations, and job interviews are no exception. As an interviewee or as an interviewer, you should expect to adapt to the culture of your communication partner. For example, many people from various ethnic and religious backgrounds find it difficult to brag about their accomplishments at a job interview, either because their culture frowns on such boastful behavior or because it violates their personal moral code. Research shows that rather than clearly state a strength ("I have extremely strong organizational skills"), African American interviewees often tell stories about themselves to illustrate their strengths (Hecht, Jackson, & Ribeau, 2003). But how might such storytelling be perceived if the interviewer is from a different ethnic background? Researchers note that European American interviewers often miss the point of African American interviewees' stories and judge the candidates to be "unfocused." Thus African Americans who adapt by directly listing their strengths for a job are perceived more positively in interviews (Hecht et al., 2003). Conversely, a European American interviewer who looks for the message behind the story an interviewee tells has competently adapted.

**CONNECT**

Consider the relational context in competent communication (Chapter 1). It is effective and appropriate to respond differently to the same question posed by your doctor and your mother, or by your boss and your romantic partner. How intimate you are with the person, your relationship history, what you know about them, and status differences between you have a profound effect on the interview situation.

## The Job Interview

In the 2006 film *The Devil Wears Prada,* young Andy (Anne Hathaway) arrives for her interview at *Runway,* a fictional fashion magazine. She is dressed in a plain and simple yet respectable outfit suitable for an aspiring young journalist on the hunt for her first job out of college. Yet when she arrives at *Runway,* she encounters an office full of sleek, stylish people dressed in expensive designer clothes. They feel quite free to laugh at her outfit and remind her that for this job, "an interest in fashion is crucial." And when she finally has the opportunity to interview with editor-in-chief Miranda Priestly (Meryl Streep), Priestly insults her for not reading *Runway,* not being familiar with the editor's reputation, and having no interest in fashion.

While such scenes make for great entertainment, in truth, most interviews are polite and diplomatic affairs. In the remaining pages of this chapter, we describe how job interviews usually go and offer solid advice on how to prepare for, engage in, and follow up on the process.

● **NOT ALL** bosses are like Miranda Priestly, and not all offices are like *Runway*'s. So don't worry that your interviewer will make fun of your cerulean polyester-blend sweater!

## Getting the Interview

The first step involves actually getting the interview! This important phase involves three interrelated tasks: locating jobs and doing homework on the organizations, preparing materials to be used in the process (the résumé and cover letter), and building realistic expectations about the interviewing process.

## The Job Search

The first element of preinterview preparation involves identifying potential jobs and then researching the field and the organizations. Although there are many strategies for locating jobs, your three best sources are likely to be people you know, placement centers, and classified advertisements.

A great place to start is with family, friends, professors, former employers, and individuals working in your field of interest. Contact everyone you know who works in your field or who might know someone who does. Let these individuals know the kind of job you are looking for, and ask for suggestions. Some may be able to connect you with specific job postings within their companies or put you in contact with their human resources departments. Others may be willing to meet with you or talk to you about potential careers in their fields or with their companies in a more general way. You can also make new contacts by joining a networking circle (such as LinkedIn.com) or an organization for professionals in your chosen field (many offer student memberships).

Placement centers are another source of jobs. Most college campuses have a centralized placement center where recruiters from major companies come to interview potential employees. These centers, as well as your school or local library, typically have a wide variety of career resources and information references.

Finally, start looking for specific job openings. Your local newspaper can be a great place to start, but you should also check out employment Web sites, such as Monster.com or Career Builder. These sites let you search through thousands of job postings by field, skill set, location, and other variables. For a more specific search, check out sites that cater to specific industries. For example, mediabistro.com and entertainmentcareers.net focus on jobs in the media and entertainment industries. You can also find job postings on the

● THERE ARE many different avenues you can explore when you begin your job hunt. Industry-specific magazines like *Variety,* job placement centers, and employment Web sites are all good places to start.

Web sites of most major companies. The corporate home page will often include a link for job openings (often labeled "Careers" or "Employment") as well as the application process.

# WIREDFORCOMMUNICATION

## Presenting Yourself: Your Online Persona

Savvy job applicants will always prepare for a job interview by doing a little armchair research. A few quick Internet searches can yield a wealth of information on a company's history, status, and corporate culture and even some insights into its future. A curious applicant might go even further, checking local and industry sources to see what has been written on, about, or by the person who will be conducting the interview.

But often, inexperienced job hunters fail to realize that those searches can go both ways. As easily as you can Google a company name, a potential employer can also do a search on your name or e-mail address. You might put forth a fantastic résumé and buy the most professional suit for your first interview, but what you've posted on online chats, blogs, Web pages, and MySpace or Facebook pages might very well be the most important factor in shaping the first impression you make on a potential employer.

Consider Brad Karsh, the president of a small company in Chicago, who was looking to hire a summer intern. When he came across a promising candidate, he did a quick online background check, taking a peek at his Facebook page. There the candidate described his interests as including marijuana use, shooting people, and obsessive sex. That the student was clearly exaggerating didn't matter. His lack of judgment regarding what to say about himself publicly, Karsh says, took him out of the running for the position (Finder, 2006). Karsh and many other potential employers are increasingly using the Web to do background checks on potential candidates. They're looking for red flags: personal information that candidates have chosen to announce to the world that makes the employer reconsider their adequacy for the position.

And so posting information about yourself on a public or semipublic electronic forum is a risky endeavor for a job hunter—or anyone else trying to make a good impression. While photos of you and your best friends being crazy at a sorority toga party might be fun to share with fellow students, such images create an immature and unprofessional impression that can be hard to shake. Likewise, postings to blogs and Web pages can reveal insights into your political leanings, religious beliefs, opinions, habits, or personal history that you might not want employers to know about. One student reported that he was having a hard time landing an interview. Upon Googling himself, he found an essay he'd posted on a student Web site a few years ago, titled "Lying Your Way to the Top." Only after he had it removed did he begin getting calls (Finder, 2006).

**THINK ABOUT THIS**

❶ Take a moment to Google yourself. Search not only for your name but also your e-mail address. What comes up?

❷ Do you have a page on Facebook, MySpace, or some other social networking site? Think objectively about the impression of you that the page conveys. Would you hire you?

❸ Do you consider the material you post on various Web sites private? Do you think it's ethical for employers to be looking at your postings?

❹ How can you create a better online image for yourself?

Preparing for a job interview is similar to preparing for a speech. In Chapter 11, we suggest studying your audience to know how to present information they'll find useful and interesting; in a job interview, you must do the same. Your goal is to learn about the organization's culture (Chapter 10). Is it a formal or informal place? What does the company value? This information helps you adapt your communication competently and impress the hiring manager.

Once you get leads on possible jobs, learn everything you can about each potential position and its organization. Check out general reference works (*Occupational Outlook Handbook, Moody's Industrial Manual, Dictionary of Occupational Titles*); use your school's alumni network to talk with employees of the organization you are interested in. Be sure to make use of the organization's Web site. Learning about the organization's mission, goals, and values will help you determine if you are a good fit for the organization.

## Prepare Your Materials

Once you've identified potential jobs, you'll need to make contact with the people in a position to hire you. As you know, first impressions are important. And as a job applicant, the first impression you will make on a potential employer will likely be via your written materials. In some cases, this might be an informal e-mail, in others, a formal cover letter and résumé. In this section, we show you how to prepare all of these materials so that they communicate the right message about you.

**The cover letter.**    A formal **cover letter**, a one-page letter indicating your interest in a particular position, is extremely important to many prospective employers. It gives you, as the applicant, the opportunity to express in writing how you learned of the position and the organization, how your skills and interests can benefit the organization, and why you are interested in applying for this particular job. The cover letter also serves as a means by which you can demonstrate your written communication skills, so make sure that you use correct grammar, punctuation, and spelling—and proofread carefully! Figure A.2 shows a strong cover letter.

Be aware that in some cases, prospective employers find that e-mails make acceptable cover letters. So when you e-mail a hiring manager or a human resource representative at an organization, your e-mail would contain the same information as your cover letter. If you are unsure of the protocol, it's always best to be more formal and include an official cover letter with your e-mail. Be sure to include a subject line and to proofread your e-mail carefully before you press Send.

**The résumé.**    You begin by pulling together a **résumé**—a printed summary of your education, work experiences, and accomplishments. It is a vehicle for making a positive first impression on potential employers. An effective résumé tells just enough about you to make employers believe they may need your skills and experience.

No two résumés look exactly alike, but most résumés should contain the following general information.

▶ *Contact information.* Include both campus and home addresses if necessary, phone numbers, and your e-mail address. Make sure that your answering machine or voice mail greets callers with a clear, professional message, and check it often. If you have an odd or cute address for your regular e-mail (partygirl@provider.com, numberonedad@provider.net), consider opening

**FIGURE A.2**

**SAMPLE COVER LETTER**

111 A Street, Apt. 2C
San Marcos, TX 78666

September 6, 2008

Taylor A. Sorenson
Director of Human Resources
Roaring Brook Press
A Division of Macmillan
175 Fifth Avenue
New York, NY 10010

Dear Director Sorenson:

I was extremely excited to see a posting for an editorial assistant position with Roaring Brook Press. I greatly admire your organization's dedication to children and youth, and I would be honored to interview for a position that would allow me to explore my interest in publishing while working on the creative editorial projects that Roaring Brook Press supports.

My publishing experience coupled with my understanding of children's education make me well suited for an editorial assistant position with your company. The summer prior to my senior year at Texas State University, I worked as an editorial intern at Chronicle Books in San Francisco. I maintained author and permissions databases using FileMaker Pro, wrote rejection letters, and collated manuscripts and artwork for review and production. I also honed my written communication skills through critiquing cookbook proposals and manuscripts, writing readers' reports on their publication potential based on analysis of the cookbook market and my editorial opinion. Balancing this task with my other daily responsibilities required me to prioritize and manage several projects simultaneously.

I have also worked with children in an educational setting. As a volunteer at the San Antonio Public Library, I have organized and conducted various informational displays aimed at getting children interested in subjects or cultures unfamiliar to them. I have also created games and other activities for children based on the books I read during story hour. Through this position, I have learned to appeal to and communicate with children in a creative yet educational way. This unique combination of skills and interests will help me excel as an editorial assistant.

I have included my résumé as requested in the job posting, and I can also provide references should they be required. I look forward to discussing my experiences and perspectives with you in person. I can be contacted at ellen.ng@serviceprovider.com or by phone at (555) 375-7111. Thank you for your kind consideration.

Sincerely,

*Ellen Ng*

Ellen Ng

another account with a more serious name for all of your professional communication.

▶ *Employment objective.* Be concise and specific about what you're looking for in a position. If you are applying for several types of jobs, it is better to create multiple résumés than to have widely diversified objectives in the same résumé.

▶ *Education.* List the institutions you have attended, their locations, and the dates of attendance. List degrees received (or date to be received), academic majors, and areas of concentration. Awards and GPA can be listed if they enhance your marketability.

▶ *Work experience.* List work experience in reverse chronological order, focusing on concrete examples of achievement or skills that you have mastered. Explain job functions as well as titles. Remember that prospective employers read this section carefully to discover how your experience, abilities, and achievements relate to their organization's needs.

▶ *Activities.* For employers, participation in a variety of academic, extracurricular, or social activities indicates that you are motivated and get involved. Include activities that are relevant to your career objective, emphasizing accomplishments and leadership roles.

▶ *Special skills.* Do you speak fluent Spanish? Are you skilled in a particular programming language? Did you climb Mount Everest? Don't be shy—let potential employers know this information. Your skills may be useful to the organization, and your accomplishments show dedication and determination.

▶ *References.* Your references are typically professors, previous supervisors, or anyone else who can confirm your employment history and attest to your work ethic and character.

A sample résumé appears in Figure A.3.

### AND YOU?

Do you have your résumé ready all the time, in preparation for any unexpected opportunities? How might pulling together a solid résumé be beneficial even when you are not on the job hunt?

## *Build Realistic Expectations*

The final component of job hunting involves developing realistic expectations about the process and preparing for "rejection shock" (Galassi & Galassi, 1978). It is important to remember that only a few résumés will make it through the screening process and that you will not be the only candidate that gets called for an interview. Therefore, you will likely face rejection at least once during the course of a job search, either because there was a better-qualified applicant or because an equally qualified candidate had some advantage (such as a personal contact in the company). You should therefore constantly remember that rejection is not uncommon and that rejection is not personal but is the inevitable result of a tight job market and a less-than-perfect selection process. Persistence pays. If you approach the job search intelligently and persistently, you will eventually get a job.

**FIGURE A.3**
## SAMPLE RÉSUMÉ

**Ellen Ng**

**111 A Street, Apt. 2C, San Marcos, TX 78666**
**(555) 375-7111 • ellen.ng@serviceprovider.com**

**OBJECTIVE**
To obtain an entry-level editorial position where I can use my strong writing and editing skills while expanding my knowledge of the publishing process.

**EDUCATION**
Texas State University, *San Marcos, TX*                                              *2006–2008*
    Bachelor of Arts, English, May 2008    GPA: 3.7/4.0
    Honors: Recipient of the Lorin D. Parkin scholarship (2007); Member of the Sigma Tau Delta honor society.

Northwest Vista College, *San Antonio, TX*                                              *2004–2006*
    Associate of Arts, Liberal and Media Arts (General), May 2006

**RELATED WORK EXPERIENCE**
Intern, Chronicle Books, *San Francisco, CA*                                          *Summer 2007*
    Wrote reports on the marketability and publication potential of cookbook proposals and manuscripts submitted to publisher. Drafted rejection letters, letters to authors, and letters requesting outstanding permissions fees. Maintained and updated author, permissions, and complimentary copy databases using FileMaker Pro. Created cost and sales figure spreadsheets using Microsoft Excel. Worked mainly on cookbooks, preparing manuscripts and artwork for production. Contacted and sent manuscripts and reviewer questionnaires to reviewers and potential endorsers for consideration.

Writing Counselor, Writing Center, *Texas State University*                    *Fall 2006–Spring 2008*
    Aided students with their academic research papers, résumés, and cover letters. Offered guidance and advice on how to rewrite poorly written papers and edited for grammatical errors. Developed exercises and writing samples to aid with college-level writing. Taught students how to recognize and solve writing problems on their own.

Writer/Editor, MyWay in Education, *Hong Kong*                                     *Summer 2006*
    Created and edited reading comprehension articles and over 300 grammar questions per week for ten different grade levels in accordance with Hong Kong public school standards for company's Web site. Oversaw and maintained Web site's 24-hour update operations during supervisor's leave of absence.

Volunteer, San Antonio Public Library, *San Antonio, TX*                    *Fall 2002–Summer 2006*
    Created themed book displays for special events, such as Hispanic Heritage Month and various national and international holidays. Read to children ages 3–5 weekly and created arts-and-crafts activities or games structured around the stories.

**OTHER WORK EXPERIENCE AND ACTIVITIES**
Cheerleader, Texas State Spirit Program, *Texas State University*             *Fall 2006–Spring 2008*

Waitress/Hostess, Applebee's, *San Marcos, TX*                                    *Fall 2006–Present*
    Waited tables three nights a week. Took drink and food orders, brought meals to tables, and cleared tables. Promoted to hostess in 2007. Take names at the host station, greet guests, and show them to their tables.

Cashier, Home Depot, *San Antonio, TX*                                          *Fall 2004–Summer 2006*
    Rang up customer purchases three nights a week. Assisted in closing up store at end of each shift.

**SKILLS AND INTERESTS**
Languages: Fluent in English, proficient in written and conversational Mandarin and Cantonese, conversational Spanish.

Computer: Word, Excel, PowerPoint, FileMaker Pro, Internet research.

Other interests: Dance, travel and food writing, cooking, cheerleading.

In Chapter 13, you learn that *state communication apprehension* is anxiety about communicating in a particular situation. Speeches cause anxiety for many people—but so do job interviews! To make sure that anxiety doesn't adversely affect your communication during an interview, try some of our suggestions for building your confidence (Chapter 13, p. 390), such as visualizing success and developing a constructive attitude toward fear.

● **SOME FIRST IMPRESSIONS** may be memorable, but that probably didn't help this *American Idol* hopeful!

## During the Interview

After a diligent job search, you've finally been called for an interview. Now what? Well, now you impress the socks off of your interviewer by making your best first impression, preparing for and anticipating different types of questions, preparing questions of your own, and following up after your interview.

### Making a Good First Impression

Salina, who works in the nonprofit world, interviewed a candidate who came forty-five minutes late to the interview. This was bad enough, but he explained his tardiness by noting that he had to "run home" to get his mom to help him with his tie. (Note: Always practice tying your tie *before* the interview.) Later, Salina interviewed a young woman who showed up and asked if she could have some friends join her during the interview. Can you imagine that? What these candidates forgot is that the face-to-face interview begins with the very first impression, even before the questions are asked.

Both verbal and nonverbal behaviors contribute to a good first impression. First of all, do your best to control your nervousness so that you don't appear hesitant, halting, unsure, or jittery (Ayers, Keereetaweep, Chen, & Edwards, 1998). The best way to accomplish this is to do your homework about the company and then arrive with plenty of time to spare so that you aren't rushed or apologetic. Keep reminding yourself that you are prepared and ready for this challenge.

As with all competent communication, in interviewing situations, you should adapt your behavior to be both effective and appropriate. Dress formally, as we've discussed; if the situation winds up being less formal than anticipated, you can always remove your suit jacket or your tie. Throughout the interview, be aware of the importance of adapting your behavior to the interviewer. Specifically, sit or stand as the other person directs; lower or raise your voice tone, rate, and pitch to fit in with the tone and pacing of the other person. And don't forget other aspects of your nonverbal communication: for example, limit gestures so that you don't distract the interviewer from your words. If you practice in front of a mirror or with an understanding friend (or even tape-record yourself), you can identify any distracting behavior before you go into the interview situation.

If you are still feeling nervous about your first impression, take a look at Box A.1, "What *Not* to Do at an Interview." Even if you wind up failing to make eye contact once or twice or you feel your voice shaking a few times, you can at least say that you weren't the candidate who brought her pet snake to the interview!

### Anticipating Common Questions

To discover whether there is a potential match between an applicant and a position, an interviewer typically explores five areas of information as they relate to the specific job:

The following are real stories about job applicants shared by hiring managers. Needless to say, they didn't get the positions. . . .

► "Said if he was hired, he'd teach me ballroom dancing at no charge, and started demonstrating."

► "Took three cellular phone calls. Said she had a similar business on the side."

► "Man brought in his five children and cat."

► "Arrived with a snake around her neck. Said she took her pet everywhere."

► "Left his dry cleaner tag on his jacket and said he wanted to show he was a clean individual."

► "When asked about loyalty, showed a tattoo of his girlfriend's name."

► "After a very long interview, he casually said he had already accepted another position."

► "After a difficult question, she wanted to leave the room for a moment to meditate."

Source: Miller (1991). Used with permission.

► *Ability.* First, based on the résumé and the interview, the interviewer needs to discover if the applicant has the experience, education, training, intelligence, and ability to do what the job requires.

► *Desire.* Second, the interviewer needs to discover if the applicant has the desire or motivation to use those abilities to do a good job. To gather this information, the interviewer is likely to explore such things as the interviewee's record of changes in jobs, schools, and majors; reasons for wanting this job; knowledge of the company; and concrete examples of prior success that indicate a drive to achieve.

► *Personality.* The third area involves an assessment of the applicant's personality and how well he or she is likely to fit into the position and the company or organization. Depending on the job, this will likely involve an attempt to discover the applicant's personal goals, degree of independence and self-reliance, imagination and creativity, and ability to manage or lead.

► *Character.* A fourth area of judgment is that of character, learning about the interviewee's personal behavior, honesty, responsibility, and accuracy and objectivity in reports.

► *Health.* This is a somewhat sensitive topic in interviews, and certain questions about your health and medical background are illegal and unethical. However, if a health issue directly affects your ability to do the job in question, the interviewer may ask. For example, if you are applying for a position at a candy factory, the interviewer may ask if you have an allergy to peanuts because if you do, you would be unable to work in a plant where peanuts are processed.

The questions asked in an interview, then, will likely relate to these five basic areas. Some frequently asked questions are offered in Table A.5. If you consider the criteria we've just explained, you'll be in a better position to anticipate the kinds of questions you will be asked and to rehearse strategies for responding to those questions.

TABLE A.5

**COMMON INTERVIEW QUESTIONS**

▶ What led you to choose your particular field (or your academic major)? What do you like about it? What don't you like about it?

▶ In which kinds of positions are you most interested? Summarize your qualifications for the position.

▶ Have you had summer employment or a volunteer position in this or a related field that you didn't mention on your résumé?

▶ What have you learned from your previous work experience?

▶ What are the most important considerations for you in choosing a job?

▶ What kinds of courses have you taken that you think prepared you for this occupation?

▶ Why are you interviewing with our company?

▶ Do you have any geographical preferences about where you work?

▶ What do you see yourself doing five years from now? Ten years from now? What are your long-range goals?

▶ What have you done that shows initiative and willingness to work?

▶ Do you have any hobbies or interests that are related to this career path or position?

▶ What would you say is your strongest attribute? What is your weakest point?

▶ Can you tell me about a time you worked through a difficult coworker situation?

▶ What can you contribute to our company that would make us want to hire you?

▶ Why do you want to leave your current employer? *or* Why did you leave your last employer?

▶ Are there any questions that you want to ask?

Source: Greco (1977). Used with permission.

## Dealing with Difficult or Unethical Questions

"What fictional character most clearly reflects your outlook on life?" This is an actual question that an interviewer asked a colleague of ours some years ago when she was applying to college. To this day, she remembers the question because she panicked. It wasn't that she lacked an answer; she simply wasn't *expecting* the question. An interviewer might use such unexpected questions to seek insights into the way candidates view themselves or to judge how well they think on their feet. Some questions are simply tricky—they offer a challenge to the interviewee but also a great opportunity to show one's strengths.

It is not uncommon, for example, for an interviewer to say, "Tell me about your weaknesses." One standard strategy for responding to such a question is to talk about weaknesses that really aren't weaknesses at all: "I tend to be very picky when it comes to details, and I have difficulty letting go of a job until I'm sure it's right." Another strategy is to think about areas that you have had difficulty with in the past and to show how you addressed the problem; for example, "I've sometimes found it difficult to manage my time. But last year I attended a great time management seminar and started using a really helpful system for time management." Such an admission shows the interviewer that you are able to evaluate yourself for weaknesses and take action to address the problem. Other difficult questions might focus on gaps in your résumé or negative experiences in the past. It can be difficult, for example, to explain why you left your last job. In such cases, it's best to be honest without being too forthcoming—avoid complaining about a previous boss or gossiping about internal politics at the last company you worked for.

Other questions are more than just difficult; they are unethical and sometimes even illegal. Questions that have no direct bearing on job performance and have the potential to lead to discrimination on the basis of race, color, religion, national origin, sex, age, disability, and marital or family status are illegal in the United States. Although an organization whose employees ask illegal questions during employment interviews can be subject to a variety of penalties imposed by the federal government's Equal Employment Opportunity Commission (EEOC), such questions continue to be asked, and applicants must consider how to answer them. Stewart and Cash (2006) suggest five tactics you can use to respond to illegal questions. By answering briefly but directly, tactfully refusing to answer, or neutralizing the question, you respond without giving too much information or inviting further inquiry. You can also consider posing a tactful inquiry—that is, asking another question in response—or using the question as an opportunity to present some positive information about yourself. These five strategies are outlined in Table A.6 (see p. 514).

## Asking Questions of Your Own

Of course, the interviewer should not be the only person asking questions in a job interview. A candidate for any job should arrive at an interview prepared to ask thoughtful questions about the position itself and related career paths within the organization, as well as about the organization itself. These questions should indicate that the applicant has done solid homework—your

**TACTICS FOR RESPONDING TO ILLEGAL QUESTIONS**

| Tactic | Sample Illegal Question | Sample Answer |
|---|---|---|
| Answer directly but briefly. | "Do you attend church regularly?" | "Yes, I do." |
| Pose a tactful inquiry. | "What does your husband do?" | "Why do you ask?" (in a nondefensive tone of voice) |
| Tactfully refuse to answer the question. | "Do you have children?" | "My family plans will not interfere with my ability to perform in this position." |
| Neutralize. | "What happens if your partner needs to relocate?" | "My partner and I would discuss locational moves that either of us might have to consider in the future." |
| Take advantage of the question. | "Where were you born?" | "I am quite proud that my background is Egyptian because it has helped me deal effectively with people of various ethnic backgrounds." |

Source: Stewart & Cash (2006). Used with permission.

preinterview research and preparation can shine here—and is able and willing to do a good job for the company.

Avoid saying things like "I really don't have any questions right now" (even if you don't have any questions), which might imply disinterest. Likewise, try not to focus on questions about your own compensation and benefits, such as "How much vacation will I get?"—at least not at the first interview. Instead, try to pose thoughtful questions that show your interest while enhancing your understanding of the position and the potential for your future. Be prepared to ask questions such as "I noticed in your annual report that you are developing a new training program. If I were hired, would I be in it?" or "If you were sitting on my side of this desk, what would you say are the most attractive features of the job?"

## Following Up After the Interview

You should continue to demonstrate good manners once the interview is over. Thank the interviewer as you leave, as well as anyone else you have met within the organization. Follow up immediately with a written or e-mailed note of appreciation. Thank the interviewer not only for the interview but also for the chance to expand your knowledge of the organization and the industry. Put in writing how excited you are about the chance to work with such a dynamic organization. Send along any support materials that you discussed during the interview (perhaps a writing sample). Since few interviewees remember to send additional materials and thank-yous, you will certainly stand out.

**AND YOU?**

Have you ever gone through an interview process to secure a job or admission to college? How prepared did you feel for your first interview? If you could do it again, what would you do differently?

# what about you?

## Your Career Preparation

Use the following grid as a starting point to assess your career strengths and goals as you prepare for job interviews. Write three descriptions of your skills, career goals, and life goals. Next, score the organizations that you plan on applying to from 1 to 5 (5 being the highest) as to how they match up with your skills and goals.

| MY SKILLS | Organization A | Organization B | Organization C |
|---|---|---|---|
| (Examples: strong writing skills, foreign-language proficiency, computer programming skills) | | | |
| 1. | | | |
| 2. | | | |
| 3. | | | |
| **MY CAREER GOALS** | | | |
| (Examples: become marketing executive, work in the Dallas area, have a job with little mandatory travel) | | | |
| 1. | | | |
| 2. | | | |
| 3. | | | |
| **MY LIFE GOALS** | | | |
| (Examples: have children, live near siblings, retire at age sixty) | | | |
| 1. | | | |
| 2. | | | |
| 3. | | | |

Now assess your results. Is there one organization that best supports your goals and skills? If not, consider which goals and skills are *most* important to you. Which organization might be the best fit?

**BACK TO** The Stephen Colbert Interview

At the beginning of this Appendix, we talked about Stephen Colbert, whose satirical "Better Know a District" interviews either tickle the funny bone or strike fear in the hearts of U.S. congressional representatives. Let's examine the nature of those interviews in the context of what we've discussed throughout this chapter.

▶ Like all interviews, Colbert's are planned and dyadic, but the process of editing them down to a few minutes makes them less interactive than a real-time interview. Comments and reaction shots are taken out of context, and during editing, Colbert is able to integrate alternative footage that was not part of the actual interview. This gives him an unusual amount of control, at the expense of the interviewee.

▶ However, a savvy interviewee can sometimes beat Colbert at his own game. When Colbert asked Congressman Hare to take up the pro-slavery side in a debate with him, Hare failed to provide the zinging line Colbert was hoping to get (Colbert: "[Slavery is] evil and wicked." Hare: "You win").

▶ Colbert makes comic use of closed questions when he offers only two possible evaluations of President Bush ("great" or "greatest"). By so blatantly limiting the interviewee's possible responses, he's making sure that he gets a response that he agrees with.

▶ The format and structure of the interview are also clear to both parties: Colbert's guests are told in advance that he will remain in character, and they are asked to play straight against his egomaniacal and satirical alter ego. Participants are well aware that their comments can and will be heavily edited and that much of what they say will be taken out of context.

▶ The goals of the interviewee and interviewer are at once similar and quite different. A congressman might appear on the show to gain exposure for his district as well as for himself with Colbert's young, politically active audience. Colbert's intentions are to offer entertaining political satire and also to mock the nature of mass media news reporting and punditry.

## THINGS TO TRY

1. Observe a press conference on television. Who is being interviewed? Who is conducting the interview? What is the goal of the press conference? How is control distributed? List five questions that are asked, and label them according to the types listed in this chapter (open, closed, bipolar, primary, secondary). Did the questioning involve a particular sequence (funnel, inverted funnel, tunnel)? What did you learn about this interview format by answering these questions?

2. A good source for seeing the subtle differences between legal and illegal job interview questions is at www.jobweb.com/Interview/help.aspx?id=1343&terms= illegal+questions. Use this site to organize a discussion with your classmates about how you would respond in a job interview. Practice and compare your responses.

3. Assess your goals for employment, and then design (or revise) a résumé accordingly. Use the guidelines in this chapter to make it clear and action-oriented. Discuss your résumé with other students in the class; ask them if your goals are clear. Compare your résumé to theirs; while the format may be similar, the content should be unique to you. Ask friends, family, and past coworkers to review your résumé too; perhaps they can suggest things to add, subtract, or reword for maximum impact.

4. Create a questionnaire to assess reactions to a topic of interest to you (parking, campus politics, community issues, the effectiveness of a group you belong to). The questionnaire must have at least twenty-five closed questions that can be tabulated (add up number of responses, yes and no answers, and so on), as well as one or more open questions that allow the interviewees to address issues that were not included in your closed questions. Interview at least twenty people, and summarize the answers to your survey in a three- to five-page report. Attach your survey, and include a summary paragraph describing what you learned about constructing questions for the interview situation.

5. Conduct an in-depth information-gathering interview, and write a report (no more than five typed pages) in which you summarize the information you received and comment on what you learned about the interview process. The interview must last at least one hour; the interviewee must be a close acquaintance older than you and must have children (consider interviewing one of your parents). The interview must cover at least two of the following topics:

   a. The person's philosophy of raising children (discipline, finances, making friends, respect for authority, character formation)

   b. The person's political beliefs (political affiliation and commitment, involvement in civic affairs, involvement in government)

   c. The person's religious beliefs, their effect on the person's life, and how these beliefs relate to family life

   d. The person's goals in life and how the person is working to achieve these goals

   e. The person's philosophy of leisure time (ideally how one should spend leisure time versus how this person actually spends it)

## IF YOU'RE INTERESTED

*What Color Is Your Parachute? A Practical Manual for Job-Hunters and Career-Changers,* by Richard Nelson Bolles (Berkeley, CA: Ten Speed Press, 2007)

Published in twelve languages, this practical guide to job-hunting is the top-selling book in its field. It deals not only with the interviewing process but also with assessments and decisions about changing careers. It gives up-to-date advice on job-hunting on the Internet, and it's an easy read too.

*Interviewing Principles and Practices: Applications and Exercises,* by Charles. J. Stewart (Dubuque, IA: Kendall/Hunt, 2002)

> This workbook is designed to guide you in the development of interviewing skills. It contains many applications and exercises to help you develop and respond to questions, as well as exercises to reflect on careers and how to get jobs in your chosen field.

*Office Space* (20th Century-Fox, 1999)

> If you want to see employees who need to do some career counseling in preparation for a job search, you'll find them in Peter Gibbons and his Initech colleagues, who suffer the defensive and condescending communication of their boss. When (after a hypnotherapy session) Peter begins to honestly speak his mind, he's inexplicably promoted, much to the amazement of his colleagues, who get downsized out of the company. Though this is a comedy, the characters deal with serious issues, such as the ethics of a high-tech embezzling scheme meant to get revenge on the company.

*Dead Man Walking* (Gramercy Pictures, 1996)

> Susan Sarandon won the best actress Oscar for her performance as real-life character Sister Helen Prejean in this powerful movie about a man on death row (played by Sean Penn). Sarandon's interviews with the killer and his victims' families illustrate effective information-gathering and counseling interviewing styles. Ultimately, her fact-finding and counseling interviews increase her empathy for both sides as the characters grapple with the ethical issues involved.

**Now that you have finished reading this Appendix, you can**

Understand the nature of interviews:

- An **interview** is an interaction between two parties that is deliberate and purposeful (p. 486).
- Interviews are planned, goal-driven, structured, dyadic (involving two parties), and interactive (p. 486).

Outline the different types of interviews:

- The **information-gathering interview** serves to transfer knowledge from one party to the other (p. 487).
- **Performance appraisals** allow you to review your accomplishments and plan your goals (p. 488).
- A **problem-solving interview** deals with problems, tensions, or conflicts (p. 488).
- In **exit interviews**, employers seek to identify organizational problems that might affect employee retention (p. 490).
- In a **persuasive interview**, questions are designed to change the interviewee's behavior or opinions (p. 490).
- **Service-oriented interviews** are designed to cull information and provide advice or support (p. 490).
- In a **selection interview**, the primary goal is to fill a position in an organization (p. 490).

Describe the three parts of a **job interview**: opening, questions, and conclusion:

- An interview should open with the three things interviewees will want to know: the topic and length (the task), something about the interviewer and how the information will be used (the relationship), and who will benefit (the motivation) (p. 491).
- Questions and answers accomplish the goals of the interview (p. 493).
- An **open question** gives the interviewee freedom in how to respond (p. 493).
- **Closed questions** restrict answer choices; **bipolar questions** can be answered with only "yes" or "no" (pp. 493–494).
- **Primary questions** introduce new topics; **secondary questions** seek clarification (p. 494).
- **Neutral questions** do not hint at a preferred answer, whereas **directed questions**, **leading questions**, or **loaded questions** may subtly or even blatantly influence the answer (pp. 494–495).

- There are three main structures for ordering interview questions: the **funnel sequence**, **inverted funnel sequence**, or **tunnel sequence**, each varying in its level of specificity (pp. 495–496).
- Interviewers use verbal and nonverbal strategies to conclude and summarize the interview (p. 498).

Devise an interview strategy from the interviewer's point of view:

- Consider potential barriers that might be disruptive (p. 499).
- Find ways to put the interviewee at ease (p. 500).
- Make sure the questions are ethical and appropriate (p. 500).
- Remember to listen well and take notes (p. 500).

Prepare for the role of interviewee:

- Have a clear idea of your personal goals, what you want to achieve in the interview (p. 500).
- Don't arrive tired or hungry, dress appropriately, and bring any documents you may need (p. 502).
- Listen and respond effectively (p. 502).
- Adapt to the situation, being particularly sensitive to cultural differences (p. 502).

Get the job interview and manage it with confidence:

- The three best sources for finding jobs are people you know, placement centers, and classified ads (p. 504).
- Write an effective **cover letter** and **résumé** (p. 506).
- Remember that rejection is not uncommon and that persistence pays (p. 508).
- Nonverbal cues are as important as what you say to make a good first impression (p. 510).
- Come prepared to answer standard questions about your abilities, desire, personality, character, and health (p. 511).
- Answer difficult questions honestly to show that you know how to evaluate your own weaknesses and take action against them, but be brief; decline to answer a question that is unethical (p. 513).
- Ask thoughtful questions about the position and the organization (p. 513).
- Follow up with a note of thanks (p. 514).

# glossary

**abstraction ladder:** A model that ranks communication from specific, which ensures clarity, to general and vague.

**accent:** Pattern of pronunciation specific to a certain upbringing, geographical region, or culture.

**accenting:** Nonverbal behavior that clarifies and emphasizes specific information in a verbal message.

**accommodation:** Changing communication behavior to adapt to other people.

**achievement-oriented leader:** A leader who sets challenging goals and communicates high expectations and standards to members.

**action-oriented listeners:** Communicators who focus on tasks; they tend to keep the discourse on track and are often valuable in meetings.

**active listeners:** People who make effective choices (about selecting, attending, and so on) when listening so as to be more competent communicators.

**adaptability:** An organization's ability to adjust to changing times and circumstances.

**adaptors:** Body movements that satisfy some physical or psychological need, such as rubbing your eyes when you're tired.

**ad hominem fallacy:** Focusing on a person rather than on the point that the person is making.

**adjourning:** The stage of group development when members reflect on their accomplishments and failures and also determine whether the group should dissemble or take on another project.

**affect displays:** Body movements that convey feelings, mood, and reactions; they are usually unintentional, reflecting the sender's emotions.

**affiliation:** The feelings we have for others.

**agenda:** A plan for a meeting that is laid out in advance and typically includes goals, participants, time restrictions, and other details.

**all-channel network:** A network in which all members are equidistant from one another and all interact.

**anecdotes:** Brief personal stories that have a point or punch line.

**antigroup roles:** Roles that serve individual members' priorities at the expense of overall group needs.

**anxiety:** A feeling of dread that comes from internal doubts about our ability to perform effectively.

**appeal to tradition:** A fallacy in which speakers suggest that listeners should agree with their point because "that's the way it has always been."

**appreciative listening:** Listening with the simple goal of taking pleasure in the sounds that you receive.

**articulation:** The clarity and forcefulness with which sounds are made.

**artifacts:** Accessories worn, carried, or used on the body for decoration or identification.

**attending:** Part of the listening process that involves focusing on a particular message or sound.

**attitudes:** Our general evaluations of people, ideas, objects, or events.

**attraction-similarity hypothesis:** The belief that the extent to which we project ourselves onto another person is the direct result of the attraction we have for that person.

**attributions:** Personal characteristics that are used to explain other people's behavior.

**bandwagon fallacy:** Accepting a statement as true simply because it is popular.

**begging the question:** Presenting an argument that no one can possibly prove because there is no valid evidence.

**behavior:** Observable communication, including both verbal and nonverbal messages.

**beliefs:** Perceptions of reality; our feelings about what is true and how confident we are about the existence or validity of something.

**biased language:** Language that has subtle meanings that influence perception.

**bipolar question:** A question for which there are only two possible responses: "yes" or "no."

**bonding:** The process of creating symbolic messages that convey the importance of a relationship between the partners and also to the outside world.

**brainstorming:** A process that entails focusing on a general area of interest, amassing information, thinking creatively, and considering problems and solutions related to the topic.

**bullying:** Unethical and harsh tactics used to acquire and keep control over a group or its members.

**burnout:** A sense of apathy or exhaustion that results from long-term stress or frustration.

**cause-effect pattern:** An organizational style that focuses on cause-to-effect or effect-to-cause relationships.

**central processing:** Thinking deeply about a message and seriously considering acting on it.

**chain network:** A network in which information is passed from one member to the next rather than shared among members.

**challenging strategies:** Tactics that promote the objectives of the individual who uses them rather than the interests of the other person or the relationship.

**channel:** The method through which communication occurs.

**channel discrepancy:** When one set of behaviors says one thing and another set says something different.

**chronemics:** The study of how people perceive the use of time.

**chronological pattern:** An organizational style that presents the main points of a message forward (or backward) in a systematic, time-related fashion.

**classical management approach:** An approach to organizational communication that likens organizations to machines, focusing on maximizing efficiency.

**cliques:** Subgroups of individuals who have bonded together, also called *coalitions*.

**closed questions:** Questions that give less freedom to the interviewee by restricting answer choices.

**clustering:** A creative technique for identifying potential speech topics in which the writer begins with a core idea and branches out into a web of related thoughts and ideas.

**co-cultures:** Groups of people within a culture who are distinguished by shared features such as race, religion, age, generation, political affiliation, gender, sexual orientation, economic status, educational level, occupation, or other factors.

**code:** A set of symbols that create a meaningful message.

**code switching:** A type of accommodation in which communicators change their regular language and slang to fit into a particular group.

**coercion:** Using threats, intimidation, or violence to gain compliance.

**coercive power:** Power that stems from a person's ability to threaten or harm others.

**cognitions:** Thoughts communicators have about themselves and others.

**cognitive forces:** Group members' thoughts, beliefs, and emotions, which influence the group's decisions.

**cognitive language:** The system of symbols you use to describe people, things, and situations.

**cognitive restructuring:** An approach to reducing communication apprehension that focuses on replacing negative self-talk with positive coping statements.

**cohesion:** The degree to which group members are bonded and consider themselves a single entity.

**collectivistic culture:** A culture that emphasizes group needs, rights, and identity over those of individuals.

**communication:** The process by which individuals use symbols, signs, and behaviors to exchange information.

**communication acquisition:** The process of learning to use language appropriately and effectively.

**communication apprehension:** Fear or anxiety associated with communication, which is often a common barrier to effective delivery.

**communication boundary management:** Reluctance to discuss certain topics with particular people.

**communication climate:** An atmosphere representative of the dominant temper, attitudes, and outlook of relational partners.

**communication privacy management theory:** The assertion that people believe they need to control their private information because it has the potential to make them vulnerable.

**communication processing:** The means by which we gather, organize, and evaluate the information we receive.

**comparative advantage pattern:** An organizational pattern that shows why one viewpoint is superior to other viewpoints on a topic.

**competent (communication):** Communication that is effective and appropriate for a given situation.

**competent communication model:** A model of communication in which communicators send and receive messages simultaneously within a relational, situational, and cultural context.

**complementing:** Nonverbal behavior that matches the verbal message it accompanies without actually mirroring it.

**compromise:** A way to resolve conflict, in which both parties must give up something to gain something.

**concerted audience:** An audience that shares a need to achieve some end with the speaker and is positively disposed to him or her.

**conflict:** A negative interaction between two or more interdependent people, rooted in a real or perceived disagreement.

**conflict management:** The way that we engage in conflict and address disagreements with our relational partners.

**connotative meaning:** The emotional or attitudinal response people have to a word.

**contact cultures:** Cultures that depend on touch as an important form of communication.

**content-oriented listeners:** Listeners who carefully evaluate what they hear; they prefer to listen to information from sources they feel are credible and critically examine the information they receive.

**contradicting:** Nonverbal behavior that conveys meaning that is the opposite of the verbal message.

**control:** The ability of one person, group, or organization to influence others and the manner in which their relationships are conducted; one of the five functional communication competencies.

**cooperative strategies:** Tactics that benefit the relationship, serve mutual rather than individual goals, and strive to produce solutions that benefit both parties.

**costs:** The negative aspects of a relationship.

**countercoalition:** A subgroup positioned against another subgroup.

**cover letter:** A one-page letter indicating interest in being hired for a particular position.

**credibility:** The quality, authority, and reliability of a source of information.

**critical listening:** Listening that involves the evaluation or analysis of information, evidence, ideas, or opinions.

**cultural myopia:** The belief that one's own culture is appropriate and relevant in all situations and to all people.

**culture:** The shared beliefs, values, and practices of a group of people.

**cyberbullying:** Abusive attacks conducted through electronic channels.

**deception:** The attempt to convince others of something that is false.

**declining stage:** The stage at which a relationship begins to come apart.

**decoding:** The process of receiving a message by interpreting and assigning meaning to it.

**deductive reasoning:** A line of thought that proceeds from the general to the specific.

**defensive climate:** A communication climate in which the people involved feel threatened.

**defensive listening:** Responding with aggression and arguing with the speaker without fully listening to the message.

**definitional speeches:** Presentations that explain to an audience what something is.

**definition by example:** An explanation that defines something by offering concrete examples.

**definition by etymology:** A definition that explains the origin of a word or phrase.

**definition by negation:** An explanation that defines something by describing what it is not.

**definition by synonym:** An explanation that defines something with closely related words.

**delivery cues:** In a speech outline, brief reminders about important information related to the delivery of the speech.

**demographics:** The systematic study of the quantifiable characteristics of a large group.

**demonstration speeches:** Speeches that show an audience how a process works.

**denotative meaning:** The basic, consistently accepted definition of a word.

**descriptive presentation:** Conveying information in a way that creates a mental picture for your audience.

**devil's advocate:** A role that involves pointing out worst-case scenarios.

**dialectical tensions:** Tensions that arise when opposing or conflicting goals exist in a relationship.

**directed questions:** Questions that suggest or imply the answer that is expected.

**directive leader:** A leader who controls group communication by conveying specific instructions to members.

**directory:** A resource that guides people to the main page of a Web site organized in a particular subject category.

**division of labor:** An aspect of the classical management approach that assumes that each part of an organization has a specific function to carry out.

**dyad:** A pair of people.

**either-or fallacy:** Presenting only two alternatives on a subject, failing to acknowledge other alternatives.

**Elaboration Likelihood Model (ELM):** A model of communication that highlights the importance of relevance to persuasion and holds that people will process the message by one of two routes: central processing or peripheral processing.

**elucidating explanations:** Explanations that illuminate a concept's meaning and use.

**emblems:** Movements and gestures that have a specific meaning for a particular group or culture.

**empathic listening:** Listening with the goal of understanding how another person feels.

**empathy:** The process of picturing oneself in someone else's place in an attempt to understand that person's experience.

**encoding:** The process of mentally constructing and sending a message.

**enthymeme:** A syllogism in which one of the premises is implicit and thus not stated specifically.

**equivocation:** Using unclear or misleading words.

**escapist strategies:** Tactics that people use to try to prevent or avoid direct conflict.

**ethics:** The study of morals, specifically the moral choices individuals make in their relationships with others.

**ethos:** A form of rhetorical proof that appeals to ethics and concerns the qualifications and personality of the speaker.

**euphemisms:** Inoffensive words or phrases that substitute for terms that might be perceived as upsetting.

**evasion:** Avoiding providing specific details.

**exit interviews:** Interviews that employers hold with employees as they leave the company, in order to identify organizational problems.

**expert power:** Power that comes from the information or knowledge that a leader possesses.

**expert testimony:** The opinion or judgment of an expert or professional in his or her field.

**explanatory speeches:** Speeches that offer thorough explanations of meaning.

**exploratory stage:** The stage of a relationship in which you seek relatively superficial information from your partner.

**extemporaneous speaking:** A style of public speaking that involves few notes but careful advance preparation.

**fact:** A statement that is true and verifiable.

**family:** A social group bound by ties of blood, civil contract (such as marriage or adoption), or an implied or explicit commitment to care for and be responsible for one another, usually in a shared household.

**feedback:** A response from the receiver to the sender that occurs when people communicate.

**feelings:** Emotions; the use of language to express emotion is one of the five functional communication competencies.

**flaming:** The posting of online messages that are deliberately hostile or insulting and usually intended only to provoke anger.

**focus group:** A set of individuals asked to come together to give their opinion on a specific issue.

**forming:** The stage of group development when group members try to negotiate who will be in charge and what the group's goals will be.

**friendship:** A close and caring relationship between two people that is perceived as mutually satisfying and beneficial.

**functional perspective:** An examination of how communication works to help us begin, maintain, and end relationships.

**fundamental attribution error:** The tendency to overemphasize the internal and underestimate the external causes of behaviors we observe in others.

**funnel sequence:** A pattern of questioning that progresses from broad, open-ended questions to narrower, more closed questions.

**genetic-similarity hypothesis:** The theory that individuals tend to help, favor, and form relationships with people from their own ethnic group.

**globalization:** The growing interdependence and connectivity of societies and economies around the world.

**goal achievement:** Relying on communication to accomplish particular objectives.

**grammar:** The system of rules of a language that guides the creation of words, phrases, and sentences.

**group:** A collection of three or more people who share some kind of relationship with one another, communicate in an interdependent fashion, and collaborate toward some shared purpose.

**groupthink:** A situation in which group members strive to minimize conflict by refusing to question ideas, analyze proposals, or test solutions.

**haptics:** The study of touch as a form of communication.

**harassment:** Communication that hurts, offends, or embarrasses an individual or creates a hostile environment.

**hearing:** The physiological process of perceiving sound, whereby sound waves are picked up by the ears and transmitted to the brain.

**hierarchy:** The layers of authority and power in an organization.

**hierarchy of needs:** Abraham Maslow's argument that an individual's motivations, priorities, and behavior are influenced by that person's needs: physiological/survival needs, safety needs, belongingness/social needs, esteem/ego-status needs, and self-actualizing needs. Lower needs (physiological) must be met before higher needs.

**high-context cultures:** Cultures that rely more on contextual cues—such as time, place, relationship, and situation—both to interpret meaning and to send subtle messages.

**high language:** Formal, polite language, used in business contexts, in the classroom, or even at formal social gatherings.

**hostile audience:** An audience that opposes a speaker's message (and perhaps the speaker personally); the hardest type of audience to persuade.

**human relations approach:** An approach to management that focuses on the human needs of organizational members.

**human resources approach:** An approach to management that considers organizational productivity from the workers' perspectives.

**human trafficking:** The coercion of people, through false promises of high wages, into exploitative situations.

**hyperpersonal communication:** A phenomenon surrounding online communication in which the lack of proximity, visual contact, and nonverbal cues results in exaggerated perceptions.

**illustrators:** Body movements that reinforce verbal messages and visually help explain what is being said.

**imagining:** The ability to think, play, and be creative in communication; one of the five functional communication competencies.

**immediacy:** The feeling of closeness, involvement, and warmth between people as communicated by nonverbal behavior.

**impromptu speaking:** Speaking spontaneously, without advance preparation.

**inclusion:** A state of involvement with other individuals.

**indirect strategies:** Tactics for obtaining information from a relational partner without directly asking for it.

**individualistic culture:** A culture that emphasizes individual needs, rights, and identity over those of the collective or group.

**inductive reasoning:** The line of thought that occurs when you draw general conclusions based on specific evidence.

**inferences:** Deductions or conclusions that we make about the facts we observe.

**informal-formal dimension:** An aspect of situational context that involves our perceptions of personal versus impersonal situations.

**informational listening:** Comprehensive listening that is used to understand the facts, ideas, and opinions communicated by others.

**information-gathering interview:** An interview that serves to transfer knowledge from one party to another.

**informative speaking:** A form of public speaking intended to increase the audience's understanding or knowledge.

**informing:** Using language to send and receive information; one of the five functional communication competencies.

**initiating stage:** The stage of a relationship in which you first make contact with another person.

**insensitive listening:** Failing to pay attention to the emotional content of a message and simply accepting it at face value.

**integrating:** The process of forging a common identity shared by relational partners.

**intensification stage:** The stage of a relationship when relational partners become increasingly intimate and move their communication toward more personal self-disclosures.

**interaction appearance theory:** A theory that explains how people change their attributions of someone's physical appearance the more they interact.

**interaction model:** Model of communication between a sender and a receiver that incorporates feedback.

**interdependence:** Relationship in which the actions of each person affect others.

**internal previews:** Extended transitions that prime the audience for the content immediately ahead.

**internal summaries:** Statements that summarize the points made in one section of a speech before moving to the next.

**interpersonal communication:** The exchange of verbal and nonverbal messages between two people who have a relationship and are influenced by each other's messages.

**interpersonal relationships:** The interconnections and interdependence between two individuals.

**interview:** An interaction between two parties that is deliberate and purposeful for at least one of the parties involved.

**intimacy:** Closeness and understanding of a relational partner.

**inverted funnel sequence:** A pattern of questioning that progresses from narrow, closed questions to more open-ended questions.

**jargon:** Technical language that is specific to members of a particular profession, interest group, or hobby.

**job interview:** A selection interview for the purpose of filling a position of employment.

**key-word outline:** The briefest type of outline; uses key words and quick headers as guideposts for a more extemporaneous delivery.

**kinesics:** The way gestures and body movements communicate meaning.

**language:** A system of symbols (words) that we use to think about and communicate experiences and feelings.

**latitude of acceptance and rejection:** The range of positions on a topic that are acceptable or unacceptable to an audience.

**lay testimony:** The opinion of a nonexpert who has personal experience or witnessed an event related to your topic.

**leadership:** The ability to influence others' behaviors and thoughts toward a productive end.

**leading questions:** Directed questions that subtly suggest or imply the answer that is expected.

**legitimate power:** Power that comes from an individual's role or title.

**library gateways:** Collections of databases and informational sites arranged by subject, generally reviewed and recommended by experts (usually librarians).

**linear model:** Model of communication in which a sender originates a message that is carried through a channel—perhaps interfered with by noise—to the receiver.

**linguistic determinism:** The idea that language influences how we see the world.

**linguistic relativity:** The belief that speakers of different languages have different views of the world.

**listening:** The process of recognizing, understanding, and accurately interpreting the messages communicated by others.

**listening apprehension:** A state of uneasiness, anxiety, fear, or dread associated with a listening opportunity; also known as *receiver apprehension*.

**listening barriers:** Factors that interfere with the ability to comprehend information and respond appropriately.

**loaded questions:** Questions that strongly suggest the answer that is expected.

**logical fallacies:** Invalid or deceptive forms of reasoning.

**logos:** A form of rhetorical proof that appeals to reason and concerns the logical nature of the message in a speech.

**love:** A deep affection for and attachment to another person, involving emotional ties and varying degrees of passion, commitment, and intimacy.

**low-context cultures:** Cultures in which individuals use very direct language and rely less on contextual cues for communication information.

**low language:** Informal language used in casual environments.

**main points:** In a speech, the central claims that support your specific speech purpose and your thesis statement.

**masking:** A facial management technique in which an expression that shows true feeling is replaced with an expression that shows appropriate feeling for a given interaction.

**matching hypothesis:** The theory that we seek relationships with others who have comparable levels of perceived attractiveness.

**media richness:** The degree to which a particular channel is communicative, based on the amount of verbal and nonverbal cues available.

**mentor:** A seasoned, respected member of an organization who serves as a role model for a less experienced individual.

**message:** Symbols (words, actions, or behavior) from one or more senders transmitted through a channel to one or more receivers.

**metasearch engine:** A search engine that scans multiple search engines simultaneously.

**mindlessness:** A state of passive processing of information, characterized by reduced cognitive activity, inaccurate recall, and uncritical evaluation.

**monitoring:** An uncertainty reduction strategy that involves observing and evaluating people as they communicate with others.

**monopolistic listening:** Listening in order to control the communication interaction.

**monotone:** Lack of variety in vocal pitch.

**motivated sequence pattern:** An organizational approach that entails five phases: attention, need, satisfaction, visualization, and action.

**multitasking:** Attending to several things at once.

**mumbling:** Omitting certain sounds in a word, running words together, or speaking so softly as to be unintelligible.

**narrative pattern:** An organizational style that ties points together in a way that presents a vivid story, complete with characters, settings, plot, and imagery.

**networks:** Patterns of interaction in a group that govern who speaks with whom and about what.

**neutral audience:** An audience that neither supports nor opposes the speaker.

**neutral questions:** Questions that provide no hint to the interviewee concerning the expected response.

**noise:** Interference with a message that makes its final form different from the original.

**nonbinding straw poll:** An informal vote on a decision that can help a group move forward when time is an issue.

**noncontact cultures:** Cultures that use touch minimally or not at all as a medium of communication.

**nonverbal codes:** Symbols we use to send messages without or in addition to words.

**nonverbal communication:** The process of intentionally or unintentionally signaling meaning through behavior other than words.

**norming:** The stage of group development in which members establish norms governing expected behavior.

**objective:** Presented in a straightforward and even-handed way, free of influence from personal thoughts and opinions.

**oculesics:** The study of the use of the eyes in communication settings.

**openness:** An organization's awareness of its own imbalances and problems.

**open question:** A question that gives the interviewee great freedom in terms of how to respond.

**operational definition:** An explanation of what something is or what it does.

**opinions:** Statements that involve personal evaluations.

**oral citations:** References to source material that are worked into the narrative of a speech.

**oratory:** A form of public speaking that involves a speech committed to memory.

**organizational assimilation:** The process by which a person figures out what behaviors are appropriate and effective in a given organization.

**organizational communication:** The interaction necessary to direct a group toward a set of common goals.

**organizational culture:** An organization's unique set of beliefs, values, norms, and ways of doing things.

**organizational heroes:** Individuals who achieve great things for an organization through persistence and commitment, often in the face of great risk.

**organizational storytelling:** The communication of the organization's values through stories and accounts, both within and outside the organization.

**organizations:** Groups with a formal governance and structure.

**organized audience:** An audience that is completely devoted to the speaker and to the speaker's purpose.

**outcome:** The product of an interchange.

**paralanguage:** Nonverbal vocal behaviors—including pauses, inflections, and the speed, pitch, and volume of speech—that communicate meaning.

**paraphrasing:** A part of listening empathically that involves rephrasing what you think the speaker has said to convey a sense of understanding.

**participative leader:** A leader who views group members as equals, invites their opinions, summarizes points that have been raised, and identifies problems that need discussion rather than proclaiming solutions.

**passive audience:** A group that is already gathered to hear the speaker, but its motivation level is not high.

**passive listeners:** People who fail to take an active role in listening, making them less competent communicators.

**pathos:** A form of rhetorical proof that appeals to emotions.

**pedestrian audience:** An audience of people who have no obvious connection with either the speaker or one another.

**peer communication:** Communication between individuals at the same level of authority in an organization.

**peer relationships:** Friendships that form between colleagues in the work environment.

**people-oriented listeners:** Communicators who listen with relationships in mind; they tend to be most concerned with others' feelings.

**perception:** A cognitive process through which we interpret our experiences and come to our own unique understandings.

**performance appraisals:** Interviews designed to review an individual's accomplishments and develop goals for the future.

**performing:** The stage of group development when members combine their skills and knowledge to work toward the group's goals.

**peripheral processing:** Dismissing a message as being irrelevant, too complex to follow, or simply unimportant.

**persuasion:** The process of influencing attitudes, beliefs, and behaviors.

**persuasive interview:** An interview in which questions are designed to elicit some change in the interviewee's behaviors or opinions.

**persuasive speaking:** Speech that is intended to influence the attitudes, beliefs, and behaviors of the audience.

**phrase outline:** A type of outline that uses key phrases as instant reminders of each point or subpoint.

**pitch:** Variations of sound and voice that range from high to low, like musical notes.

**plagiarism:** The crime of fraudulently presenting someone else's words, ideas, or intellectual property as one's own, intentionally or unintentionally.

**planting:** Limiting and controlling body movements during speech delivery by keeping one's legs apart at shoulder-width distance.

**politically correct language:** Language that replaces biased language with more neutral terms.

**posture:** The position of your arms, legs, and body.

**power distance:** The extent to which members of a culture expect and tolerate the unequal distribution of power.

**pragmatics:** The ability to use the symbol systems of a culture appropriately.

**prejudice:** Ill will toward particular groups of people, usually based on negative stereotypes and one's own feelings of superiority.

**primary groups:** Long-lasting groups that form around the relationships that mean the most to their members.

**primary questions:** Questions in an interview that introduce new topics.

**proactive strategies:** Tactics that let you obtain information about a person directly.

**probing:** Asking questions that encourage specific and precise answers.

**problem-solution pattern:** An organizational style that involves dramatizing an obstacle and then narrowing alternative remedies to the one that you recommend.

**problem-solving group:** A group with a specific mission.

**problem-solving interview:** An interview that is meant to deal with problems, tensions, or conflicts.

**process:** Any method by which an outcome is accomplished.

**productive conflict:** Conflict that is managed effectively.

**pronunciation:** The correct formation of word sounds.

**proposition:** A statement about your viewpoint or position on an issue.

**proposition of fact:** A claim of what is or what is not.

**proposition of policy:** A claim about what goal, policy, or course of action should be pursued.

**proposition of value:** A claim that discusses something's worth.

**protégé:** A new or inexperienced member of an organization who is trained or mentored by a more seasoned member.

**provocation:** The intentional instigation of conflict.

**proxemics:** The study of the way we use and communicate with space.

**proximity:** Physical nearness.

**pseudolistening:** Pretending to listen without really paying attention.

**psychological forces:** Group members' personal motives, goals, attitudes, and values.

**public-private dimension:** An aspect of the situational context involving the way physical space affects our nonverbal communication.

**public speaking:** A powerful form of communication that includes a speaker who has a reason for speaking, an audience that gives the speaker attention, and a message that is meant to accomplish a specific goal.

**quasi-scientific explanations:** Explanations that model or picture the key dimensions of some phenomenon for a typical audience.

**random selection:** A way to reach compromise that entails choosing one of two options at random (such as by a toss of a coin).

**reasoning:** The line of thought we use to make judgments based on facts and inferences from the world around us.

**receiver:** The recipient of a message.

**receptive audience:** An audience that already agrees with your viewpoints and your message and is likely to respond favorably to your speech.

**reconciliation:** A repair strategy for rekindling an extinguished relationship.

**red herring fallacy:** Relying on irrelevant information in an argument, thereby diverting the direction of the argument.

**reduction to the absurd:** A fallacy (also known as *reductio ad absurdum*) that entails extending an argument to the level of absurdity.

**referent power:** Power that stems from the admiration, respect, or affection that followers have for a leader.

**refutational organizational pattern:** An organizational style in which speakers begin by presenting main points that are opposed to their own position and then follow them with main points that support their own position.

**regulating:** Coordinating verbal interaction using nonverbal cues.

**regulators:** Body movements that help us manage our interactions.

**relational dialectics theory:** The theory that dialectical tensions arise when opposing or conflicting goals exist in a relationship.

**relational network:** The web of relationships that connect individuals to one another.

**relationships:** Interconnections or interdependence between two or more people in order to achieve goals.

**remembering:** The part of the listening process that involves recalling information.

**repair tactics:** Actions taken to save a relationship.

**repeating:** Offering a very clear nonverbal cue that mirrors the verbal message.

**responding:** A step in the listening process that involves generating some kind of feedback or reaction that confirms you have received and understood a message.

**résumé:** A summary of one's education, work experiences, and accomplishments.

**reward power:** Power that derives from an individual's capacity to provide rewards.

**rewards:** The beneficial elements of a relationship.

**rhetorical proof:** Aristotle's three means of persuasion: ethos, logos, and pathos.

**ritualizing:** Learning and following the rules for managing conversations and relationships; one of the five functional communication competencies.

**role conflict:** A situation that arises in a group whenever expectations for members' behavior are incompatible.

**running bibliography:** A list of resources you've consulted during research on a topic.

**Sapir-Whorf hypothesis:** A claim that the words a culture uses (or doesn't use) influence thinking.

**scanning:** Making and maintaining eye contact with a large group of individuals by moving your eyes from one person or group of people to another.

**schemas:** Mental constructions we use to connect related bits of information.

**search engine:** A program that indexes Web content and searches the Web for documents containing specific keywords that you've chosen.

**secondary questions:** Questions in an interview that seek clarification or elaboration of responses to primary questions.

**selected audience:** An audience that shares a common and known purpose with the speaker, but that does not necessarily agree with the speaker on the best way to achieve their shared goals.

**selecting:** Choosing one sound over another when confronted with competing stimuli.

**selection interview:** An interview in which the primary goal is to fill a position in an organization.

**selective listening:** Listening that involves zeroing in on bits of information of interest and disregarding other messages or parts of messages.

**selective perception:** Allowing bias to influence one's thinking.

**self-actualization:** The feelings and thoughts you get when you know that you have negotiated a communication situation as well as you possibly could.

**self-adequacy:** The feelings that you experience when you assess your communication competence as sufficient or acceptable but not stellar.

**self-concept:** Your awareness and understanding of who you are, as interpreted and influenced by your thoughts, actions, abilities, values, goals, and ideals.

**self-denigration:** A negative assessment about a communication experience that involves criticizing or attacking your own performance.

**self-directed work team:** A group of skilled workers who take responsibility for high-quality finished work.

**self-disclosure:** Sharing important information about yourself, as with a close friend.

**self-efficacy:** The ability to predict your effectiveness in a communication situation, based on self-concept and self-esteem.

**self-esteem:** How you feel about yourself, usually in a particular situation.

**self-fulfilling prophecy:** A prediction that causes an individual to alter behavior in a way that makes the prediction more likely to occur.

**self-monitoring:** Watching your environment and others in it for cues as to how to present yourself in particular situations.

**self-presentation:** Intentional communication designed to show elements of self for strategic purposes; how you let others know about yourself.

**self-talk:** Internal dialogues or statements that influence behavior.

**semantics:** The study of the relationships among symbols, objects, people, and concepts; the meaning that words have for people.

**sender:** The individual who originates communication, with words or action.

**sentence outline:** A type of outline that offers the full text of a speech, often word for word.

**separation:** Removing oneself from a conflict situation.

**service-oriented interviews:** Interviews that are designed to cull information and provide advice or support.

**sexual harassment:** Unwanted verbal or physical conduct of a sexual nature that affects an individual's employment, interferes with work performance, or creates an intimidating, hostile, or offensive work environment.

**signposts:** Key words or phrases that signify transitions between points, such as *however* and *similarly*.

**slang:** Language that is informal, nonstandard, and usually particular to a specific group.

**slippery slope:** A fallacy that is employed when a speaker links two events without clearly showing a causal relationship between them.

**social comparison theory:** Theory explaining our tendency to internalize our admiration for popular figures and compare what we like about them to our own self-concept.

**social exchange of costs and benefits:** The process of balancing the advantages and disadvantages of a relationship.

**social forces:** Group standards for behavior, which influence decision making.

**social group:** A group in which membership offers opportunities to form relationships with others.

**social loafing:** Failure to invest the level of effort in the group that people would put in if they were working alone or with one other person.

**social penetrational theory:** An explanation for how relational partners move their relationship from superficial levels to intimacy.

**social roles:** Roles that evolve based on members' personality traits and interests.

**spatial pattern:** An organizational style that arranges points according to their physical proximity to or direction from each other.

**speaking outline:** The final speech plan, complete with details, delivery tips, and notes about presentational aids.

**speaking rate:** How fast or slow one speaks.

**specific purpose statement:** A statement that expresses both the topic and the general speech purpose in action form and in terms of the specific objectives you hope to achieve with your presentation.

**speech repertoires:** Sets of complex language behaviors or options that we draw on to meet the demands of specific situations.

**stable stage:** The stage of a relationship when it is no longer volatile or temporary; both partners have a great deal of knowledge about one another, and their expectations are accurate and realistic.

**state communication apprehension:** An attack of communication apprehension that results from a specific communication situation.

**statistics:** Information provided in numerical form, which can be a powerful form of support for a speech.

**stereotyping:** Organizing information about groups of people into categories so that we can generalize about their attitudes, behaviors, skills, morals, and habits.

**storming:** The stage of group development in which members begin experiencing conflict over issues such as who will lead the group and the roles members will play.

**strategic topic avoidance:** Maneuvering the conversation between relational partners away from undesirable topics.

**study group:** A group that is formed for the specific purpose of helping students prepare for exams.

**style switching:** A type of accommodation in which communicators change their tonality, pitch, rhythm, and inflection to fit into a particular group.

**subjective:** Presented from a particular point of view.

**subpoints:** Points that back up your main points.

**substituting:** Replacing words with nonverbal cues.

**support group:** A set of individuals who come together to address personal problems while benefiting from the support of others with similar issues.

**supportive climate:** A climate that offers communicators a chance to explore the issues involved in the conflict situation honestly and considerately.

**supportive leader:** A leader who attends to group members' emotional needs.

**surveillance:** Monitoring employees' use of technologies such as e-mail, the Internet, and instant messaging.

**surveys:** Answers to a question or series of questions related to your topic from a broad range of individuals.

**syllogism:** A three-line deductive argument that draws a specific conclusion from two general premises (a major and a minor premise).

**symbols:** Arbitrary constructions (usually in the form of language or behaviors) that refer to people, things, or concepts.

**systematic desensitization:** A method for reducing anxiety that involves countering stress by gradually retraining individuals to react differently to stress-inducing stimuli.

**systems approach:** An approach to management that views an organization as a unique whole consisting of important members who share an interdependent relationship.

**task roles:** Roles that relate to the accomplishment of goals.

**team:** A group that works together to carry out a project or specific endeavor or to compete against other teams.

**termination stage:** The end of a relationship, generally achieved by a gradual passing away or a sudden death of the relationship.

**territoriality:** The claiming of an area, with or without legal basis, through continuous occupation of that area.

**thesis statement:** A statement that conveys the central idea or core assumption about your topic.

**time orientation:** People's personal associations with the use of time.

**time-oriented listeners:** Communicators who are most concerned with efficiency; they prefer information that is clear and to the point.

**topical pattern:** An organizational style that arranges points by topic or category.

**trading:** A way to reach compromise, which occurs when one partner offers something of equal value in return for something he or she wants.

**trait communication apprehension:** Anxiety about communication in all contexts, not just in a specific communication situation.

**transactional:** Involving two or more people in both sender and receiver roles whose messages are dependent on and influenced by those of their communication partners.

**transformative explanations:** Explanations that help people understand ideas that are counterintuitive and turn them into more accepted notions.

**transitions:** Words and phrases that connect different thoughts, points, and details in a way that allows them to flow naturally from one to the next.

**tunnel sequence:** A style of questioning in which all questions are of the same level; commonly used in polls and surveys.

**uncertain climate:** A climate in which at least one of the people involved is unclear, vague, tentative, and awkward about the goals, expectations, and potential outcomes of the conflict situation.

**uncertainty events:** Events or behavioral patterns that cause uncertainty in a relationship.

**uncertainty reduction theory:** A theory that holds that when two people meet, their main focus is on decreasing the uncertainty that lies between them.

**understanding:** The step in the listening process that involves interpreting and making sense of messages.

**undue influence:** Giving greater credibility or importance to something than should be the case.

**unproductive conflict:** Conflict that is managed poorly and has a negative impact on the individuals and relationships involved.

**verbal aggressiveness:** Attacks on individuals rather than issues.

**vocalizations:** Paralinguistic cues such as laughing, crying, or yawning that give information about the speaker's emotional or physical state.

**volume:** How loudly or quietly one speaks.

**wheel network:** A network in which all group members give their information to one central individual, who then shares the information with the rest of the group.

**working outline:** A rough draft outline used (and revised continually) throughout the preparation for a speech, a process that helps firm up the thesis statement, establish and organize main points, and develop supporting points.

**work-life balance:** The struggle employees face achieving success in both their personal and professional lives.

# references

Abhik, R., & Harwood, J. (1997). Underrepresented, positively portrayed: Older adults in television commercials. *Journal of Applied Communication Research, 21,* 39–56.

Adkins, M., & Brashers, D. E. (1995). The power of language in computer-mediated groups. *Management Communication Quarterly, 8,* 289–322.

Albada, K. F., Knapp, M. L., & Theune, K. E. (2002). Interaction appearance theory: Changing perceptions of physical attractiveness through social interaction. *Communication Theory, 12,* 8–40.

Alge, B. J., Wiethoff, C., & Klein, H. J. (2003). When does the medium matter? Knowledge-building experiences and opportunities in decision-making teams. *Organizational Behavior and Human Decision Processes, 91,* 26–37.

Alicke, M. D., Braun, J. C., Glor, J. E., Klotz, M. L., Magee, J., Cederholm, H., et al. (1992). Complaining behavior in social interaction. *Personality and Social Psychology Bulletin, 18,* 286–295.

Allen, R. R., & McKerrow, R. E. (1985). *The pragmatics of public communication* (3rd ed.). Dubuque, IA: Kendall/Hunt.

Altman, I., & Taylor, D. A. (1973). *Social penetration: The development of interpersonal relationships.* New York: Holt, Rinehart & Winston.

Amodio, D. M., & Showers, C. J. (2005). "Similarity breeds liking" revisited: The moderating role of commitment. *Journal of Social and Personal Relationships, 22,* 817–836.

Andersen, P. A., & Blackburn, T. R. (2004). An experimental study of language intensity and response rate in e-mail surveys. *Communication Reports, 17,* 73–84.

Anderson, C. M., & Martin, M. M. (1999). The relationship of argumentativeness and verbal aggressiveness to cohesion, consensus, and satisfaction in small groups. *Communication Reports, 12,* 21–31.

Anderson, C. M., Riddle, B. L., & Martin, M. M. (1999). Socialization in groups. In L. Frey, D. Gouran, & M. Poole (Eds.), *Handbook of group communication theory and research* (pp. 139–163). Thousand Oaks, CA: SAGE.

Armstrong, B., & Kaplowitz, S. A. (2001). Sociolinguistic interference and intercultural coordination: A Bayesian model of communication competence in intercultural communication. *Human Communication Research, 27,* 350–381.

Arvey, R. D., & Murphy, K. R. (1998). Performance evaluation in work settings. *Annual Review of Psychology, 49,* 141–168.

Atkinson, J., & Dougherty, D. S. (2006). Alternative media and social justice movements: The development of a resistance performance paradigm of audience analysis. *Journal of Western Communication, 70,* 64–89.

Aust, P. J. (2004). Communicated values as indicators of organizational identity: A method for organizational assessment and its application in a case study. *Communication Studies, 55,* 515–535.

Avtgis, T. A., West, D. V., & Anderson, T. L. (1998). Relationship stages: An inductive analysis identifying cognitive, affective, and behavioral dimensions of Knapp's relational stages model. *Communication Research Reports, 15,* 280–287.

Axtell, R. E. (1991). *Gestures: The do's and taboos of body language around the world.* New York: Wiley.

Ayres, J., & Heuett, B. L. (1997). The relationship between visual imagery and public speaking apprehension. *Communication Reports, 10,* 87–94.

Ayres, J., & Hopf, T. S. (1993). *Coping with speech anxiety.* Norwood, NJ: Ablex.

Ayres, J., Hopf, T. S., & Will, A. (2000). Are reductions in CA an experimental artifact? A Solomon four-group answer. *Communication Quarterly, 48,* 19–26.

Ayres, J., Keereetaweep, T., Chen, P., & Edwards, P. (1998). Communication apprehension and employment interviews. *Communication Education, 47,* 1–17.

Ayres, J., Wilcox, A. K., & Ayres, D. M. (1995). Receiver apprehension: An explanatory model and accompanying research. *Communication Education, 44,* 223–235.

Bailenson, J. N., Beall, A. C., Loomis, J., Blascovich, J., & Turk, M. (2005). Transformed social interaction, augmented gaze, and social influence in immersive virtual environments. *Human Communication Research, 31,* 511–537.

Baird, J. E., Jr. (1986). Sex differences in group communication: A review of relevant research. *Quarterly Journal of Speech, 62,* 179–192.

Baird, J. E., Jr., & Weinbert, S. (1977). *Communication: The essence of a group synergy.* Dubuque, IA: Brown.

Baker, H. G., & Spier, M. S. (1990). The employment interview: Guaranteed improvement in reliability. *Public Personnel Management, 19,* 85–90.

Baldwin, M. W., & Keelan, J. P. R. (1999). Interpersonal expectations as a function of self-esteem and sex. *Journal of Social and Personal Relationships, 16,* 822–833.

Bandura, A. (1982). Self-efficacy mechanism in human agency. *American Psychologist, 37,* 122.

Barker, L. L., & Watson, K. W. (2000). *Listen up: How to improve relationships, reduce stress, and be more productive by using the power of listening.* New York: St. Martin's Press.

Barry, D. (1996, November 7). L.I. widow's story: Next stop, Washington. *The New York Times.* Retrieved from http://www.nytimes.com

Bates, B. (1988). *Communication and the sexes.* New York: Harper & Row.

Bavelous, A. (1950). Communication patterns in task-oriented groups. *Journal of the Acoustical Society of America, 22,* 725–730.

Baxter, L. A., Braithwaite, D. O., Bryant, L., & Wagner, A. (2004). Stepchildren's perceptions of the contradictions in communication with stepparents. *Journal of Social and Personal Relationships, 21,* 447–467.

Baxter, L. A., & Erbert, L. (1999). Perceptions of dialectical contradictions in turning points of development in heterosexual romantic relationships. *Journal of Social and Personal Relationships, 16,* 547–569.

Baxter, L. A., & Simon, E. P. (1993). Relationship maintenance strategies and dialectical contradictions in personal relationships. *Journal of Social and Personal Relationships, 10,* 225–242.

Baxter, L. A., & Wilmot, W. W. (1985). Taboo topics in close relationships. *Journal of Social and Personal Relationships, 2,* 253–269.

Beam, C. (2007, July 16). Killer of Sheeple: A Toyota advergame makes you murder for a new car. *Slate.* Retrieved from http://www.slate.com/id/2170388

Beatty, M. J., & Payne, S. K. (1984). Effects of social facilitation on listening comprehension. *Communication Quarterly, 32,* 37–40.

Bellis, T. J., & Wilber, L. A. (2001). Effects of aging and gender on interhemispheric function. *Journal of Speech, Language, and Hearing Research, 44,* 246–264.

Benne, K. D., & Sheats, P. (1948). Functional roles in group members. *Journal of Social Issues, 4,* 41–49.

Berger, C., & Calabrese, R. (1975). Some explorations in initial interaction and beyond: Toward a developmental theory of interpersonal communication. *Human Communication Research, 1,* 99–112.

Berrisford, S. (2006). How will you respond to the information crisis? *Strategic Communication Management, 10,* 26–29.

Berryman-Fink, C. (1993). Preventing sexual harassment through male-female communication training. In G. Kreps (Ed.), *Sexual harassment: Communication implications* (pp. 267–280). Cresskill, NJ: Hampton Press.

Berscheid, E. (1985). Interpersonal attraction. In G. Lindzey & E. Aronson (Eds.), *Handbook of social psychology: Vol. 2. Special fields and applications* (3rd ed., pp. 413–484). New York: Random House.

Beyerlein, M. M. (2001). The parallel growth of team practices and the center for the study of work teams. *Team Performance Management, 7,* 93–98.

Biever, C. (2004, August). Language may shape human thought. *New Scientist.* Retrieved from http://www.newscientist.com

Bishop, R. (2000). More than meets the eye: An explanation of literature related to the mass media's role in encouraging changes in body image. In M. E. Roloff (Ed.), *Communication yearbook* (Vol. 23, pp. 271–304). Thousand Oaks, CA: SAGE.

Bloomberg, M. (2006, March 28). *Statement before the House Subcommittee on Crime, Terrorism, and Homeland Security.* Retrieved April 10, 2008, from http://nyc.gov

Blumstein, P., & Schwartz, P. (1983). *American couples: Money, work, sex.* New York: Morrow.

Boje, D. M. (1991). The storytelling organization: A study of story performance in an office-supply firm. *Administrative Science Quarterly, 36,* 106–126.

Booth, W. (2006, January 26). Al Gore, Sundance's leading man. *The Washington Post,* p. A1.

Borisoff, D., & Merrill, L. (1998). *The power to communicate: Gender differences as barriers.* Prospect Heights, IL: Waveland Press.

Bosman, J. (2006, May 11). User-generated content starts to take hold in advertising. *The New York Times.* Retrieved from http://www.nytimes.com

Botta, R., & Dumlao, R. (2002). How do conflict and communication patterns between fathers and daughters contribute to or offset eating disorders? *Health Communication, 14,* 199–219.

Bourhis, R. Y. (1985). The sequential nature of language choice in cross-cultural communication. In R. L. Street Jr. & J. N. Cappella (Eds.), *Sequence and pattern in communicative behaviour* (pp. 120–141). London: Arnold.

Bradac, J. J. (1983). The language of lovers, flovers, and friends: Communicating in social and personal relationships. *Journal of Language and Social Psychology, 2,* 234.

Bradac, J. J., & Giles, H. (2005). Language and social psychology: Conceptual niceties, complexities, curiosities, monstrosities, and how it all works. In K. L. Fitch & R. E. Sanders (Eds.), *The new handbook of language and social psychology* (pp. 201–230). Mahwah, NJ: Erlbaum.

Braude, J. M. (1965). *Complete speaker's and toastmaster's library.* Englewood Cliffs, NJ: Prentice Hall.

Brehm, J. W. (1966). *A theory of psychological reactance.* New York: Academic Press.

Brenneis, D. (1990). Shared and solitary sentiments: The discourse of friendship, play, and anger in Bhatgaon. In C. A. Lutz & L. Abu-Lughod (Eds.), *Language and the politics of emotion* (pp. 113–125). Cambridge: Cambridge University Press.

Brilhart, J. K., & Galanes, G. J. (1992). *Effective group discussion* (7th ed.). Dubuque, IA: Brown.

Brody, L. R. (2000). The socialization of gender differences in emotional expression: Display rules, infant temperament, and differentiation. In A. H. Fischer (Ed.), *Gender and emo-*

*tion: Social psychological perspectives* (pp. 24–47). Cambridge: Cambridge University Press.

Brown, S. L. (2000). The effect of union type on psychological well-being: Depression among cohabitors versus marrieds. *Journal of Health and Social Behavior, 41,* 241–255.

Buck, R. (1988). Emotional education and mass media: A new view of the global village. In R. P. Hawkins, J. M. Wiemann, & S. Pingree (Eds.), *Advancing communication science: Merging mass and interpersonal processes* (pp. 44–76). Beverly Hills, CA: SAGE.

Buckley, R. (1999). *Strictly speaking.* New York: McGraw-Hill.

Burgoon, J. K., & Bacue, A. E. (2003). Nonverbal communication skills. In J. O. Greene & B. R. Burleson (Eds.), *Handbook of communication and social interaction skills* (pp. 179–219). Mahwah, NJ: Erlbaum.

Burgoon, J. K., Bonito, J. A., Ramirez, A., Jr., Dunbar, N. E., Kam, K., & Fischer, J. (2002). Testing the interactivity principle: Effects of mediation, propinquity, and verbal and nonverbal modalities in interpersonal interaction. *Journal of Communication, 52,* 657–677.

Burgoon, J. K., Buller, D. B., & Woodall, W. G. (1989). *Nonverbal communication: The unspoken dialogue.* New York: Harper & Row.

Burgoon, J. K., & Hoobler, G. D. (2002). Nonverbal signals. In M. L. Knapp & J. A. Daly (Eds.), *Handbook of interpersonal communication* (pp. 240–299). Thousand Oaks, CA: SAGE.

Burleson, B. R. (1994). Comforting messages: Features, functions, and outcomes. In J. A. Daly & J. M. Wiemann (Eds.), *Strategic interpersonal communication* (pp. 135–161). Hillsdale, NJ: Erlbaum.

Burleson, B. R., Holmstrom, A. J., & Gilstrap, C. M. (2005). "Guys can't say that to guys": Four experiments assessing the normative motivation account for deficiencies in the emotional support provided by men. *Communication Monographs, 72,* 468–501.

Byrne, D. (1971). *The attraction paradigm.* New York: Academic Press.

Campbell, J. D. (1990). Self-esteem and clarity of the self-concept. *Journal of Personality and Social Psychology, 59,* 538–549.

Canary, D. J. (2003). Managing interpersonal conflict: A model of events related to strategic choices. In J.O. Greene & B. R. Burleson (Eds.), *Handbook of communication and social interaction skills* (pp. 515–550). Mahwah, NJ: Erlbaum.

Canary, D. J., & Cody, M. J. (1993). *Interpersonal communication: A goals-based approach.* New York: St. Martin's Press.

Canary, D. J., Cody, M. J., & Manusov, V. (2003). *Interpersonal communication: A goals-based approach* (3rd ed.). New York: Bedford/St. Martin's.

Canary, D. J., Cody, M. J., & Manusov, V. (2008). *Interpersonal communication: A goals-based approach* (4th ed.). New York: Bedford/St. Martin's.

Canary, D. J., Cody, M. J., & Smith, S. (1994). Compliance-gaining goals: An inductive analysis of actors' goal types,

strategies, and successes. In J. A. Daly & J. M. Wiemann (Eds.), *Strategic interpersonal communication* (pp. 33–90). Hillsdale, NJ: Erlbaum.

Canary, D. J., Cunningham, E. M., & Cody, M. J. (1988). Goal types, gender, and locus of control in managing interpersonal conflict. *Communication Research, 15,* 426–446.

Canary, D. J., & Spitzberg, B. H. (1993). Loneliness and media gratifications. *Communication Research, 20,* 800–821.

Caplan, S. (2001). Challenging the mass-interpersonal communication dichotomy: Are we witnessing the emergence of an entirely new communication system? *Electronic Journal of Communication, 11.* Retrieved March 24, 2003, from http://www.cios.org/getfile/CAPLAN_v11n101

Capozzoli, T. (2002). How to succeed with self-directed work teams. *SuperVision, 63,* 25–26.

Carless, S. A., & DePaola, C. (2000). The measurement of cohesion in work teams. *Small Group Research, 31,* 71–88.

Carter, B. (2005, March 20). *The Office* transfers to a new cubicle. *The New York Times.* Retrieved from http://www.nytimes.com

Caruso, P. (1996, September). Individuality vs. conformity: The issue behind school uniforms. *National Association of Secondary School Principals Bulletin,* 83–88.

Casmir, F. L. (Ed.). (1997). *Ethics in intercultural and international communication.* Mahwah, NJ: Erlbaum.

Cathcart, D., & Cathcart, R. (1997). The group: A Japanese context. In L. A. Samovar & R. E. Quarter (Eds.), *Intercultural communication: A reader* (8th ed., pp. 329–339). Belmont, CA: Wadsworth.

Caughlin, J. (2003). Family communication standards: What counts as excellent family communication, and how are such standards associated with family satisfaction? *Human Communication Research, 29,* 5–40.

CBS News. (2006, October 26). *Fox responds to Limbaugh accusation.* Retrieved from http://www.cbsnews.com/stories/2006/10/24/politics/main2121910.shtml

Cegala, D. (1981). Interaction involvement: A cognitive dimension of communicative competence. *Communication Education, 30,* 109–121.

Center for Science in the Public Interest. (2004, May). *Dispensing junk: How school vending undermines efforts to feed children well.* Retrieved April 2, 2008, from http://www.cspinet.org/dispensing_junk.pdf

Chaplin, W. F., Phillips, J. B., Brown, J. D., Clanton, N. R., & Stein, J. L. (2000). Handshaking, gender, personality, and first impressions. *Journal of Personality and Social Psychology, 79,* 110–117.

Chen, G., & Starosta, W. J. (1996). Intercultural communication competence: A synthesis. In B. R. Burleson (Ed.), *Communication yearbook* (Vol. 19, pp. 353–383). Thousand Oaks, CA: SAGE.

Christenson, P. (1994). Childhood patterns of music uses and preferences. *Communication Reports, 7,* 136–144.

Christians, C., & Traber, C. (Eds.). (1997). *Communication ethics and universal values.* Thousand Oaks, CA: SAGE.

Cialdini, R. B. (2004, January). The science of persuasion. *Scientific American Mind, 14*(1), 70–77.

Claire, R. (1998). *Organizing silence: A world of possibilities.* Albany: State University of New York Press.

Clark, A. J. (1989). Communication confidence and listening competence: An investigation of the relationships of willingness to communicate, communication apprehension, and receiver apprehension to comprehension of content and emotional meaning in spoken messages. *Communication Education, 38,* 237–248.

Classroom clickers make the grade. (2005, July 4). *Wired.* Retrieved from http://www.wired.com/science/discoveries/news/2005/07/68086

CNN.com. (2006, October 5). Amish grandfather: "We must not think evil of this man." *Cable News Network.* Retrieved from http://www.cnn.com/2006/US/10/04/amish.shooting/index.html

CNN.com. (2007, April 18). Massacre at Virginia Tech. *Cable News Network.* Retrieved from http://www.cnn.com/2007/US/04/17/cho.profile/index.html

CNN.com/living. (2008). *Having it all: Quiz: Are you off balance?* Retrieved May 27, 2008, from http://www.cnn.com

Coakley, C. G., & Wolvin, A. D. (1990). Listening pedagogy and andragogy: The state of the art. *Journal of the International Listening Association, 4,* 33–61.

Cohen, N. (2007, March 5). A contributor to Wikipedia has his fictional side. *The New York Times.* Retrieved from http://www.nytimes.com

Cohen, N. (2008, March 17). Open-source troubles in Wiki world. *The New York Times.* Retrieved from http://www.nytimes.com

Colbert, S. (Executive Producer). (2005, September 22). *The Colbert Report* [Television broadcast]. New York: Comedy Central.

Comer, D. R. (1998). A model of social loafing in real work groups. *Human Relations, 48,* 647–667.

Conlin, M. (2006, December 11). Online extra: How to kill meetings. *Business Week.* Retrieved from http://www.businessweek.com

Consigny, S. (1976). The rhetorical example. *Southern Speech Communication Journal, 41,* 121–134.

Conville, R. L. (1991). *Relational transitions: The evolution of personal relationships.* Westport, CT: Praeger.

Cook, G. (2002, February 14). Debate opens anew on language and its effect on cognition. *The Boston Globe,* p. A10.

Cook, K. S. (1987). *Social exchange theory.* Beverly Hills, CA: SAGE.

Cooper, L. O. (1997). Listening competency in the workplace: A model for training. *Business Communication Quarterly, 60*(4), 74–84.

Coulehan, J. L., & Block, M. L. (2006). *The medical interview: Mastering skills for clinical practice.* Philadelphia: Davis.

Cox, A. (2005, August 15). Custom made fit for school: Dress codes, student uniforms back in style. *Cable News Network.* Retrieved from http://www.cnn.com/2005/US/08/12/style.rules

Crane, D. (2000). *Fashion and its social agendas: Class, gender, and identity in clothing.* Chicago: University of Chicago Press.

Crawford, M. (1995). *Talking difference: On gender and language.* Thousand Oaks, CA: SAGE.

Crick, N. (2004). Conquering our imagination: Thought experiments and enthymemes in scientific argument. *Philosophy and Rhetoric, 37,* 21–41.

Cuda, G. (2006, April 11). Troops learn to not offend. *Wired.* Retrieved from http://www.wired.com/science/discoveries/news/2006/04/70576

Daft, R. L., & Lengel, R. H. (1984). Informational richness: A new approach to managerial behavior and organizational design. In B. M. Staw & L. L. Cummings (Eds.), *Research in organizational behavior* (Vol. 6, pp. 191–233). Greenwich, CT: JAI.

Daft, R. L., & Lengel, R. H. (1986). Organizational information requirements, media richness, and structural design. *Management Science, 32,* 554–571.

Dailey, R. M., & Palomares, N. A. (2004). Strategic topic avoidance: An investigation of topic avoidance frequency, strategies used, and relational correlates. *Communication Monographs, 71,* 471–496.

Davis, M. S. (1973). *Intimate relations.* New York: Free Press.

Davis, S., & Mares, M. (1998). Effects of talk show viewing on adolescents. *Journal of Communication, 48,* 69–86.

Day, L. A. (2007). *Ethics in media communications: Cases and controversies* (2nd ed.). Belmont, CA: Wadsworth.

Debraggio, M. (2002, October 2). President Tobin to step down. *Hamilton News.* Retrieved from http://www.hamilton.edu/news/more_news/display.cfm?ID=5095

DeClamecy, D., Wilson, S., & Philips, E. (2005, March 30). Famed attorney Johnnie Cochran dead. *Cable News Network.* Retrieved August 15, 2007, from www.cnn.com

Dewan, S. (2006, October 5). Amish school survivors struggle after killings. *The New York Times.* Retrieved from http://www.nytimes.com

Dewey, J. (1933). *How we think.* Lexington, MA: Heath.

Diener, E., & Diener, M. (1995). Cross-cultural correlates of life satisfaction and self-esteem. *Journal of Personality and Social Psychology, 68,* 653–663.

Dillard, J. P., Solomon, D. H., & Palmer, M. T. (1999). Structuring the concept of relational communication. *Communication Monographs, 66,* 49–65.

Dillon, R. K., & McKenzie, N. J. (1998). The influence of ethnicity on listening, communication competence, approach, and avoidance. *International Journal of Listening, 12,* 106–121.

DiMartino, M. D. (Writer), & Volpe, G. (Director). (2007, November 30). The day of black sun, part 1: The invasion [Television series episode]. In B. Konietzko & M. D. DiMartino (Executive Producers), *Avatar: The last airbender.* New York: Nickelodeon.

Dipper, L., Black, M., & Bryan, K. (2005). Thinking for speaking and thinking for listening: The interaction of thought and language in typical and non-fluent comprehension and production. *Language and Cognitive Processes, 20,* 417–441.

Dindi, K., & Timmerman, L. (2003). Accomplishing romantic relationships. In J. O. Greene & B. R. Burleson (Eds.), *Handbook of communication and social interaction skills* (pp. 685–722). Mahwah, NJ: Erlbaum.

Dirksen Bauman, H. (2003, Fall). Rede*signing* literature: Toward a cinematic poetics of ASL poetry. *Sign Language Studies, 4*(1), 34–47.

DiSanza, J. R., & Legge, N. J. (2002). *Business and professional communication: Plans, processes, and performance* (2nd ed.). Boston: Allyn & Bacon.

Dixon, J. A., & Foster, D. H. (1998). Gender, social context, and backchannel responses. *Journal of Social Psychology, 138,* 134–136.

Doll, B. (1996). Children without friends: Implications for practice and policy. *School Psychology Review, 25,* 165–183.

Doris, J. (Ed.). (1991). *The suggestibility of children's recollections.* Washington, DC: American Psychological Association.

Doshi, A. (with Drvaid, S., Giri, R., & David, S.). (2005, June 20). Sweep stake: Technology, television and the fast pace of modern life have dramatically altered the rules of the dating game. *India Today.* Retrieved from http://proquest/umi.com

Dougherty, D., & Smythe, D. (2004). Sense making, organizational culture, and sexual harassment. *Journal of Applied Communication Research, 32,* 293–317.

Douglas, C. (2002). The effects of managerial influence behavior on the transition to self-directed work teams. *Journal of Managerial Psychology, 17,* 628–635.

Douglass, J., Jr. (2005, January 23). Some Norwegians thought Bush was saluting Satan. *The Standard-Times,* p. B3.

Ducharme, J., Doyle, A., & Markiewicz, D. (2002). Attachment security with mother and father: Associations with adolescents' reports of interpersonal behavior with parents and peers. *Journal of Social and Personal Relationships, 19,* 203–231.

Duck, S. W. (1984). A perspective on the repair of personal relationships: Repair of what, when? In S. W. Duck (Ed.), *Personal relationships: Vol. 5. Repairing personal relationships.* New York: Macmillan.

Dues, M., & Brown, M. (2004). *Boxing Plato's shadow: An introduction to the study of human communication.* New York: McGraw-Hill.

Duncan, S., & Fiske, D. (1977). *Face-to-face interaction.* Hillsdale, NJ: Erlbaum.

Dunning, D. A., & Kruger, J. (1999). Unskilled and unaware of it: How difficulties in recognizing one's own incompetence lead to inflated self-assessments. *Journal of Personality and Social Psychology, 77,* 1121–1134.

Durham, F. (2006). Exposed by Katrina: The gulf between the president and the press. *Critical Studies in Media Communication, 23,* 81–84.

Edwards, R. (1990). Sensitivity to feedback and the development of self. *Communication Quarterly, 28,* 101–111.

Efran, M. G. (1974). The effect of physical appearance on the judgment of guilt, interpersonal attraction, and severity of recommended punishment in a simulated jury task. *Journal of Research in Personality, 8,* 45–54.

Eibl-Eibesfeldt, I. (1973). The expressive behavior of the deaf-and-blind-born. In M. von Cranach & I. Vine (Eds.), *Social communication and movement: Studies of interaction and expression in man and chimpanzee* (pp. 163–194). New York: Academic Press.

Eisenberg, E. M., Goodall, H. L., Jr., & Tretheway, A. (2007). *Organizational communication: Balancing creativity and constraint.* New York: Bedford/St. Martin's.

Eisenberg, E. M., Murphy, A. G., Sutcliffe, K., Wears, R., Schenkel, S., Perry, S., & Vanderhoef, M. (2005). Communication in emergency medicine: Implications for patient safety. *Communication Monographs, 72,* 390–413.

Ekman, P., & Friesen, W. V. (1969). The repertoire of nonverbal behavior: Categories, origins, usage, and coding. *Semiotica, 1,* 49–98.

Ekman, P., & Friesen, W. V. (1971). Constants across cultures in the face and emotion. *Journal of Personality and Social Psychology, 17,* 124–129.

Ekman, P., & Friesen, W. V. (1975). *Unmasking the face.* Englewood Cliffs, NJ: Prentice Hall.

Ekman, P., Friesen, W. V., & Ellsworth, P. (1972). *Emotion in the human face: Guidelines for research and an integration of findings.* New York: Pergamon Press.

El Ahl, A., and Steinvorth, D. (2006, October 20). Sex and taboos in the Islamic world. *Spiegel Online International.* Retrieved March 12, 2008, from http://www.spiegel.de/international/spiegel/0,1518,443678,00.html

Elliot, S. (2007, July 10). Subaru turns to the land of forbidden secrets. *The New York Times.* Retrieved from http://www.nytimes.com

El-Magd, N. A. (2006, December 3). Muslim woman gives sex advice on Arab TV. *The Washington Post.* Retrieved from http://www.washingtonpost.com

Endo, Y., Heine, S. J., & Lehman, D. R. (2000). Culture and positive illusions in close relationships: How my relationships are better than yours. *Personality and Social Psychology Bulletin, 26,* 1571–1586.

Equal Employment Opportunity Commission. (2008). *Sexual harassment.* Retrieved May 14, 2008, from http://www.eeoc .gov/types/sexual_harassment.html

Etcoff, N. (1999). *Survival of the prettiest: The science of beauty.* New York: Anchor Books.

Ewalt, D. (2005, September 17). Jane Goodall on why words hurt. *Forbes.* Retrieved from http://www.forbes.com

Farroni, T., Csibra, G., Simion, F., & Johnson, M. (2002, July 9). Eye contact detection in humans from birth. *Proceedings of the National Academy of Sciences of the*

*United States of America, 99,* 9602–9605. Retrieved from http://www.pnas.org/cgi/doi/10.1073/pnas.152159999

Federal Communications Commission. (2008, January 8). *Understanding workplace harassment.* Retrieved September 3, 2008, from http://www.fcc.gov/owd/understanding harassment.html

Fehr, B. (2001). The life cycle of friendship. In C. Hendrick & S. S. Hendrick (Eds.), *Close relationships: A sourcebook* (pp. 71–82). Thousand Oaks, CA: SAGE.

Feldman, C., & Ridley, C. (2000). The role of conflict-based communication responses and outcomes in male domestic violence toward female partners. *Journal of Social and Personal Relationships, 17,* 552–573.

Fent, B., & MacGeorge, E. L. (2006). Predicting receptiveness to advice: Characteristics of the problem, the advice-giver, and the recipient. *Southern Communication Journal, 71,* 67–85.

Ferguson, K. (1984). *The feminist case against bureaucracy.* Philadelphia: Temple University Press.

Festinger, L. (1954). A theory of social comparison processes. *Human Relations, 7,* 117–140.

Finder, A. (2006, June 11). For some, online persona undermines a résumé. *The New York Times.* Retrieved from http://www.nytimes.com

Fiske, S. T., & Taylor, S. E. (1991). *Social cognition.* New York: McGraw-Hill.

Fletcher, C. (1999). Listening to narratives: The dynamics of capturing police experience. *International Journal of Listening, 13,* 46–61.

Flynn, L. J. (2007, February 6). After long dispute, two Apples work it out. *The New York Times.* Retrieved from http://www.nytimes.com

Foels, R., Driskell, J. E., Mullen, B., & Salas, E. (2000). The effects of democratic leadership on group member satisfaction. *Small Group Research, 31,* 676–701.

Folger, J. P., Poole, M. S., & Stutman, R. K. (1997). *Working through conflict* (3rd ed.). New York: Longman.

Folger, J. P., Poole, M. S., & Stutman, R. K. (2001). *Working through conflict: Strategies for relationships, groups, and organizations* (4th ed.). New York: Longman.

Ford, W. S. Z. (1999). Communication and customer service. In M. E. Roloff (Ed.), *Communication yearbook* (Vol. 22, pp. 341–375). Thousand Oaks, CA: SAGE.

Franklin, D. (2006, August 15). Patient power: Making sure your doctor really hears you. *The New York Times,* p. F5.

Frantz, R. (2007). Groups continue to meet: Independent reviewers assess practice delineation. *Communications Magazine, 45,* 16.

Fremouw, W. J., & Scott, M. D. (1979). Cognitive restructuring: An alternative method for the treatment of communication apprehension. *Communication Education, 28,* 129–133.

French, J. R. P., & Raven, B. (1959). The bases for power. In D. Cartwright (Ed.), *Studies in social power* (pp. 150–167). Ann Arbor, MI: Institute for Social Research.

Friedman, T. L. (2007). *The world is flat: A brief history of the twenty-first century.* New York: Farrar, Straus & Giroux.

Friedrich, G. W., & Goss, B. (1984). Systematic desensitization. In J. A. Daly & J. C. McCroskey (Eds.), *Avoiding communication: Shyness, reticence, and communication apprehension* (pp. 173–188). Beverly Hills, CA: SAGE.

Galassi, J. P., & Galassi, M. (1978). Preparing individuals for job interviews: Suggestions from more than 60 years of research. *Personnel and Guidance Journal, 57,* 188–192.

Gibb, J. (1961). Defensive communication. *Journal of Communication, 2,* 141–148.

Gibson: "I am not an anti-Semite." (2006, August 2). *Cable News Network.* Retrieved from http://www.cnn.com/2006/SHOWBIZ/Movies/08/01/Gibson.dui/index.html

Gilbert, A. (2005, March 28). Why can't you pay attention anymore? *CNET News.* Retrieved from http://www.news.com/Why-cant-you-pay-attention-anymore/2008-1022_3-5637632.html?tag=item

Gilbertson, J., Dindi, K., & Allen, M. (1998). Relational continuity constructional units and the maintenance of relationships. *Journal of Social and Personal Relationships, 15,* 774–790.

Giles, H., & Smith, P. M. (1979). Accommodation theory: Optimal levels of convergence. In H. Giles & R. N. Saint Clair (Eds.), *Language and social psychology* (pp. 45–65). Oxford: Blackwell.

Giles, H., & Wiemann, J. M. (1987). Language, social comparison, and power. In C. R. Berger & S. H. Chaffee (Eds.), *Handbook of communication science* (pp. 350–384). Newbury Park, CA: SAGE.

Glover, R. (n.d.). *Executive corner: Global workforce diversity.* Retrieved May 29, 2008, from http://www-03.ibm.com/employment/us/diverse/executive_corner_vp.shtml

Goffman, E. (1967). *Interaction ritual: Essays on face-to-face behavior.* Garden City, NY: Doubleday.

Goffman, E. (1971). *Relations in public: Microstudies of the public order.* New York: Harper & Row.

Golish, T., & Caughlin, J. (2002). "I'd rather not talk about it": Adolescents' and young adults' use of topic avoidance in stepfamilies. *Journal of Applied Communication Research, 30,* 78–106.

Goodstein, L. (2006, October 4). Strong faith and community may help Amish cope with loss. *The New York Times.* Retrieved from http://www.nytimes.com

Google.com. (2008a). *Corporate information: Our philosophy* (item 9). Retrieved May 27, 2008, from http://www.google.com/corporate/tenthings.html

Google.com. (2008b). *Corporate information: The Google culture.* Retrieved May 27, 2008, from http://www.google.com/intl/en/corporate/culture/html

Google.com. (2008c). *Google jobs: The engineer's life at Google.* Retrieved May 27, 2008, from http://www.google.com/support/jobs/bin/static.py?page=about.html&about=eng

Gordon, P. (2004, October 15). Numerical cognition without words: Evidence from Amazonia [Supplementary online materials]. *Science Online.* Retrieved March 25, 2008, from http://www.sciencemag.org/cgi/content/full/sci;1094492/DC1

Goss, B., & O'Hair, D. (1988). *Communicating in interpersonal relationships.* New York: Macmillan.

Gosselin, D. K. (2007). *Smart talk: Contemporary interviewing and interrogation.* Upper Saddle River, NJ: Prentice Hall.

Gottman, J. M. (1994). *What predicts divorce? The relationship between marital processes and marital outcomes.* Hillsdale, NJ: Erlbaum.

Gouran, D. S. (2003). Communication skills for group decision making. In J. O. Greene & B. R. Burleson (Eds.), *Handbook of communication and social interaction skills* (pp. 835–870). Mahwah, NJ: Erlbaum.

Goyer, R. S., & Rickey, J. T. (1968). *Interviewing principles and techniques: A project text.* Dubuque, IA: Brown.

Grahe, J. E., & Bernieri, F. J. (1999). The importance of nonverbal cues in judging rapport. *Journal of Nonverbal Behavior, 23,* 253–269.

Granrose, C. S. (1997). Cross-cultural socialization of Asian employees in U.S. organizations. In C. S. Granrose & S. Oskamp (Eds.), *Cross-cultural work groups* (pp. 186–211). Thousand Oaks, CA: SAGE.

Greco, B. (1977). Recruiting and retaining high achievers. *Journal of College Placement, 37* (2), 34–40.

Greenhouse, S. (2006, September 3). Now bringing home the leaner bacon: Borrowers we be. *The New York Times.* Retrieved from http://www.nytimes.com

Greenwalk, A. G., Bellezza, F. S., & Banaji, M. R. (1988). Is self-esteem a central ingredient of self-concept? *Personality and Social Psychology Bulletin, 14,* 34–45.

Greulich, M. (2005, Fall). Are you a feminist? *E-Quality.* Retrieved March 25, 2008, from http://www.cbeinternational.org/new/E-Journal/2005/05fall/05fallsurvey.html

Grieves, R. (1984, January 30). Telecommuting from a flexiplace: Fans and foes take second looks at work-at-home programs. *Time.* Retrieved from http://www.time.com

Gross, B., & O'Hair, D. (1988). *Communicating in interpersonal relationships.* New York: Macmillan.

Grossman, H., & Chester, N. (1990). *The experience and meaning of work in women's lives.* Hillsdale, NJ: Erlbaum.

Grossman, R. B., & Kegl, J. (2007). Moving faces: Categorization of dynamic facial expressions in American Sign Language by deaf and hearing participants. *Journal of Nonverbal Behavior, 31,* 23–38.

Gudykunst, W. B. (2004). *Bridging differences: Effective intergroup communication* (4th ed.) Thousand Oaks, CA: SAGE.

Gudykunst, W. B., & Ting-Toomey, S. (1988). *Culture and interpersonal communication.* Newbury Park, CA: SAGE.

Gudykunst, W. B., Ting-Toomey, S., Sudweeks, S., & Stewart, L. (1995). *Building bridges: Interpersonal skills for a changing world.* Boston: Houghton Mifflin.

Guerrero, L. K., & Afifi, W. A. (1995). Some things are better left unsaid: Topic avoidance in family relationships. *Communication Quarterly, 43,* 276–296.

Hafner, K. (2007, August 19). Seeing corporate fingerprints in Wikipedia edits. *The New York Times.* Retrieved from http://www.nytimes.com

Hall, E. T. (1959). *The silent language.* New York: Doubleday.

Hall, E. T. (1976). *Beyond culture.* New York: Anchor/Doubleday.

Hall, J. A. (1998). How big are nonverbal sex differences? The case of smiling and sensitivity to nonverbal cues. In D. J. Canary & K. Dindia (Eds.), *Sex differences and similarities in communication: Critical essays and empirical investigations of sex and gender in interaction* (pp. 155–178). Mahwah, NJ: Erlbaum.

Hall, J. A., Carter, J. D., & Hogan, T. G. (2000). Gender differences in nonverbal communication of emotion. In A. H. Fischer (Ed.), *Gender and emotion: Social psychological perspectives* (pp. 97–117). Cambridge: Cambridge University Press, 2000.

Hample, D. (1987). Communication and the unconscious. In B. Dervin & M. J. Voight (Eds.), *Progress in communication sciences* (Vol. 8, pp. 83–121). Norwood, NJ: Ablex.

Harford, T. (2007, February 3). If telecommuting is so easy, why do we travel for work more than ever? *Slate.* Retrieved from http://www.slate.com/id/2158571

Harmon, A. (2005, April 14). Reach out and touch no one. *The New York Times.* Retrieved from http://www.nytimes.com

Harper, R. G., Wiens, A. N., & Matarazzo, J. D. (1978). *Nonverbal communication: The state of the art.* New York: Wiley.

Harrigan, J. A., & Taing, K. T. (1997). Fooled by a smile: Detecting anxiety in others. *Journal of Nonverbal Behavior, 21,* 203–221.

Harris, T. E. (2002). *Applied organizational communication: Principles and pragmatics for future practice* (2nd ed.). Mahwah, NJ: Erlbaum.

Hartup, W. W., & Stevens, N. (1997). Friendships and adaptation in the life course. *Psychological Bulletin, 121,* 355–370.

Harvey, J. H., Weber, A. L., & Orbuch, T. L. (1990). *Interpersonal accounts: A social psychological perspective.* Cambridge, MA: Blackwell.

Hauser, C., & O'Connor, A. (2007, April 16). Virginia Tech shooting leaves thirty-three dead. *The New York Times.* Retrieved from http://www.nytimes.com

Hayakawa, S. I. (1964). *Language in thought and action.* New York: Harcourt Brace Jovanovich.

Hebdige, D. (1999). The function of subculture. In S. During (Ed.), *The cultural studies reader* (2nd ed., pp. 441–450). New York: Routledge.

Hecht, M. L., Jackson, R. L., II, & Ribeau, S. A. (2003). *African American communication: Exploring identity and culture.* Mahwah, NJ: Erlbaum.

Helgesen, S. (1990). *The female advantage: Women's ways of leadership.* Garden City, NY: Doubleday.

Hemphill, J. K., & Coons, A. E. (1957). Development of the leader behavior description questionnaire. In R. M. Stogdill & A. E. Coons (Eds.), *Leader behavior: Its description and measurement* (pp. 6–38). Columbus: Bureau of Business Research, Ohio State University.

Hendrick, S. S., & Hendrick, C. (1992). *Liking, loving, and relating.* Pacific Grove, CA: Brooks/Cole.

Hendriks, A. (2002). Examining the effects of hegemonic depictions of female bodies on television: A call for theory and programmatic research. *Critical Studies in Media Communication, 19,* 106–123.

He said what? League's many languages complicate communication. (1999, September 27). *CNN/Sports Illustrated.* Retrieved from http://sportsillustrated.cnn.com/hockey/nhl/news/1999/09/25/language_barrier_ap

Heslin, R. (1974). *Steps toward a taxonomy of touching.* Paper presented at the Western Psychological Association Convention, Chicago.

Hinkle, L. L. (1999). Nonverbal immediacy communication behaviors and liking in marital relationships. *Communication Research Reports, 16,* 81–90.

Hirokawa, R. Y., Gouran, D. S., & Martz, A. E. (1988). Understanding the sources of faulty group decision-making: A lesson from the *Challenger* disaster. *Small Group Behavior, 19,* 411–433.

Hockenbury, D. H., & Hockenbury, S. E. (2002). *Psychology* (3rd ed.). New York: Worth.

Hoffman, L. R., & Maier, N. R. F. (1964). Valence in the adoption of solutions by problem-solving groups: Concept, method, and results. *Journal of Abnormal and Social Psychology, 69,* 264–271.

Hofstede, G. (1984). *Culture's consequences: International differences in work-related values.* Beverly Hills, CA: SAGE.

Holland, K. (2006, December 3). Under new management: When work time isn't face time. *The New York Times.* Retrieved from http://www.nytimes.com

Hollingsworth, H. L. (1935). *The psychology of the audience.* New York: American Book.

Homer, P. M. (2006). Relationships among ad-induced affect, beliefs, and attitudes: Another look. *Journal of Advertising, 35,* 35–51.

Hoover, K. (2006, February). Alumni to know: He brought Trader Joe's to Main Street. *Stanford Business Magazine.* Retrieved from http://www.gsb.stanford/edu

Horwitz, A. V., & White, H. R. (1998). The relationship of cohabitation and mental health: A study of a young adult cohort. *Journal of Marriage and the Family, 60,* 505–514.

Hott, L., & Garey, D. (2007, March). *Through deaf eyes* [Television documentary]. Washington, DC: WETA.

Howard, D. L. (2004, August 2). Silencing Huck Finn. *The Chronicle of Higher Education.* Retrieved from http://chronicle.com/jobs/2004/08/2004080201c.htm

Howard, T. (2004, February 22). "Can you hear me now?" a hit. *USA Today.* Retrieved from http://www.usatoday.com/money

Humpherys, J. (1996). Find your optimum rate of speech. *Telemarketing Success.Com.* Retrieved March 3, 2008, from http://www.telemarketingsuccess.com/predictive_dialer/optimum_speech_rate.htm

Infante, D. A. (1988). *Arguing constructively.* Prospect Heights, IL: Waveland Press.

Infante, D. A., & Wigely, C. (1986). Verbal aggressiveness: An interpersonal model and measure. *Communication Monographs, 53,* 61–69.

Ivy, D., & Blacklund, P. (2004). *Gender speak: Personal effectiveness in gender communication* (3rd ed.). New York: McGraw-Hill.

Jablin, F. M. (2001). Organizational entry, assimilation, and disengagement/exit. In F. M. Jablin & L. L. Putnam (Eds.), *The new handbook of organizational communication: Advances in theory, research, and methods* (pp. 732–818). Thousand Oaks, CA: SAGE.

Jackson, D. (2006, January 29). State of the Union address: A meshing of many ideas. *USA Today.* Retrieved from http://www.usatoday.com/news/washington/2006-01-29-sotu-speech_x.htm?POE=click-refer

Jacobs, C. D., and Heracleous, L. (2006). Constructing shared understanding: The role of embodied metaphors in organization development. *Journal of Applied Behavioral Science, 42,* 207–227.

Jacobs, T. O. (1970). *Leadership and exchange in formal organizations.* Alexandria, VA: Human Resources Research Organization.

James, C. H., and Minnis, W. C. (2004, July-August). Organizational storytelling: It makes sense. *Business Horizons,* 23–32.

Janis, I. L. (1982). *Groupthink: Psychological studies of policy decisions and fiascoes* (2nd ed.). Boston: Houghton Mifflin.

Johannesen, R. L. (1996). *Ethics in human communication.* Prospect Heights, IL: Waveland Press.

John-Steiner, V. (1997). *Notebooks of the mind: Explorations of thinking.* New York: Oxford University Press.

Johnson, A., Williams, P., Jansing, C., & Stewart, A. (2007, April 17). Worst U.S. shooting ever kills 33 on Va. campus. *MSNBC News.* Retrieved from http://www.msnbc.msn.com/id/18134671

Jones, C. (2005, May 16). Gay marriage debate still fierce one year later. *USA Today.* Retrieved from http://www.usatoday.com/news/nation/2005-05-16-gay-marriage_x.htm

Jones, D. (2004, November 30). Best friends good for business. *USA Today.* Retrieved May 10, 2008, from http://www.usatoday.com/money/workplace/2004=/=30=best=friends_x.htm

Jones, E. E. (1990). *Interpersonal perception.* New York: Freeman.

Kalbfleisch, P. J. (2002). Communicating in mentoring relationships: A theory for enactment. *Communication Theory, 12,* 63–69.

Kaplan, J. E. (2007, March 15). Emanuel tells freshmen to avoid Stephen Colbert. *The Hill.* Retrieved from http://thehill.com

Kaplan-Leiserson, E. (2005, June). Trend: Podcasting in academic and corporate learning. *Learning Circuits.* Retrieved from http://www.learningcircuits.org/2005/jun2005/0506_trends

Katzenbach, J. R., & Smith, D. K. (1993). *The wisdom of teams.* Boston: Harvard Business School Press.

Keen, R. (2004, January 6). Vending machine removal draws local attention. *Aberdeen American News.* Retrieved from http://www.asu.edu/educ/epsl/CERU/Articles/CERU-0401-186-OWI.doc

Kennedy, C. W., & Camden, C. (1983). Interruptions and nonverbal gender differences. *Journal of Nonverbal Behavior, 8,* 91–108.

Kennedy, R. (2003). *Nigger: The strange career of a troublesome word.* New York: Vintage Books.

Kenyon College. (1999). *Fly away: The great migration.* Retrieved March 3, 2008, from http://northbysouth.kenyon.edu/1999/index.htm

Keyton, J., Ferguson, P., & Rhodes, S. C. (2001). Cultural indicators of sexual harassment. *Southern Communication Journal, 67,* 33–50.

Khazzoom, L. (2005, April 19). Matisyahu keeps the faith: Rising reggae star stays true to his Hasidic roots. *Rolling Stone.* Retrieved from http://www.rollingstone.com/news/story/7265079/matisyahu_keeps_the_faith

Kline, S., Horton, B., & Zhang, S. (2005). *How we think, feel, and express love: A cross-cultural comparison between American and East Asian cultures.* Paper presented at the annual meeting of the International Communication Association, New York.

Klocke, U. (2007). How to improve decision making in small groups: Effects of dissent and training interventions. *Small Group Research, 38,* 437–468.

Knapp, M. L., & Hall, J. A. (2005). *Nonverbal communication in human interaction.* Belmont, CA: Wadsworth.

Knapp, M. L., Hart, R. P., Friedrich, G. W., & Shulman, G. M. (1973). The rhetoric of goodbye: Verbal and nonverbal correlates of human leave-taking. *Communication Monographs, 40,* 182–198.

Knapp, M. L., & Vangelisti, A. (2000). *Interpersonal communication and human relationships* (4th ed.). Newton, MA: Allyn & Bacon.

Knobloch, L. K., & Solomon, D. H. (2002). Information seeking beyond initial interaction: Negotiating relational uncertainty within close relationships. *Human Communication Research, 28,* 243–257.

Kohls, L. R. (2001). *Survival kit for overseas living* (4th ed.). Yarmouth, ME: International Press.

Kohut, A. (2007, May 9). *Are Americans ready to elect a female president?* Retrieved from the Pew Research Center Web site: http://pewresearch.org/pubs/474/female-president

Kotlowitz, A. (2008, May 4). Blocking the transmission of violence. *The New York Times Magazine.* Retrieved from http://www.nytimes.com

Kowitz, A. C., & Knutson, T. J. (1980). *Decision making in small groups: The search for alternatives.* Needham Heights, MA: Allyn & Bacon.

Kram, K. E. (1983). Phases of the mentor relationship. *Academy of Management Journal, 12,* 608–625.

Kramer, M. W., & Pier, P. M. (1999). Students' perceptions of effective and ineffective communication by college teachers. *Southern Communication Journal, 65,* 16–33.

Kraybill, D. B. (2007, October 6). Shunning: It's tough love for the Amish. *Winston-Salem Journal.* Retrieved from http://www.journalnow.com

Krcmar, M., & Greene, K. (1999). Predicting exposure to and uses of television violence. *Journal of Communication, 49,* 24–46.

Kreps, G. L., & Kunimoto, E. N. (1994). *Effective communication in multicultural health care settings.* Thousand Oaks, CA: SAGE.

Kruglanski, A. W., Chen, X., Pierro, A., Mannetti, L., Erb, H.-P., & Spiegel, S. (2006). Persuasion according to the unimodel: Implications for cancer communication. *Journal of Communication, 56,* 105–122.

Kuhn, T., & Poole, M. S. (2000). Do conflict management styles affect group decision making? Evidence from a longitudinal field study. *Human Communication Research, 26,* 558–590.

Kurdek, L. (1989). Relationship quality of gay and lesbian cohabiting couples. *Journal of Homosexuality, 15*(3–4), 93–118.

Landau, D. (2003, September). Changing the blame game: Attributional retraining as a conflict intervention. *Mediate.com.* Retrieved from http://www.mediate.com/articles/landauD.cfm

Landsford, J. E., Antonucci, T. C., Akiyama, H., & Takahashi, K. (2005). A quantitative and qualitative approach to social relationships and well-being in the United States and Japan. *Journal of Comparative Family Studies, 36,* 1–22.

Lasseter, J. (Director). (1995). *Toy story* [DVD version]. Anaheim, CA: Disney.

Lasseter, J. (2001, November 19). Regus London Film Festival interviews. *Guardian Unlimited.* Retrieved from http://www.guardian.co.uk/film/2001/nov/19/londonfilmfestival2001.londonfilmfestival1

Lauro, P. W. (2007, July 12). Bayer foes viral in Web pitch for painkiller. *The New York Times.* Retrieved from http://www.nytimes.com

Leathers, D. (1986). *Successful nonverbal communication: Principles and applications.* New York: Macmillan.

Leavitt, H. J. (1951). Some effects of certain communication patterns on group performance. *Journal of Abnormal and Social Psychology, 46,* 38–50.

Lee, J. A. (1973). *The colors of love: An exploration of the ways of loving.* Don Mills, Ontario, Canada: New Press.

le Roux, M. (2006, November 27). Let's talk about sex: Cult South African director shatters taboos. *Namibian.* Retrieved from http://www.namibian.com.na/2006/November/africa/065E8B0EB5.html

Lewis, L. (2005). Foster a loyal workforce. In *Trader Joe's adventure: Turning a unique approach to business into a retail and cultural phenomenon* (pp. 137–152). New York: Dearborn/Kaplan.

Lievrouw, L. A. (2000). Babel and beyond: Languages on the Internet. *ICA Newsletter, 28*(3), 6–7.

Ligos, M. (2001, June 20). Getting over the fear-of-speaking hump. *The New York Times*. Retrieved from http://www.nytimes.com

Lim, G. Y., & Roloff, M. E. (1999). Attributing sexual consent. *Journal of Applied Communication Research, 27,* 1–23.

Lincoln, A. (1842, February 22). Temperance address. *Repeat After Us*. Retrieved August 14, 2007, from http://www.repeatafterus.com/title.php?i=9700

Lindsley, S. L. (1999). Communication and "the Mexican way": Stability and trust as core symbols in *maquiladoras. Western Journal of Communication, 63,* 1–31.

Lipman, A. (1986). Homosexual relationships. *Generations, 10* (4), 51–54.

Lipton, E., & Shane, S. (2005, September 3). Leader of federal effort feels the heat. *The New York Times*. Retrieved from http://www.nytimes.com

Loden, M., & Rosener, J. B. (1991). *Workforce America! Managing employee diversity as a vital resource.* Chicago: Business One Irwin.

Lohr, S. (2007, October 31). Hello, India? I need help with my math. *The New York Times*. Retrieved from http://www.nytimes.com

Longley, R. (2007). From time to time: The State of the Union. *About.com: U.S. government info*. Retrieved December 31, 2007, from http://usgovinfo.about.com/od/thepresidentandcabinet/a/souhistory.htm

Lubell, S. (2004, February 19). On the therapist's couch, a jolt of virtual reality. *The New York Times*. Retrieved from http://www.nytimes.com

Lunneborg, D. (1990). *Women changing work.* New York: Greenwood Press.

Lustig, M. W., & Koester, J. (2006). *Intercultural competence: Interpersonal communication across cultures* (5th ed.). Boston: Allyn & Bacon.

Maag, C. (2007a, November 28). A hoax turned fatal draws anger but no charges. *The New York Times*. Retrieved from http://www.nytimes.com

Maag, C. (2007b, December 16). When the bullies turned faceless. *The New York Times*. Retrieved from http://www.nytimes.com

Martin, D. (2004, October 12). Christopher Reeve, 52, symbol of courage, dies. *The New York Times*. Retrieved from http://www.nytimes.com

Maslach, C. (1982). *Burnout: The cost of caring.* Englewood Cliffs, NJ: Prentice Hall.

Maslow, A. *Motivation and personality.* New York: Harper & Row, 1954.

Mast, M. S. (2002). Dominance as expressed and inferred through speaking time. *Human Communication Research, 28,* 420–450.

Mayer, R. E. (2001). *Multimedia learning.* New York: Cambridge University Press.

Mayo Clinic. (2006, June 1). Work-life balance: Ways to restore harmony and reduce stress. Retrieved May 10, 2008, from http://www.mayoclinic.com/health/work-life-balance/WL00056

McCann, R. M., Dailey, R. M., Giles, H., & Ota, H. (2005). Beliefs about intergenerational communication across the lifespan: Middle age and roles of age stereotyping and respect norms. *Communication Studies, 56,* 293–311.

McClanahan, A. (2006, March 9). What does a feminist "look" like? *Pocono Record*. Retrieved April 8, 2008, from http://www.poconorecord.com

McConnell, M. (1987). *Challenger: A major malfunction.* Garden City, NY: Doubleday.

McCroskey, J. C. (1977). Oral communication apprehension: A summary of recent theory and research. *Human Communication Research, 4,* 78–96.

McCroskey, J. C. (1997). The communication apprehension perspective. In J. A. Daly & J. C. McCroskey (Eds.), *Avoiding communication: Shyness, reticence, and communication apprehension* (pp. 13–38). Cresskill, NJ: Hampton Press.

McCullough, S., Russell, S., Behnke, R., Sawyer, C., & Will, P. (2006). Anticipatory public speaking state anxiety as a function of body sensations and state of mind. *Communication Quarterly, 54,* 101–109.

McDaniel, E., & Andersen, P. A. (1998). International patterns of interpersonal tactile communication: A field study. *Journal of Nonverbal Behavior, 22,* 59–75.

McLeod, D. N., Detenber, B. H., & Eveland, W. P., Jr. (2001). Behind the third-person effect: Differentiating perceptual processes for self and other. *Journal of Communication, 51,* 678–695.

McQueen, G. (2000, November). So you want to be in pixels: Interview with Glenn McQueen. *NOVA Online*. Retrieved from http://www.pbs.org/wgbh/nova/specialfx2/mcqueen.html

Meares, M., Oetzel, J., Torres, A., Derkacs, D., & Ginossart, T. (2004). Employee mistreatment and muted voices in the culturally diverse workplace. *Journal of Applied Communication Research, 32,* 4–27.

Media Matters for America. (2005, November 10). O'Reilly opens new front in "war" on Christmas. Retrieved April 28, 2008, from http://mediamatters.org/items/200511100014?f=s_search

Memmot, C. (2006, April 24). *Opal Mehta* author apologizes. *USA Today*. Retrieved from http://www.usatoday.com

Meyer, J. C. (1995). Tell me a story: Eliciting organizational values from narratives. *Communication Quarterly, 43,* 210–224.

Microsoft, Inc. (2005, March 15). Survey finds workers average only three productive days per week [Press release]. Retrieved April 30, 2008, from http://www.microsoft.com

Mignerey, J. T., Rubin, R. B., & Gorden, W. I. (1995). Organizational entry: An investigation of newcomer communication behavior and uncertainty. *Communication Research, 22,* 54–85.

Miller, L. C., Cooke, K. K., Tsang, J., & Morgan, F. (1992). Should I brag? Nature and impact of positive boastful disclosures for women and men. *Human Communication Research, 18,* 364–399.

Miller, R. (1991, January 31). Personnel execs reveal the truth about job applicants. *Dallas Morning News,* p. 2D.

Minkel, J. R., & Stix, G. (2005, November 21). Scientific American 50: Policy leader of the year. *Scientific American.* Retrieved from http://www.sciam.com

Molloy, J. T. (1983). *Molloy's live for success.* New York: Bantam Books.

Money is the top subject for marital spats. (2006, March 20). *Webindia123.com.* Retrieved May 1, 2006, from http://news.webindia123.com/news/ar_showdetails.asp?id=603200038&cat=&n_date=20060320

Monge, P. (1977). The systems perspective as a theoretical basis for the study of human communication. *Communication Quarterly, 25,* 19–29.

Monroe, A. H. (1935). *Principles and types of speeches.* Chicago, IL: Scott Foresman.

Montana Meth Project. (2007). Retrieved August 1, 2007, from http://www.montanameth.com

Montepare, J., Koff, E., Zaitchik, D., & Alberet, M. (1999). The use of body movements and gestures as cues to emotions in younger and older adults. *Journal of Nonverbal Behavior, 23,* 133–152.

Montgomery, D. (2006, October 25). Rush Limbaugh on the offensive against ad with Michael J. Fox. *The Washington Post,* p. C1.

Moran, B. (2003, November 18). She explores the world of language and thought. *The Boston Globe,* p. C2.

Moreland, R. L., & Levine, J. M., (1994). *Understanding small groups.* Boston: Allyn & Bacon.

Morris, D. (1977). *Manwatching.* New York: Abrams.

Morris, D. (1985). *Bodywatching.* New York: Crown.

Morris, M. W., Podolny, J. M., & Ariel, S. (2000). *Innovations in international and cross-cultural management.* Thousand Oaks, CA: SAGE.

Morrison, T., Conaway, W., & Borden, G. (1996). *Kiss, bow, and shake hands: How to do business in sixty countries.* Avon, MA: Adams Media.

Morry, M. M. (2005). Relationship satisfaction as a predictor of similarity ratings: A test of the attraction-similarity hypothesis. *Journal of Social and Personal Relationships, 22,* 561–584.

Motley, M. T. (1990). On whether one can(not) communicate: An examination via traditional communication postulates. *Western Journal of Speech Communication, 56,* 1–20.

Motley, M. T., & Reeder, H. M. (1995). Unwanted escalation of sexual intimacy: Male and female perceptions of connotations and relational consequences of resistance messages. *Communication Monographs, 62,* 355–382.

Mulac, A. (1998). The gender-linked language effect: Do language differences really make a difference? In D. J. Canary & K. Dindia (Eds.), *Sex differences and similarities in communication: Critical essays and empirical investigations of sex and gender in interaction* (pp. 127–153). Mahwah, NJ: Erlbaum.

Mulac, A. J., Wiemann, J. M., Widenmann, S. J., & Gibson, T. W. (1988). Male-female language differences and effects in same-sex and mixed-sex dyads: The gender-linked language effect. *Communication Monographs, 55,* 315–335.

Mumby, D. (2000). Communication, organization, and the public sphere: A feminist perspective. In P. Buzzanell (Ed.), *Rethinking organizational and managerial communication from feminist perspectives* (pp. 3–23). Thousand Oaks, CA: SAGE.

Murphy, D. R., Daneman, M., & Schneider, B. A. (2006). Do older adults have difficulty following conversations? *Psychology and Aging, 21,* 49–61.

Muthuswamy, N., Levine, T. R., & Gazel, J. (2006). Interaction-based diversity initiative outcomes: An evaluation of an initiative aimed at bridging the racial divide on a college campus. *Communication Education, 55,* 105–121.

National Organization for Women. (2006, March 2). *Sexual harassment remains serious problem on campus.* Retrieved May 14, 2008, from http://www.now.org/issues/harass/030206aauwreport.html

Naughton, K., & Peyser, M. (2004, March 1). The world according to Trump. *Newsweek,* pp. 48–57.

Nelson, B. (2002). Making teamwork work. *ABA Bank Marketing, 34,* 10.

Newcomb, A. F., & Bagwell, C. L. (1995). Children's friendship relations: A meta-analytic review. *Psychological Bulletin, 117,* 306–347.

Nicotera, A. M. (1997). Managing conflict communication groups. In L. R. Frey & J. K. Barge (Eds.), *Managing group life: Communicating in decision-making groups* (pp. 104–130). Boston: Houghton Mifflin.

Nomani, A. Q. (2005, December 14). Tapping Islam's feminist roots. *The Washington Post.* Retrieved March 7, 2008, from http://www.seattletimes.nwsource.com

No wrong answer: Click it. (2005, May 14). *Wired.* Retrieved from http://www.wired.com/culture/lifestyle/news/2005/05/67530

Office friends: Who needs them? (2005). *Management Today.* Retrieved May 14, 2008, via LexisNexis.

O'Hair, D., & Cody, M. (1994). Deception. In W. R. Cupach & B. H. Spitzberg (Eds.), *The dark side of interpersonal communication* (pp. 181–213). Hillsdale, NJ: Erlbaum.

O'Hair, D., Friedrich, G., & Dixon, L. (2002). *Strategic communication for business and the professions* (4th ed.). Boston: Houghton Mifflin.

O'Hair, D., Friedrich, G. W., & Dixon, L. D. (2007). *Strategic communication in business and the professions* (6th ed.). Boston: Houghton Mifflin.

O'Hair, D., & Krayer, K. (1987). *A conversational analysis of reconciliation strategies.* Paper presented at the Western Speech Communication Association, Salt Lake City.

O'Hair, D., O'Rourke, J., & O'Hair, M. J. (2000). *Business communication: A framework for success.* Cincinnati, OH: South-Western.

O'Hair, D., & Stewart, R. (1998). *Public speaking: Challenges and choices.* New York: Bedford/St. Martin's.

O'Hair, D., Stewart, R., & Rubenstein, H. (2007). *A speaker's guidebook* (3rd ed.). New York: Bedford/St. Martin's.

O'Keefe, D. J. (2002). *Persuasion: Theory and research* (2nd ed.). Thousand Oaks, CA: SAGE.

Olsen, L., & Golish, T. (2002). Topics of conflict and patterns of aggression in romantic relationships. *Southern Communication Journal, 67,* 180–200.

100 best companies to work for, 2007. (2007). *Fortune.* Retrieved May 27, 2008, from http://money.cnn.com/magazines/fortune/bestcompanies/2007/index.html

Oprah.com. (2008). *Oprah's debt diet.* Retrieved from http://www.oprah.com/money/debtdiet/money_debtdiet_main.jhtml

O'Sullivan, P. B. (2000). What you don't know won't hurt me: Impression management functions of communication channels in relationships. *Human Communication Research, 26,* 403–431.

O'Sullivan, P. B., Hunt, S. K., & Lippert, L. R. (2004). Mediated immediacy: A language of affiliation in a technological age. *Journal of Language and Social Psychology, 23,* 464–490.

Palo Alto Medical Foundation. (2005, January). *Health problems: Teen obesity.* Retrieved April 20, 2008, from http://www.pamf.org/teen/health/diseases/obesity.html

Park, C. (2003). In other (people's) words: Plagiarism by university students—literature and lessons. *Assessment and Evaluation in Higher Education, 28,* 471–488.

Park, W. (2000). A comprehensive empirical investigation of the relationships among variables of the groupthink model. *Journal of Organizational Behavior, 21,* 874–887.

Parker-Pope, T. (2008, March 25). When the bully sits in the next cubicle. *The New York Times.* Retrieved from http://www.nytimes.com

Parks, M., & Roberts, L. (1998). "Making MOOsic": The development of personal relationships on line and a comparison of their off-line counterparts. *Journal of Social and Personal Relationships, 15,* 517–537.

Parrott, R., Lemieux, R., Harris, T., & Foreman, L. (1997). Interfacing interpersonal and mediated communication: Use of active and strategic self-disclosure in personal ads. *Southern Communication Journal, 62,* 319–332.

Patterson, B. R., & O'Hair, D. (1992). Relational reconciliation: Toward a more comprehensive model of relational development. *Communication Research Reports, 9,* 119–127.

Patterson, T. (2006, November 2). *The Colbert Report:* How to beat the host at his own game. *Slate.* Retrieved from http://www.slate.com/id/2152741

Pavitt, C. (1999). Theorizing about the group communication-leadership relationship. In L. R. Frey, D. S. Gouran, & M. Poole (Eds.), *Handbook of group communication theory and research* (pp. 313–334). Thousand Oaks, CA: SAGE.

Pawlowski, D. (1998). Dialectical tensions in marital partners' accounts of their relationships. *Communication Quarterly, 46,* 396–416.

Payne, S. L. (1951). *The art of asking questions.* Princeton, NJ: Princeton University Press.

Pearson, J. C., & Spitzberg, B. H. (1990). *Interpersonal communication: Concepts, components, and contexts* (2nd ed.). Dubuque, IA: Brown.

Pearson, J. C., Turner, L. H., & Todd-Mancillas, W. R. (1991). *Gender and communication* (2nd ed.). Dubuque, IA: Brown.

Peck, J. (2007, December 29). *Top 7 tips for conquering public speaking fear.* Retrieved January 9, 2008, from http://ezinearticles.com/?expert=Jason_Peck

Perlman, D., & Peplau, L. A. (1981). Towards a social psychology of loneliness. In R. Gilmour & S. W. Duck (Eds.), *Personal relationships: Vol. 3. Personal relationships in disorder* (pp. 31–56). London: Academic Press.

Perras, M. T., & Weitzel, A. R. (1981). Measuring daily communication activities. *The Florida Speech Communication Journal, 9,* 19–23.

Petronio, S. (2000). The boundaries of privacy: Praxis of everyday life. In S. Petronio (Ed.), *Balancing the secrets of private disclosures* (pp. 37–50). Mahwah, NJ: Erlbaum.

Petronio, S. (2002). *The boundaries of privacy: Dialectics of disclosure.* Albany: State University of New York Press.

Petronio, S. (2004). Road to developing communication privacy management theory: Narrative in progress, please stand by. *Journal of Family Communication, 4,* 193–207.

Petty, R. E., & Cacioppo, J. T. (1986). The Elaboration Likelihood Model of persuasion. In L. Berkowitz (Ed.), *Advances in experimental social psychology* (Vol. 19, pp. 123–205). San Diego, CA: Academic Press.

Petty, R. E., & Wegner, D. T. (1998). Matching versus mismatching attitude functions: Implications for scrutiny of persuasive messages. *Personality and Social Psychology Bulletin, 24*(3), 227–240.

Pines, M. (1997). The civilizing of Genie. In L. F. Kasper (Ed.), *Teaching English through the disciplines: Psychology* (2nd ed.). New York: Whittier.

Planalp, S., & Honeycutt, J. (1985). Events that increase uncertainty in personal relationships. *Human Communication Research, 11,* 593–604.

Pollak, M. (2006, April 2). F.Y.I.: The beyond-this-world's fair. *The New York Times.* Retrieved from http://www.nytimes.com

Prager, K. J. (2000). Intimacy in personal relationships. In C. Hendrick & S. S. Hendrick (Eds.), *Close relationships: A sourcebook* (pp. 229–242). Thousand Oaks, CA: SAGE.

Preston, D. R. (1998). Language myth #17: They speak really bad English Down South and in New York City. In L. Bauer & P. Trudgill (Eds.), *Language myths* (pp. 139–149). New York: Penguin Putnam.

Priester, J. R., & Petty, R. E. (1995). Source attributions and persuasion: Perceived honesty as a determinant of message scrutiny. *Personality and Social Psychology Bulletin, 21,* 637–654.

Principles of public speaking (SPE101). (2004). *Using your speech power!* Retrieved May 1, 2008, from http://usingyourspeechpower.com/sample_student_intros.shtml

Public speaking. (n.d.). *Compton's online encyclopedia.* Retrieved June 10, 2000, from http://www.comptons.com/encyclopedia

Punyanunt-Carter, N. M. (2005). Father and daughter motives and satisfaction. *Communication Research Reports, 22,* 293–301.

Rabinowitz, J. (1995, July 25). *Huckleberry Finn* without fear: Teachers gather to learn how to teach an American classic, in context. *The New York Times.* Retrieved from http://www.query.nytimes.com

Ratner, L. (2007, March 5). Pow! Whap! Ka-ching! The Comic Con report. *The New York Observer.* Retrieved from http://www.observer.com

Rawlins, W. K. (1994). Being there and growing apart: Sustaining friendships during adulthood. In D. J. Canary & L. Stafford (Eds.), *Communication and relational maintenance* (pp. 275–294). New York: Academic Press.

Read, B. (2005, March 18). Seriously, iPods are educational. *The Chronicle of Higher Education.* Retrieved from http://www.chronicle.com

Reis, H. T. (1998). Gender differences in intimacy and related behaviors: Context and process. In D. J. Canary & K. Dindia (Eds.), *Sex differences and similarities in communication: Critical essays and empirical investigations of sex and gender in interaction* (pp. 203–231). Hillsdale, NJ: Erlbaum.

Relief workers confront "urban warfare": Violence disrupts evacuation, rescue efforts in New Orleans. (2005, September 2). *Cable News Network.* Retrieved from http://edition.cnn.com/2005/WEATHER/09/01/katrina.impact/index.html

Rempel, J., Holmes, J., & Zanna, M. (1985). Trust in close relationships. *Journal of Personality and Social Psychology, 49,* 95–112.

Reuther, C., & Fairhurst, G. T. (2000). Chaos theory and the glass ceiling. In P. Buzzanell (Ed.), *Rethinking organizational and managerial communication from feminist perspectives* (pp. 236–256). Thousand Oaks, CA: SAGE.

Richmond, V., & McCroskey, J. C. (1998). *Communication apprehension, avoidance, and effectiveness* (5th ed.). Boston: Allyn & Bacon.

Richmond, V. P., McCroskey, J. C., & Payne, S. K. (1991). *Nonverbal behavior in interpersonal relations.* Englewood Cliffs, NJ: Prentice Hall.

Richmond, V. P., Smith, R. S., Jr., Heisel, A. D., & McCroskey, J. C. (2001). Nonverbal immediacy in the physician-patient relationship. *Communication Research Reports, 18,* 211–216.

Ridge, S. B. (2007). Balance: The new workplace perk. *Forbes.* Retrieved May 14, 2008, from http://www.forbes.com

Rogers Commission. (1986, June 6). *Report of the presidential commission on the space shuttle* Challenger *accident.* Retrieved from http://science.ksc.nasa.gov/shuttle/missions/51-l/docs/rogers-commission/Chapter-5.txt

Roloff, M. E. (1980). Self-awareness and the persuasion process: Do we really know what we are doing? In M. E. Roloff & G. Miller (Eds.), *Persuasion: New directions in theory and research* (pp. 29–66). Beverly Hills, CA: SAGE.

Rosen, M. (2004, February). Can you truly trust an office friend? When to share and when to shy away—a guide to getting along with your workplace pals (on the job). *Good Housekeeping,* 56.

Rosenbloom, S. (2006, August 10). Please don't make me go on vacation. *The New York Times.* Retrieved from http://www.nytimes.com

Rosener, J. (1990). Ways women lead. *Harvard Business Review, 68,* 119–125.

Rosenthal, M. J. (2001). High-performance teams. *Executive Excellence, 18,* 6.

Ross, C. (2007, March 11). Hare interviewed for *Colbert Report. The Register-Mail.* Retrieved from http://www.register-mail.com

Ross, L., & Nisbett, R. E. (1991). *The person and the situation: Perspectives of social psychology.* Philadelphia: Temple University Press.

Rothman, A. J., Salovey, P., Turvey, C., & Fishkin, S. A. (1993). Attributions or responsibility and persuasion: Increasing mammography utilization among women over 40 with an internally oriented message. *Health Psychology, 12,* 39–47.

Ruben, B. D. (2005). Linking communication scholarship and professional practice in colleges and universities. *Journal of Applied Communication Research, 33,* 294–304.

Rubin, A. M., Perse, E. M., & Powell, R. A. (1985). Loneliness, parasocial interaction, and local television news viewing. *Human Communication Research, 12,* 155–180.

Rubin, D. L., Hafer, T., & Arata, K. (2000). Reading and listening to oral-based versus literate-based discourse. *Communication Education, 49,* 121–133.

Rushton, J. P. (1980). *Altruism, socializiation, and society.* Englewood Cliffs, NJ: Prentice Hall.

Rushton, J. P. (1990). Sir Francis Galton, epigenetic rules, genetic similarity theory, and human life-history analysis. *Journal of Personality, 58,* 117–140.

Russell, J. E., & Adams, D. M. (1997). The changing nature of mentoring in organizations: An introduction to the special issue on mentoring in organizations. *Journal of Vocational Behavior, 51,* 1–14.

Saeed, K. (2006). Danish cartoon controversy. *American Muslim Voice.* Retrieved February 7, 2006, from http://amvoice-two.amuslimvoice.org/html/body_cartoon_controversy.html

Salazar, A. J. (1996). An analysis of the development and evolution of roles in the small group. *Small Group Research, 27,* 475–503.

Salkever, A. (2003, April 24). Home truths about meetings. *Business Week.* Retrieved from http://www.businessweek.com

Samovar, L. A., & Porter, R. E. (2001). *Communication between cultures* (5th ed.). Belmont, CA: Wadsworth.

Samovar, L. A., Porter, R. E., & Stefani, L. A. (1998). *Communication between cultures.* Belmont, CA: Wadsworth.

Samter, W. (2003). Friendship interaction skills across the life span. In J. O. Greene & B. R. Burleson (Eds.), *Handbook of communication and social interaction skills* (pp. 637–684). Mahwah, NJ: Erlbaum.

Sapir, E., & Whorf, B. L. (1956). The relation of habitual thought and behavior to language. In J. B. Carroll (Ed.), *Language, thought, and reality: Selected writings of Benjamin Lee Whorf* (pp. 134–159). Cambridge, MA: MIT Press.

Sarich, V., & Miele, F. (2004). *Race: The reality of human differences.* Boulder, CO: Westview Press.

Sawyer, C., & Behnke, R. (1990). The role of self-monitoring in the communication of public speaking anxiety. *Communication Reports, 3,* 70–74.

Sawyer, C., & Behnke, R. (1996). Public speaking anxiety and the communication of emotion. *World Communication, 25,* 21–30.

Sawyer, C., & Behnke, R. (2002). Behavioral inhibition and communication of public speaking state anxiety. *Western Journal of Communication, 66,* 412–422.

Scheerhorn, D., & Geist, P. (1997). Social dynamics in groups. In L. R. Frey & J. K. Barge (Eds.), *Managing group life: Communicating in decision-making groups* (pp. 81–103). Boston: Houghton Mifflin.

Schenck v. United States, 249 U.S. 47 (1919).

Schillinger, L. (2006, September 20). Foreign *Office:* The French and the Germans have remade the BBC series. Why? *Slate.* Retrieved from http://www.slate.com/id/2150015

Schlenker, B. R., Weigold, M. F., & Hallam, J. R. (1990). Self-serving attributions in social context: Effects of self-esteem and social pressure. *Journal of Personality and Social Psychology, 58,* 855–863.

Schofield, H. (2003, October). Jewish dad backs headscarf daughters. *BBC News.* Retrieved from http://news.bbc.co.uk/2/low/europe/3149588.stm

Schrodt, P., & Wheeless, L. R. (2001). Aggressive communication and informational reception apprehension: The influence of listening anxiety and intellectual inflexibility on trait argumentativeness and verbal aggressiveness. *Communication Quarterly, 49,* 53–69.

Schrodt, P., Wheeless, L. R., & Ptacek, K. M. (2000). Informational reception apprehension, educational motivation, and achievement. *Communication Quarterly, 48,* 60–73.

Schroeder, L. (2002). The effects of skills training on communication satisfaction and communication anxiety in the basic speech course. *Communication Research Reports, 19,* 380–388.

Schullery, N. M., & Gibson, M. K. (2001). Working in groups: Identification and treatment of students' perceived weaknesses. *Business Communication Quarterly, 64,* 9–30.

Schulman, P. R. (1996). Heroes, organizations, and high reliability. *Journal of Contingencies and Crisis Management, 4,* 72–82.

Schweitzer, T. (2007). *Seven out of 10 employees admit to abusing office computers, phones.* Retrieved May 13, 2008, from http://www.inc.com

Scott, W. R. (1981). *Organizations: Rational, natural, and open systems.* Englewood Cliffs, NJ: Prentice Hall.

Scully, M. (2005, February 2). Building a better State of the Union address. *The New York Times.* Retrieved from http://www.nytimes.com

Secret of the wild child [Transcript]. (1997, March 4). *Nova.* Public Broadcasting System. Retrieved March 25, 2008, from http://www.pbs.org/wgbh/nova/transcripts/2112gchild.html

Seul, J. R. (1999). "Ours is the way of God": Religion, identity, and intergroup conflict. *Journal of Peace Research, 36,* 553–569.

Shannon, C. E., & Weaver, W. (1949). *The mathematical theory of communication.* Urbana: University of Illinois Press.

Shaw, M. E. (1988). Group composition and group cohesiveness. In R. S. Cathcart & L. A. Samovar (Eds.), *Small group communication* (4th ed.) (pp. 42–49). Dubuque, IA: WCB Publishers.

Sherif, M., & Sherif, C. W. (1967). Attitude as the individual's own categories: The social judgment-involvement approach to attitude and attitude change. In C. W. Sherif & M. Sherif (Eds.), *Attitude, ego-involvement, and change* (pp. 105–139). New York: Wiley.

Shultz, B. G. (1999). Improving group communication performance: An overview of diagnosis and intervention. In L. Frey, D. Gouran, & M. Poole (Eds.), *Handbook of group communication theory and research* (pp. 371–394). Thousand Oaks, CA: SAGE.

Sides, C. H. (2000). Ethics and technical communication: The past quarter century. *Journal of Technical Writing and Communication, 30,* 27–30.

Sinickas, A. (2000). How many focus groups do you need? *Total Communication Measurement, 2,* 11.

Siple, L. (2003). American Sign Language communication. *Signing Resources.* Retrieved April 26, 2007, from http://www.signingresources.net/deaf_connect_understanding_culture.html

Smith, P. (2005, February 11). Bullies incorporated. *Sydney Morning Herald.* Retrieved from http://www.smh.com.au

Smith, R., Jr. (2004). Recruit the student: Adapting persuasion to audiences. *Communication Teacher, 18,* 53–56.

Smith, R. E. (1993). Clustering: A way to discover speech topics. *The Speech Teacher, 7* (2), 6–7.

Smitter, R. (2005, November). In times of crisis, communication *is* the story. *Spectra, 4,* 2.

Snyder, B. (2003, May). Teams that span time zones face new work rules. *Stanford Business Magazine.* Retrieved from http://www.gsb.stanford.edu

Snyder, M. (1974). Self-monitoring of expressive behavior. *Journal of Personality and Social Psychology, 30,* 526–537.

Snyder, M. (1979). Self-monitoring processes. In L. Berkowitz (Ed.), *Advances in social psychology* (Vol. 12, pp. 86–128). New York: Academic Press.

Sokol, R. I., Webster, K. L., Thompson, N. S., & Stevens, D. A. (2005). Whining as mother-directed speech. *Infant and Child Development, 14,* 478–486.

Spender, D. (1985). *Man-made language* (2nd ed.). London: Routledge & Kegan Paul.

Springsteen, B. (2005, March 17). *Bruce Springsteen inducts U2 into the Rock and Roll Hall of Fame* [Transcript]. Retrieved from http://www.u2station.com/news/archives/2005/03/transcript_bruc.php

Stafford, L. (2003). Summarizing and questioning Canary and Stafford's model of relational maintenance. In D. Danary & M. Dainton (Eds.), *Maintaining relationships through communication* (pp. 51–77). Mahwah, NJ: Erlbaum.

Standage, T. (2005). *A history of the world in six glasses.* New York: Walker.

Steel, S. (2007, August 31). Missing mom: Princes Harry and William at Diana's memorial service. *National Post.* Retrieved from http://communities.canada.com/nationalpost/blogs/posted/archive/2007/08/31/missing-mom-prince-harry-s-speech-at-diana-s-memorial-service.aspx

Steil, L. K., Barker, L. L., & Watson, K. W. (1983). *Effective listening: Key to success.* Reading, MA: Addison-Wesley.

Steil, L. K., Summerfield, J., & de Mare, G. (1983). *Listening: It can change your life.* New York: Wiley.

Steptoe, S. (2006, January 8). Q&A: Defining a new deficit disorder. *Time.com.* Retrieved from http://www.time.com/time/health/article/0,8599,1147207,00.html

Sternberg, R. J. (1988). *The triangle of love: Intimacy, passion, commitment.* New York: Basic Books.

Stevens, D. (2007, March 23). Television without pity: Will corporate ownership ruin a cult Web site? *Slate.* Retrieved from http://www.slate.com/id/2162470

Stewart, C. J., & Cash, W. B., Jr. (2006). *Interviewing: Principles and practices* (11th ed.). New York: McGraw-Hill.

Stewart, L. P., Cooper, P. J., & Steward, A. D. (2003). *Communication and gender.* Boston: Pearson Education.

Stewart, R. A. (1994). Perceptions of a speaker's initial credibility as a function of religious involvement and religious disclosiveness. *Communication Research Reports, 11,* 169–176.

Stiff, J. B., & Mongeau, P. (2003). *Persuasive communication.* New York: Guilford Press.

Suler, J. (2007). The psychology of cyberspace. Retrieved December 26, 2007, from http://www-usr.rider.edu/~suler/psycyber/psycyber.html (Original work published 1996)

Sullivan, L. (2006a, July 26). At Pelican Bay, a life spent in solitary. *All things considered* [Television broadcast]. Retrieved from http://www.npr.org/templates/story/story.php?storyId=5584254

Sullivan, L. (2006b, July 26). In U.S. prisons, thousands spend years in isolation. *All things considered* [Television broadcast]. Retrieved from http://www.npr.org/templates/story/story.php?storyId=5582144

Sutton, S. R. (1982). Fear arousal and communication: A critical examination of theories and research. In J. Eiser (Ed.), *Social psychology and behavioral medicine* (pp. 303–337). Chichester, UK: Wiley.

Sybers, R., & Roach, M. E. (1962). Clothing and human behavior. *Journal of Home Economics, 54,* 184–187.

Tannenbaum, R., Weschler, I. R., & Massarik, F. (1961). *Leadership and organization.* New York: McGraw-Hill.

Tao, T. (2000, March 7). Caring for new mothers. *Shanghai Star.* Retrieved December 26, 2007, from http://app1.chinadaily.com.cn/star/history/00-03-07/l01-care.html

10 questions: Jimmy Wales. (2007, March 21). *Time.* Retrieved from http://www.time.com

Thomas, L. T., & Levine, T. R. (1994). Disentangling listening and verbal recall: Related but separate constructs? *Human Communication Research, 21,* 103–127.

Tidwell, L., & Walther, J. (2002). Computer-mediated communication on disclosure, impressions, and interpersonal evaluations: Getting to know one another a bit at a time. *Human Communication Research, 28,* 317–348.

Ting-Toomey, S., Yee-Jung, K. K., Shapiro, R. B., Garcia, E., Wright, T. J., & Oetzel, J. G. (2000). Ethnic/cultural identity salience and conflict styles in four U.S. ethnic groups. *International Journal of Intercultural Relations, 24,* 47–81.

Todd, T. L., & Levine, T. R. (1996). Further thoughts on recall, memory, and the measurement of listening: A rejoinder to Bostrom. *Human Communication Research, 23,* 306–308.

Trachtenberg, A. (2000). *The incorporation of America.* New York: Hill & Wang. (Original work published 1982)

*Trader Joe's fearless flyer.* (2008, May). Monrovia, CA: Trader Joe's.

Treaster, J. B. (2002, March 30). Home insurers frown on many dogs. *The New York Times.* Retrieved from http://www.nytimes.com

Triandis, H. C., Brislin, R., & Hul, C. H. (1988). Cross-cultural training across the individualism-collectivism divide. *International Journal of Intercultural Relations, 12,* 269–289.

Trubisky, P., Ting-Toomey, S., & Lin, S. (1991). The influence of individualism-collectivism and self-monitoring on conflict styles. *International Journal of Intercultural Relations, 15,* 65–84.

Tucker, J. S., & Anders, S. L. (1998). Adult attachment style and nonverbal closeness in dating couples. *Journal of Nonverbal Behavior, 22,* 109–124.

Tuckman, B. (1965). Developmental sequences in small groups. *Psychological Bulletin, 63,* 384–399.

Tufte, E. (2003, September). PowerPoint is evil: Power corrupts; PowerPoint corrupts absolutely. *Wired.* Retrieved from http://www.wired.com/wired/archive/11.09/ppt2.html

University of Sussex, Press and Communications Office. (2002, February 22). Cancer doctors learn how to listen [Press release]. Retrieved from http://www.sussex.ac.uk/press_office/media/media200.shtml

U.S. Census Bureau. (2005). *Poverty thresholds, 2005.* Retrieved from http://www.census.gov/hhes/www/poverty/threshld/thresh05.html

U.S. Department of Health and Human Services. (2005). *The 2005 HHS poverty guidelines.* Retrieved from http://aspe.hhs.gov/poverty/05poverty.shtml

Vangelisti, A., & Banski, M. (1993). Couples' debriefing conversations: The impact of gender, occupation, and demographic characteristics. In *Family relations* (Vol. 42, pp. 149–157).

Van Zandt, T. (2004). Information overload and a network of targeted communication. *RAND Journal of Economics, 35,* 542–561.

Vascellaro, J. (2007, August 28). Social networking goes professional. *The Wall Street Journal.* Retrieved from http://online.WSJ.com

Viewpoints: Cartoon row. (2006, February 3). *BBC News.* Retrieved from http://news.bbc.co.uk/2/hi/europe/4676632.stm

Villaume, W. A., & Brown, M. H. (1999). The development and validation of the vocalic sensitivity test. *International Journal of Listening, 13,* 24–45.

Vivinetto, G. (2004, November 30). Free your mind and name change will follow. *St. Petersburg Times,* p. E1.

Von Raffler-Engel, W. (1983). *The perception of nonverbal behavior in the career interview.* Philadelphia: Benjamin.

Waldman, S. (2004, October 26). Who knows? *The Guardian.* Retrieved from http://www.guardian.co.uk

Waldron, V. R., & Applegate, J. A. (1998). Effects of tactic similarity on social attraction and persuasiveness in dyadic verbal disagreements. *Communication Reports, 11,* 155–166.

Walker, A. (1982). *The color purple.* New York: Harcourt Brace Jovanovich.

Wallace, A., Wallace, I., & Wallechinsky, D. (2004). *The book of lists.* New York: Bantam Books.

Wallis, C. (2006, March 27). The multitasking generation. *Time,* 48–55.

Walster, E. H., Aronson, E., Abrahams, D., & Rohmann, L. (1966). Importance of physical attractiveness in dating behavior. *Journal of Personality and Social Psychology, 4,* 508–516.

Walther, J. B. (1996). Computer-mediated communication: Impersonal, interpersonal, and hyperpersonal interaction. *Communication Research, 23,* 3–43.

Walther, J. B. (2004). Language and communication technology: Introduction to the special issue. *Journal of Language and Social Psychology, 23,* 384–396.

Weisz, C., & Wood, L. F. (2005). Social identity support and friendship outcomes: A longitudinal study predicting who will be friends and best friends 4 years later. *Journal of Social and Personal Relationships, 22,* 416–432.

West, A. (2007, August 20). Facebook labeled a $5b waste of time. *Sydney Morning Herald.* Retrieved May 13, 2008, from http://www.smh.com.au

Westmyer, S., DiCioccio, R., & Rubin, R. (1998). Appropriateness and effectiveness of communication channels in competent interpersonal communication. *Journal of Communication, 48,* 27–48.

Wheelan, S. (1994). *Group process: A developmental perspective.* Boston: Allyn & Bacon.

Wheeless, L. R. (1975). An investigation of receiver apprehension and social context dimensions of communication apprehension. *Speech Teacher, 24*(3), 261–268.

Wherfritz, G., Kinetz, E., & Kent, J. (2008, April 21). Lured into bondage: A growing back channel of global trade tricks millions into forced labor. *Newsweek.* Retrieved from http://www.newsweek.com/id/131707

Why most meetings stink. (2005, October 31). *Business Week.* Retrieved from http://www.businessweek.com

The wicked stepdaughter [Letter to "Dear Prudence" advice column]. (2008, April 10). *Slate.* Retrieved from http://www.slate.com/id/2188512

Wieder, T. (2003, November 21). Wear thee well: The hosts of TLC's *What Not to Wear* speak out about style, self-image, and marabou trim. *The Boston Phoenix.* Retrieved from http://www.bostonphoenix.com/boston/news_features/qa/documents/03333644asp

Wiemann, J. M. (1977). Explication and test of a model of communication competence. *Human Communication Research, 3,* 195–213.

Wiemann, J. M., & Backlund, P. M. (1980). Current theory and research in communication competence. *Review of Educational Research, 50,* 185–189.

Wiemann, J. M., & Daly, J. A. (1994). On getting your own way. In J. A. Daly & J. M. Wiemann (Eds.), *Strategic interpersonal communication* (pp. vii–xiv). Hillsdale, NJ: Erlbaum.

Wiemann, J. M., & Knapp, M. L. (1999). Turn-taking in conversations. In L. K. Guerrero, J. A. DeVito, & M. L. Hecht (Eds.), *The nonverbal communication reader: Classic and contemporary readings* (pp. 406–414). Prospect Heights, IL: Waveland Press.

Wiemann, J. M., & Krueger, D. L. (1980). The language of relationships. In H. Giles, W. P. Robinson, & P. M. Smith (Eds.), *Language: Social psychological perspectives* (pp. 55–62). Oxford: Pergamon Press.

Wiemann, J. M., Takai, J., Ota, H., & Wiemann, M. O. (1997). A relational model of communication competence. In B. Kovačić (Ed.), *Emerging theories of human communication* (pp. 25–44). Albany, NY: State University of New York Press.

Wiemann, J. M., & Wiemann, M. O. (1992). *Interpersonal communicative competence: Listening and perceiving.* Unpublished manuscript, University of California–Santa Barbara.

Wilde, M. (2008, January). Do uniforms make schools better? *GreatSchools.* Retrieved April 16, 2008, from http://www.greatschools.net/cgi-bin/showarticle/ga/361

Williams, A. (2005, Summer). "Doing the month": Ancient tradition meets modern motherhood. *Urban Baby and Toddler.* Retrieved December 26, 2007, from http://www.urbanbaby.ca/postpartum.htm#Doing

Williams, P. (1993). Surveillance hurts productivity, deprives employees of rights. *Advertising Age, 64,* 14.

Wilmot, W. W. (1987). *Dyadic communication* (3rd ed.). New York: Random House.

Wines, M. (1995, March 15). Celebrities take art's cause to Congress. *The New York Times.* Retrieved from http://www.nytimes.com

Winston, C. (2002, January 28). State of the Union stew. *The Christian Science Monitor.* Retrieved from http://www.csmonitor.com

Witt, P., Brown, K., Roberts, J., Weisel, J., Sawyer, C., & Behnke, R. (2006). Somatic anxiety patterns before, during, and after giving a public speech. *Southern Communication Journal, 71,* 87–100.

Witteman, H. (1993). The interface between sexual harassment and organizational romance. In G. Kreps (Ed.), *Sexual harassment: Communication implications* (pp. 27–62). Cresskill, NJ: Hampton Press.

Wolvin, A. D., & Coakley, C. G. (1991). A survey of the status of listening training in some *Fortune* 500 corporations. *Communication Education, 40,* 151–164.

Wood, B. (1982). *Children and communication: Verbal and nonverbal language development* (2nd ed.). Englewood Cliffs, NJ: Prentice Hall.

Wood, J. T. (1992). Telling our stories: Narratives as a basis for theorizing sexual harassment. *Journal of Applied Communication Research, 20,* 349–362.

Wood, J. T. (2001). The normalization of violence in heterosexual romantic relationships: Women's narratives of love and violence. *Journal of Personal and Social Relationships, 18,* 239–261.

Wood, J. T., & Inman, C. C. (1993). In a different mode: Masculine styles of communicating closeness. *Journal of Applied Communication Research, 21,* 279–295.

Yandrick, R. M. (2001). A team effort. *HR Magazine, 46,* 136–141.

Yook, E. (2004). Any questions? Knowing the audience through question types. *Communication Teacher, 18,* 91–93.

York, M. (2006, December 25). A place where sign language is far from foreign. *The New York Times,* p. B1.

Zhao, S. (2006). Do Internet users have more social ties? A call for differentiated analyses of Internet use. *Journal of Computer-Mediated Communication, 11,* 844–862.

Zimmerman, D. H., & West, C. (1975). Sex roles, interruptions, and silences in conversation. In B. Thorne & N. Henley (Eds.), *Language and sex: Difference and dominance* (pp. 105–129). Rowley, MA: Newbury Press.

Zogby International Poll. (2007, August 30). *As Labor Day nears, Workplace Bullying Institute survey finds half of working Americans affected by workplace bullying.* Retrieved April 20, 2008, from http://www.zogby.com/search/ReadNews.dbm?ID=1353

# acknowledgments

## Text Credits

**Box 1.2:** National Communication Association, "Credo for Ethical Communication." Copyright © 1999 by the National Communication Association. Reprinted with permission.

**Page 42:** "The Buckets." Cartoon by Greg Cravens. Copyright © 2003 by United Features Syndicate. Reprinted with permission. Originally created by Scott Stantis.

**Figure 2.4:** "Assessing Our Perceptions of Self." Adapted from Dan O'Hair et al., *Competent Communication,* second edition. Copyright © 1997 by Bedford/St. Martin's Press. Adapted with the permission of Bedford/St. Martin's Press.

**Page 62:** M. Snyder. "Self-Monitoring Test." Adapted from "Self-Monitoring and Expressive Behavior" by M. Snyder, in *Journal of Personality and Social Psychology* 30 (1974): 526–537. Copyright © 1974 by the American Psychological Association. Adapted with permission.

**Figure 3.1:** "The Abstraction Ladder." Adapted from Dan O'Hair et al., *Competent Communication,* second edition. Copyright © 1997 by Bedford/St. Martin's Press. Adapted with the permission of Bedford/St. Martin's Press.

**Table 3.2:** "The Language of Text Messaging." Reprinted by permission of Steve Nash, www.textmefree.com.

**Table 4.1:** "The Power of Eye Contact." Adapted from Dale G. Leathers, *Successful Verbal Communication: Principles and Applications,* third edition. Published by Allyn and Bacon, Boston, MA. Copyright © 1997 by Pearson Education. Adapted with the permission of the publisher.

**Figure 4.2:** "Four Zones of Personal Space." From Dan O'Hair et al., *Competent Communication,* second edition. Copyright © 1997 by Bedford/St. Martin's Press. Adapted with the permission of Bedford/St. Martin's Press.

**Table 4.2:** "How People Touch." From Dan O'Hair et al., *Competent Communication,* second edition. Copyright © 1997 by Bedford/St. Martin's Press. Adapted with the permission of Bedford/St. Martin's Press.

**Table 5.1:** "Listening Goals." From Dan O'Hair et al., *Competent Communication,* second edition. Copyright © 1997 by Bedford/St. Martin's Press. Adapted with the permission of Bedford/St. Martin's Press.

**Page 148:** L. R. Wheeless. "Your Listening Apprehension." From *Speech Teacher* 24 (1975): 261–268. Copyright © 1975. Adapted with permission.

**Table 6.1:** "Family Communication Standards." From three studies of 1,023 undergraduate students at the University of Illinois conducted by Dr. John Caughlin. Published in *Human Communication Research* 29 (2003): 5B40. Reprinted with the permission of Sage Publications, Inc.

**Table 6.4:** "Strategies for Managing Stable Relationships." Adapted from Daniel J. Canary and Michael J. Cody, *Interpersonal Communication: A Goals-Based Approach.* Copyright © 1994 by Bedford/St. Martin's Press. Adapted with the permission of Bedford/St. Martin's Press.

**Page 214:** Dominic A. Infante. "Hitting Above and Below the Belt." From *Arguing Constructively* (Long Grove, IL: Waveland Press, 1988). Adapted with permission of Waveland Press, Inc. All rights reserved.

**Figure 8.1:** "Complexity of Group Relationships." From Dan O'Hair et al., *Competent Communication,* second edition. Copyright © 1997 by Bedford/St. Martin's Press. Adapted with the permission of Bedford/St. Martin's Press.

**Figure 8.2:** "Group Communication Networks." From W. Richard Scott, *Organizations: Rational, Natural, and Open Systems.* Copyright © 1981 by Pearson Education. Reprinted with the permission of Pearson Education, Upper Saddle River, NJ.

**Page 253:** "How Well Do You Interact in a Group Setting?" Adapted from J. C. McCroskey (1982), *An Introduction to Rhetorical Communication* (4th ed., Englewood Cliffs, NJ: Prentice-Hall). Reprinted with permission.

**Figure 10.1:** "A College or University System." From Dan O'Hair et al., *Competent Communication,* second edition. Copyright © 1997 by Bedford/St. Martin's Press. Reprinted with the permission of Bedford/St. Martin's Press.

**Table 10.2:** "Perceptions of Appropriate Ways to Handle Organizational Tasks." From Pew Internet and American Life Project Email at Work Survey (April–May 2002), N-1003. Reprinted by permission.

**Page 309:** "Are You Off Balance?" From "Having It All: Work/Life Balance" (August 1, 2007), www.cnn.com/2007/LIVING/personal/07/30/wlb.quiz.balance/index.html. Reprinted with permission.

**Page 324:** Sample Speech 11.3: Excerpts from "U2 Rock and Roll Hall of Fame Induction" by Bruce Springsteen. www.u2station.com/news/archives/2005/03/transcript_bruc.php. Copyright © 2005 by Bruce Springsteen. Reprinted with the permission of the author.

**Figure 11.1:** "Types of Audiences." Adapted from Dan O'Hair et al., *Competent Communication,* second edition. Copyright © 1997 by Bedford/St. Martin's. Adapted with the permission of Bedford/St. Martin's Press.

**Table 11.1:** "Personal Interest Topics." Adapted from D. O'Hair, R. Stewart, and H. Rubenstein, *A Speaker's Guidebook,* third edition. Copyright © 2007 by Bedford/St. Martin's Press. Adapted with the permission of Bedford/St. Martin's.

**Figure 11.2:** "Example of a Web of Associations Produced by Clustering." Adapted from Dan O'Hair et al., *Competent Communication,* second edition (New York: Bedford/St. Martin's, 1997, p. 399). Adapted with the permission of Bedford/St. Martin's Press.

**Page 339:** Copyright © 2008 by Ask.com. Reprinted with permission.

**Page 339:** Copyright © 2008 by Google, Inc. Reprinted with permission.

**Table 12.1:** "Useful Delivery Cues." From D. O'Hair, R. Stewart, and H. Rubenstein, *A Speaker's Guidebook,* third edition. Copyright © 2007 by Bedford/St. Martin's Press. Adapted with the permission of Bedford/St. Martin's Press.

**Table 12.3:** "Useful Signposts." From D. O'Hair, R. Stewart, and H. Rubenstein, *A Speaker's Guidebook,* third edition. Copyright © 2007 by Bedford/St. Martin's Press. Reprinted with the permission of Bedford/St. Martin's.

**Page 380:** Sample Speech 12.1: Dr. Martin Luther King Jr., excerpt from "I Have a Dream" (August 28, 1963). Copyright © 1963 by Martin Luther King Jr., renewed 1991 by Coretta Scott King. Reprinted with the permission of The Heirs to The Estate of Martin Luther King Jr., c/o Writer's House, LLC.

**Page 381:** "Assessing Your Speech Delivery." From D. O'Hair, R. Stewart, and H. Rubenstein, *A Speaker's Guidebook,* third edition. Copyright © 2007 by Bedford/St. Martin's Press. Adapted with the permission of Bedford/St. Martin's Press.

**Table 14.2:** "Types of Informative Speeches, Sample Topics, Informational Strategies, and Organizational Patterns." From D. O'Hair, R. Stewart, and H. Rubenstein, *A Speaker's Guidebook,* third edition. Copyright © 2007 by Bedford/St. Martin's Press. Adapted with the permission of Bedford/St. Martin's Press.

**Box A.1:** "What *NOT* to Do in an Interview." From "Personnel Execs Reveal the Truth About Job Applicants" by R. Miller, *Dallas Morning News,* January 31, 1991, p. 2D. Used with permission.

## Photo Credits

**1:** (part openers, L-R) Chris Graythen/Getty Images; © Walt Disney/courtesy Everett Collection; Karl Walter/Getty Images; Blend Images/Punchstock; (grid, L-R) Getty Images, Kelsey McNeal/© 20th Century Fox Film Corp. All rights reserved/courtesy Everett Collection, Getty Images, Stockbyte/Getty Images, © Photofusion Picture Library/Alamy, © Martin Norris/Alamy; **2:** Chris Graythen/Getty Images; **6:** (grid, L-R) © JoeFoxNewYork / Alamy, © Ramin Talaie/Corbis, © Warner Bros./courtesy Everett Collection, Dean Hendler/© NBC/courtesy Everett Collection; **7:** (top) © 20th Century Fox Film Corp. All rights reserved/courtesy Everett Collection, (bot) © Paramount/courtesy Everett Collection; **8:** © David Grossman/The Image Works; **12:** (top) Paul Spinelli/Getty Images, (bot) Brian Bahr/Allsport/Getty Images; **16:** (top) © 20th Century Fox Film Corp. All rights reserved./courtesy Everett Collection, (bot) © Paramount Vantage/courtesy Everett Collection; **18:** (top) © Fox Searchlight/courtesy Everett Collection, (bot) © Chris Pizzello/Reuters/Corbis; **21:** © HBO/courtesy Everett Collection; **26:** (L) © Mango Productions/Corbis, (R) © Robert Fried/Alamy; **32:** Chris Graythen/Getty Images; **36:** Karl Walter/Getty Images; **39:** Chris Hondros/Getty Images; **40:** David Young-Wolff/PhotoEdit; **42:** The Buckets: © United Feature Syndicate, Inc.; **44:** (grid, L-R) Keith Brofsky/Photo Disc/Getty Images, © Sean Sprague/The Image Works, Hector Mata/AFP/Getty Images, © Jack Kurtz/The Image Works; **48:** AP Photo/Eric Gay; **49:** (top) Image courtesy of The Advertising Archives, (bot) WORKING TITLE/The Kobal Collection; **50:** (grid, L-R) © LHB Photo/Alamy, Robyn Beck/AFP/Getty Images, © Peter Turnley/Corbis, Andrew Gray/onAsia; **53:** Chris Pizzello/Reuters /Landov; **55:** The Kobal Collection/NBC-TV; **56:** © Bravo/Photofest; **61:** Wathiq Khuzaie/Getty Images; **66:** Karl Walter/Getty Images; **70:** (grid, L-R) Getty Images, Kelsey McNeal/© 20th Century Fox Film Corp. All rights reserved/courtesy Everett Collection, Getty Images, Stockbyte/Getty Images, © Photofusion Picture Library/Alamy, © Martin Norris/Alamy; **73:** (L-R) Charles Shoffner/Index Stock/Jupiter Images, Charles Shoffner/Index Stock/Jupiter Images; **75:** Rubberball/Jupiter Images; **76:** © Ian Middleton/Alamy; **78:** © DreamWorks/courtesy Everett Collection; **80:** Michael Sharkey/Getty Images; **85:** (L-R) © Beathan/Corbis, © Stephanie Sinclair/Corbis; **89:** © Claudette Barius/© HBO/courtesy Everett Collection; **94:** © Foodcollection.com/Alamy; **95:** © Warner Brothers/courtesy Everett Collection; **96:** © Amit Bhargava/Corbis; **97:** (grid, L-R) Getty Images, Kelsey McNeal/© 20th Century Fox Film Corp. All rights reserved/courtesy Everett Collection, Getty Images, Stockbyte/Getty Images, © Photofusion Picture Library/Alamy, © Martin Norris/ Alamy; **100:** © Walt Disney/courtesy Everett Collection; **103:** (L-R) Simon Baker/Getty Images, AP Photo/Al Behrman; **104:** Getty Images; **105:** © Sandy Felsenthal/Corbis; **106:** Courtesy of Jessica Chesnutt and Natalie Sauro; **109:** © Warner Brothers/courtesy Everett Collection; **111:** (table, top-bot) © Ace Stock Limited/Alamy, John Henley/Getty Images, Vladimir Godnik/Getty Images, VEER Nancy Ney/Getty Images, ColorBlind Images/Getty Images, Justin Sullivan/Getty Images; **112:** © NBC/courtesy Everett Collection; **119:** © ABC/Photofest; **122:** Matt Campbell-Pool/Getty Images; **123:** Ron Sachs/CNP/Newscom; **124:** AP Photo/The Advocate Messenger, Clay Jackson; **127:** © Walt Disney/courtesy Everett Collection; **132:** Blend Images/Punchstock; **135:** (L-R) Blend Images/Punchstock,

Blend Images/Punchstock; **137:** (L-R) © Jeff Greenberg/The Image, Digital Vision/Punchstock; **139:** © Buena Vista Pictures/Photofest; **140:** Photo by Michael Ochs Archives/Getty Images; **142:** Juice Images/Punchstock; **143:** © Vikki Martin/Alamy; **149:** © Warner Brothers/courtesy Everett Collection; **150:** © Paramount/Photofest; **152:** © Fox/Photofest; **155** © 20th Century Fox Film Corp. All rights reserved/courtesy Everett Collection; **156:** Blend Images/Punchstock; **161:** (part opener, L-R) © Newscom, © NBC/courtesy Everett Collection; **162:** © Newscom; **165:** © TLC/Photofest; **167:** © Columbia Pictures/courtesy Everett Collection; **169:** (grid, L-R) Mike Powell/Getty Images, © John Birdsall/The Image Works, Hola Images/Getty Images, Zhao Yingquan/Xinhua/Landov; **171:** © JP Laffont/Sygma/Corbis; **173:** Photograph of Beatrix Potter and William Heelis at Bolton Gardens, 1913. Courtesy of Warne Archive; **174:** © TLC/Photofest; **177:** © Buena Vista/courtesy Everett Collection; **178:** © Universal Studios/Photofest; **179:** © Columbia/courtesy Everett Collection; **180:** © Columbia/courtesy Everett Collection; **186:** © Fox/Photofest; **190:** (top) © Warner Bros./Photofest, (bot) © Newscom; **194:** © NBC/courtesy Everett Collection; **198:** © MGM/courtesy Everett Collection; **199:** © Touchstone Pictures/Photofest; **200:** © Sony Pictures/courtesy Everett Collection; **204:** © SCI FI Channel/courtesy Everett Collection; **207:** © Universal/courtesy Everett Collection; **208:** © Rick Friedman/Corbis; **210:** Jennifer Durham/Jupiter Images; **215:** Creatas/Jupiter Images; **216:** © HBO/courtesy Everett Collection; **217:** John Lund/Drew Kelly/Getty Images; **219:** © NBC/courtesy Everett Collection; **225:** (part opener, L-R) Courtesy of Wikimedia, ©Getty Images, © ABC/Photofest; **226:** Courtesy of Wikimedia; **229:** © Sony Pictures Classics/courtesy Everett Collection; **231:** (grid, L-R) David Furst/AFP/Getty Images, © 20th Century Fox Film Corp. All rights reserved/courtesy Everett Collection, AP Photo/Vail Daily, Shane Macomber, © ABC/Photofest; **233:** © Bravo/courtesy Everett Collection; **235:** (L-R) © Bob Mahoney/The Image Works, AP Photo/Damian Dovarganes; **237:** © Fox Broadcasting/Photofest; **241:** AP Photo/Herbert Knosowski; **242:** © Discovery/Photofest; **246:** © Fox/Photofest; **249:** © Bettmann/Corbis; **251:** © Fox/Photofest; **252:** © WB Television/Photofest; **253:** Courtesy of Wikimedia; **258:** © ABC/Photofest; **261:** © Universal Pictures/courtesy Everett Collection; **264:** © NBC/courtesy Everett Collection; **266:** © Universal Pictures/Photofest; **267:** © 20th Century Fox Film Corp. All rights reserved/courtesy Everett Collection; **269:** (L-R) Image 100/Punchstock, Blend Images/Punchstock; **271:** Punchstock; **273:** © 2007 Getty Images; **275:** © Warner Bros./courtesy Everett Collection; **279:** © Bravo/Photofest; **281:** Jon Feingersh/Getty Images; **283:** © ABC/Photofest; **286:** © Getty Images; **289:** (top grid, L-R) Elena Rooraid/PhotoEdit, Inc., © Bob Rowan; Progressive Image/Corbis, © JimYoung/Reuters/Corbis, © Yuriko Nakao/Reuters/Corbis, (bot) © Warner Brothers/courtesy Everett Collection; **292:** © JUPITERIMAGES/Thinkstock/Alamy; **294:** Andy Kropa/Redux; **296:** © NBC/courtesy Everett Collection; **298:** AP Photo/The News Leader, Mike Tripp/Wide World;

**300:** © Corbis Premium RF/Alamy; **302:** (L-R) Image Source/Punchstock, GoGo Images/Punchstock; **305:** © Jens Büttner/epa/Corbis; **307:** KRT photograph by Bob Breidenbach/Providence Journal/Newscom; **311:** © Getty Images; **315:** (part opener, L-R) Valery Hache/AFP/Getty Images, © Paramount/courtesy Everett Collection, © NBC/Photofest, AP Photo/Peter Dejong, © 2006 Viacom International Inc "Avatar: The Last Airbender" courtesy of "Nickelodeon"; **316:** Valery Hache/AFP/Getty Images; **320:** Marie Hansen//Time Life Pictures/Getty Images; **323:** © Michael Goulding/Orange County Register/Corbis; **328:** © Jeff Greenberg/Alamy; **330:** (L-R) Frank Micelotta/Getty Images, Timothy A. Clary/AFP/Getty Images; **338:** Smirnov Vladimir/ITAR-TASS/Landov; **339:** (L-R) Courtesy of Ask.com, Courtesy of Google.com; **341:** © NMPFT/DHA/SSPL/The Image Works; **349:** Valery Hache/AFP/Getty Images; **352:** © NBC/Photofest; **355:** Comstock/Jupiter Images; **356:** © Caro/Alamy; **357:** (top) © Jim Batty/Alamy, (bot) KOBAL COLLECTION/DAVIS FILMS/BOLAND, JASIN; **360:** (L-R) InsideOutPix/Jupiter Images, © Andrea Rugg Photography/Beateworks/Corbis; **363:** © 20th Century Fox/Photofest; **370:** cartoonstock.com; **374:** THE KOBAL COLLECTION / UNIVERSAL TV/WOLF FILM; **378:** © The New Yorker Collection 2001 Jack Ziegler from cartoonbank.com. All Rights Reserved.; **380:** © Bettmann/Corbis; **382:** © NBC/Photofest; **386:** © 2006 Viacom International Inc "Avatar: The Last Airbender" courtesy of "Nickelodeon"; **390:** © Blend Images/Alamy; **392:** Jeffrey R. Staab/CBS/Landov; **393:** © CJ Gunther/epa/Corbis; **394:** © Dreamworks/Photofest; **395:** (grid, L-R) © Rick Wilking/Reuters/Corbis, Jeff Kravitz/FilmMagic/Getty Images, Monty Brinton/CBS/Landov, © Chris Kleponis/Zuma/Corbis, JJ/Getty Images, © Jeff Morgan education/Alamy; **398:** © ABC/Photofest; **401:** (top) © Sony Pictures Television/courtesy Everett Collection, (bot) Zuma/Newscom; **403:** © Reuters/Corbis; **405:** Justin Sullivan/Getty Images; **406:** Susana Gonzalez/AFP/Getty Images; **408:** created by author; **411:** © 2006 Viacom International Inc "Avatar: The Last Airbender" courtesy of "Nickelodeon"; **416:** ©Paramount/courtesy Everett Collection; **419:** © Roger Ressmeyer/Corbis; **422:** (grid, L-R) Hugh Sitton/Getty Images, Ulf Andersen/Getty Images, Mark Ralston/AFP/Getty Images, Dr. Morley Read/Photo Researchers, Inc.; **424:** (L-R) Digital Vision/Photolibrary, NASA-KSC; **425:** (L-R) AP Photo/Nati Harnik, AP Photo/Bill Haber; **427:** Courtesy of Peggy Paul; **429:** © Carlos Davila/Alamy; **432:** Claude Estebe/OnAsia.com; **433:** © factoria singular/Alamy; **435:** (L-R) George Rose/Getty Images, Sire Records/Getty Images; **439:** (L-R) © ABC/Photofest, © HBO/Photofest; **442:** © Lawrence Manning/Corbis; **446:** © Paramount/courtesy Everett Collection; **450:** AP Photo/Peter Dejong; **495:** © Bob Daemmrich/The Image Works; **456:** © Bettmann/Corbis; **459:** (grid, L-R) AP Photo/Jose Luis Magana, Getty Images, Josephine Soughan & Simon Pentleton/PYMCA/Jupiter Images, AFP/Getty Images, David Emmite/Getty Images; **462:** © Universal Pictures/Photofest; **465:** © The Meth Project; **467:** (top) © Buena Vista Pictures/Photofest, (bot) Joe Cavaretta/Wide World;

**469:** RL Productions/Getty Images; **473:** Photodisc/Punchstock; **475:** AP Photo/Gary Kazanjian; **480:** AP Photo/Peter Dejong; **484:** © Comedy Central/courtesy Everett Collection; **487:** (grid, L-R) Myra/Everett Collection, © The CW/courtesy Everett Collection, ERproductions Ltd./Getty Images, Creatas/JupiterImages; **488:** © Fox Searchlight. All rights reserved/courtesy Everett Collection; **490:** © Comedy Central/Photofest; **491:** Chris Haston/© NBC/courtesy Everett Collection; **493:** AP Photo/The News-Gazette, Robin Scholz;

**498:** © CBS/Photofest; **502:** (top) Simon Watson/Getty Images, (bot) © Spencer Grant/PhotoEdit; **503:** © 20th Century Fox Film Corp. All rights reserved/courtesy Everett Collection; **504:** (grid, L-R) © 2008 Variety, Inc. Reprinted by permission, courtesy of careerbuilder.com, Matthew Staver/BLOOMBERG NEWS/Landov; **510:** © 20th Century Fox Film Corp. All rights reserved/courtesy Everett Collection; **516:** © Comedy Central/courtesy Everett Collection.

# index